Teaching the Integrated Language Arts

Teaching the Integrated Language Arts

Shane Templeton
University of Nevada, Reno

**Houghton Mifflin Company
Boston**

Dallas
Geneva, Illinois
Palo Alto
Princeton, New Jersey

Cover illustration by Andrea Eberbach.

Chapter-opening photo credits: Chapter 1: © Paul Merideth/TSW/Click Chicago, Ltd.; Chapter 2: © Jean-Claude Lejeune/Stock Boston; Chapter 3: © Elizabeth Crews; Chapter 4: © Spencer Grant/Stock Boston; Chapter 5: © Elizabeth Crews; Chapter 6: © Elizabeth Crews; Chapter 7: © Alan Carey/The Image Works; Chapter 8: © Ursula Markus/Photo Researchers; Chapter 9: © Elizabeth Crews; Chapter 10: © Jean-Claude Lejeune; Chapter 11: © Barbara Rios/Photo Researchers; Chapter 12: © Elizabeth Crews; © Chapter 13: Bob Daemmrich/The Image Works. Photographs in Figure 8.1: (top) Robert Kristofik/Image Bank; (bottom) Ronald Sheridan, Ancient Art and Architecture Collection.

Excerpts from the following material have been reprinted by permission of the publishers.

"The Boy in the Bubble" by Paul Simon. Copyright © 1986 by Paul Simon. Used by permission of the publisher.

Macbeth. The Riverside Shakespeare (Boston: Houghton Mifflin Company), p. 1320. Reprinted by permission.

Brown Bear, Brown Bear, What Do You See? Text by Bill Martin, Jr. Copyright © 1967, 1983 by Holt, Rinehart and Winston. Reprinted by permission of Henry Holt and Company, Inc.

The Canterbury Tales, translated by David Wright. (New York: Oxford University Press, 1985). Reprinted by permission of Peters Fraser & Dunlop Group Ltd.

The Poetry of Robert Frost, edited by Edward Connery Lathem. Copyright 1923, © 1969 by Holt, Rinehart and Winston. Copyright 1951 by Robert Frost. Reprinted by permission of Henry Holt and Company, Inc.

D.R. Bear and D.M. Barone, "Using Childrens' Spellings to Group for Word Study and Directed Reading in the Primary Classroom," *Reading Psychology,* Vol. 10, #3, pp. 275–292, 1989. Reproduced by permission of the authors.

Printed in the U.S.A.
Library of Congress Catalog Card Number: 90-83028
ISBN: 0-395-48154-6

BCDEFGHIJ-H-9654321

To Katherine.
And to Jason, Gavin, and Kirstin:
Your love, support, encouragement, and patience
have made this book — and so much else — possible.

Table of Contents

Chapter 6
THE PROCESSES AND DEVELOPMENT OF READING AND WRITING 174

Chapter 7
THE TEACHING OF WRITING 216

Chapter 8
THE TEACHING OF READING   270

Chapter 9
RESPONDING TO LITERATURE THROUGH READING AND WRITING   328

Chapter 10
THE TEACHING OF VOCABULARY AND SPELLING   386

Chapter 11
THE TEACHING OF GRAMMAR AND HANDWRITING   442

Chapter 12
ASSESSMENT AND EVALUATION OF STUDENTS' INSTRUCTIONAL NEEDS   484

Chapter 13
DIVERSITY IN THE LANGUAGE ARTS CLASSROOM   516

Preface

The good teachers I had were interested in *me,* a perennially over-active student from kindergarten through high school who floundered in math from fractions to functions. Whenever stationary, however, I was reading, writing — and, of course, talking! Some of my teachers, and they were very special ones indeed, let me teach *them.*

I believe these are monumentally exciting times for language arts education. If we do it right, we can help our children come to understand themselves in deeply consequential ways. Through reading, writing, discussion, and critical reflection, they can come to make better sense of the challenges we all face on this planet. I have written this book in the hope of sharing those constants and those strategies about teaching the language arts that, over the last two decades, I have been so fortunate and honored to explore with many wonderful present and future teachers.

Audience and Purpose

Teaching the Integrated Language Arts has been written for preservice elementary school teachers. It is intended for a first course in language arts as well as for courses in which reading and language arts theory and methods are combined. The book can also serve as a foundations text for inservice teachers returning to pursue further graduate work; in this capacity it can familiarize teachers with the new thinking and developments in writing, reading, and language. For both of these groups of students, the book is intended to serve as a practical classroom resource. The text can also provide a solid grounding in the language arts — the core of the elementary curriculum — for students in educational leadership and administration who are doing coursework in curriculum and instruction.

The book's fundamental premise is that elementary students must be engaged in frequent reading, writing, and speaking throughout all areas of an integrated curriculum. Furthermore, this integrated curriculum should be based upon and occur within a real-world context that involves significant exposure to literature.

Knowledgeable teachers play a seminal role in orchestrating this involvement and in helping students to think critically. Running throughout this book is the firm belief that all teachers *can* and *must* become knowledgeable about the dynamic enterprise of teaching. Always considering the needs of the developing teacher, this text establishes an empathetic tone, anticipating and addressing directly the concerns of a novice and providing considerable practical information about the what, when, and how of teaching the integrated language arts.

Coverage

Teaching the Integrated Language Arts presents applied instructional strategies and activities and the theory behind those applications in thirteen chapters. Each of the language arts is presented and discussed with the other language arts in mind so that integration is shown in operation within every chapter.

Because teachers' instructional decisions can be informed by their knowledge of both children's language and cognitive development and of the process behind each of the language arts, background discussions and illustrations of both development and process are woven throughout the book. Equally important in the modern world is a teacher's understanding of different cultures and the special needs of diverse student populations. Thus, diversity is a theme that underlies instructional presentation in all chapters.

The first three chapters lay much of the theoretical groundwork. **Chapter 1** defines the important terms, sets up the framework of an integrated language arts curriculum, and describes the contexts in and out of school that affect children's development. **Chapter 2** presents an overview of the important concepts in the development and functioning of language and cognition, primarily during the important preschool years. The chapter emphasizes the role of social interaction in helping children *construct* their understandings. **Chapter 3** briefly presents a historical overview of spoken and written language and then concentrates on the development of the English language. The chapter suggests that even a casual familiarity with this historical picture should be of benefit to the classroom teacher, but more important, this type of understanding should help the teacher explore the history of language and its relevance to vocabulary, usage, and spelling with the elementary school student.

Chapter 4 covers organization and management within the classroom and describes the context in which integrated language arts instruction occurs effectively. This information is presented early in the text in order to give students a realistic framework within which to fit subsequent instructional information; the chapter could also be valuable used later in the course. The chapter provides in-depth discussions and an extended illustrative example of the kind of elementary classroom that provides a predictable instructional environment fostering student independence and critical thinking.

Chapter 5 addresses the oral language foundations of the language arts. The chapter demonstrates how to facilitate students' development in these areas and explains how listening, speaking, and creative dramatics establish a natural foundation for instruction and development in writing and reading.

Chapters 6, 7, and 8 work together to explore in considerable depth the topics of writing and reading. First, **Chapter 6** offers a developmental perspective on each of writing and reading and on the interaction of these two processes. Then, **Chapter 7** treats the writing process in detail. All stages — prewriting through sharing and publishing — are discussed, and specific guidelines for conferencing, questioning, and facilitating different types of writing are presented. Next, **Chapter 8** examines the nature of reading comprehension and word knowledge, from an interactive viewpoint. Guidelines for teaching strategic reading of narrative and expository texts are offered. This chapter can serve as either a comprehensive introduction to reading for the neophyte or as an excellent review for students who have already taken a course in the teaching of reading.

Chapter 9 weaves together all the instructional pieces presented thus far and demonstrates how reading, writing, and oral language can be integrated within a literature-based language arts curriculum. After providing brief overviews of the different categories of children's literature, the chapter walks students through the transition from a more traditional type of language arts classroom to a predominantly literature-based classroom. Literature response activities are offered, culminating with the presentation of two representative thematic or literature-based units.

The premise behind **Chapter 10**, which treats both vocabulary and spelling instruction, is that the topics of vocabulary and spelling are linked by a spelling-meaning connection. Within the context of the other language arts, strategies for the productive exploration of words are presented. **Chapter 11** discusses instruction of grammar, mechanics, usage, and handwriting. These traditional aspects of the language arts are presented in a functional context so that they make sense to students and have a purpose.

Chapter 12 offers a general overview of assessment and evaluation. Portfolio assessment, informal observation, other types of informal assessment, and the changing nature of formal tests are all explored. **Chapter 13** concludes the text by addressing the theme of student diversity within the elementary school classroom. The chapter is aimed at helping teachers develop awareness of the needs of multicultural and special education learners. The chapter's underlying premise is that effective teaching of special needs students is based on appropriate application of excellent regular education strategies and activities.

Features

The text includes a number of special features to help students construct their understandings of the content and apply these understandings.

- *Focusing Questions* at the beginning of each chapter address major concepts that students should acquire as they read the chapter.
- *Chapter Opening Quotations and Introductions* open each chapter and help orient students to the content while providing a realistic perspective of the importance of the topics.
- *Classroom Examples* are set off throughout the book to illustrate teaching in action. They are an integral part of the chapter and provide real modeling of effective teaching strategies for the reader.
- *Build Your Teaching Resources* are annotated bibliographies that appear directly within the chapters and that list both children's literature and professional resources.
- *Expand Your Teaching Repertoire* lists provide in-depth walk-throughs of instructional strategies and activities intended for use in the elementary classroom.

- *At the Teacher's Desk,* set-off "advice boxes" that run throughout the chapters, offer observations about a wide range of teaching and learning issues, and provide a forum for the author to share personal perspectives and insights about the topics at hand.
- *A Concluding Perspective,* summaries at the ends of the chapters, not only summarize the contents of the chapter but also act to coalesce the material and to present it as a springboard for ensuing topics.
- *Appendices* A through E conclude the book. Appendix A is a resource for Chapter 10 and should be referred to during the reading of that chapter; it lists important structural elements (prefixes, suffixes, stems) in words. Appendices B, C, and D present scope and sequence charts for the teaching of grammar, mechanics, and usage. Appendix E offers a selection of recommended computer software that effectively complements language arts instruction.

Acknowledgments

The role of reviewers in the development of a book is critical, and I wish to express my sincerest appreciation to the following colleagues for their time, thoughtfulness, advice, and criticism. I believe the book is considerably richer because of their efforts:

John G. Barnitz, University of New Orleans
Judith Cochran, Eastern New Mexico University
Jerry Converse, California State University, Chico
J. Richard Gentry, Western Carolina University
Nancy C. Millett, Wichita State University
Brenda Power, University of Delaware
Louise D. N. Wachter, Wilkes College, Pennsylvania

There are many others that I would thank by name if space permitted, but I do wish to single out the following for special acknowledgment.

Although they know it well, I nonetheless wish to acknowledge the support and encouragement I have received from my colleagues in Reading/Language Arts at the University of Nevada, Reno. I cannot imagine a more supportive, exciting, and intellectually stimulating group of colleagues: Donald Bear, Meggin McIntosh, Martha Combs, John Beach, and Stephen Lafer. And to my colleague from afar, Dave Yaden, Jr., I also extend special thanks.

I am also grateful to my University of Virginia colleagues from long ago and from recent years: Jim and Carol Beers, Tom Gill, Charlene Gill, Jean Gillet, Darrell Morris, Bob Schlagal, Elizabeth Sulzby, Bill Teale, Charlie Temple, Jerry Zutell, Mary Abouzeid, Bill Barnes, Marcia Invernizzi, Phyllis Coulter, and Bill Weber. And a special belated thanks to a departed Virginian and friend of us all, George Graham.

From those early years at Emory University in Atlanta, Jim Miller and Carole Hahn will always hold a very special place. Thanks also to Don Riechard and Jackie Irvine.

The students and classroom teachers too numerous to mention in Virginia, Georgia, Nevada, and all points in-between have taught me at least as much as I have shared with them. And thanks to those who may not realize they taught me *more* than what I shared with them: Linda Scarborough-Franks, Beth Spencer, Sharon Cathey, Diane Olds, Tamara Baren, and Nancy Kelly.

A very special thanks to Diane Barone, former doctoral student and present colleague, for everything. She read and responded at length to the first draft of this book, and when time overtook my writing schedule, she joined the enterprise and contributed two exceptional chapters.

I am extremely grateful to some wonderful people in both the School and College Divisions at Houghton Mifflin. They helped initiate the adventure many years ago; had the vision to inspire me to undertake this book; and encouraged me throughout the whole process. I also extend a very special thanks to my editor. Until one has seen it in action, there is no way to appreciate fully the work that an outstanding developmental editor can do, not only in working intensively with the author, but in coordinating all of the other million and one tasks involved in-house and out. I cannot imagine a more effective, supportive, and gentle critic.

Finally, a special acknowledgment to Edmund H. Henderson, a gentleman and a scholar in the truest sense of the expression. Professor Henderson was a very dear friend and mentor; though his untimely passing precluded the more direct recognition and expression of gratitude I had wished, it is a special honor to acknowledge his influence here. Ed was the reason I went into Education; he initiated and helped sustain my interest in language, cognition, and literacy. I earnestly hope that this book is in some small way a fitting testament to his teaching, his guidance, and his vision.

Shane Templeton

Teaching the Integrated Language Arts

1 The Language Arts: Content and Context

FOCUSING QUESTIONS

- What are the "language arts"?
- What does it mean to say that you are teaching the language arts in an *integrated* manner?
- What are the three types of knowledge that the language arts help students develop?
- Why do we classify human beings as "meaning makers"?
- What are the various types of *culture,* and how can they influence what goes on in the classroom?
- What are the implications of our multicultural society for teaching?
- What are the various sources of information with which elementary students interact, and how may they affect students?
- What are the differences between direct teaching and informal teaching?

Use your "mind's eye" for a moment and imagine yourself in an elementary school classroom. No, dissolve that first image that probably just came to you — the one of you as an elementary school student — and imagine yourself instead as the teacher. Yes, you are in a fairly typical classroom in a fairly typical elementary school building. The precise appearance of the building does not matter much, however, nor does the grade level. Focus on what is actually going on within that physical setting — the ways in which you manage and conduct the activities and the interactions in this classroom — and here I will be so bold as to help you sketch the image:

There is a low hum of voices; the room is not "so quiet you can hear a pin drop." Many students are talking with each other in groups of two, three, four, or more as they are engaged in a task. From time to time one or two students leave the classroom, a book tucked under the arm, headed toward other classrooms where each student will read to a group of younger students. At times you move about the classroom, interacting briefly with first one group and then another. At other times you call a number of students to a corner of the classroom where you carefully and directly teach them a specific strategy or skill or engage them in a lively discussion about the latest chapter in a book they have read. At still other times you talk with individual students, responding to their questions, their reading, their writing, to them as individuals that you know well.

In this classroom you see yourself throughout the day bringing the whole class together for talk, for thought, and for play. At times you are the "manager"; at other times one or more students are managers. At times there is total or near-total quiet as students listen to you read a story or poem aloud; at other times all students are either reading silently or writing. These are important times, times of critical experience and reflection.

Notably, your students are not always seated in rows, not always silent (or supposed to be silent), and not always bent over ditto sheets and workbook sheets or locked into ability groups. The traditional "so-quiet-you-can-hear-a-pin-drop" classroom may unfortunately be quite familiar to you because it is a type of classroom most Americans have experienced and that many expect. Such a classroom is not a genuine learning environment, however, and the teacher in such a classroom is not a genuine teacher.

INTRODUCTION

You are now embarked on a course of study and practice that should lead toward the realization of the first classroom image. Part of your study and practice will involve this book, in which we explore together the teaching and learning of the most critical elements of the elementary curriculum — speaking, listening, reading, and writing: the language arts. We will examine how to establish the learning environment and how to coordinate and manage the interaction that occurs within that environment.

As a teacher you will always be expanding your repertoire of activities and lessons, for there are no limits to the range of activities and lessons you can teach.

Effective teaching of the language arts, however, does not depend solely on the extent of your teaching repertoire. Also critical is your knowledge of thought, of spoken and written language, and of the interaction among these within the developing child in the context of a classroom.

You have probably already taken or will soon take at least one course in child development and/or educational psychology. The course in which you are now enrolled, and of which this book is a part, will focus on elaborating and extending this knowledge base and on bringing it to bear on the week-to-week, day-to-day, and minute-to-minute enterprise of teaching the language arts. Part of our focus will be on the nature of thought and language and the way children develop in their thinking and language abilities. It is essential that you understand this framework, for if you do, you will be able to make, as Applebee recommended, "*principled* use of the one-thousand-and-one things in [your] teaching repertoires" (Applebee, 1987, p. 269, emphasis added).

If you are studying to become a teacher, you are of course concerned about developing and expanding your own "one-thousand-and-one things." This text is designed to help you reach that goal. We will be at least equally concerned, however, with developing the principles that guide the use of each lesson or activity. Toward this end, this chapter will examine important issues, both wide-ranging and specific.

I will begin by defining the *content* of the language arts, and then discuss their bases — thought and language development. Next I will describe the *contexts* in which the language arts are applied: first, the notion of culture, the context in which and because of which the language arts are taught. Following this I will examine our "information society" and our interactions with information within this society. Based on this overview, I will suggest implications for the language arts classroom, and then consider your role as the teacher of the language arts.

Content: What Are the Language Arts?

Listening, speaking, reading, and writing: these are the language arts. Children learn about the language arts by applying them in all areas of their learning as well as by studying them directly. In fact, the language arts are being applied all the time in the classroom. In every area of the elementary school curriculum — science, math, music, social studies, art, and so forth — speaking, listening, reading, and writing occur. In a very real sense, the language arts are tools that help students better explore these content areas. Their understanding of the nature and the application of these tools will lead to deeper understanding in the content areas.

In science, for example, children can learn about the interrelationships among plants, soil, temperature, and atmosphere by discussing the reasons why more droplets form on the inside of a terrarium in the morning than in the afternoon. Children can sharpen their observations and focus their thinking by writing about their observations in a journal or learning log. Reading about the phenomenon on a large-scale basis — as it applies to a region of the country — will help your students stretch their current understanding of weather patterns.

What does it mean to talk about the *integrated* language arts? First of all, this is not integration in the sense of "to blend together or consolidate," where the identity of each separate entity might be lost. Instead, as the science example illustrates, it is an integration of all the distinct areas of the elementary curriculum. It is also an integration within your own mind — an understanding of how the pieces fit together, even when you may be focusing primarily on only one piece.

Integrating the language arts also means that speaking, listening, reading, and writing are most often addressed and used in a real or authentic context. For instance, when you are speaking naturally, you are also involved in listening; when you are writing, you are also reading what you have written. When you are reading and thinking about "what it means" or why the information on the page has been presented as it has, you are also of necessity thinking like a writer — like the author of whatever you are reading. In authentic contexts, in other words, we do not usually separate speaking from listening or writing from reading. Your teaching should reflect this, and you should explicitly inform your students of this.

When you *do* individually address and focus on a particular language art, your purpose should be clearly apparent to students — this focus should grow out of authentic purposes. You'll begin with the whole, break it down when appropriate into primarily speaking and listening, primarily writing, primarily reading, and so forth, and look carefully within each — but you will always put it back together again with the students, *re*integrate it, making sure the students know what is being done and why. As we'll explore later on, involving your students in literature units will afford the opportunity to address and apply the language arts both holistically as well as separately. Teaching in an integrated manner, often through these literature units, will ultimately help students learn and apply the language arts effectively in "real world" contexts.

Because so much of the emphasis in language arts education relates to the whole child and the whole curriculum, in recent years the term *whole language* has emerged to describe this emphasis (K. Goodman, 1987; Goodman and Goodman, 1981). Whole language educators emphasize the importance of involving children "in using [language] functionally and purposefully to meet their own needs" (K. Goodman, p. 7). Kenneth Goodman succinctly expresses the role of classroom teachers within the whole language philosophy: ". . . helping students to achieve a sense of control and ownership over their own use of language and learning in school, over their own reading, writing, speaking, listening, and thinking, will help to give them a sense of their potential power" (1986, p. 10). By teaching language arts through an integrated perspective, we can help students develop this important sense of control and ownership as they grow and develop.

Recently, researchers and educators have been drawing an important distinction between what they term "oracy" and "literacy" — that is, between those types of knowledge and abilities that apply to and support *oral* language — speaking and listening — and those that apply to and support *written* language — reading and writing (e.g., Tannen, 1982). However, as we discussed above, the learning and the teaching of the language arts affect *all* communication and thought, and some knowledge that your students develop in reading, for example, will be reflected in their oral communication.

Human beings communicate with others and with themselves through the language arts. The language arts are the bridge over which the silent thoughts of one individual cross to meet those of others, and over which the individual is able to reconstruct the meanings and intentions of others. The language arts also offer perhaps the most powerful avenues by which individuals come to know themselves.

Almost everyone is able to cross this bridge to share ideas. The quality of our innumerable journeys, however — the sense we make of ourselves, of others, and of our world — will be tremendously affected by the ways in which we can use the language arts.

There is an art to using language effectively in communication and in one's own learning. You should think of your role as a language arts teacher in part as one in which you will help your students become increasingly more competent and adept — more "artful" — in applying reading, writing, speaking, and listening to their own learning, creativity, and social development. In this sense, it is helpful to think of the language arts as *tools;* you will help your students learn the proper and appropriate use of these tools.

Thought and Language: The Bases of the Language Arts

Human beings are "meaning makers" (Wells, 1987). We cannot help but be, for this is the way we are constructed and have evolved. We have evolved in ways so that, through our thought and language processes, we organize and try to make sense of our environment. We "make meaning," in other words, and in the process, we learn. As I discuss the ways thought and language help us to make meaning, I will introduce several terms here and in the next two chapters. Do not be concerned about the number of terms; focus instead on their meaning. In every case, the terms refer to knowledge that you already possess, but you will be applying your knowledge in slightly different ways. Now, using ourselves as subjects, let's briefly consider the nature of this learning in thought and language.

Thought

We do not just passively take in the sights, sounds, and smells of our environment. We *categorize* what we experience, which helps give meaning to the experiences, and set up relationships among these categories. We interpret this information and make value judgments about it. Even if we refuse to deal with some information, by our very refusal we are categorizing it and making a value judgment about it.

The objects and processes of our thought are based on *knowledge.* Throughout this book you should see how the following types of knowledge are developed through the language arts: topical knowledge; procedural knowledge; and self-knowledge (Dillon and Sternberg, 1986).

Topical knowledge is what most people have in mind when they talk about knowledge. It is, simply, a collection of facts or information about a particular topic. Topical knowledge is extremely important, for the more we know about an area or topic, the better we are able to understand it and learn more about it.

Procedural knowledge involves how we go about studying and learning about a particular phenomenon and how extensively we study that phenomenon.

Self-knowledge helps us to determine what type of procedural knowledge we will use. It refers to our awareness of our own learning processes and our ability to monitor those processes. Also referred to as "metacognitive" knowledge (Garner, 1987; Palincsar, Brown, and Campione, 1989; Weinhert and Kluwe, 1987), self-knowledge plays a critical role in helping us to determine what we will learn and how we will go about learning it.

Understanding these different types of knowledge should help you make an extremely important distinction between knowledge "telling" — reciting facts and information — and knowledge "transforming" — changing and applying those facts and information (Scardamalia and Bereiter, 1986). This distinction is important because it underscores the difference between the ability to simply recall a bundle of facts — your students' topical knowledge — and knowing how to *use* those facts — your students' procedural knowledge and self-knowledge. The process of pulling relevant topical knowledge together and applying it appropriately is what we usually mean when we talk about *critical thinking.*

Critical thinking involves taking topical knowledge and applying it through the use of procedural and self-knowledge. When topical knowledge is applied, it becomes *transformed.* Transformed knowledge means that topical knowledge is being used to understand, to solve, to evaluate, and to define (Scardamalia and Bereiter, 1986). Transformed knowledge involves noting the implications of and interrelationships among topical knowledge. Transformed knowledge puts topical knowledge to work for us. When this happens, then, we are usually thinking critically.

At different points in the development of elementary-age children, each child will vary in the type of information about a topic he or she is capable of understanding, the ability to apply procedures to problem solving, and the awareness of how he or she goes about learning. However, almost all children are capable of developing each of these types of knowledge.

Let's consider some examples of mere topical knowledge — knowledge "telling" — as opposed to transformed knowledge and the development of what we are calling critical thinking. Your students may be able to define *characterization* as an element in stories but not know how to identify how an author is developing characterization, much less apply a knowledge of characterization to an understanding of other people in general. Your students may also be able to tell you that one should write clearly when giving directions in a letter but the students may not be able to write clearly. Your students may not understand that the reader of the directions does not have the same information as the writer and that the directions will have to be much more explicit than if the person were standing right in front of them.

With your help, your students can learn how to transform their knowledge: they can learn how to answer, for example, the question "So what?" after telling another student that some very unique creatures exist on the Galápagos Islands, or that volcanoes often occur where tectonic plates overlap.

In a nutshell, the concepts of topical knowledge and knowledge "telling," of procedural knowledge, of self-knowledge, and of knowledge transformation are all part of *critical thinking.* Teaching critical thinking in the language arts and through the language arts will be your major responsibility. Topical knowledge — knowing the facts — is important, but topical knowledge does not mean much if nothing is done with it, if the knowledge is not transformed in some fashion and if it does not help students to think critically in different areas. The knowledge must mean something to students and do something for students.

Language

Language can be spoken, written, gestured, signed, and felt. It is a powerful tool with which we make meaning. Regardless of our native language — English, Farsi, Hmong — most of us learned spoken language as very young children, with little conscious effort. If our hearing is impaired, we learned to sign with little conscious effort if others around us were signing.

We acquired our language without consciously thinking about it, in the day-to-day business of getting about and doing things. This very fact has intrigued linguists and researchers for many years. Well before children begin formal schooling they master much of the vocabulary and structures according to which that vocabulary is arranged in utterances. Still, the ability to use oral language — as is the case with so much of the rest of our learning as children — is no less than a wonderful accomplishment, one that I will examine in more depth in Chapter 2.

If individuals are to make meaning that expands and stretches their understanding, though, they need to apply their language as well as their thinking more deliberately and more productively. This is where your role as a teacher becomes so important.

In the classroom, a major goal of yours will be to help your students learn how to use language much more deliberately. Part of this learning process will involve having your students step back from time to time and think about language as a tool, in order to understand *how* it works and how it can best be applied. Thinking about language, sometimes referred to as *metalinguistic awareness* (Downing and Valtin, 1985; Tunmer, Pratt, and Herrimann, 1984; Yaden and Templeton, 1986), is an important part of learning to read and write; it helps us communicate effectively and consequentially in both written and spoken language. Moreover, it is a preeminent aspect of learning to think critically.

In Chapter 2 I will discuss the systems of language that underlie our ability to learn and use language, as well as the ways in which language can be used.

Context: The Modern World

The term *context* refers to a setting or location as well as to what goes on in that location. The context of the home, for example, includes the physical characteristics of the place where each of us lives as well as what usually goes on in the home. The context of the school includes the physical characteristics of the building and the classrooms as well as what goes on in the school. Cole and Griffin (1987) suggested that it is useful to think of "schooling" as existing within several *embedded contexts:* the classroom, the teacher, the school, the school board and administration, the community, the parents, and so forth. What goes on in schools cannot help but be affected by all of these contexts. The way you teach the *content* —

reading, writing, listening, and speaking, as well as critical thinking in these areas — will be determined in part by the contexts in which you and your students function. This is not to say that you are totally controlled by these contexts, but you should certainly be aware of the contexts if you are to teach effectively.

In this section, I will explore the influences of the broader context on the classroom by focusing on the diversity of cultures and the information that exists within and across these cultures.

Our Multicultural Society

Anthropologists and sociologists tell us that contexts are often determined by *culture*. Broadly defined, culture refers to the beliefs, values, art, literature, artifacts, and institutions of a group of people. As a nation, the United States includes a diverse range of cultures and subcultures representing various socioeconomic, ethnic, and racial groups. How children perceive themselves, others, and the broader world in which they live is affected in large part by the culture in which they live. According to the predominant culture in which they are raised, children learn, for example, (a) that they should work individually and competitively or that they should work collaboratively; (b) that they should be quiet and passive in school or that they should be active and vocal; and (c) that they should make direct eye contact with adults or that they should avoid it.

Your classroom will usually reflect this diversity. The environment and tone you establish as well as the way the language arts are applied within your classroom should allow for and respect this diversity. At the same time, keep in mind the wider world your students will have to deal with.

Throughout the course of North American history, migrations from different continents and countries have at different times significantly expanded the population. In the nineteenth and early twentieth centuries, immigrants to the United States came primarily from Europe and the Far East; more recently, immigrants have come from Southeast Asia, the Pacific Rim, Mexico, and Central and Latin America (see Figure 1.1). For many years, the influx of immigrants into the United States led to the concept of American society as a huge "melting pot," a common culture into which different peoples simply blended, keeping few if any vestiges of the original culture from which they came. In recent years, sociologists and social historians have challenged the notion of a true "melting pot" (e.g., Banks, 1981). Such a complete assimilation does not appear to be the case. Although most cultural groups do become assimilated over time into the mainstream of American culture, their language, values, art, religion, and so forth are rarely forever shed. For example, not only do African Americans, Native Americans, and Hispanic Americans value and retain aspects of their cultures, but in fact, elements of these cultures influence and enrich the broader American culture.

Although it is quite difficult to speak of an "American" culture in specific terms, there is a general culture in the United States. Most often this culture is described in terms of traditional values such as thrift, hard work, honesty, and patriotism. Our form of government, our institutions, our urban and rural areas, our literature, our language — all are expressions of the general culture. Of course, the closer we

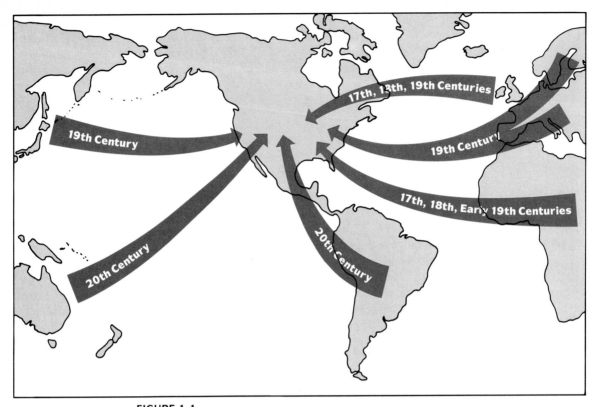

FIGURE 1.1

Patterns of Immigration from the Seventeenth to the Twentieth Century

look, the more variety we see — the effects in turn of the many different cultures that make up the United States. The concept of culture is an abstraction anyway, and whatever general sense we have of ourselves is in part a reflection of this "American" culture in which we live.

Popular culture includes the prevailing trends and attractions of the present — music, movies, clothing, attitudes, and certain books. Some aspects of popular culture become ingrained in our cultural heritage. *Huckleberry Finn,* for example, was vehemently attacked when it first appeared and was considered by many to be "trash." The book of course endured and became a significant part of our nation's cultural heritage.

This cultural heritage represents the values and more specifically the heritage of our literate tradition — the art, music, literature, and history of our nation and its people. This tradition has been to date primarily Western, representing a Greco-Roman, Judeo-Christian orientation.

Many writers and educators have emphasized that in order to be productive and informed citizens of the predominant society, it is necessary for citizens to be at least familiar with many of the names and terms associated with this cultural tradition (Hirsch, 1987). Although this is an important point, some controversy surrounds the content of this tradition because the contributions of women and of

The environment and tone you establish in your classroom should allow for and respect the diversity of your students. *(© Elizabeth Crews/The Image Works)*

groups that lie outside the traditional European sphere of influence — African Americans, Hispanic Americans, Native Americans, and Asian Americans — are not widely represented.

As a teacher, you will be the primary transmitter of the nation's cultural heritage. Your position should be realistic and well grounded. Undeniably there is an orientation toward and respect for much of the traditional American heritage, and as elementary teachers of the language arts you will prepare your students for more in-depth study of this heritage in later years. Much of this heritage is important simply because it represents the values and the ideals of the nation over the years. On the other hand, many of the nation's values and ideals are shared by cultures recently represented in the society at large, and we should expect much of the arts and literature of these cultures to become part of the more general cultural heritage of the nation. Our cultural heritage is not fixed; it is living and organic. It should represent both the ideals of our society as well as what the society is continually in the process of becoming.

When we consider the diverse cultures in our country, it is difficult to avoid considering social issues that are directly or indirectly connected to the ways in which diversity is often manifested in our society — poverty, hunger, and unemployment, the problems of the homeless, of children from single-parent homes,

AT THE
TEACHER'S
DESK:
*Moving
Beyond
Stereotypes*

There are many ways you can help students, first, to become aware of how they think about differences among people, and second, to understand the nature and value of diversity in our society. Our ultimate objective is to help students move beyond thinking in terms of stereotypes (a way of thinking that most of us fall into from time to time).

Many of the reading and writing activities I'll be exploring later on facilitate this awareness. In addition to implementing such activities, however, we can begin to sensitize our students to differences by discussing fairly simple, straightforward, and noncontroversial subjects: What differences among individuals do we find in *our* classroom? Thinking about this will bring out the obvious differences: boys and girls, different heights, eye color, hair color. Eventually, with careful guidance, discussion can address differences that unfortunately often carry negative connotations — skin color, for example, or where someone lives or the country someone came from.

In time, you can explore the concept of *stereotype* with your students, particularly in the intermediate grades. Through such discussion, students can come to realize that stereotypes are usually negative and limited to one or two particular aspects — realistic or imaginary — of a group. Because of this, they do not give a broader, realistic, fairer picture of a group or an individual. People in almost all cultures have stereotypes, not only for people of different color but for people of different economic levels. Why is laughter one frequent response when stereotypes are mentioned? What are some other common reactions?

I suggest you begin with yourself. With a small group of colleagues, explore these issues about stereotypes. Your reflection on these issues and the answers you come up with should be insightful, and you will also be better prepared for exploring these issues someday with your students.

children who are not given adequate physical and emotional support at home, and so forth. During your professional career as a teacher you will have children in your classroom from any or all of these backgrounds. Although you will want to help these children and to make a difference in their lives, often you may be left with the feeling that you have not accomplished either. Do not despair. You will probably have given these children powerful tools for thinking about and dealing with their environment: discussion; the exploration of meaningful literature, both fiction and nonfiction; writing in response to reading and for the purpose of finding out what one knows and believes; and thinking about the uses of different forms of language.

Throughout this book I will refer to the ways language arts content, strategies, and activities can involve children from diverse cultural backgrounds. These and other issues involving diversity in the classroom will be the specific focus of Chapter 13.

Our Information Society

The following lines from the Paul Simon song, "The Boy in the Bubble," capture the spirit of a powerful and influential context within which we all are living:

Medicine is magical and magical is art
The Boy in the Bubble
And the baby with the baboon heart . . .
These are the days of lasers in the jungle
Staccato signals of constant information

Ours is an information society. From the mundane to the incredible, information is everywhere. In terms of speed and quantity, our access to information is much greater now than it was a few years ago. Moreover, in contrast to previous ages, the sheer volume of the information is staggering. Information of all types is continually competing for our attention. Because of this onslaught — the "staccato bits of constant information" — any true understanding of a phenomenon is often obscured, even if it is revolutionary, like the "baby with the baboon heart" and the powerfully metaphorical "lasers in the jungle."

We have become an information processing society. Although we are not necessarily smarter than our predecessors, we have the potential to be wiser because more information is available to us. We also have the potential to become so overwhelmed by all this information that we paradoxically withdraw from it, becoming more uninformed than ever. The information society is a significantly new context in which we all now exist.

Children's access to information is also so much greater than in years past, and of course there are positive and negative aspects to this access. Although the various media make it easier for children to have access to information, the information itself may at times be of questionable value to young "information consumers." Children need to be taught how to select and receive information, how to organize it, and how to evaluate it — in other words, how to think *critically* about it.

If you were to compose a short list of sources of information for elementary students, you would probably include the following items, some of which I will highlight for separate consideration below: simple "talk" (from peers and from elders), television (from the quick and stereotypical but always resolvable programs, to MTV, to "docudramas," to advertisements), magazines, video games, cinema, and of course schooling.

More than twenty years ago, Alvin Toffler referred to our difficulties in understanding and reacting to this explosion of information and events as "future shock" (Toffler, 1970). One of the best defenses against this phenomenon is the awareness of what information is and how it is used. Once children decide to pay attention to certain information, we want the children to be in control of their own interpretations, rather than being controlled by other people who will tell them what the information means. If, by your guidance and example, your students learn how to use and understand the language arts effectively to evaluate ideas and information, your students will be much better prepared for the decisions they will have to make as adults and as responsible citizens. Because ours is an information-based society, you will need to help your students become knowledgeable consumers of information, so that they are neither overwhelmed by nor excluded from the economic, political, and educational mainstream.

A scholar once commented almost thirty years ago that the world was becoming a "global village" (McLuhan, 1964). By this he meant that, through the medium of television and of other forms of instant electronic communication, human beings the world over are brought together. This more immediate access to information carries with it the responsibility of making quick decisions. How we respond — emotionally and critically — depends in large part upon how we have been taught. Schooling, in other words, may be the one place where students can learn how to make more sense out of more information.

Elementary school children are unavoidably going to be growing up in the contexts of a variety of embedded cultures, surrounded by all the information that is coursing throughout those cultures. What will be the nature of their interactions with these contexts and their various content?

Content and Context:
Interactions with Information

Sources of information are both the *content* of language arts and the *context* within which we are formed: We are what we read and hear; what we write and speak reflects who and what we are. Information of course comes to us through direct, face-to-face contact with other individuals as well as through print and electronic media. Electronic media include television, film, radio, and computers. This section will discuss the impact of each of these sources of information and the nature of individuals' interaction with these sources.

Print

In terms of quantity, printed material is probably the most pervasive type of medium in our society. Even those individuals who choose not to read books, magazines, or newspapers are still bombarded by and must interact with information in printed form.

Print serves a variety of purposes in our society. We take it for granted that print can illuminate us, extend our knowledge and our perspectives, and instruct and assist us in any number of undertakings. In our society we have come to believe in the power of being literate and the knowledge and wisdom that this ability conveys. The language arts are tools, and the ability to read is a powerful tool indeed. More than simply being an instrument that helps us accomplish some immediate purpose, however, reading allows us to interact in significant and at times life-changing ways with situations, information, and individuals. Because of these interactions we become wiser, more understanding, and better able to deal with our world in a more meaningful sense. As we will see in Chapter 9, books such as

Charlotte's Web (E. B. White), *A Bridge to Terabithia* (Katherine Paterson), or *Tuck Everlasting* (Natalie Babbitt) can help young readers understand and perhaps deal with some very powerful ideas and emotions for the first time: the meaning of friendship, for example, of life and the acceptance of death.

The act of reading is similar to the other language arts in important ways, but it is also quite different. Notably, the reader is in control of the rate and the type of "information intake." Regardless of the type of material being read, the reader is free to vary the rate, to stop to reflect, to go back or skip forward quickly. For example, an engaging scene in a story can be read more slowly, thought about, and reread. Print gives instructions to the reader on how to construct images, but the images are unique to each reader, not already provided as would be the case with a movie or a television program.

Unlike other sources of information, print "freezes" the writer's language and the writer's ideas as expressed in language — the language is always there. Spoken language, in contrast, flows along in real time and is gone. The speaker's words can be taped for replay, of course, but spoken language remains more difficult to reflect on and analyze than printed language. Because of the permanence of print, several scholars (Havelock, 1982; Olson, 1977) have observed that print can affect *how* we think in significant ways. These researchers have noted that one of the most profound influences of print has to do with logical, analytic thinking. Exposure to the more explicit representation of ideas and relationships among ideas in print will have an effect on how readers organize ideas and more generally on how readers organize and apply their thinking skills — their procedural and self-knowledge.

In addition to providing and capturing information in a permanent form, print serves a variety of purposes in our society. The way in which printed information is read should vary depending upon the purposes for which we read. Consider for a moment the different types and contexts of print: books (modern romance novels versus *War and Peace*), newspapers (*National Enquirer* versus the *New York Times*), magazines (*Pro Wrestling Review* versus *Time* or *Newsweek*), "environmental" print such as signs or labels, and advertisements — the list goes on. Each of these examples may be read for a variety of purposes. Most students, however, do not adjust their reading strategies and their attention according to the nature of what they are going to read and what they expect to bring away from that reading. Your students should read their social studies textbook, for example, differently from the way they read a story. There are differences in the strategies for approaching these different types of reading material just as there are differences in the way we analyze, evaluate, and respond to them. One of your responsibilities will be to teach your students *directly* how to determine the purposes of reading different types of material and how to adjust their reading strategies accordingly.

Of course, we are not just consumers of print; we create it as well. Students will become better at critical reading and thinking as they write, as they come to understand how writers go about their craft, and as they come to think of themselves as authors. In presenting ideas, a writer must provide much more explicit information than if he or she is communicating face-to-face. Not only must the writer's ideas be clearly expressed, but the relationships among the ideas, how they go together, must be clear. A writer must do a better job, in other words, of creating the context for the information than if he or she were talking face-to-face with another person. In a classroom context in which lots of reading and writing is going on, your students will gradually gain control over the conventions of writing as they understand better the perspective of their audience. Your students will become readers of their own writing and discover the power of writing to extend and elaborate their own thinking. The students will develop a truer sense of themselves as they discover their own "voice" in writing — and they will discover in a basic sense who they really are.

Electronic Media and Film

Television

Television ranks as one of the most widespread and pervasive phenomena of our culture. It has unquestionably affected the way our society has viewed itself and understood other societies. Television has brought the nation and on occasion the world together in times of joy and in times of tragedy. Because it has done so with immediacy and vivid detail, its effect is immediate and powerful. Television is also the primary means by which many other nations have come to understand our nation — for better or for worse.

Of course, television is not without critics. There is no question that television has the potential to provide information of high quality. However, critics have charged that there is far too much violence on TV, that far too many questionable values are portrayed, that there are far too many misleading commercials, and far too little quality programming. Neil Postman (1979) referred to television as the "first curriculum" in children's education because of the simple fact that children spend more time watching television than they spend in the classroom. According to Postman, television is therefore *the* most influential educating medium in our society. Though a moderate amount of television viewing appears to be more beneficial to students than no television at all, research has established that students who do poorly in school watch considerably more television than do average or above-average students. This leaves less time for other activities that can engage and challenge students who do not do well in school. And of course these students are not likely to be readers, much less writers.

As with most sources of information, the critical issue with respect to television is the quality of the viewing time; this includes the quality of the programs that children actually watch as well as whatever discussion occurs before, during, and after a program is viewed. Parents and teachers can help children respond critically to programming and get them to think about what they have just seen or soon will see. As a teacher, you will probably not use television to a great extent in your classroom, but you will spend time teaching your students how to become critical viewers.

Part of understanding any medium critically involves working in that medium. Just as your students will become critical readers in part by writing, so can they become critical television viewers in part by creating their own television programs and commercials. Many schools now have portable, easy-to-use video recorders, so these projects are becoming considerably easier to do in schools.

The research into the effects of television is revealing and at times surprising. Susan Neuman is a researcher who for a number of years has studied the effects of television viewing on reading. One of her recent studies (1988) examined data from the 1984 National Assessment of Educational Progress. Although she states that more precise measures of TV viewing and reading may eventually yield different information, she did find some consistent patterns.

For example, watching two to four hours of television a day does not appear to affect students' reading test scores. Watching more than four hours does, however. Moreover, television viewing does not seem to "displace" other activities such as leisure reading, sports, or spending time with friends.

Are you surprised by the finding about leisure reading? Apparently, leisure reading and television viewing each address different needs in children. So, rather than ranting and raving about how television has infringed on time that children would otherwise spend reading (which, as the parent of three children, I certainly have done), we should heed Neuman's observation that "... children actively seek reading on the basis of perceived enjoyment rather than as a substitute for television" (Neuman, 1988). If your students are not turned on to reading, in other words, your challenge as a teacher is clear!

Film

Like television, film or cinema offers great potential for high-quality creations. The number of films that are intended for children is now greater than ever, and many of these are truly top-flight in quality. Interestingly, most of these high-quality films never reach the theaters; however, they are available on videocassette.

Just a few years ago, we either had to pay to see a film in a theater or wait until a film might appear on television, in which case it was edited and interrupted by commercials. But now — because a large number of homes have videocassette recorders (VCRs) — children have access to films on an unprecedented level. This access may be beneficial if they are able to see more quality films; it may, on the other hand, be detrimental if they see films intended for older audiences.

As with television, the quality of the experiences with film is what counts. You will probably show some movies in your classroom, either to provide students the opportunity to compare and contrast the film version with a book they have just read or to elaborate their background knowledge about a particular topic or event. Also, some films will be valuable simply because they can provide students with a truly aesthetic experience. Talk with your students before and after a viewing — beforehand priming their curiosity and observation, and afterwards engaging them in reflection on why and how a particular film influenced them.

Radio

For elementary students, radio is primarily a source of entertainment, offering music and, to a lesser degree, role models of a sort in the persons of disc jockeys. However, radio holds a great deal more potential than this. Radio continues to supply the same news and information as television and does so probably better than it has ever done before. Some of the best and most analytical news programs are on radio. Despite the attention commanded by television, we can still use radio as a valuable source of information and of learning.

As we will explore in Chapter 5, students can begin to make comparisons between television and radio and between print and radio and reflect on the differences in how they experience and react to information in the different media. Unlike print, radio controls the flow of information; however, radio is like print in that it allows the person receiving the information to construct his or her own images. Because the images are the listener's own, they are often richer and more meaningful than they would be if they had been provided by television or film. You will be able to help most upper elementary students appreciate this fact, as well as to understand its implications for their own learning apart from television and film.

As far as quality programming is concerned, radio is offering more all the time, particularly on educational or public radio stations. A few years ago, for example, an extremely entertaining production of *Star Wars* was aired on National Public Radio. On the level of critical thinking, your students can interact with an important broadcast by thinking beforehand about what they already know regarding the topic and reflecting afterwards on what was presented. This "before, during, and after" sequence is one that I will emphasize throughout the book, because students' involvement with and understanding of any medium occurs not only during the time they are actually engaged with it, but before and after as well.

Computers

It has been said that our society is in the midst of a "computer revolution." The tremendous advances in hardware design, for example, have made microcomputers widely available and laptop computers a reality. Similar advances have occurred in software design. At the elementary school level, computer programs have been designed to handle everything from reinforcing skills, teaching reading comprehension strategies, word processing, and accessing sources of information over modems to using a spreadsheet format to organize information for content area study. Computers can interface with videodiscs to help make a novel, a scientific phenomenon, a tour of a museum, or a historical period "come alive." Not only can computers function as tutors and tools in the classroom but as "tutees" as well (Maddux, 1989). That is, students can *teach* the computer to do things, and in the process extend and elaborate their own concepts. Computers have come a long way, in other words, from the early Univacs that ran on vacuum tubes and took up a whole room.

At present, most schools are caught somewhere betwixt and between the promise and the reality of computers. Although students can learn to interact with information in new ways through the application of computer technology, there is rarely enough money to buy the number of units to make regular use of computers in

the classroom feasible. Most schools have opted for a computer lab in which students are scheduled, usually as an entire class at the same time.

Even though most schools cannot purchase enough computers for every classroom, in the long run computers will certainly be one of the most powerful tools available to us as teachers. With time, prices should come down. In the meantime, as educators we should be familiar with the basics of operating and using microcomputers and should involve our students as much as possible with computers, thus preparing our students as well as we can for a time when computers will be widespread in all facets of education and the workplace. For the present, microcomputers may be most helpful to students as word processors. As your students become "keyboard literate," they will appreciate the ease afforded by word processing in all phases of writing.

Social Relationships

Much of the information that individuals glean from their environment occurs when they are talking with others. Talking is a way of finding out about what we know (Galda, 1984). In a world that increasingly involves a constant flow of information electronically conveyed in bits and pieces, students will need to learn how to work together to address the myriad challenges of a truly complex local and global society. These collaborative efforts will often depend on face-to-face communication. Children start out learning much about their world this way, of course, but schooling has traditionally redirected this natural inclination. This situation needs to change.

As Douglas Barnes noted, "Speech makes available to reflection the processes by which [children] relate new knowledge to old. *But this possibility depends on the social relationships, the communication system, which the teacher sets up*"

(Barnes, 1976, emphasis added). Barnes noted that "Through your interaction with children you will be helping them [put] old familiar experience into words in order to see new patterns in it" and "make sense of new experience by finding a way of relating it to the old" (Barnes, p. 83). The process Barnes described is what we have already referred to, in other words, as "making meaning."

A theme I will return to again and again in this text is that most learning either occurs in a social context or is influenced in some way by social contexts. As Deborah Rowe succinctly expressed it, "Social interaction acts as a frame for what and how individuals will learn" (Rowe, 1989, p. 312). Other researchers have noted that children come to understand written language better — its conventions and its meaning — through social interaction (Dyson, 1989; Rowe, in press).

Social relationships always occur in a context that is governed by certain conventions, even though these conventions are often known only tacitly or subconsciously (see Chapter 2). In addition to the context of the family and other adults, there is the context of the student's peers, and there is the context of the classroom.

Smith (1981) pointed out that, in this classroom context, children are "learning all the time" — important information is being conveyed regardless of what the teacher is doing and how he or she is doing it. Researchers have only recently begun to examine carefully the nature of the interaction among students in classrooms as well as the impact of this interaction on the nature and extent of children's learning (Cazden, 1988; Cohen, 1986; Fillion and Brause, 1987; Rowe, in press). This research underscores the observation that the more humans communicate face-to-face, the more they learn. People have more opportunities in this context to express themselves and gauge the effect on others as well as to interpret the ideas expressed by others. The exciting challenge of the classroom is to set up an environment that encourages productive interaction, so that each child's natural propensity to communicate is directed toward both the content and the processes of learning. Speaking and listening about what one knows are bridges to writing and reading, and eventually, to conversing with oneself, and thereby learning, through writing and reading.

Implications for the Dynamic Teaching of the Language Arts

Let's pull together the factors that you will be thinking about as a teacher in the elementary language arts classroom. As we have seen, your students will be operating within several embedded contexts, including that of the school and of the classroom. Each student will be bringing to the classroom knowledge and language that are shaped in part by the outside world and in part by the school. The factors that shape knowledge and language include the sources of information I have just discussed — social interaction with peers and adults, electronic media, print, and film. You will be drawing upon these shaping factors as you further develop your students' topical, procedural, and self-knowledge.

Learning and the learning environment are complex. It is not possible to try to manipulate only one of the variables in this equation; all must be considered and each one will affect the others. Part of the challenge to you as a teacher will be to

One of your challenges as a teacher will be to create a positive learning environment in which students feel free to take risks and to stretch themselves in language and in thought. (© Elizabeth Crews/The Image Works)

create a positive learning environment in which students feel free to take risks — to stretch themselves in language and in thought. Another part of the challenge will be to manage effectively the interaction among the many variables in this complex environment. You will set up the learning environment and you will conduct activities — some involving direct teaching, some indirect or informal — through which the interaction will most effectively occur.

Quite a number of language arts educators, myself included, suggest that the learning environment you create — the context of the classroom — should first and foremost involve *meaningful* speaking and listening, reading, and writing. This type of classroom environment, in which the freedom to communicate and to take risks is developed and encouraged, does not imply an unmanaged classroom, without goals or purpose. Freedom to learn in any type of social group involves respect for others, and you should manage your classroom in a way that nurtures an organized approach to learning until such time as the students are able to assume primary responsibility for their own learning. *You* should be the prime mover in this undertaking and yet do so with tact and respect. Elizabeth Cohen noted that this will free you "from the necessity of constant supervision and allow the use of professional skills at a much higher level" (Cohen, 1986, p. 52).

Part of the way you can use your skills at a higher level will involve direct and indirect, or informal, teaching. *Direct teaching* refers to the organized, systematic presentation of topical, procedural, and self-knowledge. A direct teaching format is usually understood to include modeling, practice, and "real world" application stages. As teachers, we are providing direct knowledge of a specific skill or type of knowledge and the vocabulary with which to discuss that skill or knowledge.

Direct teaching involves linking new information to what the students already know and it involves explicitly telling the students what is to be learned and why. You then model — demonstrate for your students — whatever is to be learned, involve students in applying this information under your guidance, and summarize what has been introduced. Students then practice what has been taught, gradually applying the new knowledge on their own. This sequence allows you to monitor the degree to which the students are coming to understand the new knowledge.

How detailed a direct teaching lesson is depends on your purpose and your students' needs. As we will see, the lesson may range from a simple statement to the students on through to a more systematic presentation. Direct teaching will be a powerful tool in your professional repertoire, but it should be used judiciously — far too often it is overused and applied across the board in all learning situations (Slavin, 1989). Direct teaching is appropriate for many students in many situations, but not for all students in all situations. When you determine that a direct teaching technique is appropriate, you may use it to teach topical knowledge — specific content — as well as to model or demonstrate for your students how to apply specific knowledge. The focus of direct teaching techniques can be as specific as teaching how a particular prefix combines with different base words to form new words, or as general as modeling effective strategies for reading a chapter in a textbook or organizing an essay.

You will also be teaching "indirectly," or more precisely, informally. In general, you will be doing this by arranging the environment and occasionally setting up the context in ways that are likely to lead to certain understandings. More specifically, you will respond to situations and questions as they occur, sometimes providing more information and feedback, sometimes less, and sometimes you will simply provide an appropriate and encouraging nudge along a particular learning path. Whereas direct teaching is usually planned, informal teaching is often more spontaneous, based on a student or students' needs at a particular moment. Throughout the text, I will provide examples of appropriate direct and informal teaching techniques and guidelines.

Prospective and practicing teachers often find it hard to dispel an idealized conception of what a teacher should be. Part of this idealized conception portrays the teacher as all-knowing, a fount of all knowledge and wisdom. This of course is an unattainable goal. Although they are aware of how impossible it is to realize this goal, many teachers still measure their own self-worth and ability against this myth. Obviously, teachers *should* be quite knowledgeable, and they should be able to teach much content and many strategies directly. But the teacher should also be a *learner* (Calkins, 1983, 1986; Graves, 1983; Heath, 1983).

Teachers — just like children — are learning all the time. Although we should not be reluctant to share our knowledge, neither should we be reluctant to say when we do not know or are uncertain about something. Whenever this occurs, we can provide a first-rate example of what to do when you do not know: we can demonstrate how to go about finding the answer. Moreover, when we think of ourselves as learners, we are recognizing that, by definition, our students have something to teach us. And as we now know, children learn more about what they know when they talk about what they know.

As you read in professional educational journals and books, you may notice an ongoing debate involving "student-centered" versus "curriculum-centered" instruction. This debate revolves around the role of the teacher: How much control should the teacher exercise over what the students do, and how much of a role should the students have? A related issue is the role of published instructional materials in the classroom. A teacher who uses these materials is often described as "curriculum-centered" rather than "student-centered."

These types of issues are never either/or, and it is important that you realize this from the outset. Throughout this book I will try to give you a balanced perspective on these issues — what I believe will be a *realistic* approach that will allow you and your students the opportunity to realize a maximum learning and teaching potential.

I will be advocating the type of teacher who, above all else, is tuned in to the students, allowing and supporting their active involvement in their own learning. This type of teacher invites students to take risks with their learning, to question, to wonder, to actively explore and experience the thrill of discovery. I will be advocating the type of teacher who will combine his or her developing creativity with a full understanding of when and how to select activities to address specific instructional ends. Often such a teacher creates these activities and instructional units; often he or she pulls from published materials. Such a teacher knows that many published materials offer little more

than "busy work," but that many such materials also offer important and productive tasks. Good teachers know the difference and choose accordingly.

Teachers can inadvertently become enslaved by published instructional programs and by educational fads and labels. All these will come and go, but the type of teaching I'm advocating will always be a reassuring constant.

You will find ongoing support for this type of teaching by joining one or more professional organizations; you may join as a student member. Those most directly related to your interests as an elementary-school teacher of the language arts are the following:

- *National Council of Teachers of English* (NCTE)
  1111 Kenyon Road
  Urbana, IL 61801
- *International Reading Association* (IRA)
  800 Barksdale Road
  PO Box 8139
  Newark, DE 19714-8139
- *American Library Association*
  50 E. Huron Street
  Chicago, IL 60611

As a member of one or more of these organizations, you will be exposed to the most up-to-date journals and professional books that will enable you to keep up with cutting-edge developments in theory and practice. In addition, you should attend local NCTE and IRA meetings and conferences. These are affiliations you will want to continue when you become a professional teacher.

Throughout the year, you will be demonstrating for your students how to be a good, sensitive learner. In the process, you will also be delightfully surprised how much you really can learn about your students' world and about them as individuals, which will in turn make you a more effective and sensitive teacher. The learning cycle is complete!

You will also be a reader and a writer with your students. They will see you using these abilities every day in a meaningful way. You will share with the students your excitement about a particular book or story you are reading. Much of your reading will be books appropriate for your students — good children's literature — but even though you are an adult, you will rarely fail to be excited, moved, and motivated by these books. Because such experiences demonstrably make a difference in your life, your students, however reluctantly at first, will come to appreciate how such experiences can make a difference in their lives.

With respect to reading and writing, then, you will have a dual responsibility: to teach so that your students will not only apply reading and writing skills in their day-to-day activities but so that they will use these skills to reflect on important and urgent issues, extending their awareness of the issues so they can eventually act upon them appropriately. As we will explore in Chapters 7, 8, and 9, the sense individuals make of themselves, their world, and their place in that world depends greatly upon the texts with which they will interact and what the individuals are able to make of those texts.

In a nutshell, the following three guidelines will determine how, what, and when you teach directly and informally. In other words, these guidelines should facilitate the effective and dynamic teaching and learning of the language arts.

1. Organize your classroom to facilitate meaningful interaction among your students.
2. Interact with your students so that they develop an awareness and understanding of how language and thinking affects them and their learning.
3. Help your students develop a commitment to and a stake in their own learning.

A CONCLUDING PERSPECTIVE

Your challenge as a teacher is to help your students develop the tools and the understanding so that each student can not only acquire a basic competence in the language arts but move considerably beyond this basic competence. Your students will then be able to communicate more knowledgeably and effectively. They will then be able to make sense of their world throughout their lifetimes in a considerably richer, more satisfying, and more meaningful way.

Because you are engaged in an enterprise no less complex than human beings themselves, you face a significant challenge. Your students may puzzle you and at times frustrate you, but if you approach the challenge with the necessary knowledge and a "principled" repertoire of strategies, your students will usually delight you — and you will teach them well. Moreover, the lives you will touch will be far greater in number than those who pass through your classroom. This is why, quite simply, you cannot be engaged in a more important or potentially rewarding enterprise.

A recent educational report offered the following observation:

If our standard of living is to be maintained, if the growth of a permanent underclass is to be averted, if democracy is to function effectively into the next century, our schools must graduate the vast majority of their students with achievement levels long thought possible for only the privileged few (Carnegie Forum, 1986, p. 3).

Your understanding and teaching of the language arts are essential to helping students attain these achievement levels. Does that sound like a tall order? Perhaps it is. Nonetheless, there are a great many teachers throughout the country accomplishing this goal. They are not doing it by standing in front of the classroom and lecturing day in and day out, insisting on absolute quiet and obedience, demanding the one right answer and error-free writing. Rather, these teachers are doing it by combining competent and deliberate direct and informal teaching with a learning environment in which students teach and learn from each other, in which students are shown how to take responsibility for much of their own learning, and in which students and the teacher are collaboratively engaged in seeking after and *transforming* knowledge. Teachers and students, together, are creating an environment in which the ideals of learning and understanding are actually being realized. You will not become such a teacher overnight — no one ever does. However, this book should be one resource that will help you become this kind of teacher.

I would like to close this chapter on a bit of a philosophical and encouraging note as you consider your role in the type of language arts classroom implied in this chapter. The classroom should be a place where all of your students can discern order out of their innumerable experiences and where each child can learn and take control of the strategies that will help him or her become an independent learner and thinker. *Meaningful* language must be continuously in use in the elementary classroom. All language in the classroom, verbal as well as gestural, should be conveying the right messages. Remember, children are learning all the time and we want to be sure they are receiving the right messages. Toward this end, the following general observations are offered.

When children are free to communicate, they are free to test their perceptions with others. They are able to expand and elaborate their knowledge because they are able to test it out and receive feedback. Their self-esteem and self-awareness are increased because they have the opportunity to teach their classmates and they come to respect and value the worth of their classmates as their classmates teach them.

When children are free to communicate, they are free to express their thoughts, unbridled, and to use writing in all its functions, not the least of which is as a means to understand themselves and their worlds more deeply.

When children are free to communicate, they explore whatever they read with a critical eye, yet are able to give themselves over to the richness of the world in the book and to live fully in a time and space beyond the immediate here and now.

They acquire a sense of ownership of the experience and make it a part of themselves forever; they discover that such freedom brings a perspective that is also beyond the here and now. They begin to understand actions and consequences, both trivial and significant. They gradually acquire a sense of themselves, of the world, and of their place in it.

When children are free to communicate, in other words, they are in control, and this sense of control and purpose is essential to a productive learning process.

REFERENCES

Applebee, A. (1987). Commentary: Studies of classroom practice, classroom interaction, and instructional materials: What have we learned? What needs to be done? In J. R. Squire (ed.), *The dynamics of language learning: Research in reading and English*. Urbana, IL: National Council of Teachers of English.

Banks, J. A. (1981). *Multiethnic education: Theory and practice*. Boston: Allyn and Bacon.

Barnes, D. (1976). *From communication to curriculum*. New York: Viking Penguin.

Calkins, L. (1983). *Lessons from a child: On the teaching and learning of writing*. Portsmouth, NH: Heinemann.

Calkins, L. (1986). *The art of teaching writing*. Portsmouth, NH: Heinemann.

Carnegie Forum on Education and the Economy (1986). *A nation prepared: Preparing teachers for the 21st century*. Chicago.

Cazden, C. (1988). *Classroom discourse*. Portsmouth, NH: Heinemann.

Cohen, E. (1986). *Designing groupwork: Strategies for the heterogeneous classroom*. New York: Teachers College Press.

Cole, M., & Griffin, P. (1987). *Contextual factors in education: Improving science and mathematics education for minorities and women*. Madison, WI: University of Wisconsin, School of Education, Wisconsin Center for Education Research.

Dillon, R., & Sternberg, R. (eds.) (1986). *Cognition and instruction*. Orlando, FL: Academic Press.

Downing, J., & Valtin, R. (eds.) (1985). *Language awareness and learning to read*. New York: Springer-Verlag.

Dyson, A. H. (1989). *Multiple worlds of child writers: Friends learning to write*. New York: Teachers College Press.

Fillion, B., & Brause, R. (1987). Research into classroom practices: What have we learned and where are we going? In J. R. Squire (ed.), *The dynamics of language learning: Research in reading and English*. Urbana, IL: National Council of Teachers of English.

Galda, L. (1984). The relations between reading and writing in young children. In R. Beach & L. S. Bridwell. *New directions in composition research*. New York: Guilford Press.

Garner, R. (1987). *Metacognition and reading comprehension*. Norwood, NJ: Ablex.

Goodman, K. (1986). *What's whole in whole language?* Portsmouth, NH: Heinemann.

Goodman, K., & Goodman, Y. (1981). Whole language comprehension-centered reading curriculum. Occasional Paper #1, Program in Language and Literacy, Tucson, AZ: University of Arizona.

Graves, D. (1983). *Writing: Teachers and children at work*. Portsmouth, NH: Heinemann.

Havelock, E. (1982). *The literate revolution in Greece and its cultural consequences.* Princeton, NJ: Princeton University Press.

Heath, S. B. (1983). *Ways with words: Language, life, and work in communities and classrooms.* New York: Cambridge University Press.

Hirsch, E. D. (1987). *Cultural literacy.* Boston, MA: Houghton Mifflin.

Maddux, C. (1989). *LOGO in the schools.* Haworth Press.

McLuhan, M. (1964). *Understanding media: The extensions of man.* New York: McGraw-Hill.

Neuman, S. B. (1988). The displacement effect: Assessing the relation between television viewing and reading performance. *Reading Research Quarterly, 23,* 414–440.

Olson, D. (1977). From utterance to text: The bias of language in speech and writing. *Harvard Educational Review, 17* (3), 257–281.

Palincsar, A. S., Brown, A. L., & Campione, J. C. (1989). Discourse as a mechanism for acquiring process and knowledge. Paper presented at the American Educational Research Association, March.

Postman, N. (1979). *Teaching as a conserving activity.* New York: Delacorte Press.

Rowe, D. (1989). Author/audience interaction in the preschool: The role of social interaction in literacy learning. *Journal of Reading Behavior, 21* (4), 311–349.

Rowe, D. (in press). *Preschoolers as authors.* Norwood, NJ: Ablex.

Scardamalia, M., & Bereiter, C. (1986). Writing. In R. Dillon & R. Sternberg (eds.), *Cognition and instruction.* Orlando, FL: Academic Press.

Slavin, R. (1989). PET and the pendulum: Faddism in education and how to stop it. *Phi Delta Kappan* (June), pp. 752–758.

Smith, F. (1981). *Essays into literacy.* Portsmouth, NH: Heinemann.

Tannen, D. (ed.) (1982). *Spoken and written language: Exploring orality and literacy.* Norwood, NJ: Ablex.

Toffler, A. (1970). *Future shock.* New York: Random House.

Tunmer, W., Pratt, C., & Herriman, M. (eds.) (1984). *Metalinguistic awareness in children.* New York: Springer-Verlag.

Wells, G. (1987). *The meaning makers.* Portsmouth, NH: Heinemann.

Weinhert, F. E., & Kluwe, R. H. (eds.) (1987). *Metacognition, motivation, and understanding.* Hillsdale, NJ: Lawrence Erlbaum Associates.

Yaden, D., Jr., & Templeton, S. (eds.) (1986). *Metalinguistic awareness and beginning literacy: Conceptualizing what it means to read and write.* Portsmouth, NH: Heinemann.

2 Thought and Language

FOCUSING QUESTIONS

- Why do we say that children are "hypothesis testers"?
- Describe the three patterns that characterize children's development in thought and language. Why are these characterized as "universals" in the development of children?
- How do we develop our concepts and the relationships among concepts? What is the role of spoken language in this development?
- What are the three "systems" of language and how does context influence their use?
- What can adults do to support language development in the preschool years? What are the implications of this for what adults — teachers — do in the elementary school years?

Cindy, a seventeen-month-old girl sitting in her stroller next to her mother in the line at the grocery store checkout counter, points to the male checker and squeals, "Daddy!"

Thirty-two-month-old Brian proudly announces to a visitor, "I wented to poddy by myse'f!"

Kirstin, a five-year-old girl, confidently tells her older brothers that "Tyrannosaurus rex got his name because he goes around and wrecks things!"

Michelle, aged 6, informs her mother that "Once you know someone, you can never unknow them."

INTRODUCTION

In Chapter 1, children were described as "meaning makers" (Wells, 1986) who are "learning all the time" (Smith, 1981). These excerpts from children's speech help us see how they are constructing their meaning and their language. In this chapter, we will examine how this meaning and language are made by taking a brief excursion through the nature and the development of thought, or cognition, and language. As you teach your students about the language arts and how to use them, you will be building on this foundation and stretching your students' capacities for thought and language.

I would like to suggest at least three reasons why you should examine the development of thought and language in young children:

First, in order to facilitate the development of thought and language in elementary-school children, you should know what they have already learned and how they have learned it — the content and contexts of their learning.

Second, the ways children acquire language and develop thought in the early years have strong implications for the way you should set up the learning environment in your classroom and what you should be able to accomplish in this environment.

Third, because you will understand much of *what* children learn in the preschool years, you should be able to identify several common understandings and abilities that the children appear to develop. Although individual children are very different on the surface, when it comes to learning about language and literacy, all children share some striking similarities.

Children's development is determined by their biology and by their environment. Biology ensures that the mind of a child has a tremendous potential for learning. The environment — parents or other caretakers, siblings, other children, and teachers, all of whom reflect one or more cultures (see Chapter 1) — will in large part determine the degree to which this potential is realized. The development of intelligence, in other words, is an interpersonal process (Trevarthen, 1974).

Harste, Woodward, and Burke (1984) have spoken of a fundamental challenge for language arts teachers: to develop the *communication potential* of children. This communication potential is built upon a complex and impressive network of knowledge about language and the world that all children possess. In the preschool years most of this knowledge is at a tacit or subconscious level; as children grow and develop they are able more and more to think about this knowledge — and to think about thinking — on a conscious level.

Much of this conscious knowledge will develop because of *your* efforts. The tacit knowledge the children bring to school has developed in an informal, more "natural" context. Although you will be establishing as natural a context as you can in your classroom, you will also be helping the children to extend their knowledge of language and their ability to use language in direct and systematic ways — helping your students to become aware of and reflect *explicitly* on language and on thought.

In this chapter I will present the essential information about cognitive and linguistic development. I will start by presenting some common principles — the similarities that emerge from investigations of children's development. I will then present the types and nature of various systems of language, and hope to convey an appreciation for the way in which children construct their linguistic and cognitive world. Next, I will examine the development of thought and language as they occur throughout the stages of childhood. Although this examination will be brief, it will reveal processes that will continue throughout the school years and which you will nurture.

Foundations of Thought and Language: The Communication Potential

Our brains are already "programmed" at birth to follow certain paths of development. This programming is our neurobiological heritage. However, this programming also allows for a marvelous flexibility, so that each individual can incorporate and adapt to a wide range of experiences.

What are the characteristics of our brains that help determine our early growth in thought and language? These characteristics also help determine the ways in which school-age children and adult learners act upon and learn from their world. Bussis, Chittenden, Amarel, and Klausner (1985, p. 12) have noted the following characteristics:

- The brain constructs perceptions and thought, as opposed to behaving like a sponge.
- The brain's central function is to create meaning.
- Meaning arises through the perception and interpretation of patterns, or relationships, in events.

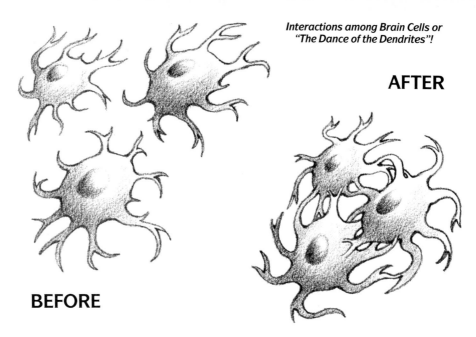

*Interactions among Brain Cells or
"The Dance of the Dendrites"!*

AFTER

BEFORE

◼ Anticipation and intention exert a directing influence on perception and interpretation.

In other words, our brains are not passive. They are always active — perceiving, interpreting, *making meaning* of what's "out there." The nature, quality, and anticipation and intention of the meaning we make critically depends on the type of information we receive — and the way it is presented. Our brains are built to organize and use information in exquisitely effective ways. Much of this information comes from the outside — from teachers — and can affect the nature of the knowledge that each one of us constructs and how we feel about that knowledge.

Learning has a very real basis in the neurobiology of our brains. After birth, a child's brain does most of its developing by the time the child is five years of age; in fact, between the ages of two and five, the child's brain will increase from 75 percent to 90 percent of its adult weight. This increase is not in number of brain cells but primarily in the *interconnections* among these cells. These interconnections are established as a result of *learning* — by actively interacting with the physical and social environment. This process, by the way, is not limited to children. As you acquire new information and construct new knowledge, you are also establishing new connections among your brain cells.

There appear to be some universal features in the development of cognition and language. Just as most children learn to crawl, walk, and run at certain ages — or at least in a fairly typical order — children around the world usually begin to talk at a certain age and to follow a similar pattern of cognitive development, regardless of their language or culture. Much of this development is biologically determined; children's initial cognitive and language development "just happens" as the children interact with their physical and social environment.

Before investigating this pattern of development, I should point out that recent research suggests that "intelligence" — the concept according to which our brains are usually measured — is *not* fixed, even though it is, to a degree, most certainly based on our biological endowment. Gardner (1983) offers a comprehensive and informed description of the nature of intelligence or, as he maintains, *intelligences*. He suggests that there are six different types of intelligences: linguistic, logical-mathematical, spatial, musical, bodily-kinesthetic, and personal. See Table 2.1 for a further explanation of these intelligences.

All of us possess each of these intelligences to varying degrees. Occasionally one of us is exceptionally endowed in one of these types of intelligence and on rare occasions an individual may be gifted in more than one type.

What are the implications of Gardner's theory of multiple intelligences for education in general and the language arts in particular?

First, our challenge as educators is to develop as much of the whole child as we are able. The cultural backgrounds of some of your students may place greater or lesser value on different intelligences (for example, on musical or on personal intelligence) than does the predominant culture. Teachers should be aware of, sensitive to, and motivated toward developing all these intelligences. In this way, more of the communication potential of each child can be developed.

Second, these multiple intelligences provide the resources that can be explored, reflected upon, and developed in large part through the language arts. As a teacher, therefore, you should be concerned with each type of intelligence. At present the prevailing culture of most schools will emphasize primarily only a few of these

TABLE 2.1 THE NATURE OF MULTIPLE INTELLIGENCES

TYPE OF INTELLIGENCE	DESCRIPTION	EXAMPLE
Linguistic	Sensitivity to language and its use	Poet; effective public speaker
Logical-mathematical	Ability to manipulate symbolic information	Mathematician
Spatial	Ability to conceptualize and mentally manipulate objects	Architect, chemist, physicist
Musical	Sensitivity to rhythm, sounds, and ability to apply this sensitivity in creating and/or performing	Violinist, percussionist, composer
Bodily-kinesthetic	Sensitivity to movement, balance, timing	Tennis player, dancer, choreographer
Personal	Sensitivity to others and an ability to relate comfortably to people; also includes a sensitivity to one's own feelings	Therapist in clinical psychology; skilled teacher; religious leader

intelligences, but each type can and should be addressed and developed within the context of a comprehensive language arts program.

Thought and Language: Some Common Principles

Bissex (1980) noted three patterns that can be observed in the development of language and thought. As I will discuss later on, these patterns are reflected in the development of reading and writing as well. The three patterns are the "acquisition of universals before culture-specifics, development from global to differentiated and integrated functioning, and movement outward beyond the immediate in time and space and beyond our personal perspective" (Bissex, p. 200). These three patterns represent what is most important to learn and to apply in your study of the development of thought and language, for the patterns appear everywhere we look.

■ *Acquisition of universals before culture-specifics.*

Example: Children the world over will scribble pretty much the same way at a certain point in development; later the scribbling will mirror the characteristics of the writing system used in the particular culture in which the children are living (see Figure 2.1).

FIGURE 2.1

Language Influences on the Scribbles of Young Children
Source: Adapted from Figs. 7.1 and 7.2, "Multicultural Writing Samples" and "Uninterrupted Writing Samples," Jerome C. Harste, Virginia A. Woodward, and Carolyn L. Burke, *Language Stories & Literacy Lessons*. Adapted and reproduced by permission of Heinemann Educational Books, Inc., Portsmouth, NH.

The uninterrupted "writing" of three-year-old English, Hebrew or Arabic speakers looks much like this:

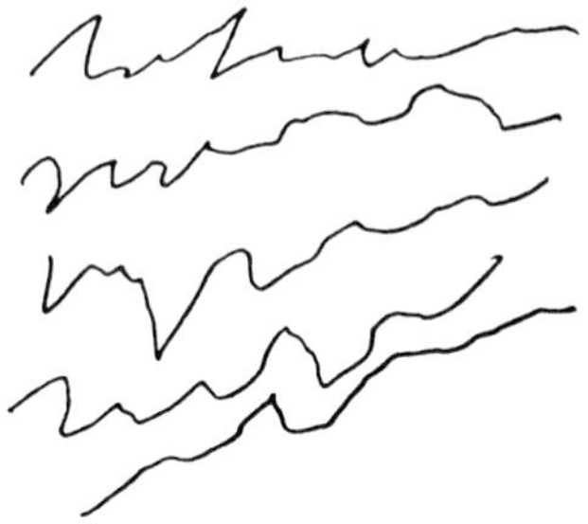

By four years of age, their writing looks like this:

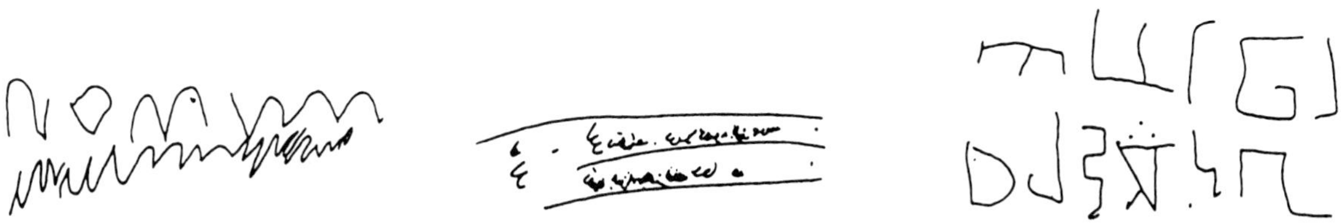

English   Arabic   Hebrew

■ *Development from global to differentiated and integrated functioning.*

Example: A young child is observed to "read" a book, though she is actually "reading" the pictures, not the print. Nevertheless, she is engaged in a "global" act of reading and, with time, she will learn about and attend to print and its function, to words, letters, and sounds. The process of reading becomes differentiated, and the knowledge about words and their letters and sounds becomes integrated, or meaningfully related.

■ *Movement outward beyond the immediate in time and space and beyond our personal perspective.*

Example: A four-year-old tells you that the moon he sees from the bathroom window is not the same moon he sees from his bedroom window. On the other hand, when he is watching the moon while traveling in the car, he will tell you that the moon is following him because it appears to be traveling over trees, fields, or buildings. Eventually, he will understand that *he* is the one doing the moving and that there is only one moon, which is relatively stationary!

Throughout these three patterns, children act as "hypothesis testers" — constructing hypotheses, trying them out, and receiving feedback about the way the language and the world around them works. Children cannot help but do so because, as we saw above, this is the way their brains work. Each child constructs his or her knowledge of the world. This process of knowledge construction begins early, with the visual, auditory, and tactile interaction between parent and child.

At first, of course, children are not consciously testing hypotheses, but at a tacit level their brains certainly are. At a later point in development this hypothesis testing will come under the child's conscious control (an important responsibility of the teacher), but it is nevertheless a universal process according to which children — indeed, all of us — make sense of our world (Smith, 1981).

Thought and Its Development

Cognitive development is quite complex, so we will touch only on the basics here. In a nutshell, this is a process that is the same for preschool children, older children, and adults: we set up *concepts* or categories; these concepts become differentiated, integrated, and come to form *schemas* (Bartlett, 1932; Pearson and Anderson, 1984), or broader mental representations of events, actions, and places.

The knowledge that young children develop is based primarily on their actions upon their world (Piaget and Inhelder, 1969). Children learn what things are and how things behave through *physically* acting upon and manipulating them. Children develop *concepts* — categories that represent their experience in the world. At first these concepts are broad — all four-legged animals are "doggie" or "bow-

Through experiences with their environment, preschool children develop knowledge, begin to establish concepts, and come to understand the actions and consequences of things happening in the world around them. *(© Patricia Reynolds/The Picture Cube)*

wow" — but with continued experience and interaction with others, children differentiate these concepts as they label the things and people in their world, and the relationships among these concepts become better integrated. This process of differentiation and integration continues throughout life. I will talk about this a bit more in the next section, on language development.

As preschool children establish and develop their concepts through interacting with their environment and the people in it, the children build up an understanding of various relationships. Some of these relationships include *causality, recurrence, nonexistence, location,* and who (the *agent*) is doing what (the *action*) to what or whom (the *object*). Children come to understand and anticipate the actions and consequences of things happening in the world around them. As Tannen (1979) expressed it, "based on one's experience of the world in a given culture (or combination of cultures), one organizes knowledge about the world and uses this knowledge to predict interpretations and relationships regarding new information, events, and experiences."

Researchers suggest that the way we organize and use our conceptual knowledge is based on *schemas.* Schemas include concepts but also extend to include actions, events, and locations — interrelated networks of concepts. Schemas reflect different ways of grouping and applying our conceptual knowledge. Here's an example: You of course have a concept of what a dog is and does, and this concept represents all of your experiences with dogs, but you also have different schemas for the actions, events, and locations in which dogs play a role: dog races, dog pounds, dog shows, walking the dog, and so forth. You have a schema for elementary classrooms, representing your experience with elementary classrooms, and this schema guides your expectations and interpretations of what goes on in such a classroom. You have a "basketball game" schema that helps you predict and interpret what goes on in a basketball game, whether you are watching a game in person, seeing one when you are changing channels on TV, or playing in the game. You have different schemas for textbooks, cooking, Ancient Egypt, space shuttles — obviously, the list is a very long one.

How many schemas you have constructed and how elaborate they are depend entirely on your experiences. Most of us do not stop to think explicitly about what we know about our schemas, but there are times when we probably should — when we deliberately set out to learn something and need to know what we *do* know so we can better understand what we *do not* know. You will be helping your students do this quite often in the classroom.

In preschool children, conscious thought is directed primarily to the world that the child has experienced directly. The child pays attention to one feature of a stimulus at a time. Toward the end of the preschool years the child is moving, as Bissex (1980) expressed it, "outward beyond the immediate in time and space and beyond [his or her] personal perspective." The child can simultaneously attend to more than one feature of a stimulus at a time: he or she can "*de*center," as Piaget termed it, to attend to *more* than one aspect of a stimulus array rather than centering on one aspect. For example, the child can attend to more than one letter in a word at a time or to another student's perspective on what is happening in a story that is being read to the children as a group. This broadening of perspective will continue well into the school years, and you will be involved in facilitating and directing it.

Because children are able cognitively to decenter, for most of the elementary school years a child is not tied to the immediate things, people, or events he or she perceives. Mentally, children can now perform operations involving sequencing, causality, and reversibility — operations that exist in the concrete, material world. Children *do* think abstractly, but the content of their abstract thinking is based on their concrete world. For example, children can understand the idea that socially inappropriate behavior has consequences, but the behavior and its consequences are tied to their concrete experience. For instance, they probably know that you do not steal from others because if you get caught you will get punished. Although the child can understand that the victim of the theft will be unhappy, the overriding deterrent is fear of punishment!

Beginning sometime during the fifth and sixth grades — from eleven to twelve years of age — a child's reasoning is applied to more truly abstract concepts. Now children are capable of mentally working out relationships and problems without seeing these relationships in the real world. In solving a problem a child is able to hold several aspects of the problem constant while varying one aspect at a time. For example, a sixth-grader can picture the planet Earth with the moon orbiting around it while he or she estimates the speed and course of a rocket launched from Earth so that it intersects the course of the moon. Children are able to apply this reasoning to moral situations as well, as for example in thinking about civil disobedience. Again, younger children would say that a civil law should not be broken because it is a law and you might get punished; older children are able to reason that it is permissible to break a civil law if it is wrong in moral terms. Older children can understand that the moral law says that all individuals have the right to eat where they wish, even though the civil law may say that certain groups may not eat in a restaurant.

Metacognition

As children decenter and develop a greater awareness of the perspectives of others, detaching themselves from the here-and-now, they are able to start becoming aware of their own thinking and of how they think. This ability is broadly termed *metacognition*. Metacognition is knowledge *about* thinking — the ability to think about thinking.

In general, metacognition becomes more important in the intermediate grades and beyond. One of our goals as teachers is to help our students develop their procedural knowledge and self-knowledge. Both of these are dependent upon metacognition, because students have to think about their thinking in order to be aware of what they need to know and how they need to go about acquiring that information. In order to *transform* their topical knowledge of the facts, to think critically, students need to be aware of the tools for such thinking and the contexts or situations in which these tools are applied.

Throughout the remainder of this text these tools or strategies are discussed. We will examine how you present, model, *teach* the process of enquiry through discussion groups, for example, and before/during/after reading and writing activities. With time, your students should internalize the nature and application of these strategic tools. As Vygotsky noted, "What the child can do today in co-operation, tomorrow [he or she] will be able to do on his [or her] own."

Language and Its Development

What Is to Be Learned?

The noted linguist Noam Chomsky attempted to explain how learners can produce and understand so many utterances that they have never before heard (Chomsky, 1965, 1975). His explanation in fact revolutionized the way scholars thought about language development. Another well-known linguist, Leonard Bloomfield, once wrote that language learning is "doubtless the greatest intellectual feat any one of us is ever required to perform" (Bloomfield, 1933, p. 29). Consider for a moment why this is so. Harste, Woodward, and Burke's description of the many ways language is used makes this quite clear:

> Language varies according to the topic, the persons involved, and whether it is written or spoken. The language used in church is different from the language used when talking with one's playmates; the language we find in books is different from the language we find on street signs. Language which sounds right at home may sound funny in church. Children learn naturally to make adjustments in their language by having many opportunities to be present in different kinds of settings where language is being used. Successful language users adjust their language to meet the demands of the setting in which they find themselves. (1984, p. xvi)

When we produce and comprehend language in natural settings, we are attuned primarily to the *meaning* that underlies speech or print. We are seldom aware of other aspects of language, even though different types of language *systems* interact to create and support meaning. These systems do not really function independently in normally developing language users, but by discussing the systems separately, we can gain a better understanding of language as a whole and better understand its development.

Language, as Harste, Woodward, and Burke (1984) point out, is a social event — it usually occurs between at least two individuals and it is learned in a social context. Of course, we can use language on our own when we think, read, and write, but its ultimate purpose is usually social — to communicate with others. Figure 2.2 represents the relationships among the different knowledge systems underlying language use.

Before we look at each system of language, let's get an overall feel for how the systems are related. All language occurs in a particular context — as Harste, Woodward, and Burke noted, this could be at church or at play, or for that matter in a college classroom. Not only does *context* refer to a setting or location but it also refers to what goes on in that location, as we saw in Chapter 1. This context can vary across spoken language situations — formal versus informal settings, for example, and whether the individuals involved are children or adults. The context can vary across written language as well — although written language shares much with spoken language, it is also different in significant ways.

Depending on our intentions, the context in turn usually determines how we use the systems of language. The socially appropriate use of language in a particular situation is termed *pragmatics* — the appropriate selection of words, sentence structure, and emphasis in speaking in a particular context.

Learning the tacit "rules" of pragmatics takes quite some time. The beginnings of this learning, however, lie in the first year of life (Halliday, 1975). Halliday identified seven interpersonal functions of language that are evident in the babblings of babies; these functions are also apparent in the utterances of older children as well as adults. In babies, the functions are identified by the context in which they

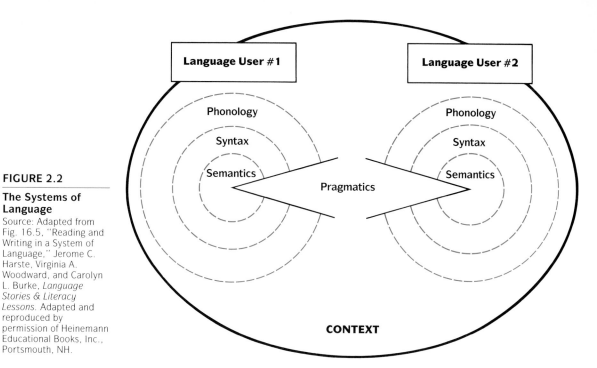

FIGURE 2.2

The Systems of Language
Source: Adapted from Fig. 16.5, "Reading and Writing in a System of Language," Jerome C. Harste, Virginia A. Woodward, and Carolyn L. Burke, *Language Stories & Literacy Lessons*. Adapted and reproduced by permission of Heinemann Educational Books, Inc., Portsmouth, NH.

occur, the baby's intonation patterns, and the babbles that the baby is producing. Halliday refers to this as a "protolanguage" and suggests that it is important for many reasons, not the least of which is its role in helping children "learn how to mean."

Paraphrasing in conventional English the child's intent within each function, Halliday suggests the following:

- *Instrumental:* "I want" (in reference to a toy that is out of reach).

- *Regulatory:* "Do as I tell you" (in reference to an action the child wishes the adult to perform).

- *Interactional:* "Me and you" (in reference to "special moments" shared between child and adult, as in tickling games).

- *Personal:* "Here I come" (in reference to the child's self and his or her "controlling" role in a particular situation).

- *Heuristic:* "Tell me why" (in reference to seeking information).

- *Imaginative:* "Let's pretend."

- *Informative:* "I've got something to tell you."

These functions of language become further differentiated as the child grows. As they develop the ability to decenter, children are capable of becoming aware of different contexts for language and the different social conventions that are considered appropriate in each context.

In Chapter 5, these functions will be examined in the context of speaking and listening in the elementary classroom.

Context and pragmatics help link the language systems together in a common purpose — they determine the ways that each speaker puts the three language systems to use (see Figure 2.2):

1. *Semantics* — How we express our meaning through words. Meaning lies at the core of the three language systems because it is always central to our intent in communication. Semantics also has to do with which features of our world are labeled with words; for example, many Native American languages of the southwestern United States have quite a number of words that refer to shades of brown, because such distinctions are important in a desert environment.

2. *Syntax* — How we structure our sentences by putting words and phrases together.

3. *Phonology* — How we pronounce the sounds, words, and phrases in our language. This includes the intonation patterns — the "ups" and "downs" — that flow across the words and phrases.

Because we will be dealing with these language systems throughout this book, I will take a little time here to explore each one further.

Semantics

As we saw in the case of children first learning about their world, the initial concepts children develop reflect their interactions with and physical manipulation of things in their real world. A child's initial definitions for objects are based very much on the physical attributes of things and, as we saw in the previous section, what the child can do to those things. As the child gains experience with language and with the world, the concepts underlying the words become refined and the child's definitions approximate more closely "standard" definitions. This does *not* mean that the child's initial definitions are "wrong" — just that we should be sensitive to how those definitions might vary from ours.

Many researchers in language development have noted children's tendency to overextend the range of things to which a particular word refers (E. Clark, 1973). For example, fifteen-month-old Gavin used his word *moont* to refer to the full moon, but he also used *moont* to refer to lamps and streetlights. These objects share common features with the moon — brightness, shape (somewhat), and being important at nighttime. With time, this large category of things becomes differentiated so that *moont* comes to refer only to the moon, and other verbal labels are used to refer to lamps and streetlights. Children may also occasionally differentiate between things in the sense that they restrict or "underextend" the meanings of words (Anglin, 1977; Carey, 1977, 1982). A child may use *fork*, for example, to refer only to small forks, not to large ones.

An important point to make about our semantic knowledge is that it is never fixed; it is always developing. As Moskowitz noted, "The meanings of words continue to expand and contract through adulthood, long after other types of language acquisition have ceased" (Moskowitz, 1978, p. 106). In the context of the classroom, this awareness should guide your introduction of new concepts and new vocabulary. Begin with familiar words for the students. In the context of a parent conference, you may say that a child is "good at figuring out words"; in discussing the same child with fellow teachers your terms will be more precise: "Sarah's knowledge of *structural analysis* is quite good, particularly of *prefixes.*"

In the next major section we will briefly explore the processes by which words are learned — the processes by which a child begins to construct a semantic network.

Syntax

Syntax usually refers to the order of words and phrases or clauses within a sentence. There are many ways in which words and phrases can be combined to form sentences, and language users already know just about all the ways. A language user knows, for example, that articles always precede nouns in English, that adverbs can precede or follow the verbs they modify, and how to turn an active sentence into a passive sentence ("Carrie squished the mango" becomes "The mango was squished by Carrie") or a declarative into an interrogative ("John broke the spatula" becomes "Did John break the spatula?"). A language user also knows how to embed a relative clause within a sentence ("I borrowed a magazine from Warren. The magazine is no longer published" becomes "The magazine *that I borrowed from Warren* is no longer published.") Language users may not always be certain of the labels for these different parts or the way the parts are assembled, but each user does have a tacit command of this knowledge.

The contexts of spoken and written language often determine the syntactic structures we use. For example, if you are speaking with a child who knows little English, you are likely to use active rather than passive sentences. When you teach writing, you will work with students whose sentences are short and rather "flat" to include more information while making the sentences "come alive": "I have three cousins" becomes, for example, "Ever since I can remember, I have had three crazy cousins who look like a bad dream."

Phonology

The *phonology* of a language refers to the sound system of that language. When we speak of the *phonological knowledge* of a speaker of that language, we are talking about how that speaker knows to articulate sounds and place stress or emphasis on words and phrases. Not surprisingly, most of this knowledge is tacit; human beings are not aware of what this knowledge is or how they apply it.

For example, chances are you are not aware that you pronounce the /p/ sound differently in the words *pill* and *spill* or the /k/ sound differently in *cot* and *keen*. In English, we treat the sounds as the same, but actually they are pronounced slightly differently. Some other languages treat these as quite different sounds. The difference between the *p* in *pill* and *spill* has to do with the way the air is released when each sound is articulated. On a tacit level you know how to pronounce these sounds differently, but on a conscious level this difference may never have occurred to you before.

The phonological knowledge that speakers of English possess about accent or stress placement within words helps the speaker to pronounce appropriately the italicized words in the following sentence: "The guitarist plans to *record* a new *record*." In the first *record* the stress is placed on the second syllable (re-CORD) and on the first syllable in the second *record* (REC-ord). In fact, with most words of more than one syllable, speakers must place stress appropriately within the word: re-DUC-tion, POP-ulate, em-PLOY.

Knowledge of stress placement within phrases and sentences, often referred to as *prosody,* allows speakers to utter such mundane sentences as "She bought a coat" with varying emphasis on the words. It is easy to become aware of how this knowledge works when you try placing stress on different words within the same sentence: Compare "She bought a *coat?*" (rather than a sweater) with "She *bought* a coat?" (rather than borrowing one) or "*She* bought a coat?" (rather than her mother buying one for her). Obviously, where you place strongest emphasis or stress reflects what you want highlighted, and it depends on your meaning as you are able to express it in particular contexts.

To summarize the relationships among the systems of language: One's intent within a particular context determines the appropriate social rules of language — pragmatics — which then influence the selection of words (semantics) and the types of sentence structure (syntax) and oral expression (phonology) used to convey meaning.

The Preschool Years

As with thought, the development of language is a marvelously complex phenomenon. Although we cannot delve into it in any type of depth here, we can get a feel for the complexity and for the general trends of language development by selectively examining aspects of this development. We can chart a child's language development by noting and studying the "errors" the child makes — by seeing how a young child's language varies from that spoken by older individuals. By studying the way a child's spoken language varies from a model, we can gain insights into the development of *written* language in young children as well. We will look at this more closely in Chapter 6.

Language development in young children seems to have a lot of the magical about it. Children continually amaze and delight us with the ways they express their ideas. We might refer to this as the "poetry" of young children's language. Some of the examples at the beginning of the chapter illustrate this. Young children have in fact been characterized as "poets" for many reasons (Egan, 1987). First, children's language often strikes us as poetic as they test their hypotheses about words and experiences. This testing helps children sort out the defining characteristics of concepts and the words that represent those concepts. For example, while riding in an old Volkswagen, Jason (age 3) pointed to the round speedometer and its needle and exclaimed, "That's a toothpick clock!" Kirstin (age 5) described a dancer's back-and-forth movements as being "backwards and thiswards."

A second poetic characteristic of young children's language is their sensitivity to rhythm and rhyme in oral language (Geller, 1985). Children enjoy repeating rhymes, often as an accompaniment to play (jump-rope jingles, for example), and making up spontaneous rhymes. Often, to adults' dismay, these rhymes have to do with "taboo" words concerning subjects such as using the bathroom.

A young child's oral language "world" can be a powerful springboard into literacy while at the same time providing a stimulating foundation throughout the elementary years for developing the child's imagination, humor, metaphorical thinking, and sense of narrative. Looking toward the elementary school years, Egan (1987) suggests that in our elementary curriculum we build on these features of "orality" so prevalent in preschool children's language. We will examine how we can in fact do this in Chapter 5.

My primary focus in this section will be on oral communication, but I will continue to remark on the interactive process between thought and language: pragmatics, semantics, syntax, and phonology all develop within and reflect this underlying interaction. In this regard, Wells (1981) commented that the first two years of life "provide the basis for breaking into language but, once acquired, language becomes a means of extending the range and complexity of thought" (Wells, p. 87). For this reason, I have divided the preschool period into birth to (approximately) two years and (approximately) two years to five years. Why end at five years? As Moskowitz has noted, "although many subtle refinements are added between the ages of five and 10, most children have completed the greater part of the basic language-acquisition process by the age of five" (Moskowitz, 1978, p. 92).

Birth to Two Years

In most babies, the first recognizable words of the native language have appeared by twelve months of age. These first words represent things and people that are important and interesting to babies: a particular child's pronunciations for the words *keys, doggie,* and *juice* are more likely to appear before words for *table, diaper,* or *chair,* the latter being things that are simply there and which are not particularly exciting objects in the young child's life.

How do children pick out the words in the stream of speech? Wanner and Gleitman (1982) suggest that *stressed syllables* are cues. The child tacitly picks up on these cues; they highlight the important words in speech and therefore the important objects in the environment. Parents also play the "name game," which involves asking "What's that?" and then providing the label (Ninio and Bruner, 1978). The name game usually occurs in the context of playing a game with the child or as an

Children learn their first words through active explorations in a social context with adults.
(© Paul Conklin/Monkmeyer Press Photo Service)

accompaniment to some other activity, such as taking a bath. Eventually the child understands at a tacit level that *things* have labels — *names* — and then the name game, and language development more generally, really takes off.

As children grasp, kick, suck, crawl, and eventually toddle about, their actions and the consequences of their actions represent *relationships* — location, causality, recurrence — and these various relationships come to define the early language structure of the child. Roger Brown (1973) described these relationships in terms of *agent-object, location, attribution,* and so forth. The terms that fill the agent-object or agent-action slots "map" or reflect the underlying relationships. Jerome Bruner (1975) suggested that it is this close correspondence between actions in the world and the language relationships that represent those events that help the child construct this early syntax. Lindfors (1980) gives a succinct example of this process: The "differentiation of actor and action is one that comes about through the child's increasingly varied physical interactions with an increasing range of objects and people" (Lindfors, p. 167).

Note the role of other *people.* These active explorations occur in a *social context.* Early on in the child's development the adult caretaker and the child jointly focus on the same object, and the young child is tacitly picking up on the following idea: "*You* (the adult) and *I* (the baby) are talking about *it* (whatever the adult and baby are jointly focusing their attention on). This is an important communication "triangle" that lays the foundation for language development within a social context.

Here are some characteristic utterances by children at this period: "Hat on ... Wear hat ... All gone." This period, toward the end of the second year, is termed (for obvious reasons) the "two-word" stage. Out of this stage, in which each word maps the relationships mentioned above, the "telegraphic" stage will develop. At that point, most children are into their third year.

Two Years to Five Years

"Telegraphic" speech is an appropriate label because, as in a telegram, only the content words are evident. *Function words* — those words that "glue" the content words together and express relationships among the words (for example, *the, and,* and *of*) — are usually not used, nor are inflectional endings such as *-ed, -ing,* and the plural *s.*

As children continue to experience their world, their utterances expand and change in marked ways and include the use of function words — the speech is no longer telegraphic. For example, expressions of relations that would have stood by themselves earlier, such as "I play" and "My game," are now combined: "I play my game." Moreover, each of these single-relation statements may be expanded: for example, "I can play" and "my own game."

Here is where we see the beginnings of language "extending the range and complexity of thought," as Wells put it. *What* children notice, *how* they notice it, and *why* and *when* they pay attention to it will usually depend on the conversations the children have with adult caretakers and with other children.

We should add to this the possibility of changing *organization* of the language on the part of children. Because the growth of a child's language between ages two and five is so much more complex syntactically than earlier and does not map real-world actions and reactions nearly so straightforwardly as in the "telegraphic" period, some researchers have suggested that this later language is based on a quite different organization within the brain. This reorganization results from "neurological changes in the learner that cause him to reinterpret linguistic evidence" (Wanner and Gleitman, 1982). Gleitman (1981) characterizes this as a "metamorphosis" view of language development — kind of like a tadpole's metamorphosis into a frog — rather than an evolutionary view.

Up to this point, the child's development has clearly been evidenced by increasing length of the child's utterances. Toward the end of the preschool years, however, you will notice that the key feature of language development is not length so much as increasing economy of expression. As they approach kindergarten age, children are better able to "enfold" syntactic structures within each other.

In general, children from ages two through five become increasingly sophisticated in their use of both semantics and syntax:

■ *Continuing growth in vocabulary.*

Even apart from all other language development, growth in vocabulary is astounding. By the time a child begins first grade, he or she has learned, on

*AT THE
TEACHER'S
DESK:
Observing
Language
Grow*

I would like to share a couple of personal observations. You might call them "home movies" because they involve two of my children. The observations illustrate some aspects of how children go about learning language and can offer implications for us as teachers of the language arts.

When my family and I first moved to Reno, Nevada, several years ago, we were struck by the beauty of the surroundings: the Sierra Nevada mountains, Lake Tahoe close by, and the Truckee River, originating in Lake Tahoe and flowing through the city. One morning we happened to be talking about this river as we were riding in the car. As we turned onto another street and the Truckee River came into view, a squeal burst from our 34-month-old daughter.

"Look!" she exclaimed. "There's the Turkey Liver!"

She had sufficient semantic knowledge in this context; what she still needed was the phonology!

Following is a different example illustrating semantic and syntactic distinctions. About eight months after my first child, Jason, was born, I began advanced graduate work. It seemed a wonderful, serendipitous opportunity to observe the development of thought and language first-hand as I studied about it in my coursework. Young children, I learned, "test hypotheses" about how language works, until they get it "right." Usually, this process takes some time, but with the pride and conceit of a first-time parent, I figured *my* child would somehow be different, and that *I* could move matters along more rapidly.

I well recall one of many such attempts. Jason had just stated, "My go outside," and I figured I could get him at least to say "*I* go outside." The interchange went something like this:

DAD: "Oh, *you* go outside?"
JASON: "Uh-huh. *My* go outside."
DAD: "No, Jason: *I* go outside." (About this time, I realized this was going to be harder than I at first thought!)
JASON: (excitedly): "*Daddy* go outside?"
DAD: "No, Jason. You should say '*I* go outside.'"
JASON: (impatiently, starting for the door): "*My* go outside!"

Oral language development among preschoolers holds many implications for learning in the elementary school years. What these two examples remind us is that children first assimilate information according to *their* theory of how the world works. The second example also reminds us that the process of children's testing a theory and then modifying it often takes quite a while. As teachers, therefore, we should keep in mind that, although we may think we are providing the best possible example of a concept — modeling it perfectly, providing appropriate feedback, and so forth — it may still take more time and more exposure before the child's hypothesis is truly modified.

the average, 5,000 to 6,000 words. Many of these words are learned through requests ("What that called?") and the "name game," but most are learned in the business of day-to-day interaction with the environment and with others.

As more and more words are acquired, children begin to include function words as well as inflectional endings such as -*ed, ing,* and the plural *s.* The -*ing* inflectional ending, which is pronounced pretty consistently in the language, appears first; it is followed by the past tense -*ed* and the plural *s.* As a child acquires expertise in using these forms in conventional ways, he or she is apt to overextend their application, just as is done with many words. For example, a child may pronounce *watched* correctly in the sentence "I watched TV this morning" but next week pronounce *watched* as *watchded;* the child may use *went* correctly this week but say *goed* or *wented* next week.

Such errors are evidence of growth. They do *not* mean the child is regressing. Rather, the errors are evidence that the child has moved beyond a single memorized item to a level at which he or she is now applying a rule that covers a number of words.

■ *The continuing expansion and development of utterances or sentences.*

From ages two to five, children learn how to phrase questions and express negative relationships. For example, the child now says "I *don't* want that" instead of the earlier "I *no* want that," and later still overextends the use of negatives in expressions such as "He can't have nothing" and "I never have none"). The child can also express more complex statements about relationships.

Questions, or *interrogatives,* can be fairly complex. Questions serve different functions, and the child must tacitly learn the distinctions among these functions. For example, questions can elicit yes/no responses, information, or express "polar" relationships ("Did Herbie sleep over last night, or the night before?"). Moreover, questions can be identical syntactically but represent more complex underlying relationships. As an example, Lindfors (1980) lists the questions "Where did you go?" "Why did you go?" and "When did you go?" Children will master these relationships in this order at different times in their development.

Language from this point on will allow children a means by which they can not only act upon their world but *reflect* upon those actions. Not coincidentally, this is when most children begin their formal schooling.

Herein lies the role of the teacher: You will play a pivotal role in facilitating this action and reflection. There is adventure but also inadvertent pitfalls in this role, for as Bridges, Sinha, and Walkerdine (1981) point out: "School as a context of learning not only provides new opportunities for developing knowledge and language; it can also be the occasion for mutual lack of comprehension between teachers and children" (Bridges, et al., p. 155). At all costs you will avoid this situation.

As Harste, Woodward, and Burke (1984) comment, "As teachers we can organize the social environment of the classroom to support the language user's perception, organization, and presentation of texts in reading and writing" (Harste, et al., p. 206). Such a social environment will guarantee that *meaningful* language use is going on — and that children are free to communicate.

The Contexts of Early Language Learning

Wells (1986) states that learning to talk should be thought of "as the result of a partnership between parents and other members of the community" and the child. Let's turn our attention more specifically to the contexts or situations in which this partnership occurs — in which young language learners interact with more knowledgeable language users — because these contexts and how we respond within them have definite implications for the elementary classroom as well.

Heath (1983), Au (1980), Wells (1981, 1986), and others have studied the characteristics of language use in homes reflecting different racial and socioeconomic groups. These researchers have found that the ways parents and other adults interact with children do differ. The social appropriateness of certain types of interactions — the *pragmatics* — differ from group to group. The *types* of interaction also vary. For example, in asking children to retell an event, some parents expect simply a literal account of what happened. On the other hand, other parents may ask for an explanation of the reasons underlying what happened. Still others, by their responses to the child, may encourage him to embellish the story by adding events and actions that were not a part of the original event.

On one hand, it is important to note that these differences in contexts do not lead to "better" language in some groups than in others. On the other hand, we must be aware of these differences because, as teachers, we must be aware of how we respond to children from cultural backgrounds different from ours. This issue will be explored in depth in Chapter 13.

Many studies have been conducted into the types of language caretakers *should* use with young children — should they restate what the child has said, for example, or expand and elaborate upon it? Such questions are usually too narrow, however. Roger Brown correctly defined the situation when he observed that "There is no set of rules of how to talk to a child that can even approach what you unconsciously know. If you concentrate on communicating, everything else will follow" (Brown, 1977). Similarly, Gordon Wells noted that "These are the conditions that foster language development: when one has something important to say, and other people are interested in hearing it" (Wells, 1986, p. 107).

Within this situation, what general factors facilitate language growth? Reviews of the research (Snow, 1977; Wells and Robinson, 1982) yield four recommendations:

- The amount or quantity of interaction between the child and adults is important.
- As much as possible, interaction should be one-to-one and should concern things that are important to the child.

- Clarity of expression should be attempted. Adults should rephrase and adjust the length of their utterances when necessary to ensure that they understand what the child is trying to say and can then respond appropriately and effectively to the child.
- In order to accomplish the preceding suggestions, adults absolutely must be good *listeners*.

Parents of young children and teachers of preschool children should be aware of these guidelines. However, because the recommendations are equally applicable to later years, they should be applied in elementary classrooms as well. Toward this end, Wells offered the following excellent guidelines (1986, p. 50):

- When the child appears to be trying to communicate, assume he or she has something important to say and treat the attempt accordingly.
- Because the child's utterances are often unclear or ambiguous, be sure you have understood the intended meaning before responding.
- When you reply, take the child's meaning as the basis of what you say next — confirming the intention and extending the topic or inviting the child to do so him- or herself.
- Select and phrase your contributions so that they are at or just beyond the child's ability to comprehend.

This last guideline may need further comment. So often we are at pains to make sure the child understands us that we oversimplify what we say. Remember, however, that the young child needs to hear where his or her language will be going, and by "stretching" the child's understanding a little — but not too much — we are providing this opportunity.

Written Language in Oral Language Development   In recent years, several researchers have investigated the role of written language in oral language development (for example, Olson, 1984). In addition to exposing the young child to written language in a comfortable and supportive context and laying the foundation for literacy development, these interactions, or "literacy events," involve parent and child in meaningful exchanges in which oral language is developed. Books serve as a "prop" for such interchanges (Sulzby, 1985; Yaden, et al., 1989). For example, parents point to pictures in the books, talk about the pictures, ask the child questions about the pictures, and discuss the story before, during, and after the reading.

These early literacy events are not necessary for the development of language, but they certainly do afford the valuable "partnership" time to which Wells refers. And perhaps more important in a literacy-based culture, these experiences introduce children to the *metalanguage* — the "language about language" — that eventually helps children become metalinguistically aware of these important concepts. Let's close this discussion of language development with a brief discussion of metalinguistic awareness.

Metalinguistic Awareness

Metalinguistic awareness is an important part of metacognition, or thinking about thinking (Downing and Valtin, 1984; Tunmer, Pratt, and Herrimann, 1984; Yaden and Templeton, 1986). Simply put, metalanguage is language that is used to talk about language. Most children will be able to talk about language for quite some time before they can think metalinguistically — that is, before they can think about language as an object.

Much of what usually goes on in kindergarten and first grade — indeed, throughout the primary grades during formal reading and writing instruction — involves using language to talk about language. Consider, for example, the terms *word, letter, sound, sentence, rhyme, vowel,* and *consonant.* These labels in effect let children know that there is a concept out there they need to pay attention to. Metalinguistic awareness will play an important role in children's developing knowledge about language and its various uses, both general and subtle.

A CONCLUDING PERSPECTIVE

It is important to spend time looking at the development of thought and language in the preschool child simply because the way that the brain is "wired" and the underlying processes at work in the construction of thought and language during these years continue throughout life. We must understand the beginnings of these processes if we are to understand how they function when the child begins formal schooling.

As they learn language and develop thought, children are meaning makers. Children cannot help but be, because that is how their brains work. In large part, because of their interaction with their world and their "partnership" with adults, children construct systems of knowledge that underlie their understanding of language and of their world. These systems become more differentiated and organized as time goes by and the children continue to interact with their world.

Thought and language development are complex phenomena that interact with each other throughout life. Though a child's potential is determined in part by biology, this potential is realized in a social context. What children do through interaction will over time become internalized to nurture their capacity for thought and language. Different contexts determine the social rules of language that will apply in a given situation, and these in turn determine how language users' systems of meaning (semantics), word order (syntax), and oral expression (phonology) are applied. In responding to the communications of children, we must be sensitive to what they are saying — making sure we understand their intentions as best we can. We can encourage a child to "stretch" a bit in terms of both thought and language in these communications, but in order to do so we must be attuned to the nature of the information the child can handle.

As preschool children become more familiar with oral language, they are also learning about written language, and the contexts in which this learning occurs in turn provide opportunities for oral language development.

In building on this foundation in the elementary grades, we must work not only toward expanding and elaborating our students' thinking and language but toward helping our students "step back" — decenter — from their language, to think about it as an object of study, and from their thinking, in order to control and direct it more effectively. In the following chapters, we will probe this issue to much greater depths — into the foundations for language as it is used, heard, read, and reflected upon.

Prior to passing through the kindergarten classroom door, children have learned how to communicate and they can certainly think. But the gap between simply being able to speak and think and *applying* and developing speech and thought is wide: as wide as the gap between simply running, and running a four-minute mile; between simply seeing, and painting what we see in a way that others will see differently; between simply hearing, and transforming what is heard into a symphony. The gap is as wide as that between powerlessness and empowerment. In other words, the tools of language and thought must be firmly grasped, understood, and put to use.

In the next chapter we will see how the use and purposes to which the English language has been put over the centuries have created a powerful tool indeed.

REFERENCES

Anglin, J. M. (1977). *Word, object, and conceptual development.* New York: Norton.

Au, K. H. (1980). Participation structures in a reading lesson with Hawaiian children: Analysis of a culturally appropriate instructional event. *Anthropology & Education Quarterly, 11,* 2, 240–252.

Bartlett, F. (1932). *Remembering.* New York: Macmillan.

Bissex, G. (1980). *GYNX AT WRK: A child learns to write and read.* Cambridge, MA: Harvard University Press.

Bloomfield, L. (1933). *Language.* New York: Henry Holt and Company.

Bridges, A., Sinha, C., & Walkerdine, V. (1981). The development of comprehension. In G. Wells, *Learning through interaction: The study of language development.* Cambridge: Cambridge University Press.

Brown, R. (1973). *A first language.* Cambridge, MA: Harvard University Press.

Brown, R. (1977). Introduction. In C. E. Snow & C. A. Ferguson (eds.), *Talking to children: Language input and acquisition.* New York: Cambridge University Press.

Bruner, J. (1975). The ontogenesis of speech acts. *Journal of Child Language, 2,* 1–19.

Bussis, A., Chittenden, E., Amarel, M., & Klausner, E. (1985). *Inquiry into meaning: An investigation of learning to read.* Hillsdale, NJ: Lawrence Erlbaum Associates.

Carey, S. (1977). The child as word learner. In M. Halle, J. Bresnan, & G. Miller (eds.), *Linguistic theory and psychological reality.* Cambridge, MA: The MIT Press.

Carey, S. (1982). Semantic development: The state of the art. In E. Wanner & L. R. Gleitman (eds.), *Language acquisition: The state of the art.* New York: Cambridge University Press.

Chomsky, N. (1965). *Aspects of the theory of syntax.* Cambridge, MA: The MIT Press.

Chomsky, N. (1975). *Reflections on language.* New York: Pantheon Books.

Clark, E. (1973). What's in a word? On the child's acquisition of semantics in his first language. In T. E. Moore (ed.), *Cognitive development and the acquisition of language*. New York: Academic Press.

Downing, J., & Valtin, R. (eds.) (1984). *Language awareness and learning to read*. New York: Springer-Verlag.

Egan, K. (1987). Literacy and the oral foundations of education. *Harvard Educational Review, 57*, 445–472.

Gardner, H. (1983). *Frames of mind: The theory of multiple intelligences*. New York: Basic Books.

Geller, L. (1985). *Wordplay and language learning for children*. Urbana, IL: National Council of Teachers of English.

Gleitman, L. R. (1981). Maturational determinants of language growth. *Cognition, 10*, 103–114.

Halliday, M. (1975). *Learning how to mean*. London: Edward Arnold.

Harste, J., Woodward, V., & Burke, C. (1984). *Language stories and literacy lessons*. Portsmouth, NH: Heinemann.

Heath, S. B. (1983). *Ways with words: Language, life, and work in communities and classrooms*. New York: Cambridge University Press.

Lindfors, J. (1980). *Children's language and learning*. Englewood Cliffs, NJ: Prentice-Hall.

Lindfors, J. (1987). *Children's language and learning* (2nd ed.). Englewood Cliffs, NJ: Prentice-Hall.

Moskowitz, B. A. (1978). The acquisition of language. *Scientific American, 236*, 92–110.

Ninio, A., & Bruner, J. (1978). The achievement and antecedents of labeling. *Journal of Child Language, 5*, 587–590.

Olson, D. (1984). See! Jumping! Some social antecedents to literacy. In H. Goelman, A. Oberg, & F. Smith (Eds.), *Awakening to literacy* (pp. 185–192). Portsmouth, NH: Heinemann *Educational Books*.

Pearson, P. D., & Anderson, R. C. (1984). Reading comprehension. In P. D. Pearson, et al., *Handbook of Reading Research*. New York: Longman.

Piaget, J. (1977). *The development of thought: Equilibrium of cognitive structures*. New York: Viking.

Piaget, J., and Inhelder, B. (1969). *The psychology of the child*. New York: Basic Books.

Rosch, E., & Lloyd, B. B. (eds.) (1978). *Cognition and categorization*. New York: Academic Press.

Smith, Frank (1981). *Essays into literacy*. Portsmouth, NH: Heinemann.

Snow, C. E. (1977). Mothers' speech research: From input to interaction. In C. E. Snow & C. A. Ferguson (eds.), *Talking to children: Language input and acquisition*. New York: Cambridge University Press.

Sulzby, E. (1985). Children's emergent reading of favorite storybooks: A developmental study. *Reading Research Quarterly, 20*, 458–481.

Trevarthen, C. (1974). Conversations with a two-month-old. *New Scientist, 2*, 230.

Tunmer, W. E., Pratt, C., & Herrimann, M. L. (1984). *Metalinguistic awareness in children*. New York: Springer-Verlag.

Vygotsky, L. S. (1962). *Thought and language*. Cambridge, MA: The MIT Press.

Wanner, E., & Gleitman, L. R. (eds.) (1982). *Language acquisition: The state of the art*. New York: Cambridge University Press.

Wells, G. (1981). *Learning through interaction: The study of language development.* Cambridge: Cambridge University Press.

Wells, G. (1986). *The meaning makers.* Portsmouth, NH: Heinemann.

Wells, G., & Robinson, P. (1982). The role of adult speech in language development. In C. Fraser & K. Scherer (eds.), *Advances in the social psychology of language.* Cambridge: Cambridge University Press.

Yaden, D. B., Jr., Smolkin, L. B., & Conlon, A. (1989). Preschoolers' questions about pictures, print convention, and story text during reading aloud at home. *Reading Research Quarterly, 24,* 188–214.

Yaden, D. B., Jr., & Templeton, S. (eds.) (1986). *Metalinguistic awareness and beginning literacy: Conceptualizing what it means to read and write.* Portsmouth, NH: Heinemann.

Our Language Heritage

FOCUSING QUESTIONS

■ How will having some knowledge of language history help you in your teaching of the elementary language arts?

■ Why is knowing about the Indo-European language important in understanding the English language?

■ Why has the alphabet been so important in the evolution of written language?

■ Why is the English language unique in its development? How have other languages influenced the development of oral and written English?

■ What influences have changed English as it is spoken in North America?

Questions students ask about the English language:

Why do we have two words — like street *and* road *— when they mean the same thing?*

How come words like island *have silent letters?*

How are we really supposed to spell theater: *theater* or *theatre?**

To these questions I will add some that students often ask about language in general:

Why are languages around the world so different?

Do chimpanzees and dolphins have language?

Do we have to learn Latin to understand our language better?

Why do some languages look so strange when they are written down?

INTRODUCTION

If you are involving elementary students in meaningful reading and writing, the chances are good that your students will become curious about language. The questions above are just a few of the sort you are likely to encounter. You will not always know the answers, but in the elementary classroom a little bit of knowledge can be a good thing where language history is concerned — at least good enough to send an inquisitive student on an informed search for an answer.

Although you can teach language arts without it, some understanding of the origins and historical development of language in general and of the English language in particular can be an important and enjoyable part of your knowledge foundation. Having this background can make you a more confident teacher and help you infuse your students with wonder and enjoyment of all aspects of language. Moreover, you will find this knowledge base a welcome part of your teaching repertoire when you are focusing on spelling and vocabulary development (see Chapter 10).

In this chapter we will explore the following topics from a historical perspective: first, the development of spoken and written language; second, the development of spoken and written English; and third, the processes that work to create new words in our language.

The Development of Oral Language

Other species besides humans can communicate, and some — such as chimps — can be taught to do so rather creatively. No species, however, has developed the capacity to use language in as complex, intricate, and creative a manner as have humans. How has this ability developed?

*(Tomkins and Yaden, 1985)

In our dim and distant past, the ancestors of humankind enjoyed an advantage over other species in toolmaking and hunting. This allowed early humans more possibilities for vocalization with each other, and with this most likely came the development of other social customs. Advantages of this development were many: During toolmaking, humans could *explain* the process, and this would extend to other areas of learning. The complexity and creativity of thought and language evolved together. As early humans developed more facility with spoken language, they were able to construct more intricate sentences. Instead of stringing together simple sentences ("The man is old," "The man once killed mammoth"), the separate events were blended into a single, more complex sentence: "The old man once killed mammoth."

From this point on, language, thought, and culture played increasingly intricate and interdependent roles. It is with one of these prehistorical languages and cultures, the Indo-European, that we are able to pick up the thread of the origins of English as well as of many other modern languages.

The Grand Ancestor: Indo-European

Beginning in the eighteenth century, language scholars found marked similarities in form and meaning among many languages; these similarities were so numerous that scholars concluded they could not be based merely on chance, on borrowing between one language and another, or on certain features that are likely to be found in any spoken language. Instead, the evidence suggested that these precise similarities could only arise from a source common to all of the languages — a single language that existed at a much earlier point in time.

Eventually, similarities were noted among languages from "Iceland and Ireland in the west to India in the east, and from Scandinavia in the north to Italy and Greece in the south" (Watkins, 1985, p. xiv). Scholars realized that these languages must indeed have come from one common source. This earlier language came to be called Proto Indo-European, or simply Indo-European, and today it is acknowledged to be the parent language of the Indo-European family of languages.

Why is Indo-European of such interest? For educators, there are two primary reasons: first, the languages in this family comprise those of half of the Earth's population; second, more than half of the basic roots found in Indo-European exist in some form in present-day English (Watkins, 1985, p. xii). By understanding something about how Indo-European works, you can gain insight into the structure of many languages, as well as be able to help your students understand the origins and the vocabulary of a large number of words in English. Also, there is always a bit of a thrill in realizing that the language we speak as we near the twenty-first century links us to a people who existed approximately 7,000 years ago.

You may be able to gain an idea of the effects of the Indo-European language (IE) by examining "cognates" from several different modern languages. For example, *mother* was *mater* in IE; it is *madre* in Italian, *mère* in French. *Three* was *trei* in IE; it is *tres* in Spanish, *trois* in French.

Historians believe the Indo-Europeans lived somewhere in the area from the Balkans in eastern Europe to the Russian steppes north of the Black Sea. Over time, groups that spoke Indo-European moved beyond their original location to settle in other areas. Without contact with the original culture, the language spoken by these groups began to change. Eventually, these languages became quite different from the original Indo-European. Further change occurred when members of this newer culture in turn moved on, and their language inevitably changed as well. Given enough time, peoples who spoke these new languages spread far and wide and their languages were in turn influenced by the languages of those people they met in the areas in which they settled. Over the past 7,000 years, then, this process has resulted in many different branches of languages, nine of which still exist today; one of these, Germanic, includes the English language.

In your classroom, you can give intermediate students a real feel for the role of Indo-European and subsequent language development in the histories of a word or group of words by walking your students through the word's development from a single IE root. Sometimes you get into this development quite serendipitously by checking on the etymology of a single word — say, *famous;* first you go back in time to the Indo-European and then you wind up exploring the many other words that have sprung from the same root as *famous.* You do not need any special talents to trace the development of a word or words from Indo-European because the dictionary will provide enough information to engage you (see Chapter 10). Should you become intrigued and wish to investigate the particulars of certain words further, however, then the resources mentioned at the end of this chapter will provide more than enough material for you.

Tracing diagrams (Tompkins and Yaden, 1985) can help guide your exploration of single words. As Figure 3.1 illustrates, a diagram can be adapted to explore many words. Figure 3.1 presents a few of the derivations from the single Indo-European root, *bha.* Based on this diagram and a little background, you could walk through a few words in this fashion.

CLASSROOM EXAMPLE

"Boys and girls, I've got a challenge for you: What do *fables, telephones, infants,* and *blame* all have in common? Kind of a toughie, isn't it? Well, we're going to find out in a little bit. First of all, we've talked about the Indo-European language before and its importance for the English language. Let's take a couple of minutes and really follow through on the development of words from a single Indo-European root." [Display the left-hand side of the diagram, showing the root *bha* and the Latin and Greek "nodes" L, GK, and GK.]

"Starting with just one Indo-European word, *bha,* which meant 'to speak,' several related Greek and Latin words developed. [Now reveal the top half of the diagram, showing all the derivatives from Latin.] From these Latin roots we get *fate,* which for the Romans meant what was spoken by the gods, and *affable,* a word that means a likable person — someone who is easy to speak to. This next Latin word [pointing to *fabula*] meant a *spoken* story, and from it we get *fable* and the word *fabulous,* which originally described the incredible beasts that appeared in fables.

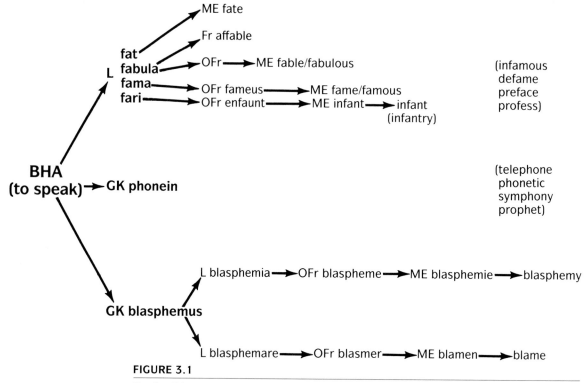

FIGURE 3.1

Tracing Diagram for Indo-European Root *Bha*

"This Latin word [point to *fama*] originally meant 'rumor' or, literally, what people are *saying* about you. Eventually the notion of being talked about by a lot of people developed into *famous,* but we also have the related word *defame,* which means someone can harm your character by spreading lies about you.

"Notice these other words I've put off to the side? *Preface* belongs to the same family as the words we've just mentioned; it means literally "to say before." In a book, the preface is the short part that comes before the book itself. *Professor* also is related; literally, *profess* means 'to speak foward,' or publicly. Isn't that what professors do?

"The last word on the diagram that comes from the Latin roots is *infant,* which literally means 'no speech.' [At this point you may ask your students how they think *infantry* is related to *infant;* if necessary, you can help them solve the mystery: The infantry were foot soldiers, the *youngest* members of the military. Indeed, Italian cavalrymen referred to them as "the babies"!]

"You can trace the words *blasphemy* and *blame* back to their Greek root *blasphemus,* using the diagram. The other Greek word — *phonein* — is not mapped out but words that developed from that base — *telephone, phonetic, symphony,* and *prophet* — are included." [As soon as possible, you should get your students involved in discussing why they think certain words developed as they did; as each student realizes how words have developed, he or she will be less hesitant to generate more creative possibilities. After all, *infantry* does have a fascinating derivation!]

This type of "wordplay" is most appropriate for intermediate students, and usually in small doses. I can guarantee that some of your students will be hooked on this degree of etymological searching, and become quite involved in it — they can become your "resident wordsmiths."

The Development of Written Language

Most of us take for granted the most technologically and culturally important invention of humankind: the alphabet. In most Western languages, the alphabet is a system of twenty or so symbols that allows us to write virtually anything that we can say and to read virtually anything that can be written. It was not always so.

Humankind has been experimenting with ways to encode information symbolically for well over 30,000 years before the alphabet as we know it was finally developed. Fairly advanced civilizations existed and conducted their business without as effective a tool as the alphabet. Why was the alphabet a relatively late development in the history of humankind?

Our response to this question should underscore the incredible feat accomplished by most seven-year-olds: They master in approximately seven years what it took humankind approximately 30,000 years to accomplish.

The development of writing can be discussed in terms of the following stages: *pictographic, logographic* (sometimes referred to as *ideographic*), *syllabic,* and *alphabetic.* It is important to keep in mind, however, that the shift from one type of representation to the next is usually a gradual one, with characteristics of each type overlapping at any one time.

Strictly speaking, *pictographic* representation is not written language, but it is an important predecessor of it. Cave drawings and paintings attest to humankind's desire to represent experience and to control one's environment as best as one could. As early as 30,000 years ago, cave dwellers may have used notches on tools and weapons to signify or symbolize important aspects of their world; for example, crescent notches on a tool may have represented a primitive moon calendar, a means of keeping track of time over the passing of a year (Marshack, 1972).

Writing has its beginning in these prehistoric efforts. The symbolic representation of the real world in cave drawings also served important purposes. At first, the drawings or pictographs simply represented events, as for example a particular hunt or fishing expedition. The following pictographs stand for "Man catches fish":

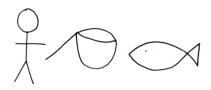

Pictographic representations, by the way, are not merely a historical artifact. If anything, we see them more and more often today in the form of international road signs, for example, and even in fashion. "Pictographs, in internationally agreed form, decorate our roads and our underwear, warning against falling rocks or dry-cleaning" (Henderson, 1982, p. 14).

Gradually, pictographs became more stylized and less true to the original. At this point they ceased being strictly pictographic and came to stand for one word or idea in a particular language — they became *logographic* systems:

This now means "Man catches cow." The net has become a *logograph,* still meaning "catches" but not specifically limited to the catching of fish. Its meaning has become extended to the more general sense of "catching things." In the next stage, the graphs have lost any obvious pictorial reference, though they still mean "Man catches cow":

One of the best-known and most influential logographic systems was developed by the ancient Sumerians. Their logographs were written as *cuneiforms;* the writer impressed soft clay tablets with a stylus, leaving wedge-shaped imprints (the word *cuneiform* comes from the Latin word *cuneus,* meaning "wedge").

In a logographic system, the intended meaning of a sign depended on the context — the meaning — of the particular text being read. The sign for the sun, for example, could also mean "bright," "white," or "day." This posed a potential problem for this type of writing system. Eventually, therefore, logographs came to represent sounds that were independent of their meaning. This process probably began with the need to indicate the personal names of individuals. Gelb (1963, p. 67), offered an example of how the name "Neilson" might be written in such a system: The sign for *kneel* would be combined with the sign for *sun;* together, the signs would phonetically render "Neilson." The signs, though, would no longer represent their original logographic meaning — they no longer represent *ideas* but rather *sound.*

Once begun, this process spread rapidly. It provided the spark that led to a writing system based on *syllables,* the next significant development in the history of writing. Spurred by trade and commerce, syllabic writing in turn spread rapidly, from Sumeria to Egypt and to the east, quite possibly stimulating the development of Chinese writing. One drawback to the Sumerian syllabic system was the number of signs — more than 600 were necessary to represent the syllables in the language. In addition to this, as with logographic systems, the reader had to rely heavily on context — knowledge of what the text probably was about. These drawbacks would lead to further refinements of this type of system, the most notable being the Egyptians' adaptation. Figure 3.2 illustrates some influential ancient writing systems.

Another syllabic system used by the Phoenicians was eventually borrowed by the Greeks. The Phoenician system, however, did not work well when applied to the Greek language. How could a syllabic-based alphabet intended for a language with a simpler syllabic structure be applied to a language that was quite complex syllabically? The Greeks answered this question, and in doing so accomplished what some have referred to as the most significant technological advance in the last 2,500 years.

What was so distinctively different — indeed revolutionary — about the Greeks' alphabet?

The Greeks solved the problem of trying to represent their own language with the Phoenician system by separating the consonants from the vowels, and giving separate symbols to each sound. This allowed them to write whatever they wished clearly and unambiguously, thus making the task of reading much easier. In contrast to most syllabic-based systems, speakers of Greek who had never before seen a particular text in Greek but who understood the sound equivalents for each of the symbols or letters in the alphabet could easily decode the message.

Eric Havelock, a scholar who has studied the development of the Greek alphabet, suggested that the Greeks "did not just invent an alphabet; they invented literacy and the literate basis of modern thought" (Havelock, 1982, p. 82). Literacy was not in the hands of only a few in the society; it could be acquired by most individuals in childhood. The number of written works and their availability increased, leading to "an immense expansion of knowledge available to the human mind" and, most important, the alphabet "made possible the production of novel or unexpected statement, previously unfamiliar and even 'unthought'" (Havelock, pp. 87, 88). The long-range consequences of this "were new inventible ways of speaking about human life, and therefore of thinking about it, which became preservable and extendable in the alphabetic literatures of Europe" Havelock, p. 88).

Investigating interesting features of the development of spoken and written language is one way to hook your students into an ongoing interest in and appreciation for the origins of language — and therefore much of their thought. This legacy is a common heritage shared by all humankind.

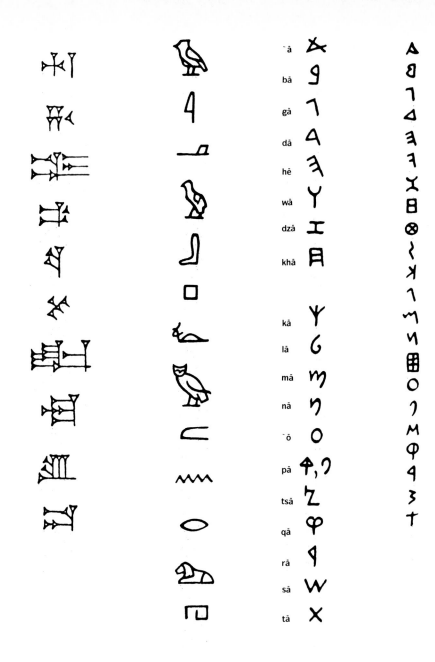

Sumerian Cuneiform	Egyptian	Phoenician	Early Greek

FIGURE 3.2

Ancient Writing Systems

Source: Sumerian Cuneiform from Gelb, I., *A Study of Writing* (Chicago: University of Chicago Press, 1963), p. 70. Egyptian, Phoenician and Early Greek from J.P. Hughes, *The Science of Language* (New York: Random House, Inc.).

The English Language: A Brief History

Since Shakespeare's time, the English language has grown from being the native language of approximately five million people to one that is spoken as a first language by 350 million and as a second language by 400 million. In many respects, English is unique as languages go, because its history and sources are more diverse than most of the other 2,700 languages that are spoken in the world today. In this section, I will offer a brief survey of the development of spoken and written English. As is the case with a knowledge of the history of language in general, your knowledge of the development of English will be an invaluable resource as you help your students understand the nature and the fascination of English vocabulary and spelling.

Old English

Over the centuries English has been shaped by Latin and Greek and by early German, Danish, and French.

A history of the language should begin, however, with the roots of the legendary and somewhat mysterious people who built Stonehenge, the Celts. The Celts occupied the British Isles more than 2,000 years ago, and resisted Roman invasion until around 50 A.D. The Romans occupied Britannia for almost 400 years, and absorbed much of the Celtic culture. Around 410 A.D., however, the Romans left, and Britain was left vulnerable to the invasions of the Germanic tribes — the Angles, Jutes, and Saxons. Brutal in their conquest, these tribes spoke the language that was to become English, and the Angles became the namesake of the land (Angleland) and the language.

Old English seems like a foreign language to us today — see Figure 3.3 to get a sense of how this language looks in print. However, the core vocabulary in Modern English comes directly from Old English: All of the 100 most frequently used words are from Old English, and of the second 100, eighty-three are from Old English. It is virtually impossible to utter a sentence without using some of this vocabulary. For example, simple words like *the, is, on, we,* and *in* are all Anglo-Saxon.

Some of the earliest words reflect the agricultural orientation of the Anglo-Saxon society: *sheep, earth, wood, work, dirt, tree,* and the verb *rake.* Around 600 A.D., Latin began to influence the Old English language, due in large part to the establishment of monasteries, which became cultural and intellectual centers. Some words contributed by Latin during this time include *psalm, angel, talent,* and *temple* — not coincidentally, terms of the church.

In the late eighth century the Vikings invaded, but their conquests were eventually halted by Alfred the Great. Eventually, the Viking culture and vocabulary mingled with the Old English. The Danish vocabulary added considerably to Old English. Scholars have suggested that the intermingling of the peoples and the languages led to the capacity to express finer and finer distinctions among concepts. For example, to indicate that one *desired* something there was the English word *wish* and the Danish word *want;* over time, these words came to represent

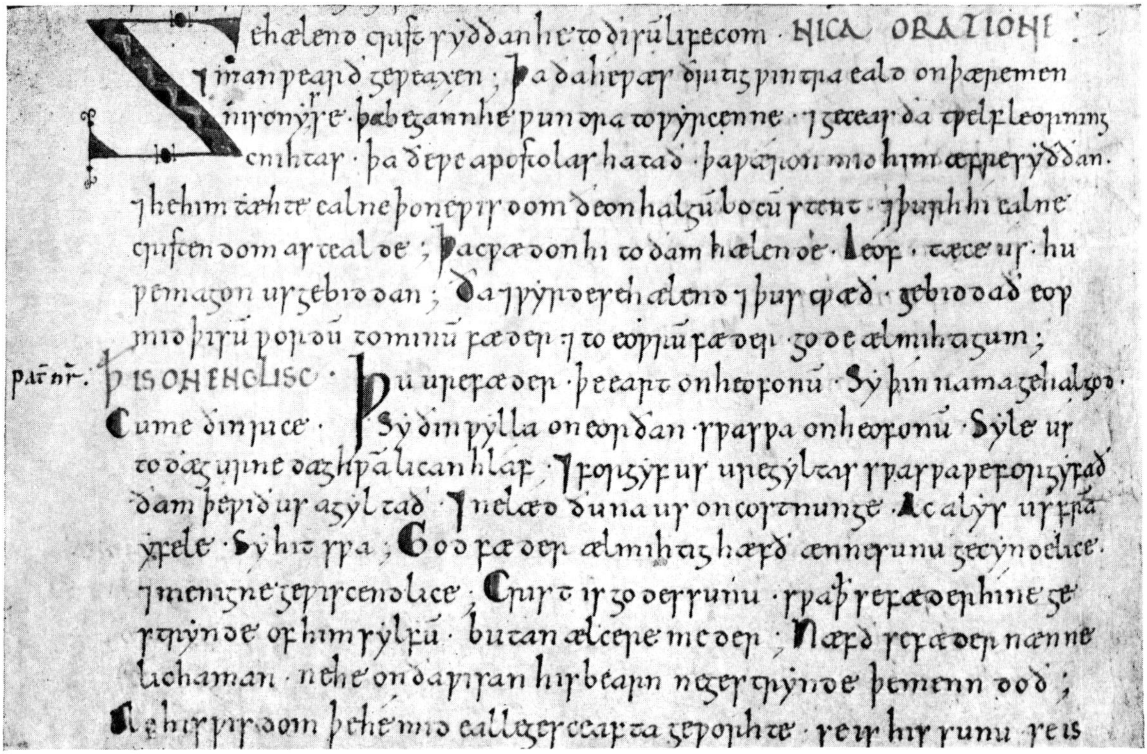

FIGURE 3.3

Old English Manuscript

Source: Ælfric, *Homily on the Lord's Prayer,* Cambridge University Library MS Gg 3 28 (circa 1000) fol. 56v lower half. Passage i (p. 9) begins nine lines from the bottom. Reprinted in Scragg, D.G. (1974). *A History of English Spelling.* Manchester, G.B.: Manchester University Press.

different aspects of desiring something. Similarly, *craft* (English) and *skill* (Danish) came to represent different aspects of the more general concept of "ability." Other examples: You could *rear* a child (English) or *raise* a child (Danish); you could wear a garment referred to as a *shirt* (English) or a *skirt* (Danish) — originally the words indicated the same type of garment but the words came to refer to different types.

By the end of the ninth century, a remarkable consistency had been achieved in the spelling of words, and English scribes were producing books for both England and the rest of Europe at a tremendous rate. The English language had grown over the course of some 500 years in its vocabulary, its structure, and its capacity to express meaning. It was the language of intellectuals throughout medieval Europe. Then, after 1066 A.D., written English virtually disappeared for some 200 years.

Middle English

With the Norman king William the Conqueror's victory over the English at the Battle of Hastings in 1066 A.D., the rule of England passed into French hands. Norman French became the language spoken by the rulers. It was used in the royal court, in parliament, and in legal matters. Written correspondence was usually in French except writing regarding religion and scholarly matters; for these, Latin was used. The long-range consequences of the Norman invasion for the English language were to infuse a large segment of French vocabulary into the language, and through French, quite a number of Latin terms as well. Approximately 40 percent of modern-day English has French origins. Throughout the Middle English period, from 10,000 to 12,000 new words were added to the language.

As was the case in Old English when Latin and Danish vocabulary were added to the Anglo-Saxon base, the addition of the French vocabulary further developed the capacity of English to express finer shades of meaning. To illustrate, consider the Old English word *ask*. During the Middle English period, the French *question* and the Latin *interrogate* were added to the language, each reflecting a different shade of meaning when contrasted with the original single word *ask*.

Regarding Middle English, the language scholar Jespersen made the distinction between English as the provider of "colloquial" terms and French as the provider of "literary" vocabulary (Jespersen, 1938, p. 104). The following pairs illustrate this distinction. The first part of each pair is English and the second part is French: *begin/commence, hide/conceal, feed/nourish, inner-outer/interior-exterior*. To highlight the distinction further, Jespersen observed that "While the names of several animals in their lifetimes are English, they appear on the table with French names" (Jespersen, p. 92). He cites the examples *ox, cow, calf, sheep, swine, boar, deer/beef* (English) versus *veal, mutton, pork, bacon, venison* (French).

In the latter part of the fourteenth century, Middle English received its finest expression in the writing of Geoffrey Chaucer. Best known for *The Canterbury Tales* (see Figure 3.4), Chaucer worked the language in such a way that today readers can still be moved, delighted, and amazed at this brilliance.

Surnames emerged around the time of Chaucer in the 1300s. Their origin was usually based on four factors:

1. "Son of" someone; for example, *Johnson, Thomson.*
2. Where someone lived; for example, *Brooks, Rivers.*
3. Occupation; for example, *Butcher, Hunter, Miller, Mason.*
4. Continental names; for example, *French, Fleming, Holland.*

The fourteenth century was also notable for the founding of universities and the more liberal expansion of education throughout English society. The wealth of the merchant class was increased, paper was introduced on a widespread basis, and these phenomena together led to an increased demand for books. The monasteries, where books had been produced by scribes for centuries, could not fill the demand, and book production passed to the "scriveners" — professional scribes who were not monks or members of the clergy. With the coming of the printing press in the next century, printers would meet the need for books even better.

The new professional scribes had a spelling standard they could aim for. By about 1430, the "chancery" or court in England issued its documents in English;

SCHOOL OF EDUCATION
CURRICULUM LABORATORY
UM-DEARBORN

The Canterbury Tales

Fragment I (Group A)

GENERAL PROLOGUE

■

Here bygynneth the
Book of the Tales of Caunterbury.

Whan that Aprill with his shoures soote
The droghte of March hath perced to the
　　roote,
And bathed every veyne in swich licour
Of which vertu engendred is the flour;
Whan Zephirus eek with his sweete breeth　　5
Inspired hath in every holt and heeth
The tendre croppes, and the yonge sonne
Hath in the Ram his half cours yronne,
And smale foweles maken melodye,
That slepen al the nyght with open ye　　10
(So priketh hem nature in hir corages),
Thanne longen folk to goon on pilgrimages,
And palmeres for to seken straunge strondes,
To ferne halwes, kowthe in sondry londes;
And specially from every shires ende　　15
Of Engelond to Caunterbury they wende,
The hooly blisful martir for to seke,
That hem hath holpen whan that they were
　　seeke.

Fragment I (Group A)
GENERAL PROLOGUE

When the sweet showers of April have pierced
The drought of March, and pierced it to the root,
And every vein is bathed in that moisture
Whose quickening force will engender the flower;
And when the west wind too with its sweet breath
Has given life in every wood and field
To tender shoots, and when the stripling sun
Has run his half-course in Aries, the Ram,
And when small birds are making melodies,
That sleep all the night long with open eyes,
(Nature so prompts them, and encourages);
Then people long to go on pilgrimages,
And palmers to take ship for foreign shores,
And distant shrines, famous in different lands;
And most especially, from all the shires
Of England, to Canterbury they come,
The holy blessed martyr there to seek,
Who gave his help to them when they were sick.

FIGURE 3.4

Chaucer's Prologue to *The Canterbury Tales*
Source: From Benson, L.D. (Gen. Ed.), *The Riverside Chaucer,* Third Edition. (Boston: Houghton Mifflin Company, 1987), p. 23. Reproduced with permission. Modern English translation from *The Canterbury Tales*, translated by David Wright. (New York: Oxford University Press, 1985). Reprinted by permission of Peters, Fraser & Dunlop Group Ltd.

French had been finally abandoned. The spelling style of the chancery became the spelling of the professional scribes, and rapidly spread with the increased book production.

The continuing demand for books led an enterprising William Caxton to set up a printing press in London in 1476. He realized the advantage he would have over professional scriveners and despite the inferior quality of his product, it *was* less

To give you more of a flavor of the changes in English spelling exerted by French and Latin, let's consider the following more notable examples.

1. The letter *c* replaced *s* in many words: *cinder, ice* (from the Old English *sinder, is*).

2. The letter *o* replaced *u* in many words: *come, some, monk, son, tongue, wonder, dove, love.* In some cases, the motivation for this change was to make reading easier. The strokes in the letter *u* were very similar in appearance to those in the letters *n* and *m*. By using the letter *o*, these words were visually easier to distinguish. In other cases, the change reflected the scribes' confusion among French, Latin, and English spelling.

3. English or French words were modified in light of later Latin words. For example, the French word *perfit* (perfect) entered the language in the thirteenth century; later, during the Renaissance, the word *perfection* was borrowed. The Latin root in each word was now spelled in two different ways, *fect* and *fit*, so to keep the same visual/meaning relationship between the two words the spelling of *fit* in *perfit* was changed, and the word *perfect* — with the same meaning but now a different spelling — was created.

---

expensive than the books of the scriveners, and inevitably their days — and their products — became numbered. The printing press indisputably affected the growth and structure of the English language, but toward the end of the fifteenth century another phenomenon was to have a tremendous influence — the Renaissance, which literally means "re-birth."

Throughout Europe, the Renaissance was actually a time of rediscovery of the legacy of classical Greece and Rome. This legacy encompassed the arts, literature, and language. The Latin language was admired for its precision and its structure, and many English scholars believed it was vastly superior to their own language. Jespersen observed that the influence of Greek and Latin in English "has been stronger than in any other language, French perhaps excepted" (Jespersen, p. 119).

Both Latin and Greek lent themselves well to the formation of new words, and language scholars and scribes began to change the spelling of a great many English words so as to reflect what they believed were the original classical roots of the English words. For example: ver*dit* changed to ver*dict,* from the Latin *dicere; dette* changed to *debt,* from the Latin *debitum; doute* changed to *doubt,* from the Latin *dubitare; egal* changed to *equal,* from the Latin *aequalis; bankrout* changed to *bankrupt,* from the Latin *ruptus* ("to break"); *sisourses* changed to *scissors,* from the Latin root *cid-* ("to cut"). Note that in several of these examples, the changes had the effect of adding a silent letter (as in *debt* and *scissors,* for example). As we will see in Chapter 10, these changes actually provide the opportunity for some powerful vocabulary instruction.

A significant change in pronunciation occurred during the later Middle English period. Termed the "Great Vowel Shift," this change affected the ways in which certain long vowel sounds within words were pronounced. The pronunciation of the italicized vowels in the following words will give you some idea of the nature of this change: ser*e*ne (ME: /seRAnə/); n*a*me (ME: /NAMə/); div*i*ne (ME: /dəVENə/). Significantly, the spelling did not usually change to reflect this change in pronunciation.

By the end of the fifteenth century the English language had changed tremendously when compared to Old English. In writing and in speech, it resembles very closely the English spoken today. For this reason, the year 1500 A.D. is often cited as the demarcation between Middle and Modern English. The real power and poetry of the language, however, was still to come.

Modern English

Modern English is often broken down into two periods: Early Modern (1500–1700) and Late Modern (1700 to the present).

The forces and events that were at work during the latter part of the Middle English period continued to influence English after 1500. Apart from the Renaissance, the astounding advances in science and world exploration were to have a profound effect on the development of English. As we have seen, the Renaissance brought a renewed interest in Greek and Latin. In addition to having an effect on the spelling of English, Latin, together with Greek, provided the building blocks for creating new words to describe the new discoveries in science and in exploration.

Science provided new phenomena to name and explain. The voyages of discovery by many European explorers revealed new lands, new plants and animals, and new human societies and cultures, causing an anonymous sixteenth-century Englishman to observe that there were "more things than words to name them with." In response, hundreds of new words were created by combining Latin and Greek word parts or by adding certain prefixes and suffixes to these parts: for example, *atmosphere, thermometer,* and *gravity.* In addition, many old words came to be used in new ways.

From the beginning of the reign of Elizabeth I in 1558 to the death of James I in 1628, the English language grew and changed at a rate unparalleled at any other time in history. One individual, William Shakespeare (1564–1616), single-handedly contributed a significant share to that growth. At a time when the language was growing at a rate that even people of the time marveled about, Shakespeare used the language in ways and to serve purposes that may never again be realized by a single writer. He stretched words to new connotations and coined phrases that have formed the bedrock of Modern English. The first edition of Shakespeare's collected plays, *The First Folio,* was published a few years after his death; the title page of this Folio is shown in Figure 3.5. This established the traditional three categories of Shakespeare's plays — comedies, histories, and tragedies.

In addition, because of his love of words and his habit of using them in new ways, Shakespeare was able to speak to a variety of audiences — which in part explains his popularity during his lifetime. Smith (1966) offers an excellent illustration of this in the following four lines from *Macbeth:*

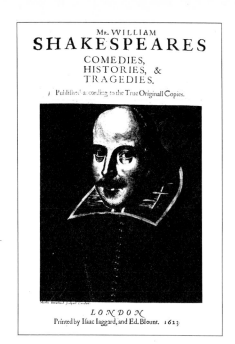

> Will all great Neptune's ocean wash this blood
> Clean from my hand? No; this my hand will rather
> The multitudinous seas incarnadine,
> Making the green one red.

The last two lines express two ways Shakespeare explains how the blood of the king whom Macbeth has murdered will mix in the sea. The third line uses Latinate vocabulary; the fourth uses Anglo-Saxon vocabulary. Shakespeare was thus able to communicate with learned and less-educated audiences alike. Perhaps more than any other writer, Shakespeare offered proof of the power and the poetry of the English language.

In those days people spelled pretty much as they pleased and it was not uncommon for someone to spell the same word several different ways in the same document. Around the time of Shakespeare, *spelling books* appeared, helping to establish the concept of correct versus incorrect spelling. The momentum for standardized spelling began with the publication in 1582 of a book by Richard Mulcaster, in which he argued for stabilizing the spelling system and called for a comprehensive dictionary of the English language. The last fifty-five pages of Mulcaster's book presented a recommended list of spellings for a large number of words. For example, he was probably the first to recommend regularizing the final *e* to indicate that the preceding vowel is long (for example, mak*e* instead of mak or maak). In short, Mulcaster had a profound influence on the stabilization of English spelling.

By 1700, the stabilization of English spelling was just about complete; some fine-tuning of the language remained to be done, though, and this task was magnificently accomplished by Samuel Johnson. In 1745 Johnson began writing his *Dictionary of the English Language;* ten years later his project was completed and published. Although other dictionaries had been published earlier, none approached the comprehensiveness of Johnson's, and none was as elegantly written. In a tremendously influential way, Johnson answered Mulcaster's call for a comprehensive dictionary of the English language.

Another dictionary to which scholars refer along with Johnson's was published in 1828, seventy-three years after Johnson's. It was published by Noah Webster, and it too exerted a significant influence on the language. There is an important difference between the two dictionaries, however: whereas Johnson's was a dictionary of the English language, Webster's was a dictionary of *American* English. Had two distinctively different languages developed by the nineteenth century? To answer this question, we need to return to the European explorers' voyages of discovery.

American English

Throughout the 1500s, the English as well as the Spanish, Dutch, and French explored the New World first accidentally encountered by Columbus in 1492. Because several European peoples eventually established settlements in the New World, all of their languages would come to influence English. England began to establish settlements in earnest in the early 1600s, and from that time on, the English language was in turn influenced by the languages of the Native Americans.

The English adopted many of the Native American names for the new animals and plant life that were encountered. Some of these words remained intact: *hickory, hominy, totem, moccasin, igloo.* Others became changed over time: *raccoon* from *raughroughouns, skunk* from *segankn, squash* from *isquontersquash.*

By 1828, when Webster's dictionary was published, the descendants of the early English settlers had of course established a new nation. Most French colonists had been pushed to the West and north to Canada. In Canada the French established a nation in an uneasy alliance with the loyalist English who had fled north after refusing to renounce their allegiance to the British crown during the Revolutionary War.

In the late 1700s and early 1800s there was a strong sense of nationalism and patriotic pride in the United States, and these feelings extended to the language as well. The individual who did more than anyone else to advance this pride in the language was Noah Webster.

In particular, Webster wanted to reform many English spellings. In his *American Dictionary of the English Language,* he made some spelling changes that to this day distinguish British from American spellings. A few examples follow (the first spelling is British; the second is American): *honour* versus *honor* and *colour* versus *color; theatre* versus *theater; defence* versus *defense; benefitted* versus *benefited; axe* versus *ax; phantasy* versus *fantasy; publick* versus *public* (in the latter two examples the British spelling would later change to the American!).

As the new nation grew in territory and in outlook throughout the nineteenth century, Spanish and Native American vocabulary increasingly were incorporated into the language. Over the past century, in fact, of all the languages, Spanish has exerted the most influence on English.

Of course, the growth of the new nation was not without some wrenching soul-searching and conflict. The American Civil War and the related issue of slavery are the two most critical examples of this. The "peculiar institution" of black slavery, however, nonetheless left an indelible linguistic mark on the English language.

Originally, the languages of West Africa blended with the English spoken in the American colonies. According to J. L. Dillard (1972), the first step in this process was the development of a *pidgin* English — a variety of English that allowed Africans who spoke different languages to communicate. Pidgin English was a form of simplified English in which features of the language that were least important for minimal mutual understanding were omitted; for example, verbs like *is* and the present-tense inflectional endings. These are features that in fact still characterize the dialect of American English referred to as Black English. As with other dialects and languages that have contributed to Modern English, Black English dialect and the literary and artistic culture it represents have profoundly influenced the development of American English, and in general, American society.

In the latter part of the nineteenth century, the general phenomenon known as the Westward Movement exerted still another strong influence on the development of American English (Dillard, 1985). From the language of the riverboats on the Mississippi River to that of the railroad, the cowboy, and the gold rush, the American lexicon expanded tremendously with terms and phrases such as *gambling, gold rush,* "bite the dust," "the real McCoy," *sidetracked,* and "to reach the end of the line."

As in earlier centuries, immigration was an important phenomenon. Throughout the nineteenth century and the early part of the twentieth, millions of immigrants came to begin new lives in the United States: Irish, Chinese, Germans, Scandinavians, Central Europeans. All of these groups brought their native languages, and as they learned English, their native languages in turn influenced American English.

For a multitude of reasons, new immigrants were rarely welcomed with open arms, and the history of the accommodation of these groups to American society is often an unpleasant one. Nonetheless, with time the animosity lessened and the nation as a whole benefited immeasurably from the knowledge, culture, and language brought by each group of immigrants.

The trend of immigration continues. The new immigrants from Central and South America, from Mexico, and from the Pacific Rim bring still more linguistic and cultural perspectives to a continually evolving American society, language, and culture.

The course of English in Canada has followed a different path than in the United States. Although the influences on English were of course the same prior to the English loyalist colonists' migration north during and after the Revolutionary War, after that migration there was and continues to be a remarkable similarity across the speech of "Standard English"-speaking Canadians. To the best of language scholars' knowledge, the word *Canada,* by the way, came from an Iroquois word that was distilled through French: *kanata,* meaning "village."

Processes Affecting English Vocabulary

For your elementary students, the vocabulary of English provides the most obvious illustrations of the changing language. Now that we have briefly considered the nature and change of the English language over the past 1,500 years, it should be helpful to examine the processes that have given us our words today and that continue to exert an effect (Jespersen, 1938; Marchand, 1974; Strang, 1970).

- *Derivation: adding something to words*

  Beginning in Old English, suffixes such as *-er, -en, -ster* (songster), and *-stress* (seamstress) became commonly used to create new words. In Middle English, the noun-forming suffixes *-ness* (goodness), *-dom* (kingdom), and the adjective-forming suffixes *-ly* (cowardly), *-less,* and *-ful* were added to create new words. Also in the Middle English period, the prefixes *un-, mis-,* and *be-* entered the language.

- *Functional shift: adding nothing at all*

  In many cases, words that had been used as nouns eventually were extended to function as verbs. For example, *crown* came to refer to the *procedure* by which someone was given the crown. *Love* similarly was extended to refer to the *act* of loving as well as the concept of love itself.

- *Compounding*

  This process occurs whenever we combine two words to create a new word, as in *river + boat = riverboat* and *basket + ball = basketball.* The process also applies to the compounding of word parts, or morphemes, of Greek or Latin origin. For example, *tele* (far, distant) + *meter* (measure) = *telemeter; tele + photo* (light) = *telephoto.* Several such elements can be combined, as in *electroencephalograph:* "Instrument that records (graph) electric current (electro) within (en) the head (cephalo)."

- *Back formation*

  As illustrated in the first list item above, if new words are derived from existing words, this normally follows the trend whereby a new word is derived from a base word by adding a prefix or a suffix. The opposite process, referred to as *back formation,* has also occurred. In this case a word that you would think is the original base word is actually created from the earlier form of the word — and this earlier, original form looks like it was derived from the base word. In the process, the syntactic function that the new word served was often different than that served by the parent word. For example, in each of the following word pairs the first word is the later form: *beg/beggar; edit/editor; burgle/burglar; donate/donator.*

- *Clipping*

  This process creates new words by "clipping off" parts of the original words. For example, *bus* from *omnibus, phone* from *telephone, vet* from *veterinary* or *veterinarian, perks* from *perquisites, caps* from *capital letters, exam* from *examination, cab* from *cabriolet, fad* from *fadaise, mob* from *mobile vulgus.*

- *Blending*

  Through this process, new words are created by putting together parts of existing words. For example, *smoke + fog = smog.* In his famous poem "Jabberwocky," Lewis Carroll creates many of these words and has Humpty Dumpty call them "portmanteau" words: *chortle* is from *chuckle* and *snort; slithy* is from *lithe* and *slimy.*

■ Build Your Teaching Resources

Language Heritage

Books for Teachers

Clairborne, R. (1988). *The roots of English.* Time/Life Books.

Dale, E., O'Rourke, J., & Bamman, H. (1971). *Techniques of teaching vocabulary.* Palo Alto, CA: Field Educational Enterprises.

Davies, P. (1981). *Roots: Family histories of familiar words.* New York: McGraw-Hill.

Editors, American Heritage Dictionary (1986). *Word mysteries and histories: From quiche to humble pie.* Boston: Houghton Mifflin.

Funk, W. (1954). *Word origins and their romantic stories.* New York: Grosset and Dunlap.

Laird, H., & Laird, C. (1957). *The tree of language.* Cleveland, OH: World.

Logan, R. (1986). *The alphabet effect.* New York: Simon and Schuster.

McCrum, R., Cran, W., & MacNeil, R. (1986). *The story of English.* New York: Viking.

Partridge, E. (1983). *Origins: A short etymological dictionary of modern English.* New York: Outlet Book Company.

Skeat, W. (1984). *A concise etymological dictionary of the English language.* Oxford: The Clarendon Press.

Tompkins, G., & Yaden, D., Jr. (1986). *Answering students' questions about words.* Urbana, IL: National Council of Teachers of English.

Watkins, C. (1985). *American Heritage dictionary of Indo-European roots.* Boston: Houghton Mifflin.

Weekly, E. (1967). *An etymological dictionary of modern English.* New York: Dover.

Books for Students

Azimov, I. (1961). *Words from the myths.* Boston: Houghton Mifflin.

Azimov, I. (1968). *Words from history.* Boston: Houghton Mifflin.

Burningham, J. (1984). *Skip trip.* New York: Viking.

  See also several other titles by Burningham, all published by Viking.

Cox, J. (1980). *Put your foot in your mouth and other silly sayings.* New York: Random House.

Davidson, J. (1972). *Is that Mother in the bottle? Where language came from and where it is going.* New York: Franklin Watts.

Hall, R. (1984). *Sniglets.* New York: Macmillan.

Hazen, B. (1979). *Last, first, middle and Nick: All about names.* Englewood Cliffs, NJ: Prentice-Hall.

Lambert, E., & Pei, M. (1959). *The book of place-names.* New York: Lothrop, Lee and Shepard Books.

Katan, N. J. (1981). *Hieroglyphs: The writing of ancient Egypt.* Boston: Houghton Mifflin.

Pickles, C., & Meynell, L. *The beginning of words: How English grew.* New York: G. P. Putnam's Sons.

Robinson, S. (1989). *Origins* (2 vols.). New York: Teachers and Writers Collaborative. (Vol. 1: *Bringing words to life;* Vol. 2: *The word families.*)

Sarnoff, J., & Ruffins, R. (1981). *Words.* New York: Scribner's Sons.

Spier, P. (1971). *Gobble, growl, grunt.* Garden City, NY: Doubleday.

Wolk, A. (1980). *Everyday words from names of people and places.* New York: Elsevier/ Nelson Books, 1980.

A CONCLUDING PERSPECTIVE

Language is so much a part of everything we do that we scarcely pay it any attention. Moreover, we know that most students are not in the habit of stepping back and taking a look at their language, much less considering where that language has come from. We realize the value of such a perspective, however, and will need to entice the students to enjoy the fruits that such study can offer. A sense of the nature and the source of the language in general and English in particular not only gives students these valuable insights into their language, but it gives them a sense of who they are and of the cultures from which they have come.

We know that wordplay and word curiosity lead to growth in communication potential and meaning potential — in language ability and in thought. In Chapter 10 we will examine the content and the processes for such involvement.

REFERENCES

Dillard, J. L. (1972). *Black English: Its history and usage in the United States.* New York: Random House.

Dillard, J. L. (1985). *Towards a social history of American English.* New York: Mouton.

Gelb, I. J. (1963). *A study of writing.* Chicago: University of Chicago Press.

Havelock, E. (1982). *The literate revolution in Greece and its cultural consequences.* Princeton, NJ: Princeton University Press.

Henderson, L. J. (1982). *Orthography and word recognition in reading.* London: Academic Press.

Jespersen, O. (1938). *Growth and structure of the English language.* Garden City, NY: Doubleday.

Marchand, H. (1974). *The categories and types of present-day English word-formation.* Munchen: C. H. Beck'sche Verlagsbuchhandlung.

Marshack, A. (1972). *The roots of civilization: The cognitive beginnings of man's first art, symbol, and notation.* New York: McGraw-Hill.

Smith, P. L. (1966). *The English language.* Oxford: Oxford University Press.

Strang, B. (1970). *A history of English.* London: Methuen.

Tompkins, G., & Yaden, D., Jr. (1985). *Answering students' questions about words.* Urbana, IL: National Council of Teachers of English.

Watkins, C. (1985). *American Heritage dictionary of Indo-European roots.* Boston: Houghton Mifflin.

4 Classroom Organization and Management

FOCUSING QUESTIONS

- How and why are the characteristics of risk taking, talking, and integrated instruction important in your considerations of classroom management?
- What are the central issues related to establishing the physical environment of the classroom?
- What are the strengths and weaknesses of the three discipline systems discussed in this chapter?
- What are several strategies that you might use to involve parents?
- How should you go about determining goals for the academic environment?
- What are the different group configurations possible in the classroom and what are the reasons for each particular organization?
- What are the characteristics of the different types of cooperative groups?

In Ramona the Pest, *Beverly Cleary writes about Ramona's first encounter with a substitute teacher. Ramona and Howie, her friend, arrive at the kindergarten door one morning and discover a stranger. Howie, obviously aware of whom this stranger might be, says, "I bet the substitute won't even know the rules of our kindergarten." Ramona responds to Howie with concern about the expertise of this stranger. She replies, "Miss Binney said following the rules of their kindergarten was important. How could this stranger know what the rules are? A stranger would not even know the names of the boys and girls. She might get mixed up." Faced with the dilemma of the substitute teacher, Ramona abandons kindergarten and hides behind the trash cans. Eventually, she is discovered and returned to her classroom. This scenario ends with Ramona's remarks about the ineptness of the substitute. Ramona grumbled, "Here it was seatwork time, and Mrs. Wilcox was not even having the class do real seatwork, but was letting them draw pictures as if this were the first day of kindergarten. . . . Things were not supposed to be this way."*

INTRODUCTION

Ramona, like other elementary school children, had a clear understanding of the management and organization of her classroom. How did Ramona develop this understanding? Certainly Miss Binney considered the classroom environment and her kindergarten students when she decided upon the organization of her classroom. Most likely during the first few weeks of school, she instructed her students in the expectations for behavior and the procedures for classroom routines. What exactly were the behavioral expectations or the classroom routines? Although we cannot enter Miss Binney's imaginary classroom, we can look into your future classroom and discuss the elements necessary in establishing a well-tuned classroom environment that supports integrated language arts instruction.

In this chapter we will take a look at the planning behind the organization and management of an elementary classroom. Though this chapter is often focused on language arts instruction, it is not limited to just management and organization within the language arts instructional portion of the school day. As we have discovered in previous chapters, language arts instruction often extends into other content areas such as social studies, science, and even math. This chapter will help you establish a smoothly running classroom in which your students have become so familiar with the rules and regulations that they can be fully involved in all of the learning activities. At the end of this chapter we will visit a fifth grade classroom to see how one teacher organized his room at the beginning, middle, and end of the school year. This visit will give you an in-depth look at the management and teaching/learning considerations you will deal with as a teacher at various times throughout a school year.

Note: This chapter was contributed by Dr. Diane Barone, University of Nevada, Las Vegas.

Special Characteristics of
Classrooms That Support Learning

The classrooms I will describe in this chapter are a departure from what is often considered to be the "ideal" classroom, a room where all of the children are quietly working at their desks — alone. In our proposed classroom the children often share and discuss as they work together. This model language arts classroom is complex in organization and management. Often when visitors walk into an active, integrated language arts classroom, they have difficulty determining what the underlying organizational patterns are. Children are busy reading, writing, painting, and conferring with other children or the teacher. Instruction is not separated into discrete periods; the reading and writing activities, for instance, are intermingled. The most notable characteristic of the classroom is the variety of activities that are usually going on at one time.

How does a teacher manage and organize such a complex environment? Before we analyze how to manage this type of classroom, let's visit a complex classroom in operation. We will drop in on Mrs. Webb's first grade classroom in October, just as the students have arrived at the classroom door.

CLASSROOM EXAMPLE

Each child enters the class, puts away personal belongings, and quickly moves to his or her desk. Before school, Mrs. Webb placed each child's journal on his or her desk so that the journals would be ready when the children arrived. Jim opens his journal and reads Mrs. Webb's response to the entry he made yesterday: "I remember getting a sunburn too. It was hard to sleep. I hated being all red and having my skin peel." Jim leans over to Mary and asks if she can help him read some of the words in Mrs. Webb's message. Children throughout the class are helping each other read. Once the messages have been read, the children write another entry into their journals. As the children are reading and writing, Mrs. Webb moves around the room offering support if children require it. Heather asks Mrs. Webb how to spell *balloon.* "Well, how do you think it is spelled, Heather?" Heather replies, "It begins with a *b* and I'm not sure of the rest." Mrs. Webb says, "That's a fine beginning, Heather, why don't you put a line after the *b* to show that there are other letters and just go on with the next word."

The children continue writing for about fifteen minutes. Then a few children share their journals with the whole class. At this point a transition from the journal writing activity occurs. Mrs. Webb takes a few minutes to give directions to the children before they begin a new activity. First, she reminds the children that their journals need to be turned in before lunch. After this brief reminder, several groups of children are given specific directions: "Those of you who have just read *Rosie's Walk* need to continue working on your mural. All the materials are under the back table where they were left yesterday. If you read *The Jigaree* yesterday, please go to the listening center and listen to the story one time, then join in and read the story with the tape. After you have listened and read, take a piece of paper from the listening center and draw a picture of the Jigaree and write about your Jigaree. Mary and Jeff, please go to

Mrs. Hamilton's table. She will be listening to you read and you will write a new story with her. And I will be working with Pat, Jill, John, Chris, Anne, and Sam. Please bring your word banks* with you today. Don't forget to check the chart on the board so that you know when it is time to switch activities. Those of you working on the mural will not work with me until last today, so you have a large block of time to paint. Does anyone have any questions? Okay, Jigaree and mural people please get started. Those people working with Mrs. Hamilton or me, please move."

◆ ◆ ◆

This vignette provides a glimpse of the organization beneath the exterior activity evident in the room. The journal writing had everyone involved in the same activity at the same time. The children could share their writing with a neighbor and talking was definitely present, but it was not out of control and it did not interfere with the children's journal writing. The talking certainly enhanced this activity and provided a real audience for the children's reading and writing. Mrs. Webb then provided a few direct instructions about this morning's particular activities. If we had entered the class after Mrs. Webb had given the directions, we might have been surprised at the variety of activities occurring in the classroom. Yet, after listening to the directions, we have a clearer understanding of exactly what all the children are doing. We have a more thorough grasp of Mrs. Webb's organizational scheme for language arts instruction.

Integrated language arts classrooms have certain key characteristics that support this more complex teaching and learning environment. These characteristics were present in Mrs. Webb's first grade classroom. Notably, when the children were reading and writing in their journals, they were free to *talk* with their neighbors about this activity. Journal writing, creation of a mural following reading, listening to a story and the follow-up drawing and writing, and word bank activities illustrate the way Mrs. Webb *integrates* all the components of the language arts in her teaching. Though not so obvious, Heather's attempt at spelling *balloon* illustrates the risk taking she was willing to engage in while learning to write. These three critical characteristics — risk taking, talking, and integrated instruction — are present in integrated language arts classrooms.

Risk Taking

Children and teachers need to be free to make errors while teaching and learning. Perhaps it seems strange to include teachers in risk taking, but as a teacher, whenever you try something new you are taking the risk that it might not work out. These risks are not just academic — you will also take risks when the children in your class are given the freedom to make decisions about their learning. By giving them choices, you are relinquishing your position as the person in charge and

*For a description of word banks, see Chapter 8.

sharing this role with your students. At first, you may find that you feel a little uneasy about this new role.

Harste, Woodward, and Burke (1984) elaborate on an environment that supports risk taking. They say that, "In order to learn we must allow ourselves to be vulnerable to the situation, to others' perceptions, and to our own past experiences. The sharing of half-baked ideas is an integral part of language, learning, and teaching" (Harste, et al., p. 130). When we become troubled or confused about something we are trying to learn, then after a period of turmoil, we make the connections to a new level of understanding. An example from outside the classroom will help clarify this idea of risk taking. Picture yourself on a ski slope. You have had a great day — you skied the same trails all day and never had a fall. This might be quite an accomplishment for most of us, but if your goal is to improve your skiing, then on this day you have not improved much. In order to get better, you are going to have to ski some steeper slopes and you probably will fall quite often. If your friends laugh and make fun of your efforts on the difficult slope and if you are like most of us, you will probably retreat and head for the bunny hill. If, however, your friends support and encourage you and maybe even give you a clue about how to negotiate the hill better, you will try again. And through this effort, you will reach a new level of skiing proficiency.

Let's move from the ski slope to the classroom, where the analogy should become apparent. If children are allowed to keep turning in safe, correct, neat work, are they really growing as learners? What happens if children, in their attempts to solve a problem, are scorned and ridiculed by their peers? Neither of these situations will provide an environment where children will struggle to reach new levels of understanding about a story, a math problem, or a science experiment.

Harste, Woodward, and Burke (1984) discuss this same point and include the work of Vygotsky to support the importance of risk taking in literacy learning. They state:

> . . . under known conditions the language user's responses are predictable and hence safe. Under such conditions, rather than learn new rules, what the language user is doing is confirming old rules. Only when things go wrong, that is, when the expected relationships or known rules do not hold, is the language user forced to develop new rules and new responses in order to cope. To live within existing rules and predictable patterns is not to grow. It is only under conditions in which all of the relationships are not known that language users must scamper to outgrow their current selves." (p. 136)

In essence you will be taking the idea of carefully examining children's "mistakes" and expanding this view to all the areas of your curriculum.

Talking

Barnes begins his book, *From Communication to Curriculum,* with this sentence: "Schools are places where people talk to one another" (Barnes, 1976, p. 11). He then lets us eavesdrop on a teacher in a classroom.

There is only one adult in the room, she seems to be talking more than all the children together. She is the centre of everybody's attention: she asks many questions, and demands answers that are right. "What other ways are there of measuring it?" she asks, and goes on urgently, "Come on. More hands up. Have you all gone to sleep?" In spite of the urgency, she seems to know the answer already, for she dismisses several suggestions until one comes which she greets with, "That's it. Good answer, John." Her young pupils ask hardly any questions, except for permission to fetch ink from the cupboard. When one or two children shout answers without first being named by her, she checks them with a cryptic "Hands?" which they seem to understand as a re-proof. (pp. 11–12)

This scene might be familiar to many of you. It is the scene that often comes to mind when visualizing a classroom during instruction. Barnes is criticizing the proportions of talk by the teacher rather than the students. He wants students to be real participants in discussion. The students should be questioning and refining their thoughts about consequential issues, not merely filling in the blanks left in the air by the teacher.

Barnes is not alone in his worries about who is really talking in the classroom. Several authors mention the necessity for students to talk to teachers and to other students for learning to occur (Carducci and Carducci, 1984; Harste, et al., 1984; Hawley and Hawley, 1975; House and Lapan, 1978; Hubbard, 1986; Torbe and Medway, 1981). Torbe and Medway argue that teachers should realize "that we learn by talking, and that learning is an act of creation by which we make and shape the very world we inhabit ... the pupils [have] to do the talking, not the teachers" (Torbe and Medway, 1981, p. 9). Perhaps the most convincing argument Torbe and Medway offer in support of student discussion comes from quotes provided by children:

GIRL, 14: Mrs. X's lessons are really good. You have these discussions and really you don't think you're learning anything, but at the end of the lesson you know ever so much more than you did before.

BOY, 14: When you started working like this I hated it. All this having to decide what we were going to do, I wished we were in Mr. X's class, he tells them what to do. But I think we've learned more than them now, they're all saying how boring he is. (p. 96)

The students have discovered that talking through a situation helps with understanding. The fourteen-year-old boy also realized that this type of discussion is hard work.

The idea of the quiet classroom really does not fit the way we know that students learn. When you think about the many language arts activities described in this book, most of them require thoughtful discussion on the part of the students and the teacher. How will you manage a not-too-quiet classroom?

Later in this chapter we will more fully address your concerns about establishing and managing a classroom where you cannot hear the sound of a pin drop. What is important to remember now is that the students' talking should be *meaningful*. Their talk should be focused on the important issues related to a topic or project. You can use the content of their talking as a gauge to determine the appropriateness of the discussion.

You can integrate talking into the classroom quite simply. Your students might start their day with sharing, sometimes better known as show-and-tell or bring-and-brag. Here children can practice talking to the whole class and the class can practice listening. You will encourage your students to exchange ideas with the person who is sharing. They might ask that person questions or discuss a personal experience that is related. For example, your students could ask a child who has brought in a special rock where he found the rock and why he determined that it was special. During these types of activities, the children are learning the social conventions of dialogue. Most important, the children are learning that it is difficult to listen to more than one person at a time.

Another simple way to encourage student talk in class is to have students form partnerships. Two children can read together, research together, do math problems together, and so on. There are other times when larger groups can be formed. Writing workshop is a natural time for these groupings. Three children can work together in a response group. Several children can co-author a book. Other children can participate in a mini-lesson. You will want to model these groups, so your students will have clear expectations about what should be accomplished. Your demonstration might include the type of discussion that is expected and the appropriate volume level for talking. (See the grouping section later in this chapter for a fuller discussion.)

Eventually, you will be comfortable with a hum of voices in the room, even when you are teaching a small group or an individual child. You will quickly develop a sense for on-task noise and noise that signals a problem. Because of your modeling, children will know when they may talk to a neighbor and when this behavior is inappropriate.

Integrated Instruction

Let's review the concept of *integrated instruction* for it will provide the context for all the organizational and management ideas discussed in this chapter. As we already know, it implies teaching and learning activities that include all of the components of the language arts. For example, the *Jigaree* activity from Mrs. Webb's class clearly involved reading, writing, speaking, and listening. The children listened to the story and then read along with the tape. Following these reading activities, the children were asked to draw a Jigaree and write about this special Jigaree. Most likely the children were talking and listening to each other's comments while these activities were occurring. So in fact all of the language arts elements were incorporated into this single activity. One other area of the curriculum was also integrated into this lesson: by having the children draw a Jigaree, Mrs. Webb also brought in art.

When your teaching is integrated, it is often difficult to discretely, subject by subject, describe exactly what you are teaching and what the children are learning.

Were you teaching reading? Was this a writing lesson? Were you working on listening skills? Or was this a lesson in artistic creativity? Probably it was a lesson that fostered all of these objectives. Later in this chapter I will give you some examples of lesson planning in this type of complex, overlapping curriculum. Most likely you have already guessed that separate blocks of time for each subject area will no longer work effectively. Subject areas will flow into each other and generally longer blocks of time will be required for this type of learning and teaching.

Just as Mrs. Webb used the Jigaree activity to integrate art along with the components of the language arts, you can include other subject areas besides the language arts in your integrated teaching approach. Art activities often correlate with reading and writing lessons. You might not think of music as readily, yet many books and writing activities can be enriched by including appropriate music. For example, Chinese music would enhance the Chinese "Little Red Riding Hood" story *Lon Po Po*. Periodically science and social studies texts might be shared during directed reading-thinking lessons so that children learn the strategies necessary in comprehending these books. You can include writing instruction during a science lesson so that children learn to record their observations. For example, your students could keep a daily record of the growth of seeds.

Integrated instruction does involve all of the subject areas. Pappas, Kiefer, and Levstik (1990) describe integrated classrooms as places where the teachers do not consider reading, writing, listening, and talking as separate subjects.

> **Instead, they are used together as tools, as means for learning other things. In the process, students learn both the other things *and* the language. Activities and projects span the curriculum so that there is enough time for children to engage in systematic and reflective inquiry on a range of topics. As children use language to learn, teachers collaborate, respond, facilitate, and support their efforts. (p. 1)**

Organizing and Managing the Physical Environment

What exactly should an elementary classroom look like? Should all classrooms look the same? What are some of the critical elements of the physical environment? What is the best way for us to begin to organize our classrooms?

Arranging the furniture is a task that many teachers use as a beginning step in setting up their classroom each year. Evertson (1989) indicates that "effective teachers plan for the arrangement of furnishings to accommodate different types of activities, to minimize problems with disruptive movement in the classroom, and to facilitate monitoring of student work and behavior" (Evertson, p. 60). You can arrange and rearrange the furniture within the room to facilitate your particular learning environment. You will find that certain configurations of furniture facilitate particular types of instruction. The desks may sometimes be arranged in a circle for a large-class discussion. This arrangement works particularly well when input is needed from the whole class. When the students are brainstorming potential writing topics, for example, you would want the students to hear all of the topics offered so that they can provide other possibilities.

On most occasions, three or four desks might face the same number of desks to form small learning groups within the classroom. These arrangements facilitate small-group discussion. If some of your students are completing word sorts, for example (see Chapters 8 and 10), the children in the group would be able to hear what a friend is doing and offer comments. A third arrangement might be to have the desks in rows for those few times when students need to work alone, perhaps during testing of one sort or another. This type of arrangement limits talking and only facilitates activities that need to be done individually.

Because you will need to provide for a wide variety of activities, there should be stable areas within the room such as the library, supply areas, and art center. These areas should remain stable so that children are not constantly searching for materials. Many classrooms have library corners with an old sofa or pillows so that the children can get comfortable while they read. For young children, a bookcase where the covers of books can be displayed is a good idea. Young students often choose books based on their cover illustration.

The supply areas are critical to a classroom, especially if you expect your students to be independent when they are not working directly with you. Think about where the supply centers might be placed. They need to be distant from where most of your lessons will be conducted and away from areas of the room that have a lot of traffic, like the drinking fountain or pencil sharpener. Some teachers have one supply center, typically a bookcase, filled with various sizes and types of paper, scissors, glue, staplers, markers, pencils, rulers, and maybe even ink-correcting liquid. Another supply center could store many of the art materials, such as construction paper, paint, colored chalk, yarn, and collage materials. You might have one other supply/storage area for your classroom collection of unifix cubes, pattern blocks, and other math manipulatives.

Maybe you are feeling uneasy about having all of these materials freely available to children. Will they break the stapler, squirt the glue, or waste paper? The answer is they probably will. Remember, however, that before your students visit the supply centers, you will discuss the rules related to using supplies. We will talk more about classroom rules soon and how to reduce the number of glue squirters in your room.

In addition to setting up supply areas for the students, you should designate certain places where work is turned in or stored while it is being completed. Some teachers use stacking files to hold students' work. Often each container is labeled with subject headings so that the teacher can collect and correct just the math papers, for instance. If you set up a place where papers are to be turned in, the students can accomplish this task independently. You should also contemplate possible short-term locations to store unfinished projects. For example, remember the group of students working on a mural for the book *Rosie's Walk*? They will need a place to store this project until it is completed. Some subject areas may have special storage requirements too. Where will children keep their writing folders with works in progress, word-study notebooks, published stories (stories that have been written by the children, photocopied, and distributed), science observations, and so on? You will need to set up places for these materials, so your students can retrieve and put away their work on their own.

Think about the placement of your desk and the table where you will be working with small groups. Some teachers use their desks as a place to store materials necessary for teaching. If this is the way you plan to use your desk, then place it near the spot where most of your teaching will occur. If you feel that you will be working at your desk when children are in the room, then you should position your desk so you can observe your students.

The table or floor space that you will use for most of your small-group work needs to be away from congested areas; make sure that you can also observe the other students in the class. Think about where you will stand or sit in relation to the small group. It is important to have eye contact with the students in your small group and at the same time be able to oversee the other children in the classroom. It is generally better not to sit with your back to the classroom. In that position you will only be able to hear, not see, what all those other children are doing. Finally, don't forget to interact with the students sitting right next to you. Because these children are sitting to either side of the teacher, they are often neglected in favor of the children sitting across the table.

Now that you have the furniture arranged, what will you do about the bulletin boards? How complete will the boards be before the children arrive? Some teachers have the whole room decorated before the children arrive; other teachers put up background paper and captions only on the bulletin boards. These unfinished boards are waiting for the children to complete them. The second approach seems more appealing as a way to bring the children into the class. These incomplete bulletin boards give an underlying message that the room is not just *your* classroom — your students own it too. What an important message to share with children on the very first day of school. You can have your students change the boards monthly or at the end of a thematic unit. Traditionally, most classrooms also have an alphabet, number line, and calendar as part of the permanent display.

Evertson, Emmer, Clements, Sanford, and Worsham (1989) caution that a classroom has minimal space available for as many as thirty persons working throughout an entire school day. They provide four keys to good room arrangement:

1. **Keep high-traffic areas free of congestion.**
2. **Be sure students can be easily seen by the teacher.**
3. **Keep frequently used teaching materials and student supplies readily accessible.**
4. **Be certain students can easily see instructional presentations and displays. (pp. 4–5)**

Many different physical arrangements of classrooms are possible. Figure 4.1 shows two examples. In both of these rooms the teacher can view the entire class during small-group or whole-class instruction. The high-traffic areas in the room are not near teaching-learning centers. The supplies are accessible and the students

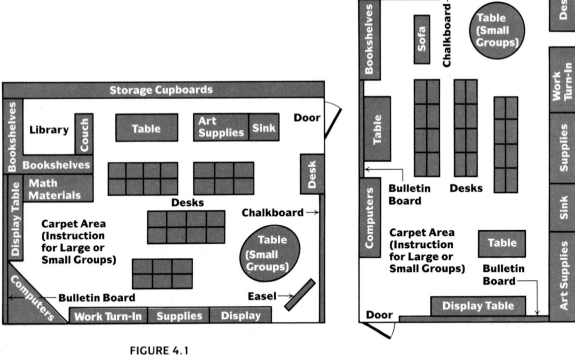

FIGURE 4.1

Possible Classroom Arrangements

should have no difficulty observing the teacher during a lesson. Storage for long-term projects is solved by using the space under the tables.

Organizing and Managing the Social Environment

The physical environment of the classroom is more concrete and easier to manipulate than the social environment. It is simpler to move chairs, desks, and tables than it is to envision the social structure within the room. Change in the physical environment is less disruptive to the students. If your first room arrangement doesn't work, it's not very difficult to move the furniture. The children may turn the wrong way at first, but they will quickly adapt. This is not the case for the social environment. The rules and regulations of classrooms are abstract. Children are expected to internalize these rules and once this happens, it is difficult to change the rules — after children have learned the rules of their room, they will expect them to be maintained.

Many of you have probably been more anxious about management and discipline issues than you have been about academic concerns. How does one person manage students' behavior and teach concepts or skills?

In the final section of *Becoming a Nation of Readers,* the authors discuss the need for quality teachers and the concerns of new teachers. They state that "the first year or two of teaching are extremely difficult for newcomers to the profession. Beginning teachers are often overwhelmed by having the complete responsibility for a class, anxious about maintaining discipline, and concerned about their effectiveness" (Anderson et al., 1985, p. 109). In a classroom, the teacher is in the unique position of being responsible not only for his or her own behavior but also for the behavior of the students in the class.

As a new teacher, you will undoubtedly worry about establishing all of the nuances of a well-managed classroom. McDaniel (1984) reports that a developmental progression exists in the establishment of classroom management and discipline. The first concerns of a new teacher are in mastering the elements of instruction. New teachers focus on motivation, sequencing the parts of the lesson, preparing the materials, and actively involving the students. Next in McDaniel's hierarchy are concerns centered on management and discipline. At this stage, teachers consider the physical arrangement of the room and its relationship to behavior. A new teacher usually implements a more structured discipline system.

Once you have had several years of positive experience in the classroom and when many of the routines have become automatic, you will have the energy to expend on more complicated ways of considering children's behavior. As a more experienced teacher, you will move into the third and most complex stage in McDaniel's developmental continuum of classroom management and discipline. This stage involves a humanistic approach to teaching and management. You will encourage your students to be independent and responsible in managing their own behavior. At that point, your classroom can best be described as a community of learners based on mutual respect and reasonable expectations.

Evertson (1989) states that effective teachers plan their classroom rules and procedures before the students arrive. You might wonder about what type of rules and procedures need to be decided. Shouldn't the teacher and students discover all of these rules together? Some rules can certainly be derived through a cooperative effort between the students and the teacher. Teachers and students could participate in a discussion group to talk about how the whole class will manage waiting in line for lunch, or how the students will decide who plays on the soccer field. You and your students can also meet to discuss specific decisions about the interior space of the classroom. Often this type of discussion focuses on revisions of rules that were put in place at the beginning of the year. For instance, you may decide to reevaluate a rule or policy that only three children can work together at any one time when six children decide to co-author a newspaper. There are other rules and regulations, however, that need to be in place before the students arrive. For example, you will need to decide the regulations for bathroom use, sharpening pencils, and dismissal from the classroom. If there are no regulations in place for these routine behaviors, chaos often results. Every child may want to run to the pencil sharpener to sharpen that brand-new school pencil at the same time. Having every child in line waiting for a turn hardly supports learning.

Although some rules should be carefully thought out before the school year begins, these rules should be kept to a minimum and should be overtly shared with the students very early on the first day of school. When situations arise in the classroom or in the school, classroom meetings should be called so that a resolution of these problems can be arrived at through the joint efforts of every member of the class. The key is to have a few rules in place to begin and to then add or revise rules with the full participation of the students.

Classroom Procedures and Routines

You may think that in order to keep your classroom creative and your students free from boredom, you will need to change the routine daily. Calkins (1986) described this process in her own classroom. She constantly changed the plans so that her classroom would be exciting for her students. She states that:

> **My days were full of planning, scheming, experimenting, replanning. Meanwhile, my children waited on my changing agendas. They could not develop their own rhythms and strategies because they were controlled by mine. They could not plan because they never knew what tomorrow would hold. They could only wait. (p. 12)**

Calkins's realization of the children's dependency on her organization led her to create a classroom that had predictable routines — routines that the children internalized so that they were able to expend their energy on academic pursuits.

Although a class may enjoy breaks from the routine, continual disruptions interfere with purposeful learning. You would be remiss if you did not share a learning opportunity that might occur spontaneously, like a hot air balloon landing in the playground. However, if you never superimpose a structure around the activities, your students will always be left to wonder, what next? Hubbard (1986) expands on this idea of structure within the classroom: "Teachers, too, provide needed structure in their classrooms, then open choices to their students limited only by the students' experiences and imagination, which they constantly work to expand" (Hubbard, p. 180).

Hubbard reached these conclusions after she had observed two classrooms over a lengthy period of time. Both teachers she interviewed discussed the underlying structures that the children had internalized. Early in the year the teachers had articulated many of the routines so that the students were aware of these patterns. These teachers also commented on the changes in the way they originally structured classrooms and what they are doing now. Hubbard reports that each teacher discovered that "the teacher is not the initiator of all activity; instead he or she has the responsibility to create a structure and an environment conducive to learning, provide resources, present options, and demonstrate strategies to help children become independent learners" (Hubbard, p. 185). The teachers Hubbard observed attributed changes in their curriculum to their new philosophy about teacher and student roles. Each teacher was currently organizing their reading and writing curriculums around literature-based reading and process writing. These changes resulted in more integrated instruction and more student input about the activities that they were engaged in.

Brophy (1986) concurs with Hubbard's conclusions. In writing about teachers who are effective managers, he mentions that they have "clear behavioral expectations and install effective routines and procedures at the beginning of the year" (Brophy, p. 189).

When you consider the whole school day, you will notice that most of the classroom routines and procedures repeat themselves. This means that there are several key times during the day when you will need to establish — and convey to your students — clear expectations about procedures. These routines might include leaving the classroom, pencil sharpening, and transitions between lessons and groups. You should explain your expectations surrounding these behaviors explicitly to your students. Let's examine some of these procedures more closely.

You will need to set up some procedures for allowing children to leave the classroom during the instructional portion of the day. How many children may leave the classroom at one time? How do the children indicate that they are leaving? How will you know who has left the class? Are there times when children should not expect to leave the classroom? For example, will you want Joe and Jed to leave for a drink at the crucial part of a science experiment? Your school will have some rules already in place about leaving the classroom, and how many students may be out of the class. You will need to formulate rules in your classroom that will result in minimal distraction to all involved.

Besides making trips to other places in the school, children need to get supplies, turn in work, work at centers, put trash in the wastebasket, and get drinks, among other things. How do you want the students to manage these tasks? Some teachers have established times during the day when students can get drinks and sharpen pencils. Other teachers not only have designated times; they limit the number of students at any one of these locations. You will need to decide if your students will perform these behaviors informally or if there will be specific expectations. Combinations of structured and less structured routines might also be realistic. For instance, during small-group time, when you are not working with all the students, these routines might be accomplished at the discretion of the students. When you are working with the whole class, however, the students would not be free to visit the wastepaper basket or get a drink, for example.

Transitions

Transitions — short time periods at the beginning and end of the day, before and after recesses, and between lessons — need to be carefully planned. McGreal (1983) estimates that "80 percent of all classroom management problems occur during off-task times in the classroom" (McGreal, pp. 90–91). The majority of this unstructured time occurs during transitions, when children are not focused on specific tasks.

One transition time occurs when children arrive at school. The children often bring notes for the teacher, lunch money, homework, book orders, and other things of importance that need to be managed just as the school day is beginning. What will you expect the children to do with these items? While you are collecting these tidbits from one child, what will the other children be doing? If we think back to Mrs. Webb's class, she had the children start the day by writing in their journals. Once the children were comfortable with this routine, she could focus on the individual children who needed her attention.

You can also resolve this dilemma by building specific routines into the school day. When children arrive at school, their first routine could be to place their homework in a designated location. You could also have a special place for notes to be turned in. These simple routines will allow your students to move quickly into the academic portion of the day. If all the students come into the class at the same time and you are concerned about bedlam as various items are turned in, you could set a limit on the number of students who may do these tasks at one time. The groups might be rotated until all of the children have had a turn. While the children are waiting for their turn, they can read books at their desk or write in their journals.

Following these tasks, some ritualized beginning to the day should occur. This is the time for the pledge of allegiance, calendar activities, and perhaps sharing. Children really enjoy a sharing time at the beginning of the day. It is an easy entry into the school day and it also allows the children to get to know each other better. At the start of a school year, the children take pleasure in sharing their new school things. You might find, for example, that one child is surprised and thrilled to see that another child has a similar folder with a popular cartoon character on the cover. These simple discoveries build links between children and foster friendships. At the completion of these activities the children should be eager to start the more academic activities of the day.

Other important transitions are the closing or cleaning up at the end of a lesson and the preparation for the next lesson. Imagine that you are coming to the end of a language arts block of time. One group of students is working on a mural using tempera paint, one group of students is scattered at various centers, and a third group has just completed a word-study activity with you. You expect that the students should clean up and be ready for lunch in five minutes. This type of clean-up is relatively typical when integrated instruction is occurring. How will you accomplish this?

Your students should know when lunch is, especially if you have encouraged them to monitor the duration of their activities by the amount of time scheduled. About five minutes before clean-up is expected, you can remind the students that there are ten minutes left in which to work and clean up. With five minutes left, you can stop all activities with some predetermined signal such as blinking the light on and off or playing a piano chord. At this point, your students should clean up and return to their desks. If you take time at the beginning of the year and explain very carefully to your students about clean-up procedures, you will find that cleaning up can be accomplished quickly and efficiently. Be patient and introduce only one messy activity at a time. When children have mastered the handling of the materials for one center or activity, it's time to introduce another.

Other aspects related to transitions are the collection of work and the distribution of materials. When the students are working in a whole-class activity, you can designate several students to pass out and collect materials. You might also have a room-helper chart, so that these tasks are rotated throughout the classroom and each student knows when he or she is to perform these tasks. At other times, your students might be involved in small-group or individual activities. When this is the situation, your students can turn in any independent assignments when the work is completed. In addition to having specific routines for work collection and distribution, your students, with your input, will need to brainstorm appropriate activities that might be engaged in when assignments are completed.

The last transition occurs at the end of the day. How will you bring the school day to closure? Students can participate in an informal discussion about what they have learned or something special that happened during the day. One book that could be used as a model for this discussion is M. Brown's *The Important Book*. Each child might quickly say what was important about this particular school day. Hayden (1981) shares another special activity that she used in the closing exercises of her classroom. Hayden often told her students made-up stories about the "kobolds," creatures very much like fairies. One day she brought a box into the classroom that was to hold messages from the kobold. She told her students that "every time he saw a kind deed done, he would leave a message in the box" (Hayden, p. 55). At the end of each day Hayden would read the messages to her students. After a few days, as she expected, there were so many good deeds that the kobold needed assistance. Naturally, Hayden enlisted the help of her students. Each time they noticed a positive behavior, they would drop a note into the kobold box. The notes were shared at the end of the day. Imagine the pleasure on a child's face when he or she heard that their classmates appreciated the act of kindness.

Activities similar to these provide a closing to a school day that parallels the informal entry into the day. The children have a chance to reflect on the special behaviors of classmates and to consider some of their new understandings. These routines help build a community of learners within the classroom.

Classroom Rules and Discipline

You will have to make some decisions about the behavior you expect from your students before they arrive. Many teachers, experienced and inexperienced, often share a common phenomenon in August — the August nightmares. Some teachers wake up in the middle of the night after dreaming or having nightmares about the disruptive behaviors of their new students. Among other things, teachers dream about kids running around the room paying no attention to the teacher's pleas to be quiet. In the majority of cases these nightmares quickly dissipate once the school year has actually begun. Most children come to school excited about learning and willing to cooperate with the rules that are necessary when large numbers of students are working together. A few students may have a harder time adjusting to the classroom. How exactly does a teacher control students' behavior and teach new concepts or skills?

Kounin (1970) suggests, as does Brophy (1986), that effective teachers prevent difficulties from occurring rather than always responding to problems. Kounin observed teachers and their interactions with students and noticed several patterns of behavior. These patterns included "withitness," by which the teacher communicated to the class that he or she knew what the students were doing even when the teacher was not directly involved with the student. Perhaps you remember "withitness" as a teacher's claim to have eyes in the back of his or her head — the ability (or so you believed) to know what you were doing even while facing the chalkboard. A second pattern is called *overlapping.* Overlapping is the ability of a teacher to handle two situations at the same time. This ability is very important, particularly when several groups of students are working on different projects.

Brophy (1986) expands on Kounin's observations with the inclusion of *continuity* and *momentum* in lessons. These terms convey the idea that the teacher has thought out and prepared lessons that are taught at a brisk pace. The teacher provides clear directions and monitors the work that is included in or is a follow-up to the lesson. Because of the momentum the teacher's directions have created, the students can successfully complete the assignment without the teacher's help.

In a well-managed classroom, the students have a clear understanding of what is expected of them. The students know that the teacher is aware of their activities even if it appears that he or she is busy with another activity. Students realize that the classroom is a place to learn and that the teacher has provided, through careful planning, appropriate instruction and independent activities.

If you adopt these techniques, on most occasions you can expect that through your careful planning, your classroom will function as you expect. Infrequently, you will need to intervene more directly to encourage or discourage certain types of behavior. What will you do if a student chooses to misbehave in the classroom and disrupts the teaching/learning environment?

A Range of Discipline Systems

Effective classroom discipline requires that you reflect on how you will respond to these disruptions before an incident occurs. Perhaps you remember what happened to your fellow students in elementary school when they misbehaved. Maybe you recall a more recent visit to a classroom and the method a teacher used to discipline a student. Do these discipline methods fit your personal style or philosophy about the way students should be treated? There are a variety of discipline strategies that can be used with students after they have misbehaved.

Discipline systems include a range of approaches, from very structured to less structured. Some systems suggest that all children be treated the same way; other systems support consideration of the individual when determining consequences for behavior. While three discipline systems will be discussed, we hope that you will quickly move to a system of managing behavior that considers the students in your class as individuals. This type of discipline system fosters respect and trust between you and your students.

A very structured, systematic approach to discipline has been labeled *Assertive Discipline* by Canter (1979a, 1979b). When a teacher uses this system, he or she generally establishes four or five rules with the students. In conjunction with these rules are lists of escalating consequences for more serious or repeated misbehaviors and a corresponding list of possible rewards. Consequences for problem behavior range from warnings to detention, and all students in the class are aware of other students' punishment. Usually whole schools support this discipline strategy, so that all teachers are coordinated and consistent in the way that they treat students.

One of the potential problems associated with this system is that students depend on the teacher to solve all of the problems. Students have little opportunity to solve problems collaboratively or to explore the origins of problems. Another concern is that most of the rewards are material incentives. Deci and Ryan (1985) and Lepper and Greene (1978) state that extrinsic incentives may cause students to become more concerned with the rewards than with the tasks they are doing. This shift in emphasis may result in decreasing academic performance. In addition, the emphasis on extrinsic, material rewards may lessen the students' intrinsic motivation to do well in school (Good and Brophy, 1987; Orlich, et al., 1985).

Canter's system has become very popular and is frequently observed in schools. New teachers in particular find this system attractive, as it is easy to implement. Philosophically, however, there are drawbacks to this approach because of the public nature of punishment and the limited input allowed children. Also, as the classroom becomes more complex, with more varied activities occurring at one time, and as children become active participants in the classroom, this behavioral reward-punishment approach will not match the teaching and learning environment.

Gordon's *teacher effectiveness training* (1974) is a less structured system. This system is based on communication between the teacher and students. Teachers are not expected to eliminate all problems exhibited by the students. The students themselves accept the ownership of the problem and develop, with the help of the teacher, strategies to resolve a problem. A difficulty with this behavior-management system is the amount of time required in discussing and working through a problem with a student. This process can be very time-consuming, especially when you consider the number of students in your classroom. However, usually there are only one or two children who are really having difficulty adjusting to the classroom rules and regulations, so this system is quite possible to implement. Gordon's system supports your students as individual learners and builds trust among all of the members of the class. A very important benefit of a system like Gordon's is that students' behavior changes are long term. The student gradually changes and is responsible for his or her behavior even when you are not present.

A third system is Dreikurs's *logical consequences* approach (1957, 1982). As in Gordon's teacher effectiveness training system, the teacher is not expected to solve the student's behavior problems alone. The responsibility for correcting the problem rests with the student. The teacher and students develop many rules together. If a rule is broken, there is a logical or natural consequence as a result. Logical and natural consequences can be confusing terms. *Natural consequences* are those events that happen as a result of behavior. For example, if the rule is that students may not return to the classroom during recess and a child forgets his coat inside on a cold day, then the natural consequence would be for the child to be cold for a recess. *Logical consequences* are determined by teachers as suitable punishment for an inappropriate action. A logical consequence might be the separation of two children who are working together because, for instance, they are building towers with their unifix cubes rather than solving math problems. The difficulty with this system is twofold: one, most adults don't want to see a child freeze and then get sick because his or her coat was withheld; and two, logical consequences are difficult to develop. If you choose to implement a discipline model similar to Dreikurs's, you can solve the coat problem by having some old lost-and-found coats near the door. Children aren't thrilled about wearing them, but the coats will keep the children warm. In this example a natural consequence has been changed into a logical consequence. Developing logical consequences is often more difficult than this coat-and-separation example would suggest. The strength of this approach is that misbehavior infrequently reoccurs.

As teacher, you will first need to check with your principal to determine if any particular discipline system is mandated in your school. If a system is used school-wide, then decide how you will implement this system in your classroom. If no system is adopted schoolwide, then think through what system or combination of various elements from systems will work best for you. Remember that you want to treat children as worthwhile individuals. This means that your classroom management system should allow serious input from your students through either private writing and discussion or through open class meetings. You *and* your students should be responsible for managing behavior in a class — not you alone. We recommend that you extend the atmosphere of open discussion that you maintain about academic issues to discipline concerns so that a true partnership in creating and maintaining a learning environment is built.

General Guidelines

Callahan and Clark (1977) suggest some general tips that will help you manage your classroom, no matter which discipline system you choose.

■ *The proximity of the teacher helps control behavior.*

When a student is misbehaving or not paying attention while you are teaching, move nearer to that student. You might even want to touch the student's desk or shoulder. Usually the child will stop misbehaving before you get to his or her desk.

In addition to moving nearer to a student who is misbehaving, it is a good idea to not just teach in front of the classroom. If the students are participating in a discussion, move among them. Make sure that you visit all the areas of the classroom where students are sitting. This movement throughout the room will keep students focused on the lesson.

Don't forget about eye contact. Eye contact lets your students know that you are listening to each and every one of them. Good eye contact with students even in the back of the class will keep them involved. You can also use a glare to stop a student's misbehavior.

■ *Let the students know that you care about them.*

Your smile each morning as the children arrive will signal that you are happy to see them. If you make a personal comment to a student who seems upset, you can help ease that child into the school day. Don't forget those personal comments written in the students' journals and on their papers. These comments will let each student know that you are interested in him or her as an individual.

A search for an appropriate discipline system for your class can be difficult, particularly during your first years of teaching. If you choose an approach and you find it uncomfortable, change. Talk to the children about why you find it necessary to revise a procedure. They will probably offer suggestions as to how the system or particular rule can be improved. Don't forget to monitor yourself as you use a discipline system. Are you disciplining only a few children who seem to be driving you crazy? If so, now would be the time to reflect on exactly why these children are being disruptive to the learning environment. Is the work that you are assigning possible for these children to do successfully and independently? Has the child been sick lately? Could the child be suffering through a major adjustment at home, perhaps a move, a divorce, or a new baby? When discipline isn't working, check with the child to find out why. Children will usually be very forthright in their explanation.

Teachers have often noticed that discipline concerns dissipate when children participate in written dialogues with the teacher. These conversations, carried out through journals, build a personal relationship between the child and the teacher. Once the child knows that the teacher really cares for him or her as an individual as demonstrated through these dialogues, the child ceases to act out in the classroom. What a wonderful benefit that comes with the use of journals!

■ *Expect positive rather than negative behavior.*

Focus on the students who follow directions when you have asked students to get ready for a lesson or to line up. In most cases, the rest of the students will soon comply.

■ *Expect that you and your students will make mistakes.*

Most teachers are becoming comfortable with the idea that all learning is accompanied by errors. For example, children often "invent" spellings before they spell accurately. Accepting mistakes related to behavior is sometimes more difficult, though. You might have a classroom rule to not yell out answers. Let's suppose Billy has been working on remembering to raise his hand and to wait for you to call on him before he talks, and he is improving. However, when the discussion becomes very exciting, he spontaneously blurts out his idea. How seriously will this mistake be considered? Will you ignore this lapse because of the excitement of the lesson, or will you discipline Billy?

■ *Provide a helpful hand at a crucial time.*

Some students really do have good reasons for having a terrible day. You might try dealing with the student individually. If this private talk doesn't help, the child may need to leave the class for a short time. You might arrange with another teacher to have this student sit in his or her classroom for a while. This strange environment will usually calm the child. When the child feels ready, able to control his or her behavior, then he or she may return to the classroom.

■ *Ignore certain behavior when appropriate.*

Sometimes the best solution to problem behavior is just not seeing it. Callahan and Clark point out that "the relatively inexperienced teacher tends to believe that he has to do something about everything or things will get out of hand. There are times, however, when just 'not seeing' is the best thing you can do" (Callahan and Clark, p. 120).

Here is an example of when ignoring behavior might be the best strategy. During a writing workshop, the students are usually expected to be busy with story writing. During one workshop, John is having difficulty getting started. He decides to spend the morning drawing and then looking through books. As the teacher, you have two choices. You might confront John and strongly suggest he get busy writing. John might then pick up a pencil and make a half-hearted attempt at his writing. You might also choose to observe John for a day or two instead, to see if he is using these activities as a way of preparing for writing. If John begins a story after a few days, a forceful nudge really isn't necessary.

■ *Have fun with your students.*

Laugh with the children in your room, especially when something really silly happens. When a lesson falls apart, you probably should all have a laugh and not take it all that seriously.

In one class, a teacher was involved in an integrated science, art, math, and reading lesson. The children were reading a recipe on how to make salt dough. In small groups, the children measured the ingredients, mixed the dough, and made salt-dough bunnies. The lesson was well planned out, all of the groups followed directions, and the expectation was that beautiful bunnies would be the result. The lesson disintegrated because of an unplanned-for element — it was unusually humid outside. The dough was sticky and couldn't be formed into anything because of the humidity. After ten minutes of watching children attempt to mold this sticky goo into something, the teacher recognized defeat and called the lesson to a halt. When the students and teacher looked at each other, there was nothing anyone could do but have a good laugh and clean up.

■ *Have a signal for attracting attention.*

When students are all involved in small-group work, it is sometimes difficult to get their attention. Before they begin working, you and the students should decide on a signal for students to be quiet and refocus on you for further directions.

Classroom discipline is not as straightforward to implement as we might desire. What works for one teacher and one classroom might not work for another teacher or class. The discipline system that you select will need to match your personal philosophy about behavior and will need to conform to your school's guidelines. It is important to remember that any system can be modified when the situation requires it.

Home and Community Involvement

Another way to help keep a complex classroom running smoothly is to bring in other adults. Many teachers have solicited the help of parents, either through direct participation in the classroom or indirectly through involvement at home. Figure 4.2 illustrates a form that was distributed to parents during a back-to-school parents' night. Parents want to participate in their child's education, but they often are not sure what they should do. By using a form similar to the one in Figure 4.2, you can communicate clearly that parents are a welcome part of their child's education.

Although including parents in your classroom will require some additional planning on your part, this planning does not need to be very complex. Initially, you might schedule a meeting for all of your class parent volunteers. Your agenda for this meeting might include these items:

1. Greeting; express appreciation for volunteering.
2. Discussion of what parents will be doing with students.
3. Establishment of a place where parents will be working with students.
4. Discussion of the rules and routines of the classroom. (These parent volunteers will be managing a child or small group of students, so they will need to know your behavior expectations.)
5. Establishment of a schedule so that parents know when to arrive at school. (A list of other volunteers and their phone numbers should be provided so that when a parent is unable to come, he or she can call a substitute.)

At the beginning of the year, your parent helpers could listen to the students read or read to the children. Eventually, the activities conducted by parents can be expanded. Parent volunteers can take individual dictations from students and participate in word-study activities.

The parents are particularly helpful in providing additional small-group time for individual students. Parent volunteers also make overall classroom management easier because they are directing the teaching and learning of several students. Fewer students are functioning in the classroom without direct supervision, so potential discipline problems should be reduced. Additional benefits of having parent volunteers are the support you will gain as a teacher and the clearer understanding the parents will gain of the complex requirements of the teaching and management of many children.

Some parents will be unable to volunteer in school, perhaps because of young

Source: Diane Barone.
Used with permission.

Our classroom needs your support. If you are interested in volunteering extra time for our class, please complete and return this form.

NAME_____

CHILD'S NAME_____

I am interested in the following:

_____ one hour per week working with children in the classroom

_____ room parent (help with parties and special events)

_____ baking for parties

_____ special projects (art, cooking)

_____ field trip chaperone

_____ working at home making and compiling books

_____ I need more information before I volunteer. Please call

me at this number _____.

Thank you,

FIGURE 4.2

Parent Volunteer Sheet

children at home or job commitments. These parents might still be willing to prepare materials at home for the classroom. Perhaps these parents could assemble small booklets so that each child can create his or her own book after hearing a story. For example, after hearing *The Bus Ride,* a group of first graders could create their own individual bus books, if someone could take the time to cut and prepare thirty bus-shaped booklets. On an occasional basis, parents enjoy creating these materials, but if you enlist parents' help with an idea like this, make sure the parents will have at least two weeks to prepare the materials.

Not only parents but foster grandparents and older students can serve as helpers in the classroom. Many communities already have programs established so that foster grandparents can volunteer in the classroom. Senior citizen centers often coordinate these programs. Their role would be similar to that of the parents. These more mature helpers particularly enjoy reading and discussing stories with children. In one kindergarten the foster grandfather became the primary resource for a unit on grandparents. It was a delight to observe his very serious discussions with children when they asked him what it was like when he was a child.

Many teachers have also had great success with using older students as classroom volunteers. The teacher of these older students could establish a rotating schedule so that all the students get a chance to help in your classroom. You could also create a small pool of student helpers from several classrooms. You might even request the students who always seem to be in trouble and/or are not the best academic achievers. Some experienced teachers may initially consider this plan idealistic and greet it cynically, but these "problem" kids usually turn into excellent tutors. These older students know exactly what children do to drive other people crazy and they won't tolerate these behaviors from the children they tutor. The younger children build a bond with these older students and both students become friends. Often an older student is seen protecting a younger student on the playground or bus. An added advantage is that the older child, who is always close to trouble in his or her own classroom, becomes a surrogate teacher in the second classroom. This sense of responsibility often has long-term positive effects on the older student's academic and social skills.

Organizing and Managing the Academic Environment

Goal Setting

When you have observed or worked in classrooms, you most likely have seen teachers conduct either small-group or whole-group lessons. Perhaps you were so intent on the lesson that you didn't consider a larger issue: How did the teacher know what to teach, how to teach, and when to teach that particular lesson? These are the questions that will shape your classroom curriculum and organization.

School districts develop curriculum guides in all subject areas and for all grade levels that reflect the state's requirements, the community's concerns, and the teachers' and principals' interests. These curriculum guides specify what the district expects students to learn and what attitudes and habits the students are expected to acquire within each grade level.

You should refer to these curriculum guides as a starting point in establishing what you will be teaching. Next, you will want to see the textbooks that will be used at your grade level. Check the scope and sequence charts that are printed in the teacher's editions of your textbooks. These charts indicate which concepts and skills are to be taught and learned by your students. Compare the goals, skills, and concepts set forth in these charts to your district's guidelines. Do the skills and concepts overlap? If so, then you will not have to supplement your core set of materials to teach these skills. However, if these lists deviate and if your school district expects more teaching of skills or of specific concepts, then you will probably need to supplement your materials.

During your first year of teaching, you will probably rely heavily on the material and order of presentation of your textbooks. Once you become more familiar with a grade level and the concepts and skills that are taught at that level, you will move beyond your textbooks. Even experienced teachers who rely less on textbooks still plan around the curriculum guides and the textbooks' scope and sequence charts. You can use these resource materials as a guide for your departures from more traditional teaching methods.

After your classroom has been arranged, you will want to spend several days looking over your textbooks and guides and making a yearly plan. This plan can be very brief — an outline often works best. Establish the content that will be taught in each subject area and a possible sequence. Naturally, this plan will be modified because of the children you teach and unplanned-for changes in scheduling. As you make your plan, consider the length of the school year. Will you be able to fit in all the topics that you want to teach? If not, which content areas are most important and must be scheduled? Is there any way that some content areas can be integrated with other subjects so that these topics can be worked into the schedule? It is important to consider these questions before you begin the year, not in April when half of the science curriculum still needs to be taught. This type of organization also allows you to order films and other materials that will support the teaching of a topic. If you wait too long to request your materials, you may find that they have been checked out by another teacher.

Once you have made a tentative yearly plan, you will want to take a narrower focus, perhaps on the first month of school. What do you hope to accomplish academically during this month? What concepts, skills, and content will you introduce to these students during this month? Remember to check the curriculum guidelines and your textbooks to help you with these decisions.

If you choose a more general theme for your classroom, you can use that theme as the focus of most of the bulletin boards in the classroom. For example, you can use a welcoming theme to help your students get to know each other. One of your boards might have all of the students' names on it. On another board, the children could list facts about themselves, such as number of brothers and sisters, color of eyes, distance of home from school, hot or cold lunch, and so on. Throughout the year, having an informal theme can help you plan art, music, and physical education activities. In art, for example, you could group your students in pairs and have them create portraits of each other. Later in your teaching career, you might organize all of your curriculum around broad thematic units. We'll explore more about this type of organization shortly.

Scheduling

After working out your yearly and monthly plans, you will want to focus on one week at a time, and the days within that week. What do you want to accomplish by Friday afternoon? What materials need to be prepared? How will the day be scheduled? This is the planning that is most often recorded in the teacher's plan book. As you begin to work in the plan book, the schedule for each day should be considered. List the times when school begins and ends. Block out recess and lunch time. Check each day so that special classes are included. For instance, your class might be scheduled into the library only on Thursday at 2:00. Here is an example of this type of schedule for a second grade class:

Daily Schedule

Regular

8:30–9:00	Children arrive
	Journal writing
	Record keeping
	Group discussion
9:00–10:00	Writing (including English mini-lessons)
10:00–10:15	Recess
10:20–12:00	Reading (whole group, small groups, and individuals)
12:00–12:45	Lunch and recess
12:50–1:15	Silent sustained reading and teacher-read stories
1:15–2:15	Math (integrate with science one day per week)
2:15–3:00	Science, social studies, and physical education
3:00–3:10	Get ready for dismissal

Special

Monday	2:30–3:00	Library
Tuesday	9:45–10:15	Music
Friday	1:15–1:45	Music

Now you are ready to work in the lesson plan book. This general schedule should be recorded in the book. Any special classes in which your students will participate should also be marked, and certainly any assemblies or special programs should be indicated. If you have read many teachers' plan books, you have noticed that their plans are often abbreviated. Don't be dismayed if their plans don't resemble the more involved plans that you have been writing for your classes. During your first year, and most likely for many of your years after the first, you will still want to complete more detailed plans. This means that the boxes in the plan book will probably not be sufficient. You can attach extra sheets with your more carefully structured plans to your book. Another strategy is to have two books. One book could be for reading and writing activities; a second book could include the plans for other subject areas. Or your two books might be divided by morning and afternoon: morning plans would be in one book, afternoon plans in another. Figure 4.3 shows the first week of school in a first grade teacher's plan book.

These plans are relatively abbreviated. The teacher who used these plans had more extensive details relating to the lessons on supplementary sheets. When you are planning, don't forget about transition time. There will always be time lost between subjects and before and after recess. The children will be slower at these transitions during the first month of school. You will need to remind your students how these transitions should be accomplished. If you take time at the beginning of the year to carefully establish the routines associated with transition times, the children will become more efficient and fewer problems should occur as the year progresses.

A brief aside is in order here. During the first few weeks of school, try not to

	8:30	9:00	10:20	12:50	1:15	2:15
MONDAY journal record keeping calendar sharing	WRITING draw pictures of themselves illustrate whole-page dictated stories about themselves	READING teach Sam, Sam poem DLTA Hairy Bear create Big Book	SSR Bear book poem – share after SSR	MATH graph shoes explain tubs unifix cubes pattern blocks cubes kids at these tubs	kids do cover of booklet with pictures + stories about themselves 2:30 library
TUESDAY journal record keeping calendar sharing	Share some of published stories from previous year brainstorm possible topics for writing 9:45–10:15	review Sam, Sam reread Hairy Bear concept sort toys, clothing music	SSR Bear book poem	people pattern explain tubs jewels geoboards junk boxes kids at any one of 6 tubs	science curly hair straight hair microscopes (get at media center)
WEDNESDAY journal record keeping calendar sharing	Discuss writing folders – how kids will store folders begin writing	1) evaluate concept of word 2) tape of Hairy Bear 3) drawings of Hairy Bear	SSR Bear book poem	graph clothing explain tubs stamps macaroni 2/3 at tubs 1 group patterning	social studies Who are the people in our school? list + discuss roles
THURSDAY journal record keeping calendar sharing	have students share some of their writing – continue writing	1) spelling inventory 2) cut pictures from magazines school things home things 3) listening center letter center	SSR Bear book poem	graph birthdays 2/3 at tubs 1 group patterning rotate	p e working with partner mirrors – kids take turns being mirror
FRIDAY journal record keeping calendar sharing	have students share some of their writing – continue writing close with discussion	1) Brown Bear 2) find brown things in magazines cut - paste 3) listen to Brown Bear – draw pictures	SSR Bear book poem	graph bedtime 2/3 at tubs 1 group patterning rotate 1:15 – 1:45 music	art children with partners They draw their partner.

FIGURE 4.3

Plan Book
Source: Diane Barone.
Used with permission.

worry about how little actual teaching you are accomplishing. This month is the time to establish the procedures; if you do a good job here, the children will be able to focus on teaching and learning for the remaining months of school. Remember too what Calkins had to say about establishing a predictable routine. When the children know what content area comes next and roughly when to expect it, they will anticipate when they need to clean up and get ready for the next lesson.

During this first month, you will spend more time doing *perception checks.* These checks require that you stop during a lesson or between lessons and ask several children how they did. Questions you might ask are:

■ "How are things going?"

■ "What story are you working on? Did you get much accomplished today?"

■ "Did you have any problems? How might you solve this problem in the future?"

■ "What did you do when you finished your work? Did you have any problems cleaning up?"

Ask all the children to stop whatever they are working on while these questions are being asked and answered. The questions let students know that you care about what they are doing even if you are not actively involved at the moment. The students will also listen in as other students talk about how they solved problems. Many times these discussions will reinforce procedures that are expected of the students — procedures that some children may have forgotten.

When observing in a classroom, you may have noticed that the teacher allocated short times for each subject. Perhaps he or she taught math for a half-hour and then moved to a fifteen-minute spelling lesson. The day was divided into many short blocks of time in which discrete subject matter was taught. As you *integrate* various subject areas, however you will discover that large blocks of time generally work best. For instance, your students might spend five minutes getting settled into writing. Then they will reread what they wrote yesterday. After this reading, they might start writing, stop, reread, and write. This process will most likely be repeated several times. Midway through a student might need to confer with a friend about a specific part of the story. These activities take time. If only thirty minutes had been allocated, some children might not have even started writing.

The plan book illustrated in Figure 4.3 demonstrates the larger blocks of time that have been allocated for more integrated instruction. Separate blocks of time are earmarked for writing and reading during this first week of school, but it is easy to visualize how these time blocks will eventually merge and overlap with one another. For the first week of school, the teacher has planned a small integrated unit that focuses on getting acquainted and building a classroom community. On Monday, each student will dictate a story about himself or herself and draw a picture to accompany the story. Later in the day, during math, the children will build a bar graph detailing the shoes that they are wearing. Finally, the children will design a cover for their own book about themselves. The first entries in this book will be their individual dictations and self-portraits. On Tuesday, the children will investigate the differences between curly and straight hair. As part of the science lesson, the children will study their own hair and these discoveries will be added to their book. Other discoveries about self occur during math lessons on Wednesday, Thursday, and Friday. The children will be graphing clothing, birthdays, and bedtimes. Physical education is brought into the unit by having the children take turns being a mirror to each other. As one child moves, the other child tries to mirror the movement of the other child. Art is included as a parallel to the mirror activity. Each child observes a partner and then draws a portrait of the partner. While the teacher has begun to integrate instruction of different subject areas, other blocks of time are reserved for more discrete activities. Instructional blocks in math and reading include assessment and procedural issues. That is, the teacher uses many of the initial subject-related instructional sessions to informally assess literacy and math development (see Chapter 12) and to establish procedures for selecting and cleaning up materials. This blend of integrated and more discrete subject matter instruction often occurs in classrooms, particularly at the beginning and end of the school year.

Let's consider this weekly plan a second time with a new perspective, focusing now on the time allocation for each subject area. An hour has been allocated for math and an hour and a half for reading. The teacher has divided her class into three groups during both of these blocks. Sometimes these groups will be homogeneous — with children of the same ability level — and at other times the groups will be heterogeneous — with children of varying abilities. In this case, the children are heterogeneously grouped for math and homogeneously grouped for reading. The teacher has divided students into three groups for math. One group will work with the teacher, another group will be building patterns with the math manipulatives, and the third group will investigate manipulative math materials with a partner. After twenty minutes, the groups will rotate. The group working with manipulatives will now be with the teacher. The pattern group will move to the manipulatives. Finally, the group working with the teacher will move to building patterns with the manipulatives. After twenty minutes the students will again rotate, so that all children have completed all three of the activities. The chart below shows how this rotation schedule might work:

	Group 1	*Group 2*	*Group 3*
1:00–1:20	Teacher	Manipulatives	Patterning
1:20–1:40	Patterning	Teacher	Manipulatives
1:40–2:00	Manipulatives	Patterning	Teacher

This organizational plan can also work during reading. The time periods might be slightly longer, but the same rotations would occur. One group might be doing a Directed Listening-Thinking Activity (DLTA) for the book *Hairy Bear;* another group might be learning the poem "Sam, Sam" for concept of word assessment (see Chapter 8); and a third group might be creating a Big Book based on *Hairy Bear.* At the end of a designated period, the children would rotate so that they would be able to participate in all of the activities.

There are several ways to let students know when and where they will be moving. You might have a chart on the board similar to the one shared above. This chart might be combined with a signal from you for changing activities. One teacher had a chart on the board without the times. The signal for students to move was when the group that she was working with left the small-group area. While the transition time was extended in this circumstance, it gave her a chance to move around the room and check up on the students before she began working with the next group.

This type of rotation organization might not be appropriate with older students. These students are often involved with projects that require large blocks of time for completion. Group or individual contracts might better match the learning needs of the students. When a contract is drawn up, it means that the teacher and a student or a group of students have jointly decided on a project; the details of the project such as specific components and time limit constraints are recorded on the contract. These contracts allow older students to be more independent as learners and to study topics in more depth.

However you choose to organize the day, children need extended periods of time to work on projects that are a part of integrated instruction. In addition, they need to know that writing or reading time, for instance, will recur on a regular basis so that they can plan their activities. That means that these time blocks should be predictable in their time slot within the day and their frequency during the week.

Grouping

The first grade teacher described above organized her students into several grouping patterns. She chose to have both *homogeneous groups* and *heterogeneous groups* within her classroom. Her plan book shows that she has also considered other grouping configurations for her students. For example, during physical education the children are paired off, and during silent sustained reading and writing workshops the whole class is working together. How were these groupings determined by the teacher? What rationales were used to form groups?

Purposes of Grouping

As teacher, you will want to consider each learning episode and consider the optimal form of organization. If you contemplate the learning needs of the approximately thirty students in your class, it seems reasonable that there will be times when teaching the whole class will not be appropriate. For instance, after the children have been evaluated for competencies in reading and math, you will want to form small ability groups for specific instruction. Here is an example that should clarify why these ability groups are most efficient for some instruction. After using a spelling inventory to evaluate students' word knowledge, the teacher realized that some children were representing words with only initial consonants (*b* for *bed*), others were including short vowels (*bad* for *bed*), and a few children were using long vowel markers (silent letters) in words (*trane* for *train*). (See Chapters 6 and 10 for an explanation of these spellings.) The teacher then formed groups based on this information for direct teaching in word study. One group investigated initial consonants, one group studied short vowel patterns, and a third group considered long vowel patterns. If the group using initial consonants to represent words had been included in the long vowel pattern investigation, they would not have been able to participate, as this material would have been at a frustration level for those children and therefore beyond their comprehension. Certainly, teachers do not want to have all of their groupings organized on the basis of ability, but as the above example demonstrates, this type of grouping makes sense for certain instruction.

Besides grouping students on the basis of ability, teachers often use smaller groups when teaching material that requires direct involvement of the students. When children are conducting a science experiment, the teacher would organize groups of three or four students to work together. These smaller groups allow each child to have the opportunity to participate in the investigation and discuss the process and results. Informal small groups often naturally evolve during reading and writing time. Children seek out other children who are willing to listen as they read a passage from a book or who will provide a critical ear to a portion of a story that has just been written.

During certain instructional portions of the day, you may see a teacher use many

Throughout the school day, you will make use of a variety of groups — for example, to give students an opportunity to pursue special interests in greater depth. (© Ned Haines/Photo Researchers)

types of groupings. Writing workshops generally contain several different types of groups. The workshop often begins with a mini-lesson that includes all of the students. Following this brief lesson, children may work on a story on their own, with a partner, or in a small group. The teacher might also assemble a group of children to present a specific skill such as the use of quotation marks. Individual children may request the assistance of the teacher through conferences about the content of a story. At the end of each writing workshop, all of the children might meet in a large group to share published stories.

In each classroom, there will generally be a variety of groups. An observer should see whole-group, small-group, and individual instruction. During the majority of the time, students should be working informally in heterogeneous arrangements. For some direct teaching, children should be organized into homogeneous groups. Before organizing students into groups, review each learning situation to determine which type of organization is most appropriate.

Role of Evaluation

Evaluation is an *ongoing* process that helps teachers determine specific abilities and characteristics of their students. Teachers use the information from these informal evaluations at the beginning of the year to group children for some instruction. The plan book in Figure 4.3 revealed that this teacher would be evaluating her students for concept of word in print by using the poem "Sam, Sam" and for word knowledge as demonstrated through each child's performance on a spelling inventory. Teachers can also supplement their initial evaluations and observations of students with information included in the students' cumulative folders. These are folders that follow children as they move through a school. Many teachers are reluctant to read these folders before the students arrive at school. They don't want to be biased about a child before they meet him or her. Teachers know that students act differently in different environments. A child who was disruptive in a third grade setting might never exhibit this behavior in the fourth grade. Although you may not want to read every folder diligently before school begins, you should scan the folders to determine if a child has a health problem. If a child is allergic to a particular food or insect or is asthmatic, you will want to be aware of this.

Remember that your groups are flexible and that many of your students will be rusty after that long summer vacation, so don't worry that you might not place them accurately. Children can easily be moved from one group to another and these movements should happen routinely during the year. These initial groupings will just help you get started into the organization that you will maintain during the school year. The advantage of screening so early is that children can quickly be brought into the organizational patterns that you have set up for your class, such as a rotation schedule during reading and math.

Teachers use informal observation to determine characteristics of children beyond academic ability. When you form heterogeneous groups, consider characteristics such as shyness, impulsiveness, and the ability to complete tasks. These groups should include a variety of students so that children will derive maximum benefit from working together.

Periodically throughout the year, you will revise your assessments and include other informal measures so that your evaluation of a student is current. In conjunction with these evaluations, you will update information about a child through routine daily observation.

Forming Groups

Teachers generally form groups based on a teaching or learning objective. So far we have focused primarily on homogeneous groups resulting from evaluation of students' abilities in certain subject areas. However, there are many situations in the class that lend themselves to other grouping arrangements.

Special Interest Groups   Many groups are formed on the basis of a special interest. These groups usually come together for a short duration of time to accomplish a special assignment. Several children might decide that they want to write a classroom newspaper, for example. These children would write together until this project was complete and ready for distribution to the class. Another group of children could plan a bulletin board display of the information that they discovered about dinosaurs. Eeds and Wells (1989) described another type of interest group called a *literature study group*. Children in this group read the same book independently and came together on a daily basis for discussions. Each literature study group stayed together until they finished reading and discussing the book. The types of interest groups that might be formed are endless.

Cooperative Groups Another way of looking at groups is to focus on the interaction patterns — the social dynamics — that occur within the groups. Students can basically interact in three ways. As Kohn (1986) noted, students can compete, work individually, or work cooperatively. Typically, competition is the dominant pattern of interaction in schools. Recently classroom teachers have included and encouraged cooperative groupings among their students. Notably, cooperative groups are characterized by positive goal interdependence as well as individual accountability. *Positive goal interdependence* requires the children to work together to achieve a goal. You can probably remember group work where one student did the task and all of the students were equally rewarded. In cooperative groups each child must participate in order for the group to be rewarded; each child is *held accountable* for his or her unique contribution. An example of this type of group work is seen when three children are given the task of helping each other learn spelling words for the weekly quiz. Each child may have some different words to learn and a different goal as to success on the quiz, but the way the group is rewarded is by having each child in the group reach his or her goal (Johnson and Johnson, 1975).

There are several ways that cooperative groups can be formed. The most widely used method is *student teams achievement divisions,* or *STAD* (Slavin, 1980). Teams are formed to study the material that was presented by the teacher. The students eventually take a quiz when the team feels that each student is ready to succeed. Teachers have predetermined goals for each student's performance on the quiz. If each student in a group attains this goal, then the group is rewarded.

Another method is the *jigsaw approach* (Aronson, 1978). In this organization a small group of students meet and become experts on some bit of information. Some of the students might become experts on one section in a chapter about reptiles, for instance. Other students in other small groups would be developing expertise on other sections of this chapter. The students would then regroup so that one expert on each section of the chapter would be included in each new group. The experts would now be responsible for teaching their group their special knowledge. As a concluding activity, the students would take an individual test, and, as in the STAD approach, the group would be rewarded if each member achieved his or her goal.

A third method of cooperative organization is called *Learning Together* (Johnson and Johnson, 1975). In this system, the students in each group are expected to complete a single assignment. Each student has a specific responsibility. For instance, one child might be a reader, another the discussion leader, a third the recorder, and a fourth the checker to make sure that all the participants are fulfilling their role. All of the group members would be assigned the same grade for the completed task.

One other method has been described by Sharan (1980) as *Group Investigation*. This method is the most complex, as it places the total organization and responsibility for learning on the part of the students. The members of each group assume responsibility for what they will learn, how they will organize themselves, and how they will communicate what they have learned to the class. Certainly, this is not an approach that you will want to try in your first expeditions into cooperative learning.

Teachers and parents, in particular, are sometimes concerned about the learning benefits of these cooperative groups. Sometimes parents feel that bright children are penalized by having to facilitate the learning of other students. Slavin (1986) addressed this question head on. His research shows that the "tutors" often show greater learning gains than the "tutees." Slavin explains that these students gain a more thorough understanding of the subject matter through their attempts at teaching this material to other students. The added benefit to this more complete understanding is the social status that comes with being a surrogate teacher. A summary of the research (Kohn, 1986) indicates that cooperative learning enhances academic achievement across all age groups. In addition, students are more positive about school, curriculum, and teachers. Most important, students are positive and supportive of one another regardless of differences in abilities, physical handicaps, or ethnic backgrounds (Slavin, 1979).

Other Considerations

When you are deciding on group arrangements, a few other issues should be resolved. The first issue concerns *physical space*. Children need room to work in groups. Sometimes group work deteriorates because two groups are simply too close together. Perhaps the talking of one group interferes with the thinking of another group. A general principle is to have groups scattered throughout the class. Think about the spaces in your room and try to arrive at three or four possible locations for group work. Consider these locations from two perspectives: one, when all of the students in the class are working in groups, and two, when only one or two special interest groups are functioning. If only one or two groups are busy, they need to be separated from the other students so that their tasks do not interfere with the other teaching and learning occurring in the room.

The second issue concerns the *social dynamics* of the group. As mentioned above, the personalities of the students play an important role. Each group should have both quiet and verbal children. Children who always come up with great ideas should be scattered throughout the groups. Planners and organizers should also be evenly distributed. Usually there are one or two special children — children who have difficulty controlling their behavior, have a handicapping condition, or are significantly below grade level in academic functioning — in the class. These children should certainly not be placed in the same group, and group membership in general should be rotated for these children. Students are usually willing to work with these more difficult children if they are not included in every group.

Thematic Units

Earlier in this chapter we discussed how to use the district guides and your textbooks to plan a curriculum. A suggestion was also made about selecting a theme to help with bulletin boards, art, and music. As you gain confidence in your teaching, you will want to experiment with more involved thematic units (see also Chapter 9). Theme studies integrate the various disciplines of study and thereby provide additional time for extended explorations of subject matter.

Children's literature is often a central element in the development of a theme unit. Moss (1984, 1990) has described several units of study that can be developed from children's literature. Her units center on topics like toy animals, pig tales, or the night. She recommends books and related writing activities for large groups and small-group story sessions. Coody (1983), Gamberg, et al. (1988), Hains (1982), and Johnson and Louis (1987), among others, have written books that can help you develop thematic units.

Literature provides a beginning place for teachers to organize subject matter. For example, a book like *People* (Spier, 1980) provides the impetus for a second grade teacher to create a large theme study of the similarities and differences among people. The curriculum that had been mandated by the school district required second graders to study graphing in math and health in science, as well as to consider character analysis in literature, and develop respect for different cultures in social studies. This teacher decided to combine all of these requirements under one large thematic topic centered on people.

As the core text, therefore, *People* was selected. This book by Peter Spier looks at all of the people in the world. Spier carefully represents the similarities and differences among people. Each page of his book is filled with comparisons and contrasts of physical and social characteristics. On one page, he illustrates how fashions differ from country to country; on another, he shows people's need to write and all the different methods of representing words. The teacher began this unit by having children build bar graphs based on many of the characteristics shared in the book. Then the teacher asked parents and students to supply lists of favorite foods, vacation spots, countries of origin, and so on. This information was used to form additional graphs. The children then began to investigate themselves. They studied the foods that they usually ate and compared these to the foods eaten by other children living in other places. The students studied their own and each others' hair type, eye color, and skin color. During reading and writing, the children investigated the characters in stories that they were reading. The children developed charts that compared the physical and personality traits of the characters in various stories. The teacher and the students invited guests to school to share some of the unique aspects of their particular culture. The students then researched their own families to discover personal traditions. This unit could also be shifted slightly to consider family members and a generational theme might be included. Students could investigate the roles of babies and grandparents in stories, for instance. Clearly, with a little brainstorming, a theme unit can be created that provides more in-depth coverage of a topic while at the same time fulfilling the curricular requirements of a district.

Once you have decided upon which elements of your curriculum can be combined into one unit, you should visit the library. You will want to check out a large quantity and variety of books related to the topic. These books should be at various reading levels, so that all of the children in your class can enjoy them. After selecting the books and referring to various teacher resource books, you will want to plan the activities that will occur during your unit. A teacher planning sheet for a fairy-tale unit is provided in Figure 4.4. The teacher used this sheet to make sure that all the areas of the curriculum were included.

Many teachers find the integration of diverse subject matter a complex task. They become overwhelmed with the planning. This task can be simplified if you rely on curriculum guides and grade-level textbooks. Then develop a form similar to the one presented, so that you are assured about teaching the important aspects of your curriculum. These organizing strategies will help you focus and more easily plan a thematic unit.

FIGURE 4.4

Teacher Planning Sheet

Source: Diane Barone. Used with permission. Some of the ideas adapted from *The WEB: Wonderfully Exciting Books*. The Ohio State University, Columbus, OH.

```
The Jolly Postman - Ahlbergs
    letters to characters
Dialogue journals
    children will write in notebooks
    as they read fairy tales
Write a fairy tale
Word Study
    collect size words (giant,huge)
    collect "wee" words (sweet,sweep)
    collect character words (elf,goblin)

                    WRITING
```

```
Fairy-tale museum
    collections of real objects that
    accompany fairy tales
Fairy-tale homes
Murals of fairy tales
Fairy-tale quilt
    quilt blocks representing
    original fairy tales
Bread-dough figures
ABC book of fairy tales

                    ART
```

```
Storyteller
    shares tradition of fairy tale
Grandparents, parents, teachers,
    principal share favorite fairy tale
Fairy-tale party
    dress as character
    food from stories
    dramatize stories
Mark on world map where fairy tales
    originate

            SOCIAL - STUDIES
```

```
Cooking
    foods from fairy tales
Cooking transformations
    (bread, Jello)
Use magnifying glass (small to big)
Plant bean seeds

                    SCIENCE
```

```
Surveys to discover
    favorite fairy-tale character
    scariest fairy-tale character
    most disliked fairy-tale character
.Measurement--capacity
    fairy cupfuls to giant-sized
    container
Working with threes

                MATH
```

```
Tape-recorded noises made by big and
    small creatures
Listen to
    The Witch's Sabbath - Berlioz
    The Peer Gynt Suite - Grieg
Creative movement to music
    selections and to an entire fairy
    tale

            PE & MUSIC
```

AT THE TEACHER'S DESK: Creating Units

Developing thematic units is simpler if you work with other teachers. The brainstorming activities centered on books and activities are richer when several people are participating. Same-grade-level teachers often work in teams to develop these units and then share the units. In this way the amount of background research is shared by all of the teachers.

When you or a group of teachers gather to participate in this brainstorming activity, be willing to include any idea. Sometimes the best thematic units develop around ideas that seemed very strange at first. The idea of exploring size words from fairy tales and comparing stories with magic items began this way.

There are many resource books that can help you develop theme units. Use them. In addition to the books already mentioned, a book by Pappas, Kiefer, and Levstik, *An Integrated Language Perspective in the Elementary School* (1990), provides many suggestions for creating thematic units and offers sample units. This book is an excellent resource that will help you develop your own thematic units.

Evaluating Learning

A critical academic concern faced by teachers is how to evaluate students' work. Flood and Lapp (1989) discuss the complexity of evaluation:

> **The question of evaluation is a messy one with few answers that happily satisfy students, parents, and teachers. A single score, whether it is a course grade or a percentile score from a norm referenced test, almost always fails to accurately report students' overall progress. Sometimes the problem is more one of parents' and students' misunderstandings and misperceptions than of measurement or evaluation per se. (p. 509)**

We will examine the evaluation of students' work in more detail in Chapter 12. Here are some of the issues that need to be considered: Do you evaluate everything? If you choose to, then when do students get to practice what they are learning? Do you take grades every week, or just after students have practiced and you designate this assignment a test? Do students have input into what is graded? First check with your principal to see if there is a school policy about recording grades. Some schools want teachers to record at least one grade per subject each week. These grades are then averaged for the report-card grade. Your school may allow you more flexibility in collecting grades. For example, you may not need to report any grades in math for one week while you are introducing a new concept. Then, after the children have practiced, you could record grades from two assignments. However you collect these grades, they are usually averaged for the one grade that will appear on the report card. A difficulty that you might face with this procedure is how to grade the child who is really trying but is below grade level in skills. Sometimes by talking to your principal and the parents of this child, you can negotiate to avoid giving letter grades. You might just give an S (for *Satisfactory*) in each subject, and have additional conferences with parents to explain what their child is doing academically.

Most teachers find that report cards are not sufficient for informing parents about their child's progress. Teachers usually schedule parent conferences at least twice during the year. Flood and Lapp (1989) suggest that teachers share a *comparison* or *assessment portfolio* with parents during these conferences. This portfolio might include standardized test scores (see Chapter 12), informal testing measures, writing samples, reading program reports, self-assessments, and samples of materials used in school. The samples of materials might represent what a child was able to read in September and now what he or she can read. In this way a parent has concrete evidence of how much their child has improved. These portfolios will facilitate a parent's understanding of a child's growth. Their perspective will be broadened beyond the reporting of a single grade.

Involving Parents

Earlier in this chapter we discussed ways that parents and other volunteers could be included in the class to help with teaching and management of students. Parents, whether or not they are volunteering in the classroom, need to be involved with the academic concerns of the classroom from the very first day of school. One way to facilitate this involvement might be for you to develop a short booklet that addresses the immediate concerns of parents. Your booklet might include a letter to parents describing a typical day, a school calendar, necessary supplies, a sample report card, and an invitation to the first parents' meeting.

It is important to have a parents' meeting early in the year — the earlier the better, so that parents will not ask you to confer about their child. (If they do make this request, you can honestly say that you do not know the child well enough to have a conference yet.) During this meeting, you should discuss your expectations, both academic and behavioral. Many teachers also share their feelings about "invented" spelling and how they will evaluate writing. A strategy that you might incorporate at this meeting is to have your parents perform many of the activities that their children accomplish during a school day. For instance, each parent can be given a schedule of activities and a starting place for rotation among activities. The parents might

1. read a Big Book.
2. read a child's published story.
3. write a letter to their child and place it in the child's writing folder.
4. look at the books about frogs and toads and write down two facts or questions that they have. Leave these in a folder for their child.
5. participate in a word-study activity. Sort pictures by school things and home things. Write ten words related to school on word cards. Sort these. (Provide an example.)
6. do some math on the computer.
7. add and subtract with the unifix cubes.
8. make a pattern with the pattern blocks.

9. make a prediction and graph the prediction. For example, how long will it take a candle to burn out?

10. enjoy a treat.

After participating in all of these activities, the parents will have a clearer understanding about their child's learning. Many of your parents will now have had their first experience in learning without completing a worksheet. Perhaps this experience will help enlist parent support for your departure from a dependency on worksheets.

Another way you can involve parents is to periodically send home student gifts to parents or booklets that include samples of all the students' work. Often your theme will provide direction as to the form of a booklet. For example, during a unit on vehicles, your students might interview their parents about when they learned to drive. These interviews can be used as the basis for stories about learning to drive. When these stories have reached the publishing stage, each story could be photocopied. These photocopies can then be collated so that every parent receives a booklet that includes one story from each child in the class. The same procedure could be used for other stories or poems written about a particular theme. The children could also create a newspaper that reports what is happening in their class. The class could also put together a calendar with several child-created stories for each month as a holiday gift for parents.

Another way to include parents in the academic curriculum is to foster their participation in word-study activities. You might be exploring words related to vehicles or fairy tales, for instance. For homework, children might ask their parents to help them jot down five words that correspond to the topic. The following day the children could work with you or in small groups and sort the words that they brought from home. Parents and children have fun with this activity. Searching for words is an easy way for parents to help with homework. Children who haven't done their homework are left out when the sorting is done in class. Most students won't want to be left out more than once — another logical consequence that will result in more students completing their homework.

A final suggestion for keeping parents involved with the academic curriculum comes from the classroom of Kathy Perrone. Perrone teaches the academically talented students in her school. She asks one child from each group of students to write a note to parents about what they have done in class that week. These notes are then photocopied and distributed to the parents. A sample from Perrone's class is displayed in Figure 4.5.

These methods, along with others that you will create, will keep parents aware of exactly what is happening in class. That way when children arrive at home and their parents ask, "What did you do in school today?" they won't believe the traditional answer, "Nothing."

As we conclude this chapter, we will visit a fifth grade teacher's classroom. We will visit Mr. Young's class on the first day of school, in the middle of the year, and toward the end of the year. As you read these observations, consider the teacher's planning both for management and academic concerns. Notice how the structure of the classroom is internalized by the students as the year progresses.

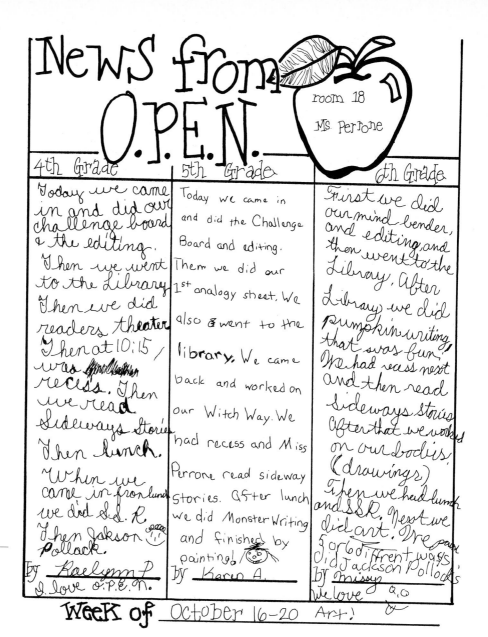

FIGURE 4.5

News to Parents about Class Activities

Source: Kathy Perrone, Bakersfield, CA. Used with permission.

The handwritten newsletter reads:

News from O.P.E.N.

room 18
Ms. Perrone

4th Grade

Today we came in and did our challenge board & the editing. Then we went to the Library. Then we did readers theater. Then at 10:15 was recess. Then we read Sideways Stories. Then lunch. When we came in from lunch we did S.S.R. Then Jakson Pollock.

by Kaelynn P.
I love O.P.E.N.

5th Grade

Today we came in and did the Challenge Board and editing. Then we did our 1st analogy sheet. We also went to the library. We came back and worked on our Witch Way. We had recess and Miss Perrone read sideway Stories. After lunch we did Monster Writing and finished by painting!

by Karen A.

6th Grade

First we did our mind bender, and editing, and then went to the Library. After Library we did pumpkin writing, that was fun! We had recess next and then read Sideways Stories. After that we worked on our bodies. (drawings) Then we had lunch and SSR. Next we did art. We did 5 or 6 different ways. We did Jackson Pollocks. we love

by missy

Week of October 16-20 Art!

One Fifth Grade Classroom

First Day

The room is ready. Mr. Young is pleased that all of the bulletin boards are prepared. Several of the boards are waiting for projects that the students will complete on the first day. He has carefully thought about where the supply areas should be and where the students will be able to store projects in progress. His students will work on projects related to the curriculum rather than at learning centers on most days, so these supply and storage areas are very important. Mr. Young has indicated with little notes which desk belongs to which student. Each desk has construction paper on it, so that each child can create his or her own name tag.

Mr. Young escorts his students to the classroom. He welcomes the students and gives directions about designing their name tags. As they are doing this he calls the roll and asks about lunch. "Tomorrow, I will assign a student to call roll and take lunch count. Don't worry, I'll show you what to do." In about fifteen minutes, he asks the students to stop working on their name tags. "We'll have time to finish the name tags later. When you are finished, I want you to put the tags in the file on the bookcase near my desk. After school, I will laminate them and we'll put them on our desks tomorrow."

Next Mr. Young begins a discussion about rules and goals. He tells his new students about the rules he has developed and asks for their thoughts. They agree with the rules and suggest a few others. Mr. Young adds these to the class-room rules chart. He then talks about goals. His goals for this year are to set up the room so that students work with other students and to teach math, writing, science, reading, and social studies. He also talks about his goals as a university student. "I want to learn to speak Spanish. I'm taking a class twice a week. I might even practice with you." Mr. Young passes out writing paper and drawing paper. "I want you to draw yourself. After your picture is the way you want it, I want you to write your goals for this year. Try to come up with four or five." Periodically, throughout the year the children will look back at these goals and write about how they are doing in achieving them. When the children finish, a few are willing to share. Paul wants to read and spell better. Jason wants to stay out of trouble. Mr. Young collects these goals and self-portraits and stores them in a safe place.

Mr. Young talks about the daily schedule with the students as he writes it on the board. "We'll begin the day with SSR — Sustained Silent Reading. Please find a book in our class library or bring one from home. You will need one every day. Next we'll have math. After math, writing and reading. Remember, we don't have morning recess anymore. If you need to visit the restroom, sign out on the chalkboard. When you return erase your name. Only two people may be out of the room at one time. You may leave for the restroom, sharpen your pencil, turn in work, and get supplies when I am not teaching you directly. In the after-noon, we'll have science, social studies, p.e., and music. We will be doing art in our projects so we usually won't have a special art time. That's the way most days will be."

Mr. Young moves to the front of the room and asks the students to tell him all the math words that they know. He quickly builds a list of many words. He and the students begin to sort them: multiplication words, subtraction words, meas-urement words, and so on. He then asks his students to create a worksheet that has an example of all of the problems the students know how to do. He adds that they also need to solve the problems. Mr. Young will use this information and the textbook placement tests in planning his math groups.

It's the fifth graders first full morning without a recess break. Mr. Young is pleased with how well they have worked through this first morning. Now it's time for lunch and recess. He hasn't squeezed in everything he had planned, but the children seem to be developing an understanding of the classroom environment.

The students come in noisy from the playground. It takes several minutes for them to settle into the classroom. When the students are quiet, Mr. Young discusses their behavior. He wants them to know that they need to be quiet in the halls so that they won't disturb other classes, and that they are to come into the room ready to learn. At this point, Mr. Young has the students get in line and practice coming into class. No more is said about the matter. Mr. Young is then able to begin the afternoon as he had planned, by reading a chapter from *Dear Mr. Henshaw.*

Mr. Young explains that for the first two weeks of school the class will be working on a social studies project. Then for two weeks the students will study science. Following this overview, Mr. Young begins the social studies lesson. "We're going to start by studying our school. Let's list the people in our school." When the list is quite large, Mr. Young points to the word *principal.* "What do you think the principal does?" The children come up with several ideas. "We are going to create a book that tells about all of the people in our school. We'll discuss their jobs here, then we'll interview them. We'll practice with each other before we really do the interview. Today, we'll each work with a neighbor and brainstorm what this person might do." Mr. Young assigns different people to each pair. The pairs work for fifteen minutes on deciding what the people in the school do. Then the pairs work for another twenty minutes developing questions that they might ask each individual. Mr. Young ends the lesson here. Tomorrow the students will share questions and role play to see which questions result in the best answers. Then it will be time to revise the questions, making sure that each question is very open-ended.

Mr. Young hands each child a paper. The paper has the names of four people who work in the school. "Tonight, I want you to talk with your parents about these people. Ask Mom or Dad what these people do and what questions we should ask them. We'll use this information tomorrow." Mr. Young answers a few questions about the assignment and the students are dismissed.

Discussion

Looking back at Mr. Young's first day of school, we get a clearer picture of how he organized and managed the academic environment. He had thought about the *goals* for instruction by checking the district's guidelines and textbooks and by deciding himself what he thought would be important for students to learn this year. On the first day of school he shared some of these goals with the students and then he offered a personal goal — learning Spanish — that related to school and to his personal life. In addition to these goals, Mr. Young encouraged the students to develop individual goals for the school year. These goals will be referred to throughout the school year so that students can measure their own progress in accomplishing them.

Immediately after this discussion and activity, Mr. Young explained the *daily schedule.* He let the students know the daily routine and that this routine would be repeated on most days. Included in this discussion were the rules that students would need to know right away. The students quickly knew that they needed a book, how to leave the room, and how to gather supplies.

During this first day Mr. Young predominantly used *whole-class grouping*. The goal-setting activity and the math lesson were primarily organized this way. The math evaluation sheet indicates that during math instruction Mr. Young will sometimes group by ability. When the students brainstormed for their upcoming interviews, they worked in pairs. Mr. Young will be busy observing while these pairs work and will use this social interaction information to form other groups.

Mr. Young has decided to not start his year with a full integrated *thematic unit*. He has developed a small unit in social studies that centers on the occupations of the school personnel. This unit will eventually move into math and art when the students design replications of the school and then design their "ideal" school.

The only *evaluation* that is obvious in this first day is the math evaluation. This evaluation is unusual in that the students are creating the evaluation tool themselves. Mr. Young had the students brainstorm math terms and then categorize them. This activity served as a review. Then he asked students to create a worksheet that samples all of the problems the students can solve. These worksheets should provide some interesting information about each child's math proficiency.

And finally, Mr. Young has incorporated the *parents* into instruction from the very first day of school. Each child has been asked to use their parents as an expert about the people who work in a school. The parents and their child will work jointly at developing interview questions.

Middle of the Year

The children are reading at their desks. SSR usually lasts for 30 minutes. Mr. Young indicates that the children should finish up the paragraph that they are reading, put their books away, and get ready for math. Today, Mr. Young has planned for two math groups. One group will work on double-digit multiplication with regrouping and the other group will work on two-step word problems. Mr. Young teaches a lesson to one group while the other students work in their math books. The students rotate after a half hour.

When the math lesson is completed, Mr. Young directs the students to move into reading-writing workshop. The students are divided into three groups, even though each group is basically doing the same activity. Mr. Young wants every child to be able to participate in the discussion that will accompany his lesson, so small groups are needed. All of the students are reading biographies and writing in a literature log. They read the stories independently and freely write their thoughts in the log. As a connection between their reading of biographies and writing, the students are all working on their interviews of people in the community. These interviews will eventually be published in a class book and copies will be sent to the parents. Mr. Young is conducting lessons with three small groups of students on types of questions and how to determine the answers. He is using a story in the basal text for this lesson. The reading-writing workshop lasts for two hours and the students rotate among these three activities. At the end of this workshop, the children leave for lunch and recess.

When the students come in from lunch, they write in journals. Mr. Young gives them about fifteen minutes for this writing. He then reads to them from *In the Year of the Boar and Jackie Robinson* (Lord, 1984), a biography about a Chinese child and her new life in New York.

The next hour is spent on science. The students are studying the ocean. Today several small groups of students are doing an experiment about wave action with a ball and a tray of water. After participating in and observing the experiment, the children write in their science notebooks their observations and why they think the waves formed the way they did. Mr. Young finishes the science block of time by conducting a content Directed Reading-Thinking Activity (DRTA) with the section in their textbook on ocean waves. Many of the children have a clearer understanding about their experiment after reading this portion of text.

The day ends with a music lesson with the music teacher. Mr. Young dismisses the children at its conclusion.

Discussion

Mr. Young is pursuing the academic goals that he established at the beginning of the year. Clearly his students are progressing in math, reading, and writing. On this day we can observe his teaching of multiplication, story problems, wave action, and a content DRTA. He also has provided time for reading and has encouraged both writing about the biographies being read and more personal writing in journals.

Mr. Young's schedule is basically the same as the one he established at the beginning of school. One difference is that reading and writing have been connected and form one very large instructional block. As Mr. Young planned, the students have rotated between science and social studies instruction.

This visit shows the flexibility in grouping patterns that Mr. Young has incorporated into his class. He has used *whole-group instruction* when the students are reading and writing in response to the biographies. He has also used whole-group instruction for the content DRTA in science. During math he has formed two *ability groups* for instruction. Each group participates in direct teaching with Mr. Young and then works independently on related problems. Mr. Young has included *small heterogeneous groups* during reading instruction. He has divided the class into three groups so that each child will have a chance to participate during a lesson on types of questions.

Mr. Young and his students appear to be studying *two thematic units* concurrently. The students are investigating the genre of biography and are reading biographies. Mr. Young has planned to have the students write biographies about a member of the community. This writing activity will build on the skills related to interviewing that the students developed early in the year. The second theme centers on the ocean. The students are investigating various aspects of the ocean. As a tie between these units, Mr. Young plans to have an oceanographer visit the class. This interview will be included in the interview book that will represent the culmination of this unit.

There are no clear examples of *evaluation* in this visit. We can observe the results of evaluation by noting the math groups. These groups are certainly dealing with two very different topics. Although we cannot directly observe the biographies that the students are reading, we should assume that Mr. Young provided a wide range of materials that vary in difficulty. In this way every child will be able to participate in the biography reading and discussion.

Mr. Young has again thought about *parent involvement* and in this case, about community involvement as well. The children will be interviewing community members and writing about them. These interviews will eventually be shared with the parents and the interviewed community members.

End of the School Year

Jeremy is calling the roll and Mark is taking the lunch count. Most of the children are reading silently at their desks. Every so often a giggle breaks the silence. Mr. Young ends SSR after thirty minutes. The children, without any directions from Mr. Young, prepare for math.

Mr. Young is teaching a lesson about long division to the whole class today. He begins the lesson with a quick mental math review. Each student writes his or her answer on a scrap of paper after completing the mental calculations. Mr. Young moves from this activity to overhead examples of many of the long division problems that the class had worked on yesterday. He has the calculations accompanying the problem so that the students can see them. "Now, I want you to be the teacher. One of your students has just turned in this paper with many problems done incorrectly. We'll go through each problem and discover what the student did wrong. That way we'll know what to do to help this student correct his errors." Mr. Young and his students work through five problems in this manner. He then writes a new problem on the overhead. "I want each of you to solve this problem with a partner. One person will work the problem and say everything that he or she is doing out loud. The other person will listen carefully and offer help if it is needed. The person with the longest pencil solves the problem first. Get going." When the students have solved the first problem, Mr. Young puts a new problem up and the other half of the pair solves this one, using the think-aloud procedure. The students repeat this procedure one more time. Mr. Young passes out one worksheet with long division problems for each partnership to complete. The pairs are expected to complete the sheet by using the think-aloud procedure described above. Both students will receive one grade for their combined efforts.

As the students finish, they turn in their worksheet and either work on their story or continue reading Katherine Paterson's *Bridge to Terabithia*. Each day, after reading, they write about what has happened in the book or how they are feeling about it. While the students are reading or writing either responses or stories, Mr. Young confers with individual students about their revised drafts of friendship stories. The students continue on these projects for the remainder of the morning. Some students read and then work on their story. Other students choose the opposite sequence. Several students hold conferences with each other about their friendship stories. There is a busy, calm pace throughout the morning workshop.

The afternoon begins with the students writing in their journals. Once most of the journals are closed, Mr. Young reads *Charlie and the Chocolate Factory* by Roald Dahl. He has chosen to read this book because the students are studying machines. *Charlie and the Chocolate Factory* contains the descriptions of some very unusual candy machines. These machines are fanciful and an extension for the more realistic machines that the children are studying.

The unit on machines began when a student brought in David Macaulay's *The Way Things Work.* The students were glued to the book, so Mr. Young decided to take advantage of this enthusiasm. He quickly went to several libraries and collected as many books as he could about machines. He called several repair shops to see if they had any small appliances that were beyond repair. These, without their cords, were brought into the classroom. He also located tools that the students could use to take the appliances apart. Each day, Mr. Young would lead a mini-lesson and small-group experiments on several topics described in the book, such as levers, gears, and pulleys. The students kept logs of all the experiments. About a week into the unit, each student chose one particular topic mentioned in Macaulay's book. The students researched their topic during the second half of the afternoon. Each student and Mr. Young negotiated a contract for a project that included a report — either oral or written — about the topic and some sort of visual presentation to accompany the report. Mr. Young contacted many businesses in the area that were willing to send speakers to help the students understand particular machines. The students particularly enjoyed the speaker who talked about repairing computers. A field trip was also arranged so that the students could see an assembly line in action. Mr. Young is particularly pleased that he followed the students' direction with this unit. In many cases, he is learning with the students about several of the machines.

The students work right to the dismissal bell. They quickly clean up and are heard talking about computers and microchips all the way to the bus.

Mr. Young will be staying late this afternoon as he has scheduled parent conferences for several of the students. He will be sharing evaluation information collected throughout the school year. Each parent will take a final look at their child's portfolio and note the child's academic growth.

Discussion

The goals that Mr. Young established early in the year have been accomplished. The students are working on long division in math. In reading and writing they are experimenting with the inclusion of feelings as a response to reading. And Mr. Young has felt comfortable enough with each student's accomplishments to deviate from the planned unit of study to one initiated by the students, on machines. The students are also handling the housekeeping chores associated with the class. This is seen as Jeremy and Mark take roll and the lunch count.

Scheduling remains the same. Mr. Young has consistently provided an environment that can be predicted by the students so that they know how to plan their activities. The students have internalized this routine. Mr. Young no longer has to indicate when students should prepare for the next block of instruction. They do this on their own, as seen in the preparation for math.

Mr. Young has again used a variety of groups during the school day. This time he organized math with *whole-group instruction*. For guided practice he utilized *partnerships*. These partners used a think-aloud strategy to facilitate the learning of long division. Then these partners participated in a more formal *cooperative grouping* to complete a math worksheet. During the science unit about machines, each child was responsible as an individual to research a topic, develop a report, and then present this information.

The students developed the *theme unit* during this visit. Mr. Young decided to respond to the students' enthusiasm about the way machines work and build a unit of study around it. This unit will eventually find its way into every aspect of the curriculum. The students will need to measure to create a model of their machine. Reading and writing are certainly involved as the students research their topic. Art is necessary in the presentation and as they create their machine. And this whole unit centers on science and the people who work with these machines.

As in the mid-year visit, no direct evidence of *evaluation* is evident. Mr. Young has evaluated the students throughout the year, both formally and informally. He has developed portfolios for each student and will share these at the final parent conference. The parents will see new worksheets with sample math problems that their child feels competent to do. These sheets will be compared with those completed on the first day of school. Several samples of writing are included. Mr. Young has even photocopied some of the children's responses to stories. The results from the district's criterion testing and national standardized testing are included in the portfolios.

Mr. Young has carefully involved the *parents and the community*. Many of the speakers that have been included in this unit are parents of the students in the class. These adults feel very important to be sharing information that the students are so interested in. The parents are very excited to be invited to the final machine presentations. Mr. Young has also made sure that each parent will be coming to an end-of-the-year conference. He wants the parents to be aware of the academic growth of their children.

◆ ◆ ◆

A CONCLUDING PERSPECTIVE

This chapter provided an overview of classroom organization. We began by planning for the physical, social, and academic environment of the classroom. Although each segment of the classroom was discussed separately, remember that these elements are all interrelated in the classroom. Each element helps or hinders the functioning of the others. The chapter ended with a snapshot of a fifth grade teacher's classroom at the beginning, middle, and end of the year. The visit gave us a chance to see the classroom application of many of the theoretical issues discussed.

Mr. Young moved quickly to establish an environment that would allow children to participate in the process of learning. This meant establishing the rules and routines of the classroom within the first few weeks of school. When you move into your own classroom, spend time just getting used to it before the students arrive. Then arrange it the way it seems best to you, depending on what you and your students will be doing. Don't panic when an "experienced" teacher visits and states that children can't sit at tables until at least January. Just smile and say you are experimenting and thanks for the information. Don't worry if you begin the year by being very traditional; make one small change at a time. You don't need to have five cooperative groups working together during the first day of school. Partnerships are an easier way to begin. During the year, you will gradually move from your traditional beginning to an environment more in accord with your expectations of an integrated language arts classroom. Be patient with yourself — these changes will take time, require determination, and demand lots and lots of outright physical energy.

REFERENCES

Anderson, R., Hiebert, E., Scott, J., & Wilkinson, I. (1985). *Becoming a nation of readers: The report of the commission on reading.* Washington, DC: The National Institute of Education.

Aronson, E. (1978). *The jigsaw classroom.* Beverly Hills, CA: Sage.

Barnes, D. (1976). *From communication to curriculum.* New York: Penguin.

Brophy, J. (1986). Classroom management techniques. *Education and Urban Society, 18*(2), 195–210.

Brown, M. (1949). *The important book.* New York: Harper and Row.

Calkins, L. (1986). *The art of teaching writing.* Portsmouth, NH: Heinemann.

Callahan, J., & Clark, L. (1977). *Teaching in the elementary school.* New York: Macmillan.

Canter, L. (1979a). *Assertive discipline: A take-charge approach for today's educator.* Los Angeles, CA: Canter and Associates.

Canter, L. (1979b). Taking charge of student behavior. *National Elementary Principal, 58*(4), 33–36, 41.

Carducci, D., & Carducci, J. (1984). *The caring classroom.* Palo Alto, CA: Bull Publishing.

Cleary, B. (1968). *Ramona the pest.* New York: Dell.

Cleary, B. (1984). *Dear Mr. Henshaw.* New York: Dell.

Coody, B. (1983). *Using literature with young children.* Dubuque, IA: Wm. C. Brown.

Cowley, J. (1980). *Hairy bear.* San Diego, CA: The Wright Group.

Cowley, J. (1983). *The jigaree.* San Diego, CA: The Wright Group.

Dahl, R. (1964). *Charlie and the chocolate factory.* New York: Knopf.

Deci, E., & Ryan, R. (1985). *Intrinsic motivation and self-determination in human behavior.* New York: Plenum Press.

Dreikurs, R. (1957). *Psychology in the classroom: A manual for teachers.* New York: Harper and Row.

Dreikurs, R., Grunwald, B., & Pepper, E. (1982). *Maintaining sanity in the classroom: Classroom management techniques.* New York: Harper and Row.

Eeds, M., & Wells, D. (1989). Grand conversations: An exploration of meaning construction in literature study groups. *Research in the Teaching of English, 23*(1), 4–29.

Evertson, C. (1989). Classroom organization and management. In M. Reynolds (ed.), *Knowledge base for the beginning teacher.* Oxford: Pergamon Press.

Evertson, C., Emmer, E., Clements, B., Sanford, J., & Worsham, M. (1989). *Classroom management for elementary teachers.* Englewood Cliffs, NJ: Prentice-Hall.

Flood, J., & Lapp, D. (1989). Reporting reading progress: A comparison portfolio for parents. *The Reading Teacher, 42*(7), 508–514.

Gamberg, R., Kwak, W., Hutchings, R., & Altheim, J. (1988). *Learning and loving it.* Portsmouth, NH: Heinemann.

Good, T., & Brophy, J. (1987). *Looking in classrooms.* New York: Harper and Row.

Gordon, T. (1974). *T.E.T.: Teacher effectiveness training.* New York: Peter H. Wyden.

Hains, M. (1982). *A two-way street: Reading to write — writing to read.* Rochester, MI: Council of Teachers of English.

Harste, J., Woodward, V., & Burke, C. (1984). *Language stories and literacy lessons.* Portsmouth, NH: Heinemann.

Hawley, R., & Hawley, I. (1975). *Human values in the classroom.* New York: Hart Publishing.

Hayden, T. (1981). *One child.* New York: Avon Books.

Hoban, R. (1976). *Best friends for Frances.* New York: Harper and Row.

House, E., & Lapan, S. (1978). *Survival in the classroom.* Boston: Allyn and Bacon.

Hubbard, R. (1986). Structure encourages independence in reading and writing. *The Reading Teacher,* 180–185.

Hutchins, P. (1968). *Rosie's walk.* New York: Macmillan.

Jackson, P. (1968). *Life in classrooms.* New York: Holt, Rinehart, and Winston.

Jaggar, A. (1989). Teacher as learner: Implications for staff development. In G. Pinnell & M. Matlin (eds.). *Teachers and research.* Newark, DE: International Reading Association.

Johnson, D., & Johnson, R. (1975). *Learning together and alone: Cooperation, competition, and individualization.* Englewood Cliffs, NJ: Prentice-Hall.

Johnson, T., & Louis, D. (1987). *Literacy through literature.* Portsmouth, NH: Heinemann.

Kohn, A. (1986). How to succeed without even vying. *Psychology Today, 20,* 22–28.

Kounin, J. (1970). *Discipline and group management in classrooms.* New York: Holt, Rinehart, and Winston.

Lepper, M., & Greene, D. (eds.) (1978). *The hidden costs of reward: New perspectives on the psychology of human motivation.* Hillsdale, NJ: Erlbaum.

Lobel, A. (1972). *Frog and toad together.* New York: Harper and Row.

Lobel, A. (1976). *Frog and toad are friends.* New York: Harper and Row.

Lord, B. (1984). *In the year of the boar and Jackie Robinson.* New York: Harper and Row.

Macaulay, D. (1988). *The way things work.* Boston: Houghton Mifflin.

McDaniel, T. (1984). Developing the skills of humanistic discipline. *Educational Leadership, 11,* 71–74.

McGreal, T. (1983). *Successful teacher evaluation.* Alexandria, VA: Association for Supervision and Curriculum Development.

Moss, J. (1984). *Focus units in literature.* Urbana, IL: National Council of Teachers of English.

Moss, J. (1990). *Focus on literature: A context for literacy learning.* Urbana, IL: National Council of Teachers of English.

Orlich, D., Harder, R., Callahan, R., Kravas, C., Kauchak, D., Pendergrass, R., & Keogh, A. (1985). *Teaching strategies.* Lexington, MA: D.C. Heath.

Pappas, C., Kiefer, B., & Levstik, L. (1990). *An integrated language perspective in the elementary school.* New York: Longman.

Paterson, K. (1979). *Bridge to Terabithia.* New York: Avon.

Renner, J., Shephard, G., & Bibens, R. (1973). *Guiding learning in the elementary school.* New York: Harper and Row.

Sharan, S. (1980). Cooperative learning in small groups: Recent methods and effects on achievement, attitudes, and ethnic relations. *Review of Educational Research, 50,* 241–271.

Slavin, R. (1979). Effects of biracial learning teams on cross-racial friendships. *Journal of Educational Psychology, 71,* 381–387.

Slavin, R. (1980). Cooperative learning. *Review of Educational Research, 50,* 315–342.

Slavin, R. (1986). Learning together. *American Educator, 10,* 6–13.

Spier, P. (1980). *People.* New York: Doubleday.

Torbe, M., & Medway, P. (1981). *The climate for learning.* Montclair, NJ: Boynton/Cook Publishers.

Wagner, J. (1976). *The bus ride.* Glenview, IL: Scott, Foresman.

Young, E. (1989). *Lon Po Po.* New York: Philomel Books.

5

The Teaching of Listening, Speaking, and Creative Dramatics

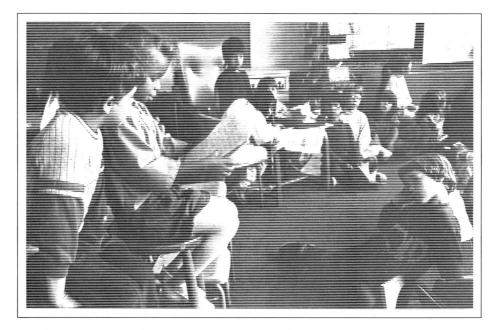

FOCUSING QUESTIONS

- Why does oral communication form the foundation for thinking throughout all the language arts?
- How can the teacher initiate and maintain the types of experiences that fully develop the "communication potential" of each student?
- How will books play a significant role in the development of listening and speaking?
- What are the ways in which creative dramatics can develop thinking and language in the elementary grades?

Have you ever hurt about baskets?
I have, seeing my grandmother weaving for a long time.
Have you ever hurt about work?
I have, because my father works too hard
and he tells how he works.
Have you ever hurt about cattle?
I have, because my grandfather has been working on the
cattle for a long time.
Have you ever hurt about school?
I have, because I learned a lot of words
from school,
*And they are not my words.**

INTRODUCTION

School becomes meaningful to children — it teaches them *their* words —
when teachers heed what Bernstein pointed out several years ago: "If the culture
of the teacher is to become part of the consciousness of the child, then the culture of the child must first be in the consciousness of the teacher" (Bernstein,
1971, p. 149). In this chapter, you will see how you can set up an oral communication system — a system that is sensitive to both the predominant and minority
cultures of the children — thus creating a context for language heard, spoken,
read, written, and reflected upon.

For most individuals, oral communication is the primary means of communication. It is also the foundation for acquiring and applying the language arts of
reading and writing. Skills developed through listening will be directly applicable
to reading; those developed through speaking will be directly applicable to writing. As we anticipate the speaker, so we will anticipate the writer; as we plan what
we will say in light of our listeners, so we will plan what we will write in light of
our readers. And there are mutually beneficial connections through the many
possible interrelationships among speaking/listening/reading/writing, so that instruction in one aspect will almost always have an effect on the other aspects, as
the diagram in Figure 5.1 suggests.

Because we must give considerable attention in the elementary classroom to
the elaboration and expansion of children's oral communication base and, conse-
quently, their thinking, the first major part of this chapter will explore strategies
and activities for developing oral communication in the classroom.

Your overriding objective in the classroom will be to facilitate the use of oral
language as a means of *communication* and of *learning*. In order to do this, you
will be teaching in order to:

*Poem by an Apache child in Arizona, as quoted in *Classroom Discourse: The Language of Teaching
and Learning* (1988) by Courtney Cazden, Heinemann Educational Books, Inc., Portsmouth, NH.

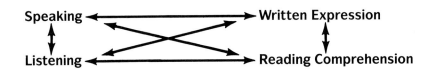

FIGURE 5.1

Developing the
Interrelationships
among the Language
Arts

- expand and elaborate children's production and comprehension of oral language.
- help children develop the ability to apply effectively the several different language *functions* so that their language is appropriate for the context and for their intentions.
- involve children in discussion groups that will help them move beyond egocentricity to cooperative and collaborative problem solving.
- help children become increasingly aware of and able to control their listening and speaking abilities throughout the elementary years.
- expose children to the oral tradition in different cultures through storytelling and reading aloud, so that the children may develop an appreciation of the forms, styles, and content of narratives.

In this chapter, we will address these objectives by considering the role of oral communication in the classroom and your role in facilitating this development, reading aloud to pupils (of all ages!) and the Directed Listening-Thinking Activity (DLTA), storytelling, sharing, the analysis of propaganda, and small-group discussion.

The second major part of the chapter will deal with *creative dramatics*. I will present a sequence of organization designed to allow you a realistic, effective, and rewarding transition into creative dramatics activities you can use in your classroom.

In addition to addressing many of the same objectives as does oral communication, creative dramatics are concerned with the following objectives:

- the stimulation of imagination
- the stimulation and growth of critical thinking
- growth in understanding the motivation underlying human behaviors, including the understanding of oneself

Although it is difficult to separate the effects of creative dramatics on all the language arts, let's take the diagram in Figure 5.1 and see where creative dramatics plug into it (see Figure 5.2).

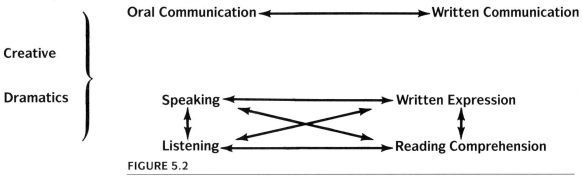

FIGURE 5.2

Developing the Interrelationships among the Language Arts through Creative Dramatics

The Role of Oral Communication in the Classroom

In Chapter 2 we considered the development of language and thought, focusing primarily on the preschool years. Competence in oral language enables us, as Vygotsky noted, to control thought. With this in mind, we can now consider the "relevant functions, meanings, and structure" of language (Wells, 1986) in the context of the classroom. We must provide children with opportunities to hear the appropriate use of these functions, meanings, and structures and with opportunities to use them appropriately. This is an important responsibility, for as Wells observed, "what is learned and the order in which it is learned becomes progressively more dependent on *experience* . . ." (Wells, 1986, emphasis added).

As we saw in Chapter 2, the experiences we provide as teachers become increasingly important for children's development during the elementary school years. As Barnes noted: "In order to learn, students must use what they already know so as to give meaning to what the teacher presents to them. Speech makes available to reflection the processes by which [students] relate new knowledge to old. *But this possibility depends on the social relationships, the communication system, which the teacher sets up*" (Barnes, 1976, emphasis added).

Remember, the absolutely quiet classroom is the antithesis of a productive environment that supports integrated learning, but so is a raucous, noisy classroom. Your goal will be to establish a midpoint between these alternatives, an environment where all functions of language can be used to develop effectively the *communication potential* (Harste, Woodward, and Burke, 1984) of each student. Because of the balance you will establish, your students will understand and respect the underlying classroom organization, which will allow them to communicate purposefully about common tasks in which they are engaged. As we began to see in the last chapter, this midpoint will be attained as a result of your direct efforts and your types of teaching, from direct through indirect. For example, you will teach directly the process of group discussion, so that students will learn more effectively through this medium as well as be able to monitor the process on their own.

Because most children already understand and can use spoken language, oral communication is going to be the foundation of your instruction. Although you must begin, realistically, where the children are, you will be able to show them how to expand and elaborate upon their oral communication skills. Through your interaction with children, you will help them "[put] old familiar experience into words in order to see new patterns in it" and "make sense of new experience by finding a way of relating it to the old" (Barnes, 1976, p. 83). Instructionally, we don't begin with the new but with the familiar. Only if children understand the familiar well can they make sense of the new.

We will begin with the examination of familiar experiences in part so that children will learn *how* to examine what is new. By directing children's attention to everyday objects and processes that engage their minds and exercise their language in the everyday world, you can help the children develop a better sense of who they are and where they are. This is important because, as noted in Chapter 1, children are the recipients of the "information explosion." Much of this information onslaught, coming primarily from television, is in the form of visual images. Removed from the immediate here and now, these images swirl about and lodge in children's minds, where their visual impact is amplified but their meaning little understood. We must try to balance this information by helping the reality and the images from everyday life — here and now — become equally powerful and comprehensible. Oral communication plays a primary role in this process.

As philosophers through the ages have observed, not without reason, the *examined* experience (or life) is central. Egan (1987) has underscored the importance of this for young children, primarily in the context of *experiences*. He suggests, for example, that children in the primary grades begin with "the close and systematic observation of some particular natural object or process — a tree, rain, a spider's web, a patch of grass" (Egan, p. 467). As the teacher, you can use oral language to help children with their close and systematic observations, so that they can better talk about, reflect on, and organize their thinking about the object or process.

Oral communication is extremely important in the classroom because it is not only a means of learning but a means of going about other types of learning. I've already mentioned the interrelationships among *all* the language arts (see Figures 5.1 and 5.2). Children will learn to apply skills developed in listening and speaking to the other language arts and as a *means of learning* in the other language arts. Here's a concrete example: Writing and reading conferences, discussed in Chapters 7 and 8, rely upon effective oral communication among students. So does group work on a particular science project. Moreover, these activities rely upon specific procedures that have themselves been taught through oral communication. If students have not learned how to apply their oral communication skills effectively, then their effective learning in reading, writing, and different content areas will suffer.

One final important note: As we reflect on all the children for whom the Apache child speaks, it is apparent that our schools are incorporating a greater diversity of students at a greater rate than ever before in our history. We also realize teachers cannot be experts in all cultures and languages represented by the students in their classrooms. As teachers we must, however, be sensitive to, value, and encourage the diversity we see as we strive to help the students adjust to and understand the predominant culture. The environment of the classroom and the *kinds of language* that are used there will establish the context in which this kind of learning can occur.

Your Role in Developing Oral Communication Skills

Recall from Chapter 1 that teaching can be characterized as more "direct" or more informal ("indirect"). In this section, we will explore this instructional continuum from the perspective of oral communication skills.

Direct Teaching

In Chapter 1, we discussed direct teaching in terms of the explicit presentation of purpose and technique by a teacher. There are a number of learning strategies involving speaking and listening that you may teach or model directly. Later, for example, we'll walk through an example of direct teaching about propaganda techniques and the reasons why such knowledge is important. Through such instruction, students will learn important critical listening skills. The process of how a discussion group works, for example, may be directly taught by the teacher, working with one group of students at a time.

Modeling

The most important part of direct teaching is the *modeling* that you do as a teacher. Regardless of how much or how little you emphasize other aspects of the direct-teaching format, the modeling phase should be clear and straightforward. Demonstrate for your students: "This is what I do when I listen to a speaker . . . ." Or, "Have you noticed? When I tell a story the first thing I try to do is create a mood for you. I do this by turning down the lights and putting on my old shawl. Next, I lower my voice slightly to draw you in . . . ." Or, "After you have determined what information you're going to give in your oral presentation, you need to think about what props you might need. If you're doing a science experiment, make sure you have containers for your water . . . ." Just as you will be directly teaching your students to do so, you will always try to be sensitive to the explicitness of your "modeling" discussions — to the language, voice, and pacing. When necessary, you can use additional props to illustrate whatever is being taught.

Informal Learning Situations

Less structured but equally effective instructional situations will involve your minute-to-minute responses to students as they are engaged in activities, as well as informal demonstrations of what you are teaching. This informal teaching often takes place on a one-to-one basis, or with a small group. Rather than teaching a skill or process directly to a group, your role is to respond most effectively to what is happening at that particular moment.

Demonstrating the Functions of Language

In the context of speaking and listening, let's consider some situations in which you are informally demonstrating the various functions of language (adapted from Pinnell, 1985):

Instrumental   Be available, receptive, and responsive to your pupils' requests. Encourage them to make their requests in an appropriate and effective manner, however.

Regulatory   It is important to monitor yourself so that you use less regulatory language. This is the language function most used and abused by teachers! When you *do* use it, be as clear as you can be and usually say things *one* time. This way, most pupils will understand, and those that don't — if it's because of not paying attention — will need to ask their peers. This is not a popular tactic, so most children will soon learn to "tune in" first time around!

Interactional   Take advantage of those serendipitous opportunities throughout the day to simply talk with your pupils, singly or in a group. This is purely *social* talk, usually outside of an instructional context, but it goes a long way toward establishing you as a real person, as well as demonstrating for your students an important aspect of the wider world's social talk.

Personal   Much like interactional language, personal language is between two or sometimes more individuals. A significant difference, however, is that personal language deals with the concerns, worries, and fears of your pupils. Your sensitive listening, understanding, valuing, and occasional advice are extremely important.

Imaginative   You should take obvious delight in the sounds, rhythms, and meanings of words and phrases. Talk about them. Tell and read to the children stories that can effectively create vivid and occasionally powerful images for them.

Heuristic   Make your curiosity obvious; wonder openly about things. This may be done as simply as by uttering "I wonder why . . ." It is important, though, that your "wonderings" should be genuine and not contrived. Contrived musings are quite transparent and can quickly become stale and ineffective.

Informative   You will elicit effective use of informative language through the types of questions you ask and the questioning techniques you use. Your questions will lead your students to more critical and effective reflection and action. This is quite often one of the most difficult aspects of teaching — learning how, when, and what type of question to ask. We will address questioning explicitly in Chapter 8.

Listening

Developing Skills from the Simple to the Complex

There is little question that listening is the language art least attended to — not only in school but probably in our society as well. Start by being a good listener yourself. As Wells observed (Chapter 2), you must be the model of a good listener and assume your students have something important to say.

For many years, educators have made an important distinction between *hearing* and *listening:* Hearing is simply receiving the sounds, including oral language, from the environment; for non-hearing-impaired individuals, hearing happens effortlessly. Because hearing *is* so effortless, in the case of speech, we assume that what went in was understood as the speaker intended it to be understood. Of course, we should know better! The actual sounds may have been received, but it is another matter entirely whether and to what degree the speech was processed — and this is where *listening* comes in. If the listener is attentive, he or she must *construct* the message. Construction is an active process that depends on the context of the situation, the listener's mood, interest, expectations, and knowledge. Truly active listeners try to approximate as closely as they can the intended meaning of the speaker; depending on the context, this approximation or construction of meaning may seem almost effortless, or it may be quite challenging, even difficult.

Let's sketch a practical example. Picture yourself in a college class for one of your more challenging subjects. The professor is lecturing, and you know that you are hearing the same sounds as the other students — you understand the words — yet you're still struggling to comprehend the professor's intended meaning. As we pointed out in Chapter 1, meaning does not directly move from one individual to another — it travels, with varying degrees of success, over bridges, and in our present situation, oral communication is the bridge.

Range of Instructional Situations

We already know that our primary focus in the classroom should be on meaningful activities and projects; much of the deliberate, attentive listening and speaking we seek will occur because the children are motivated. We still must turn the children's attention to the process of communicating orally — to help them become *aware* of how they communicate through oral language — and this can be done across the continuum of more direct to more informal contexts.

Effective communication will depend on topical knowledge, surely, but also on procedural knowledge (being aware of how to go about communicating orally more effectively) and self-knowledge (being aware of how well one is *applying* procedural knowledge). Real-world listening usually incorporates some or all of the different features and strategies of listening. To be effective listeners, though, students should learn these features and strategies *explicitly* and put them to use often enough so that they become automatic.

Described below is a series of instructional formats that represent a range of situations. These activities first get children thinking about sound *per se,* then build on successive levels of awareness and ability. Their purpose is to help children actively direct attention to sound by attending to it and responding to it in successively more complex ways. Although these categories are arranged in order of complexity, you need not try to exhaust the possibilities in one format before proceeding to the next.

Natural and Created Sounds   Direct children's attention to the sounds that are naturally occurring around them. If you can hear the sounds of the outdoors, so much the better. Begin by having children close their eyes and *listen;* for beginners and young children, one minute is long enough. Then ask the children what they heard. At first the class will simply list the sounds; later, you can ask children to *describe* the sounds.

Both you and individual children can *create* sounds for other children to identify; as with naturally occurring sounds, everyone will need to close their eyes for a brief period of time. Nails drummed on a table top, erasers clapped together, paper wadded — these and more exotic sounds can be identified and described by the children. As you might expect, children's descriptive vocabulary may not be extensive, so here you can help by subtly playing your role as model. You should introduce descriptive terms and apply these terms after they have appeared. For example, you may use the words *scratchy* and *grainy* after playing part of an old 78-rpm recording; *liquid,* to describe a particular bird song, and *ticklish,* to refer to a giggle. You can help your students move beyond description of a single sound or phrase to *comparison* with other sounds: "this sound is a little like a jackhammer"; or "the air coming through the vents reminds me of when the heater comes on at home and I feel snuggly in my bed."

Voices   After focusing on natural and created environmental sounds, children enjoy attending to the identity and the quality of voices. The setting is the same: eyes closed, ears alert. As you move about the room, tap different children. At each tap, that child will say a brief phrase or sentence; then have the class guess the child's identity. As Stewig (1983) noted, this listening exercise will allow you to introduce terms having to do with the "structure" of sound; for example, *pitch* (high or low), *timbre* (harsh, buzzy, raspy), and *duration.*

This sequence and these simple activities are surprisingly powerful in their objectives. Not only do they direct children's attention exclusively to sound; they help the children become aware of their own listening efforts, and thus better able to control and direct them.

Sequence   With younger children, ask them simply to recall a sequence of different sounds; for example, tapping, closing of a book, opening a drawer. Eventually they can recall more involved sequences, including remembering events in a story or directions — from two- or three-step directions to sequences that are quite a bit longer.

Anticipation   The types of information for which children listen in anticipation are limitless. They can vary from listening to fill in a missing word or phrase in a poem or a predictable text (see Chapter 8) to listening for and remembering key events or bits of information. When children are going to listen to a speaker, an important anticipatory activity should involve learning something about the speaker's background and qualifications as well as asking the students to reflect on what they already know about the topic and what new information they think they might pick up.

Critical Listening   This broad category covers important subcategories as well as a world of responses — and obviously is a part of our overall concern with teaching critical thinking. It depends in large measure on the types of questions you model and with which you elicit information from students, based on what they have heard. Your primary objective is to stimulate your students' thinking beyond the immediate information in order to help them recognize relationships among ideas, analyze them, and make judgments about them.

Your students are carrying around in their heads many of the cognitive underpinnings that allow for critical listening. Again, your task is to elicit the application of these abilities and to make your students aware of them, so they can apply them appropriately. For example, in many instances they will tell you without hesitation whether a situation on television is "fake," or whether a commercial is realistically portraying a product. Clever programmers can get around this *unless* the children are shown how to apply to more subtle media presentations the information they possess. Ask your students: What technique is being used? How can you tell? What types of information are you not being given (or, how is the information being presented to skew your thinking)?

In the next section of this chapter, we will examine specific propaganda techniques and the way they are used. Later, you and your students can apply the types of knowledge developed through the analysis of propaganda to more "objective" presentations of information, such as newscasts, documentaries, "docudramas," and informational oral presentations. And, just to drive home the point one last time, I'll mention that these skills — developed in an oral communicative context — will be equally applicable to reading and to writing!

■ Build Your Teaching Resources

Sources of Activities

For extensive discussion of this range of activities as well as additional activities, the following two sources are recommended:

Hennings, D. G. (1990). *Communication in action: Teaching the language arts.* Boston: Houghton Mifflin.

   See Chapter 4: Listening for Meaning.

Stewig, J. (1983). *Exploring language arts in the elementary classroom.* New York: Holt, Rinehart, and Winston.

   See Chapter 3: Oral Language.

Examining Propaganda

At heart, the primary language function of propaganda is *regulatory* — to get someone else to do something (in a great many cases something that the individual would not normally do) or to refrain from doing something. Most of the terms that have been used to describe and label propaganda techniques have been around for a long time. Your purpose in introducing propaganda techniques, talking about them, and having students apply them is primarily to show your students how language is used *on* them in order to influence them. You will want your students to be able to step back and think about how language can be used to persuade, entice, and convert. It is the *reasoning* underlying propaganda to which students need to become sensitive. The purposes of propaganda should be examined not only in commercials and advertisements but in everyday communication as well.

I'm addressing propaganda in the context of speaking and listening primarily because this is where we first encounter it, and oral communication is the primary mode in which we continue to encounter propaganda throughout life. As you will see, once students become aware of and understand propaganda through oral communication, they can apply this knowledge to other media such as print and electronic communications. Quite often students are in fact aware of the purpose of propaganda — and this is good — but they will need to understand *how to apply* this awareness in their day-to-day lives. As Tutolo expressed it, "We must make our students aware of the empty promises of hope, vitality, prestige, and athletic prowess hidden in the ads for beauty cream, orange juice, automobiles, and tennis shoes" (Tutolo, cited in Rudasill, 1986). And beyond these ads, the students must know how these subtle techniques can be used just about anywhere, including in serious discussion and writing.

Following are the major categories of propaganda:

1. *Glittering Generality.* This type of statement is obviously true, obviously positive — and way too general! It is worded in order to influence listeners, but the meanings of the words are usually vague. The politician states that he is in favor of "a free country, without prejudice, with opportunity for all." We may agree with that statement — it's often hard to disagree with glittering generalities — but merely saying that he stands for these goals is hardly the same as telling us how he might *realistically* attain them.

2. *Bandwagon.* "You don't want to be left out, do you? Simply *everyone* is buying Skyhigh athletic shoes!" This approach works especially well on both younger and older adolescents. The key is to stress that everyone is involved, and you don't want to be left behind.

3. *Testimonial.* If a well-known and well-respected personality supports something, then — we are urged to conclude — it *must* be good. Support can be verbal, as in a commercial, or subtle, as when a picture of a sports star appears on cereal boxes.

4. *Deck Stacking.* "Crunchy Munchies cereal is loaded with vitamins." You are not told what the vitamins are, how much of a dosage is included, and that Crunchy Munchies actually has more sugar than any other cereal on the market! This approach "stacks the deck" with supportive evidence in favor of

whatever is being offered, and conveniently leaves out the detracting evidence.

5. *Positive Association.*   Something or someone is presented in a situation that has a positive, pleasant, favorable connotation. There is little if any *realistic* association between the two, however. For example, a magazine ad shows an attractive woman in an evening gown standing next to a lawnmower.

6. *Plain Folks.*   Products or people are presented as down-home, salt-of-the-earth. The subtle message is that high-falutin', university-educated, big-business type individuals are somehow not as honest, hard-working, and bedrock-values-oriented as the rest of us. In a recent presidential election, for example, both candidates seemed to go out of their way to ignore, if not disavow, their Ivy League university educations.

7. *Snob Appeal.*   This is the other side of the "plain-folks" and "bandwagon" techniques. The attempt is to convince the hearer that he or she is special, unique, and somehow more intelligent, perceptive, or attractive than most other people. Some illustrative slogans: "There aren't many who've worked as hard as you have — you deserve the very best"; "*You* know the meaning of speed and performance — that's why the Super XYZ Sportcoupe takes you out ahead of the crowd . . ."

8. *Name Calling.*   As the term suggests, this technique aims at establishing an association with individuals or ideas that have negative connotations. The association is unfair because there is no evidence to support the name-calling — for example, referring to someone's beliefs as "neo-Nazi" or to a reporter as a member of the "left-leaning liberal press."

The direct teaching lesson presented here is appropriate for many third-graders and most students from fourth grade on up. It lends itself particularly well to a whole-class instructional format.

1. Talk about different commercials that the students have seen on television. Ask questions such as: Is what they present absolutely true? Do you entirely believe them? What is their purpose? How do you think the people who make the commercials try to influence you — to get you to want what they are selling?

   After discussing these questions with the students, explain that you're going to be looking very closely at *propaganda* — types of techniques that people use to influence the opinions and desires of others. Commercials are one very important part of propaganda, but the techniques of propaganda can be used anywhere.

   Discuss with the students *why* they think being aware of propaganda techniques is important. Here you are highlighting *what* your students are going to learn and *why.*

   Depending on how much you feel would be appropriate to cover at first, present the different types of propaganda with their definitions. If you have taped commercials that illustrate each type, this works best. Magazine advertisements also work extremely well, and in most instances are more convenient for you to use, anyway.

2. Using new commercials or advertisements, discuss what you notice about the language and the pictures. Relate this to the definitions you have given for each propaganda type, then tell the students what type each commercial or ad best illustrates. At some point in your modeling, the students will probably join in as they catch on, and this is fine.

3. Have the students work in pairs to go through advertisements, categorizing each one. Give feedback where appropriate; often an ad will in reality illustrate more than one type of propaganda, and this is all right — ask the students which *single* type the ad best illustrates, or go ahead and label it with the different types.

   An excellent follow-up after working in pairs is to have the students share and discuss with the whole group what they have found.

4. Restate the purpose of studying the different techniques of propaganda, and discuss with the students how an awareness of propaganda techniques can apply to everyday life, including reading and writing.

5. If necessary, follow up with independent practice. The students can make a group book illustrating different types of propaganda with illustrations cut from magazines. Your students can catalog different types as viewed in commercials on television or heard on the radio at home. An excellent writing activity involves them in composing their own commercials; their scripts should include a description of the setting as well as directions. If possible, follow up with actual videotaping and involve the students in analyzing and identifying the propaganda techniques used.

Reading Aloud to Children

There is a type of magic in the air when stories are read aloud. Reading aloud is not just for younger students — there are some important reasons why we should read to students throughout the grades. There is a rhythm and cadence to the language of books. Reading aloud is also an excellent way to help young children develop a sense of story (Applebee, 1978) from hearing how stories are conveyed in texts.

CLASSROOM EXAMPLE

The setting is a fifth grade classroom. The teacher is reading *Tuck Everlasting* by Natalie Babbitt to the students, one chapter per day. This is a wonderful and powerful book for upper elementary children. It intertwines several themes, perhaps the two most powerful ones being the whirling emotions and physical turmoil of Winnie, a twelve-year-old girl on the verge of womanhood, and death and its meaning, including the prospect of immortality. The Tuck family is immortal, having discovered and drunk from a spring that could be characterized as a fountain of youth. Winnie, a girl from a nearby village, has discovered the secret of the spring. In the following excerpt the patriarch of this immortal family, Tuck, tries to explain to Winnie why she shouldn't drink from the spring. His explanation is simple, beautiful, and riveting. It should be read in its entirety, of course, but the following excerpt captures a bit of its power:

> Everything's a wheel, turning and turning, never stopping. The frogs is part of it, and the bugs, and the fish, and the wood thrush, too. And people. But never the same ones. Always coming in new, always growing and changing, and always moving on. That's the way it's supposed to be. That's the way it *is* . . . . That's what us Tucks are, Winnie. Stuck so's we can't move on. We ain't part of the wheel no more. Dropped off, Winnie. Left behind. And everywhere around us, things is moving and growing and changing. You, for instance. A child now, but someday a woman. And after that, moving on to make room for the new children. . . .

> [When Winnie fully realizes for the first time that she *will* die someday]:

> She raged against it, helpless and insulted, and blurted at last, "I don't want to die."

> "No," said Tuck calmly. "Not now. Your time's not now. But dying's part of the wheel, right there next to being born. You can't pick out the pieces you like and leave the rest . . . ."

All the power of language, ideas, and emotions that spring from a story read aloud is clearly evident in the faces of the roomful of fifth-graders transfixed by a tale such as *Tuck Everlasting.*

As a teacher, yours is a significant charge: For those children who may not hear it at home, where else will these children have the language of books modeled? Only in one place, school — your classroom. In short, *you* will be the sole source of this language; in a very real way, you will provide the model for the "silent voice" within each child's head, the voice the children will hear when they read for themselves — a factor that is important for older students as well as younger ones.

The value and importance of reading stories to young children in particular has been convincingly described by Heath (1982) in her article "What No Bedtime Story Means." Put directly, no bedtime story means that children are not prepared for the types of literacy experiences and expectations that occur in school. Kindergarten experiences, for example, are based on the assumption that children are familiar with stories in the predominant culture.

Children who have not been read to have a sense of story that is based upon the television programs they have seen, programs that are at best only approximately related to written narratives. Especially for these children, your read-alouds are critical. For almost all kindergarten and first grade children, by the way, "predictable" books or "Big Books" will be popular books to read aloud, but your use of them and *how* you read them will differ from simple read-alouds. These types of books will be discussed in Chapter 8.

Depending on your personality, you will feel more or less comfortable with dramatizing the story you are reading. Some teachers love to assume different voices with each character. Some children's literature authorities suggest that you avoid such dramatization, leaving the obvious characteristics of the speech of characters to the children's imagination. As in all such matters, of course, there is a midpoint. A little bit of "hamming it up" is fine; too much may tend to distract children from the overall story itself. As we discussed above, storytelling is the place where you can, if you are so inclined, display your more theatrical qualities!

The best reference for reading aloud to children of all ages is *The Read-Aloud Handbook* by Jim Trelease. The book contains a "treasury" of read-alouds, some of which are listed later in this chapter. Part of the information Trelease provides for each book is whether it requires "experienced" listeners; this is a good guide to gauging the appropriateness of the books you wish to share with your students. We will talk about this book again later, because it contains a world of information above and beyond the specifics of how to read to children; for the moment, however, we will pull a few suggestions from it primarily to offer some guidelines for reading aloud, culled from children's literature authorities:

1. Make sure you have read or at least skimmed the book yourself. This will prevent the occasional embarrassing or awkward instances when you encounter language or situations in the book that really ought not to be shared with a whole class of children. More important, though, skimming will give you the sense of the story that you will need to read effectively.

2. Read a book that *you* enjoy!

3. Have a particular time each day that you read to the children, and *read every day.* If you fall into the habit of skipping days, your commitment and the students' interest will be diluted.

4. Allow some time for students to get settled down and back into the story.

5. Sit so that your voice will project out to all of the students. If you are reading a picture book, sit so that when you hold the book for students to see, *all* will be able to do so.

6. This is a time *for listening only.* Although some teachers allow pupils to complete unfinished work or work on whatever they please during read-aloud time, this will at best only approximate your read-aloud objectives.

Now is an excellent time to begin your own "bookfile." This will be a 3 × 5 filebox or a file you keep on a microcomputer. For every children's book you read, fill out a 3 × 5 card or type in information listing the author, title, publisher, date of publication, and the type of book — more about this in Chapter 9. In addition, write a brief summary of the book, *your* reaction to the book, and the age range and type of children for whom you believe the book would be particularly enjoyable and beneficial (see Figure 5.3). Eventually, you will be classifying the books in different sections of your file when the numbers become too great for alphabetization. You might also note the type of literature and thematic units for which the book would be appropriate (see Chapter 9). Then, when the time comes to organize a unit, a quick search through the file will yield a number of titles.

If you're already aware of the many fine references for children's literature that contain this kind of information and more, you may wonder about the necessity of keeping your own file. Your own file will still be quicker. Besides, you will soon have read so many books that you will forget certain titles and authors; if you have taken the time to write in the information mentioned above, the book — and your reaction — will be "logged into" your long-term memory much more efficiently and lastingly.

I strongly recommend that you store your file on a microcomputer or floppy disk. Not only will your file be more efficient and easy to access, but you will also be able to do a number of things with it. For example, your search for appropriate titles for a unit is swift because you simply use the "search" function on your word processor — once you type in the important terms ("historical fiction," "biography," "siblings," "detectives," and so forth), *everything* in your file will be searched, including your comments about the books. A list of the books that are identified may be dumped into a separate file and then run off when you're finished. You now have your list of titles to choose from. From time to time you will also wish to run off information from your file for your students; you can create any list they may need easily and efficiently. Over time, invite your students to offer comments that you can include in your file — this is important for you to know, and it is extremely helpful for students who will browse through your list. As we know, the students' comments about a book will often carry far more weight than those of an adult, or a review written by an adult. Students' comments, by the way, can be coded differently in your file, so that only their comments and not yours will appear when you run off lists for other students.

Doodling or drawing, however, is another matter — particularly for very active children.

7. Read more slowly rather than faster. Listeners need time to construct their pictures "in the mind's eye." This visualization is important not only in listening but in reading as well — a critical aspect of reading comprehension is the ability to visualize as one reads. Reading more slowly also helps to establish the rhythm and the cadence of the language.

FIGURE 5.3

Bookfile Entry Run Off on a Computer

O'Dell, Scott. <u>Sign Down the Moon</u>. Houghton Mifflin, 1970. Historical fiction.

<u>Summary</u>: Through the eyes of a Navajo girl, Bright Morning, we witness the forced removal of a band of Navajo from their homeland to Fort Sumner in 1864. O'Dell's prose really captures the physical and spiritual defeat of the Navajos. The book also demonstrates the power of the individual spirit and will, as Bright Morning persuades the disillusioned brave she has married to escape with her and return to their homeland. There they will raise their young son. The book ends with an uplifting sense of renewal.

The book is powerfully written and will be a real eye-opener for most students. We also get a realistic and identifiable portrayal of Bright Morning, who has the same feelings most girls experience, regardless of time and place. Upper elementary.

8. Always stop at a suspenseful point. As Trelease counsels, "Leave the audience hanging; they'll be counting the minutes until the next reading" (Trelease, p. 59).

9. There should be time for discussion and reaction after reading. Reaction can take the form of drawing and/or writing, *if the students wish to do so.*

10. *Gradually* ease into longer and more complex stories. For students either not in the habit of listening or returning from a long break, you should begin with shorter, more attention-grabbing selections.

11. Read a variety of selections throughout the year.

12. Occasionally read material that will stretch the children intellectually.

Trelease also offers a list of practices that should be avoided. Here are two that are of most significance for teachers:

1. Don't continue reading a book that is clearly not working.

2. Don't go into your own ideas about interpretations of the book; too often this becomes didactic and the kids adjust their responses accordingly.

Recommended Read-Aloud Books

The books listed below are categorized *very* generally according to primary, middle, and upper elementary grades. Please keep in mind, though, that for particular students or classes, a book in the primary category will often be quite appropriate for third or fourth grade as well, and vice versa.

Because the books listed here are recommended for read-alouds, you may be wondering if we should save them for this purpose and steer young *readers* away from them. Of course not. They are marvelous books for children to immerse themselves in; they are mentioned here as read-alouds because their language, format, and content lend themselves particularly well to sharing orally. Also, as our guidelines above indicated, many of these books — particularly at the primary grade levels — can easily be understood and enjoyed by the children if read aloud, whereas if they read them on their own, the going might be slow because of unrecognized words. *Hearing* these books first will facilitate the children's reading of them later.

■ Build Your Teaching Resources

Read-Alouds

Primary (K, 1, 2)*

Aardema, V. (1978). *Why mosquitoes buzz in people's ears: A West African tale.* New York: Dial Books. **CC****

Allard, H. (1974). *The Stupids step out.* Boston: Houghton Mifflin. **T**

de Paola, T. (1975). *Strega Nona.* Englewood Cliffs, NJ: Prentice-Hall. **CC**

Erickson, R. (1974). *A toad for Tuesday.* New York: Lothrop, Lee and Shepard. **CM**

Fisher, R. (ed.) (1986). *Ghosts galore: Haunting verse.* London: Faber and Faber.

Freeman, D. (1968). *Corduroy.* New York: Viking. **T**

Gag, W. (1928). *Millions of cats.* New York: Coward, McCann and Geoghegan. **CE, T**

Heide, F. (1971), *The shrinking of Treehorn.* New York: Holiday House. **T**

Kennedy, R. (1975). *The contests at Cowlick.* Boston: Little, Brown. **T**

Lobel, A. (1985). *Frog and Toad are friends.* New York: Harper and Row. **CC, T**

Michels, B., & White, B. (1983). *Apples on a stick: The folklore tales of black children.* New York: Coward, McCann and Geoghegan/Putnam, 1983.

Milne, A. A. (1926). *Winnie the Pooh.* London: Methuen. **CC**

McCloskey, R. (1976). *Make way for ducklings.* New York: Penguin. **CC, T**

Pinkwater, J. (1983). *The cloud horse.* New York: Lothrop, Lee and Shepard.

Potter, B. *The tale of Peter Rabbit.* New York: Frederick Warne. **CC**

Sendak, M. (1984). *Where the wild things are.* New York: Harper and Row. **CC, T**

Steig, W. (1969). *Sylvester and the magic pebble.* New York: Simon and Schuster. **CC, T**

Viorst, J. (1975). *Alexander who used to be rich last Sunday.* New York: Atheneum/Macmillan. **T**

Waber, B. (1975). *The house on East 88th street.* Boston: Houghton Mifflin. **T**

Waber, B. (1975). *Ira sleeps over.* Boston: Houghton Mifflin. **CC, T**

Williams, V. (1982). *A chair for my mother.* New York: Greenwillow. **CC, T**

Zolotow, C. (1972). *William's doll.* New York: Harper and Row. **CE, T**

Grades 2, 3, 4

Barrett, J. (1982). *Cloudy with a chance of meatballs.* New York: Atheneum. **T**

Blume, J. (1986). *Freckle juice.* New York: Dell. **T**

Cleary, B. (1982). *Ramona the pest.* New York: Dell. **CM**

Dahl, R. (1978). *Danny, the champion of the world.* New York: Bantam. **T**

Kennedy, R. (1979). *Inside my feet: The story of a giant.* New York: Harper and Row. **T**

*Some titles were originally published years before the date given here; in most cases the most recent edition and publisher are listed here to make it easier for you to locate these books, if you wish.

Many books appear on the California list of recommended readings (*Recommended Readings in Literature, Kindergarten through Grade Eight,* California State Department of Education). They may be designated as **CC (*core* list), **CE** (*extended* list), or **CM** ("*motivational*" list). Those also appearing on Trelease's lists are designated with a **T**.

Miles, M. (1971). *Annie and the old one.* Boston: Little, Brown. **CC**
Mosel, A. (1972). *The funny little woman.* New York: E. P. Dutton. **CE**
Ness, E. (1966). *Sam, Bangs, and Moonshine.* New York: Henry Holt. **CC**
Parish, P. (1983). *Amelia Bedelia.* New York: Harper and Row. **CM, T**
Peterson, J. (1986). *The Littles.* New York: Scholastic. **T**
Smith, D. (1976). *A taste of blackberries.* New York: Scholastic. **T**
Van Allsburg, C. (1988). *Jumanji.* Boston: Houghton Mifflin. **CC, T**
White, E. B. (1952). *Charlotte's web.* New York: Harper and Row. **CC, T**

Grades 4, 5, 6

Andersen, H. (1970). *The fir tree.* New York: Harper and Row.
Armstrong, W. (1972). *Sounder.* New York: Harper and Row. **T**
Asborjornsen, P., & Moe, J. (1938). *East of the sun and west of the moon.* New York: Viking. **CC, T**
Babbit, N. (1975). *Tuck everlasting.* New York: Farrar, Straus and Giroux. **CE, T**
Bellairs, J. (1974). *The house with a clock in its walls.* New York: Dell.
Brink, C. (1970). *Caddie Woodlawn.* New York: Macmillan. **CE, T**
Burnett, F. (1962). *The secret garden.* New York: J. B. Lippincott. **CE, T**
Byars, B. (1981). *The 18th emergency.* New York: Penguin. **T**
Carroll, L. (1977). *Alice's adventures in wonderland.* New York: Delacorte.
Carroll, L. (1977). *Through the looking glass.* New York: St. Martin's Press.
Cleary, B. (1984). *Dear Mr. Henshaw.* New York: Dell. **CC, T**
Dahl, R. (1986). *Charlie and the chocolate factory.* New York: Bantam. **T**
Dahl, R. (1977). *Charlie and the great glass elevator.* New York: Bantam.
Dahl, R. (1983). *James and the giant peach.* New York: Penguin. **CC, T**
de Saint-Exupery, A. (1982). *The little prince.* New York: Harcourt Brace Jovanovich.
Fitzgerald, J. (1971). *The great brain.* New York: Dell. **CE**
George, J. (1975). *My side of the mountain.* New York: E. P. Dutton. **CM, T**
Gipson, F. (1956). *Old Yeller.* New York: Harper and Row. **CE**
Juster, N. (1961). *The phantom tollbooth.* New York: Random House. **CE**
Knight, E. (1978). *Lassie, come home.* New York: Holt, Rinehart, and Winston. **T**
Konigsburg, E. (1986). *Jennifer, Hecate, Macbeth, William McKinley and me, Elizabeth.* New York: Dell.
Lawson, R. (1973). *Ben and me.* New York: Dell. **CC**
L'Engle, M. (1986). *A wrinkle in time.* New York: Dell. **CC, T**
Lewis, C. S. (1986). *The lion, the witch, and the wardrobe.* New York: Macmillan. **CC, T**
Norton, M. (1986). *The borrowers.* New York: Harcourt Brace Jovanovich. **CE**
O'Brien, R. (1971). *Mrs. Frisby and the rats of NIMH.* New York: Atheneum. **CE, T**
O'Dell, S. (1987). *Island of the blue dolphins.* New York: Dell. **CC, T**
Paterson, K. (1977). *Bridge to Terabithia.* New York: Thomas Crowell. **CC, T**
duBois, W. (1947). *The twenty-one balloons.* New York: Viking. **T**
Rawls, W. (1961). *Where the red fern grows.* New York: Doubleday. **CC, T**
Selden, G. (1970). *The cricket in Times Square.* New York: Dell. **CE**
Silverstein, S. (1964). *The giving tree.* New York: Harper and Row. **T**
Silverstein, S. (1974). *Where the sidewalk ends.* New York: Harper and Row. **T**
Singer, I. (1984). *Zlateh the goat and other stories.* New York: Harper and Row. **CE, T**
Steig, W. (1976). *Abel's island.* New York: Farrar, Straus and Giroux. **CC**
Taylor, T. (1983). *The trouble with Tuck.* New York: Avon. **CE**
Twain, M. *The adventures of Tom Sawyer.* New York: Harper and Row. **CE**
Wilder, L. (1953). *Little house on the prairie.* New York: Harper and Row.

Directed Listening-Thinking Activity (DLTA)

An excellent activity that adds a very effective interactive twist to the teacher's read-alouds is the *Directed Listening-Thinking Activity,* or DLTA. We already know that children are active processors of information — their brains ensure that they are. Over the elementary years children will need some direction in *how* they process and use information, and the DLTA provides a solid foundation for that direction. We also know that children will comprehend more and better if "new" information is related to "known" information — to children's existing schemas. The DLTA does this quite efficiently and naturally for the children, providing the foundation for more explicit instruction later on about comprehension strategies in reading and about critical thinking.

The Directed Listening-Thinking Activity builds on what children already know and shows them how to apply this prior knowledge in new situations. It is a variation on another strategy that you will use with your students — the *Directed Reading-Thinking Activity,* or DRTA (Stauffer, 1969, 1980), which will be described at length in Chapter 8.

Listed below are the basic steps in the DLTA. Keep in mind that these steps are the same regardless of grade level; the only difference is in the *way* in which the teacher discusses the story.

1. Select an appropriate storybook to share with your students. With young children, there may also be pictures.

2. After reading the title of the book to the students and showing them the first picture, ask the children, "What do you think this story might be about?": [To the classic response, "I don't know," Edmund Henderson (1981) suggests that you respond: "I *know* you don't know; what do you *think?*" This will draw them out almost every time!]

3. Read to a predetermined stopping place. This should be a point in the story where the plot and/or action has been raised to a high level of suspense and excitement. Then say to the students, "*Now* what do we think? We thought that [such and such] would happen. Is that how it has turned out so far?" After discussing the predictions the children made, say, "Now what do you think's going to happen?" You may ask "Why?" or "Why not?" (Note: You *may* ask! Exercise good judgment in this so it is not overdone.) Then, say, "Well, let's listen and find out!" and continue with the reading.

4. After the reading, you may ask questions such as, "How did you know that . . ." and, "Would *you* have done the same thing?" "How is this like an experience you have had?" and so forth. (Guidelines for asking good questions are presented below.)

I suggest you do the following:

1. Avoid using the terms "right" and "wrong" in referring to predictions; if children haven't done so already, they quickly contract "right/wrong-itis" in school and will be reluctant to make predictions.

2. You may also wish to avoid referring to the specific children who made the

predictions and simply ask the children in general about whether or not what was predicted later occurred.

Like all effective teaching strategies, the DLTA has been used for years by good teachers, even though they probably did not really have a name for what they were doing. It is especially effective with young children in kindergarten and first grade, but should continue to be used throughout the grades.

Let's see how the steps of the DLTA are applied early in the year in a first grade classroom; the teacher is going to read Judith Viorst's *Alexander and the Terrible, Horrible, No Good, Very Bad Day*. The book is about Alexander and everything that goes wrong with him, from the time he gets up in the morning to bedtime that night. Everyone has days like this, and Alexander's is a classic!

CLASSROOM EXAMPLE

TEACHER (showing the front cover of the book to the children): "Boys and girls, we're going to listen to a story written by Judith Viorst, called 'Alexander and the Terrible, Horrible, No Good, Very Bad Day.' What do you think this story might be about? Jason?"

JASON: "He gonna have a *bad* day!"

TEACHER: "It *does* sound like it, doesn't it? Yes, Annie?"

ANNIE: "He's gonna be sick."

TEACHER: "Okay! What else might happen? Yes, Glen?"

GLEN: "I think he'll have to clean up his room!"

PATRICIA: "I think he's gonna get blamed for something he didn't do."

TEACHER: "Let's find out! Listen as I read and we'll see what will happen to Alexander."

The teacher reads the first four pages in which Alexander has trouble getting ready for the day, does not get a prize in his cereal box (both his brothers get great prizes), and does not get to sit by the window in the car on the way to school. The fourth page ends with a refrain that will occur throughout the book: "I could tell it was going to be a terrible, horrible, no good, very bad day." The teacher stops after the fourth page and says, "*Now* what do we think? We thought that Alexander might get sick, he might have to clean up his room, or get blamed for something he didn't do. Is that how it has turned out so far?"

GLEN: "Well, we don't know yet, but *I* think he's gonna have trouble at school!"

TEACHER: "How about the rest of us? Do we agree with Glen about not knowing whether something will happen or not?"

CONNIE: "I don't think he's gonna have to clean up his room, 'cause he's not at home anymore."

MONICA: "Yeah, me too!"

MATT: "I still think he's gonna be sick."

TEACHER: "Why do you think so, Matt?"

MATT: "'Cause things will probably just get worse and that's one of the worst things that can happen to you at school."

BONNIE: "I think the car's gonna get a flat tire."

SAM: "Prob'ly not . . . , but we don't know for sure yet."

TEACHER: "That's true. How about being blamed for something he didn't do? Might that still happen?" (Several pupils chorus: "Yeah!" "It could . . . .") "Well, let's listen and find out if the car will have a flat tire, Alexander will have trouble at school, get sick, be blamed for something he didn't do — or maybe something else."

◆ ◆ ◆

This is the format for the remainder of the reading; some predictions are gradually rejected and others confirmed. With this particular book, the things that *might* happen are almost unlimited, but what the children are able to do fairly well is reject predictions that they realize couldn't happen, given the time frame of the story and the location. (If you haven't read the book yet, you must! But to give you an idea of what else goes wrong — Alexander believes his drawing is rejected by the teacher, his best friend shuns him, everybody else has dessert in their lunch except him, he goes to the dentist and has a cavity, and on and on through other mishaps. Even when Alexander is literally in bed that night, he is wearing the railroad train pajamas he hates and feeling dejected because the cat wants to sleep with his brother rather than with him . . .).

After the story is finished, you may ask a few questions — just a few — using the guidelines discussed below. A story such as *Alexander* has great potential for tying in with children's own experiences, but also for talking about the perspectives of *other* individuals — in this case, Alexander's mother and father, and his friend at school who shunned him. For example, you could ask, "I wonder . . . Do we sometimes behave toward our friends the way Paul behaved toward Alexander?"

It is important to understand that the format is not followed rigorously but as the situation suggests. You should not ask "Why do you think so?" for *every* prediction; the important point is that this is done often enough so that pupils eventually become comfortable with thinking about their rationale and justifying it.

Now, let's anticipate some problems you may encounter when you sit down with what you believe is a great book only to learn that a) someone says they've already heard it, b) they've seen the movie, or c) they've heard another version! In all three instances, you can tell such children that they can enjoy listening, but that you'd like them to keep the story to themselves when you ask the others what they think is going to happen. In the case of the movie and hearing another version, you can also tell them that they may enjoy seeing how the book is different from the movie or how *this* version may be different from the one they have already heard. Rather than spoiling your plans, these children will now be exercising some important critical listening skills. They can share the similarities and contrasts *after* the reading is finished. Here's a suggestion about interacting with the children: Notice that you do *not* need to respond orally after every child has said something. We often fall into that habit, and it's not necessary. Were we in the classroom, we would see that the teacher *is* acknowledging each child's contribution with a smile, a nod of the head, raised eyebrows, and so forth. In most interactions in which the teacher is involved, the discussion should not be teacher/pupil/teacher/pupil, but rather teacher/pupil/pupil/pupil/teacher, etc.

The Directed Listening-Thinking Activity allows children *actively* to anticipate what might occur in stories. This anticipation is based on their own experiences and knowledge of the world. The DLTA allows children to refine their predictions as they listen to a story and to reflect in consequential ways on what they have heard. This active listening and responding is critical to all communication, and the DLTA lays the foundations for effective interaction with all kinds of texts later on through reading, writing, and discussion.

Storytelling

Ramon Ross has spoken persuasively of a role for storytelling in our modern society: "There is a humanism inherent in sharing language, sharing stories, dancing and singing in the old ways. These are kindly approaches to learning about yourself and those around you ... there needs to be, I think, a strong and vital strain of tenderness, love and slippery feeling stuff in our lives. And that's where storytelling comes in" (Ross, 1980, p. 5).

Storytelling is enjoying a renaissance in education because it is a truly entertaining art form and because, for young children, it powerfully conveys information that will be essential in the development of their world in general and literacy in particular. With regard to literacy, storytelling conveys the structure or form of *narratives* and the forms and rhythms of effective language. In addition to motivating children to read, storytelling can introduce them to the values and literary traditions of different cultures.

The concept of stories and the roles they play are etched deep in all civilizations and cultures. Although the conflicts and characters in stories may arise from common psychological roots (Bettelheim, 1976; Jung, 1953), the form and substance that stories or narratives assume are shaped by the particular cultures in which they are shared. As we will explore in more depth in Chapter 9, in the predominant Western conceptualization of narrative, stories have a beginning, middle, and an end. They are often told or read in one sitting. In many other cultures, stories do not reflect this organization and may seem to be "looser," without definable beginnings and endings — and they may be told in *many* sittings.

Even quite young children can be transfixed by a fairly long story when spun by a storyteller. One technique a storyteller uses is to provide "hooks" or refrains along the way, for example — the repetition of a significant or catchy verse. Remember the Billy Goats' "trip trap, trip trap" on the bridge? Jay O'Callahan (1986), for example, tells a delightful story of Herman and Marguerite — the former an earthworm, the latter a caterpillar who later changes into a butterfly. In what is a major creative effort for him, Herman the earthworm manages to write his own song, sung shyly at first, with gusto later on:

My name is Herman,
and I like squirmin',
and I like bein' close to the ground, grum, grum.

Storytelling can be a powerful tool for the teaching of literacy as it conveys the forms and rhythms of language and simultaneously introduces children to the literacy traditions of different cultures. *(© Loren Santow/TSW/Click Chicago Ltd.)*

This song grows from a silly giggle for children to, believe it or not, an inspiring affirmation of Herman's self and purpose. It comes to be anticipated and, each time it appears, causes delight.

Many teachers are uncomfortable when they first attempt storytelling. Whether you'd rather "debut" in front of peers or children, debut nevertheless — you will most likely find yourself hooked! Following are some guidelines for storytelling, adapted from Stewig (1983):

1. Choose a story *you* enjoy.
2. Partition the story into "units of action"; that is, identifiable action segments.
3. Write a brief summary of each unit of action on a card; as you prepare to rehearse the storytelling, you can carry the cards around as aids to remembering.
4. Do *not* attempt to memorize the story exactly as it is written in a book. Rather, tell it in your own words. There is one exception to this suggestion: important *repeated* words, phrases, or lines — such as "My name is Herman," and so on — *should* be committed to memory.
5. Many storytellers like to use a prop every time they tell a story — an instant

mood-setter, letting the pupils know a story is about to begin. Examples are a storyteller's shawl, a candle, a particular hat, and so on.

The younger the children, the easier to draw them into storytelling — and, the more astray the story is likely to go. In the type of classroom we are describing, though, the children have many, many opportunities to see "storying" modeled — both the form and the coherence or organization of material. This modeling will occur through your storytelling and your "read-alouds" and as we will see in Chapter 7, will provide much of the foundation for your students' *writing* of stories.

■ Build Your Teaching Resources

Books about Storytelling

A number of excellent storytelling books are now available, and articles are appearing frequently in journals such as the *Reading Teacher,* the *Hornbook,* and the *New Advocate.* The following books have come to be considered classics of storytelling:

Baker, A., & Greene, E. (1977). *Storytelling, art and technique.* New York: R. R. Bowker.
Bauer, C. F. (1977). *Handbook for storytellers.* Chicago: American Library Association.
Colwell, E. (1965). *A storyteller's choice.* New York: Henry Z. Walck.
Shedlock, M. L. (1951). *The art of the storyteller.* New York: Dover.

Sharing and Oral Presentations

Sharing

Sharing, or "show-and-tell," may be one of the most underappreciated and perhaps underused activities in the elementary grades. Sharing time, however, is an excellent context in which each of the functions of language can be further developed. The skills that students develop through sharing provide the foundation for other, more complex oral speaking situations, as for example presenting a report orally. As we'll see in later chapters, these skills will also support children's development in reading and in writing, because the kinds of thinking required in sharing will also be applied to the other language arts. There are two types of situations in which sharing can occur: teacher-directed and student-directed.

Teacher-Directed Sharing

Teacher-directed sharing time will serve two functions: First, it allows you to model the ground rules for the activity. Second, it allows you to demonstrate language that helps to encourage elaboration and better organization of information to be shared.

For both primary and upper elementary students, the ground rules are simple and straightforward. Drawing on Moffett and Wagner (1983) and Michaels and Foster (1985), I suggest the following guidelines:

1. One person at a time will share.
2. A designated "leader" for that day will choose who gets to share (in the beginning, the "leader" is the teacher).
3. Children must raise their hands if they wish to contribute.
4. If children misbehave, they get one warning from the leader — a second warning sends them back to their seats.
5. When the sharer has finished sharing her initial information, listeners may question and contribute.

As we've already said, you will model good listening behavior. You will ask follow-up questions that draw the sharer into elaboration; these should reflect natural interest and curiosity. For example, "'When did they give it to you?' 'What happened to the wing there?' 'What's the red button for?' 'What do you do if you want to get the money out again?' 'Where do you keep it?' 'Do you let your brother use it?'" (Moffett and Wagner, p. 84). Over a period of time, these kinds of requests help children anticipate what others may want to know, thus helping them grow beyond a primarily egocentric perspective.

You should model your interaction with sensitivity. As Cazden (1988) reported, teachers must realize *why* children wish to share something and not completely change the children's agenda and make it the teacher's. For example: A second-grader brings in his pet kitten. His focus is on his new, cuddly pet; he wants to share with the class when it was born, how it behaves, his love for it, and so forth. After he shares, the teacher decides that this might be an appropriate time to talk about the difference between domesticated and wild animals. He asks the child if there are cats that are much bigger than the size his kitten will grow up to be, intending to expand the thinking and talking to lions, tigers, mountain lions, and so forth. Even if the child takes the teacher's lead, the talk is now off on another tack entirely — away from the child's excitement and pride in his new pet and toward an abstraction that is, at least at this particular time, of little concern to the child and somewhat uncomfortable. Again, be sensitive: Your questions can involve children in elaboration without changing their focus.

If you feel students need help in selecting topics for sharing, or simply if you want to change the prevailing focus from time to time, ask students to bring something that "(1) has a good story behind it, (2) they made or grew, (3) means a great deal to them, or (4) moves or works in a funny or interesting way" (Moffett and Wagner, 1983, p. 84). Again, these criteria are just as appropriate for older students as for younger ones.

In the teacher-directed mode, as well as in the student-directed mode discussed below, two types of sharing presentations will be evident — the "lecture demonstration" and the "performed narrative." The first is object-related; the second is related to an event or situation that is not presently going on. The *lecture demonstration* usually involves passing around something of interest and telling about it. The *performed narrative* is an account of something that has happened. In these narratives, younger children are often given to going on and on, frequently without an obvious or coherent organization. This is where well-chosen questions on the teacher's or the student-leader's part are invaluable, because the children's questions will help the sharer to focus or perhaps clarify information.

Student-Directed Sharing

There are more similarities than differences between teacher-directed and student-directed sharing. You have already established the ground rules, so the format of student-directed sharing time is set. There is one very significant difference, however: the *context* is quite different, because you are not there — the students are on their own.

The student-directed mode allows the students to develop independence in effective interaction by applying the general procedure you have modeled and to sort out any glitches on their own. The groups are small: six to eight students at a time. Although you have provided a model for how much time one sharer may take and have responded to what you feel is inappropriate behavior, you have not given a list of rules to the students — it is up to them to decide. Different leaders may have different criteria, but in figuring these out, the students are engaged in purposeful interaction.

As we'll see in Chapters 7 and 9, many of the language functions and questions modeled and used in sharing time will be used in writing conferences as well. Michaels and Foster (1985) observed that "through discourse activities such as sharing time, teachers help children develop valued language skills and literature discourse strategies that are required in written communication" (Michaels and Foster, p. 156) and, they add, in oral language as well. Developing a sensitivity to one's audience is critical in all facets of the language arts, and this sensitivity is well exercised in both teacher-directed and student-directed sharing groups.

Oral Presentations

The process of sharing helps students feel more comfortable and less inhibited in speaking before an audience — even of their peers — and prepares them for the next big step: presenting an oral report before a group. Preparing the content of oral reports is quite similar to preparing content for written reports, so this aspect will be discussed in Chapter 7. I'll focus here on the *delivery* of oral reports.

Presenting oral reports accomplishes several objectives: First, students apply skills in organizing material for clear presentation. This is an important paring-down process, involving the identification of what is *most* important — thus requiring students to think critically about their content. Second, students learn how an oral presentation can be effectively delivered using oral and body language as well as supporting materials. Third, students' confidence is developed. Fourth, oral presentation skills can be very useful throughout the school years, and of course, eventually in the workplace as well. Although it is to be expected that each new speaking situation will create a certain amount of anxiety, if students have a previous experience with successfully discussing something before a group, then they will have skills they can draw upon. Rather than being terrified, then, they should at worst be just a little nervous!

Students should first present their reports before a small audience. Later on, as they gain confidence, students may present reports before a larger group. Their initial presentations may in fact be one of several oral reports by a committee that has worked together.

As with sharing, oral reports should involve the use of visuals or props of some type to which children can refer: transparencies on an overhead projector, maps, or the materials for a science experiment. These provide important supports for presenters and also help their audience understand the presentation.

In preparing to deliver the report, students should at least audiotape their presentation. This allows them to try out different speech mannerisms, as for example the speed with which they talk and how they can vary their pitch. If possible, videotaping works best, particularly if students are working together with a group and each student will be presenting orally. The students can help each other out by constructively evaluating the taped presentation.

Students should be aware of and attend to the following skills of oral presentation: They should speak clearly, make eye contact with their audience, gesture and move smoothly, use space effectively, and make appropriate and effective use of visual aids.

Small-Group Discussions

We have been emphasizing the importance of helping students become independent learners as well as cooperative workers. Both of these objectives will be addressed in the small-group work the students undertake. The collaborative and cooperative learning that such group work allows will underlie most of the learning that occurs in your classroom; many of the small-group activities you read about in Chapter 4 are excellent examples of this. In that chapter we explored the procedure for setting up small groups and teaching the process of how to work in small groups. In this chapter we will address *discussion* activities in the context of the small group, and in subsequent chapters we will explore small groups for reading and writing activities.

Discussion groups provide an opportunity for systematically identifying issues or problems, defining their parts, and working through a problem-solving process to arrive at a conclusion. The process of discussion involves critical thinking; one of our goals is to have this process become internalized by the students so that they can apply this reasoning in their independent problem-solving. As Moffett and Wagner summarized:

All these are part of an external social process that each member of the group gradually internalizes as a personal thought process: she begins to think in the ways that the group talks. Not only does she take unto herself the vocabulary, usage, and syntax of others and synthesize new creations out of their various styles, points of view, and attitudes, she also structures her thinking into mental operations resembling those of the group interactions. Good discussions by groups build toward good thinking by individuals. (1983, p. 79)

Getting Underway

As we saw in Chapter 4, when grouping was discussed, small-group work must be phased in gradually. Here are some guidelines for beginning discussion groups in your class:

■ *Start slowly, with one group at a time.*

Whether you begin with new groups or with existing groups, for example, you should "walk through" a group discussion with one group at a time, discussing the procedure and modeling it for the students.

■ *Start with simple topics.*

You should set the students up for success as much as possible. Especially at first, you will probably select most discussion topics. For example, topics such as the advantages and disadvantages of staying up late or open campus in elementary school may be more likely to generate discussion at first, although your students may surprise you. Your students may get as involved and excited about discussing topics such as famine and what to do about it, or whether or not there is a drug problem at school.

   Later on, questions or topics to be discussed can come from just about anywhere — your groups can discuss current concerns as well as ideas and conflicts in the literature the students will be reading. Interpersonal problems in the classroom — children simply not getting along with certain other children — are often best addressed and resolved through discussion.

■ *Focus on the process at first.*

At first, keep the time fairly brief — fifteen minutes or so. The first few times, you and the students should spend a fair amount of time evaluating how well the discussion group went and how it might go better next time around. If you are straightforward and honest in your feedback, your students will be with theirs. The content is still important in the beginning, but you need to focus on the process so that all subsequent discussion group work can focus exclusively on the task or topics at hand.

Procedural Guidelines

Morris (1977, cited in Cohen, 1987) offers the following "basics" as discussion group guidelines:

1. Decide what the question to be discussed *means,* then discuss the meaning with the rest of the group.
2. Make sure the group decides on one meaning.
3. Say your own ideas.
4. Listen to others; give everyone a chance to talk.
5. Ask others for their ideas.
6. Give reasons for your ideas and discuss many different ideas.

When all class members are involved in small-group discussions, pull them together afterwards for a wrap-up (Barnes, 1976; Cohen, 1987). This also allows the opportunity to have one child who has grasped a major concept or idea "run through" it for the rest of the class. Conclude with feedback on the *process* as well — how well the discussions went.

The Teacher's Role in Small-Group Discussions

As stated in the *English/Language Arts Framework* for the state of California (1987, p. 18), through discussion "students learn how to respond to each others' insights and observations, how to listen attentively, how to rephrase and clarify a point, and how to disagree tactfully." Barnes (1976) summed up the teacher's role in discussion well: "The quality of the discussion — and therefore the quality of the learning — is not determined solely by the ability of the pupils. The nature of the task, their familiarity with the subject matter, their confidence in themselves, their sense of what is expected of them, all these affect the quality of the discussion, *and these are all open to influence by the teacher*" (Barnes, 1976, emphasis added).

Your mission is to facilitate the *process,* and you do this generally in the way you interact all day long with the pupils as well as specifically during discussion times. As a result, we expect that the pupils will be familiar with the task and that they are developing confidence in themselves.

During times when the whole class is engaged in small-group discussions, you should roam about, alert for those times when it is wise — not just convenient — for you to dip into a discussion to "facilitate." You will do this sparingly; for example, let's say you overhear two students quarreling about how many people living in poverty there are in the United States; the discussion has bogged down over this issue and the rest of the group is getting squirmy. Kneeling next to the group, you excuse yourself for interrupting and say, "Based on your discussion, I wonder if you're all agreeing on the same definition of *poverty*? Janet, how are you defining *poverty*? Jeremiah, how are you defining it?" The students — and the

AT THE
TEACHER'S
DESK:
Small-Group
Discussion
in Action

Discussion in small groups can facilitate the solution to significant problems, whether the problems are in the classroom, the school, or the community at large. Brainstorming is one specific application of small group discussions that can be an excellent way to address such problems. The objective is for the group to generate a number of ideas or solutions that immediately come to mind. Each group should have a "scribe" or recorder who writes down the ideas as fast as they come (see Figure 5.4). There is no comment or evaluation — that will come later. After the ideas are brainstormed, then the group goes back and determines how realistic each suggested idea or solution is. Each idea proposed should be considered in terms of whether or not it is immediately feasible, may take a longer period of time, or perhaps is simply unusable. A more involved extension of brainstorming spreads the problem-solving sessions over five days. Each day a different question is brainstormed:

1. What is the issue, problem, or goal?
2. What has caused this situation or keeps us from accomplishing our goal?
3. What could we do to solve the problem or reach our goal?
4. Is there anything that will prevent us from doing this?
5. What should be our next steps?

group — then realize why they were going round in circles. This means of clarification should stick in their minds the next time there is a similar hitch.

Your role will usually be to ask questions that require the students to elaborate, clarify, and qualify (Moffett and Wagner, 1983). In the example with Janet and Jeremiah, your questions were aimed at *clarification. Elaboration* entails considering additional information or possibilities: "Are there any other ways of accomplishing that?" "What else could they do to address the problem?" *Qualification* involves looking again at a statement or belief, usually one that is overgeneralized: "Do you think *all* fifth-graders would feel that way?" "Is there a time when this *wouldn't* work as fast?"

We would be unrealistic if we did not acknowledge that a few pupils do not seem to work well in small groups; in fact, some will consistently behave negatively (Cohen, 1987). As we saw in Chapter 4, most behavior problems in the classroom arise from inappropriate instructional demands and unclear ground rules for interaction and work. If you carefully set up the groups and ease into this mode of student-to-student work, you will be able to head off most of the behavior problems that might arise. Those that remain reflect insecurities and perhaps emotional maladjustments. These are the children that you want dearly to help but often wind up feeling more at wit's end about. The problems may be deep and the solutions complex, but many of these children simply need to be perceived in a positive light, however faint it may at first be! The application or simple variation of questioning and helping techniques should go a long way toward changing the behavior.

Give such children specific responsibilities within the group. For example, for

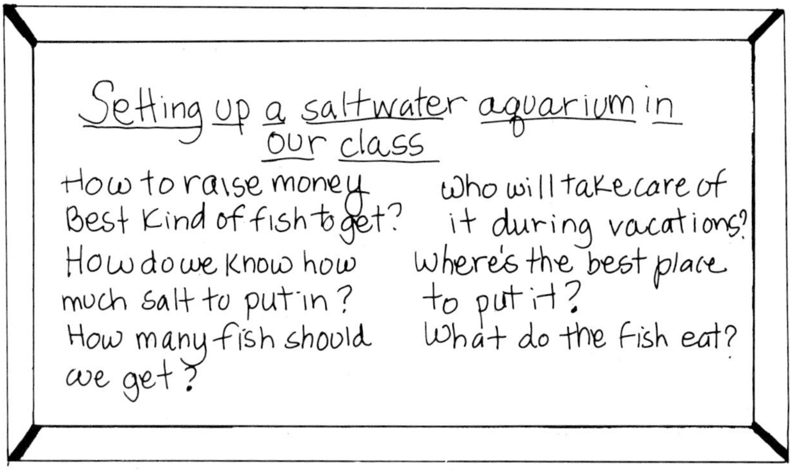

FIGURE 5.4

Ideas Generated by
Small-Group
Brainstorming

**Setting up a saltwater aquarium in
our class**

How to raise money
Best Kind of fish to get?
How do we know how
much salt to put in?
How many fish should
we get?

Who will take care of
it during vacations?
Where's the best place
to put it?
What do the fish eat?

the chronic interrupter and naysayer, being group "scribe" or recorder for a short period of time should help. This role *requires* the student to listen to what others say and to withhold comment. The student will get positive reinforcement from the group at the end of his or her stint as recorder.

Children who misbehave to get attention — even negative attention — are more likely in a small-group situation to begin to receive some *positive* reinforcement. The reason is simple: the group is small, so there is more opportunity to get to talk. If these opportunities for talk become egocentric monologues, however, a subtle comment or question from you may be of help: "Rick, it sounds like you are restating what Karen said . . . ." "Gina, are you disagreeing with Mark's statement, then?" Such prompts from you are gentle reminders that there *is* a group discussion going on, and perhaps the student ought to pay more attention.

I have tried to cover the basics of small-group discussion here; we will return to this topic several times over the next few chapters as we explore the ways in which discussion can be a springboard to many other activities.

Creative Dramatics

Consider the following scenes from different classrooms, both of which are examples of students who are engaged in creative dramatics.

**CLASSROOM
EXAMPLE**

An entire class of second-graders has been arranged into pairs. The children in each pair are facing each other, apparently moving in the same fashion. It becomes apparent that they are trying to "mirror" each other, but one is the "mover" and the other is the "reflection." Occasionally there is a burst of giggling from one or two pairs, but most are intently moving almost in unison, as each "reflection" becomes better attuned to the movements of the other child.

The reflections and movers will switch roles soon, but it is obvious that these seven- and eight-year-olds are becoming quite adept at "reading" another individual — putting all their energies into anticipating what the other will do. This is an important exercise in losing one's egocentricity by trying to make connections, through movement, with another mind.

Now let's walk over two buildings to the upper elementary wing and observe a group of sixth-graders. In their class, they periodically interrupt the reading of *Summer of My German Soldier* to interpret or to improvise through spontaneous drama aspects of Betty Greene's novel about the summer of 1943. Today, the children are improvising reactions of the citizens of a small town in Arkansas, after the townspeople have just discovered a young Jewish girl has been sheltering an escaped German prisoner of war. The "citizens" are outraged at the girl, but the scene takes a novel and riveting turn when one of the students exclaims, "We're doing exactly what the Nazis are doing — and we're fighting a war with them because of the way *they* are treating people!" Suddenly, fully, the impact and understanding of the irony revealed in this insight is realized by the other children.

Unless you have been involved in theater and drama, just the term *drama* may be a bit intimidating to you. You may envision actually performing and directing children in plays, memorizing lines, and making costumes. This *is* a part of drama, but it is certainly not the only aspect of creative dramatics activities. Intuitive teachers have always made use of creative dramatics to help their students understand all manner of concepts at a basic, visceral level. Through creative dramatics, students can become aware of a broad range of concepts and emotions, from the noblest of ideas to the function of a part of speech. And very little of it will be "rehearsed."

What are creative dramatics? I will offer a brief definition here, then share objectives for elementary students. In the subsequent elaboration of these objectives I will be drawing upon the landmark work in this area by Geraldine Siks, Dorothy Heathcote, and Betty Jane Wagner, as well as on the fine work of a new generation of creative dramatics educators. My objective for you, by the way, is that you become convinced of the power of this too-often-neglected aspect of the language arts and make it a mainstay of your curriculum.

Creative dramatics cover a broad range of activities from informal movement and pantomime on through interpretation and improvisation activities. The key word here is *informal*. Through creative dramatics children become spontaneously aware of themselves and of others. Perhaps less obtrusively than in any other domain, creative dramatics begin where the children need to begin. Why? Because at heart creative dramatics are an *extension of play* (Verriour, 1989). They build on what children already know how to do. As Heinig and Stillwell pointed out, creative dramatics usually aim for "growth and development of the players rather than entertainment of an audience" (Heinig and Stillwell, 1977, p. 5).

Because creative dramatics are a fairly direct extension of play, they facilitate children's thought about themselves and others. These activities involve *action* upon the environment and in concert with others. In the process, experience is transformed into language and related to other knowledge and experiences. The adage about "walking a mile in someone else's shoes" before making a judgment about another person is particularly apt; Verriour (1989) has remarked how creative dramatics can allow children to *live* other roles in order to understand these roles better. He has characterized succinctly and effectively the role of drama in the classroom: "Drama has the power to place children in a position to take risks in their learning without fear of penalty, to face and deal with human issues and problems, again without penalty, as well as to reflect on the implications of choices and decisions they may have made in the dramatic context" (Verriour, 1989, p. 285). In a review of the research investigating the effects of drama on learning, Wagner (1988) observed that "drama has a positive effect on personal attitudes often associated with language growth: self-confidence, self-concept, self-actualization, empathy, helping behavior, and cooperation" (Wagner, 1988, p. 48).

Because creative dramatics tap so many different modes of expression, they reflect each of the "intelligences" described by Gardner. From the linguistic through the spatial, personal, kinesthetic, and so on (see Chapter 2), each intelligence is drawn upon and exercised. Wagner made an observation that is particularly relevant for young children: "Since the acquisition of literacy is dependent on the manipulation of symbols and increasing decontextualizing of language, social symbolic play provides a useful bridge to literacy" (Wagner, 1988, p. 49).

Before we begin we must set the stage. Remember our earlier discussion of managing transitions, including moving students into small discussion groups? In your classroom, *all* new procedures and activities will require this transition time, with careful preparation of the students. In the rest of this chapter I will present a sequence of organization and activities designed to allow you to make a realistic, effective, and rewarding transition into creative dramatics in your classroom. I will explore creative dramatics through the following three topics: first, the best use of space and materials; and second, the "basics" of creative dramatics, including relaxation techniques, focusing concentration, building trust, simple movement activities, and "quieting down." We'll finish with fingerplay and puppetry, pantomime, and spontaneous and planned drama.

Space and Organization

As far as space is concerned, it seems there is never enough. There will be occasions when you will want to have your students use the multipurpose room or a classroom that is not in use (depending on where you are in the country, however, either you have never *seen* an unused classroom or there is one in every wing of the school!). Most of the time, though, your students will use space that is right in your classroom. You should set up a corner or open area that is available for these activities. (See Figure 4.1 on p. 86 in Chapter 4.)

In order to accommodate whole-class activities, you should have either an existing space or be able to arrange conveniently a space that will allow twenty or more students to move around on their own without restriction.

Materials will be kept in the drama area for small-group work and are readily available if needed for large-group work. Essential materials for all grade levels

include large blocks, both cube- and L-shaped, fabrics of different colors and textures and of different widths and lengths. Essential for younger students is a variety of hats, gloves, discarded and laundered coats (oversized ones work marvelously). Siks (1977) lists as "useful but not necessary" old bedsheets, towels, and drapery materials. If these are available, you should also have on hand a supply of clothespins to be used for on-the-spot fastening together of fabrics. Not *absolutely* necessary but certainly helpful are a couple of small tables. For younger students, collections of empty cereal boxes and safe containers from the supermarket are invaluable; they will be used in creating constructions of different types and in role playing.

A word about *grouping* for these activities: Besides whole-class grouping, there are other possibilities for creative dramatic activities. Students can work together in pairs, independently, and in groups of four to five. At times your class will be "half and half," with half involved in an activity and the other half observing. Remember, in case you are concerned about the excitement generated at the beginning of whole-class activities, that the students usually will know ahead of time what they will be working on. Allow a few minutes for the laughing and talking that will naturally occur among the students; then your students will usually be ready for concentrating. If they are *not* "settling down," however, this is the time to remind them that your "starting signal" (discussed below) will be given when everyone is quiet and concentrating. Your patient waiting then reinforces the message.

The "Basics" of Creative Dramatics

Relaxation

Before beginning a creative dramatics activity, you often will need to guide the students through some relaxation exercises. Certainly at the beginning of the school year you will need to do this; later, the students will apply these techniques on their own. These low-risk techniques or "warm-ups" relax and limber up children while getting them in the mood for other types of creative dramatics. They will also help the students become more aware of their muscles and sources of control, an awareness students will need as they experience and interpret that experience primarily through their kinesthetic intelligence.

I recommend that you start with the following activity (Siks, 1977) that will help the students become aware of how muscles can be tensed and then relaxed: Have the students sit in a circular formation on the floor, then tell them to put their arms at their sides, their hands on the floor, and their legs and feet straight out in front of them. Then, have them tilt their heads upward. Tell them to sit up even straighter and lift their heads even higher, while still being sure that their hands are firmly on the floor and their legs are straight out in front of them. Of course, this is going to increase tension in all the muscles, and you may even hear some mock groans from some students! Then, tell the students to relax *slowly* by letting the tension go in each body part, one at a time, until they are in a comfortable sitting position with no unnecessary tension. Your final step is to have the students discuss with a partner the differences between the tense and the relaxed feelings.

Once your students consciously understand the contrast between being tense and being relaxed, they will appreciate the value of relaxation activities. Here are some activities that you can use with the whole class and which the students can also use on their own (Moffett and Wagner, 1983):

- Have your students gently rock their heads from side to side.
- Have them pretend to yawn until they *do* yawn.
- Have them scrunch up as much as they can, pretending they are trying to fit into a tiny space, tightening every muscle and then slowly open up, expanding into as much space as they can.
- While lying on the floor, have the students alternately tighten up and relax their muscles, beginning with their toes and working all the way up to their foreheads. They should then lie still with their eyes closed. When they open their eyes, have them take a deep breath.

Concentration

In addition to learning how to relax, students also need to develop their ability to concentrate. Children are certainly capable of concentrating. The task in the classroom, of course, is to focus their abilities on the upcoming task at hand. In preparation for creative dramatics activities, *you* will provide the information about focus. The following activities (Siks, 1977; Moffett and Wagner, 1983) are excellent for focusing concentration:

- You throw an imaginary ball to a student, and the student then throws it to another, and so forth. Everyone "watches" the ball as it is thrown and flies through the air. After a while, tell the students that the ball is getting heavier and heavier; later still, tell them that it is not only getting heavier but *tinier* — "it is like a tiny marble made of lead." The ball can change to a balloon, a porcupine, a piece of wood, and so on.

- Remember the second-graders who were "mirroring" each other? That was a concentration activity. As the students work in pairs, the one who is moving — the "mirror" — must move slowly and with concentration. He or she can move as if carrying out a familiar activity (putting on a shirt or blouse, for example), or move in a free-form fashion. The other student, who is the "reflection," must try to pick up on the movements and move so that an observer would not be able to tell who is the "mover" and who is the "reflection."

- Ask your students — again working in pairs — to take turns in concentrating, to see how each one tenses and relaxes his or her body in response to changes you suggest. For example, you may suggest the students change from an apple to applesauce, uncooked spaghetti to cooked spaghetti, or from a snowman to soft snow.

Trust

Like concentration, trust is something that most children develop naturally, but it must be directly facilitated by you so that creative dramatics activities can flow more naturally. Your overall classroom environment is arranged to establish trust, of course, but now we are going to address it directly.

One of the best ways to develop trust is to have students select a partner for a "walk for the visually impaired." The partner is at first usually a good friend — later, partners can be less familiar students. The students will take turns being blindfolded so that one of them cannot see. The seeing partner will guide the blindfolded partner around the room, stopping occasionally to help the latter "see" a particular object by using other senses — touch, smell, and sound. By having to rely so closely on each other, the students become explicitly aware of the concept of trust. This activity can be expanded to include a walk through the school — as we'll note in Chapter 13, it also helps sighted children appreciate the world of the visually impaired student.

An activity that should probably be undertaken after students have engaged in the visually impaired walk is one that helps to build *group* trust. In a group of four or five students, one student is blindfolded and then goes "limp." He or she is held up by the group as the members gently push the student around from one to another. Of course, the group encircles the blindfolded student closely enough so that there is no danger of falling! As with most activities you do, this is one that you will model for the whole class first, by demonstrating with a group of students (Moffett and Wagner, 1983).

Simple Movement

When you begin creative dramatics, your whole-class sessions will probably involve movement activities. The main reason for this is that students will be much less self-conscious when everyone is moving en masse; students who are reluctant, inhibited, or who simply want to watch to see how other students are going about the activity will not usually stand out in this type of situation. Low-risk movement activities are particularly good for young children, and are well worth engaging in two or three times a week.

Before we look at a couple of different movement activities, a word about music, the usual accompaniment to movement. If you know an instrument, you're set — you don't have to be a virtuoso. Even if you know only a few chords on the guitar, for example, there still is much you can do. The type of instrument really doesn't matter, although the piano probably offers most possibilities. There is always the autoharp, and even a harmonica has promise! Of course, you might also use recorded music. Ways to vary the music include alternating between high and low notes, the length of the notes, and how much stress is placed on the notes. Importantly, as Moffett and Wagner (1983) comment, "Learning to discriminate various auditory dynamics will sensitize children to pattern and structure in other media, including literature" (Moffett and Wagner, p. 102).

When your students engage in whole-class activity simultaneously, begin with *herd movement.* Arranged in a circle and accompanied by music, the students can run, skip, tiptoe, hop, leap, slide-step, or jump, depending on what the music tells them. To encourage *individual invention,* have each student remain in a small area. Again in response to music, the students will move different parts of their body while standing or sitting. Urge them to "try motions that are twirling, angular, smooth, jerking, [or] gliding." You can then ask each student to think about the following questions: "What is happening? Who are you? Where are you?" (Moffett and Wagner, p. 103).

Have a starting signal for your activities that everyone knows. For example, you can strum or play a particular chord once to mean "start," and play the same chord twice to mean "stop." Similarly, you could use one drumbeat to begin the activity, and two drumbeats to end it.

"Quieting" Activities

Quieting activities are appropriate after whole-class creative dramatics activities. They have two purposes: (1) To calm the students down before they move to other types of activities; and (2) to allow the experiences, ideas, and emotions that arose during the activities to be absorbed. Heinig and Stillwell (1974) suggest the following:

1. Narrate a very quiet selection, such as a poem, in which the characters are relaxed or tired. The children should close their eyes as they listen, perhaps resting their heads on desks or tables. Excellent poems for this purpose are "Fatigue," by Peggy Bacon; "Lullaby," by Robert Hillyer; "Slowly," by James Reeves; and "Sunning," by James S. Tippett (Heinig and Stillwell, p. 38). To these I would add "Slumber Song," by Louis Ledoux; "The Little Girl Lost," by Barbara Taylor Bradford; and "Shop of Dreams," by Mary Jane Carr.

2. For older students, the teacher can request that [the students] pretend they are "floating on a sea of tranquility" (Heinig and Stillwell, 1974, p. 38).

3. The old standby: as children rest their heads, play quiet, calming music.

From Fingerplays to People Plays

When creative dramatics activities take on a story line, however spontaneous or contrived, they move into a wide range of possibilities. In this section we discuss a few of the prominent possibilities.

Fingerplay and puppetry are small-scale extensions of ourselves, as natural as the movements of an animated child's hands. While surveying a kindergarten classroom one afternoon during rest period, I noticed one boy, lying on his back, who seemed to be having a "conversation" between his hands. Holding them over his face, he had each hand "talking" in turn. The conversation was growing more animated; each hand seemed to reflect a definite personality. Before long, however, these "hands" had a falling out, and they went to "biting" at each other!

While this lad was certainly amusing himself during the rest period, I was struck by the naturalness with which his hands came alive. They were personalities, certainly, yet still very real extensions of himself. In fact, if he were to put a sock on each hand and continue the exchange, we would then call them "puppets."

Fingerplay

Simple fingerplays help young children think directly about language and actions. Fingerplays are sequences of finger and arm motions that accompany a short narrative, poem, or song. They work extremely well when you have explicitly planned for them, as well as when they can help fill some "down time" in the classroom — while students are waiting for a bus, waiting to go to lunch, or there are a couple of extra minutes at the end of the school day. Here are a couple of classics that lend themselves to fingerplay or arm motions (Heinig and Stillwell, 1974):

Rhyme	*Motions*
Hickory dickory dock	One arm swings like a pendulum.
The mouse ran up the clock	Fingers "run" upwards.
The clock struck one	Hold up index finger.
The mouse ran down . . .	Fingers "run" downwards.
I'm a little teapot	Bend over slightly.
short and stout	
Here is my handle	Place arm on waist.
Here is my spout . . .	Extend right arm outward from shoulder, bent upward at elbow, with hand extended outward.

Puppetry

Puppets provide an excellent medium through which young children can express themselves creatively. The children can act out moods and emotions without really being personally responsible. The charm and effectiveness of puppets is in their link with the child's play. How many times have you drawn out an otherwise reluctant young child with puppets, dolls, or stuffed animals? It is no coincidence — these "alter egos" are safe because, from a young child's point of view, no one

Puppets provide young children with a liberating means through which they can act out moods and emotions and express themselves creatively. (© Will McIntyre/Photo Researchers)

really knows that the child is still in control. For those children who may be more reluctant than most to engage in other creative dramatic activities, puppetry provides an excellent transition. The *act* of manipulating a puppet can be liberating, particularly if children have made the puppet themselves.

As I've already suggested, puppets can be as simple as hands and socks. Although hand puppets — commercial ones or those made with socks — are most common, other popular puppets in the classroom are made from paper plates (attached to rods), paper bags (both sandwich and shopping size), and work-type gloves (see Figure 5.5). Siks and others have remarked that puppets have personalities: the paper-plate-attached-to-rod puppets are more dignified, while the hand puppets are the "clowns" (Siks, 1977). Children will come to choose the appropriate puppets depending on the particular performance that will eventually take place.

For kindergarten and primary-grade children, it is best to begin using puppets in simple play, followed closely by some type of short presentation. In preparation for such a presentation — illustrating a nursery rhyme or simple story, for example — have the children practice how their puppets would move or behave to express different emotions, such as sadness, happiness, exhaustion, or anger, and talk about this. You can then talk about using voices and have each child try out different voices in order for their puppets to express different feelings. Hennings (1990) suggests that, when young children are ready to put on a puppet show, they should use a tape-recorded sound accompaniment, so they can concentrate on their puppet's actions. For older students, the script should be attached to a surface where it can be easily read — on the back of the puppet stage, if one is available, or on the back of a table serving as a stage.

FIGURE 5.5

Types of Puppets

Sock Puppet

Paper Plate Puppet

Paper Bag Puppet

"Finger" Puppet
(Cut-off glove finger)

Pantomime

It is through pantomime that feelings, ideas, and stories are portrayed silently by using gestures and actions. Recall the discussion of kinesthetic intelligence in Chapter 2? A mimetist, often called a "mime," is someone who actively applies this type of intelligence. Few will rise to the heights of a Marcel Marceau, of course; regardless, pantomime is an activity with rich rewards.

I witnessed the power of a simple pantomime and how it could engage young children in my second-grade classroom one year. It was an autumn day, and I (who at that time regrettably did not do much in the way of creative dramatics!) was talking with the children about falling leaves. Chris, who was having some difficulty describing how leaves fall, asked if he could *show* us how a falling leaf felt. Pleasantly surprised, I agreed. Chris's facial expression, his arms, and his general motion all coalesced into a strikingly touching portrayal of a leaf — twisted, dry, near death, torn from its home and tossed chaotically, whimsically, and in the end, pathetically by the wind. I was struck by the pathos of Chris's pantomime and by the class's reaction — the pupils were engrossed, moved, enlightened. What we were only groping at with language, Chris had flawlessly captured in movement and expression.

Pantomime helps children turn a conscious lens on past experience in order to analyze that experience, and then to form images that they can represent through action. Pantomime activities can be done in unison, in small groups, or in pairs. They can run the gamut from simple to complex actions, from everyone knowing ahead of time what will be pantomimed to everyone trying to guess the action a particular student is pantomiming. I suggest the following sequence for pantomime activities:

1. *Whole Class in Unison.* While the whole class moves in a circle, you or a student suggest actions. You allow a fair amount of time for each suggested action to be developed before suggesting another. Begin with simple ones and develop into more imaginative ones. For example:

    a. You are walking through thick mud.

    b. You are walking barefoot across a hot parking lot in the summertime.

    c. You are fighting your way through dense tropical vegetation.

    d. You are walking on the moon, in light gravity.

    e. You are trudging across the bottom of the ocean when you see a shark but you cannot swim away. Suddenly you are whooshed up through the water and are sailing along on a jetstream that whisks you across the country and you come down on a ferris wheel at a state fair.

2. Once students are used to pantomiming in unison — like whole-class movement activities, group pantomimes are low-risk and safe — they can pantomime individually. Moffett and Wagner (1983) call these "pretend to be" pantomimes. Simple individual pantomimes include imitating animals (a timeless favorite with younger children). As children develop confidence, they can pretend to be a favorite character from a storybook, a particular type of community helper, a common household appliance, or whatever. Your list of possibilities will grow as your students get into this type of activity.

3. "Pretend to do" — a variation on "pretend to be" — involves pantomime of familiar and not-so-familiar actions: washing dishes, tying shoes, combing or brushing hair, wrapping a present, peeling onions, a bird listening for a worm, responding to a drink machine (the kind that slides a paper cup under a stream of beverage) that has gone haywire and will not stop dispensing the beverage. The context for "pretend to be" and "pretend to do" activities can vary; students can try to guess what action someone is pretending. The actions can grow to represent more symbolic actions or features; to suggest the possibilities, Heinig and Stillwell (1974) offer "dancing a question mark."

Narrative Pantomime

Narrative pantomime entails the teacher or a student reading a poem or story and other students acting it out in pantomime. Stewig (1983) makes a distinction between what he terms *interpretation* and *creative pantomime:* In his view, narrative pantomime would be interpretive rather than creative because children are not adding anything to the story or poem. If they were to "spin off" of the narrative and generate new events or situations, however, they would then be creative. It is important to know that some educators make this distinction and it is probably an important one to keep in mind, but don't get bogged down in terms and lose sight of doing both types of activities in your classroom.

When you introduce narrative pantomime, you should have the students do it either individually or in pairs; they can concentrate better and will probably be more focused than if they begin in a larger group. When each child is engaged individually, he or she is allowed to play any imaginable character, as opposed to being assigned a character.

An effective variation on narrative pantomime involves students acting out problematic or confusing situations they have encountered in their reading. This is an excellent alternative way to reconstruct meaning when the purely verbal track has bogged down.

Children's Storytelling

Children will pick up much about the art of storytelling from your storytelling and from any other storytellers they may see and hear. Of course, children are in a real sense natural storytellers themselves, but they should have the opportunity to be storytellers in class as well.

To help provide structure to the children's storytelling, encourage them to use props such as wordless picture books, flannel boards (see Figure 5.6), and as we saw above, puppets, if they so wish. Children should at first plan for telling short stories. These short versions may be told to a small group or perhaps just one other student. Through the process of storytelling, children learn how to abstract and sequence important information. These are important skills for reading and writing as well. Children will quite naturally begin to use the language in books read to them and in stories they have heard. You will notice certain words and phrases that creep in. This type of language will in turn help comprehension in reading and expression in writing. When my oldest son was a kindergartner, for example, he used the phrase, "It is my command," several times in a composition — a phrase that occurred repeatedly in a story being read to him at home.

As children become more comfortable in storytelling, there are many possibilities for elaborating on this form of expression. As one or two children relate a story, for example, others can act it out wordlessly in narrative pantomime. Although he does not label it as such, Verriour (1990) describes another variation that is in effect a type of Directed Listening-Thinking Activity:

- The teacher either reads or tells a story to the class.
- When he or she stops at certain points, children meet in prearranged groups for several minutes to predict what might happen next.

FIGURE 5.6

Using a Flannel Board as a Prop for Storytelling

■ While they meet, the children may fall into the storytelling mode themselves, taking turns in telling the story according to how they believe it might develop.

Improvisation

The rudiments of improvisation are learned through movement activities and through narrative pantomime. As students gain confidence and expertise in these foundational activities, they can branch out into interesting variations that involve true improvisation.

For example, Moffett and Wagner (1983) suggest that students write on separate slips of paper a character, a setting, and a problem. The "character" slips are placed together, as are the setting and problem slips. After the students are divided into small groups, each group draws a setting and a problem, and each student draws a character. Then each group improvises a skit.

Another variation involves giving each small group a line that can be either at the beginning or the end of a situation. For example: "They will never try that around here again," or "You get what you pay for." These lines can be improvised in a skit in different forms — as a drama, a dance, or a comedy.

Improvisation can enfold much larger chunks of the curriculum and available time, but do so while addressing curricular objectives. Cecily O'Neill (1989), for example, describes a situation involving kindergarten and first grade children in which she and the children discussed the fears many children have about beginning school for the first time. O'Neill was the "principal" and the children were the "teachers" who would help allay the anxiety of the new "children" — who were played by real-life parents and teachers. An example at the intermediate level is offered by Erickson (1988), who presents a lively scenario: The teacher greets a fifth grade class one morning as an aging Irish personality who owns a castle but who wishes to sell it. Sensing they are in for an adventure of sorts, the children engage in conversation with this new personality, who is obviously *not* the teacher. The children are drawn more and more into the situation until they find themselves in a full-fledged unit that will involve them in the exploration of medieval castles, ghosts (dead Vikings!), cartography, and legends.

Dorothy Heathcote has described this type of improvisation as involving the "mantle of the expert" and "teacher-in-role," but emphatically *not* teacher-as-entertainer. Children are deemed "experts" in a particular area, they may act as the experts, and they are responded to as such, while the teacher leaves behind his or her usual role and assumes the role of another individual involved in the improvisation. For teachers who are concerned with management, O'Neill notes that "It may be more worrying for teachers to lose control of the ideas in the classroom than to lose control of children's behavior" (O'Neill, 1989, p. 151).

Drama

As students engage in, reflect on, enjoy, and learn from creative dramatics, you may wish to entice them further. In the process, you will probably be quite impressed with their ability to stretch themselves. Cox (1980, 1985), for example, has described activities for involving elementary students in Shakespeare. Of course, most elementary children cannot at first sustain their interest and attention through heavy doses of Shakespeare. There are snatches, however — such as the witches' scene from the beginning of *Macbeth* — that will definitely engage them and give them a feel for the rhythm and fullness of Shakespeare's language. The opportunity to merely enjoy the sound and feel of Shakespeare's work will help set the stage for later appreciation of Shakespeare and many other dramatists and writers.

Students can adapt plays in children's magazines for radio plays or for reader's theater (see Chapter 8), as well as for more full-scale productions (see Kohl, 1988). These situations will allow children to reflect on *how* language is expressed and how individuals move to convey meaning. If an entire play is used, take the opportunity to discuss briefly the elements of a play and how they are developed — such as plot (the unifying factor behind characters, theme, and action) and characterization. This will support your instruction about story elements (see Chapter 9), which of course overlap with the elements of a play. *How* the elements are developed in a play, though, is different in important ways from the way they are developed in written narratives, and these differences should be explored with the children. For example, explore questions such as "How is characterization similar in plays and in stories? How is it different? How is setting similar or different?"

A CONCLUDING PERSPECTIVE

For most children, oral communication — listening and speaking — is the foundation for learning and for communication of all types. As children's language expands, so expands their thinking, and vice versa. Children also become aware of what they say and how they say it. In today's society, this is an important awareness and a very real fact of life: *How* a person speaks determines as much if not more how he or she will be perceived as much as what the person has to say. However disturbed we may be by this fact, it is a fact that is timeless. We must teach the importance of valuing other dialects and other languages, but we must not be blind to the realities of the way speech is perceived by a great many people in our society and other cultures. It is as true in Spanish, Chinese, and Urdu as it is in English. Because language is the most "visible" expression of a culture, it is the most obvious expression of its speakers as well. As educators, we can work to raise awareness while helping our students to understand and acquire the features of the predominant dialect and its nuances. In other words, we can wear our idealistic cloak as well as our practical cloak.

By examining their experiences and the language that accompanies those experiences, and by interacting in groups in a meaningful way with judicious help from us as educators, students will internalize the language and the strategies of the learning environment and make them their own. All that we will be considering and learning how to facilitate from here on — meaningful reading, writing, and responding — will stem from this social interaction and social learning, from language and learning strategies heard, used, and reflected upon.

Creative dramatics link all the language arts in a type of symbolic expression that is, for children, perhaps easiest to identify with and understand. Beginning with simple props and movements, creative dramatics can express the full range of expression and allow critical thinking through that expression. In our rush to help children learn about and use the symbol system of written language, though, we often lose sight of the value of creative dramatics as a meaningful and motivating foundation for learning to use written language. As we expressed at the outset, creative dramatics can stimulate imagination and critical thinking, as well as help children understand themselves and the motivation underlying human behavior. More involved dramatics experiences, as in the improvisation that led to a unit of study, help students understand "how the power of drama [can] enhance and enrich their learning" (Verriour, 1989, pp. 284–285).

I hope you have become convinced of the power of creative dramatics, a too-often-neglected aspect of the language arts, and plan to make it a mainstay of your curriculum. I also hope I have dispelled any misconceptions you may have about the role of "teacher-as-entertainer," because that is not what creative dramatics are all about — they are about the *students*.

REFERENCES

Applebee, A. (1978). *The child's concept of story.* Chicago, IL: University of Chicago Press.

Barnes, D. (1976). *From communication to curriculum.* Harmondsworth, England: Penguin.

Bernstein, B. (1971). *Class, codes, and control (Vol. 1).* London: Routledge and Kegan Paul.

Bettelheim, B. (1976). *The uses of enchantment.* New York: Harper and Row.

California State Department of Education. (1988). *Recommended readings in literature, kindergarten through grade eight.*

Cazden, C. (1988). *Classroom discourse: The language of teaching and learning.* Portsmouth, NH: Heinemann.

Cohen, E. (1987). *Designing groupwork.* New York: Teachers College Press.

Cox, C. (1980). Shakespeare and company: The best in classroom reading and drama. *Reading Teacher, 20,* 125–130.

Cox, C. (1985). Stirring up Shakespeare in the elementary school. In C. Carter (ed.), *Literature — news that stays news.* Urbana, IL: National Council of Teachers of English.

Edmiston, B., Enciso, P., & King, M. L. (1987). Empowering readers and writers through drama: Narrative theater. *Language Arts, 64*(2), 219–228.

Egan, K. (1987). Literacy and the oral foundation of education. *Harvard Educational Review, 57,* 445–472.

Erickson, K. (1988). Building castles in the classroom. *Language Arts, 65*(1), 14–19.

Genishi, C., McCarrier, A., & Nussbaum, N. (1988). Dialogue as a context for teaching and learning. *Language Arts, 65*(2), 182–191.

Greene, B. (1973). *Summer of my German soldier.* New York: Dial.

Harste, J., Woodward, V., and Burke, C. (1984). *Language stories and literacy lessons.* Portsmouth, NH: Heinemann.

Heath, S. B. (1982). What no bedtime story means: Narrative skills at home and school. *Language in Society, 11,* (2), 49–76.

Heinig, R., & Stillwell, L. (1974). *Creative dramatics for the classroom teacher.* Englewood Cliffs, NJ: Prentice-Hall.

Henderson, E. (1981). *Learning to read and spell: The child's knowledge of words.* DeKalb, IL: Northern Illinois University Press.

Hennings, D. G. (1990). *Communication in action: Teaching the language arts.* Boston: Houghton Mifflin.

Jaggar, A., & Smith-Burke, M. T. (eds.) (1985). *Observing the language learner.* Newark, DE: International Reading Association, and Urbana, IL: National Council of Teachers of English.

Johnson, L., & O'Neill, C. (eds.) (1984). *Dorothy Heathcote: Collected writings on education and drama.* London: Hutchinson.

Jung, C. (1953). *The collected works of C. J. Jung.* (ed. by F. Fordham). London: Routledge and Kegan Paul.

Kohl, H. R. (1988). *Making theater: Developing plays with young people.* New York: Teachers and Writers Collaborative. [for grades 3–9]

McCaslin, N. (1974). *Creative dramatics in the classroom.* New York: David McKay.

Michaels, S., & Foster, M. (1985). Peer-peer learning: Evidence from a student-run sharing time. In A. Jaggar & M. T. Smith-Burke (eds.). *Observing the language learner.* Newark, DE: International Reading Association, and Urbana, IL: National Council of Teachers of English.

Moffett, J., & Wagner, B. J. (1983). *Student-centered language arts and reading, K–13: A handbook for teachers.* Boston: Houghton Mifflin.

Morris, R. A. (1977). *A normative intervention to equalize participation in task-oriented groups.* Unpublished doctoral dissertation, Stanford University. Cited in E. Cohen (1987). *Designing groupwork.* New York: Teachers College Press.

O'Callahan, J. (1986). *Herman and Marguerite* (video). West Tisbury, MA: Vineyard Video Productions.

O'Neill, C. (1989). Dialogue and drama: The transformation of events, ideas, and teachers. *Language Arts, 66*(2), 147–159.

O'Neill, C., & Lambert, A. (1982). *Drama structures: A practical handbook for teachers.* London: Hutchinson.

Palincsar, A., Brown, A., & Campione, J. (1989). Discourse as a mechanism for acquiring process and knowledge. Paper presented at the American Educational Research Association, March, San Francisco, CA.

Pinnell, G. S. (1975). Language in primary classrooms. *Theory into practice, 14* (December), 318–332.

Pinnell, G. S. (1985). Ways to look at the functions of children's language. In A. Jaggar & M. T. Smith-Burke (eds.), *Observing the language learner.* Newark, DE: International Reading Association, and Urbana, IL: National Council of Teachers of English.

Rosen, H. (1986). The importance of story. *Language Arts, 63*(3), 226–237.

Ross, R. (1980). *Storyteller.* Columbus, OH: Merrill.

Rudasill, L. (1986). Advertising gimmicks: Teaching critical thinking. In J. Golub, Chair, & the Committee on Classroom Practice (eds.), *Activities to promote critical thinking.* Urbana, IL: National Council of Teachers of English.

Siks, G. (1958). *Creative dramatics: An art of children.* New York: Harper and Row.

Siks, G. (1977, 1983). *Drama with children.* New York: Harper and Row.

Spolin, V. (1963). *Improvisation for the theater.* Evanston, IL: Northwestern University Press.

Stauffer, R. (1969). *Directing reading maturity as a cognitive process.* New York: Harper and Row.

Stauffer, R. (1980). *The language experience approach to the teaching of reading.* New York: Harper and Row.

Stewig, J. (1983). *Exploring language arts in the elementary classroom.* New York: Holt, Rinehart, and Winston.

Verriour, P. (1989). Creating worlds of dramatic discourse. *Language Arts, 63*(3), 253–263.

Verriour, P. (1990). Storying and storytelling in drama. *Language Arts, 67*(2), 144–150.

Viorst, J. (1972). *Alexander and the terrible, horrible, no good, very bad day.* New York: Atheneum.

Wagner, B. J. (1976). *Dorothy Heathcote: Drama as a learning medium.* Washington, DC: National Education Association.

Wagner, B. J. (1988). Research currents: Does classroom drama affect the arts of language? *Language Arts, 65*(1), 46–55.

Wells, G. (1986). *The meaning makers.* Portsmouth, NH: Heinemann.

C H A P T E R

The Processes and Development of Reading and Writing

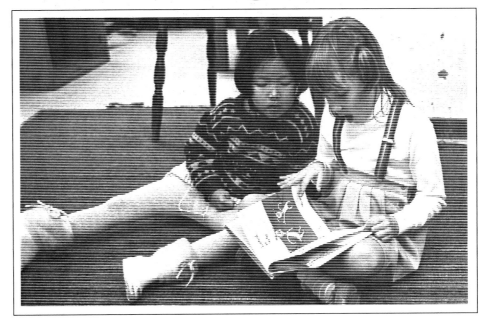

FOCUSING QUESTIONS

■ Why are writing and reading "two sides of the same literacy coin"?

■ What types of knowledge about written language do children acquire throughout the elementary grades?

■ Why is the application of knowledge about reading and writing such a complex process? Why is it necessary for much of this knowledge to become "automatic"?

■ What are the characteristics of most children's writing and reading knowledge during each of these periods: the preschool years, the primary school years, and the intermediate school years?

"Reading is stand up, sit down."

"When I read out loud the words go out my ears and are gone but when I read silently they stay in my head."

"I can't write 'cause I don't know how to read yet."

"How can I know what I think until I see what I say?"

INTRODUCTION

The first three observations are from primary-grade children; the fourth is from the writer E. M. Forster. The children's insightful observations reveal as much about how they are being taught as about what they think reading is. The first child went on to explain that when his turn came in reading group, he stood up to read until he made a mistake, then he had to sit down (Johns, 1986). The second child was explaining why, for him, reading silently was better than reading orally. The third comment, made by a first-grader, is telling, because most children will not make this observation without some coaching; here one senses the influence of a teacher's ideas. More positively, Forster's concluding comment represents what writing or composition can become for students — a true exploration in which they discover things about themselves, who they are and what they think, that they didn't know before.

Chapter 1 outlined many challenges to education and to teaching. Higher literacy levels in both reading and writing are at the top of the list. These levels will be realized in part as children come to understand better the functions and nature of written language — and insofar as we can avoid giving them the sorts of impressions voiced above in the first and third observations. Your students will understand and attain higher levels of literacy primarily through *meaningful* experiences with reading and with writing.

In contrast to much teaching in years past, *your* teaching will focus on reading and writing as being two sides of the same literacy coin. Both activities call upon many of the same skills, and children can apply the understandings they develop in one area to the other. As children write, they learn how authors think; as children read, they learn how authors write. In other words, as children come to think of themselves as *authors,* their insights into the purposes, form, and content of print develop in critical and exciting ways.

This chapter lays an important cornerstone in the foundation you will build to successfully provide integrated reading and writing in your classroom. In the first section, I will outline and describe briefly the nature of written language. The second section looks at the *processes* of writing and reading. The third section presents an overview of the developmental stages through which children proceed as they understand the nature and processes of reading and writing.

What Is to Be Learned: The Nature of Written Language

The Purposes of Written Language

The purposes or functions of written language are many. Written language can entertain, instruct, inform, label, remind, persuade, or warn, as well as perform any combination of these functions at once. It thus serves the same purposes or functions as those we discussed for oral language in Chapters 2 and 5: instrumental, regulatory, interactional, personal, imaginative, heuristic, and informative. In this chapter and the next I will refer to these purposes or functions using the traditional terms more common in the professional literature and in the classroom: poetry, narrative (interactional, personal, imaginative), description, exposition, persuasion (instrumental, regulatory, heuristic, informative).

What do writers want their writing to do? How should it affect the reader? The writer's *purpose* usually determines in large part what the writer wishes to say and the form in which he or she wishes to say it — by means of a letter, a poem, an essay, and so forth. Let's examine how the writer's purpose may be realized.

The Content and Form of Written Language

Because it represents much more information than we usually realize, the nature of written language invites a good deal of analysis. For now, however, we'll keep to fundamentals, and consider the information in written language in terms of *content* and *form*. From here on, you should refer to Figure 6.1 as a good "organizer" of the terms and concepts I'll be addressing in this section.

On one hand — *content* — written language represents the purposes and the intended meaning of the writer. What the writer wants to say and his or her purposes for saying it determine whether the writing will be more formal or more informal, whether it will be less "removed" from the present time and situation. Content, in other words, influences the writer's choice of *genre scheme*. As we'll see below, the genre scheme selected will in turn affect the content, molding and organizing it. There is a reciprocal relationship, then, between content and form.

On the other hand — *form* — written language represents information about spoken language: phrases, words, and sounds. This information is arranged linearly on the page — in English, left to right and top to bottom. Sentences organize ideas and relate to each other in a coherent whole. Separate paragraphs signal main ideas, major or minor topical changes, and turn-taking in conversation. And, as I've just mentioned, the particular genre schemes writers select will affect decisions they make about how to organize and express the content. The two major categories of genre are *narrative* and *expository* or informational. As Figure 6.1 illustrates, these two major categories can be further partitioned according to specific purpose and form (for example, poetry, description, persuasion) and format (son-

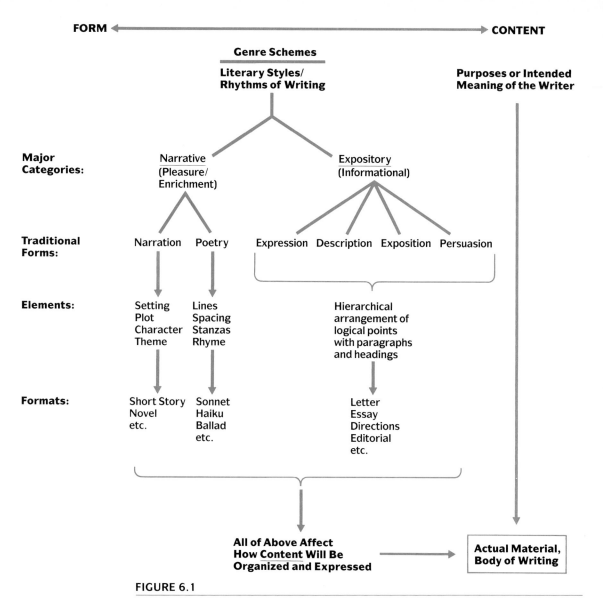

FORM ◄──────────────────────────────────────► **CONTENT**

Genre Schemes

**Literary Styles/
Rhythms of Writing**

**Purposes or Intended
Meaning of the Writer**

**Major
Categories:**

Narrative
(Pleasure/
Enrichment)

Expository
(Informational)

**Traditional
Forms:**

Narration   Poetry   Expression Description Exposition Persuasion

Elements:

Setting   Lines   Hierarchical
Plot   Spacing   arrangement of
Character   Stanzas   logical points
Theme   Rhyme   with paragraphs
                              and headings

Formats:

Short Story   Sonnet   Letter
Novel   Haiku   Essay
etc.   Ballad   Directions
               etc.   Editorial
                              etc.

**All of Above Affect
How <u>Content</u> Will Be
Organized and Expressed**

**Actual Material,
Body of Writing**

FIGURE 6.1

The Structure of Written Expression

net, essay, editorial). However, I'd like to begin our analysis at the level of the two major categories, narrative and expository structure.

Narrative Structure

The roots of narrative content and form — of stories — reach beyond the medium of written language, almost to the dawn of humankind. Seated around the fire of the clan, for example, elders told stories that helped unite the clan and protected it from the unknown. The earliest narrative forms may have been more poetic or lyric because they would then be easier to recall verbatim.

Stories are metaphors for our existence and our experiences (Bruner, 1988; Rosen, 1985). In most cultures stories follow a predictable format or structure. Story writers follow this format, and as we'll soon see, readers set up their expectations according to this format.

Several researchers have investigated the structure or "grammar" of stories and the effect it has on readers' recall of stories (Mandler and Johnson, 1977; Stein and Glenn, 1977). Stories have beginnings, middles, and endings, and each of these parts has its own characteristics. For example, the beginning of a story usually states a problem or a goal (say, a magical good-luck stone is stolen from a village), and the protagonist or protagonists begin a series of actions directed toward achieving the goal (a boy and girl set out to find the stone). The middle of the story usually comprises one or more attempts to achieve the goal (the boy and girl have to pass through three trials, each of which tests their cunning and their resolve, but each trial successfully moves them toward their major goal of finding the stone), and the ending provides the resolution (face to face with the villain who stole the stone, the boy and girl outwit him, seize the stone, and return to their village, where they receive a tumultuous welcome). When readers undertake the reading of a story, they subconsciously or tacitly expect to find these basic components, and this expectation helps to guide their comprehension.

Nested within this story structure are the traditional elements of stories that breathe life into the structure: setting, plot, characterization, and theme. *Setting* refers to the historical and geographical location(s) of the story, and *plot* "is a chart by which a story is navigated" (Taylor and Taylor, 1983, p. 313). Plot deals with what happens and why in the story. *Characterization* refers to how the characters are described and developed, and *theme* in effect sums up the story and is often expressed as a moral — for example, "love conquers all," or perhaps less loftily, "waste not, want not." By the end of the elementary school years, students should be familiar with these four elements of narratives.

Poetry is classified as a part of narrative structure. As we'll see in the next chapter, poetry presents language, form, and meaning in a unique way; it invites a special type of awareness or reflection that may not be experienced through any other kind of reading or writing. Children's sense of what poems are and what they can do comes from being around poems. As Heard (1989) commented, "After hearing many poems, students begin to know what different kinds of poetry sound like, and they come to their own understanding of what makes a poem a poem" (p. 3).

Expository Structure

Although on its surface expository text often looks very much like narrative text, its structure is quite different. Rather than telling a story, it explains facts and ideas by organizing them in terms of their logical relationship to one another (Taylor and Taylor, 1983). This organization is usually presented straightforwardly and arranged hierarchically. At the topmost level in the hierarchy are major ideas or topics, often signaled by headings; important supporting topics are signaled by subheadings. Nested within each major idea are paragraphs, each with a topic sentence that is in turn supported by other sentences that clarify, elaborate, and extend the topic sentence. At the most basic levels are the logical relationships among these sentences, referred to as *coherence* (Halliday and Hasan, 1976): are the sentences clearly related, flowing one from the other, with the referents for pronouns clearly understood as well as sequence and cause/effect relations clearly expressed? The format of expository texts often includes diagrams, pictures, or maps that support and elaborate on the text and may feature special emphasis for important terms by printing them in boldface or italics.

Writing within the traditional form of *description* conveys the observations of a detached observer; it relates aspects of some present situation by detailing the attributes of a person, object, or event. Within the form of *exposition,* writing usually explains something, as, for example, the steps involved in a particular task or procedure. *Persuasion* attempts to convince the reader to hold a certain opinion or attitude. *Expression* focuses on the writer's own attitudes and beliefs. Most early writing efforts take this latter form, and it can later be engaged in more mature writing. (Because expressive writing comes more naturally for most children it does not usually need the instructional attention that the other types require. For this reason, I will focus later on the other three types of expository writing and how they may be taught.)

Perhaps you're wondering why there are discrete categories of expository structure for features of writing that in reality occur in many different types of written expression. For example, can't description occur in a persuasive piece, or persuasion in a descriptive piece? For that matter, doesn't description occur in a narrative story? The answer to each of these questions is *yes*; these labels are not meant to suggest that a piece of writing is exclusively one type or another.

The reason we have these labels is two-fold. Historically, educators have made these distinctions, and they have become part of our traditional writing terminology. More important, instructionally the distinctions can be helpful and can allow students to focus their writing. Students can be shown that their main *purpose* in writing a particular piece is critical, and that they will need to structure the composition differently according to whether their primary aim is to describe, direct, or persuade.

Through reading and writing, elementary school students will come to understand, appreciate, and appropriately use narrative and expository forms and their various formats. Although our discussion of these forms has been necessarily brief, we'll focus more closely on the ways in which children develop a sense of written forms, and how to teach these forms and their formats through reading in the rest of this chapter and the next three chapters.

The Processes of Writing and Reading

As we discuss the processes of writing and reading, you will notice similarities between them. There are also important differences, of course, and it is necessary to understand these commonalities and differences in order to facilitate children's learning. Chapters 7 and 8 explore in depth the teaching of these processes; in this section we examine the way they function.

The following list, adapted from Bussis, et al. (1985), gives the types of knowledge that individuals draw upon when they read and write:

- background knowledge (concepts and schemes) about the content of the topic to be written about or the book to be read
- knowledge of grammatical structure, or *syntax*
- knowledge of "genre schemes" or text schemas, including literary styles and rhythms of writing
- knowledge of the information encoded in writing itself (This knowledge has two aspects: *word knowledge,* which includes letter/sound relationships, spelling patterns, and vocabulary knowledge; and *punctuation.*)
- prerequisite understandings about the nature of writing and reading and the conventions of writing and print

Let's examine how these types of knowledge are brought to bear during the processes of writing and reading.

The Process of Writing

There is no mystique about writing — it requires effort and is usually a very deliberate process. There are very few writers who can sit down and have ideas, words, syntax, sentences, and organization all flow from their minds through their hands and onto the page in "final form." Instead, writing is a *process* that involves a continual interplay among these aspects. Whether the result is a one-shot draft or multidraft effort, writing is a complex process that requires an interaction with the language systems and with information about the world. Though this process is often challenging, it can also be exhilarating, liberating, and sometimes life-changing. Usually it is somewhere in between.

What must be going on when we plan for and engage in writing? We must coordinate the planning of a host of factors — the form and content of the composition, both short and long term — with the actual mechanics of composing. All these factors further depend on our intentions and our expected audience. Scardamalia (1981) described this process well.

> Even a casual analysis makes it clear that the number of things that must be dealt with simultaneously in writing is stupendous: handwriting, spelling, punctuation, word choice, syntax, textual connections, purpose, organization, clarity, rhythm, euphony, the possible reactions of various possible readers, and so on. To pay conscious attention to all of these would overload the information-processing capacity of the most towering intellects. (p. 81)

The trick for writers, of course, is to automate many of these aspects so that they can direct conscious attention to the most important concerns. Scardamalia,

Bereiter, and others have used the term *information processing* to help describe the ongoing process of writing (Lindsay and Norman, 1974); more recently, the term *verbal efficiency* (Perfetti, 1985) has gained popularity. Borrowed from experimental psychologists, both of these theories of mental functioning analyze the ways in which individuals balance automated functions and conscious functions. For the process of writing, the theories describe how focus must be placed on the types and nature of the demands made on writers' attention as they write — what information must be "processed," and the effects of giving more conscious attention to some information at the expense of other types. Sometimes the task of handwriting will be foremost in the writer's mind; at other times spelling; at still other times content and form, as when writers are focusing on concepts or characters to be developed and points to be made.

By considering writing in terms of the efficient processing of different types of information, we are able to think about the time it takes to perform certain aspects of writing as well as how much "room" these aspects take up in our thinking or cognitive "space" as we write. What the writer is able to focus on depends on development and purpose: from a developmental perspective, younger children don't have many aspects of writing automated, so they must consciously attend to handwriting, for example, and their mastery of content will therefore not be as developed. Children in first and second grade often need to give a significant amount of time to figuring out the spelling of words, forming the letters and so forth, and this may not leave much cognitive space for attending to an elaboration of the topic or the consideration of a possible reader's point of view. As these "lower-order" skills become more automatic, however, then more processing time, cognitive space, and downright energy is available for attending to other types of important information. Later on, handwriting and spelling shouldn't and won't take up as much time or cognitive space during the initial drafting. At the appropriate point in the writing process, the students may turn conscious attention to these matters, but this time their purpose may be to prepare their composition for publishing. Their composing has already been fine tuned.

It's important to remember that before we even set about the task of putting pencil or pen to paper (or fingers to keyboard!), we are operating according to a high-level scheme that will direct the writing in accordance with our purpose. In the same way that humans organize other aspects of knowledge and experience, writers have schemas, or "genre schemes," for different types of writing. We've already discussed genre schemes briefly above; as we will see further in Chapter 9, the source of these schemas lies in the type and amount of reading in which we have engaged. To a considerable extent, these genre schemes establish the types of information and the strategies that we will employ as writers. Finally, the types of information available to us affect the words, phrases, and other aspects of the language that we select to actually write down on the page.

Let's walk through an example of this process — purpose/genre scheme/information — with Greg, a second-grader. Greg hopes to persuade his parents to allow him to stay up until eleven o'clock so that he can see a particular movie on television.

First of all, Greg's purpose is to stay up to watch TV. To convey what he wants to say, he must engage the appropriate genre scheme, which in this case is probably a letter. Greg has neither read nor written many letters, but he does have an idea of their structure and their purpose. He is unlikely, however, to write a story or a poem about a boy named Greg and how he tried to get his parents to let him stay up; although this might strike us as a particularly creative approach, it would probably not appeal as an option to most second-graders.

Greg's purpose and "letter scheme" help him select only the specific information that will help his cause. He is of course aware of the evidence his parents will marshall to support their position — he has heard it on innumerable occasions! The information that will support his cause and refute his parents' arguments will guide his selection of the appropriate language or wording.

At this point Greg is now writing, selecting language that will best represent his purpose and cast his intentions in the best possible light. As he is writing, there is a complex interaction among the lower-order aspects of writing (spelling, punctuation, and so forth) and these other types of information that he is processing — his fundamental purpose and language choice. If Greg is overly concerned with correct spelling, then his thinking "space" will be taken up with this concern and his message will suffer. He will not be thinking nearly as much about those persuasive statements that might weaken his parents' resolve!

The product of Greg's "information processing" before and during writing is shown in Figure 6.2. The process of writing need not result in a substantial text in terms of content and length. As Greg's effort attests, the interactive characteristics involved in the process are at work in any effort. In his composition the traces of genre scheme, intention, information, and language are all in evidence.

The process of writing can occur in a comparatively short burst of time, as in Greg's letter. For more significant efforts, though, the process will extend over some period of time and will involve more deliberate planning during the prewriting phase, followed by the actual initial draft, revising of that draft, and editing of the final draft. Throughout the remainder of this text, we'll discuss the process of writing using these more convenient and perhaps more congenial terms: *prewriting, drafting, revising,* and *editing.* We'll further explore the nature and teaching of these aspects of the writing process in Chapter 7.

FIGURE 6.2

The Product of Greg's Writing Process

```
DEAR MOM AND DAD:

    CAN I PLESE STAY UP AND WACH INVASHUN FROM MARS ON T.V.? I

KNOW IT IS ON LATE BUT I WILL TAKE A NAP FOR A WEEK. I PROMISS

I WILL PICK UP MY ROOM AND I WILL TAKE OUT THE GARBIJ. I LOVE

YOU VERY MUCH.

    LOVE,

    GREG
```

The Process of Reading

One way of conceptualizing written language is in terms of a blueprint. Texts — and these include any written material — are "blueprints" for the construction of meaning. Recall Wells' assertion (see p. 6) that children are "meaning makers"; this is as true for reading and writing as for language development. It is easy enough to see how writers can construct meaning, but readers do so as well. Meaning is not completely "in the text" or "on the page," but is constructed by readers, who use the text as a blueprint in combination with what they bring to the page by way of background knowledge and understanding (Iser, 1976; Pearson, 1985; Rosenblatt, 1978).

Reading — the process of constructing meaning suggested by a text — has been described as the "patterning of complex behavior" (Clay, 1979) and as a "complex skill" involving the "orchestration" of a set of simpler skills (Bussis, Chittenden, Amarel, and Klausner, 1985). These skills enable readers to appropriately apply the types of knowledge presented at the beginning of this section as they try to (1) maintain satisfactory comprehension or understanding while (2) moving through a selection with reasonable fluency or rate and (3) maintaining accuracy to the text — the words that the author used.

The application of knowledge to a text involves each reader's interaction among the language systems and background information about the content addressed by the text — the underlying schemas that represent how concepts are organized into broader mental representations of events, actions, and places (see Chapter 2). Again, much in the process must be automated if the process is to work efficiently (Bussis, et al., 1985; Perfetti, 1985; Rayner and Pollatsek, 1989).

The Interactive Nature of the Reading Process

Let's examine the reader and the text a little more closely before discussing how they come together to create a *text model* — the meaning that results from this interaction.

The *text* presents readers with words arranged according to the conventions of print, in an overall format that suggests how the words, sentences, and paragraphs should contribute to the construction of meaning. The writer has arranged these elements in such a way as to help the reader construct the writer's intended meaning.

The *reader* draws upon his or her knowledge of language — syntax and phonology — as well as upon background knowledge and knowledge of different contexts to interpret what is on the page. In the same way that listeners respond to oral language, readers draw upon their knowledge of language, their prior knowledge, and their knowledge of different contexts in different reading situations depending on what they are reading, where they are reading, why they are reading, and how they feel about the reading (Rosenblatt, 1978). The same is true for children learning to read, although of course the information upon which they draw is not as extensive as is the mature reader's.

Different models of the reading process highlight or emphasize primarily the *text,* the *reader,* or the *interaction* between the two. The models tend to be based on different assumptions about "who's in control here — the text or the reader?" Models that suggest the text is primarily in control and drives the reading process are often referred to as "bottom-up" theories; those that maintain the reader is primarily in control and contributes most to the reading process are called "top-down." Of course, you've gathered by now that I am suggesting the issue is not either text *or* reader but a combination — an interaction — between the two. From an educational standpoint, this *interactive model* best describes what probably goes on during the reading process.

I will adapt the model of communication that I presented in Chapter 2 to illustrate the interaction between the text — representing an absent communication partner — and the knowledge in the reader's head that he or she will use. For a diagram of this interaction, see Figure 6.3. The context of situation is the "what, where, and why" of reading, and determines in part the "pragmatics" — the rules — that determine how the reader in this particular context of situation will apply the rest of his or her knowledge. (For example, you are likely to interact with a certain text differently depending on whether you are reading it on the beach during spring break, reading it during a coffee break on your job, or skimming a chapter to find a particular paragraph that supports a point you just made — and the professor has asked you to read it out loud to the rest of the class!)

As we move through a text, we must identify the words appropriately (print information) and understand the meaning of the words in the particular context in which they occur (interplay among print information, syntax, and semantics).

FIGURE 6.3

Reader/Text/Context

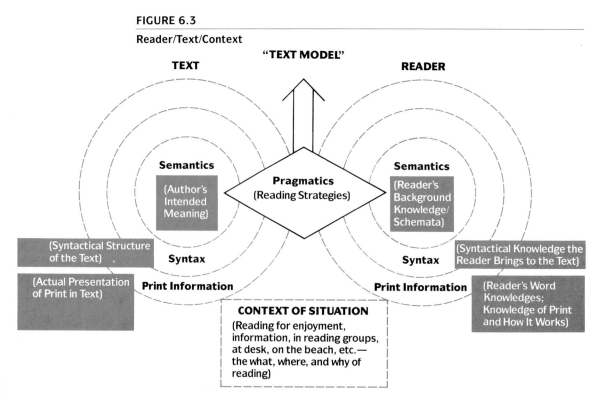

The Processes and Development of Reading and Writing

We must construct the underlying relationships among the concepts that the words represent, both within and between sentences (syntax and semantics). And we must construct an overall "model" of the text about which we are reading. This model represents the constructed meaning or text world we create as a result of reading this text; it did not exist prior to our reading. As we go along in our reading, this model becomes more elaborated while at the same time it helps to guide further meaning construction.

This process proceeds in light of what Perfetti (1985) calls the *verbal efficiency theory*. Simply put, this theory states that the quality of the reading depends on the efficient — and therefore effective — use of processing resources. These resources include not only knowledge about words, syntax, and semantics but also the information-processing capacity of the brain itself — the type and amount of information that the brain uses at any given instant. The reader is making effective and efficient use of these resources if understanding is occurring with good fluency and accuracy to the text.

There are a number of things that can go awry in this process, however, in which case the quality of the reading suffers. For example, a disproportionate amount of processing "space" in the brain may be taken up trying to identify words, in which case the sentence-to-sentence comprehension bogs down and, in turn, the overall text model cannot be adequately constructed. On the other hand, identification of individual words may be fine but the appropriate overall meaning that the words represent in a particular context cannot be accessed — too much processing "space" is taken up trying to construct context-appropriate meanings. Appropriate comprehension at both the sentence and the text level breaks down, as would be the case if this author were attempting to read a text on nuclear physics!

Components of the Reading Process

Although we will be examining rather closely in later chapters the knowledge, skills, and strategies involved in reading, these components are usually grouped under two headings: comprehension and word knowledge. *Comprehension* refers to the reader's understanding of the text being read — the construction of an appropriate "text model." The ability to construct appropriate understanding in turn depends on the application of strategies for reading a particular text, and these strategies may be engaged before, during, and after reading. *Word knowledge* refers to an understanding of the structural and semantic (meaning) features of words.

Traditionally, three categories or types of comprehension are identified (Barrett, 1976; Pearson and Johnson, 1978): *literal* comprehension, *inferential* comprehension, and *critical* comprehension. Occasionally a fourth, *creative* comprehension, is added. I will stay with the traditional three categories primarily because these are the categories referred to most often by the professional literature and by instructional materials.

The best way to think about the differences among these categories is to consider the degree to which the reader needs to rely upon *prior knowledge* in constructing meaning. Prior knowledge operates in every category, even literal (for example, you must know the meaning of the actual words on the page). Literal comprehension involves understanding what is explicitly stated in the text — what is "right there." Inferential comprehension involves understanding what is implied by the text — it is often referred to as "reading between the lines." In inferential comprehension, prior knowledge helps you to draw among the ideas represented within the text relationships that are not explicitly stated. Critical comprehension involves understanding how to go beyond the information on the page, either to connect the information with what you already know or to realize that you don't have enough information in your head to make a connection — in which case you will need to go elsewhere to get that information ("beyond the lines") (Raphael, 1983, 1986).

Students must learn how to construct the intended meaning of a text in order to go beyond that text and relate the constructed meaning to the real world. Stated somewhat differently, our charge as teachers is to address how meaning can best be constructed (the *reading*) and how that meaning connects with the real world (*critically thinking* about the reading).

Let's summarize. The more we know about a topic (background knowledge/schemas) and the genre scheme of the text we are reading (text schemas), the more efficient our reading will be, because we will be able to construct a text model that is clearly organized. We cannot bring these types of knowledge to bear, however, unless we understand how information is encoded in writing (word structure) and how print "works." We must understand the "blueprint" so that we will construct a solid text model.

The Development of Reading and Writing

As we have noted, reading and writing are processes that share much in common. Children's developing understandings about reading influence their developing understandings about writing, and vice versa. Psychologically, reading and writing are not completely different processes.

In the real world, reading and writing occur together much of the time. Just as we saw with the development of oral language, the development of print literacy — in reading and writing — occurs in a *social* context. Children learn about written language — its features and its functions — in an environment filled with examples of written language and with people using and talking about written language; in turn, children ask questions about written language (Yaden, et al., 1989).

Recent research in the development of literacy has mapped part of the terrain that all children must traverse in becoming literate (Bissex, 1980; Bussis, et al., 1985; Goodman and Goodman, 1978; Langer, 1986; Lomax and McGee, 1987; Mason, 1980; Teale and Sulzby, 1986). Different children may explore the contours of this terrain in different ways, but there appear to be some important common understandings that most children share in their development. Bussis and her colleagues have observed that children in first, second, and third grade "displayed much greater uniformity in what they knew about reading and print than in how they brought their knowledge to bear on text ... Many differences ... turned out to be *more a matter of how they used knowledge than of knowledge acquisition or knowing per se*" (Bussis, et al., p. 65, emphasis added). In other words, the nature of this knowledge and how it develops will be quite similar from one child to the next. For this reason and for your teaching, it is important that you know the general outline of this development.

The Preschool Years: Birth Through Kindergarten

Much of the wonder and complexity of early literacy development has been explored by researchers investigating what has come to be called "emergent literacy" (Holdaway, 1979; Strickland and Morrow, 1989; Teale and Sulzby, 1986). As we examine the nature and course of emergent literacy in the preschool years, we will see again two of the three patterns noted in Chapter 2 that characterize development: (1) from universal to culture-specific; and (2) from global to differentiated and integrated functioning (Bissex, 1980).

Written language is everywhere. How and how often children's attention is directed toward it will importantly influence their emerging concepts about literacy. In addition to general language and cognitive development that children will draw upon in reading and writing, along with their *background knowledge* about their world, preschool children can learn the following about written language:

■ *The beginning development of "genre schemes"*

The basic understandings developed here are the concepts of "story" and often of "nursery rhyme."

■ *Knowledge of grammatical structure, or syntax*

This is related to the development of genre schemes. The nature and structure of the language of books, or "book talk," is different from normal conversational talk in that it is often expressed through a fuller, more complete syntax. As we will elaborate below, this grammatical structure also reflects a different prosodic flow: book talk *sounds* different in important ways from everyday talk.

■ *Prerequisite understandings about the nature of reading and writing and the conventions of writing and print*

It stands for speech.
It reads left to right and top to bottom.
It exists within the concept of "book" — and this concept includes front and back, beginning, middle, end, and so forth.

■ *Knowledge of the information encoded in writing*

The minimal units of writing are *letters,* and there is a limited number of letters that are used over and over.

In this section we will examine the development of these different types of knowledge through reading and writing.

Reading

In the early years, children's experience with books may not teach them much about print at first, but it *is* beginning to teach them about visual, two-dimensional representations that are different from their usual experience with a three-dimensional world. They learn that the real world can be graphically portrayed and that this portrayal can be organized in a format we call "books."

Throughout this early development, children are in the presence of written language. The type and the degree of exposure vary, usually depending upon the adult caretakers. It is almost impossible for a child to be cut off completely from print; it is evident on signs, doors, shelves, cereal boxes, and automobiles. Print is used and attended to in many contexts in the home: storybooks, newspapers and magazines, TV guides, grocery lists, phone messages, checks, recipes or microwave cooking directions, and on and on.

Adult caretakers (usually parents) play an extremely important role in helping children learn to mediate between print and speech and to negotiate the different contexts in which written language occurs. Print therefore occurs in social contexts, and these social contexts will also be important in preparing children for the culture of the school. Although some children can learn to read from the "environmental print" that surrounds them, most do not. This is because the print with which we interact most in our society — that is, in books and booklike materials — does not have as much contextual support as does environmental print. For example, many preschool children who can recognize the word "McDonald's" in the context of the actual fast-food restaurant cannot recognize it out of context on a plain sheet of paper (Masonheimer, 1983; Hiebert, 1986). However, environmental print is nevertheless critical, because it provides the foundation for children's dawning awareness of the form and function of print literacy.

Of all the ways in which young children are exposed to print, the context of the storybook is one of the most important. The experience that adult and child share while reading together contributes to the development of literacy *and* oral language in general (Olson, 1984; Yaden, 1988; Yaden, et al., 1988). Children will learn much about "reading" itself, as well as develop concepts and vocabulary, as adults point to and discuss objects, characters, and actions represented in the storybook's pictures.

Reading to Children Most preschool children enjoy being read to by adults. The most effective approach is to sit the child in your lap or right next to you so that he or she can see the pages. This simple, comfortable context of shared storybook reading will allow the child to develop many of the understandings and information about print literacy I listed at the beginning of this section. Before we investigate these more specifically, let's consider some of the ways young children respond when they are read to.

Little children love to latch on to a favorite book, and to parents' chagrin, it so often seems to be one that lacks any real redeeming value or literary merit. Regardless, children will want you to read the same book over and over, and for a parent of a firstborn who wishes to oblige the child, this situation can go on literally for weeks. Such was the case with my first child. He requested the same book repeatedly, and his mother and I grew extremely weary obliging him. Finally, I told him a "white lie" — I said I couldn't find the book anywhere! Then, "miraculously," it was discovered several months later, at a time when he was interested in other books.

Parents needn't despair, however, because the desire to hear the same story or book over and over is a natural phenomenon with young children. *This repetition is critical.* It allows children to memorize, almost effortlessly, a number of texts. With time, as the child recites the story while turning the pages, he or she will read it exactly as the adult did, turning the pages exactly at the right point. Further, the child is developing a simple concept of story. In the preschool years, this understanding is quite basic and will include the narrative elements we discussed earlier: setting, plot, characterization, and theme.

Such children have had the "language of books" revealed to them. Although in one sense writing is "speech written down," in many others it is not. As we have seen, speech is usually less formal and more context-dependent, allowing for back-and-forth communication. The storybook is different. It tries to create its own world, and much of this world is signaled by the way the story is read to young children. Imagine for a moment how an adult's voice changes the instant he or she begins to read aloud the words "Once upon a time." There is more inflection in the voice and it usually changes noticeably depending on whether the adult is reading dialogue or a descriptive passage.

Children whose parents read to them have also developed a basic knowledge of how nursery rhymes work and, importantly, enjoy the rhythms and rhymes of them. Several scholars have suggested that such rhymes lay the earliest foundations for children's sensitivity to the sounds of language, a sensitivity that will be extremely important later on during the beginning of conventional literacy learning (Bradley and Bryant, 1985; Chukovsky, 1971).

Children who have been exposed to storybooks have begun to develop a knowledge of the "conventions" of print. In the beginning, young children do not pay much attention to the print on the page as a book is being read aloud. As you would expect, the child is examining the pictures. Gradually, however, children begin to attend somewhat to the print, and it is probable that adults are the cause of this. As adults read to children, they occasionally point to the lines of print, sliding a finger from left to right, with a return sweep to the beginning of the next line. In this way they are modeling the *directionality* of print for the child: left to right and top to bottom. Because they point to the print and say the same thing every time they read the book, the child will come to understand that these marks "contain" the story somehow — that each time around they will represent the same thing. Gradually, the child will understand that these marks represent spoken language.

Writing

Most of us are not accustomed to thinking about preschool children actually writing. A common response to this notion, even from many educators, is something like, "How can they write? They don't even know how to *read* yet!" (Templeton, 1980). One of the most dramatic findings from the recent research into preschool literacy development, however, has been the discovery that little children do indeed form ideas about writing, its function, and its conventions and characteristics. Children learn much at a general level about how print "works" before they can begin to learn the specifics.

Scribbles and Drawing   Quite early on in development, for most children anywhere from fifteen months to twenty-four months of age, scribbling begins. Young children seem innately to enjoy making marks — and anything is fair game as a writing surface! In the early stages, the marks appear to be random; it is as if the action and its effect is all that is important to a child. Later on, however, the scribbles are identifiable as pictures. Later still, drawings and scribblelike writing will co-exist in the same picture.

Young children are excellent observers. They attend to the way adults interact with written language as well as what adults read, and take their cues accordingly. Children will imitate the act of writing and the appearance of the writing as best as they are able. Figure 6.4 illustrates the contrast between the same child's writing in a grocery list, for example, and a "story": the general appearance of the writing represents the child's global perceptions of the print. The "list" does not go all across the page, whereas the "story" does. The child does not draw pictures of items to be bought, but writes them in a list format. As the children are writing, they may even be observed to construct their text from left to right and from top to bottom.

FIGURE 6.4

A Child's Uninterrupted Writing — Grocery List and Story
Source: Fig. 12.2, "Uninterrupted Writing: Shopping List & Story (Hannah, Age 3)," Jerome C. Harste, Virginia A. Woodward, and Carolyn L. Burke, *Language Stories & Literacy Lessons*, p. 157. Reproduced by permission of Heinemann Educational Books, Inc., Portsmouth, NH.

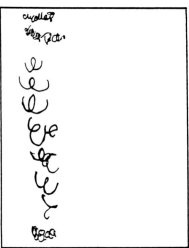

Approaching Alphabetic Writing   Children do not begin their attempts at writing by matching up letters with sounds; such alphabetic writing is preceded by and built upon a strong foundation of experience and experimentation with written language. Long before children focus on figuring out letter/sound relationships, they must first develop an understanding of how information is represented visually in two-dimensional space.

Young children's writing grows out of their drawing and early scribbling (Ferreiro and Teberosky, 1984). For most children it seems that when letters and letterlike characters first begin to appear, they are parts of a picture; the child includes them in the drawing mainly because they are features of what he or she has seen elsewhere on paper: they belong there, whether or not they relate to the drawing (see Figure 6.5). If you were to ask four-year-old Jeremy, the creator of this figure, "What do these letters *say*?" he would most likely respond, "Letters!" This is because young children do not perceive these forms to stand for anything else — like other objects and features of the real world, they are simply there, being themselves (Ferreiro, 1984; Ferreiro and Teberosky, 1982; Bissex, 1980).

Somewhat later, letters come to stand for the picture's name, because children see that the picture itself cannot be a "name"; they recognize that "name" is a feature of writing, not of pictures. At about this point, it appears that children begin to establish a type of relationship between the letters they write and the objects to which the letters refer. Writing appears more often by itself, not merely as an

FIGURE 6.5

Young Child's Drawings Incorporating Letterlike Characters
Source: Reproduced by permission of Victoria University from E. Ferreiro, "The Underlying Logic of Literacy Development," *Awakening to Literacy,* eds. Hillel Goelman, Antoinette Oberg, and Frank Smith (Portsmouth, NH: Heinemann Educational Books, Inc., 1984), p. 159.

embellishment of a picture. Gavin's "dinosaur" story in Figure 6.6 is one such example.

Fascinatingly, "children may use more letters if the object whose name is going to be written is bigger, heavier, or older than other objects" (Ferreiro, 1984, p. 166). When my daughter was four, for example, I observed her tearing up pieces of paper and using them to label different items in her bedroom. Both the dog, a collie, and the cat happened to be there, so she chose a larger slip on which she wrote several letterlike characters to stand for the dog's name ("Angie"), and a smaller slip on which she wrote fewer characters to stand for the cat's name ("Faux Pas"). The animals' names were each two syllables, so we can see by the number of "letters" used that at this stage children do not attend to the characteristics — the syllables or length — of the spoken word or name. This soon changes, however.

FIGURE 6.6

Gavin's Dinosaur Story

When children begin to relate letters to speech, they do not match letters with individual sounds, but rather with *syllables*. At this stage, the dog ("Angie") and cat ("Faux Pas") are now each represented in print with two characters because each name has two syllables. Interestingly, the characters may be the same but arranged differently, or different characters altogether.

Let's take stock of what children know at this point. First, the child has a concept of directionality. Second, the child clearly understands that writing is separate from pictures and is meant to convey information. Third, the child is developing a foundation for understanding how alphabetic characters are used and combined, even though there is not a correct correspondence between the characters and sounds. Clay (1975) has described this foundation as being composed of two important principles in writing: the *recurring* principle and the *generativity* principle. Children understand that a limited number of characters (letters) recur again and again, and these characters are combined in different ways to generate many different forms. In addition, these characters reflect what Clay called the *flexibility* principle: They may appear as *a* or *A* or *a* and they will always be understood to be the same letter "a" (Clay, 1975).

These understandings must be in place and children must evidence a command of them if they are to understand in a more formal sense the ways in which letters correspond to sounds. Children's awareness of these principles develops over a period of time, and most children who have acquired them have gone through a developmental process in which writing has to be distinguished from drawing, letters distinguished from other types of characters, and directionality firmly established.

You will also notice that, occasionally, young children experiment with form apart from content. For example, when my daughter was five, her usual writing contained distinguishable letters, but one day she wrote the following:

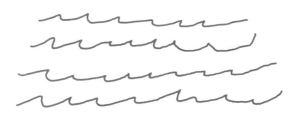

Upon completion, she showed me the piece, declaring, "I wrote a story!" When I asked her if she would read it to me she replied, "I can't. I haven't made it up yet!"

Children will now in their writing begin to include letters that, while still corresponding to syllables, more closely relate the sounds of syllables to the names of letters. An excellent example of this is the message written by my son, Gavin, when he was five years old: BBCUS. When asked to read this, Gavin pointed to each letter as he read, "Bye-bye, see you soon."

By now you can probably appreciate the distance children have come in their development. Although "BBCUS" appears somewhat primitive and simple to the naive adult, it represents a long process that has been nurtured by immersion in a print-rich environment *and* encouragement to attend to and explore that environment. Children engage in a complex interplay between the information that print represents in the environment and their own developing concepts about how print works. Ferreiro (1984) expressed this interplay so well: "Children pose deep questions to themselves. Their problems are not solved when they succeed in meaningfully identifying a letter or string of letters, because they try to understand not only the elements or the results but also, and above all, the very nature of the system" (Ferreiro, p. 172).

In the preschool years children have learned much about writing and reading in the "universal to cultural-specific" sense I mentioned earlier. Through processes of increasing integration and differentiation they have developed the basic understandings that underlie writing systems in general, and they have moved toward an understanding of the specifics of our own alphabetic system.

The Primary School Years: First Through Third Grade

Recall the list earlier in the chapter of the types of knowledge that individuals draw upon when they read and write. Let's consider more specifically the types of information within these categories that will develop throughout the first three grades:

- *Background knowledge*

  Simply by virtue of living, children will be developing concepts and schemas about their own world and the world beyond them. They will begin to bring this knowledge to bear on what they read and write about, and in turn be better able to use what they are reading about to expand and elaborate their own world.

- *Knowledge of grammatical structure, or syntax*

  While children are growing in their syntactic knowledge — learning to "fine-tune" their syntactic competence by handling more sophisticated and lengthy constructions — they will learn how to read the longer sentences they are able to use orally. In the first grade, much of this ability will develop if these longer sentences are their own oral language, written down exactly as they have said it.

- *Knowledge of genre schemes*

  At first, the "story grammar" that children construct at this stage is primarily sequential: problems in the story are addressed and resolved but in a straightforward, linear sequence. ("Flashbacks," for example, are understood to occur not earlier in the story but wherever they actually are located in the sequence.) A bit later, children will elaborate their understanding of the concept of *story*; episodes will become more involved and time sequences may be switched around (the story may begin at one point, then shift to an earlier point in time). The children will begin to understand how "chapter books" work — as longer stories broken into parts. They will learn that a fictional account could be real (contemporary realism; see Chapter 9). They can begin to explore informational books and simple poetry.

With respect to comprehension in these different genre schemes, children will grow in their ability to (1) identify relevant information in texts and understand how this information is related, and (2) respond to this information — that is, make judgments about it or evaluate it.

The genre schemes that children experience in reading will subtly begin to influence their "voice" in writing. As Figure 6.7 shows and as I'll elaborate below, these voices are expressive, poetic, and transactional.

■ *Knowledge of the information encoded in writing itself*

Children's understanding of word structure follows an identifiable sequence. First, children will conceptualize words as comprising letters that match sounds in a straight left-to-right or *alphabetic* fashion: *bat* is spelled B-A-T, but so is *bait*! Second, children will come to understand that sounds within words do not always work in a straight left-to-right fashion. There may be "silent" letters that influence how other letters are pronounced: *bait* has a "long *a*" because there is a silent vowel letter that follows the letter *a*; *bike* has a "long *i*" because there is a silent *e* at the end of the word that "makes" the *i* have a long sound. Letters now work in *patterns* to represent sound. Most of the printed words children will learn during the primary years will be those that they already use in oral language.

Children will acquire a basic knowledge of simple *punctuation* conventions — the use of periods, capital letters at the beginning of sentences, and some comma usage.

For children the primary years can be a time of tremendous excitement and discovery in writing and reading. I will often stress how important your knowledge and understanding of children's development in literacy will be, because this knowledge is your firmest instructional foundation and guide. Although children vary in how they apply their developing knowledge about literacy, there are none-theless commonalities in the ways that knowledge is represented in their heads and in their reading behavior. If you teach at the primary levels, an understanding of these commonalities will help you tremendously in providing the right type of instruction and context for each pupil.

Our overview of developing literacy in first through third grade will look at the writing and reading behaviors that accompany the period just before beginning conventional literacy on through the "word-by-word" stage of word knowledge and then the "transitional" stage. Throughout this discussion, use Figure 6.7 as a guide to what children learn and the general developmental sequence in which they learn it.

FIGURE 6.7

Reading and Writing from a Developmental Perspective

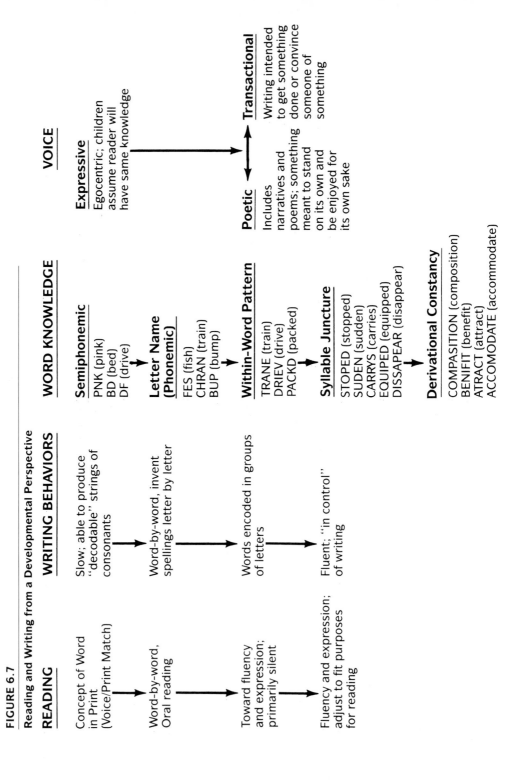

Beginning Conventional Literacy and the Development of Word Knowledge

I will explore below how children acquire an understanding of the alphabetic nature of words. Our consideration of beginning conventional literacy, however, must begin with the more global picture: children's reading and writing.

Children's Reading   Children now begin to examine words letter by letter and slowly but steadily acquire a *sight vocabulary*. Sight words are words that a child can identify without having to sound them out or guess. Unless otherwise noted, whenever we are discussing sight words in this text they will have this definition.

As you observe children's reading at this point, you will usually notice most of the following behaviors: (1) they may mark their place with their finger as they read; (2) they will read out loud — usually loud enough for you to hear — or softly, under their breath; and (3) they will read quite slowly and choppily, in more or less a monotone, a phenomenon often described as "word-by-word" reading or "voice pointing" (Clay, 1985). At first, they often need guided support in their reading — a word that they do not know is immediately supplied by the teacher or another student. If they are reading material in which they know most of the words by sight, their literal comprehension is good and they can reflect on what they have read and draw inferences.

Children's oral, choppy reading at this stage is natural. This is because they have to examine almost every word they encounter carefully; as they gain more experience with print, they will quickly identify more and more words. In time, this process becomes almost subliminal, or "automated," and the children will not need to direct as much deliberate attention to it.

Children's Writing   From a developmental perspective, the orientation and function of writing can be described as moving beyond egocentric to audience-considerate writing and to writing that advances one's own thought and awareness in creative ways. Dyson (1989) has described the complexity of the beginning writing process in the school setting, and in so doing helps place the social context of writing in appropriate focus. When children write stories, Dyson observes, "the gist — the challenge —" … is not simply to create a unified text world but to resolve tensions between the real and the imaginary, between self and others, and among images, sounds, and written words" (Dyson, p. 331). Dyson refers to these as "multiple worlds" consisting of (a) the child's imaginary world — consisting of and based on talk, pictures, and text; (b) the child's ongoing social world — involving others in one's own task and involving oneself in others' tasks; and (c) the child's wider experienced world of people, places, objects, and events. Though this resolution of tensions is largely tacit, it nevertheless aptly portrays some of the challenges the beginning writer faces, apart from getting the words down on the page!

Refer to Jesse's story in Figure 6.8. The story's focus is not as extensive or its language as elaborate as it would be if Jesse had told us orally about the accident, but again this is because of the processing time that must be given over to "lower-

As they begin to read, children will read out loud and may read quite slowly and choppily.
(© Elizabeth Crews)

level" processes. The nature of the processing at this time has very important instructional implications that we will examine more closely in the next chapter. However, you can certainly already see why it is probably *not* a good practice to say to most children at this point, "Is that all you can write?" or "Can you write a little more for me?" or "Try to use words that really paint a pretty picture for me."

As already noted, the children will be developing their knowledge of different genre schemes, and over time their writing will be influenced by this knowledge. Britton (1970) described this process of differentiation in terms of *voice*. An ability to engage appropriate genre schemes really grows out of the child — out of his or her "voice." Voice is where the writer places himself or herself in relation to the writing. Britton suggested a development from *expressive* or personally oriented writing (a somewhat "self-centered" voice) to *poetic* or primarily narrative writing (a "storytelling" voice) and *transactional* or primarily expository writing (a more matter-of-fact, usually objective voice).

Refer again to Figure 6.7 and notice how "voice" fits into the developmental sequence. Britton suggested that "conventional" writing — writing that we can more or less read — is first characterized by an expressive voice. This voice is personal because children write down what they are thinking about and are concerned about; at this early stage the writing is usually egocentric in that it tacitly assumes the reader or listener has the requisite background knowledge about the writer's life and world in order to comprehend what the young author is saying. The poetic voice (which includes narratives as well as poems) develops out of

I SO A CAR ACCEDET
in Fot if My HOOS No win
Gif hrt

(This story reads: I saw a car accident in front of my house. No one got hurt.)

expressive writing, as does the transactional voice. Poetic writing creates something that is meant to stand on its own and usually be enjoyed for its own sake. Transactional writing is usually not intended to stand on its own as a "creative" act.

Development of Word Knowledge in Reading and Writing   What is the nature of the word knowledge that underlies children's reading and writing? Actually, in order to understand this knowledge, we need to begin just before children become the "word-by-word" readers I just described. Children must first develop a concept of word in print. Simply put, a concept of word in print means that children understand that *a word is a group of letters with spaces at both ends.*

There is a striking similarity between the historical development of written language and children's developmental awareness of written language. When most preschool children's attention is directed to individual words, they tend to notice and remember the words as *logographs.* That is, children take the visual representation for the writer's idea as a whole. The internal structure of the visual representation — the word — does not really have that much meaning for the young "reader": it is the whole that counts. As we have just seen, by the end of kindergarten, writing for many children consists of letters, letterlike characters, and perhaps numerals randomly aligned on the page. Many other children will be writing "syllabically."

There comes a point, though, when children do begin to examine the internal structure of words. Recall that preschoolers can easily, almost effortlessly, remember favorite texts. As they begin to examine these texts and notice some groups of letters with spaces at both ends, they are able to match up their memory for the sounds in the texts with some of these letter groups. The children may realize that the first letter group on one page stands for the first sound they hear when this page is read to them — let's say *three* at the beginning of the rhyme "Three blind mice." This group of letters comes to correspond to the spoken unit "three," and the children begin to realize at a tacit level that the visual unit *three* matches up with the spoken unit "three." The children are on their way toward the understanding that Henderson (1981, 1986) termed a tremendously important event in literacy development: the development of a *concept of word in print.*

At the point when children develop a concept of word in print, their "invented spellings" — their application of knowledge of letters and sounds in writing — will appear very much like the writing in Figure 6.9. They use single consonant letters to stand for consonants and vowels: "bird" is spelled *BD;* "worm" is spelled *WM.* Note also that there are no spaces between "words." This type of word

FIGURE 6.9

Semiphonemic Spelling

VBDZE TGVWRM

(This sentence reads: A bird is eating the worm.)

knowledge in spelling is referred to as *semiphonemic,* because children are show-ing us that they are capable of attending to more than one "sound" within a single syllable — but as yet they are not able to discern all the sounds. Notably, the vowels are usually missing. Again, we see a parallel with the historical development of writing. Just before full alphabetic, letter-to-sound or "phonemic" writing appears, consonants are represented and they stand for a consonant *and* a vowel sound.

The next step for the children (as it was for the Greeks) is to split the vowel sound from the consonant sound, thus having two letters where before there was one. What are the characteristics of young children's writing and invented spelling at this point, soon after they have acquired a concept of word in print? When you observe children actually encoding their oral language you will see how slowly the operation proceeds — they are "word-by-word" writers as well. Much of their pro-cessing time and space must be given over to figuring out how to represent the sounds within the words they have decided to write. They are now spelling pho-nemically or according to what we call *letter name:* they select a letter of the al-phabet whose name is closest to the sound they need to represent.

Let's look again at Figure 6.8, which is a good example of a letter-name or pho-nemic stage writer. Early in this stage, even though they have a concept of word in print as they read, children will often run several words together in their writing. Spaces in writing usually come later, after children understand the function of spaces from their reading. (We can certainly see that the children have something they wish to express, however, as Jesse's "story" attests.)

Whereas at the previous stage (Figure 6.9) invented spellings consisted primarily of consonants, now you will see vowels included, because children are represent-ing almost every sound they perceive in a word with a letter. In Jesse's story, *saw* is spelled SO; *accident* is spelled ACEDET; *front* is spelled FAT. You will also see children begin to spell correctly many of the words they are encountering in their reading, although most of the children's spellings will still be invented.

Jason wrote a longer story (see Figure 6.10). Although still in the letter-name stage — sounding out words from left to right — he is farther into this stage than Jesse, as the quality of his invented spellings attests.

We will explore the marvelous logic underlying these invented spellings when we examine the development of word knowledge more closely in Chapter 10. Although there has been considerable debate over the years about whether and how to study words and word parts, research has consistently demonstrated that knowledge of letter/sound correspondences facilitates conventional literacy learn-ing at the primary grade levels (Chall, 1989; Ehri and Wilce, 1987; Stuart and Coltheart, 1988). As we'll see in Chapter 10, the teacher can directly facilitate much

You can assess the degree to which children have a concept of word in print by asking them to point at the words as they recite a short poem, nursery rhyme, or story that they have already memorized (Morris, 1980, 1983, in press). If they do not know such a text, however, you may teach them orally a short rhyme, such as "One, two, button my shoe/Three, four, out the door," and then ask them to point to each word as they say the two-line poem.

Most preschool and many beginning first grade children have little or no concept of word in print. They may slide their finger across a whole line as they are saying one or two words; they may jab randomly at the text as they re-cite; they may point to individual letters, right to left, matching each letter up with each syllable they pronounce. Most children, though, will reach a point where they exhibit the following "pointing" behavior. They may do just fine pointing to words of one syllable; it appears as if they are "really reading." As the child points to and recites the "one, two" rhyme, she may point to "one, two" as she says each word, then point to *button* as she says "buh" and then to *my* as she says "ton." Can you tell what she is doing? At this point children are matching the words in print with *syllables* in speech. Actually, this is a pretty advanced notion for a child, and it should not be long before she is pointing to *button* and saying "button."

of this knowledge, but much of it also can develop through the children's own efforts at sounding out words on their own. We must encourage and support them in these invented spellings.

Transitional Reading and Writing

The term *transitional* is used here to represent the period during which children are making a transition from beginning to more specialized, diverse reading. This developmental benchmark starts for most children in second grade and continues through the third grade. Importantly, children at this point in development are able consciously to "decontextualize" information. They are better able to take an objective stance and understand information about print as well as the content expressed through print. In terms of the model presented at the beginning of this chapter, they have the ability to think consciously about the context of the situation and adjust the "pragmatics" — the rules — more appropriately. Children's vocabulary knowledge reflects the ability now to deal with puns and simple metaphor. They are more metalinguistically aware — they can think about language *as* language. Earlier, they could not distance themselves enough to realize the different senses in which the same word or phrase can be understood.

Children at this stage are moving beyond themselves to consider at a more conscious level the viewpoints and needs of others (see Chapter 2). This developing awareness combines with children's exposure to stories: their structure, their language, and (more subtly) their phrasing and their nuances. Children are also

(This story reads:

The Story About An Ostrich That Lost a Feather

One day an ostrich lost a feather. She was so angry she stamped her feet. And she picked it up. She tried to put it on. She could not put it on. When she woke up the next morning she found another feather. The End)

FIGURE 6.10

Story by a Child Well into the Letter-Name (Phonemic) Stage

developing a budding awareness of expository texts — their structure, language, and means of addressing and presenting information. This combination of experience with potential helps children negotiate the "multiple worlds" within which their storywriting occurs, and which will become more of a factor in the following stage.

Children's Reading Most children now read silently. They rarely point to mark their place while reading, and when they do read orally, it is with more natural expression. Children's reading rate or *fluency* is more rapid, and their comprehension in reading comes to be more in line with their listening comprehension. All of these developments occur because many of the lower-level word identification processes are now becoming automated, leaving more cognitive "space" for constructing the ideas suggested by the text — for *thinking* while reading. In constructing a text model, children draw more from their own experiences and from the information expressed in the material they read. This ability corresponds generally to the students' advancing cognitive and linguistic development.

Children's Writing and Spelling   Just as with fluent reading, fluent writing depends on "automatic" functioning. Writing is more rapid because the encoding of words is more rapid — more automatic, with only occasional conscious reflection on spelling. As fluency grows, writers can allocate more attention to how and what they want to express and to begin understanding and incorporating conventions of style and mechanics in the writing. Children are now much more aware of the audience for their writing and of that audience's expectations in terms of writing content and mechanics. This is not to say, however, that children's sensitivity to their audience is fully developed; there is still much more to learn in this regard later on!

In second grade, compositions are often characterized by a complete rendering of "what happened"; Calkins (1986) has referred to them as "bed-to-bed" stories. If not literally beginning with "First I got up" and ending with "And then I went to bed," children are including all the information that occurred during the event or time period on which they're focusing. There is little differentiation in the attention they give to varied bits of information; they weight them all equally. An example of this feature is Kirstin's story, "Let's Go on a Walk, Buster" in Figure 6.11.

For second-graders, longer stories that seem to cover an interminable list of information may result from the desire simply to "write more," to have one's own composition go on for pages — just as in "real" books. If the children wish to revise a composition, however, they are certainly capable of doing so, as we will see in the next chapter. Kirstin's final draft, shown in Figure 6.11 in its final "published" version — run off on a word processor (with invented spellings corrected), illustrated, and laminated — differs from the first in that she realized her story would be more enjoyable if she substituted different words for "*said* Buster."

Third-graders continue in much the same mold as second-graders, although they may be persuaded to trim their lengthy accounts somewhat. They are still controlled for the most part by the topic they are writing about, rather than the other way around. They will experiment with form, though, as Gavin's "pigons" poem attests (Figure 6.12).

The "pigons" poem is a good example of a child primarily experimenting with form; the forced rhyme nonetheless creates some engaging images! Children's increasing cognitive sophistication allows for this interest in and attention to differing form, although children may also decide to "play it safe" with writing and keep to predictable formats, using words they know how to spell. As we'll see in Chapter 9, exposure to a variety of appropriate texts at the third grade level can "stretch" children to the challenges that new literacy experiences can offer — and they will very likely respond.

Notice the spellings in Figure 6.12. This child is in the *within-word pattern* stage of spelling or word knowledge. As a proportion of total words in the composition, more words are spelled correctly in terms of conventional spelling than at the letter-name stage. And the spellings that *are* invented still reflect conventional spelling patterns; notably, silent letters are usually included to indicate long vowels. As noted earlier, we'll look at the logic underlying these invented spellings in Chapter 10.

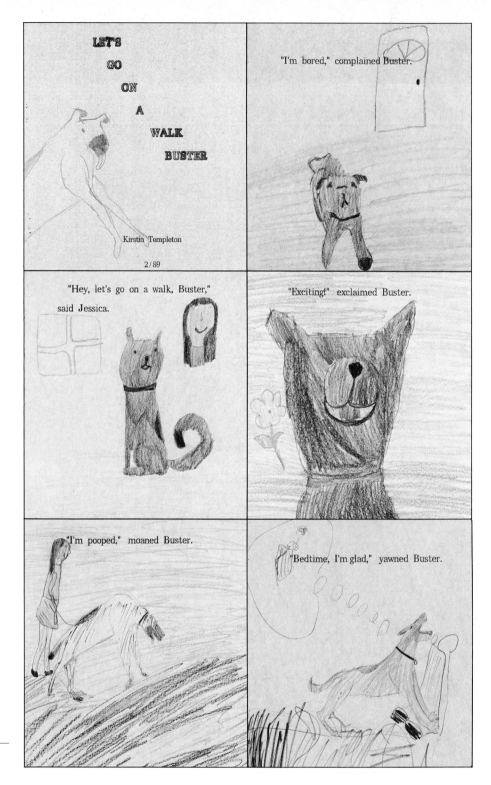

FIGURE 6.11

A Second-Grader's "Published" Story

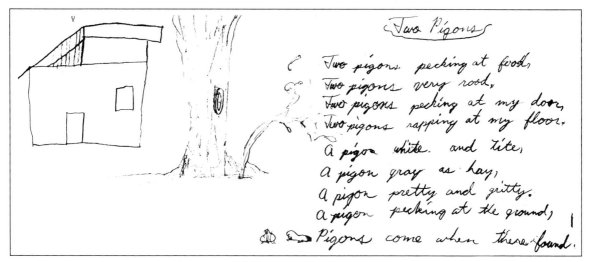

FIGURE 6.12

Child's Poem Showing Experimentation with Form

The Intermediate School Years: Fourth Through Sixth Grade

During this time the knowledge and experiential bases that underlie reading and writing are more developed and interrelated than at the primary school years. Because lower-level tasks involved in processing the print are becoming even more efficient and automated than at the transitional stage, readers have more cognitive "space" available not only to follow the "blueprint" in the text but to draw from their own knowledge of the world. During these years, children demonstrate a striking advance in their powers of reasoning. This advance allows them to interact in important and critical ways with what they read, be it published material or peers' compositions. These are also the years during which students can explore their interests through reading and writing, truly becoming "experts" — certainly to the extent that they will know more about a particular area than the teacher!

Newkirk (1987) fittingly described the awareness that develops as elementary students explore the world of books. His observation applies equally to the awarenesses that develop through writing: particularly at the intermediate grades, students come to understand "the emerging self-consciousness of the main characters, their ability to monitor their own thoughts and feelings, as well as their ability to penetrate those of others. With this ability comes a sense of independence — of self" (Newkirk, 1987, p. 118).

By the time most students are in the intermediate grades, they will primarily draw upon three types of knowledge: background knowledge, knowledge of genre schemes, and knowledge of the information encoded in writing itself.

Background Knowledge or Content Schemata

In these grades children's expanding cognitive sophistication holds the potential for an informational and conceptual explosion. They are capable of bringing much more background knowledge to bear on their encounters with new texts and new material. In fact, quite often the major instructional challenge for teachers at this level is reassuring the students that it is okay and even desirable to do so! Strategic reading is an important focus here; this is the point at which *metacognition* — thinking about thinking — comes into play, as students learn how (*procedural knowledge*) and why (*self-knowledge*) different strategies and purposes for reading are applied (see Chapter 2). In other words, the reader is "monitoring" the reading (Cooper, 1986).

Many skills and strategies that will develop in the intermediate years rely on the reader's conscious awareness of what he or she is trying to do and the ability to ask the following kinds of questions: How should I approach this next bit of reading I have to do? When I'm reading, what do I do when I don't know a word or am having difficulty in locating a specific answer? How do I know when I don't know, and what do I do when I don't know? When I'm finished with the reading, how do I deal with the information I've obtained in the reading? Metacognition in reading involves the application of *procedural knowledge* (what do I do?) and *self-knowledge* (when do I do it?).

We have two main objectives in bringing together intermediate students and expository texts, and they should be addressed in this order: First, students must learn how to read these texts and how these types of texts are structured and organized. Second, students must learn how to learn from these texts; although books will certainly not be their sole source of information, they will be a very important source, now and throughout the students' school lives.

Knowledge of Genre Schemes or Text Schemas

Because of their increasing cognitive sophistication, students in their reading have the potential to follow and to understand more elaborate text schemas. For example, they understand and even enjoy strange and unexpected twists in stories. They can handle more complex characterization, plot structure, and themes. In the latter instance, background knowledge is also called upon because the children's life experiences provide the raw data of understanding.

As we will explore in some depth in Chapter 8, *expository* texts play a much bigger role in instruction in the intermediate grades, and most students will need to be taught explicitly about their structure and organization. Otherwise, many if not most of your students will apply the very same strategies for reading narratives to the reading of informational material. Part of the information they will come to learn about has to do with how major and supporting ideas are linked together. These patterns of organization in most expository texts are *description, sequence, comparison, cause and effect,* and *problem and solution* (McGee and Richgels, 1985).

The National Assessment of Educational Progress has shown over the years that there are definite gains in the quality of students' writing throughout the intermediate grades. Notably, toward the end of this period, students' length and quality of written expression can surpass the length and quality of spoken expression (Loban,

1976). This also is a time of experimentation with different forms and with different types of elaboration. Rather than generating a topic or theme and then deciding in which genre it would best fit, pupils often decide that they will write a play, for example, or a newspaper, and then come up with the content. Writing in the intermediate or upper elementary grades will reflect pupils' real-world experiences and their literary experiences and knowledge.

As an example of the type of written creations of which students at this level are capable, consider fifth-grader Danielle's poem (Figure 6.13) written in response to Richard Garcia's "The City Is So Big." Garcia's poem describes trains rushing by and house demolitions and concludes with an image of ". . . Elevator doors opening and closing" and people disappearing within. Danielle has certainly grasped a "sense" of poetry, going beyond mere form, and she has engagingly incorporated her reaction to particular ideas expressed in Garcia's poetry within her own creation.

Figure 6.14 is the first draft of a composition co-authored by two fifth-graders on a word processor. They have been reading Alfred Hitchcock's *Three Investigator* books. Only the first page (of three) is reproduced here. Already, though, we can see inclusion both of real-world experiences — in the interchange with the mother

FIGURE 6.13

A Fifth-Grader's Poem Written as a Response to Poetry

One day, Jimmy Gordon was sitting on the front porch steps with his sister, Katie Gordon. "I'm bord," said Jimmy. "Me too!" said Katie. "Nothing exiting happens around here any more." Jimmy agreed. "That is unless your counting the time when Mrs. Waterman had the minnows coming out of the kitchen faucet!" Jimmy said. "No" said Katie "I mean like a safe cracking or something." Jimmy said "We haven't had one of those since 1924! And I don't think we"ll have one of those for a long time. Because the guy, I think his name was Jonathan Henry or something like that, served a 20 year sentence in prison!"

"Well, I still think there's going to be some kind of a crime around here soon, I can feel it in my bones," said Katie.

"Don't get your hopes up," said Jimmy. "And besides, Christmas is coming so we'll have something to play with," Jimmy said.

Just at that moment their mom came out. "Jimmy and Katie, it's almost dinner time."

Jimmy and Katie both said together "Oh, mom." Jimmy said "By the way, what is for dinner?" His mom answered "We're having pizza..." "Goodie!" Jimmy and Katie interupted.

"Wait, let me finish" said their mom "Your father and I are having pizza, and you're having liver." "Yuck!" said Jimmy and Katie. "Can't we skip dinner tonight?" said Jimmy.

"No, but I suppose you could have a couple of pieces of pizza," said there mom. Jimmy and Katie looked relieved. And right at that point they heard a cry of pain from next door, Mr. Gunman's house. Jimmy and Katie rushed over to help him. "Wait!" cried

FIGURE 6.14

A Mystery Story by Two Fifth-Graders

— and of literary knowledge about how to establish setting and foreshadow an exciting event.

Students in the intermediate grades acquire control of and flexibility with their writing, rather than being controlled by it. They have passed through the stage where entire compositions, for example, are written as dialogues, and they are now able to use dialogue more judiciously. What before they had to write out in full to see if it worked they can now examine first in their heads.

At the intermediate levels, children develop a set of "codes and strategies" for their writing (Calkins, 1986). They have internalized questions that may be asked of their writing and, significantly, can become "readers of their own writing." Students have the potential to read their own compositions as others would read them — becoming aware in a much more sophisticated sense of their audience. Another way of describing these internalized features is to say that they represent for students an "intuitive" sense of their own writing. As Bereiter described it, in this type of writing, "One does not merely write to entertain the reader but also to please oneself. One does not argue simply to convince the reader but also to present an argument that oneself finds convincing" (Bereiter, 1980). Writing at this level can truly become a *craft*.

Engaging in reading and then discussing what is read contributes to this development. As students think critically about their reading, they incorporate this knowledge into the composing process (Langer, 1986). Eventually, just as reading plays a significant role in the development and elaboration of knowledge, so does writing. Although you will be encouraging children to record their observations in journals — which certainly will reinforce their learning — at this level students can become aware of new and important insights. For example, while writing about a stepparent he is not fond of, a student may suddenly realize *why* he has been feeling the way he has, and move toward a resolution for himself. The writing in Figure 6.15 hints at this type of writing; taken from a sixth-grader's response journal (see Chapter 8), this piece was the student's spontaneous reaction written just after finishing Katherine Paterson's *Bridge to Terabithia*. In a very simple, straightforward way this student has voiced the realization — and the wisdom — that many students reach after reading this book: after the loss of a very close friend, life must go on.

Bereiter (1980) called this level of writing *epistemic* writing (related to *epistemology,* the study of how knowledge is acquired). For older students, epistemic writing in an expository mode has the potential for creating extended and involved

FIGURE 6.15

A Sixth-Grader's Response to a Story (Journal Entry)

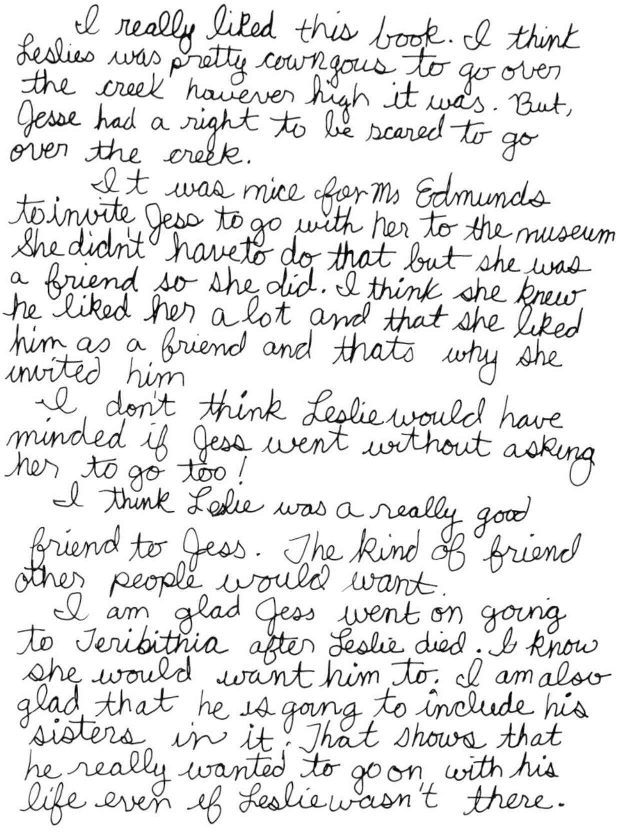

I really liked this book. I think Leslies was pretty courageous to go over the creek however high it was. But, Jesse had a right to be scared to go over the creek.

It was nice for Ms Edmunds to invite Jess to go with her to the museum. She didn't have to do that but she was a friend so she did. I think she knew he liked her a lot and that she liked him as a friend and thats why she invited him

I don't think Leslie would have minded if Jess went without asking her to go too!

I think Leslie was a really good friend to Jess. The kind of friend other people would want.

I am glad Jess went on going to Teribithia after Leslie died. I know she would want him to. I am also glad that he is going to include his sisters in it. That shows that he really wanted to go on with his life even if Leslie wasn't there.

thought that, as Olson (1977) suggested, is almost impossible without writing. Why *is* this type of thought almost impossible without written language?

The answer lies in the structure and the complexity of the reading that students will do — the number of ideas that are expressed, as well as the length of this type of writing. All of this is rarely modeled in oral language. Even in those rare instances where it is partially modeled — in a good lecture, for example — this form is not available for examination unless it is somehow preserved for convenient review after the oral language "record" has faded from memory. And the best means for such convenient review and examination is a written transcript.

In addition to its more obvious role in putting thought "out there" to be examined over time, writing at this epistemic level allows writers to have intensive and extended conversations with themselves. As writers read more examples of texts that reflect this type of writing, then their "conversations" increasingly take on the form of these models. This interactive process involving writing and reading leads to growth and development in the extended and involved thought to which Olson referred.

Although the types of writing we have described here are extremely useful in helping to understand the development of writing, it is important to place them within a classroom perspective. First, pupils need not master all of the characteristics of one type of writing before "moving on" to the next type; each student will bring different levels and types of skills to bear. Research by Graves (1983) and Calkins (1983, 1986), for example, demonstrates that third-graders are capable of being "readers of their own writing" as well as coming to understand a subject more deeply as a consequence of writing about it. On the other hand, some sixth grade students who are regularly writing at a higher level may also write occasionally in an "expressive" voice.

Second, keeping these types of writing in mind will help you to consider each pupil in terms of the type of writing he or she *is* producing versus the type of writing he or she is *capable* of producing. Why is this distinction important? Gradual movement from one type of writing to the next means not only that students are growing in writing ability but that they are growing in quality and sophistication of thought as well. Being aware of development, in other words, will keep you alert to students' potential at any point.

Knowledge of the Information Encoded in Writing Itself

Here we are considering students' word knowledge, an issue we will explore more in Chapter 10. For the moment, however, know that students at this level will be learning much about the *structure* of words — their syllabic structure, but even more important, their *morphemic* structure. Structural or "morphemic" analysis is the study of how *morphemes* (the smallest units of meaning in words) combine to represent the meaning of words; this analysis includes *some* principles of syllabication, as these aid in determining the possible meaning of unknown words encountered in reading. Far and away the most important aspect of structural analysis is the systematic exploration of the ways in which prefixes, suffixes, base words, and word roots combine to create meaning. The resulting knowledge serves students very well in both their reading and their writing.

Briefly, here are the elements of structural analysis that students have the potential to understand and apply in their reading and writing:

- *Concept of "base word"* After removing any prefixes and/or suffixes, if the element that remains can stand by itself as a word, then it is referred to as a *base word.*

- *Syllabication* This process refers to the partitioning of unfamiliar polysyllabic words into single syllables for purposes of sounding them out and identifying them.

- *Common prefixes and suffixes* These elements, collectively referred to as "affixes," amplify or change the meaning of the base words or word roots to which they are attached. Examples are *un-, re-;* and *-er/-or, -ment.*

- *Concept of "word root" and common word roots* After removing any prefixes and/or suffixes, if the element that remains *cannot* stand by itself as a word, then it is referred to as a *word root* (in + *spect* + ion = in*spect*ion; in + *cis* + ion = in*cis*ion).

At the intermediate grade levels, research supports the value of examining important structural or morphemic elements as part of structural analysis or vocabulary study. Such examination of words and word parts can facilitate vocabulary development as well as support more efficient, fluent, and text-appropriate reading (Templeton, in press; White, Power, and White, 1989). As has been indicated here, however, and as we will see in Chapter 10, the real question for teachers is not *whether* to study words and word parts, but *when* to study *which* word parts. The bottom line, though, is this: *the more students know about words and word structure, the better readers they will be.*

We can trace the nature of students' understanding of word structure by examining their invented spellings during these years. Figure 6.7 illustrates spellings representative of the last two stages of word knowledge, *syllable juncture* and *derivational constancy.* In the intermediate grades, most children generally will be in one of these two stages.

Students in the syllable-juncture stage have a very good command of patterns within single syllables, but the errors they make most often occur at the juncture of syllables: *sudden* may be spelled *suden, carries* (carry + s) may be spelled *carrys,* and *equipped* may be spelled *equiped.* As students acquire a larger reading and writing vocabulary and enter the derivational constancy stage (in the upper elementary years), a majority of their errors will reflect what they are learning about the primarily Greek and Latin base of English vocabulary. As at the syllable-juncture stage, the errors that students commit will occur often at the juncture of syllables (*interupt, atract*), but most errors will occur within the unstressed syllables of the more complex words that they are learning: *compasition* (composition), *benifit* (benefit).

A CONCLUDING PERSPECTIVE

Many years ago, a chapter of this nature would not have appeared in a language arts textbook. The fact that it does now reflects what we have learned about development and how development affects instruction. I have attempted in this chapter to present a synthesis of what appears to be the most significant work in developmental literacy. My aim has been to give a general framework for conceptualizing the development of literacy — a framework that will guide your thinking about children's development and provide you with a firm foundation for making instructional decisions. Your knowledge of children's advancing development in literacy will be your cue to instructional strategy — you will know better how to stretch your students while at the same time helping them to consolidate their new and existing knowledge.

We looked first at *what* will be learned: the form and content of written language — broadly speaking, the nature of narrative and expository structure. We then examined the processes of reading and writing; specifically, students' understanding of and experiences in both reading and writing will be grounded in background knowledge (concepts and schemas), knowledge of syntax, genre schemes (text schemas), word knowledge, and punctuation. Next we considered *how* this would be learned — the characteristics of literacy development in the preschool, primary school, and intermediate school years.

The next several chapters will explore in depth how you as a teacher will be able to facilitate your students' literacy development. We'll focus first on writing, then reading, and finally pull these together within the context of a learning environment rich in children's fiction and nonfiction literature.

REFERENCES

Barrett, T. C. (1976). Taxonomy of reading comprehension. In R. Smith & T. C. Barrett (eds.), *Teaching reading in the middle grades*. Reading, MA: Addison-Wesley.

Bissex, G. (1980). *GYNX AT WRK: A child learns to write and read*. Cambridge, MA: Harvard University Press.

Bradley, L., & Bryant, P. (1985). *Rhyme and reason in reading and spelling*. Ann Arbor, MI: University of Michigan Press.

Britton, J. (1970). *Language and learning*. London: Penguin Press.

Bruner, J. (1988). Life as narrative. *Social Research, 54*, 11–32.

Bussis, A., Chittenden, E., Amarel, M., & Klausner, E. (1985). *Inquiry into meaning: An investigation of learning to read*. Hillsdale, NJ: Lawrence Erlbaum Associates.

Calkins, L. (1986). *The art of teaching writing*. Portsmouth, NH: Heinemann.

Chall, J. S. (1989). The uses of educational research: Comments on Carbo. *Phi Delta Kappan, 71*, 158–160.

Chukovsky, K. (1925/1971). *From two to five*. Edited and translated by M. Morton. Berkeley, CA: University of California Press.

Clay, M. M. (1975). *What did I write?* Auckland, NZ: Heinemann.

Clay, M. M. (1979). *Reading: The patterning of complex behaviour.* Portsmouth, NH: Heinemann.

Cooper, J. David (1986). *Teaching reading comprehension.* Boston, MA: Houghton Mifflin.

Dyson, A. H. (1989). Research currents: The space/time travels of story writers. *Language Arts, 66,* 330–340.

Ehri, L. C., & Wilce, L. S. (1987). Does learning to spell help beginners learn to read words? *Reading Research Quarterly, 18,* 47–65.

Ferreiro, E. (1984). The underlying logic of literacy development. In H. Goelman, A. A. Oberg, & F. Smith (eds.), *Awakening to literacy.* Portsmouth, NH: Heinemann.

Ferreiro, E., & Teberosky, A. (1982). *Literacy before schooling.* Portsmouth, NH: Heinemann.

Goodman, K., & Goodman, Y. (1978). Learning to read is natural. In L. B. Resnick & P. Weaver (eds.), *Theory and practice of early reading: Vol. 1.* Hillsdale, NJ: Lawrence Erlbaum Associates.

Halliday, M.A.K., & Hasan, R. (1976). *Cohesion in English.* London: Longman.

Heard, G. (1989). *For the good of the earth and sun: Teaching poetry.* Portsmouth, NH: Heinemann.

Henderson, E. H. (1981). *Learning to read and spell: The child's knowledge of words.* DeKalb, IL: Northern Illinois University Press.

Henderson, E. H. (1985). *Teaching spelling.* Boston: Houghton Mifflin.

Hiebert, E. (1986). Issues related to home influences on young children's print-related development. In D. B. Yaden, Jr., & S. Templeton (eds.), *Metalinguistic awareness and beginning literacy: Conceptualizing what it means to read and write.* Portsmouth, NH: Heinemann.

Holdaway, D. (1979). *The foundations of literacy.* Sydney, Australia: Ashton Scholastic.

Iser, W. (1976). *The act of reading.* Baltimore, MD: Johns Hopkins University Press.

Johns, J. (1986). Students' perceptions of reading: Thirty years of inquiry. In D. Yaden, Jr., & S. Templeton (eds.), *Metalinguistic awareness and beginning literacy: Conceptualizing what it means to read and write.* Portsmouth, NH: Heinemann.

Langer, J. (1986). *Children reading and writing.* Norwood, NJ: Ablex.

Lindsay, P. H., & Norman, D. A. (1977). *Human information processing: An introduction to psychology.* New York: Academic Press.

Loban, W. (1976). *Language development: Kindergarten through grade twelve.* Research Monograph No. 18. Urbana, IL: National Council of Teachers of English.

Lomax, R. G., & McGee, L. M. (1987). Young children's concepts about print and reading: Toward a model of word reading acquisition. *Reading Research Quarterly, 22,* 219–256.

McGee, L., & Richgels, D. (1985). Teaching expository text structure to elementary students. *The Reading Teacher, 38,* 739–748.

Mandler, J. M., & Johnson, N. S. (1977). Remembrance of things parsed: Story structure and recall. *Cognitive Psychology, 9,* 111–151.

Mason, J. (1980). When *do* children begin to read: An exploration of four-year-old children's letter and word reading competencies. *Reading Research Quarterly, 15,* 203–227.

Masonheimer, P. (1983). Information used by preschool readers and nonreaders. Paper presented at the biennial meeting of the Society for Research in Child Development, Detroit, MI.

Morris, D. (1980). Beginning readers' concept of word. In E. H. Henderson & J. W. Beers (eds.), *Developmental and cognitive aspects of learning to spell: A reflection of word knowledge*. Newark, DE: International Reading Association.

Morris, D. (1983). Concept of word and phoneme awareness in the beginning reader. *Research in the Teaching of English, 17,* 359–373.

Morris, D. (in press). Concept of word: A pivotal understanding in the learning to read process. In S. Templeton & D. R. Bear (eds.), *Developmental orthographic knowledge and the foundations of literacy: A memorial Festschrift for Edmund H. Henderson.* Hillsdale, NJ: Lawrence Erlbaum Associates.

Strickland, D. S., & Morrow, L. M. (1989). *Emerging literacy: Young children learn to read and write.* Newark, DE: International Reading Association.

Mason, J. (1980). When *do* children begin to read: An exploration of four-year-old children's letter and word reading competencies. *Reading Research Quarterly, 15,* 203–227.

Newkirk, T. (1987). On the inside where it counts. In J. Hansen, T. Newkirk, & D. Graves (eds.), *Breaking ground: Teachers relate reading and writing in the elementary school.* Portsmouth, NH: Heinemann.

Olson, D. (1977). From utterance to text: The bias of language in speech and writing. *Harvard Educational Review, 17*(3), 257–281.

Olson, D. (1984). See, jumping! In H. Goelman, A. Oberg, & F. Smith (eds.), *Awakening to literacy.* Portsmouth, NH: Heinemann.

Pearson, P. D. (1985). Changing the face of reading comprehension instruction. *The Reading Teacher, 38,* 724–738.

Pearson, P. D., & Johnson, D. D. (1978). *Teaching reading comprehension.* New York: Harper and Row.

Perfetti, C. (1985). *Reading ability.* New York: Oxford University Press.

Raphael, T. E. (1983). Question-answering strategies for children. *The Reading Teacher, 36,* 186–190.

Raphael, T. E. (1986). Question-answer relationships revisited. *The Reading Teacher, 39*(6), 516–522.

Rayner, K., & Pollatsek, A. (1989). *The psychology of reading.* Englewood Cliffs, NJ: Prentice-Hall.

Rosen, H. (1986). The importance of story. *Language Arts, 63*(3), 226–237.

Rosenblatt, L. (1978). *The reader, the text, the poem: Transactional theory of literary work.* Carbondale, IL: Southern Illinois University Press.

Scardamalia, M. (1981). How children cope with the cognitive demands of writing. In C. H. Frederiksen & J. F. Dominic (eds.), *Writing: The Nature, Development, and Teaching of Written Communication.* Hillsdale, NJ: Lawrence Erlbaum Associates.

Stein, N., & Glenn, C. G. (1977). An analysis of story comprehension in elementary school children. In R. O. Freedle (ed.), *Discourse processing: Multidisciplinary prespectives.* Norwood, NJ: Ablex.

Stuart, M., & Coltheart, M. (1989). Does reading develop in a series of stages? *Cognition, 30,* 139–181.

Taylor, I., & Taylor, M. (1983). *The psychology of reading.* New York: Academic Press.

Teale, W., & E. Sulzby (eds.). (1986). *Emergent literacy: Writing and reading.* Norwood, NJ: Ablex.

Templeton, S. (1980). Young children invent words: Developing concepts of "word-ness." *The Reading Teacher, 33*(4), 454–459.

Templeton, S. (in press). Theory, nature, and pedagogy of higher-order orthographic development in older students. In S. Templeton & D. Bear (eds.), *Development of orthographic knowledge and the foundations of literacy: A memorial Festschrift for Edmund H. Henderson.* Hillsdale, NJ: Lawrence Erlbaum Associates.

White, T. G., Power, M. A., & White, S. (1989). Morphological analysis: Implications for teaching and understanding vocabulary growth. *Reading Research Quarterly, 24*(3), 283–304.

Yaden, D. B., Jr. (1988). Understanding stories through repeated read-alouds: How many does it take? *The Reading Teacher, 41,* 556–560.

Yaden, D. B., Jr., Smolkin, L. B., & Conlon, A. (1989). Preschoolers' questions about pictures, print convention, and story text during reading aloud at home. *Reading Research Quarterly, 24,* 188–214.

7

The Teaching of Writing

FOCUSING QUESTIONS

■ Why must the teaching of writing combine characteristics of *both* "natural" and "structured" environments?

■ How can students effectively help one another with their writing? What is the teacher's role in facilitating this interaction?

■ What are the components of the writing process? How can you develop students' understanding of each in narrative writing? In expository writing?

■ What is unique about poetry? Why is attention to students' learning to write poetry so important?

■ What roles can microcomputers play in students' writing?

We believe that writing can play a significant part in a child's development. For that reason we have sought a way to release freer, more genuine self-expression and at the same time to cultivate the skill necessary for writing with correctness and ease. . . . We have become clearly certain that this concept of writing brings children deep personal satisfaction as well as effective control of its essential mechanics. . . . If a child is to be an effective, poised personality, he must have an awareness and an appreciation of his own power. Such self-knowledge comes only through frequent opportunity to experiment. . . . The satisfaction he has had in what he has made [his writing] — that momentary kinship with creative power — makes him seem worthy to himself.*

INTRODUCTION

So Alvina Truet Burrows and her colleagues conceptualize the role of written composition in their classic book on the teaching of writing titled *They All Want to Write* (1939). This affirmation of the value of writing is not unrealistic. Beginning in the mid-1930s, Burrows and her colleagues' classroom studies — and the many investigations since that time — have demonstrated that it is indeed possible to have the best of both writing worlds: a command of correctness — spelling, punctuation, and grammar — and a richness and fluency of creativity and expression. Not until recently, however, has consistent documentation across a wide range of pupils demonstrated the potential for writing both to address deep personal needs and to meet standards of correctness. Most of the significant research on writing has been conducted within the past two decades, but as the above excerpt shows, significant insights into the teaching of writing have existed for years.

In this chapter, we will be exploring the writing process and the many ways in which you will be able to facilitate students' learning of this process as well as other aspects of writing. In Chapter 9 we will more directly address the integration of writing activities with literature.

As we move through the chapter, Figure 7.1 should help you keep in mind the relationships among the terms and the concepts involved in the teaching of writing, all of which we discussed in the last chapter. Most of the time I will be talking about the more general level of *genre schemes* — narrative and expository texts. Recall, also, that children's *voices* arise from within themselves and eventually come to reflect the types of texts to which they are exposed. Figure 7.1 shows the relationship of these voices to the major genre schemes of narrative and expository and the traditional forms of expression, narration, poetry, description, exposition, and persuasion. These in turn are illustrated by examples of different formats.

*(Burrows, et al., 1939, 1952, p. 1)

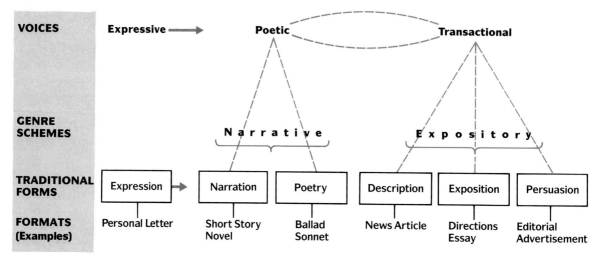

FIGURE 7.1

Relationship of Voices, Genre Schemes, Traditional Forms, and Formats of Writing

Framework for the Teacher: How Can Writing Be Taught Effectively?

"Natural" or "Structured" Process?

What does the research say about the effectiveness of instruction in writing? Applebee (1986) and Hillocks (1986) have offered recent comprehensive reviews, and they are clear on one point: children do not learn to write as a result of working exclusively on exercises in grammar texts — they learn to write by writing. Besides doing lots of writing and reading, however, is anything else required? Emphatically, yes.

Applebee made a distinction between "natural" and "structured" process writing. Hillocks (1986) described natural process writing as being primarily student-centered, with pupils writing about what is of most interest and concern to them, getting feedback from their peers, and revising in light of their interaction with peers. Though including natural process writing is an extremely important part of creating a supportive writing environment, Hillocks found that the teacher should also select materials and activities as well as be involved in the frequent presentation and modeling of those activities. The students, however, carry out the activities, often with interaction among themselves. In structured-process writing, then, there is more of a balance between the teacher's role and the pupil's role.

What is the nature of the type of environment in which effective writing instruction can occur? Nancie Atwell (1987) cites Donald Murray (1982) in this regard: "it is our job as teachers of writing to create a context that is as appropriate for writing as the gym is for basketball" (Murray, in Atwell, p. 54). Toward this end, the environment and the context of situation must be supportive and appropriate. Within this context students should have the opportunity to write frequently and for different purposes. All of the stages in the writing or composing process should be addressed: prewriting or "rehearsing" (see p. 232); drafting (p. 239), revising (p. 240), editing (p. 243), and sharing or publishing (p. 245). Conferences or small response groups in which the writing of individual students is received, valued, and responded to provide a very supportive and effective context. Over time, instruction should respond to and facilitate children's natural writing development, from primarily personal or expressive writing to more expository and narrative forms. Direct teaching of individuals and of groups by the teacher — and sometimes by the students themselves — is important. This strategy provides opportunities for appropriate instruction in all stages of the writing process, from global aspects such as getting started and drafting to specific matters of sentence structure and sentence combining, spelling, and punctuation. Assessment and evaluation should be as nonthreatening as possible and include the holistic evaluation of writing.

As in other areas of the language arts, there is no one best approach or technique; rather, a judicious coordination of several instructional features is most effective. The issue for you to address is always one of the degree to which your students will explore and interact with their peers. Toward establishing a sense for that judicious coordination, I will here outline briefly the techniques and strategies you will be using with your students as you guide and teach them in their writing. The balance of the chapter will provide in-depth illustrations of their use. As you consider your teaching of writing keep in mind this rule of thumb expressed by Nathan, Temple, Juntunen, and Temple: "The child's purposes come first, but the teacher deliberately creates a setting in which writing in different forms can be perceived as useful" (Nathan, et al., 1989, p. 93).

Conferencing

As we have already seen, much of learning is a social activity. An extremely important aspect of this learning is the kind of social interaction that goes on between you and your students and among the students themselves. Referred to as "conferencing," this interaction — whether it be teacher/student or student/student — entails a type of question-response format in which the writer is helped to identify aspects of his or her writing that could be clarified, expanded, or elaborated. Student/student conferences are often referred to as *response groups.* The foundation for interaction within them can be established and supported within sharing and discussion groups (see Chapter 5).

In conferencing, the focus is notably not only on developing a more refined piece of writing but on elaborating and refining students' thinking as well. A conference provides yet another context in which to facilitate critical thinking. And, as we'll explore below, conferencing is often a context for direct teaching mini-lessons. The questions and feedback that make up a large part of student interaction are instructional in their own right. In turn, conferencing skills can be modeled through a direct teaching format.

Direct Teaching

Much of your students' learning about writing will grow through actually doing it and through feedback about it in conferences with others. However, many specific strategies and skills, such as word choice, grammar, punctuation, format, and spelling, as well as steps in the process of writing, are often effectively addressed in a direct teaching format. Students too can assume the role of "teacher" in this context.

Depending on your students, some skills are best addressed explicitly when the need for them arises, and others are best addressed appropriately in advance. Of the latter type, you will find that many skills lend themselves to whole-class or small-group instruction. Nathan, Temple, Juntunen, and Temple (1989) refer to such instruction as "focus lessons"; Calkins (1986) uses the term "mini-lesson"; Goodman and Burke (1980) refer to "strategy lessons." Although you may address these skills in a teacher-student conference, Nathan and her colleagues suggest that you regularly conduct a direct teaching lesson rather than waiting for the need to arise in a conference. Importantly, they note the need to "balance the concerns of maintaining the child's initiative and authority as a writer on the one hand with the efficiency of direct teaching on the other" (Nathan, et al., p. 68). You will always be planning your instruction with the objective of maintaining this balance.

In Chapter 1 I outlined direct teaching techniques. Recall that there are many variations, but at its heart direct teaching is this: the systematic presentation of a specific piece of information. ("In this particular context, this is what you should do," etc.) We provide direct knowledge of a specific skill and the vocabulary with which to discuss that skill (for example, "This is a weak *closing statement* [or *lead*]"). How detailed each direct teaching or "focus" lesson is depends on our purpose and our students' needs. As we will see, these mini-lessons may range from a simple statement you make to students on through a more systematic model as described by Cooper (1986).

Modeling

First and foremost, *you* must write yourself. Modeling the writing process means simply that you show the students how writing is done. As you walk through the process for them, you "think aloud" and describe each step.

You may not feel you are a writer, or you may not really like to write, but you should try not to let these misgivings become an obstacle. By learning, applying, and then modeling, teaching, and facilitating the writing process you will find that you can overcome your own doubts — particularly as you see the process transforming the way your students think and respond. Many teachers have in fact first "liberated" themselves with respect to writing when they began modeling the process of writing for their students (see, for example, Calkins, 1983).

How does modeling bring about this liberating effect — and why is it so important to your students? As we will see below, by modeling the process of writing, you are showing your students not only that they can write — that in fact *anyone* can write — but you are taking the "mystery and mystique" out of writing. Most students believe that published writing somehow springs full blown from authors' pens. By modeling the full process, you will be showing them that writing — *all* writing — takes time and effort to evolve. The finished product on the printed page was all many of us ever saw when we went through school, but modeling shows the process behind that product.

Textbooks and Prepared Materials

Your planning and your students' needs will determine the place of textbooks and other prepared materials in your teaching framework. You can directly teach and/ or reinforce many written language skills in conjunction with textbook exercises and other prepared materials. The advantage to these materials is that they are readily available and that the lessons do not require your preparation time. One important disadvantage, however, is that many of the activities are not based on the writing that *your* students are generating.

Particularly in your first year or two, there are a couple of reasons why such materials should probably play a supportive role in your classroom. First, assuming that you have given your students a context for why they are learning a particular skill, the reinforcement provided by well-structured exercises is beneficial. Second, prepared materials represent a format similar to one that students will often meet in testing situations.

The Writing Process: Putting Understanding into Practice

Components of the Writing Process

For years, one of the greatest shortcomings of American elementary schools was teachers' lack of knowledge about the teaching of writing. As recently as 1985, a study in *Elementary School Journal* indicated that most elementary school teachers thought writing was a skill that could be learned from an English textbook; most also believed writing instruction ought to emphasize penmanship and standards of correctness. However, after many years of research and effort, these beliefs are beginning to change.

Much of our knowledge of how to go about teaching and guiding students' growth in writing is based on the work of many researchers and educators including Nancie Atwell, Lucy Calkins, Donald Graves, James Gray, and Donald Murray. Recent emphasis on understanding and teaching the writing process may be traced to the Bay Area Writing Project (BAWP) at the University of California at Berkeley. James Gray began this project in 1973 in order to train practicing teachers in writing instruction, primarily by involving the teachers themselves in writing and in talking about their writing. This was the same technique that the teachers would in turn use with their students, regardless of grade level. The popularity of the project grew, and it soon became known as the National Writing Project. To date, the NWP is conducted in more than one hundred centers in forty-four states.

Conferencing with peers is one of the linchpins of learning how to write. To help students learn conferencing skills, the teacher models questions that the students can ask of their own writing and that of their peers. Through sharing one's writing with peers and responding to their questions about it, a student grows in writing competence and in sense of audience. Proponents of this approach maintain that it allows spelling, grammar, punctuation, and so forth — the "basic skills" of writing — to be mastered in a context in which their use has real meaning and significance. During what Harste, Short, and Woodward (1989) have termed the "authoring cycle," each experience before, during, and after the writing process provides a student with new data upon which is based more general growth — and further writing. Reading and discussion are critical variables that fuel the cycle, helping to develop the student's knowledge and experiential base for further writing.

Most writing researchers and educators have described the process of writing as a continual interaction between the writer and the piece he or she is composing. Part of this interaction may be free flowing and relatively unstructured; part of it can be quite structured and deliberate. For purposes of instruction, the writing process is usually broken down into five main components: *prewriting, drafting* or *composing, revising, editing,* and *sharing* and *publishing.* As we consider each component, keep in mind that these stages not only lead to growth in writing development but also represent a process by which students can hone critical thinking and problem-solving skills.

Prewriting

Prewriting is the first stage in the writing process. It refers to whatever students need to do in order to get thoughts out of their heads and down on paper. Since the purpose of prewriting is to record ideas for later use and elaboration, students needn't use complete sentences but can express these thoughts in as simple a form as possible. During prewriting students also begin to consider what they will want their audience to gain from reading their composition.

A number of strategies and practices exist for presenting prewriting. Teachers should model and facilitate each one so that students will not get bogged down with the age-old questions "What do I write about?" and "How do I get started?" It is important for students to understand that a composition usually begins not with sustained writing but with ideas. An effective prewriting activity will result in a feeling of readiness to write, that telltale moment when the writer knows he or she should move on to the drafting or composing stage (Rico, 1983).

Drafting

During the drafting, or "composing," stage the expression of *meaning* and *intent* are foremost. Although punctuation and spelling certainly play a part, they should not at this stage be the primary focus; this allows students to allot more cognitive space to the expression of meaning. As we will explore later in this chapter, however, even for young children the urge to express meaning through writing is strong enough to sustain their effort on both fronts — the sounding out and the encoding of words as well as the expression of a meaning or intent.

The lion's share of the writing is usually undertaken during the drafting stage. This is the point at which mature writers have a "conversation" with themselves. For students, interactions with the teacher and with peers will develop this ability to carry on an internal conversation and help them learn to write on their own. As with the development of thought, *internalization* of such social interactions contributes to the content and the nature of these conversations with oneself. The language, emotions, and content the student experiences through reading also add to the conversation. Obviously, there won't always be an external "ear" — an audience or editor — during this drafting stage. One of the important transitions to maturity in writing is the development of one's own ear, rather than continuing reliance on conferences and teacher input.

Students must acquire an important understanding about the drafting stage: drafts are usually *first* drafts. By definition, therefore, they are incomplete and tentative — a time to try things out and take risks. All too often, students get the message that what is valued in writing is good handwriting, proper spacing between words, correct spelling, correct margins, thorough erasure of mistakes, and so forth. This leads to compositions that are usually wooden and dull. "Older children often want to know what topics you expect," Donald Graves pointed out, "correct spelling, how to line off the page. It is only right that they ask. This has been the pattern in previous years. They don't want to be censured for their mistakes. Many will need weeks or months to be convinced you seriously wish to know what they have to offer" (Graves, 1983, p. 19). As you'll see, however, with appropriate and sensitive guidance, such students can be turned around.

Revising

Once the writer has a first draft in hand, the process of revision may begin. A little bit of revision goes on during the actual drafting of a composition, but significant revision is a reworking of the first draft. This "re-vision" (literally, "seeing again") involves making whatever changes are necessary in the first draft so that the purposes and intentions of the writing will be more precisely met. Substitutions, additions, re-ordering, and deletions of ideas can be made at any level — word, phrase, sentence, paragraph, and so on.

First drafts rarely achieve the level of precision and comprehensibility their authors intend, so the process of revision allows authors the opportunity to determine not only the strengths of their first drafts but also what can be elaborated, clarified, omitted, and re-ordered. While revising, students will come to think critically about writing and the eloquence and precision with which they are communicating to their audience. Revision depends upon a clear understanding of the purpose of the writing, because only then will the writer be able to judge the effect the writing will have on the intended audience.

Editing

At this stage the writer gives explicit attention to the mechanics — spelling, punctuation, and grammar — for final "fine-tuning" of the composition. Although the mechanics remain pretty much in the background during the previous stages, these aspects are nevertheless important. Peter Elbow aptly describes their importance this way: "When you meet strangers, you can hardly keep from noticing their clothing before you notice their personality. The only way to keep someone from noticing a surface is to make it 'disappear,' as when someone wears the clothes you most expect her to wear. The only way to make grammar disappear — to keep the surface of your writing from distracting readers away from your message — is to make it right" (Elbow, 1981, p. 168).

In the editing stage, the writer has reached a point where he or she is at least satisfied if not outright pleased with the composition, and probably will make no further changes to its content. The writing is then ready to be prepared for publication. The major task of readying a composition for publication is a careful reading of the manuscript.

Editing becomes something other than a dull, routinized, and mildly irritating duty when students appreciate the sense of Elbow's metaphor — that is, when they see a clear and worthwhile purpose for editing. This purpose usually occurs to them when they realize that their writing is going to be published — publicly shared — in a consequential fashion. This means, quite simply, that there will be an interested and appreciative audience for the writing.

Skill in editing will develop along with expertise in writing if, from the primary grades on, teachers gradually and appropriately introduce the concepts underlying the mechanics of writing, thus requiring greater precision in editing as the competence of the writer develops. This is the realm of the "basics" in writing, and we will explore the best way to handle this gradual introduction later. Chapter 10 presents and discusses a general scope and sequence for spelling patterns, and Chapter 11 and Appendices C, D, and E do so for elements of grammar and punctuation.

Sharing and Publishing

By now it is obvious that students' writing has a much broader readership than the traditional "audience of one" that was the teacher. Writing may be shared as it is being developed — as in response sessions — and it may be shared when it is finished, through the "Author's Chair" concept (Graves and Hansen, 1983). The *Author's Chair* is a privileged place; both the students and the teacher will occupy it at different times. The students may read their own writing or from a favorite trade book (see Chapters 8 and 9); importantly, questions are always asked after the piece is read. If they wrote the piece, the students respond as authors, and if they read from a trade book, they respond as they believe the author would if he or she were there. In this manner the students will come to think as writers when they read, and think as readers when they write (Smith, 1983). Your students will begin to consider *themselves* authors, perhaps kindred spirits with the absent authors who have written their trade books.

Often students' writing will be published to be shared with the whole class and occasionally even a wider audience. The publication of writing simply means that the writing will be prepared so that it will be available for reading by this wider audience. Publishing can take many forms, as we will see later in this chapter.

In summary, the process of writing comprises five stages: prewriting, drafting or composing, revising, editing, and sharing or publishing. These stages certainly do not represent discrete, exclusive tasks, but overlap. What distinguishes one stage from another is the degree of focus placed on particular tasks at different points in the evolution of a composition. Discussing each stage with students as their need for understanding and guidance arises is the teacher's challenge.

How do you introduce these stages to your students? The illustrative dialogues that follow demonstrate how your initial discussions might proceed. Later in the chapter we will explore what will happen as you build on these beginnings and your students learn, with your help, how to take more control of their writing.

Helping Young Children Become Comfortable with Writing

Our primary concern with children in kindergarten and first grade is to make them fairly comfortable with the act of writing. When the children are not hesitant about writing and are no longer awkward in their handling of writing implements — pencils, crayons, managing the paper — we can then move along to revising and editing. But let's look at the very beginnings: how can we get young children to start writing?

First of all, most young children entering first grade seem to believe they *can* write, although they will admit that they may not know how to read (Graves, 1983). Early on we will let them draw, and if they choose to include letters or letterlike characters, so much the better (see Chapters 6 and 10). As we saw in Chapter 6, many children will spontaneously sound out whatever they want to say, using their knowledge of the names of the letters in the alphabet. Many other children, for any number of reasons, do not spontaneously make these attempts and will deny that they know anything about how to write or print. (It is important, by the way, to determine whether a child interprets "writing" to mean *cursive* handwriting, rather than the process of writing. If you suspect so, try using the word "printing" to see how the child responds.) If children have at least a beginning concept of word in print (Chapter 6), then they can benefit from a little encouragement by you. If they are not developmentally at this point, then hold off until later.

When you do need to offer encouragement — let's say for a reluctant six-year-old, Camille — your wording may go something like this:

CLASSROOM EXAMPLE

TEACHER: "Camille, tell me about your drawing here."
CAMILLE: "It's a elephant."
TEACHER: "What's the elephant doing?"
CAMILLE: "Nothin' much — he's just standing there."
TEACHER: "Well, you've done a good job of drawing him. Why don't you label your drawing by printing *elephant* underneath the picture?"
CAMILLE: "I don't know *how* to write!"
TEACHER: "I bet you know a lot about how to write; in fact, you might surprise yourself! You know the names of a lot of the letters, and they will help you write down what you want to say. Let's try it with *elephant*. What's the first sound you hear in *elephant*?"
CAMILLE: "L?"
TEACHER: "Good! Write down the letter that makes that sound." [Teacher points to the place on the drawing where Camille can begin to write.] "What's the next sound you hear?" [Teacher pronounces the word carefully and slowly by syllables: "el-e-phant."]

CAMILLE: "A?"

TEACHER: "Okay! Write that down . . . What's the next sound?" [Teacher again pronounces *elephant,* slightly emphasizing the '*f*' sound.]

CAMILLE: "F?"

TEACHER: "Good! Write that down . . . What else do you hear?" [Usually by this point children have caught on; Camille finishes her writing: LAFNT. Teacher continues:] "Good, Camille! How about that? You've written *elephant*!"

Children such as Camille will probably need continuing support of this sort; an excellent means of reaching several such children at once is to work with a group. Sounding out a word in a group is a particularly effective means of showing even the most reluctant child "how it's done." A child who may not respond at all to sounding out when you try it one-on-one will, in the comfort of the group, at least hear and remember how other children are approaching the task.

What if Camille had asked, after spelling *elephant* as LAFNT, "Is it right?" She knows enough about print to realize that it looks different from *her* writing! The most effective and satisfying response is something like "You know, you'll see it spelled differently in books, but I really like the way *you* sounded it out!" This sends two important messages: (1) Yes, words are often spelled differently in books, and (2) you appreciate and support the child's spelling, even if it is different. This skirts the "right/wrong" mindset and encourages the children to keep up their attempts.

As we'll discuss further later on in this chapter, journal writing is an excellent means of keeping young children writing in a nonthreatening context. With continued development, they will come to write more and in time will be ready for plugging in the rest of the phases in the writing process. However, it is extremely important that you do not attempt to engage all aspects of the writing process with children who are at the letter-name stage (see Chapter 6), because they are giving it their all in just getting down a few lines.

Teaching, Modeling, and Applying the Writing Process

Using Conferences in Writing Instruction

Vivid understandings and appreciation of the elements of the writing craft come about most often when students closely examine their own writing or the writing of their peers. Conferences, which may be used at any stage in the writing process, are a forum for such close work. In this section, I'll present general guidelines for conferencing, along with questions that will facilitate students' thinking and revision throughout a composition.

Teachers can model the format of conferencing through the following sequence:

1. The student reads his or her draft to you.

2. Focusing on content and then (if necessary) on order, your questions probe

what the student means, feels, likes best, and may be having difficulty with, and ask where he or she will be going next with the composition. Calkins suggests that the best way to begin is with the simple questions, "How's it going?" "Where are you with this?" or "How can I help you?" (Calkins, 1986, p. 121).

3. Respond to the students' questions, but do not take over the process for them.

4. Emphasize only one or two aspects at a time in a single conference.

Your conferences with students may be informal — a word or two here and there to keep things moving along as the children write — or formal, in which you set aside several minutes to confer one-to-one with a student about his or her writing.

Small-group or student/student conferences adapt the teacher's basic format (Calkins, 1986; Millett, 1990; Nathan, Temple, Juntunen, and Temple, 1989). These guidelines are appropriate beginning with the first draft of a composition:

1. The writer reads his or her composition out loud.

2. The listener(s) respond to the piece. If there are parts that are confusing, listeners may ask questions for clarification.

3. Focus is on the *content* of the writing; in response to questions, the writer elaborates on the content and "teaches" the listener(s) about the topic.

4. Finally, emphasis returns to the composition itself: "what will the writer do next and how will he or she do it?"

As writers conference more with each other and with you, their questions seeking feedback and help will become more precise — because they are more aware of what their audience may want or need. Not surprisingly, their questions often will have originated with you in individual conferences. Your challenge is to be the effective listener (remember Chapter 5?); if you work at this, then you will find that your questions flow more easily and appropriately.

The specific questions that you ask in individual conferences will vary, depending on where the student is with his or her composition and what the nature and purpose of the composition is. Before we look at the types of questions you may ask in conferences, let's watch a response group in action, so that you can get a sense of how it functions. Notice how the teacher highlights what is going to be done and why, and how she illustrates through her questioning how students might respond.

CLASSROOM EXAMPLE

The setting is a third grade classroom. The teacher has already asked one pupil, Mike, if he would share his story with the class. The teacher asks the students to come up and sit in a semicircle around the Author's Chair. Seated beside the chair, the teacher begins.

TEACHER: "Boys and girls, we will be sharing a lot of the writing we will be doing this year — my writing as well as yours. Whether we share in a group or with a partner, we will usually respond to one another's writing in a similar way. Mike is going to share his story with us, and together we're going to learn how we will be responding to each others' writing. Okay, Mike, as an author you are going to sit in the Author's Chair."

[Mike then reads his composition to the group.]

MIKE: "My story is called 'The Snake and Me.'

"One day my friend and I were shooting goals in my basketball goal. My brother was kicking balls against the wall in the garage. He wanted to play basketball with us so he got a ball out of our ball bucket. When he leaned down to get a ball he saw a black gold kind of snake. He ran very fast over to me and shouted, 'Mike, there is a snake behind the ball bucket.'

I yelled, 'Dad! Matt found a snake.'

Dad shouted, 'Where is the snake?'

I said, 'In the corner behind the ball bucket.'

He got one of his sharpest rakes and ran where the snake was. He got him out from behind the bucket. It was hard work getting him out, but we did. He started along on the brick that was sticking out. He was slithering along the bricks. My dad picked up his rake and ran over and used the rake to push the snake off the bricks sticking out. When we got him off the bricks my dad asked me to step on its head so it would not turn and bite my dad. When I got my foot down where it was supposed to be, my dad chopped its tail off, then its middle, and then finally its head. My friend asked my dad if he could keep its tail so he could take it apart. I said, 'How in the world are you going to do that?'

He said, 'Simple. All I have to do is put it in acid.'

We went walking down the street house to house asking if they had any acid and if we could borrow some of it. Everybody said 'NO!'

A few days after we found the snake, I went over to my friend's house. The snake had been taken apart and was laying in acid! I said 'OH WOW!' and that was the end of the snake."

TEACHER: "Thank you, Mike! Kids, who listened really well and can tell Mike what you heard in his story? Mike, you may call on whomever you want."

MIKE: "Okay. Dreanne?"

DREANNE: "I heard that you and your brother were shooting baskets and then your brother saw the snake behind the ball bucket. You called your Dad and he came with a rake and he killed him while you held him down with your foot. I liked that part — where your dad was chasing the snake! And then, umm, then you went looking for acid to keep the tail in."

TEACHER: "Okay! Let's tell Mike what else we liked about his story . . . [Wait several seconds — it may take a little while this first time around, but eventually students will respond.]

BRYAN: "I like the part where you and your dad are trying to kill the snake!"

HEATHER: "I like how you told about the snake after you found him — when you said it *slithered* I could see it trying to get away."

DANNY: "I really like when your dad got the snake off the bricks; it was like I could see him running after the snake who was going really fast!"

TEACHER: "Is there anything you'd like to ask Mike about his story?"

YOLANDA: "Weren't you scared when your dad told you to put your foot on the snake's head?"

MIKE: "Kind of, but I wanted to show my dad how brave I was!"

TERRY: "I wasn't sure what you meant when you said about the bricks sticking out."

MIKE: "There's these bricks along the front of our house, from the ground to about halfway up. At the top, they are laid different so they stick out more from the side of the house."

LEWIS: "I got kind of confused at the end when you said you went looking for acid and couldn't find any and then you and your friend found the snake but it sounded like your friend had him in acid — how could he have done that if he was out with you *looking* for acid?"

MIKE: "No, that's not what I meant. When I said 'we' found the snake I meant my brother and me over at my friend's house."

LEWIS: "Oh, *that* makes sense!"

TEACHER: "Mike, if you were to change your story, can you think of a way that would make that last part clearer?"

MIKE: "Yeah, I see that if I probably just said, 'Me and my brother found the snake at my friend's house,' that could do it."

TEACHER: "That's an excellent idea. Mike, when you write more on your story why don't you change that part and then the end would be clearer. Thank you *very* much for sharing your story with us!

"Kids, when we share our writing with each other we'll usually do it just like Mike did. Someone will read their piece to us, we'll listen, and we'll tell them what we heard them say. Then, we'll tell them what we liked and then ask questions about anything we need more information on. That will help all of us with our writing."

And that's it for the first time around. Keep it simple, but let the "author" call on and interact with the other students as you gently guide the process. You can close out the sharing by reiterating what the group just did, and why.

Questioning in Teacher/Student Conferences   Most students reach a point in their development as writers where they have a feel for whether an idea or topic is worth continued attention. If they decide it is not, they will put it in their writing folder for possible future use. When students first begin the writing process, however, they need guidance in sustaining a topic or idea long enough to expand, elaborate, and develop it. The questions you ask them in individual conferences, both formal and informal, will provide this guidance. Much of your students' realization in the first few days and perhaps weeks of school will be that the writing is not finished once the first draft is finished. In this sense, you are teaching not only writing but also thinking through writing.

To build the following list of questions for use in teacher/student conferences, I have drawn upon the questions suggested by several specialists in the teaching of writing (Calkins, 1986; Graves, 1983; Millett, 1990; Murray, 1982; Nathan, et al., 1989). I've categorized these questions according to the ways in which they will direct the students' thinking about their writing: (1) getting the writing "off the ground"; (2) identifying the central focus of the writing; (3) expanding and elaborating on the writing (often in combination with questions that identify the central focus); (4) establishing the sequence of information; (5) refining sentences, word choice, and phrasing; and (6) helping students see their own development as writers. Because children respond differently to questions, the varied phrasings given below offer different ways of reaching the main objective for each category.

■ *Getting the writing "off the ground"*

How's it going?
Where are you with this?
How can I help you?

■ *Identifying the central focus of the writing*

What part is most interesting to you?
What is the most important thing in this piece?
How do you feel about this?
Which idea matters most to you?
What made you decide to write about this topic?

■ *Expanding and elaborating on the writing*

Tell me more about . . .
Is that important to add?
Do you think others might have more questions about this?
How did you get to this part in your draft?

■ *Establishing the sequence of information*

Did this happen before or after?
Where could this new idea go?
Which parts talk about the same thing?
How might you put these parts together?
Are there parts you could save for another piece of writing?
Why did you put these things in this order?
How about your beginning and/or ending? Are you happy with them? Does your beginning really grab your reader?

■ *Refining sentences, word choice, and phrasing*

Could you break this longer sentence into shorter ones?
How could you combine two or three of these short sentences?
How would changing this statement into a question work?
Which sentences do the best job of *showing,* not just telling?
How could you *show* instead of *tell* about this?
Could you be more specific here?
What action words have you used? Could you use others?
How does this draft sound when you read it out loud?
Show me where I can really tell it's *you* writing this piece.

■ *Helping students see their own development as writers*

What did you learn from this piece of writing?
How does this piece compare to others you have written?
What did you try that was new in this draft that you haven't tried before?

At first you may have some difficulty remaining loose enough in conferences to go with your true and honest reaction rather than thinking about what question you should ask. This is natural. Eventually, however, you will feel more relaxed. Calkins (1986) offers an excellent example. When a teacher asked eleven-year-old Sumi, "How's it going?" Sumi showed her the composition she had been working on; to that point Sumi had written a short paragraph about her father who died when she was three. The last line she had written was "When I see other kids with their fathers, I wonder what it would be like to be his daughter." The teacher could have asked questions that would have expanded on what Sumi had written, but wisely — and fortunately — chose to respond as she truly felt at that instant: "Sumi, I'm glad you are writing about this. I can tell how special your father is to you, even though you never got the chance to know him." After Sumi briefly told about how she felt cheated — even though she pretended it all didn't matter — the teacher said, "I'm going to leave you now because I don't want to get in the way of what you are doing. It is so important, the things you have been saying. I'll be back, my friend" (Calkins, 1986, pp. 125–126).

Questioning in Student/Student Conferences   As students internalize both the procedure for responding in groups and the types of questions you ask in teacher/student conferences, they become better at responding to one another's compositions while working in pairs. At this point you may provide guidelines for both authors and responders. At first these should be kept simple, but in time — particularly with older students — they can be expanded. Following are your basic conference guidelines:

1. Read your draft to your partner.
2. Ask your partner what he or she likes or thinks is interesting about your draft.
3. Read your draft again to your partner.
4. Ask your partner if he or she has any questions about your draft. Your partner may also write down any questions for you.

Notice that these guidelines reflect strategies and issues that the teacher would already have addressed and modeled. In keeping with the "gradual release of control" perspective on instruction, these issues will eventually be internalized and be part of students' independent and ongoing assessment of their own writing. However, students should also understand that they can always benefit from sharing their writing with others and getting their feedback prior to final publication of the writing.

When your students are more comfortable with the writing process, you may provide additional, more specific questions that they can ask one another. These questions will reflect the questions you are asking in teacher/student conferences, as well as whatever particular skill or strategy you may be working on at the time:

1. Read your draft to your partner.
2. Ask your partner what he or she likes or thinks is interesting about your draft.

Although students may at first put on a show about not wanting to share their writing with others, most of them — deep down — are really delighted to do so. However, for various reasons (fear of criticism, exposing themselves to potentially unkind or negative comments), a few other students really are reluctant to share before others. Respect this; with time, the reluctance usually fades as they see how supportively others' writing is received. Then, when they are feeling more confident, ask them to share with a small group rather than making their "debut" before the whole class!

3. Ask your partner any one or more of these questions:
   a. Is my lead interesting?
   b. Am I too wordy?
   c. Do you have trouble following me?
   d. What is unclear in my draft?
   e. Do I get off my topic anywhere?
   f. How's my ending?
4. You may discuss these questions with your partner and/or he or she may write down responses for you to take back with you for your revisions.

In both simple and more advanced student/student conferences, you may provide formatted sheets for response when students do write down their questions. Figure 7.2 is an illustration of such a form.

Prewriting

The classic response from students when you announce, "Let's write!" is "I don't know what to write about." In time, your students won't respond this way; their purposes will easily dictate the form and content of their writing.

The overriding aim of prewriting activities is to free up the students' thoughts and feelings — the cognitive and the affective realms — and to generate ideas that they can elaborate upon in the subsequent writing. At first the prewriting phase will address the basic issue of identifying a topic to write about. With time, this phase can help writers identify concepts they may use in the writing, and knowledge they may want the audience to gain from their writing. The techniques you will introduce and how much you will encourage students to use them will depend upon the age of the students, their developmental level, and their purposes for writing.

Children have much to call upon for writing topics, but in the beginning we must encourage them to tap this wellspring: ". . . children cannot leave their lives, like rain boots, at the door to the classroom to be retrieved on their way home" (Guilbault, 1988, p. 464) — nor should they be expected to.

With time, the prewriting phase will come to include any type of activity that precedes and helps give focus to a written composition. These types of activities,

Sample Peer Evaluation Master

Your name _Carrie R._ Date _Oct. 19_

Writer's name _Sarah H._

★ · ★ · ★ · ★ · ★ · ★ · ★ · ★ · ★ · ★ · ★ · ★ · ★

Write one or two things you like about this writer's paper.

1. Sarah has used really good words to describe what she did. When she talked about how cold the water felt when she dove into it, I could really feel that!

2. The story makes me want to read more. To find out what happens when the water starts to pull her down.

Write one or two ideas for making the paper better.

1. Maybe you could describe more about how scared you were when you knew you couldn't keep your head above water.

2. _____

presented throughout this book, can range from show-and-tell to reading different types of literature, to journal writing, to field trips, to interviews, to films, to class discussions — and so on. More prewriting techniques are discussed below.

Drawing   This is the most natural type of prewriting activity, and is most effective in the primary grades. In first grade, writing is usually merely a "comment" on the drawing; with time the two processes will better complement each other, and soon, the writing will usually surpass the drawing in complexity and effort. You can follow up on a child's drawing by asking questions to elicit more information — for example, what the child is illustrating and why. You may encourage the child to add to the drawing, if appropriate, and/or to identify perhaps one element in the drawing that he or she may now wish to write about.

Clustering   *Clustering* refers to a technique that has variously been called "webbing" and "mapping." Interestingly, it closely mimics the ways in which, as information processing theorists have described, information is organized in our brains (see Chapter 2). The technique of clustering allows us to access associations to a particular idea in a free flowing, nonlinear manner. Clustering helps writers to identify specific topics or twists on topics that they may wish to pursue and to realize when the "moment to write" has struck: when they have shifted from "randomness to a sense of direction" (Rico, 1983, p. 10). Eventually, students will use clustering individually, as you will in the "At the Teacher's Desk" section on p. 236. At first, however, it is done with a group or the whole class as follows.

The teacher writes a word or phrase in the middle of the chalkboard or on a piece of chart paper. He then draws a circle around it and asks the students what comes to mind when they think of this idea. As students offer suggestions, he writes them around the central "idea" and draws a circle around each. In the course of offering ideas, at least one, and usually more, specific areas will develop as spin-offs of the general idea.

Figure 7.3 shows a cluster generated by a class of second-graders. The main idea here is "gerbils." The class first contributed the words connected by lines to the main idea. Notice, though, that after "cages," the teacher has drawn arrows to connect the circles; this shows how other ideas were spun off from "cages," eventually winding up with a child's comment about "Noises I hear from the gerbil cage at night." At this point, the children are ready to write, having had their schemas and

FIGURE 7.3

A Second Grade Class's Cluster

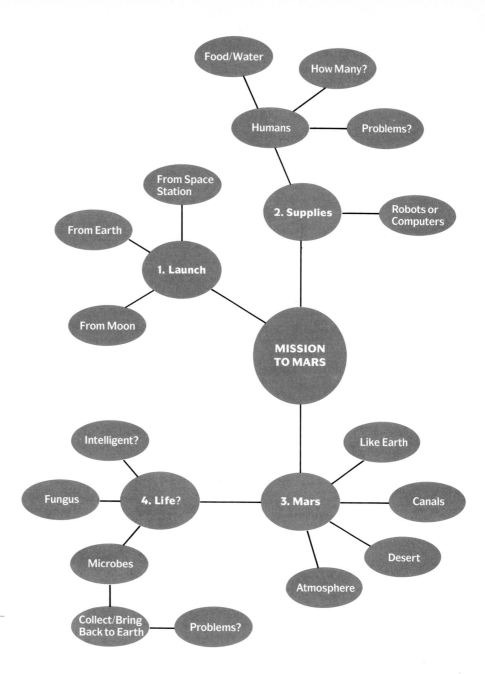

FIGURE 7.4

A Fifth Grade Class's Cluster

perhaps their imaginations stimulated. They may use the words on the cluster if they wish, but they certainly should not be required to do so. And if a few or many students are stimulated to write about something other than gerbils, so be it!

Figure 7.4 shows a cluster generated by fifth-graders. Notice that it is not only more elaborate than the previous one but that, given its complexity, the teacher has numbered major concepts so as to illustrate how order can be brought to the cluster as a first pass at organizing the main ideas.

If you have never used clustering to "uncork" your own mind to generate ideas for writing, you should try it out. The following procedure, adapted from Rico (1983), will get you going.

Begin by writing a word, such as *afraid,* in the middle of the page. Circle it. Then rapidly write down any other words or phrases that enter your mind, circling each and "radiating out from the center in any direction they want to go" (p. 35). Draw lines from one circle to the next and when an idea occurs to you that does not fit with the words you've been writing down, go back to the central word, *afraid,* and start again, spinning out as far as that association will take you.

Don't stop to think about what is coming to you; keep writing down the words or phrases. If your mind goes momentarily blank, then simply trace over the circle around *afraid* until your mind gets going again. Usually, quite suddenly, you will realize the direction you want your writing to go and you are ready to write.

Look over your cluster, and you will realize how to go about writing your first sentence. You are on your way. Write for a few minutes. Then look back at your beginning and relate your ending to it. This should not be difficult at all; the words will occur to you.

Brainstorming   Like clustering, brainstorming usually involves a group of students and taps the ideas associated with a particular idea. The idea may be represented by a word, a phrase, or a picture. Originally intended as a group problem-solving technique, brainstorming can be adapted for prewriting by having individuals call out ideas that a "scribe" then writes down on a chalkboard or chart paper. The scribe — initially this is usually the teacher — accepts all suggestions without evaluation. That will come later in the problem-solving process. As a prewriting activity, brainstorming usually stops after many ideas have been recorded, and these may or may not be a part of the subsequent writing.

If the ideas have been written down in a list, you can extend brainstorming by asking the students if any item in this list catches their interest. If so, that idea can be pulled off to the side and a list of "specifics" brainstormed for it. Or the idea can be used as the focus for clustering. You can also ask students if they sense any connections among the items in the list. If they do, these can be circled and connected with a line or arrow. This connection can be the starting point for a piece of writing, especially if you encourage more brainstorming or clustering around it.

Stream-of-Consciousness Writing   Most effective for the intermediate grades and above, this type of prewriting activity can not only result in identifying ideas for writing, but also ease students into the flow of writing. Your instructions to the students are simple: "When I say 'begin,' start writing down whatever comes into your head. You do not have to write in complete sentences or be concerned with spelling or punctuation. Just *keep writing*! If you find that there are no new thoughts in your head, just keep writing the last word you wrote until a new thought does come along."

Stream-of-consciousness writing is an activity that many published authors have found to be successful. The technique helps to break through the self-editing that even professional writers succumb to at the prewriting stage. When a thought pops into our head we will often say to ourselves, "That idea is unimportant" (or silly, or dumb, or weird) and won't write it down, thereby editing out ideas that might be developed. Stream-of-consciousness writing helps to break the self-editing habit and save all the ideas. It should most definitely be kept personal, so that students do not avoid writing down certain thoughts for fear others will read them.

The following Classroom Example illustrates the prewriting phase in action — as a teacher engages in a variant of the brainstorming technique and frees herself to write by homing in on her topic.

CLASSROOM EXAMPLE

The teacher begins the lesson in front of the class, standing at an overhead projector. On the projector is placed a clear transparency. Notice that she is going to be "thinking aloud" for the students, modeling for them how she comes up with a topic to write about.

TEACHER: "Boys and girls, I'm going to be writing today — in fact, *all* of us will be writing — but I first need to decide what I'd like to write about. Do any of you ever have trouble figuring out what you'd like to write about?" [Many heads nod and several "yeahs" are heard.] "What do you do when that happens? Yes, Brian?"

BRIAN: "Well, most of the time I wind up writing about something I'm not too interested in — but I get the assignment done!"

TEACHER: "Do you enjoy writing when you do that?"

BRIAN [shaking his head]: "Nope!"

TEACHER: "Sometimes it's true that we have to write things that we're not very interested in, but most of the time we can enjoy whatever we are writing about.

"I'd like to show you one technique that *I* use when I am planning to write and need to think of something that I want to write about. First, I think of the things that are on my mind right now or that I have been thinking about all day — these are the things that I'm more concerned about, and any of them could be a topic or a theme for my writing.

"Right now, there are several things on my mind. I'm thinking about showing all of you how I get started in writing, but I've also been thinking about going to the balloon races this weekend. I've been thinking about how I need to go shopping for groceries this evening . . . Okay, I'm ready to make a list of these things that I have been thinking about. After writing them down I'll decide what I'm *most* interested in, and then that will be my topic.

"First, there is my showing you how I get started . . ." [Writes "Getting started in writing" on the transparency.] "Then, there are the balloon races . . ." [Writes "Balloon races" on the transparency.] "Next, there are the groceries I need to buy . . ." [Writes "Groceries" on the transparency.]

"Let's see — what else is on my mind? I guess that's about it. Well, now I need to choose which one of these three things I want to write about . . ." [Several children call out, "Balloon races!"]

"You know, I agree with you! Writing about the upcoming balloon races this weekend will be more fun for me right now than my other possible topics." [Removes transparency and places another blank transparency on the overhead projector.]

"Next, when I have a topic that I want to write about, I start another list. This time, I simply write down anything that comes to me that has to do with my topic. This gets me in the mood to write about my topic, and it also gets many of the ideas that I will use when I'm writing down on the page for ready reference if I need them. The important thing about this list, and something that you will need to keep in mind when you do this on your own, is to write down whatever comes to your mind, no matter how silly or unimportant it may seem to you.

"Okay, when I think about the balloon races I think about blue skies [writes "blue skies" on the transparency], dragonlike sounds of the balloons when their burners are turned on [writes "dragonlike sounds" on the transparency] . . ."

[Teacher continues in this fashion for approximately one minute. When she is finished, the transparency contains eight ideas. Figure 7.5 shows the completed transparency.]

"You know, I've just gotten a feeling that I'm ready to get started with my actual writing. You will usually get this feeling too; sometimes it comes almost right away and sometimes it takes a while, but it usually comes . . . To me, it's simply a feeling that I want to get going with my writing — I want to say more about these first few ideas that have come to me.

"I've got to hold off right now, though, because it's time for each of you to get the feel of coming up with a topic and listing ideas about it."

The teacher then asks the children to think for a moment about what's on their own minds and to list these possible topics. She then encourages the children to brainstorm ideas about the most appealing of these topics. During this prewriting experience she circulates about the classroom, helping out and encouraging those children who still are uncertain about the task or, more likely, are reluctant for whatever reason to put their thoughts down on paper.

◆ ◆ ◆

FIGURE 7.5

Brainstorming about Balloon Races

blue skies
dragonlike sounds
a party
excitement

huge wicker baskets
early morning
wet grass
balloons blocking
out the sun

Drafting

Because it is difficult, for obvious reasons, to model the entire composing of a first draft, teachers usually model both the beginning — the "getting-started" phase — and how to keep the writing going. A primary objective at the getting-started stage is to help the children realize that they do not have to sit and wait for just the right sentence or just the right words to pop into their heads. When they feel they're ready to write they can begin, working from the ideas they jotted down during the prewriting phase.

CLASSROOM EXAMPLE

Once again, the teacher is at the front of the classroom, standing next to the overhead projector. She places the list of ideas based on the balloon races shown in Figure 7.5 on the projector.

TEACHER: "Kids, yesterday when we were thinking about what to do before starting our writing, I told you I felt I was ready to write after jotting down these ideas about the balloon races." [Turns on overhead projector.] "Today I'd like to show you what I do when I get started writing, when I am actually ready to write what we call the first draft.

"Well, now. Okay . . . I'll start with this idea." [Writes, "I always look forward to the balloon races each year." Pauses, looking down at the transparency.]

"That's an okay start, but where do I go from here? What should I say next? Hmm . . . Okay, I've got another idea . . . [While pronouncing each word softly but loud enough to be heard, she writes: "The first time I went to the races, I wasn't sure if I would really enjoy them. I had never seen balloons like that up close before." Pauses, still looking down at the transparency, then continues writing, still pronouncing words softly as they are written: "But when I saw them being inflated and heard the hissing sound of the burners when flame came out, I was reminded of dragons. I was hooked! I had never seen anything like them before." Another pause.]

"I'm not sure exactly where I want to go now, so I'm going to look back at my list of ideas." [Places the list quickly on the transparency and exclaims, "Oh! I've got it!" Returns to writing: "All around me, it felt like one large party. People were shouting as the balloons went up. One minute the sun was shining brightly. The next minute, it was blocked by one of the balloons."]

"Well, class, now I feel as though I'm really rolling with this particular piece of writing. I feel most comfortable right now with describing what my first experience at a balloon race was like, and I'm going to continue to develop this main idea when I go back to my writing.

"What you've seen me doing is exactly what I do when I write by myself — I may not talk out loud while I write — but I'm thinking the kinds of things I've been saying out loud to you.

"Let's think back about what I've done. When I started writing, did I know *exactly* what I wanted to say when I began writing? Charles?"

CHARLES: "I don't think so . . ."

TEACHER: "How did I begin to get an idea of the direction I wanted my piece to go in? Tamatha?"

TAMATHA: "I think it happened while you were writing . . ."

TEACHER: "Good! That's exactly how it happened. I knew I wanted to write about the balloon races, but I wasn't sure about what to focus on. It became clearer as I moved along in my writing.

"A lot of your first drafts will begin this way. With other first drafts, you will have a pretty good idea about what your main focus is going to be. Often though, when you want to write and you feel like you're ready, but you're not sure exactly where your piece is going to go, then just begin writing with your first ideas in your list as a guide. The focus will usually come along, just as the feeling that you were ready to write came along.

"Well, now that I've got *my* composition started, the rest of you need to get *your* pieces underway!"

As before, the teacher offers encouragement and support as she circulates about the room.

As we saw in Chapter 6, when writers write, they usually have a purpose, and this purpose will determine the genre scheme and particular format they will select. The teacher has just pointed this out to the students. Nevertheless, in the beginning your purpose is simply to get the students writing, and what this teacher has modeled is an excellent way to get students off the ground.

Revising

Teachers play an extremely important role in helping students to "see their writing again" in light of their audience. It is not uncommon, incidentally, for a child to be his or her own most demanding and severe audience. When a child has invested much in a piece, the compulsion to "get it *right*" — wording, structure, focus, or whatever — may take over.

An extremely important process comes into play during the revision stage. Teachers model response strategies for their students and show the students how they in turn can facilitate the revision of each others' writing by responding to the first draft as the teacher will do. This process of response will become a most effective type of *collaborative learning,* facilitating critical thinking that arises out of the questions that will be asked both during the initial drafting and during the follow-up reaction to that first draft.

After students have decided to revise a draft, they do not have to worry about copying it over as they make changes. Rather, they can use proofreader's marks to indicate the changes they want. Figure 7.6 shows the common marks that elementary students will find helpful. Students may also do a bit of "cutting and pasting," moving sentences or perhaps paragraphs around.

When the teacher first models the revision stage, she is able to model *how to respond* to a piece of writing as well. Based on the paragraph in Figure 7.7, let's examine how a teacher might model the process of revision for students. Notice how the teacher addresses different aspects of the elements of writing, all within the context of revision.

Proofreading Marks

Mark	Explanation	Example
¶	Begin a new paragraph. Indent the paragraph.	¶ We went to an air show last Saturday. Eight jets flew across the sky in the shape of V's, X's, and diamonds.
∧	Add letters, words, or sentences.	The leaves were red ∧_and_ orange.
ℓ	Take out words, sentences, and punctuation marks. Correct spelling.	The rain passed ℓ quickly. The sky is bright ~~blew~~ _blue_ now.
/	Change a capital letter to a small letter.	The /Fireflies blinked in the dark.
≡	Change a small letter to a capital letter.	New York ≡city is exciting.

FIGURE 7.6

Proofreading Marks
Source: From *Teaching the Writing Process: A Guide for Teachers and Supervisors* by Nancy Carolyn Millett. Copyright © 1990 by Houghton Mifflin Company. Reprinted by permission of Houghton Mifflin Company.

CLASSROOM EXAMPLE

TEACHER: "What I am going to be doing, class — thinking about what we like and about what we would change in this piece of writing — is called revision." [Writes *revision* on a clear transparency.] "If we want to continue working with a piece of writing in order eventually to publish it, then there are almost always some changes that can be made to make our piece more effective — to say what we want to say more precisely and to affect our reader a bit more powerfully. When we think about our writing in these ways, we are talking about *revision.* Revision usually leads to second drafts and sometimes third and fourth drafts, depending on how important we feel a particular piece of writing is. In order to learn about revision, we're going to be continuing to share our drafts with one another.

"I've put the first paragraph of a composition on this transparency. The paragraph is from a story written by a sixth grade student last year. Listen as I read it aloud to you." [Teacher reads out loud to the class.]

"Okay, kids, the first thing we do when we work with another's writing in the revision stage is to tell what the writer has done *well.* I'm going to point out to you some things that I think this particular writer has done well. As I read over this piece, I especially like the way the author talks about the flat surface and then curling up at the end — it shows how she feels that's pretty unusual or

When Pam looked out at the ocean, she wondered how that kind of flat serface could wind up cureling into waves at the end. The end was where it reached the shore. She had read about the sun and the moon and how they were important in making the waves but she didn't really understand it. It seemed like magic, she thought. Suddenly, she saw a dark object just above the water. She looked closer but it was gone.

FIGURE 7.7

Paragraph from a Sixth-Grader's Story — Showing Revision

strange. We usually take for granted how the tides work, but she's showing us that she's really *thinking* about it. It's complicated, and it really does seem like magic when you think of it that way.

"Something else that I like is how she grabs our attention when she writes, 'Suddenly, she saw a dark object just above the water.' She doesn't tell us what she thinks it is yet, and that's good — it really creates a sense of excitement and anticipation. She's also able to create this because she puts it in right after a really quiet, thoughtful part, where she's wondering about the waves. It has more of an effect on you than if she simply began with something like 'Pam thought she saw a dark object above the water.' She has set us up in kind of a thoughtful mood, and then . . . pow! She hits us with the exciting, suspenseful part . . . The writer has done some things well, some things that get our attention as readers.

"Now let's change our focus on this piece. Our next step in revision is to think about anything that might need to be changed. It's important, though, that we ignore spelling and punctuation and concentrate on the *meaning* of the piece — on anything that is unclear or confusing to you.

"Look at the beginning of the piece, where she's talking about the end of the ocean and she says, 'The end was where it reached the shore.' That kind of seems stuck out there by itself, really, cut off from the first part. We could change it by connecting it to the sentence before it, and seeing how that would sound. Here's how I would make that change: I put a delete mark through the period after *end.* [Does this on the transparency.] Then I put a comma after *end* at the end of the first sentence, and then, so it won't sound odd, I cross out 'The end was.' Now the sentence reads, 'When Pam looked out at the ocean, she wondered how that kind of flat surface could wind up curling into waves at the end, where it reached the shore.'

"That's a nice change, isn't it? It pulls the thought, the *flow,* together more tightly. I've noticed something else. It seems she left a *the* out before *sun.* This is how I would insert it." [Writes the caret mark in, then writes *the* above it.]

"There's one last revision I would make to this fine composition. Remember how we've been talking about paragraphs lately? It seems like there should be two paragraphs here, because the author is talking about two different things. She's gone from just sort of looking at the ocean — sort of peaceful and calm — then there's this pretty dramatic change. I would start the second paragraph where she writes, 'Suddenly, she saw a dark object just above the water,' but since I don't want to have to rewrite this over again, down at the bottom in a separate paragraph, I'm simply going to put this mark [Draws a ¶ in front of the word *Suddenly*], which means, begin a new paragraph here.

"Okay! That does it for now. In this revision stage, then, I've done two important things. I've shown what I like about what the writer has done — she has written her beginning in such a way that we are really drawn into the piece and interested right away — and I've pointed out how some unclear places can be made clearer."

Editing

Editing refers to the preparation and proofreading of the final manuscript. The nature of editing is quite similar to that of revising in that students can use the proofreading symbols presented in Figure 7.6, but the writer's attention now focuses more on mechanics than on content. Whatever skills students have learned with respect to "fine-tuning" a composition may now be brought into play. Handwriting now assumes a more important role, because students know that its quality — its legibility — is what readers will first notice (see Chapter 11).

A general rule for editing is to have students read for one or two new aspects at a time. For example, the first feature of punctuation they can check is that each sentence ends with a period. At the same time we can ask them to make sure each new sentence begins with a capital letter. Much of your direct teaching will focus on the fine points involved in editing. With time, of course, students' awareness of these fine points should become automatic.

Editing is modeled in very much the same fashion as is revision. Students will come to understand, however, that the difference between the revision stage and the editing stage lies in the amount of attention they pay to *content* versus *mechanics.*

The teacher in the following scenario has previously modeled how to read through a piece with an "editing" eye. This time she is engaging the students in the process before turning them loose on their own. She uses the story shown in Figure 7.8.

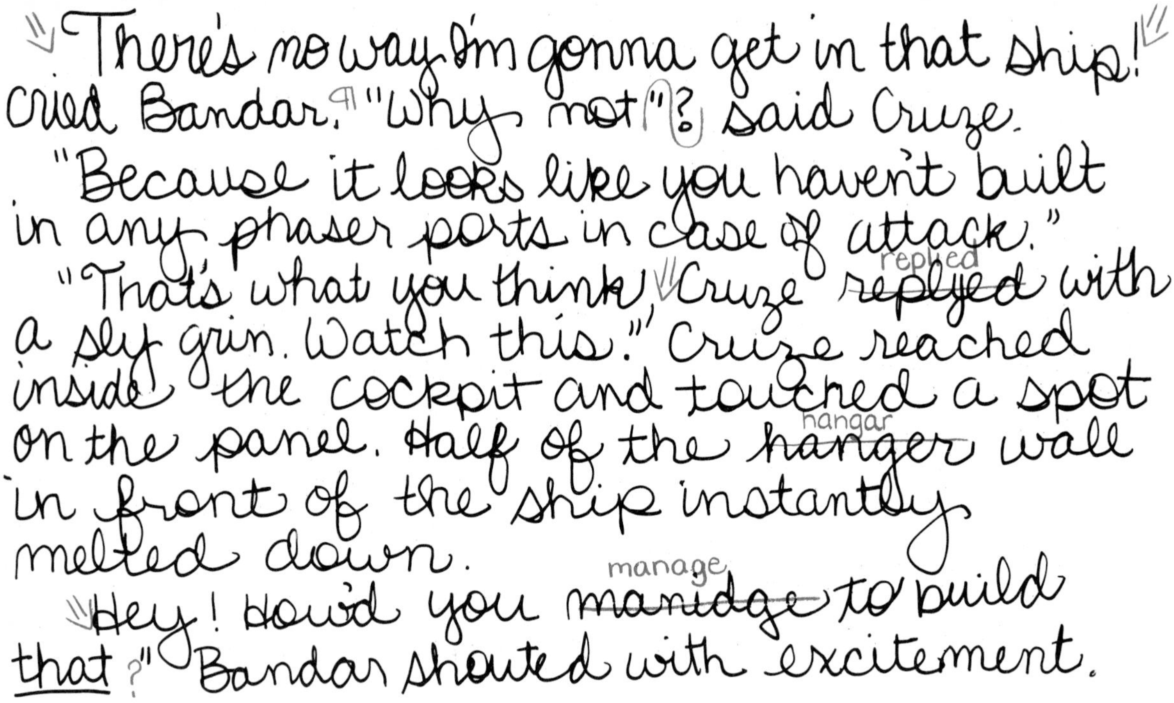

> *There's no way I'm gonna get in that ship!"* cried Bandar. *"Why not?"* said Cruze.
> *"Because it looks like you haven't built in any phaser ports in case of attack."*
> *"That's what you think, Cruze"* ~~replyed~~ [replied] with a sly grin. *Watch this."* Cruze reached inside the cockpit and touched a spot on the panel. Half of the ~~hanger~~ [hangar] wall in front of the ship instantly melted down.
> *"Hey! How'd you* ~~manidge~~ [manage] *to build that?"* Bandar shouted with excitement.

FIGURE 7.8

Sixth-Grader's Story — Showing Editing

CLASSROOM EXAMPLE

TEACHER: "We've been discussing quotation marks a bit lately. When we edit our finished drafts this week, let's pay particular attention to these marks. I suspect that most of you will need to be on the lookout for when you've used them and how you've used them, because most of you have been writing stories in which there's a fair amount of dialogue!

"One of your classmates has kindly given me permission to make a transparency of part of his story. Let's look at this part and proofread it, looking in particular for how he has used quotation marks."

[Teacher and students silently read the story shown on the transparency.]

TEACHER: "Okay, I know it's obvious one of your classmates has a real thriller going here, but let's tear our attention away from the melting hangar and check for his use of quotation marks! Yes, Chris?"

CHRIS: "In the very first sentence, where Bandar is talking, it should begin with quotation marks and — let's see — should end after *ship*."

TEACHER: "Right after the word or after the exclamation point?"

CHRIS: "After the exclamation point."

TEACHER: "Good! Okay, anyplace else where we should be concerned with quotation marks? Yes, Michon?"

MICHON: "In the third paragraph, he needs a mark after *think* and before *Watch*."

TEACHER: "Okay . . . exactly where should the mark go after *think* — after the word or . . ."
MICHON: "After the comma!"
TEACHER: [making change] "Right you are!"

And so it goes. In addition to discussing the placement of the quotation marks in relation to other punctuation, students point out where there are misspellings. The teacher makes the appropriate changes on the transparency. After complimenting the students on noticing other errors that good editing can catch, she reminds them that, for a while at least, they will need to pay particular attention to quotation marks. She underscores this point because quotation marks are a recent topic for her students, and she wants to make sure the students gain a feel for the use of them. This balancing of older and newer aspects of mechanics is a crucial part of teaching editing.

When you first begin teaching, or early in the school year, you may opt to model revision and editing in the above manner. This method allows you to involve the students while you are in control at the overhead projector. With time, however, and as your students become accustomed to writing, discussing, and conferencing, you can seat them in the "Author's Chair" for purposes of instruction. In the next section we will discuss how you can make this important accommodation.

Publishing and Sharing the Finished Work

The excitement — if not outright exhilaration — students feel when their work truly reaches and is appreciated by a larger audience is perhaps the best motivator for writing and inevitably for further growth in writing. The value of sharing work with other students in the classroom is inestimable, but the audience beyond the classroom will come to play a larger role as your writing program develops over the course of the year.

Early on in this chapter we discussed the "Author's Chair." This is the valued place in your classroom where in-progress works as well as published works may first be shared with the class as a whole or with a group. The Author's Chair will continue to be a preeminent place in the publishing and sharing phase of your writing program, but what are the more long-term possibilities for publishing completed work? Following is a partial list:

- Bulletin boards (featuring several students or an "author of the week")
- Books written by individual students or a group of students, which may be assigned reference numbers (e.g., Dewey Decimal System) by the librarian or media specialist (including books for primary students written and illustrated by intermediate students)
- Radio scripts, plays for actual performance, puppet shows
- Books written on specific topics that can be placed in waiting rooms in the community (Nathan, et al., 1989)

A highlight of your students' engagement in the writing process will be the students' sharing their writing with an audience. (© *Gale Zucker/Stock Boston*)

- Compositions read aloud by students in homes for the elderly and other institutions, then left for residents to read
- Classroom and/or school newspaper
- Book with pictures and illustrations of class field trips
- Writing contests sponsored by children's magazines, local newspapers, and television and radio stations

Several short-term publication possibilities exist as well, such as sending notes home, putting up schoolwide bulletin board displays, writing lyrics for original songs, and making greeting cards.

A marvelous way to celebrate the best of a semester's or of a whole year's publications (class, school, or districtwide) is through a *Young Authors Conference* (Millett, 1990). Students share their best published work in different categories through exhibits in a fairlike setting with booths and entertainment. The categories include fiction, nonfiction, poetry, and drama (including puppetry). Readings are held, as well as panel discussions. Awards may be given, but it is often best to award certificates of participation rather than first-, second-, and third-place ribbons.

Predictably, books remain one of the most popular formats for publication, in part because of their permanency. This is particularly true if the students' books are to be coded just like all the trade books in the media center and placed in their

Directions for Book Binding

Materials:

Heavy cardboard or covers from old books
White construction paper or typing paper
Large tapestry needle
Heavy-duty thread
Wallpaper, contact paper, or shelf paper (for cover)
Rubber cement
Colored construction paper (slightly smaller than cardboard covers)
Colored tape 1½″ wide

Procedures:

1. Fold sheets of either construction paper or typing paper in half to form pages of book. Trim to ½″ smaller than cardboard cover.
2. Sew sheets of paper together along fold as shown, using a back stitch.

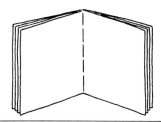

3. Cement cardboard to plain side of cover paper (wallpaper, contact paper, etc.) as shown, allowing ½″ between pieces and a 1″ border around the edge.

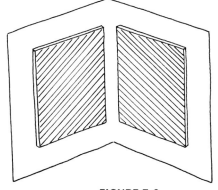

4. Cut out corners of cover paper. Fold in edges and cement them to cardboard. It might be better to fold top and bottom edges first, and side edges last, rather than folding in the sequence illustrated.

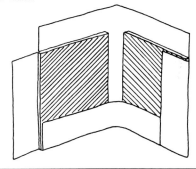

5. Position sewn book pages so that the fold is between the cardboard pieces. Use colored tape to attach the first page, at the folded edge, to inside front cover as shown. Tape the last pages to inside back cover in the same way.

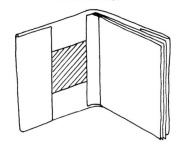

6. Cement colored construction paper to inside front and back covers to finish inside covers.
7. Reinforce outside spine of book with colored tape.

FIGURE 7.9

An Easy Way to Bind Students' Books

Source: Reproduced by permission of the publishers from Nessel, Denise D. and Jones, Margaret B., *The Language Experience Approach to Reading: A Handbook for Teachers.* (New York: Teachers College Press, © 1981 by Teachers College, Columbia University. All rights reserved.), pp. 157–159.

company on the shelves. There are many ways in which to bind books, and students may wish to experiment with different styles. Figure 7.9 illustrates a simple way of binding students' books that will stand the test of time (and many readers) quite well.

Using Journals

Journal writing has become a tremendously popular aspect of the total writing program, with good reason. A journal — usually a spiral-bound notebook —

provides students with a nonstructured and usually ungraded opportunity to write just about anything. Journals can become an effective and enlightening type of diary, providing students with a means of seeing themselves and how their thoughts unfold over time. When students — when any of us — read what we wrote two months ago, we confront what was really going on for us then. The impressions and ideas have not been recast in the light of subsequent experience; this is critical in coming to see ourselves more objectively and maturely. Journals can also function as a useful "learning log" in which students write down summaries of their observations in science, social studies, and mathematics.

Many teachers have come to realize that some guidelines for journal writing are usually necessary, since many children who simply are told every day to "write in your journals" will run out of stimulating ideas. There are a number of variations you may employ, but don't change emphases too frequently. For starters, you may need to model in a "think-aloud" format the type of writing one can do in a journal. In addition, you should write regularly in your own journal as well, because students will value what they see you valuing. Your writing may simply be a general listing of the anticipated highlights of the day, something more retrospective about yourself, or analytical notes about a student or two.

Occasionally ask the students to respond to something you have put on the board: a puzzler, an open question, a poem, an interesting trivia fact, or the like. In addition to responding to what they are reading (see below and Chapter 9), they can brainstorm possible topics for writing. Start a list that can be posted and added to throughout the year. For starters, you might consider the following possibilities (Atwell, 1987; Tchudi and Tchudi, 1984; Tompkins, 1990):

- Write about dreams you've had.
- Write as though you're a character in a book you're reading.
- Record observations about new places or people you've met.
- Write about something that may be worrying or bothering you.
- Write about how you thought about things when you were younger.
- Write to another student in class about whatever you've been reading.
- Write down favorite quotes.
- React to TV programs, movies, articles you've read.
- Write down conversations you've overheard.
- Make lists and categorize interesting words (see Chapter 10).

Dialogue Journals   In dialogue journals students write to their teacher about anything that interests them; the teacher then responds (Atwell, 1987; Fulwiler, 1987; Gambrell, 1985; Barone, 1989). In effect, the teacher has an ongoing conversation with each student. Among her many uses of dialogue journals, Barone found that students' responses to what they were reading in the dialogue journals was quite productive and insightful. She then responded to the students' responses; her responses most often reflected Atwell's objectives of *affirming, challenging,* or *extending* her children's thinking (Atwell, 1987). The following example is from a journal by Anna, a second-grader, as she was reading *Danny, the Champion of the World* (Dahl, 1975):

Dear Mrs. Barone,
My favorite part in the chapter was when he said, "What are we doing, playing twenty questions?" I liked it because I thought that it was a very brave thing to do.
Your student,
Anna

Dear Anna,
I agree. It was a very brave thing for them to do. The keeper must have been very surprised by their questions.
Mrs. Barone

(Barone, 1989, p. 89)

Barone adapted a form used initially in college writing courses (Berthoff, 1981) for use in primary students' dialogue journals. Referred to as the *Double Entry Draft* (DED), this adaptation also tapped students' responses to what they were reading. On the left side of the page, they would write down a sentence or phrase from whatever book they were reading that particularly engaged, puzzled, or delighted them. On the right-hand side of the page they would write their response, and the teacher would write her response below. Following is an example of a DED from Sarah, a third-grader who was reading *Ramona Quimby, Age 8:*

Sunday morning Ramona and Beezus were still resolved to be perfect until dinner time.	I know why they were trying to do that. They didn't want to make dinner. Don't you think Ramona and Beezus are a little tricky?

[Teacher's comment: I think they are a lot tricky. I wonder if they will get out of cooking dinner.] (Barone, 1989, p. 90)

Many teachers have students write in their journals first thing each day. In the meantime the teacher can write briefly in his or her own journal, and then turn attention to "housekeeping" duties such as collecting lunch money, book club orders, permission slips for the field trip, and so forth.

In summary, journals can be an extremely effective way of getting students to write, generating ideas for types of writing, and keeping them writing. They can connect students and teachers through important and meaningful dialogue. A good many topics may first surface in journals! As we'll see later on in this chapter, journals can be part of writing and learning across different areas of the elementary curriculum.

Applying the Process: Different Purposes, Different Forms

When you first begin writing instruction, your main concern will be finding ways to get the students to write. The thinking aloud illustrated earlier in the chapter, in which the teacher modeled how to identify topics to write about, is one of the most effective. It will usually result in *expressive* writing, which allows students to get the feel of writing. In first and second grade this may be the only type that concerns you, but eventually you should entice your students to try other kinds of writing. Our next goal is to involve students in trying out simple narrative and expository styles, and eventually fine-tuning each of these.

Teaching Expository Writing

After you have pulled students into the swing of writing during the first few weeks of the school year, you can move to simple expository writing. In the past this has usually meant writing a "report" — quite likely about a topic in which students have little if any interest. However, if you make a point of tapping into their existing interests and if you provide them with clearcut purposes, some first- and second-graders can generate expository writing early in the year, and most students from third grade on can definitely create it on a regular basis.

Guidelines for Generating
Major Types of Expository Writing

Students will be exploring the three major types of transactional writing: *description, exposition,* and *persuasion.* The process of composing (not surprisingly) does not significantly differ among these forms, but what the writer focuses on and how the writer organizes and presents the information does change. Remember, of course, that students have been reading and listening to examples of these types of writing all along; now they'll attempt to generate them themselves.

Description

1. Description is such a basic component of writing it is often taken for granted, but its purpose is quite important — it helps the reader construct the appropriate picture or idea. The words must be as precise and fitting as the writer can make them. To initiate descriptive writing, generate lists of objects, events, or people to describe. Usually these ideas come from the writing that you are already doing. Then tap into your senses: vision, hearing, touch, taste, smell. Anything can be described well, regardless of how important or trivial it may appear.

2. Brainstorm/cluster whatever words and phrases come to mind as you think about what you wish to describe. Be as free and crazy as you want, because by exaggerating you are more likely to capture the real sense of what you're describing. Remember to call upon all your senses; if you are describing how something looks, think also about how it feels to the touch. If you are describing a place, think about the smells in the air when you were there, how the air felt on your skin, and so forth.

3. You're ready to write!

Exposition

1. What do you want to explain — how to do something or why a situation has come to be or an event has happened? (For example, what are the steps to

follow in making and launching a model rocket? Why does your mother never believe you when you really *are* telling the truth? How did the jam get all over your sister's new shoes?)

2. When you have decided what you want to explain, brainstorm or cluster whatever comes to mind about the "how" or "why." Don't worry about the order of things yet — that will come in the next step.

3. Now decide the order in which you are going to explain your idea.

4. You're ready to write! Remember that your reader may not have much background information about your topic, so you will want to avoid gaps in your explanation. When you finish your draft, make sure your sentences and paragraphs clearly relate to each other.

Persuasion

1. What do you want to have happen or be accomplished that will require agreement and maybe participation from other people? (For example, do you want to stay up later than usual? get more for an allowance? be allowed to ride your bike on busy streets? Do you want to raise money for a special project?)

2. Brainstorm or cluster reasons for supporting your request.

3. Now put your reasons in order, from strongest to weakest, or vice versa.

4. Select one or two reasons and try them out with a partner. In the process, write down any additional evidence — details and examples — that you could use to support your argument.

5. You're ready to write! Keep your audience in mind, because this will help you select the appropriate wording to convince them. For example, is formal, polite language more appropriate, or informal and chatty language?

Unlike simple story structure with a clear beginning, middle, and end, expository writing offers the challenge of determining how ideas are ordered and related. Quite simply, apart from reading expository texts for models, students need to be shown how to plan for, identify, and organize their information. The key to teaching expository writing is to balance effectively the demands of the task so that they do not overwhelm the students. It is extremely unwise to begin instruction on "reports" by teaching the use of reference materials, organization of bibliographic information, outlining, organization of the writing, and so forth all at once. Rather, we begin with the students' interests and address one aspect at a time.

Keep in mind that for many students you may wish to have oral presentation of reports precede the written presentation. Regardless, the steps in preparation are quite similar. In each of the progressively more "abstract" steps below — from the self, to others, to print resources — notice how the writing process is at work.

A Three-Step Process

The Student as "Expert"   Whether you are dealing with primary or intermediate grade students, when you first undertake the writing of a composition that is meant to inform the reader, writing experts suggest beginning with the students' domain of expertise (Beach, 1983; Graves, 1983). The use of reference materials can come later. Here's how you may go about it (adapted from Harste, Short, and Woodward, 1989):

1. Distribute several slips of paper or tagboard slips to each student.
2. Tell your students that they are all "experts" in something. Ask them to think about one thing that they are an expert in and to write it on one slip of paper.
3. Next, tell them to think of other things or ideas that relate to their area of expertise (this may be a good time to teach this word because it's related to *expert;* see Chapter 10). They write each related idea on a separate piece of paper; each will be a "heading" or "main idea" for the area of expertise.
4. Ask the students to write on the other cards ideas and information that will elaborate on their headings — one piece of information on a card.
5. The students then arrange the cards sequentially. This ordering may change, and in fact you may wish to encourage them to try different orderings until they feel pretty good about one.
6. Using the cards as organizational "handles," the students can then write about their area of expertise. The "reports" need not be long; one or two pages will do nicely at first. The development of these compositions can follow the drafting/revision/editing phases of the writing process.

Figure 7.10 shows one "expert's" arrangement of her cards.

The notion of "expert," by the way, is a productive concept. Students enjoy being considered an expert in something, and may not want to rest on their laurels but continue to pursue a particular area of interest extensively throughout the year. This desire for more knowledge will lead them, as we will see in the next two chapters, into extensive reading in a variety of texts.

Using Other Resources: Interviews   Once they use the "expert" strategy, students are on their way to developing an understanding of the organization of this type of transactional writing. You can now add another aspect: the collection of information. Collecting information involves making decisions about what is relevant and important and then relating that information. When the students are working from print resources, you have the additional responsibility of helping them learn how to use these resources as well as understanding about direct copying (adults of course call this *plagiarism*!).

An excellent way to help students focus on collecting and gathering information without having to use print resources yet is to rely on *interviews* as a source (Haley-James and Hobson, 1980; Wiggington, 1971). In fact, Eliot Wiggington's *Foxfire* books provide probably the best example not only of interviewing techniques but of an entire curriculum based on such information sources. Following is a suggested plan for such prewriting and drafting:

1. Discuss with students that they are going to be writing an informational composition, but that instead of using themselves as experts, they are going to be

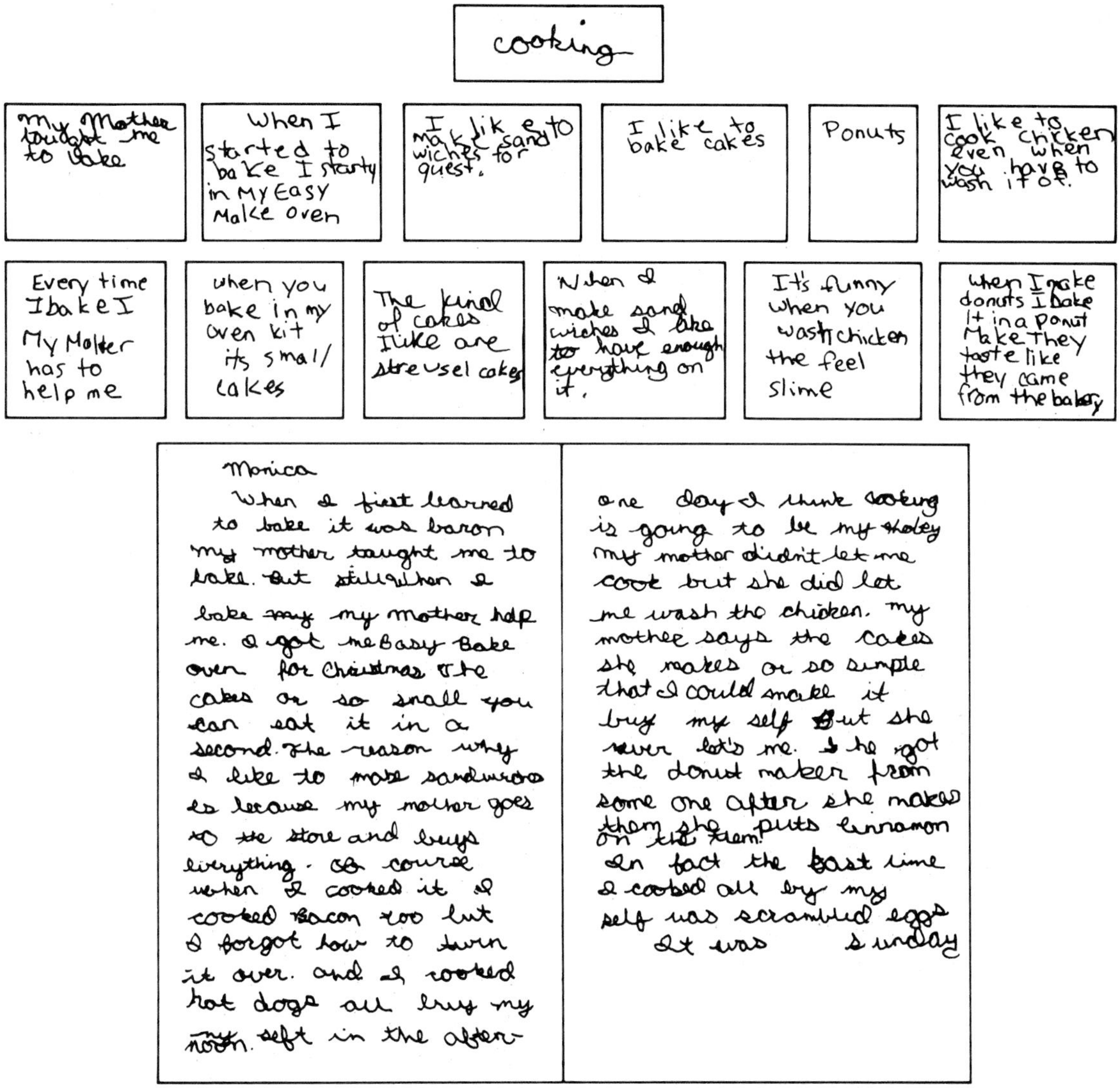

cooking

my Mother taught me to bake	When I started to bake I starty in My Easy Malke oven	I like to make sandwiches for quest.	I like to bake cakes	Ponuts	I like to cook chicken even when you have to wash it off.
Every time I bake I My Molter has to help me	when you bake in my oven kit its small cakes	The kind of cakes I like are streusel cakes	When I make sand wiches I like to have enough everything on it.	It's funny when you wash chicken the feel slime	when I make donuts I bake It in a ponut Make They taste like they came from the bakery

Monica

When I first learned to bake it was baron my mother taught me to bake. But still when I bake my ~~my~~ my mother help me. I got me Easy Bake oven for Christmas the cakes or so small you can eat it in a second. The reason why I like to make sandwichs is because my mother goes to the store and buys everything. Of course when I cooked it I cooked Bacon too but I forgot how to turn it over. and I cooked hot dogs all buy my ~~with~~ self in the after

one day I think cooking is going to be my ~~shofey~~ my mother didn't let me cook but she did let me wash the chicken. my mother says the cakes she makes or so simple that I could make it buy my self But she never let's me. I he got the donut maker from some one after she makes ~~them she them~~ puts cinnamon on it In fact the last time I cooked all by my self was scrambled eggs It was Sunday

FIGURE 7.10

Using Cards to Organize Expository Writing

Source: Fig. CC12.1, "Notes and Article Using Generating Written Discourse," Jerome C. Harste and Kathy G. Short, *Creating Classrooms for Authors*, p. 271. Reproduced by permission of Heinemann Educational Books, Inc., Portsmouth, NH.

interviewing other experts on a particular topic. These interviews are going to be conducted outside of school, so practice in conducting the interview and taking notes is probably advisable first!

2. Have students brainstorm different topics that they could write about after interviewing someone. Just as with the "self-as-expert" prewriting, they will write topics and related ideas on separate pieces of paper. The difference is that the paper is regular size, and they will put the idea at the top.

3. On each separate sheet of paper, students will list what they already know about that particular idea. Later, they will list questions for each idea that represent what they do not know but would like to know. These questions will then be pared down to become the interview questions.

4. Students then conduct their interviews, taping them if possible, and then transpose the information from their interviews onto their separate sheets. They organize the sheets sequentially and compose the report, again following the writing process for drafting, revising, and editing.

Using Other Resources: Print Material   The next step in this progression is the use of *print material* as resources. You must have plenty of books on hand in the classroom. The interview strategy will then be modified as follows:

1. After the students write ideas on separate pieces of paper, the questions they ask will represent what they don't know but would like to find out. They now have a purpose for delving into the books for information.

2. At this stage, students will often think that every bit of information that might answer their questions is important and should be written down; here copying could be a problem. Burrows, et al. (1939) offered an excellent suggestion for avoiding this: students may copy specific data and facts, for example — such as the average rainfall in their state — and note the page and book where they found that information, but as for other information, no such direct copying is advised. Instead, students should write down only the page number and source next to their question so they know where to go to find the material again. They will not only save time but learn how to paraphrase, because they'll remember the information but not the exact wording.

3. Once again, they organize the information and draft the writing. The use of print resources will be taught and reinforced throughout the intermediate grades, and students will become increasingly knowledgeable about where to go for what types of information. How to read these books effectively is addressed in Chapter 9.

Teaching Narrative Writing: Stories

Children readily understand story structure or grammar, but as Applebee discussed (1978; see Chapter 6), the expansion and elaboration of the structure and the elements of the structure can be quite complex. The primary grades lay groundwork for these story elements: plot (what happened?), setting (where did it happen?), and characterization (what were the characters like?). *Plot* is subdivided into *problem,* whatever the characters must deal with; *tension,* the point in the story where there is the greatest climax; and *resolution,* the solution to the problem.

Although we hear from authors who write stories that they often do not truly know how their story is going to turn out, we would probably be wise to help students initially to be somewhat more specific. They can be led to grasp the characters, the overall sequence of events, the problem that will be addressed, and the

The Writing Process
How to Write a Personal Narrative

Step 1: Prewriting—Choose a Topic

Robin made a list of some of the things she had done. Then she thought about her list.

Trying out for a play — She had done this recently, so she remembered a lot.

My trip to England — This might be too long, but she might want to write about just one part.

Taking the train to Mom's work — This was interesting, but not much happened.

Being in the hospital — This was also too long.

Moving to our new house — She had really enjoyed this.

Robin circled *moving* on her list.

On Your Own

1. **Think and discuss** Make a list of some things that you have done. Use the Ideas page to help you. Discuss your ideas with a partner.
2. **Choose** Ask yourself these questions about each of your topics.
   Would this make an interesting story to write and read?
   Do I remember enough details to hold a reader's interest?
   Would this story be too long? too short?
   Circle the topic you want to write about.
3. **Explore** What will you write? Do one of the activities under "Exploring Your Topic" on the Ideas page.

Ideas for Getting Started

Choosing Your Topic

Topic Ideas

My first try at ——
My favorite mud story
A race to remember
The art contest
The shopping trip
The camping trip
My best birthday
Spring cleaning day
The new baby

Brainstorm and Cluster

Brainstorm ideas for a story. Think of experiences you've had. Jot them down in any order. Let your mind roam freely. Do not screen out ideas.

Use **clustering** to think of ideas. In the middle of your paper, write a word, like *water*, and circle it. What word comes to mind when you think of experiences you've had with water? Write the word, circle it, and join it to the previous word, using an arrow. Keep going.

Exploring Your Topic

Beginnings

How will you grab your reader's interest? Don't write one beginning —write three! Pick your favorite for your first draft. Here are Robin's:

We moved into our house in winter.
Moving to our house was a disaster.
Nothing went well on moving day.

Talk About It

Have a friend interview you about your story. What parts did your friend like best? What would your friend like to know more about?

FIGURE 7.11

The Prewriting Phase of Story Writing, as Presented in a Textbook for Sixth-Graders
Source: From *Houghton Mifflin English,* Level 5. Copyright © 1990 by Houghton Mifflin Company. Reprinted by permission of Houghton Mifflin Company.

resolution that might occur. After modeling how to brainstorm and list these aspects, you can provide a "thinksheet" for students to use in planning the following: where the story will take place (*setting*); who the characters will be; what the *goal* will be; what problems the main character will encounter; and how the story will end. Figure 7.11 illustrates how a textbook for sixth-graders presents this prewriting phase for story writing.

As we will see in the next chapter, reading and talking about stories are the activities that best motivate children to create their own stories. By writing their own stories, children in turn can become sensitive to the elements of narrative structure and better able to comprehend and benefit from the structure and content of narratives that they read.

The elaboration of Applebee's developmental phases will occur as children continue to read and have read to them engaging stories. The *organization* of story writing is one aspect that you will be able to teach most directly (see Chapter 8); the following suggestions will help you more generally nurture students' development.

1. As students listen to stories in kindergarten and first grade — often in the Directed Listening-Thinking Activity (DLTA) format (see Chapter 5) — they will be developing a "sense of story." Although their command of the writing basics is not yet developed to the point that they can write a lengthy narrative on their own, they *are* capable of dictating such a story. After listening to fairy tales or folk tales, for example, the students can compose their own tale together, by dictating it to the teacher. This dictated composition can entail more than one sitting and can undergo revision as the children hear it reread each time.

2. You may develop a literature unit (see Chapter 9) around a particular story element, reading aloud stories that represent excellent examples of that element. Discuss with the students how the author develops the element; this reinforces the issues you are discussing in writing conferences (and reading conferences; see Chapter 8).

3. After intermediate students have been composing narratives for a while, experimenting with elements, and in some cases sticking with the same type of subject for an inordinate amount of time (as, for example, in writing about a particular cartoon character or characters), stretch them by pointing out and perhaps teaching lessons on the following aspects of writing good stories:

   a. They should write what they know — what they have themselves experienced. As Atwell (1987) reminded her middle grade students, most authors' first published novels are autobiographical.

   b. They should create one main character and develop him or her.

   c. They should keep to the same point of view to develop a consistent "voice": third person, for example, or first person.

   d. They should experiment with different leads (Atwell, 1987). Stories can begin with action (a character doing something), with dialogue, or with reaction (a character thinking about something).

Teaching Narrative Writing: Poetry

In Chapter 2 I mentioned that young children's developing language has often been characterized as poetic. Children naturally play with sounds and words in the preschool years and delight in doing so. In the elementary grades, we can sustain this delight and interest by developing an environment in which children continue to play with words (Geller, 1985). Such a context nurtures the type of reflection and sensitivity to language that poetry can tap. We'll explore this environment in Chapter 10; here we'll turn our attention to the motivation for poetry writing and the manipulation of language — the "poet's paint" (Heard, 1989).

Poetry turns a very special lens on the world, making the ordinary special and, oftentimes, the special ordinary. Appropriately presented, it can inspire in children singular reflection on the way things are, on themselves and other people, and on language. "Poems," Georgia Heard points out, "come from something deeply felt" (Heard, 1989, p. 14). Specifically, poetry focuses on whatever causes us to feel "something *move* inside" (Heard, 1989) and on the language that best creates the images, and expresses them precisely and rhythmically. "Poetry does not spring from satisfaction with things as they are but rather from our doubts and desires and fears. It searches out new possibilities; it would change things" (Rouse, 1983, p. 713).

Poetry grows naturally out of whatever you may be studying: sea chanteys, for example, when you focus on the sea, and *haiku* for natural science. In such contexts children can most easily and readily appreciate poetry. In this section I will focus on ways of beginning poetry writing and explore some common yet effective forms that elementary children can learn and use.

Getting the Poetry Going

Poets who teach how to write poetry suggest the following basic guidelines for getting going (Heard, 1989):

1. Start by reading poetry to the students and having them read poetry. In the next two chapters I will be emphasizing reading to students of all ages; this is as true for poetry as for any other form.
2. Tell students that poets can write about anything — not just the "flowers and love" that so many students believe is the only stuff of poetry. They can write about things they've worried about, thought about, and know a lot about, their family, their memories. You may find that emphasizing big issues — things of real consequence and concern to them — is most productive.
3. When you wish the students to write, have them first close their eyes for a minute or two and focus on the mental image that their topic suggests — then begin.

Don't feel that you must know a lot about poetry or be a poet to motivate and keep your students writing poetry. Tell the students you're learning right along with them, and think aloud for them as you model how you generate ideas, begin writing, revise, and so forth.

"Structured" Formats

Many children are in fact more freed up to write poetry if they are given a structure or format. Poetry teachers often differ sharply on this issue, but you may find it easier to move some children into poetry writing by trying out different structures. Let's consider some of the more effective formats.

Collaborative Poetry   Collaborative composition of poetry is a very effective way to begin to develop an appreciation of and interest in poetry. The students together, as a whole class or within smaller groups, compose a poem. Two such possibilities are offered here.

1. *Transforming prose into poetry.*   The very form of poetry does things to language. Ordinary prose recast in poetic form can acquire an extraordinary or singular sense. Jennifer's following descriptive piece on "Change" was recast into the form of a poem as a result of a discussion by a group of third grade children:

> *People can change*
> *in many ways.*
> *Children change their size*
> *as they grow older.*
> *When the seasons change*
> *the temperature changes.*
> *Green grass changes*
> *to brown*
> *in very hot or cold weather.*
> *Pumpkins change*
> *to happy, mean, monstrous,*
> *and funny jack-o-lanterns.*
> *Snow changes*
> *to water*
> *And lava changes*
> *to rock.*
>
> *We can see many changes*
> *All around us.*

Jennifer's original composition was certainly a thoughtful piece as it stood. However, through experimenting with changing the structure — breaking up the linearity of the sentences — the children realized that images and ideas were somehow highlighted even more. They realized that as readers they focused on the individual images because now they stood out, and that the final sentence — Jennifer agreed — became much more final and forceful when set apart in the poem.

2. *"Original" collaboration.*   Students agree on what content they want in each line of a poem, and they each compose a line on their own. For example, they may decide they want to include a sports figure, a food, and a type of clothing in each line, and that each line should begin with "I would never ..." After the students have been given time to compose their lines on separate slips of paper, the slips are collected and selected at random to assemble into a poem. A class of fifth-graders composed the following poem this way:

> *I would never be Bo Jackson eating broccoli wearing Spandex*
> *shorts*

I would never wear sweaters with cheese and a picture of
Michael Jordan on them
I would never try always to play Steffi Graf after eating
burritos in my pajamas

And so it goes. Silliness, perhaps, but once the lines are assembled, students are often impressed by the structural and thematic patterns that emerge. For students it is a short step from the excitement of group composition to the motivation to write their own poems. Philip Lopate (1975) suggested a variation on the above format, with more structure in terms of content. Children can assume the personality of someone else — for example, an elderly woman — and each child can offer a line as it may be spoken by her.

Repetitive Beginnings   An extremely popular strategy for helping students to generate original poetry was first explored by Kenneth Koch and described in a book that has since become a classic: *Wishes, Lies, and Dreams: Teaching Children to Write Poetry* (1970). Koch encouraged children to create their own poems, using the same "stem" for each line in the poem. For example, he originated the "I wish" poem format, now well known. This superficially simple beginning proved to be quite powerful in eliciting poetry from children. Why? Koch suggested that "I wish" was a simple phrase that all children have used frequently and easily; it was not "unusual," as the language of poetry often appears to be to elementary children. In addition, the simple repetition is engaging, providing its own structure without insisting on rhythm and rhyme, which children also too often believe is characteristic of all "good" poetry. Note how the following poem by a fifth-grader establishes its own "feel" through the repetition:

I wish I were someone with money and happy
I wish that all people were bluish and fun
I wish I could do math without any thinking
I wish I could fly and leave math far behind.

Other similar formats that release children's thinking and serve to motivate them are "I used to . . . /But now . . ." and "I used to think . . . /But now I know . . ."

Incidentally, an interesting but important twist to Koch's experiments with poetry was his use of Spanish words and the way he encouraged children to think about them. He chose Spanish because so many of the students in the New York school in which he worked were Spanish-speaking, although they all did know English. He realized two objectives: (1) the Spanish-speaking students were thrilled to have their language included and valued; and (2) the native English-speaking students were intrigued by the sounds and images of the unfamiliar words. For the latter type of student, Koch probed for what colors and moods the words suggested and encouraged the students to use the words in their own poems, even though they might be uncertain about the meaning.

Cinquains (pronounced "SIN kanes") A *cinquain* is a five-lined poem (from the French word for five, *cinq*). The formula for a cinquain not only produces an engaging poem, but perhaps more important, it directly channels children's attention and observation and helps them choose with more precision the words that best evoke the images they are striving to represent. Here's the formula for a cinquain:

Noun	(the title)
adjective, adjective	(describing the title)
three-words expressing action	
four words expressing feeling	
Noun	(repeating the title or giving another word related to it)

Here's the formula put into action by a sixth-grader:

Worry
scary, tight
writing, guessing, erasing,
hoping, fearing, risking, uncertain
Test!

Diamantes (pronounced "DEE uh MAHN tays") *Diamantes* are a variation on cinquains. Named after their "diamond" shape, they can tell a story or contrast two concepts, and may be introduced when children have a good concept of and enjoy working with cinquains. Here is the format:

Noun	
adjective, adjective	
three participles	
four nouns having to do with the subject	
three participles	
adjective, adjective	
Noun	(usually opposite of the first noun)

The diagonal in the third line indicates the point at which the contrast begins, as the following diamante illustrates:

Desert
sandy, windy
baking, hardening, drying
coyotes, cacti, rattlesnakes, yucca
rising, cooling, changing
fresh, crisp
Mountains

Haiku   *Haiku* is a fascinating form not only because of what it accomplishes but because of its application to English. Its rather rigid structure, adhering to certain numbers of syllables in each of the three lines, springs from the nature of the Japanese language, in which syllables correspond more straightforwardly to morphemes than in English. Nonetheless, applying the form to English gives striking results. *Haiku* is not meant to be abstract or necessarily symbolic but as concrete as possible, focusing awareness on only one thing or action — thus attempting to capture its essence.

The traditional structure of *haiku* is as follows: first line = five syllables; second line = seven syllables; third line = five syllables. It is also perfectly fine not to focus on the number of syllables in each line but simply to capture an impression in three lines, while keeping the effective visual form of haiku. Two examples of *haiku* by fifth-graders appear below; the first follows the syllable format and the second does not.

Baseball won't be hit
comes too fast you'll swing and miss
Strike out sit and watch.

The cat hunches
Scrunches and twitches
Grasshopper gone.

Now that we have observed a few of the ways in which students can begin to generate poetry, I'd like to mention a concern that some educators share. The strict format of cinquains and *haiku* — not to mention the rhythm and meter of other verse forms — is precisely what can stifle children's attempts at poetry or at best lead to "poetry by formula." This worry is justified if teachers rigidly insist on adherence to a format and discourage experimentation. But what about the kind of classroom that we have been considering all along, in which you are not going to be this type of teacher? Will you inadvertently be stifling creativity? Probably not. In fact, many children seem to want this type of guideline at first; it gives them a place from which to start. Your objective is to "hook" the children on the writing, and you can later address reliance on one or two formulas — if this even in fact becomes a concern in your class.

Revising Poetry

When poets revise, the following strategies work well (Heard, 1989):

- Have someone else read your poem to you.
- Put the poem away for a while until it feels new when you read it again.
- "Try memorizing your poem, then reciting it. Places that are unclear, or that you can't remember, usually need attention" (Heard, p. 51).
- Reorganize by switching lines around, and experiment with line breaks.

- Write "tired" words in the margin and brainstorm other words and/or use the thesaurus.

■ Build Your Teaching Resources

Teaching Poetry to Children

The following list contains titles that are excellent resources for you to have as you begin to expand your background in teaching poetry:

Carpenter, J. (1986). *Creating the world: Poetry, art and children.* Seattle: University of Washington Press.

Collom, J. (1985). *Moving windows: Evaluating the poetry that children write.* New York: Teachers and Writers Collaborative.

Hopkins, L. (1987). *Pass the poetry, please.* New York: Harper and Row Junior Books.

Koch, K. (1970). *Wishes, lies, and dreams: Teaching children to write poetry.* New York: Harper and Row.

For an interesting and dissenting critique of Koch's approach, see Myra Cohn Livingston's "But is it poetry?" in two issues of *The Horn Book:* December 1975, 571–580, and February 1976, 24–31.

Koch, K. (1974). *Rose, where did you get that red? Teaching great poetry to children.* New York: Random House.

Mathews, D. (ed.). (1981). *Producing award-winning student poets: Tips from successful teachers.* Urbana, IL: National Council of Teachers of English.

More excellent annotated references addressing the teaching of poetry to children may be found in:

Stewig, J. (1988). *Children and literature.* Boston: Houghton Mifflin.

Expository and Narrative Writing Across the Curriculum

Temple observed that "to limit the content of the writing program to personal, out-of-school experiences is to pass up the great contribution writing can make toward sharpening our powers of observation and deepening our powers of reflection, especially as they relate to the natural, the social, and the cultural world — in other words, as they relate to the content of the school curriculum" (Nathan, Temple, Juntunen, and Temple, 1989, p. 124). Writing has the potential to integrate learning across different areas of subject matter, as well as to explore the many avenues of learning within a particular subject matter. It can help students understand that curriculum exists in important and significant ways beyond textbooks.

Journals, for example, can become "learning logs" as students summarize, list, or describe in their own words what they have learned as the result of a particular learning experience (Fulwiler, 1987; Tchudi and Tchudi, 1983). Ongoing observations in science, a written description of a procedure or process in math, original word problems — all of these may be included as a meaningful part of learning log writing. The role of writing in learning can be very effectively illustrated, for example, when students undertake a project wherein they collect oral histories, hear and read good children's literature, and write in response to these models. We will explore this world beyond the textbook in greater depth in Chapter 9. For the moment, I'll offer the following as a partial list of writing possibilities that you can use in just about any curricular area:

Autobiography

Biography

Editorials

Personal letter

Formal letter

Report writing (different subject matter areas)

Invitations

Letters to important individuals

Record keeping

Letters requesting information and/or free materials

Minutes of a meeting

Book reports (or reviews)

Filling out forms

Diary

News story (sports, social/political events)

Essay

Evaluating Written Composition

We will be investigating evaluation in writing and reading in Chapter 12, but here are a few points that I'd like you to keep in mind until then. The very first question that should occur to you when you think of evaluation in writing is "Evaluation for *what*?" What you evaluate — as well as how and when you evaluate — depends on your purpose.

In the context of your classroom, two types of evaluation will concern you: *self-evaluation* by each student and *teacher evaluation*. Self-evaluation occurs as each student revises and proofreads a piece of his or her own writing, usually working from questions you have provided. Items not checked signal the student to attend to that particular aspect of the writing. Self-evaluation can also occur as students respond in pairs and in small response groups to one another's writing. For most students this type of self-monitoring or peer-monitoring of progress can be quite effective: once these students are aware of what they need to work on, they can attend specifically to those aspects. For other students, you will need to address specific areas of need in teacher/student conferences. At first or perhaps for a while they will need your guidance in learning to monitor themselves.

Your evaluation of students is the delicate and challenging issue. When the objective is to assign a grade for a report card that must include one, there is no easy technique. Any time the individual who is offering support, guidance, and understanding is also doing the bottom-line evaluation, there is potential for conflict and discomfort, and you should recognize this (see Chapter 12). Even if you must give a letter grade, however, your primary evaluation of your students' writing should focus not on that grade but rather on the development and growth that you observe in a number of areas.

You should be sensitive to two aspects of your students' growth in writing: (1) their progress in applying the process of writing and (2) the content and form of their products — their completed compositions. You should discuss both aspects with your students and make sure they are quite clear about what will be evaluated and what the criteria will be. In grades one and two, your evaluation will emphasize primarily the process. When children are in what we termed in Chapter 6 the *transitional* stage of reading and writing development, all phases of the writing process will be addressed. When you evaluate the process by which children write, you attend broadly to how they go about selecting ideas for writing, how they approach the writing and stick with it, and if they are beyond the beginning conventional literacy stage, how they go about revising and editing. In grades three through six, your evaluation will emphasize both process and product.

Organizing the Classroom for Writing

In Chapter 4, you saw a host of writing activities in action. How can you set the stage for these activities in your classroom?

Eventually, purposeful writing will be going on every day in your classroom. You may feel more comfortable starting out with two or three days a week for writing time, or in one subject area. Even experienced teachers who have not done much writing in their classrooms seem to prefer some type of transition time before fully implementing a daily writing curriculum.

Planning the Writing Time

As I noted earlier, it is usually easier to get primary students to write than it is intermediate students. If you teach at the intermediate level, you will probably need to make a careful transition to writing with your students, because often they will not be used to the kind of writing curriculum you are going to implement. At first your major objective will be getting your students "freed up" to write. Importantly, the emphasis from the outset for both primary and intermediate levels should be on keeping the writing atmosphere and expectations fun and nonthreatening.

As you plan your time for writing, keep in mind that no one plan works best for all students all the time. Whatever organizational plan you choose, however, you should stay with it for a while — so long as it seems to be working. Your designated writing periods may be combined with reading instruction, alternated with it, or held just before or just after reading time (see Chapter 4). A common framework for writing time is: (1) stimulus/discussion or "mini-lesson"; (2) sustained writing; (3) conferences, both formal and informal; and (4) sharing of writing. The time allotted to each activity will vary. Within your schedule, you also will have the opportunity to provide mini-lessons as needed.

During sustained writing, it is important that *you* write as well, at least for the first several minutes. Yes, I know — it seems like such an excellent opportunity to review students' work and so forth, but the students need to see you purposefully engaged in writing. Remember, if you wish, you can use your own developing draft to model the different steps in the writing process.

You should discuss your organizational plan with the students so that they are clear about your expectations and their own responsibilities. Students should also know that they may work on a writing project at other times of the day, during free time or when other work such as a math assignment is finished.

Materials and Physical Space

There should be at least one centralized location for writing materials and, if possible, several places around the room that store necessary supplies. Each location should include the following: pencils and pens, magic markers, crayons, scissors, stapler and staple remover, plenty of paper — both rough-draft quality and "good" quality. Many teachers have discovered the value and popularity of another writing center implement: the "DRAFT" or "WORK IN PROGRESS!" stamp. Stamped at the top of a composition, this message clearly indicates to students (and parents!) that a particular composition is not a finished product.

A writing center should also be a place where students' writing folders — an important feature of your writing program — are kept. Writing folders answer the question of how you and your students will keep track of all those drafts and completed manuscripts we've been referring to throughout the chapter. You may keep one or two folders for each student; I prefer to keep two folders, one for completed drafts (published and unpublished, filed oldest to newest) and one with current ongoing work. In the latter folder students can also keep a list of possible ideas or topics. You may wish to include your evaluations in this folder as well — as, for example, when you've observed a student correctly using quotation marks and you write this observation on a small gummed label, which will later be affixed to the inside cover of the folder or to an evaluation sheet for the student to see. Journals and learning logs may also be stored at this location.

Microcomputers, Word Processing, and Writing

As we saw in Chapter 1, microcomputers are making inroads in the schools. In the language arts, their promise at the present time and in the near future is primarily in the area of writing, or *word processing*.

In the third edition of his classic work *On Writing Well*, William Zinsser begins his chapter on writing with a word processor by making the following observation: "There's nobody more filled with anxiety than a writer who has been told that he should start writing with a word processor . . . And there's nobody more evangelistic than a writer who has made the leap" (Zinsser, 1985, p. 205). I'll try to avoid being evangelistic, but I would like to add a personal note before we consider microcomputers and their role in writing in the elementary classroom: this book has been written entirely on a microcomputer and the feedback from my editor has been on floppy disk, which has allowed us to correspond on-line as we have revised each chapter. The computer has made all phases of my writing process — drafting, revising, and editing — more efficient.

Microcomputers can be a great aid to children who are learning to write — especially as they revise and edit their first drafts. *(© Spencer Grant/The Picture Cube)*

I've offered one more testimonial for the value of microcomputers and word processing in adults' writing, but what do we know about children, microcomputers, and writing? The research in this area is still quite new. This is because microcomputers themselves are fairly new, their availability in schools is fairly limited, and when they are available, teachers are often reluctant to use them. In those situations in which microcomputers have been used in written composition, though, three fundamental observations consistently seem to emerge: (1) the social context in which computer use occurs may significantly affect children's awareness of their writing and how it communicates with an audience; (2) in the early stages of computer use, motivation to write can be enhanced; and (3) revising and editing can become easier and perhaps more effective on the microcomputer than on paper.

At present, most elementary schools locate their microcomputers in labs, and individual classes come in to use them at scheduled times during the week. Some individual classrooms have at most one or two micros. Given these limitations, how can you make the best use of the access you and your students do have?

At first, it's most practical to have students prepare handwritten drafts before going to the computer. This will save time, since beginning writers are more fluent on paper. When the draft is displayed on the screen or printed out, its different appearance often leads students to notice parts to revise. Quite often students realize they wish to make changes as they are typing the draft into the computer.

Although we do not yet know how the ability to delete, add, and move blocks of text around may facilitate writing among elementary students, we at least know that word processing makes the simple aspects of editing easier for children. And research does suggest that it isn't so important to spend time on keyboarding in the elementary grades. Rather than separately learning the layout of the keyboard and practicing the keystrokes for different letters, students are better off becoming keyboard literate through the "hunt and peck" method. Spending valuable computer time on keyboarding is the equivalent of trying to teach excellent penmanship before allowing children to compose their own written texts.

An almost unavoidable aspect of word processing in schools is its public nature — it's nearly impossible for children not to notice one another's writing on the screen. Most of the time this is not a problem — just another example of the social nature of writing in the classroom. As students become more familiar with conferencing and questioning, you will notice these activities going on around the computer.

If you have at least one computer in your classroom, you can take advantage of some special features that facilitate writing. For example, some programs include an electronic mail system such as the "Mailbag" feature in QUILL (Rubin and Bruce, 1984) and through the Minnesota Educational Computing Consortium (MECC). Electronic mail allows students not only to write and access messages within the classroom and school but between schools, states, and even countries. "E-mail" allows penpals across the country or on different continents to communicate within hours rather than days or weeks.

An additional word about the eventual role of computers in writing: they will continue to be extremely helpful, but they will not replace pen and paper. For some time to come, and for many reasons, handwritten communication will continue. A widespread "etiquette" in our written communication somehow demands this. For example, thank-you notes, sympathy cards, and so forth should not be run off on a printer; they should be handwritten as neatly as the writer can manage.

A CONCLUDING PERSPECTIVE

Writing is a developmental phenomenon in which, over a period of many years, children move from basic understanding of the differences between written and spoken language through a more elaborate unfolding of abilities, knowledge, and feelings expressed through writing. Britton (1970) described this process of differentiation as a development from *expressive* or personally oriented writing, to *poetic* or primarily narrative and *transactional* or primarily expository writing. Over time, through reading, writing, and conferencing (discussion), students gain control over the basic conventions of writing and develop an awareness of the audience for the writing. They come to view their writing more objectively, becoming "readers of their own writing." They learn to use *epistemic* writing as a tool to extend and elaborate their thinking.

Unquestionably, writing has tremendous communicative value. It allows the development and nurturing of a growing "momentary kinship with creative power" of which Burrows (1939) spoke. It helps us to discover not only what we know but also how much we know or don't know; it helps us to examine what we believe in and the degree to which we believe in it. Through it we develop, refine, and better express our "voices" — our own identities and sense of ourselves. In short, writing helps us come to know our world and ourselves much better, and for many of us, it offers one of the few ways through which we can truly and honestly communicate with ourselves.

Teachers must be sensitive to this developing competence. By understanding what children do as they learn the conventions and the purposes of writing, we will be better able to view what our students can do in their writing rather than what they cannot do. We will then be good teachers of writing — and our students will grow as writers, as thinkers, and as learners.

REFERENCES

Applebee, A. (1978). *The concept of story.* Chicago, IL: University of Chicago Press.

Applebee, A. et al. (1986). *The writing report card: Writing achievement in American schools.* Princeton, NJ: Educational Testing Service.

Atwell, N. (1987). *In the middle: Writing, reading, and learning with adolescents.* Upper Montclair, NJ: Boynton/Cook.

Barone, D. (1989). *Young children's written responses to literature: Exploring the relationship between written response and orthographic knowledge.* Unpublished doctoral dissertation, University of Nevada, Reno.

Beach, J. D. (1983). Teaching students to write informational reports. *Elementary School Journal, 84,* 213–220.

Britton, J. (1970). *Language and learning.* London: Penguin.

Burrows, A., Ferebee, J. D., Jackson, D. C., & Saunders, D. O. (1939, 1952). *They all want to write.* New York: Prentice-Hall.

Berthoff, A. (1981). *The making of meaning.* Upper Montclair, NJ: Boynton/Cook.

Calkins, L. (1983). *Lessons from a child.* Portsmouth, NH: Heinemann.

Calkins, L. (1986). *The art of teaching writing.* Portsmouth, NH: Heinemann.

Cooper, J. D. (1986). *Teaching reading comprehension.* Boston, MA: Houghton Mifflin.

Elbow, P. (1981). *Writing with power.* New York: Oxford University Press.

Fulwiler, T. (1987). *The journal book.* Upper Montclair, NJ: Boynton/Cook.

Gambrell, L. B. (1985). Dialogue journals: Reading-writing interaction. *The Reading Teacher, 38,* 512–515.

Geller, L. (1985). *Wordplay and language learning for children.* Urbana, IL: National Council of Teachers of English.

Goodman, Y., & Burke, C. (1980). *Reading strategies: Focus on comprehension.* New York: Holt, Rinehart and Winston.

Graves, D. (1983). *Writing: Teachers and children at work.* Portsmouth, NH: Heinemann.

Graves, D., & Hansen, J. (1983). The author's chair. *Language Arts, 60*(2), 176–183.

Guilbault, J. (1988). Between the lines: An affective look at real-life writing in the classroom. *Language Arts, 65*(1), 461–464.

Haley-James, S., & Hobson, C. (1980). Interviewing: A means of encouraging the drive to communicate. *Language Arts, 57,* 497–502.

Harste, J., Short, K., & Burke, C. (1989). *Creating classrooms for authors: The reading/writing connection.* Portsmouth, NH: Heinemann.

Heard, G. (1989). *For the good of the earth and sun: Teaching poetry.* Portsmouth, NH: Heinemann.

Hillocks, G. (1986). *Research in the teaching of composition.* Urbana, IL: National Council of Teachers of English.

Koch, K. (1970). *Wishes, lies, and dreams.* New York: Harper and Row.

Lopate, P. (1975). *Being with children.* Garden City, NY: Doubleday.

Millett, N. (1990). *Teaching the writing process: A guide for teachers and supervisors.* Boston, MA: Houghton Mifflin.

Murray, D. (1982). *Learning by teaching.* Montclair, NJ: Boynton/Cook.

Nathan, R., Temple, F., Juntenen, K., & Temple, C. (1989). *Classroom strategies that work: An elementary teacher's guide to process writing.* Portsmouth, NH: Heinemann.

Rico, G. (1983). *Writing the natural way.* Los Angeles, CA: J. P. Tarcher.

Rouse, J. (1983). On children writing poetry. *Language Arts, 60,* 711–716.

Rubin, A., & Bruce, B. (1984). *Quill: Reading and writing with a microcomputer* (Report No. 5410). Cambridge, MA: Bolt, Beranek and Newman.

Smith, F. (1983). *Understanding writing.* New York: Holt, Rinehart and Winston.

Tchudi, S. N., & Tchudi, S. J. (1983). *Teaching writing in the content areas: Elementary school.* Washington, DC: National Educational Association.

Tompkins, G. (1990). *Teaching writing: Balancing process and product.* Columbus, OH: Merrill.

Wiggington, E. (1972). *Foxfire.* New York: Doubleday.

Zinsser, W. (1985). *On writing well.* New York: Harper and Row.

The Teaching of Reading

FOCUSING QUESTIONS

- What experiences with print best facilitate beginning reading?
- What role can conferences play in helping you develop and keep track of students' reading?
- How can you facilitate reading comprehension? What are some general and specific strategies you can teach to ensure students' successful interaction with different types of texts?
- What is the role of word knowledge in the context of reading instruction?

Dylan Thomas, the Welsh poet and playwright, once observed that as a child he thought that books were magical things, "like eggs laid by tigers," and he was amazed when he realized that "books were made by people." A good many people have similar recollections about books and reading; somehow in the early years it is all "magic."

What are your early memories of reading and of books? Are they pleasant and magical in their own way? Or are they overcast by the dull gray of tedious, seemingly meaningless drills? In our teaching we aim to sustain and, when need be, create a sense of magic and delight with books — for their own sake and because they represent some of the finest thinking and most rewarding experiences to which young people can be exposed.

INTRODUCTION

How should we conceptualize your responsibilities as a teacher of reading? Recall the classrooms we examined at the beginning of this book — not the "so-quiet-you-can-hear-a-pin-drop" ones, but the other ones. These are classrooms in which learning and teaching are integrated, meaning that the relationships among what is discussed, written about, and read are clear and meaningful to the students. As we have seen in the preceding chapters on listening and speaking, on creative dramatics, and on writing, integrated instruction also involves working directly and primarily from time to time on a specific language art.

Reading is the language art that has traditionally been given the most attention in the classroom. Although this emphasis has been well intentioned, educators in recent years have identified some gaps in the way reading has been addressed in most elementary classrooms. Our knowledge about the process of reading and the development of this process has advanced considerably over the last two decades. This understanding, though by no means complete, nevertheless powerfully supports the types of instruction we will be discussing in this chapter. In contrast to much reading instruction in the past, we will see that learning to read throughout the grades is not simply a matter of learning discrete skills, adding them together, and coming up with proficient reading. Skills are certainly a part of proficient reading, but they are not the focal point of instruction.

In this chapter, therefore, we will be exploring ways in which students can learn and refine the process and skills of reading. In so doing, we will be looking at the context in which reading occurs, and at the few reading skills and strategies that should probably receive attention at the primary and intermediate grade levels; these are grouped generically under two headings: word identification and text comprehension. *Word identification* refers to the ability to recognize at sight or to analyze and identify words in print. *Comprehension* refers to the ability to construct an appropriate understanding of the text being read; constructing appropriate understanding in turn depends on the ability to apply strategies for reading a particular text. These strategies may be engaged before, during, or after the reading.

It is perhaps a cliché — but nonetheless true — to say that children learn to read by reading. Perhaps above all, therefore, you will be developing students' desire or motivation to read. You can do this by allowing the students to read often and widely (and much of the time to choose themselves the texts they wish to read), and by reading to them, thereby enticing them to try new authors and titles. Embedding reading and reading instruction in meaningful contexts — just as with writing and writing instruction — is also vital. Students must come to understand that not only the content of the reading but the reading strategies you are helping them develop are meaningful and applicable in a broader context, including all areas of the curriculum. Knowledge of the skills and strategies is not an end in itself, as many children have believed of reading instruction in the past.

Students' enjoyment of reading and their understanding of reading skills and strategies, in other words, will occur within the integrated language arts or whole language context we have been establishing thus far. We will probe this context in some depth in the next chapter, which covers literature units. I build a foundation for that discussion in the present chapter, where I examine the specifics of the language experience approach, direct teaching, conferencing, comprehension, and word identification strategies and methodologies.

Direct Teaching

You will be teaching directly in such a way that your students will develop the necessary knowledge underlying reading as well as the knowledge of how to apply appropriate reading strategies. You will be allowing them to try out their wings as readers by exposing them to different texts of varying complexity, watching and giving feedback, and gradually letting go as they master approaches to different types of texts in different types of contexts.

Modeling

One of the most effective ways you can demonstrate how to negotiate challenging texts or to apply new skills is through modeling "think-alouds." We saw in the last chapter how modeling (teacher demonstrations) can demystify writing; it does the same for reading. As we will see, strategies for approaching different types of reading have different types of purposes. We will not leave our students to discover these strategies on their own, because most of them won't. Rather, we will forthrightly show them. For example, you can effectively model out loud for students the way to determine the main idea or most important point of a text.

We also model reading itself, not only during read-alouds with the children, but also by reading ourselves during *Sustained Silent Reading* (SSR) time (see page 320 for a full discussion of SSR). Just as with sustained writing time, sustained silent reading is a time during which everyone is involved, including you.

AT THE
TEACHER'S
DESK:
Skills, Context,
and
Knowledge

The subject of "skills" has been surrounded by a long-standing controversy in education. Often the issue is phrased in "either/or" terms: *either* we should teach in a skills-driven, highly organized manner *or* we should let all learning be more "natural," letting students discover necessary knowledge and information for themselves. Some respected philosophers and educators line up with each of these positions. Don't be caught up in the endless roundabout of these arguments, however; the real question for teachers on the front lines in the classroom is how to effect a realistic marriage between the two extremes.

Much of the criticism of "skills" over the years has been fair. Often skills were taught in isolation — for instance, in brief paragraphs and exercises that had no relation to anything the students were really reading. Also, too much attention was given to the teaching of the skills themselves, with the false assumption that this would somehow develop the underlying knowledge as well.

Once we get the relationships between skills and context and skills and knowledge in proper perspective, however, the teaching of skills makes considerable sense and is in fact necessary. For instance, it makes sense to teach the skill of outlining a chapter, but only when students already understand the characteristics of expository structure. And it makes the most sense to teach this skill in the context of a real content-area book that students are actually studying from.

To sum up — the teaching of skills is valuable, but only in an information-rich environment that provides for full presentation, modeling, discussion, and application. This is the kind of environment that you will find demonstrated in the activities in this chapter.

Conferencing

What we noted when discussing teacher/student writing conferences applies to teacher/student *reading* conferences as well: your focus is not only on developing students' reading knowledge and strategies but also on elaborating and refining their thinking. As in writing conferences, this is a suitable time for some direct teaching. You should get a sense of where students are in their reading of a particular text, what they think about it, and what they may need help with; you can also update your ongoing evaluation. You may obtain similar information from students' response journals (see Chapter 9), but perhaps not as thoroughly as in individual conferences.

There are several ways of going about teacher/student reading conferences. The steps in the following basic structure are common to all variations (see, for example, Hancock and Hill, 1987; Hornsby, Sukarna, and Parry, 1986):

■ *Sharing*

Each student knows ahead of time that he or she will share a response or reaction to a particular element of the book. You may request a particular element or leave it up to the student. When you meet with the student, this is what he or she will share with you first.

- *Questioning*

  Ask a question or two about the book's theme, what the characters are like, and from whose point of view the story is being told.

- *Oral Reading*

  The student will read orally a passage from the book that he or she would enjoy sharing with you. This is one context in which you may be able to note fluency and application of knowledge. This passage will be longer than the passages children read in groups to answer questions and to support ideas. You will be able to pinpoint areas in which certain skills may need to be taught or reinforced.

- *Planning*

  Just as in the writing conference, you should discuss where the child will go from here with the reading. If the student will continue to read the same book for a while, what will he or she be primarily interested in, and why? If the reading is finished, what is the student planning to read next? If the student is going to base some extension activity or project on the book, discuss what this will entail. Show that you are genuinely interested in the student's plans and that you will respond and help accordingly.

- *Records*

  Immediately after meeting with the student, you will note in your records any relevant information. In addition to indicating the book the student is reading or has just completed, you will indicate where the student sees himself or herself going next. You will also note here the skill areas in which the student may need work. Specific observations about reading progress will be addressed in Chapter 12.

  You will have a separate file, log, or notebook for reading records, although it is not unreasonable to include all information in one notebook. Just be sure to plan ahead for appropriate space. A critical point to keep in mind about your reading records notebook, no matter how uninformative your entries may appear at first, is to stick with it. After a while, you will realize and fully appreciate the wealth of information you have on each child. You will also be grateful for having a permanent record to check, because as you will discover if you haven't already, when you teach there is simply too much going on to remember everything you would like to remember. The reading record is a permanent check on the impermanence of your overburdened memory! Because you will be evaluating students' growth in the *process* of reading, there is really no other way to document this growth.

Textbooks and Published Materials

Elementary school reading instruction in the United States and in many other countries has traditionally depended upon and been defined in terms of *basal reading series*. Historically, there are many reasons for this (Goodman, et al., 1988; Shannon, 1988). When basals first took hold earlier in this century they reflected a behavioristic model of learning that was prevalent at the time and that still holds sway in much of education. Basals also reflected the "product" orientation of the American marketplace — if Henry Ford could train workers to produce a better automobile more rapidly, couldn't the same model be incorporated into an instructional program? School administrators have traditionally believed that basals better "control" and systematize the teaching of reading so that it is uniform throughout a school district, thus making testing more uniform and "accountability" easier.

Basal reading series are used in almost every elementary school in the United States. This does not mean that these textbooks are used exclusively (without supplemental books) in every school, but they probably do define the curriculum in at least 90 percent of the nation's schools (Winograd, Wixson, and Lipson, 1989); Flood and Lapp (1986) suggest that 98 percent of the nation's teachers use basals. Indeed, McCallum (1988) comments that "basal series partially fill the gap between research and practice by translating research findings into instructional practices which meet the constraints under which teachers operate. Given the traditional gap between theory and practice, this is no small feat" (McCallum, pp. 204–205).

Traditionally, basal reading programs have reflected primarily a "skills approach" to teaching reading, the underlying philosophy of which is: teach skills in a certain order and eventually the students will be readers. During the last decade or so, several major publishers of basal reading series began to incorporate more directly the implications of reading research in the development of their programs. As we have seen, these implications strongly suggest that reading does not develop by simply teaching or building one skill upon another. Despite these efforts, some educators argue that basal programs still fall far short of the mark (e.g., Goodman, et al., 1988). Quite recently, though, partly in response to the California Reading Initiative (1986), some publishers have offered what are termed "literature-based" reading series, incorporating the content and the techniques of a literature-based reading program (see Figure 8.1).

What you should be aware of is that the schools in which you will student-teach and someday have your own classroom will most likely have a strong published reading series component — "traditional basal" or "literature-based" — underlying their reading curriculum. This usually does *not* mean that you should base your own reading instruction entirely on the program. Rather, you should feel you have the flexibility to use whatever you choose from the program. If you find during your first year or two of teaching that you are more comfortable drawing more from the program, fine. As you gain experience and confidence, you will feel more comfortable using only certain selections and certain lessons you have found to be particularly effective.

Winograd expressed the situation aptly when he observed that "basal readers are most effective when they are used flexibly and as part of a comprehensive, balanced program of reading instruction" (Winograd, et al., 1989, p. 1). You will find that,

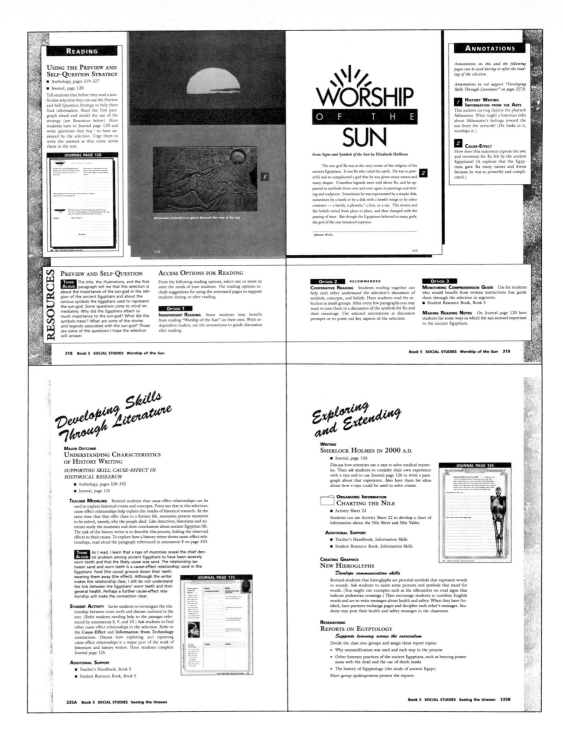

FIGURE 8.1

Pages from a Literature-Based Reading Series — Teacher's Edition (Sixth Grade)

Source: *Houghton Mifflin Reading: The Literature Experience,* Grade 6, Teacher's Book. Copyright © 1991 by Houghton Mifflin Company. Reprinted by permission of Houghton Mifflin Company.

when used flexibly, a good basal program can play an important role in at least the following four areas:

1. Most basal reading series provide a scope and sequence in comprehension and word study that interestingly and importantly matches more closely the developmental competencies we see students exhibiting.

2. Most basals include better lesson formats for direct teaching of important skills. When you wish to teach about *characterization,* for example, you can go to a basal both for a focused lesson and for a corresponding selection that highlights the understanding of characterization particularly well. You can then spin off from there.

3. Most basals provide better types and sequences of questions that facilitate reading comprehension. For example, the newer editions of most basals have questions for the teacher that follow a recommended sequence (e.g., setting, characters, problem, steps toward solution, resolution), which as research has shown facilitates overall comprehension of the text and supports development of the underlying schema for narrative genre.

4. Most series now include rather extensive lists of suggested related readings to accompany selections that appear in the basal. Some series now include multiple copies of books, excerpts of which have appeared in the basal. Unfortunately, in the past these excerpts were often rewritten to conform to readability formulas; most series now excerpt *original* segments as the authors actually wrote them.

Beginning Reading

As we saw in Chapter 6, preschool children's emerging literacy concepts grow out of experiences with print that include being read to from favorite texts. Eventually, children remember what is written in these texts; together with their explorations in writing and drawing, this knowledge supports development in the following areas:

Prerequisite understandings about the nature of reading and writing and the conventions of writing and print:

■ It stands for speech.

■ It reads from left to right and from top to bottom.

■ "Books" have a front and back, beginning, middle, end, and so forth.

Knowledge of the information encoded in writing:

■ The minimal units of writing are *letters* and there is a limited number of letters that is used over and over.

For children who have not had these experiences with written language, or have not derived much information from the experience (Combs, 1987), you must provide such experiences in your classroom. For children who *have* had these experiences, you should probably begin with the approaches I will discuss here. Through these approaches you will very quickly learn how much about writing all of your children know. The approaches we discuss here are appropriate for children in kindergarten and in first grade.

Remember, learning occurs in a social context. As we will see, this context underscores the importance of written language and of reading *making sense*. As Combs (1987) aptly observes, "Before we segment the reading process into what we think are logical instructional tasks, let's be sure that we give children an opportunity to develop concepts about the whole process so that they understand where to put each of the pieces that we teach them" (Combs, p. 426).

"Predictable" Texts

Predictability in language and in story — in syntax and semantics — can play a seminal role in beginning conventional reading (Holdaway, 1979; Yaden, 1988). Beginning readers need *support;* predictability inherently provides a good deal of it. Importantly, the predictability of texts aids *memory* for that text, and as we saw in Chapter 6, memory for specific texts underlies the development of much of the rest of a child's knowledge about print.

In recent years the phenomenon of "predictable literature" has gained popularity. As Heald-Taylor observed, predictability is reflected through "strong rhythm and rhyme, repeated patterns, refrains, logical sequences, supportive illustrations, and traditional story structures" (Heald-Taylor, 1987, p. 6). Predictable literature can cover a wide range of texts, not only the ones addressed here, which apply to beginning literacy.

"Big Books" (Holdaway, 1979) are usually predictable literature. Their fundamental feature is their size. Often referred to as "enlarged texts," Big Books are quite large, with large illustrations and large print. They are designed for reading activities with both large and small groups. Their size allows the teacher to model many prerequisite understandings about print, such as directionality (left-to-right and top-to-bottom) and the correspondence between spoken and written language, including concept of word in print.

Probably the most famous predictable text, one that eventually was published as a Big Book, is *Brown Bear, Brown Bear* (Martin, 1983). It is an excellent book to use on the very first day of first grade and is also appropriate for kindergarten. Following are the first three lines:

> **"Brown bear, brown bear, what do you see?**
> **I see a red bird looking at me.**
> **Red bird, red bird, what do you see?"**

The recurring pattern is highly predictable and the pictures support both content and language.

There are a number of things you can do when using predictable texts in an enlarged format. Depending on your students' experience and interest, much can be worked into a ten-minute session. First read the book all the way through. You may wish to pause before a word that seems to be heavily cued by the picture and

A word to the wise: many publishers are hopping on the "Big Book" bandwagon. You now see Big Books everywhere, including the grocery store. All big books are not alike, however; many have no features of predictability but are merely reprints of regular-sized books in an enlarged format. Of course, the size is not the critical feature so much as the predictability.

As you talk with parents about the types of books they may wish to obtain for their children — your students — be sure to point this out to them. Remind them that for their reading time at home with their child, regular-sized books will usually be preferable. Suggest sources of books to them (see Chapter 5), and remind them that the quality of these books will probably be higher than that of the big books available in the supermarket.

text, to allow the children the chance to fill the word in. In the case of a book such as *Brown Bear, Brown Bear,* the text is so predictable that the children will most likely be joining in during the very first reading.

You may then go back and model the reading, using a pointer to point briefly to each word as it is read, to demonstrate directionality. You may make comments about the print and its placement on the page. Take care not to try to work in too much the first time around; keep the experience fun and appropriate. At another time you can include additional readings and encourage questions and comments. As the children experience more books, you can model how to confirm an answer or prediction from the text, using illustrations and/or the text.

After they have read and reread in class several predictable, enlarged texts, children love to create their own enlarged texts (Trachtenberg and Ferrugia, 1989). These will usually be based on the original — the text has been dictated by the children — and the children will do the illustrations for each page. The teacher prints the text on each page for the children, and the book is then laminated and placed in the classroom library.

■ Build Your Teaching Resources

Predictable Texts

Articles about Predictable Texts

Following are excellent articles that describe the use of predictable texts:

Combs, M. (1984). Developing concepts about print with patterned-sentence stories. *The Reading Teacher, 85,* 171–181.

Heald-Taylor, G. (1987). How to use predictable books for K–2 language arts instruction. *The Reading Teacher, 40,* 656–661.

Jalongo, M., & Bromley, K. (1984). Developing linguistic competence through song picture books. *The Reading Teacher, 37,* 840–845.

Rosner, N., & Wilson, G. (1987). Books for reading about reading: Read-alouds for children learning. *The Reading Teacher, 40,* 282–287.

Strickland, D. S. (1988). Some tips for using Big Books. *The Reading Teacher, 41,* 966–968.

Strickland, D., & Morrow, L. M. (1989). Interactive experiences with storybook reading. *The Reading Teacher, 42*(4), 322–323.

Trachtenburg, P., & Ferruggia, A. (1989). Big books from little voices: Reaching high-risk beginning readers. *The Reading Teacher, 42*(4), 284–289.

Predictable Books

Following are excellent, highly predictable books that will get your predictable literature resource list under way:

Ahlberg, J. and Ahlberg, A. (1978). *Each peach pear plum.* New York: Viking.

Brown, M. W. (1947). *Goodnight moon.* New York: Harper and Row.

Carle, E. (1971). *The very hungry caterpillar.* New York: Crowell.

Charlip, R. (1964). *Fortunately.* New York: Parents.

Dabcovich, L. (1982). *Sleepy bear.* New York: Dutton.

Emberley, B. (1967). *Drummer Hoff.* Englewood Cliffs, NJ: Prentice-Hall.

Gag, W. (1929). *Millions of cats.* New York: Coward-McCann.

Galdone, P. (1968). *Henny penny.* New York: Scholastic.

Galdone, P. (1961). *The house that Jack built.* New York: McGraw-Hill.

Hoberman, M. A. (1978). *A house is a house for me.* New York: Viking.

Hutchins, P. (1968). *Rosie's walk.* New York: Macmillan.

Krause, R. (1970). *Whose mouse are you?* New York: Macmillan.

Martin, J. (1983). *Brown bear, brown bear, what do you see?* New York: Henry Holt.

O'Connor, J. (1986). *The teeny tiny woman.* New York: Random House/Step into Reading.

Sendak, M. (1962). *Chicken soup with rice.* New York: Harper and Row.

Sendak, M. (1962). *Alligators all around.* New York: Harper and Row.

Shulevitz, U. (1967). *One Monday morning.* New York: Scribner's.

Thayer, E. (additional text by P. Polacco). (1988). *Casey at the bat: A ballad of the Republic, sung in the year 1888.* New York: G. P. Putnam's Sons.

West, C. (1986). *"Pardon?" said the giraffe.* New York: Harper and Row/Harper Trophy Books.

Zemach, M. (1972). *The teeny tiny woman: A folktale illustrated by Margot Zemach.* New York: Scholastic.

Before we move on to another powerful beginning reading approach, let's remind ourselves of the broader "beginning reading" picture. You will be varying your students' experiences with books: you will read to them so they can simply listen and enjoy, you will read to them in the context of Directed Listening-Thinking Activities (DLTA), and you will model the reading process through modification of the DLTA procedure using Big Books. And through all of this, you will be allowing your students to *write.*

The Language Experience Approach

The *language experience approach* (LEA) is a marvelous way of integrating children's language and background knowledge with beginning reading and writing. LEA draws upon the language and the experiences of children, tailoring written material to where *they* are coming from. If you were to poll primary grade teachers across the country about LEA, most would probably say that it is a procedure in which you write down on chart paper what children say — and that's about it. As described by Hall (1980), Stauffer (1969, 1980), Nessel and Jones (1981), and Henderson (1981), however, LEA is a comprehensive beginning reading method in its own right. It is this more comprehensive picture that I will portray in this chapter.

The language experience approach (LEA) provides a more natural way in which children come to understand the features and the functions of written language. As with predictable texts, it affords teachers the opportunity to model "how print works" for children, yet it is even more natural because it is based on children's language and children's experience.

In a nutshell, here is how LEA works: Building on an experience the children have had, you will write down *exactly* what the children dictate or say about the experience. In Chapter 5 we explored ways in which oral language can be developed — through sharing, through response to Directed Listening-Thinking Activities, through discussion and the examination of first- and secondhand experiences, and so forth. Any and all of these activities can serve as the experience from which will stem the dictation. After writing down several contributions, you then read the dictated account to the children, as naturally as possible, while pointing to each word. Repeat this one or more times, and then read the account with all of the children in chorus, leading them gently with your voice, fading in and out as necessary. Individual children may then "read" the sentence they contributed.

Group Experience Charts

The following extended Classroom Example, with accompanying textual discussion, illustrates the use of the language experience approach with the whole class.

CLASSROOM EXAMPLE

Getting Underway: Day 1

Writing the Dictated-Experience Chart.
Let's say our stimulus is a basket of newborn kittens. Although the children's temptation to pick them up will of course be great, the teacher cautions the children to "look but not touch." Still, there will be much excitement and much to talk about. The whole class can be involved in the talk about the kittens — how they look, smell, behave, and so forth.

After five to ten minutes of discussion the teacher puts the basket of kittens up on a table. Seated next to an easel on which are tacked several sheets of chart paper, the teacher begins the "dictation" phase of the experience:

TEACHER: "Boys and girls, we have been talking about the kittens and now we're going to write about them. You will tell me what you would like me to write down, and I will write it exactly as you say it. Let's begin by writing a *title* for our piece up here at the top of the page. Because we're going to be writing about the kittens, let's title our piece, '*The Kittens*.' [As she pronounces each word, she writes *The Kittens* and then underlines the title.]

"Let's think about the things we said about the kittens. Who would like to say something and then have me write it down? [Several hands shoot up.] Yes, Cory?"

CORY: "I think the kittens are cute."
TEACHER: "Okay! I'll write that down, and everyone watch and listen as I do it."

Using a broad-tipped felt marker, the teacher begins printing. Starting at the left margin, she first writes "Cory said," and then puts down exactly what he said. She pronounces each word naturally as she writes it, trying to read with as much expression as she can. When she finishes Cory's line, it appears as follows:

Cory said, "I think the kittens are cute."

TEACHER: "All right! What else can we say about the kittens? Yes, Bernadette?"
BERNADETTE: "They're furry."
TEACHER: "Okay!" [She then writes *Bernadette said, "They're furry."*] Yes, Adrianna?"
ADRIANNA: "Their eyes are closed."
TEACHER: "Okay! Let's write that down . . ."

The teacher continues in this fashion; the completed dictated-experience chart appears as follows:

The Kittens

Cory said, "I think the kittens are cute."
Bernadette said, "They're furry."
Adrianna said, "Their eyes are closed."
Blaine said, "They look real soft."
Angela said, "They be good pets."
Derek said, "I thought they would smell."
Marcie said, "They sleep a lot."

Thus far, the teacher has modeled how print "works" for the children — it reads left to right, top to bottom. Moreover, she has pronounced each word as she has written it. She has modeled the formation of letters. Of course, the children are not going to learn much about the specifics of spelling and letter formation by watching just this once, but if the process is repeated many times, they will.

Before we continue, let's discuss the rationale behind what the teacher has done so far. Why didn't the teacher let the children choose the title? Because the children may not be familiar with the concept of title (a metalinguistic term; see Chapter 7), this was a gentle way to introduce the word and the concept. In a week or two, once children understand the concept, she may ask them for ideas about a title. The group will then vote for the title they prefer; conveniently, this also addresses the concept of main idea.

Why did the teacher stop after only seven children had contributed sentences? She didn't want a text that went on at length, because most of the children would have forgotten what the text said. Keep in mind the role that memory is going to play in learning to read in a conventional sense (see Chapter 6).

Why did the teacher write "Cory said," "Adrianna said," and so forth at the beginning of each line? She knows that most children in the beginning of first grade are able to read their own name, so this enables them to use this word as a "locator" for finding their sentence later on.

Why did the teacher always begin each sentence on a separate line? At this early phase, it is easier for each child to locate his or her own sentence if the children's names are at the left-hand margin.

If only seven lines from seven children are used, won't all the other children who were unable to contribute to the dictation be upset that they weren't included? There may be a momentary disappointment for some, but as we will see, opportunities for everyone to be involved will arise.

Having reviewed the teacher's rationale to this point, let's see how the teacher now proceeds.

"Reading" the Dictated-Experience Chart.
The teacher continues: "Boys and girls, now that we've *written* about the kittens, we're going to *read* what we've written. First, watch and listen as I read this back to you, because we're soon going to read it all together." Using a pointer so that she does not block the chart with her arm or body, the teacher then reads the composition aloud as naturally as possible, pointing to each word as she reads it. If she feels it is necessary, she reads the chart a second time for the children.

Next the teacher says, "Boys and girls, let's read what we've written *all together.*" She then reads as she did the first time, as naturally as possible, letting her voice lead the children if necessary as they choral-read, dropping her voice slightly if the children seem to be recalling the lines fairly well on their own. If the teacher feels it is necessary, she leads a second and perhaps a third choral reading.

Finding out What Children Know about Print.
The teacher now probes to find out what some of the children know about print. She is also mentally noting (to jot down a bit later) the children who are

attending and those who are "wandering," perhaps rolling around on the fringe of the circle. She invites children to do any or all of the following: locate their name, read what they said, read what someone else said, locate specific words — it all depends on how much they know about print and how comfortable they seem to be.

Children who did not dictate a sentence are of course free to locate another child's sentence and "read" it. For most first-graders a fifteen- to twenty-minute session is possible; this includes the "stimulus" and the accompanying discussion as well as the dictation writing and reading.

Illustrating the Experience.
When the children return to their seats, they each will draw a picture of the kittens. As they are drawing, the teacher will walk about and write "The Kittens" at the bottom of each child's drawing. The power of this simple labeling is considerable; the children will be "reading" by the end of the day when they take their pictures home — and adults at home will be impressed! (If the children wish to write on their own, fine.)

Day Two

The teacher has temporarily split the class into two groups. Her rationale is this: she wishes to engage as much as possible the students who were reluctant yesterday to be involved in the discussion and/or in the dictation. With those children who were more involved, she wishes to probe further.

For the first group, the teacher brings out the kittens again to stimulate discussion. Depending on how it goes, she may spend a good ten to fifteen minutes just talking with the students. She may feel they are ready to dictate their own story today; otherwise, the time just spent talking is well spent. Time permitting, the teacher may also read a Big Book with the children.

For the second group, Day Two is a more intensive probe into the students' knowledge about reading and print. The teacher again brings out the dictated-experience chart, reads it for the children, and has a choral reading with them. Next, she does the same sorts of "checking" she did on Day One. That is, she asks different children to come to the chart and read different sentences and perhaps locate different words. Now the teacher probes more deeply into which children perhaps already have a concept of word in print. Remember the procedure described in Chapter 6 for determining this? The dictated-experience chart is by now a memorized text and the teacher can check whether particular children can

1. point to words as they say them.
2. locate specific words within a line of print. If so, they will be able to do this by
    a. immediately pointing to the word, or
    b. returning to the beginning of the line and reading up to the target word.

The teacher makes note of which children seem to have a concept of word in print *and* of which specific words she thinks the children may be able to identify in isolation on Day Three. She makes the decision about the words based on how rapidly the children were able to identify certain words in the context of the dictated chart. If she has any doubts about a child's ability to identify a particular word, she does not select the word — she will be aiming for almost certain success.

Day Three

The first group will create their own dictated-experience chart if they have not done so on Day Two. If the "story" was dictated on Day Two, then this group will reread it today and the teacher will check for those children who can locate their names, read the title, and "read" what they dictated. Lots of modeling is important here. As on the second day, the teacher may also read a Big Book with this group during this time. The teacher checks the other, more "advanced" group on the words she believes the children will be able to identify in isolation. She has printed the words on separate cards and proceeds in this fashion:

Displaying the word card for *sleep,* the teacher asks, "Marcie, can you tell me what this word is?" If Marcie responds correctly (as the teacher is almost certain she will!), the teacher hands the card to her as she says, "Wonderful! Marcie, this is *your* word." The teacher in effect makes a "big deal" about this to emphasize the importance of Marcie knowing the word: it really does belong to her now.

The basic three-day dictation and follow-up cycle is thus completed. On the next day the cycle can begin again. The two groups may be changed into three, and there is nothing sacred about three days. The teacher may decide one group can generate dictations and remember words in isolation every two days; perhaps another group will need four days to work with a dictation. It is important, though, that you keep this basic three-day cycle in mind as a standard.

Many teachers reproduce the dictated-experience chart in a format suitable for placing in a sturdy composition book. These books will play an extremely important role throughout language experience instruction. The print should be primer sized. The story may be run off on a ditto machine or on a printer, if you have access to a microcomputer and a printer (Smith, 1985; Dudley-Marling, 1985). The children will place the composition on the right-hand page and the illustration on the left-hand facing page. Figure 8.2 illustrates how "The Kittens" appears in such a format.

These books should not be confused with writing journals, which were discussed in the previous chapter. The journals include the children's original writing; these books include their dictations but in standard spelling.

Here are some questions about the "how-to's" of LEA that even experienced teachers often raise:

1. *What about the child who dictates a "sentence" that goes on and on, linked by "and . . . and . . . and . . ."?* Tell the child that you'd really like to write down all he or she said, but that it will be easier to take just a part of it. Which part would the child like you to write down?

2. *What about children who speak a variant dialect or use a developmentally earlier form of grammar (e.g., saying "wented" instead of "went")?* This is a controversial issue for a number of reasons, as we will explore in Chapter 12. For the present, however, I will suggest a fairly straightforward rule of thumb to follow when beginning LEA: do not at first change children's language to conform to the standard dialect. There will be time later to address the differences between the variant dialect that a child may speak and the nature of the standard dialect. Right now the job is to begin conventional literacy, and changing what a child says will not only retard that development but quite possibly confuse the child as well.

3. *What is the advantage of beginning with LEA and not simply moving into the basal reading program or making available lots of trade books that may be of interest to the child?* By virtue of the immediacy of the child's experience and language, the print in dictated stories is more familiar to him or her. It will be more natural than the language patterns in preprimers. The type and range of potential sight words is greater as well; Stauffer (1969) pointed out some years ago that children may learn many more sight words through LEA than through the preprimer, primer, and first reader of a typical basal series. This sight-word vocabulary can also set the stage for moving into more trade books sooner than children might otherwise. In addition, the high-frequency, low-content words such as *of, the, was,* and so forth — potential "toughies" when encountered in isolation — are usually mastered through LEA simply because they also occur with great frequency in dictations.

4. *Why has the term "dictated* story" *not been used here?* It was frequent in the earlier writings on LEA. Sulzby (1980) makes the case that, when we are developing the child's concept of story, we should avoid using the term *story* to refer in effect to a counterexample of story-ness.

Individual Dictations

After a few cycles of group dictated-experience charts, many children are consistently able to identify isolated words taken from the chart. This consistency is a sign that such children should be moved into *individual* dictations. Children who are ready for individual dictations will have these written in the sturdy-covered composition book mentioned above. As with the group-dictated chart, children's dictations will be entered, numbered, and illustrated.

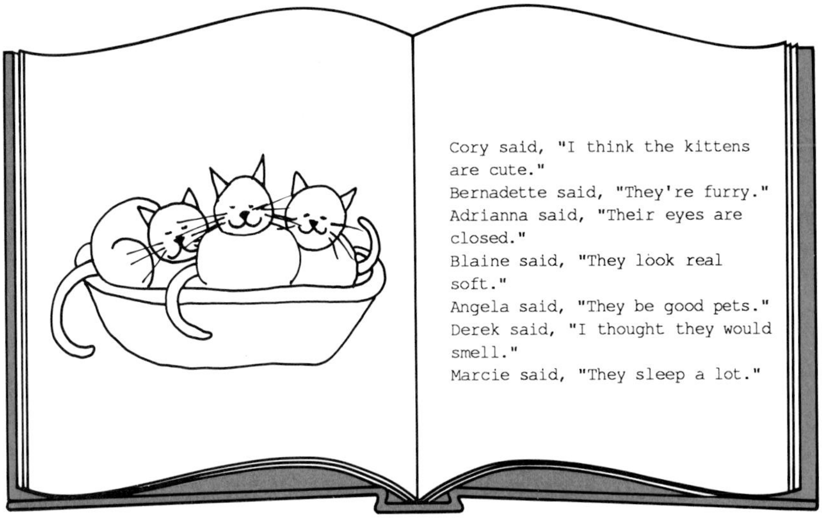
Cory said, "I think the kittens
are cute."
Bernadette said, "They're furry."
Adrianna said, "Their eyes are
closed."
Blaine said, "They look real
soft."
Angela said, "They be good pets."
Derek said, "I thought they would
smell."
Marcie said, "They sleep a lot."

FIGURE 8.2

"The Kittens" – Individual Book Version of a Story Dictated Through the Language Experience Approach

Word Banks

Each word that a child has learned to immediately identify during language experience approach lessons can be deposited in the child's word bank, which is simply a collection of all the child's known words. A word bank can be just about any type of small container; 3″ × 5″ plastic file card boxes usually work best, and their alphabetical divisions will come in handy later. The word bank will be a source of words for subsequent word study, so only the words that the child can immediately identify should go into it. Children should review their word-bank words about once a day, by themselves or with a buddy. They should check any words that they forget in the story from which the word came. Finally, the teacher or another adult should check each child on their word-bank words about once a week; any words the child does not immediately identify should be removed.

How about children who are still doing the group dictated-experience charts with you? They will be acquiring sight words at a slower rate, but you can and should certainly begin word banks with them as well. When their developing knowledge supports more rapid sight-word acquisition, then they, too, will move into individual-dictated stories.

Following are just a few word-bank activities:

Expand Your Teaching Repertoire

1. *Word Sorts:* We will discuss these in more depth in Chapter 10. In word sorts, word-bank words can be sorted or categorized according to their structure (e.g., words that begin with *m*), their sound (words that rhyme with *flat*), or their meaning relationships (words that stand for things you can play with). The format of categorization can expand to include more than one

concept per sort. When you are focusing on word beginnings or vowel patterns, the word bank can be an excellent source of words for phonics instruction (see p. 291): Students dump out a bunch of words, arrange them in columns, and search them for a particular phonic element that you target.

2. *Alphabetizing:* As noted above, alphabetization will necessarily come to play a role in word-bank activities. For first-graders who are regularly maintaining a word bank, alphabetization should probably not exceed the first two letters. When they study consonant digraphs (e.g., *ch, th*) and blends (e.g., *st, pl*), they can add separate labeled envelopes for each to the word bank.

3. *Card Games:* Students can play any number of card games with word-bank words (Gillet and Kita, 1979). One of the most popular is "Go Fish," a variation on the popular game: "Do you have a word that begins like *boat* . . . that has the same vowel sound as *tape*?"

4. *Timed Word-Bank Review:* A variation on self-checking word-bank words or checking them with the teacher or another adult, is to time the review. This can be done with students working in pairs. An egg timer or stopwatch can be used — one student can handle it while the other races against the timer. Students should find that, even though their word-bank holdings are increasing, their ability to read through all of them decreases. When they have many words in their banks, then they should be timed in groups of, say, twenty-five words.

5. *Sentence Construction:* After arranging many words in columns (for easier visual search), students can construct sentences using the words. A challenge is to see how many different sentences they can construct using a set number of words. To keep track, each sentence may be written down after it is constructed.

6. *Board Games:* Different types of word features can be reinforced within the basic board-game format. A board with a winding path that students can follow from start to finish can be used for consonant and vowel elements. Laminate the board, then write a different word on each square; the words will represent whatever phonic element or elements you want to highlight. Each student throws the dice, lands on a particular word, and looks to see if he or she has a word-bank word that fits the pattern (a word that begins the same, has the same vowel pattern, etc.) in order to advance. Later on, this task can be complicated by requiring students to *recall* a word that fits the target pattern.

■ Build Your Teaching Resources

Books about the Language Experience Approach

Excellent texts that present a comprehensive treatment of the language experience approach are:

Hall, M. (1980). *Teaching reading as a language experience.* Columbus, OH: Merrill.

Henderson, E. (1981). *Learning to read and spell: A child's knowledge of words.* DeKalb, IL: Northern Illinois University Press.

Nessel, D., & Jones, M. B. (1981). *The language experience approach to reading.* New York: Teachers College Press.

Stauffer, R. (1980). *The language experience approach to teaching reading.* New York: Harper and Row.

A book that describes a classroom that follows a procedure that could be called language experience is Sylvia Ashton-Warner's *Teacher* (New York: Simon and Schuster, 1963). The book is a classic and is a "must read" for future primary grade teachers. Ashton-Warner describes in effective and gripping detail her work teaching Maori children in New Zealand.

One of the best comprehensive treatments of LEA for remedial readers appears in

Stauffer, R., Abrams, J., & Pikulski, J. (1978). *Diagnosis, remediation, and prevention of reading disabilities.* New York: Harper and Row.

Identifying Words

Although there has been considerable debate over the years about whether and how to study words and word parts, research has consistently demonstrated that knowledge of letter/sound correspondences facilitates conventional literacy learning at the primary grade levels (Adams, 1990; Chall, 1990; Ehri and Wilce, 1987; Freebody and Byrne, 1988; Stuart and Coltheart, 1988). At the intermediate grade levels, recent research has supported the value of examining important structural or morphemic elements as part of structural analysis or vocabulary study. Such examination of words and word parts can aid vocabulary development as well as support more efficient and fluent reading and help readers appropriately construct the meaning the author intended (Templeton, in press; White, Power, and White, 1989). As I've indicated here, however, and as we will see later in this chapter and in Chapter 10, the real question for teachers is not *whether* to study words and word parts, but *when* to study *which* word parts. The more students know about words and word structure, the better readers they will be.

Recent research has identified a developmental sequence according to which children learn about aspects of phonics and structural analysis (Henderson and Beers, 1980; Templeton and Bear, in press). We touched on this sequence briefly in Chapter 6 and will discuss it in more detail in Chapter 10. This sequence, which follows elementary school children's conceptualization of word structure, will guide your more systematic instruction about words. Generally, conceptualization develops this way: children understand words first as comprising letters, then as comprising letters in certain patterns within single syllables, then as comprising more than one syllable, and finally as comprising definite *morphemes* (see p. 292).

Development of word identification skills requires students (1) to learn to recognize whole words and then (2) to learn word analysis skills including phonics, structural analysis, and context clues. We have already seen in our discussions of the language experience approach and of word-bank activities how students can begin to accrue a store of known words, primarily by repeated exposure to these words in printed format. Developing a store of immediately recognized words will be important as children learn to read, for it will help them to feel that they are actually "reading," without having to stop and analyze each word.

Ultimately, as children gain fluency, virtually all words they encounter will be known words (think of your own reading at this moment). However, during the primary years children will come upon many words whose meanings and pronunciations they know but whose printed form they have not yet learned to recognize. Often these words will need to be analyzed through use of letter/sound correspondence clues and/or context clues. In the intermediate years students will come upon words whose meanings and pronunciations they do *not* know, and these words will need to be analyzed through structural analysis and some context clues.

You are helping students to develop their word-knowledge base every time you talk about words and get the students to look at and to think about words. Make it clear to students that whatever work you do with words will help them in reading and writing, but also make it clear whenever you are dealing with different *applications* of this word knowledge. Tailor your instruction and discussion to the appropriate task and context at hand. For example, when your purpose is to help students learn what to do when they encounter an unknown word in their reading, this is not the time to talk about whether or not a final consonant is doubled when a suffix is added. That discussion is more appropriate for examining word structure at another time, when you help students attend to words for purposes of correct spelling, or to see how words are related in "families" because they have similar meanings and spellings.

Be clear, in other words, about why you are dealing with words. When you are discussing *reading* strategies, make this clear. When you are discussing word structure for its own sake or because of its role in correct spelling in writing, make this clear.

In the following section we will summarize what you have already learned about the presentation of whole words and then consider each of the word analysis skills. First, however, let's think a little further about *metalinguistic awareness* — the knowledge about language *as* language that allows children to begin word analysis (Templeton, 1986; Yaden and Templeton, 1986). As we saw in Chapter 2, this means that children need to be able to think about language as an object, to consider it apart from its meaning.

For example, a child must have a certain amount of metalinguistic awareness to be able to successfully handle this request: "Keith, can you tell me if the words *ball* and *box* begin the same?" Unless Keith simply guesses, he will have to understand the following in order to respond:

- what a *word* is
- what "beginning" means
- that words are made up of individual sounds

These seem to be simple points for us to understand, but if Keith is not ready for beginning conventional literacy, they may be too abstract for him at this point.

Whole Words

You already know how children come to identify whole words in print: by repeated exposures to a familiar text that they already know by memory. Of course, they learn some words out of connected text, as these words naturally occur in the environment (*stop; exit*). Children learn most words, however, more efficiently and in greater numbers as they naturally occur in connected print — thus the value in beginning reading of predictable books and doing language experience activities.

Word Analysis

Children's learning to read whole words is strongly supported by their learning of the names of letters, their writing, and their invented spelling of words. As the children develop a store of sight words (words they can immediately recognize in print), they are ready to turn their attention to the structure of the words. Our focus in this section, therefore, will be on word analysis in the context of reading instruction, and how word knowledge can be applied in identifying unknown words during reading.

Phonics

Phonics refers to the study of letter/sound (or *grapheme/phoneme*) relationships. These relationships are first studied as they apply within single-syllable words; the sounds or phonemes are divided into *consonants* and *vowels*. Over the years, the terms used to refer to certain sounds have come to refer to letters that represent these sounds; in other words, you will frequently hear the terms *consonant* and *vowel* used to refer to sounds *and* to letters.

In the beginning conventional literacy stage, how do you know when children are ready for phonics — the first level of explicit word analysis? If they know several sight words, have learned the names of the letters of the alphabet, and have a concept of word in print, then they are ready. In the past there has been a fair amount of debate about what kind of phonics to teach, analytic or synthetic. *Analytic* phonics begins with the whole word and then examines individual sounds, whereas *synthetic* phonics begins with individual sounds and blends or synthesizes them into words. Children actually can learn and benefit from operating on words in both ways. When they are inventing spellings, they are sounding the word out and selecting the letter they believe appropriately matches each sound, thereby winding up with a word that blends these sounds together. When children have the prerequisite knowledge of sight words, letters, and a concept of word in print, then they will have little problem in breaking whole words down into their sounds. What they will yet have to learn is the way these sounds are represented in printed English. Teachers — and children — encounter problems when an intensive phonics program is begun *before* children have this prerequisite knowledge.

Apart from their reading and their writing, children learn about conventional letter/sound correspondences by comparing and contrasting words that share particular letters. Beginning with sound, teachers can ask children to examine a column of words, for example, in which all the words sound as if they begin the same way. The students then look at the beginning of the words to see if there is anything similar about how they look. Of course, the teacher guides them to the realization that words that begin with a particular letter usually begin with the same sound.

This active type of examination, in which students search for and examine features of words, as opposed to simply being told about phonics correspondences, usually leads to deeper processing and learning.

■ Build Your Teaching Resources

Books about Word Identification

Some of the best treatment of word identification at the beginning stage of reading may be found in the following two texts:

Henderson, E. (1990). *Teaching spelling.* Boston: Houghton Mifflin.
   This text is one of the best available for addressing how phonics — as well as spelling — should be taught.
Henderson, E. (1981). *Learning to read and spell: The child's knowledge of words.* DeKalb, IL: Northern Illinois University Press.

Structural Analysis

When students examine the structure of words that consist of two or more syllables, they are involved in *structural* or *morphemic analysis. Morphemes* are the smallest units of meaning in words; a morpheme can be a prefix, a suffix, a base word, or a word root. As I've already indicated, much of what a reader learns about structural analysis has to do with meaning elements and falls more into the realm of vocabulary. We will cover the basics here, again working from the perspective of how to give students a leg up on identifying unfamiliar words during reading.

Teachers can establish the concept of structural analysis using *compound words,* such as *rowboat, cowboy, cottonball,* and so forth. Compound words are, of course, words of more than one syllable. They illustrate how words can consist of smaller, meaningful elements.

Syllabication   Syllabication refers to the knowledge of how to break up words into syllables. Once they are able to break unfamiliar words into syllables, students should then be able to sound out the individual syllables using phonics knowledge. This should be the only reason for addressing syllabication in the context of reading. Too often, however, the importance and amount of work invested in this skill is carried way too far. Students are given worksheets and told to divide the words into syllables; they are given rules to memorize, such as "if a vowel in one syllable is long, divide the word after that vowel." How quickly the whole purpose is turned around! If a student knows that a vowel is long, then why is she being asked to divide the word up? The reason we teach syllabication in reading at all is so that students can determine the pronunciation, not the other way around!

Prefixes, Suffixes, Base Words, and Word Roots   The fact that morphemic (meaning) elements combine in various ways to form words is the central understanding students need to gain from structural analysis. These meaning elements are prefixes, suffixes, base words, and word roots.

Students develop their knowledge of meaning elements throughout the intermediate years and beyond. As with phonics, the active search of a group of words that share a common element is the key. When students first examine an element, they look at parts of known words, and they move on from there. Continual examination of the structure of words in this fashion is an extremely powerful strategy.

Context Clues

Before you explicitly address how to use context clues in word identification, you have given children the feel of using such clues during your shared book experiences with predictable texts. Now let's examine how you directly address this strategy.

CLASSROOM EXAMPLE

Displaying the following sentence, the teacher explains to the children, "Girls and boys, I've left the last word out in order to get some ideas from you about what word would fit. What are some words that would go in here?"

I went to the store to get some _____.

[The teacher writes the possibilities that the children offer above and below the line.] "Wow! There are quite a few, aren't there? Do we have any way of knowing which one is correct? Of course not! They all could be . . . Well, let's see what happens when I change the sentence a little." [Displays the following sentence:]

I went to the store to get some m_____.

"*Now* what are our possibilities?" [As before, the teacher writes them down above and below the line.] "Do we have fewer possibilities this time? Right! Let's do one more." [Displays the following sentence:]

I went to the store to get some m_____k.

[The children will realize there is now only one choice: *milk*. The teacher resumes:] "Kids, what we've done here is use the other words in the sentence, together with a little bit of information from the word, to determine what the word in the blank is. You can do the same thing in your reading. When you come to a word that you don't know, use whatever sound/letter clues you *do* know to figure it out, together with the words in the sentence and sometimes from other sentences as well.

"Let's try this out now with a word that I'm pretty sure you don't know how to read yet." [Displays the following paragraph.]

Bryan did not know what he had tripped on in the dark. It made a scary sound. He turned the light on and looked at the room. He felt better when he saw it was only a *bucket.*

"Okay, we don't know what this word is [pointing to *bucket*] but we still know something about it. We know how it begins and ends, and together with the rest of the information we may be able to figure it out. Let's read this and find out." [Rereads the paragraph.] At *bucket,* the teacher reads it this way: "... when he saw it was only a *buh* ..." The teacher pauses on this last sound, and this is usually enough to cue the word; at least one if not more students will call out "Bucket!"

"Excellent! Why were you able to figure that out?" [Here the teacher is probing to get the students to restate, in their own words, her description about beginning, ending, and the rest of the information.] The teacher then continues: "Kids, sometimes when you're reading and you come to a word you don't know right away, you can use what you know about words together with the meaning of what you're reading to try to figure it out. Now, if you simply *cannot* figure it out, don't worry. You can check with someone later."

Comprehending Narrative and Expository Texts

The Nature of Reading Comprehension

We have been talking all along in this text about comprehension, although most of the time we haven't labeled it explicitly. When we discussed Directed Listening-Thinking Activities, read-alouds, discussion, and questioning in Chapter 5, we were dealing with comprehension. When we discussed responding to writing in Chapter 7 we were dealing with comprehension.

Students of course "comprehend" or understand what's happening most of the time, because they are able to make sense of their world. Your facilitation of their comprehension in reading will help them make the explicit link between the ways they think about concepts and situations expressed in oral language and how such information can be realized in reading. As Pearson and Johnson (1978) so aptly expressed it several years ago, comprehension in reading is a process of building bridges between the "new" and the "known." Comprehension in reading is different from comprehension in other communication acts, however, because the reader must be able to apply skills and knowledge appropriately to the text offered by an absent communicator in order to reconstruct or comprehend the appropriate message.

Reading comprehension involves building bridges between knowledge that the reader already has and new information he or she encounters in the text. (© Spencer Grant/The Picture Cube)

What Should Be Taught: Skills and Strategies

In the past, comprehension has been broken down into a great many subskills. Teachers all too often have found themselves busily working on the subskills and practically ignoring any real, sustained reading (Durkin, 1978/79; Winograd, et al., 1989). There *are* certain skills and strategies that you should try to develop, but it is possible to reduce them to a manageable, comprehensible number and to address them systematically throughout the elementary grades. You will see these skills and strategies labeled with different terms, but the underlying concepts will usually be the same, based on whether they focus primarily on information in the text or on information that comes from the reader's own background, and when they are put to use in reading — before, during, or after.

At the most general level, we can characterize the focus of comprehension instruction to be on the following:

- Vocabulary
- Identifying relevant information in texts and understanding how this information is related
- Knowing whether a particular reading strategy is necessary
- Responding to this information — that is, making judgments about it or evaluating it

We will address vocabulary in its own right later on. Here we will focus on the remaining three areas.

Recall from Chapter 6 that educators traditionally refer to three categories or types of comprehension: *literal* comprehension, *inferential* comprehension, and *critical* comprehension. Here is a list of terms, both formal and colloquial, that are frequently used in reading instruction to describe the different categories of comprehension:

literal	inferential	critical
explicit	implicit	applied/applicative
"right there"	interpretive	"beyond the lines"
	"between the lines"	

Most discussions of the categories of comprehension will be in the terms we have presented here, so this is why you should learn them. In Table 8.1 I've presented a fairly fine-grained analysis of different types of questions related to the

TABLE 8.1 TYPES OF QUESTIONS AS A FUNCTION OF COMPREHENSION CATEGORY

COMPREHENSION CATEGORY	TYPE OF QUESTION
Literal Comprehension	*Memory* (the reader is asked to simply *remember* what was explicitly stated in the text)
Inferential Comprehension	*Translation* (in answering, the reader must rephrase or express differently what was explicitly stated)
	Interpretation (the reader is asked to infer relationships among explicitly stated information)
Critical Comprehension	*Application* (in answering, the reader must relate what is read to information *beyond* the text)
	Logical Analysis (in answering, the reader must determine the degree to which the ideas in the text follow a logical format; the understanding of *how* to make this determination comes from the world "beyond the text" itself)
	Synthesis (in answering, the reader must use original, creative thinking)
	Evaluation (the reader is asked to make judgments based on certain evaluation criteria that are clear to the reader; these criteria come from "beyond the text")

three major categories. These types are based on Sanders' (1969) classification scheme. My purpose in presenting them here is not for you to memorize them so you can label any question you run into. Instead I'd like to suggest how you can tap and encourage successively more critical thinking from your students — directed to the text, to the relationship between the text and the real world, and to the real world in and of itself.

Note that four of the seven types of questions fall in the category of critical comprehension. This is as it should be, because we do, after all, want critical thinkers. If the critical comprehension questions based on students' reading are to generate quality thinking, however, we must be certain that students are comprehending adequately in the literal and inferential categories.

Thus we have come full circle: students must learn how to construct the intended meaning of a text in order to go beyond that text and relate the constructed meaning to the real world. Stated somewhat differently, our charge as teachers is to address how meaning can best be constructed (from the *reading*) and how that meaning connects with the real world (*critically thinking* about the reading).

■ Build Your Teaching Resources

Books about Reading Comprehension

The following book offers a complete treatment of the nature of comprehension from the perspective of cognitive science and information-processing theory, yet because it is written by reading educators, it is directly applicable to classroom instruction:

Pearson, P. D., & Johnson, D. (1978). *Teaching comprehension.* New York: Holt, Rinehart, and Winston.
    See particularly Chapters 4–8.

Another text that explores specific theoretical and teaching issues and techniques within the domain of reading comprehension is

Flood, J. (ed.) (1984). *Promoting reading comprehension.* Newark, DE: International Reading Association.

A third text that emphasizes practical teaching strategies is

Cooper, J. D. (1986). *Teaching reading comprehension.* Boston, MA: Houghton Mifflin.

In the sections below we will examine different reading strategies students can use, depending on the text they are going to read and on their purposes for reading the text. The major determinant of different strategies is whether the text to be read is *narrative* or *expository*.

Narrative Texts

The Directed Reading-Thinking Activity (DRTA)

The *Directed Reading-Thinking Activity* (DRTA) is a means of "thinking about and organizing reading instruction that ties together the components of good teaching" (Cooper, 1986, p. 55). It is often referred to as simply a *Directed Reading Activity.*

Originally developed by Russell Stauffer (1969, 1975), the DRTA is a teacher-facilitated process in which students combine their prior knowledge with information in the text to predict, confirm, or revise predictions (Davidson and Wilkerson, 1988; Haggard, 1988). As Haggard notes, the DRTA "is frequently identified as an exemplary instructional activity for developing comprehension and critical thinking" (Haggard, 1988, p. 527). One reason for this is that it occurs in a social context, in which a group of students is involved in reading and responding to the same text — not necessarily to determine right or wrong answers but to deal critically with the material. Students wind up in an intense discussion (Chapter 5). From the beginning of reading instruction, the DRTA reinforces the *active,* as opposed to passive, role that readers must play. Because readers are actively engaged, they maintain a forward momentum in their reading.

The narrative DRTA is an excellent activity for most first, second, and third grade children; however, it is important to remember that it can be used on just about any story; as we saw in Chapter 5, during the Directed *Listening*-Thinking Activity (DLTA), young children are certainly capable of thinking critically about information. As you will see, the primary differences between DRTAs at the primary level and those at the intermediate level are (1) the use of *stories,* (2) the length of the material, (3) the extent to which you require the students to focus on the process of reading, and (4) the range and type of your postreading questioning.

Here is the recommended basic format for narrative Directed Reading-Thinking Activities:

■ *At the outset, students set purposes for reading a story.*

These purposes are based on their predictions as to what will happen in the story. You may wish to tell the children the following: "Just as detectives use clues to figure out how to solve a crime, when we read we also use clues to help us figure out what might happen in the story. If we make guesses about what might happen in a story before we read, we will enjoy the story more and be better able to pick up on the clues. In other words, we are 'reading detectives.'"

As with the DLTA, after reading the title of the book and looking at any accompanying pictures, you will ask the children, "What do you think this story might be about?" Write their predictions on the chalkboard or on chart paper. Take down several ideas; a half dozen or so is good for starters. In moving the children to predictions about a story, notice that you focus the children's attention on the story *in relation to* their prior knowledge ("What do you think a story titled *Lost in the Marshes* might be about?") rather than *on* their prior knowledge ("Have any of you ever seen a marsh?"). This is a subtle but important difference between DRTAs and the way stories usually are introduced; unless you focus on the story, you are likely to get a lot of personal testimony about marshes (often with one child trying to outdo another child!) and to wind up with all of the children thinking about their own adventures rather than the story.

■ *Tell the children to read to a predetermined stopping place.*

At first, this point should probably be at the end of the first paragraph or the first page. When they reach this stopping point, they should mark their place in the book with a thumb or forefinger and close the book — this is to prevent reading ahead.

When you are just beginning DRTAs with primary students, you may wish to tell them to raise their hands if they encounter any words they do not know and you'll tell them what the word is. Later on, when they have developed some word analysis skills, you may wish to remind them, "If you come to a word that you don't know, try to figure it out as best you can. If you cannot, just read ahead and we'll figure it out later." After they've read the story, you can turn attention to unknown words.

Stopping this soon in the reading allows quick feedback for the children, and they can revise or maintain their predictions as necessary. You will ask, "*Now* what do you think?" and "Why do you think so?" Cross out rejected predictions and place a question mark by those that cannot yet be verified or rejected. After revising and/or sticking with predictions, say, "Well, let's read on and find out!" Have the students read to the next predetermined stopping place — you may tell them what it is or write it on the board — and close their books when they reach it.

■ *Subsequent stopping places should occur at points in the story where the plot and/or action has been raised to a high level of suspense and excitement.*

At each point, your questions are "*Now* what do you think is going to happen?" and "Why?"

■ *After the reading, you may ask a number of questions that will help to refine the students' reading and thinking skills.*

For example, ask, "How did you know that Timothy would probably tell his brother about the plan?" Such questions require students to recall, integrate, and apply information from the story and from their own backgrounds. You have the opportunity to reinforce reading skills by asking children to "find the place in the story where it says Hobie wasn't afraid, and read that for us." Remind the students that — just like the detective — they were using clues from their reading to stick to, to change, or to throw out their predictions.

If appropriate for the students, after you have dealt with your questions and their reactions to the reading, you may ask, "Were there any words in the story you didn't know? How did you try to figure them out?" By getting students to talk through their strategies, you are reinforcing what you have been teaching about analyzing unknown words: letter/sound knowledge and/or structural knowledge and how to use contextual clues. It may also give you the opportunity to model how to use context clues.

Even experienced teachers often raise some questions about the Directed Reading-Thinking Activity. Let's address these questions briefly here.

■ *How often do you do DRTA's with the children?*

There is no magical number of times, but you will probably conduct them more often during the first few months of school than later on. They are like reading "scrimmages"; close to the real thing but still monitored by the teacher. On the average, plan for at least one DRTA every two weeks.

■ *Students read at different rates or speeds. What about those who reach a stopping point before others?*

Usually, several seconds will separate the students' finishing times. You can take advantage of this time by leaning over and, in a whisper, asking a student who has finished for a prediction. Ask if there were any words the student did not know and whether and how he or she figured them out. Just a few seconds spent with a student this way will accomplish much.

You should also realize that students who are placed appropriately but who still read more slowly than necessary (and whose finishing times may be quite a bit behind the others') have probably just fallen into a habit of slow reading, which you can address separately.

■ *The usual way of reading a story in a teacher-directed group involves presentation of new words before the reading. In the narrative DRTA this is usually not done (see above). Why not?*

You save lots of time by not doing so! In addition, though, once children have learned a few word analysis skills, they should have the opportunity to *apply* these skills in actual reading. When we preteach words, we deny them that opportunity. Occasionally you may believe you simply must preteach a word; this is okay if the word is crucial to understanding the story, and if you believe the students do not know enough about words and how to use contextual clues to figure out the word on their own. Given these criteria, you will probably not be preteaching many words!

■ *Don't the students "peek" ahead to see what's going to happen, so their predictions will be "right"?*

This is a definite possibility! You can help prevent it by setting a tone that stresses the purpose is not always to be right but to think divergently and creatively about possibilities. But just to make sure, Stauffer (1969) recommended that, if you are using a set of basals, you keep them "off-limits," on a shelf in your reading circle area. Be up-front with the children; tell them these books will be used a lot for their DRTAs so they will be kept on a shelf and read from only at certain times. Remember, this assuredly does not deprive the students of reading, because there will be innumerable other reading materials in the classroom.

■ *What about that rare occasion when a student (for whatever reason) has read the story?*

Simply tell that student that this one time he or she will have to "sit back" during prediction times, or the student could write the predictions down for you. From time to time, some children may already be familiar with the story you are going to read, particularly if it has appeared in a number of versions (such as fairy tales and fables, for example). Although they will refrain from making predictions, you can ask them to keep in mind as they read how *this* version may be different from the one with which they are familiar.

■ *What if students are reluctant to offer predictions?*

This is often the case with students who have been in school for a while — they aren't sure what you *really* want or how you'll react, so they play it safe. In such cases, it is okay for you to offer a prediction to see what the group thinks about it; this is usually all that's required to spark the group. You may have to work on this in some cases, but it will be well worth the effort. Whatever you do, don't fall back on what was for years the mainstay of "setting purposes" in Teacher's Editions: "Read to find out [such and such]," with the teacher telling the students what to "find out." This takes the initiative and impetus away from the students and makes them dependent on you for their reading goals and purposes; thus, they have no "ownership" of their reading. (See also Kimmel and MacGinitie, 1985.)

Story Maps

A number of researchers (e.g., Beck, 1984; Reutzel, 1985) have noted the usefulness of *story maps* for both the teacher and students. These graphic aids serve two purposes: (1) for the teacher, constructing the story map assists in identifying the important elements in a story that the children will be reading, thereby delineating aspects on which the teacher can focus questions; (2) for the students, viewing the story map helps them to focus on the significant elements of narratives — setting, characterization, plot, problem and resolution — and on the relationships among these elements.

As with any visual or graphic aid, story maps should not become ends in themselves; students should not spend a lot of time constructing them and then being graded on them. Rather, the story maps should be a means to an end. You should introduce them after students have been reading and enjoying stories for some time and are ready to deal with them analytically.

In their simplest form, story maps include only the essential information in a story. As such, they help students distinguish the most important information and elements from other information. This "other" information is still important insofar as it affects the reader, but story maps will help in identifying the "skeleton" of the story.

Focusing on Specific Elements

When students are off and running with their reading of stories, and later of "chapter" books, they can focus on particular elements in order to explore and appreciate how writers develop characters, plot, resolution, and so forth (see Chapter 9). You will have discussed these elements with the students during your read-alouds, and as we saw in the previous chapter, they will be applying their understanding in their own *writing* of narratives.

Expository Texts

When was the last time you curled up by the fireplace with, say, a mathematics text — or perhaps more realistically, enjoyed the text as bedtime reading? Probably you haven't, but don't feel guilty. In part you did not do so because your purpose and motivation for reading a mathematics text is quite different from your purpose and motivation for reading a novel. Curiously, though, a lot of people think they should somehow remember as much from the math text — or any content area text — as they do from a novel. The beginning of strategic reading is the realization that these are different texts. Therefore, each text — the narrative and the textbook — should be read differently and for different purposes. Moreover, students should start learning about these differences in the elementary grades. They can then learn how to use different strategies in their reading — something that most adults have not learned!

The Content Directed Reading-Thinking Activity (CDRTA)

As we will see below, basic approaches to expository or content reading have some variations. In the intermediate grades, mainly you will be teaching students strategies for negotiating expository texts. Together with more direct teaching about the structure of these texts, this instruction will teach students how to learn from texts. The bedrock of your instruction will be the informational or *Content Directed Reading-Thinking Activity* (CDRTA).

If you have ever taken study-skills workshops or courses, you will probably recognize some common features among the strategies that were recommended there and the Content DRTA. That is hardly coincidental, because there are some basic ways readers can significantly increase their reading efficiency, retention, and recall. You can help your students build a strong foundation for these strategies in the intermediate grades by teaching them the techniques and the application of the Content DRTA.

I will outline the process of the Content DRTA as if it were the first time that you were conducting it with students; as you'll see later, you can adjust it to fit specific content objectives. Your purpose is first to teach the *process* of interacting with a content selection. When students understand and can apply the process of the Content DRTA, then you can change the focus to the actual content of what is read.

Because you initially will be focusing on the process, it is important that the

In the past, we too often assumed that simply because upper elementary students could read narratives, for example, and identify words, they could make the transition to reading textbooks. Not necessarily so! In my own case, I didn't truly learn how to read textbooks until graduate school; my usual method in college was to lay back on the bed with a textbook balanced on my stomach (say, *Western Civilization, Prehistory to 1648*) and begin reading on the first page of the chapter dealing with the Byzantine Empire. Several pages later I'd realize that, although my eyes had gone over every word, I really didn't recall much of what I'd "read." It's not that I didn't know there were other ways to read, but awareness was not enough. I needed to be put in situations where I would have been *required* to read texts in a more productive fashion in earlier years.

One could argue that I should have taken more responsibility for my own learning; knowing that there was a better way, I should simply have disciplined myself to do it. That's true, but I suspect I was more like most other students — if I wasn't required to do it, I wouldn't!

The purpose of this remembrance is to drive home a point: students should be taught how to read expository texts, and this teaching should continue until students almost automatically apply appropriate strategies. The Content DRTA is an extremely important first step in this process.

---

selections you use are well organized and logically constructed. Later, you can help your students deal with selections that are less well constructed.

1. The selection you choose to introduce the CDRTA should not be too lengthy. The number of words on the page at the intermediate grade levels varies tremendously, depending on the subject of the text and the publisher. Try, however, not to choose a passage that is more than eight pages long. You may have a selection in a textbook that seems very appropriate for this activity except for its length; that's fine — just ask your students to read only half of it.

2. When you have determined that your selection is appropriate, then read through it to determine the major concepts and organization. If these concepts are presented in terms that will be unfamiliar to your students, and if the context does not offer sufficient support for determining the meanings of these terms, you may wish to introduce these in advance. Try to limit the number of words to preteach, however.

3. You're ready to conduct the CDRTA with the children. As in the direct teaching model at the beginning of this chapter, when you conduct your first CDRTA, tell the children that they're going to be learning a strategy for reading informational selections. Especially tell them *why* you are teaching them this strategy. Explain that, just as with a story, they will make predictions about the information they are likely to encounter in the reading. Tell them that we do this type of reading usually because we need information, and that

making predictions and thinking about what we *do* know about the topic will help us to read and to hold on to the new information much better than if we simply read through from the first to the last page.

4. Explain that the very first step when reading informational material is to *preview* the selection. After reading the title, go through the selection, reading each heading as well as the captions for any pictures or diagrams, if included.

5. After the preview, help the students use the chapter title, headings, and sub-headings to make predictions as to the content of each section (in other words, they will be setting purposes for reading). In the process, you will of course be drawing out what the students already may know about the topic and getting insight into the extent of their knowledge base. Ask your students, "What information do you think we'll find in a section with the heading 'The Great Basin'?" Focus on only one heading at a time — have the students read *only* that heading and no farther.

    As in the narrative DRTA, you will write the predictions down where the students can see them.

6. Read the first section under the first heading. Then stop and review the predictions, confirming or rejecting any. At this point ask the students if there is any important new information they could add to their predictions.

    Continue in this format: read each heading, make predictions, read the section, check the predictions, and add new information. As you can see, one reason you should avoid a lengthy selection this first time around is so this cycle doesn't become redundant.

7. When you have finished reading the selection, review the major points that were covered by way of summary. Then, let the students know you are finished with the reading and that now you are going to tell them about the process in which they were just engaged. The teacher in the Classroom Example below is conducting such a review.

CLASSROOM EXAMPLE

"Boys and girls, what we have just done is read an informational selection the way it should be read. When your purpose is to really get a lot of information out of a book, you should read this way. Eventually you will be reading like this on your own, but we are going to do it as a group many times this year so that you will get better and better at it.

"When you read this way, you will preview the whole selection in order to get a general idea about what's going to be covered, then predict what you think you're going to find when you read a section. After you have read each section, you will stop and check your predictions and add new information if necessary, then go on to the next section. I can guarantee you that you will read better, get more information out of what you read, and remember it longer if you follow this method. Sounds like a commercial, doesn't it? But it's true!"

One adjustment you may need to make in teaching the CDRTA, ironically, arises from the fact that many textbooks are now better written and organized than in years past. Textbooks now usually include a list of objectives and/or prereading questions that really do help the students focus on important concepts. These can supplement and even provide a foundation for the predictions that the students will make, but don't let them take the place of students' predictions. If you do, the students will fall back into a more passive role and be lulled into believing that the text is going to do all the work for them.

Students who are introduced to the CDRTA after they have been reading informational texts for a while may complain that it takes much longer to read a textbook this new way. Initially, it does. Eventually, though, they will find that actually they *save* time by reading this way instead of having to reread the selection many times over, as they did in the old way. Let's get personal: If *you* have never read this way you will probably not wish to change now. But give it a try, ideally with a friend or a study group (like jogging or exercise, it's easy to skip if you're doing it alone but harder if you have a partner). If you are going to teach your students to do this, then you had better believe in it and do it yourself. Perhaps the best reinforcement is seeing the results on your next exam — particularly if the exam is in a subject in which you are not tremendously interested. This reinforcement also works for younger students too, by the way!

■ Build Your Teaching Resources

Books and Articles about CDRTAs

Procedures that are based on the concept of the CDRTA and that you should also try are described in the following articles:

Shoop, M. (1986). InQuest: A listening and reading comprehension strategy. *The Reading Teacher, 39,* 670–674.

Ogle, D. (1983). K-W-L: A teaching model that develops active reading of expository text. *The Reading Teacher, 39,* 564–570.

Excellent and extensive discussion of content DRTAs may be found in

Nessel, D., Jones, M., & Dixon, C. (1989). *Thinking through the language arts.* New York: Macmillan.

Stauffer, R. (1975). *Directing the reading-thinking process.* New York: Harper and Row.

The Prereading Plan (PReP)

Whenever students make predictions in a DRTA, they are actively preparing themselves for the reading, and you are gaining insight into how much they know about the topic. When you are pushing off into new waters for the most part — particularly before undertaking more extensive study of a new topic — you will want to organize more systematically and appropriately your instruction and the students' reading. You will need to get the students "hooked" by making connections between the new topic and what they already know, and you will need to find out *how much* they know about the topic. For example, you'll need to determine the degree to which the instructional materials you are organizing for your unit of study are appropriate and how you may need to adapt or adjust them for particular students. You'll also need to figure out which activities to use to facilitate learning for different students.

With all of these concerns in mind, Judith Langer (1981) developed the *prereading plan* (PReP), a common-sense approach to these objectives. The plan is actually an umbrella for many types of prereading activities. Briefly, here's how it works:

1. Let's say the major topic you are about to study in your fifth grade classroom is the solar system. Most students know *what* the solar system is by this time; just in case, though, to avoid putting them off with an unfamiliar or perhaps not-too-exciting term, you ask them, "Tell me whatever comes into your mind when you think of Earth and the other planets." You are poised at the chalkboard, ready to take down your students' associations. You may record in list format or in a cluster (see pp. 234 and 235). During these initial associations, you may ask other questions to keep the information coming — for example, "Why do you suppose most of the outer planets are made of gas?" and "Why are the inner planets so small?" After summoning a fair number of associations, ask the students to expand on them. Ask them why they thought of what they did — probe beneath the surface, in other words. This allows students to examine what they thought as well as to hear what other students have to offer, so that their thinking about the overall concept of the solar system is well stimulated. This is beneficial even for the students who did not offer any associations.

2. Now categorize the responses (Vaughan and Estes, 1985). This will help the students organize all the information that has come out. Ask the students how you might do this: "Now let's think of categories we can use to organize all this information we have." Initially, you may have to suggest some categories, such as "smaller planets," "larger planets," "moons," "asteroids," and "sun."

3. Beginning with the first category, ask if there is anything else that the students can add to each category. Because this activity is "evolutionary," in the sense that new ideas are building upon one another, by this phase you may find that several of the students' responses are a bit more sophisticated than in the first phase.

Now that you've activated the students' prior knowledge and they're sufficiently interested in the topic, you are ready to begin the new unit of study the next day. You'll use your planning time tonight to make any necessary adjustments.

Reading "Road Maps" and Interactive Reading Guides

To reinforce the different approach to reading content area material, as well as to help students who are not reading up to their potential negotiate a content selection, Wood and Mateja (1983) and Wood (1988) recommend the reading *"road map."* The idea of using a road map to traverse the reading terrain is a particularly

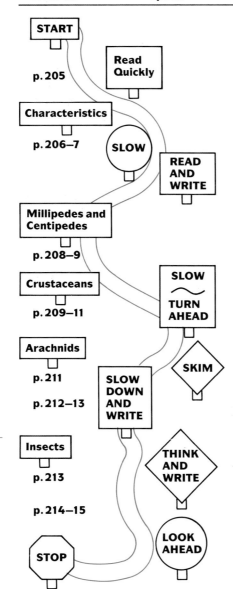

Chapter 13: Arthropods

Overall Mission: You are about to take a tour of the world of the arthropods

SKIM 1st

READ AND WRITE 2nd

Location   Speed   Mission

START

Read Quickly

p. 205

Characteristics

p. 206–7

SLOW

READ AND WRITE

Millipedes and Centipedes

p. 208–9

Crustaceans

p. 209–11

SLOW ~ TURN AHEAD

Arachnids

p. 211

p. 212–13

SLOW DOWN AND WRITE

SKIM

Insects

p. 213

THINK AND WRITE

p. 214–15

STOP

LOOK AHEAD

FIGURE 8.3

A Reading "Road Map" for a Chapter in a Science Text

Source: Fig. 2, "Guiding Students Through Informational Text," Karen D. Wood, *The Reading Teacher*, May 1988, p. 916. Reproduced with permission of Karen D. Wood and the International Reading Association.

1. Name three major characteristics of arthropods.
2. a. What does *arthropod* mean? Find at least 2 other words with the root *pod* in them.
   b. Why is the exoskeleton so important?
   c. Briefly describe the molting process. Why does it take place?
   d. How are arthropods grouped?
3. a. Recall three traits of millipedes; of centipedes.
   b. How do millipedes protect themselves?
   c. Why are centipedes called "predators"? What other animals are predators?
4. a. How would you know a crustacean when you saw one? Where would you look for one?
   b. In your own words, tell how barnacles can be harmful.
5. a. How could you recognize an arachnid? (paragraphs 1 & 2)
   b. How and what does a spider eat? (paragraph 3)
   c. Retell the second paragraph on page 213 in your own words.
6. a. In what ways are insects different from the other arthropods?
   b. Fill in the following information:
      I. Insects
         A. Beetles
            1)
            2)
         B.
            1)
            2)
         C.
            1) social
            2)
7. What have you learned from looking at the pictures on pages 214–215?
8. Reflect back on the four types of arthropods. See how much you can remember about each type: millipedes, centipedes, crustaceans, insects.

effective analogy to use with intermediate students. You can explain it to your students this way: "Before taking a trip, you plan where and how you're going, right? The same holds for reading, and this is where the reading road map comes in."

Figure 8.3 illustrates such a map; note the features that highlight what is particularly important and when students can "speed up" through certain portions of the selection (i.e., not read as carefully).

The *interactive reading guide* (Wood, 1988) is a particularly effective procedure to use with selections that are especially challenging or with texts that are not that well organized. Figure 8.4 illustrates one such guide. Notice the key to the number of individuals that will be involved at each step in the reading. In preparing such

FIGURE 8.4

An Interactive Reading Guide

Source: Fig. 3, "Guiding Students Through Informational Text," Karen D. Wood, *The Reading Teacher,* May 1988, p. 918. Reproduced with permission of Karen D. Wood and the International Reading Association.

Interaction codes:
    ○ = Individual
    ◍ = Pairs
    ⊛ = Group
    ◯ = Whole class

Chapter 12: "Japan — An Island Country"

⊛ 1. In your group, write down everything you can think of relative to the topics listed below on Japan. Your group's associations will then be shared with the class.

○◍ 2. Read page 156 and jot down 5 things about the topography of Japan. Share this information with your partner.

○ 3. Read to remember all you can about the "Seasons of Japan." The associations of the class will then be written on the board for discussion.

◍ 4. a. Take turns "whisper reading" the three sections under "Feeding the People of Japan." After each section, retell, with the aid of your partner, the information in your own words.
    b. What have you learned about the following?
       terraces, paddies, thresh, other crops, fisheries

⊛ 5. Put two pencils together and allow each person in the group to try eating with chopsticks. Discuss your experiences with the group.

◍ 6. With your partner, use your prior knowledge to predict if the following statements are true or false *before* reading the section on "Industrialized Japan." Return to these statements *after* reading to see if you've changed your view. In all cases, be sure to explain your answers. You do not have to agree with your partner.
    a. Japan does not produce its own raw materials but instead gets them from other countries.
    b. Japan is one of the top 10 shipbuilding countries.
    c. Japan makes more cars than the U.S.
    d. Silk used to be produced by silkworms but now it is a manmade fiber.
    e. Silkworms eat mulberry leaves.
    f. The thread from a single cocoon is 600 feet long.

○⊛ 7. After reading, write down 3 new things you learned about the following topics. Compare these responses with those of your group.
       Other industries of Japan
       Old and new ways of living

○⊛ 8. Read the section on "Cities of Japan." Each group member is to choose a city; show its location on the map in the textbook, and report on some facts about it.

○◯ 9. Return to the major topics introduced in the first activity. Skim over your chapter reading guide responses with these topics in mind. Next, be ready to contribute, along with the class, anything you have learned about these topics.

guides, you should keep in mind what students may be able to negotiate by themselves and what they should negotiate in pairs, triads, or larger groups.

Yes, these activities require additional preparation time and effort on your part. Trust the voices of experienced teachers here: you may not be able to prepare many of these reading guides your first year, but those you do prepare should pay off handsomely.

Graphic Post-Organizers

In addition to your post-reading questions, other activities can help the students organize and retain the information they have encountered in their reading. One of the most effective of these activities is what we will call the *graphic post-organizer.* Working together in a small group, students arrange 3″ × 5″ cards on which they have written important ideas and concepts from the previous reading so that the important relationships among the concepts are visually apparent. Groups can then compare their arrangements and discuss them; Figure 8.5 shows two such arrangements by fifth-graders.

Notice how the arrangement may also parallel the organization of the concepts in the reading! Years ago, educators suggested that the teacher use the graphic organizer as a *pre*reading tool, but research has since more strongly supported its use *after* reading. You can probably see why: this way the students are actively engaged in manipulating the concepts as they talk about how best to organize them.

Outlining

In a sense, outlines should play a valuable role in organizing and retaining information from expository texts, but let's face it — outlining is one of students' least favorite activities. If you are like most of your students, you did not enjoy doing outlines and you may be hard-pressed to appreciate their value even now. Outlining is an invaluable skill, though, and thus one that merits teaching. What are its purposes?

1. Outlining helps to reinforce students' learning of expository text structure.
2. Outlining helps students organize and understand the relationship among information in expository texts.
3. Outlining helps in studying and retaining important information.
4. Outlining helps to establish good note-taking skills for lectures, a mode of information presentation used sparingly in the upper elementary grades but extensively beginning in the middle grades. All too often, middle grade teachers assume students know how to outline while listening to a lecture, thus outlining winds up seldom being taught at *any* level.

The reason outlining is not appreciated is because outlines are usually introduced too soon and employed inappropriately. Students are not conceptually prepared for the abstractions that outlining involves. When outlining is presented as an aid to writing a report, for example, the criteria are usually too rigid: Students

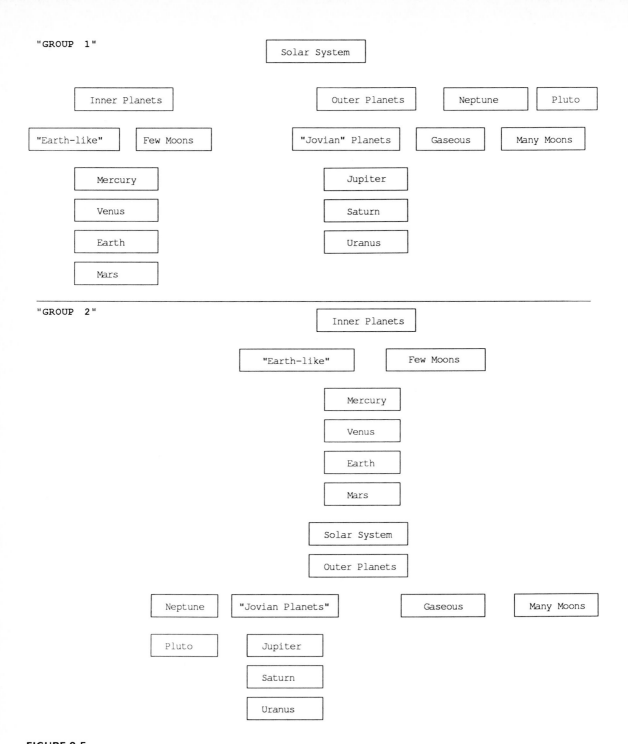

FIGURE 8.5

Student-Constructed Graphic Post-Organizers for a Chapter on "The Solar System"

are left with the impression that they must put everything that they plan to write about in outline form *prior* to actual drafting; moreover, if they find they are varying from the outline during the drafting, they are led to believe this is wrong because they are not following the outline. As we know from examining the process of writing, however, we rarely stay with the same writing plan with which we begin.

When and how should you teach outlining? Some fourth grade students and most fifth- and sixth-graders are definitely ready for outlining. Introduce it after students have been reading expository material for quite some time and after they are comfortable using the Content Directed Reading-Thinking Activity (CDRTA). They should by this time be familiar with graphic aids to reading and writing, such as webs or clusters, and with graphic post-organizers.

Although students understand by this point that authors of expository texts structure their writing in ways that highlight the most important information and supporting detail, they may not have a clear mental schema of this organization. As a prelude to teaching outlining, then, you should show students a visual schematic that clearly represents the levels and relationships among the main ideas. Figure 8.6 shows such a visual schematic for a chapter in a fifth grade science text. The teacher would display this schematic on a transparency and explain why each level occurs where it does: "Life Forms of Earth," at the top, is the main idea, with other important supporting ideas or concepts one level down; specific examples of each subdivision are at the next level, and so forth. This schematic shows relationships among the topic, supporting main ideas, and so forth, rather than simply a collection of facts arranged one after another throughout the chapter.

The visual schematic is more concrete because the levels of information are explicit. This is not as obvious in an outline, which represents the levels of information by labeling and indentation rather than by a progression from top to bottom. Thus, it is important for students to have a firm grasp on the concept of hierarchical organization before introducing the concept of outline.

Figure 8.7 shows an outline of the same chapter used for the visual schematic (Figure 8.6). Notice that the topmost idea in the visual schematic, which is the title of the chapter, is not included in the outline, but that all the other information is.

When you introduce the concept of outlining make sure that you begin with a well-organized chapter. Walk your students through the chapter, constructing the

FIGURE 8.6

Visual Schematic for a Chapter in a Science Text

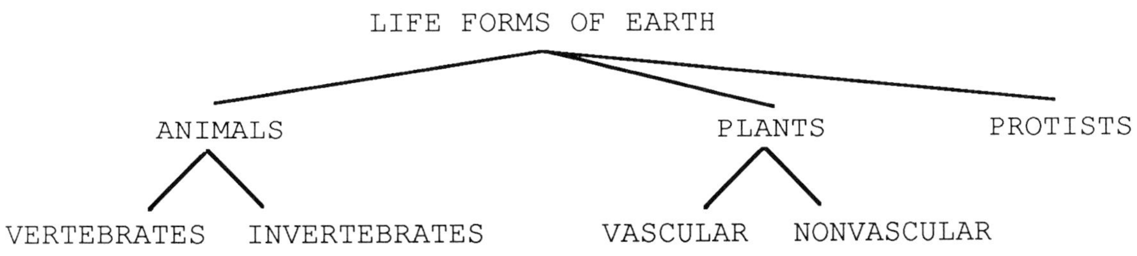

```
      I. ANIMALS

         A. VERTEBRATES

         B. INVERTEBRATES

     II. PLANTS

         A. VASCULAR

         B. NONVASCULAR

    III. PROTISTS
```

FIGURE 8.7

Outline for a Chapter in a Science Text

outline as you proceed. Explain how the outline represents the main ideas, supporting ideas, and details within each level: main ideas are the section headings and are designated by Roman numerals; supporting ideas and details are represented by capital letters and arabic numerals, respectively. When drawing up an outline, students should be assured not to worry excessively about maintaining proper form throughout. It is recommended that you work with students, however, until they have mastered the hierarchical concept of main idea/supporting idea/details.

An excellent extension of outlining is for students to use it as a note-taking strategy while listening to a lecture — a particularly important point in sixth grade, given that students are soon to be passed on to the middle grades. You begin by listing your major points (in Roman numerals) on the chalkboard. Following these, students then fill in the rest of the information at each level of the outline as you deliver a brief lecture. Afterwards, students compare and discuss their outlines with a partner or with a small group. You conclude by showing the students *your* outline on a transparency so that they can see how closely they approximated it (of course, make sure you follow your outline as you talk!). Explain why you have covered the material the way you have, thinking aloud as you go.

■ Build Your Teaching Resources

Reference for Outlining

If students need additional concrete examples of the logic underlying outlining, the following reference is extremely helpful:

Van Allen, R. (1976). *Language experiences in communication*. Boston: Houghton Mifflin.

Questioning in Reading

As I've emphasized throughout this book, questions are of the utmost importance in teaching and learning. Appropriate questions facilitate students' critical thinking as well as their topical, procedural, and self-knowledge. Questions also help you assess the degree to which students are comprehending as they read. We already know that you will be working on your questioning techniques and on the types of questions you ask. In addition, however, you will be helping your students understand better the relationships between questions and the information on which the questions are based.

We know that most students need to develop this understanding. For example, when students respond to questions based on their reading, they often think all the answers are in the book. If they can't find an answer, then they don't know what to do. In our emphasis on developing *active* and *strategic* readers, we will be helping the students realize that some answers are easy to find right there in the text; some answers require putting together information given in the text; some answers come from the students' combining their own knowledge with information in the text; and still others come from the students' own background information or from sources outside the text.

In addition, we will want to help students understand that questions work at different levels (for the types of questions, see Table 8.1). This does not mean we should teach our students the label for each type; it simply means we help them understand that some questions tap details, other questions tap higher-order information, and still others require them to manipulate this information in different ways in order to come to new understandings. Questions, in other words, will play a far greater role than simply as a check to see if the students know the information.

When can you start teaching the metacognitive aspects of questions and reading? Here's a general rule of thumb: start when children are reading more or less on a first grade level, have been enjoying books during Sustained Silent Reading, and have been reading stories with you in the context of DRTAs. We will now examine a very effective strategy you can use to help students become aware of the source of information in reading and how this information relates to questions about the reading. This strategy will in part help students learn they are in control, not at the mercy of the text they are reading. It is not always their fault, in other words, if a text is too complicated and/or they cannot find the answers.

"Question-Answer Relationships" (QARs)

Raphael (1982, 1986) has discussed the importance of students understanding the relationships between questions they are asked based on their reading and on their own prior knowledge. She has termed these relationships "Question-Answer Relationships," or "QARs." The way in which Raphael has characterized these relationships has not only been shown to be extremely effective in teaching about questioning, but also quite effectively helps to delineate the differences among the three major types of comprehension: literal, inferential, and critical (see p. 296). We will spend some time with Raphael's work, because it is one of the best examples of how our theoretical understanding of reading comprehension can be applied to effective classroom instruction.

As Raphael has explained, the value of QAR instruction "lies in the way it clarifies how students can approach the task of reading texts and answering questions" (Raphael, 1986, p. 517). Basically, Raphael makes a distinction between "In the

Book" and "In My Head" sources of information for answering questions; that is, between information that comes primarily from the text itself and information from the students' own background knowledge. If students understand this distinction, they are on their way to becoming more strategic readers and thinkers, unlikely to rely excessively on either their own background or on the text (Raphael, 1986).

Let's first examine how this basic distinction — "In the Book" and "In My Head" — is introduced in first or second grade.

CLASSROOM EXAMPLE

The teacher displays the following passage on a transparency:

Jerry picked up his bat, his ball, and his glove. He went to the playing field. Some boys were already hitting and catching fly balls.

The teacher now asks the following questions:

1. What did Jerry pick up?
2. Where did Jerry go?
3. What game is Jerry going to play?

After the students respond to the questions, the teacher asks, "How do you *know* Jerry picked up his bat, ball, and glove?" and "How do you *know* where he went?" The students will respond with something like "Because it says so!" or "It's right there!" The teacher underscores this, saying, "Good! You got that information from what you read. That is one place for finding answers to questions — in what you read. Now, how about the last question? How do you know they are going to play baseball? Does it say so?" The teacher helps the students understand that they had to rely on what they already knew to answer the question, because the answer was obviously not in the reading. He is then able to say, "You just used another good source of information besides what you read to answer the question: your *own* knowledge! A lot of times when you are reading and answering questions you will need to think about information that you already have up here, in your head."

As Raphael (1986) commented, it is important to keep the focus not necessarily on the correctness of the answers but on the *source* of the answers.

Beginning in second grade for some students, and in third grade for most, Raphael suggests that "In the Book" comprehension can be broken down into the categories of "Right There" and "Putting It Together." This captures the difference between *literal* ("reading the lines") and *inferential* ("reading between the lines") comprehension. The "In My Head" category, which often represents *critical* ("reading beyond the lines") comprehension, is broken down into "Author and You" and "On My Own."

For primary students who understand the "In My Head" and "In the Book" distinction, you will not present the rest of these distinctions all at once but begin with "Right There" versus "Putting It Together." Later on you can present the "Author and You" and "On My Own." For intermediate students, you may be able to present all four categories together as a review (assuming these have been introduced at the primary level); otherwise, present them separately, as is recommended at the primary level.

Presented in a direct teaching format, the following script illustrates how a fourth grade teacher might present and teach an awareness of these five categories.

<table>
<tr><td>CLASSROOM
EXAMPLE</td><td>

What Is to Be Learned

TEACHER: "Kids, you have been answering questions about what you read for quite some time now. Many times, though, it's important to know *how* and *where* to look for the answers to questions. This will help you better understand what you read. The key is to think about the wording of the question itself, because this will determine how and where you will look for the answer.

"Sometimes the answer to a question may be right there in your reading; other times you may have to come up with it by putting other information together. Still other times, the answer really isn't in your reading at all and you have to rely on information in your own head to come up with the answer.

"Today we're going to learn how and where you can look for the answers to questions based on your reading. We're going to use the labels you see here to talk about answers we can get in the book." [Displays the following diagram:]

</td></tr>
</table>

TEACHER: "Answers that are 'In the Book' are of these two types — they are either right there, where you can see them easily, or you may have to put the 'Right There' information together to get the answer.

"Now let's look at the labels we will use to talk about answers we *can't* get in the book." [Displays the following diagram:]

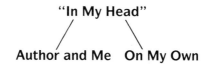

TEACHER: "Answers that are not in the book but come from your head are of these two types. In the 'Author and Me' type you need to think about what you already know and what the author tells you in order to come up with the answer. 'On My Own' answers come entirely from what you know or need to find somewhere else; you can often answer this type of question without even reading the text."

Modeling

TEACHER: "Let's read this paragraph [Displays it on a transparency] and then consider the questions that follow."

> Voyager II, which was launched in 1977, flew by Neptune in 1989. Scientists estimated that it should be able to continue to send messages back to Earth for another twenty-five years. Built to last for just five years, Voyager II was intended to send back information about only two planets. It lasted for twelve years and sent back information on four planets. The computer on board Voyager II is its only means of communication with Earth and is less powerful than the simplest microcomputer we use today for videogames and word processing!

The teacher then places a transparency with questions written on it below the passage and displays one question at a time:

TEACHER: "Okay, here's our first question based on this passage. [Displays "When did Voyager II fly by Neptune?"] Okay, what's the answer to this one? Dianne?"

DIANNE: "1989."

TEACHER: "How do you know?"

DIANNE: "It says so right there!"

TEACHER: "Right you are! So we would say that the answer to this first question is 'In the Book' — in this case, on this page — and is 'Right There.' You can tell because the wording of the question and the wording of the information in the book are the same.

"Now let's try another one. [Displays the question "How long should Voyager II be able to send messages back to earth?"] Yes, Keith?"

KEITH: "Twenty-five years."

TEACHER: "How do you know?"

KEITH: "It's just like Dianne's question — the answer's right there."

TEACHER: "Good. Again, you know it's right there because the wording of the question and the wording of the information in the book are the same. We're doing well so far. How about this question? [Displays "Has Voyager II lasted longer than scientists expected?"] Dreanne?"

DREANNE: "Yes!"

TEACHER: "Okay — how do you know?"

DREANNE: "'Cause it says it was 'built to last for just five years' and that it lasted for twelve years instead."

TEACHER: "Good! Dreanne, although the answer was 'In the Book,' in order to answer it you had to *put together* those two pieces of information. Kids, when we look at the wording of the question, it asks about Voyager lasting longer than scientists expected. When we look at the passage, nowhere do we find where it says 'Voyager has lasted longer than scientists expected.' So, we have to *put together* information that is supplied for us to answer the question.

"All right; here's another question. [Displays the question "What year will Voyager II probably stop sending messages?"] Suzanne?"

SUZANNE: "2014."

TEACHER: "Wow! How do you know?"

SUZANNE: "Well, it says it flew by Neptune in 1989, and that scientists estimate it can continue for another twenty-five years. So, I just added 25 onto 1989."

TEACHER: "Okay! So the answer was *not* 'Right There,' was it? You had to put some information together to come up with the answer. The information Suzanne put together was exactly the information she needed. The answer was 'In the Book,' so to speak, but Suzanne needed to put the information in the book together to come up with the answer.

"Here's another one. [Displays "Did the Voyager visit all the planets in our solar system?"] Okay, Lindie?"

LINDIE: "No, it didn't."

TEACHER: "Okay! But how do you *know* that it didn't?"

LINDIE: "'Cause there's nine planets in the solar system and it says Voyager only visited four."

TEACHER: "Did it say there are nine planets in our solar system?"

LINDIE: "No . . ."

TEACHER: "Then how'd you know that?"

LINDIE: "I just *knew* it already!"

TEACHER: "Good for you. In order to answer this question you needed to combine the information in your own head — there are nine planets — with the information that the author gave you about Voyager visiting four planets.

"Kids, Lindie's answer is what we call an "Author and Me" answer, because there is no way she could have come up with it unless she called on information she already has in her head and related it to the information in the reading.

"Let's do one last question, just for fun." [Displays "If it were possible, would you like to be a traveler on Voyager?"]

[At this point, several voices are heard at once, some saying "Yeah!" and others "No way!"]

TEACHER: "Okay, okay! We obviously have a difference of opinion on this one! But let's think for a moment about where our answers come from. Did you need any help from the author of this passage to answer the question or were you 'on your own'?" [Several students say "On our own."] "Right! You were on your own because you could answer such a question really without even reading the passage. Either you would enjoy long space flights or you wouldn't!"

Practicing

At this point in the lesson, the teacher will have the students each work on a task, under the teacher's supervision, that will require them to apply what has just been presented. The most straightforward task would be a sheet with another reading passage followed by questions; students would answer each question and label the QAR it represents: is it "Right There," "Putting It Together,"

"Author and Me," or "On My Own"? In this phase of the lesson, the teacher is free to give feedback to the students on their performance and do on-the-spot reteaching if necessary.

When the task is completed, it can be reviewed in the group.

Summary and Application

The teacher's summary will highlight the way to know how and where to look for the answers to questions, because it will help the students better understand what they read. It will also help them a lot when they're reading on their own and are looking for the answer to a question — the question may be one that *they* have asked and really need to know the answer to. This *application* of their knowledge of Question-Answer Relationships will occur in the context of "real" reading, when children are able to apply this knowledge as they explain, justify, or adjust their conclusions while moving through a piece.

Raphael (1982) presented an even more structured format in which to teach QARs. You may find her suggested format more beneficial for students who require a more systematic "walk-through" of the reasoning underlying "In the Book" versus "In My Head" relationships, or for students who are reading well below their potential. Regardless, as Pearson (1985) observed, in this instruction you will monitor the students' understanding and application as you "gradually release control" and require more performance and justification from the students.

Asking the Appropriate Questions

Now that we have discussed the relationship between questions and the texts on which those questions are based, let's examine another important feature of questioning. You already know you should ask different *types* of questions that stimulate students' thinking in developing topical knowledge and applying topical knowledge, but how do you generate these questions?

First of all, remember that well-designed literature-based reading series will supply a fair amount of good questions, because the publishers are responding to the recent research in questioning and reading. In other words, you won't have to begin on Day One with all original questions! As you examine many of these questions for their appropriateness, you will be applying criteria that you in turn will use in generating your own questions. Formulating effective, appropriate questions is a skill that you will continue to develop throughout your career as a teacher.

When to Ask the Questions

As we've seen, questions may be asked at several points: before reading, in the Directed Reading-Thinking Activity, where students' predictions are in effect questions; and both before and after reading, as in the questions textbooks may contain. You might now be wondering — is there any continuity or guideline for when *you* ask good questions that help the students comprehend what they are reading? As we saw in the last chapter, teacher questions can (and should) be genuine and often have no further objective than expressing true interest in what a student is pursuing in his or her writing. But of course you also have a responsibility to facilitate the development of critical thinking in your students' reading.

When you are working with a group of students in the context of reading a story or chapters in a novel (see Chapter 9), there are some basic guidelines you should follow.

1. Your questions should usually come after the reading of the story or chapter rather than interrupt the reading, although exceptions to this rule of thumb do occur from time to time. In the case of many first and second grade students, you may find that judicious questioning by you throughout the story does help for a while; this may also be the case with older students who are significantly behind their peers in reading.

2. Questions you ask during and after the reading should guide the students in developing or fleshing out a mental "map" of the story (Beck, Omanson, and McKeown, 1982; Reutzel, 1985). Students can use this "map" deliberately to reflect on the reading; this in effect raises to a conscious level and elaborates what we have in earlier chapters referred to as the "text model." For example:

    a. "Where (or when) did the story happen?" (setting)

    b. "What does (character name) do and say that makes him/her like (another character name)?" (characterization)

    c. "What is the problem (character name) faces?" (main idea; topic)

    d. "What does (character name) do first, second, etc?" (details of the plot)

    e. "What is the moral of this story — what's it *really* about?" (theme)

3. Next, questions that you ask help students apply the skills you have been teaching. For example:

    a. "What were you thinking Barb would do when you were on page 37?" (identify relevant details)

    b. "Why would Barb do that?" (identify cause/effect relationship)

    c. "What did the writer do to win you over to her point of view?" (detecting bias)

It is important to remember that often you can facilitate the application of skills, particularly those dealing with details, by asking higher-order questions. Then, when students are required to support their answers, they necessarily have to attend to the details — the lower-order relationships. Using higher-order questions thereby makes the context relevant rather than simply checking to see if the students remember specific details.

The Role of Free Reading

In a literature-based approach students are operating *all along* with a lot of "real" reading. That is, they are freely reading genuine, authentic literature. Ironically, however, in years past teachers often spent more time on trying to teach individual reading skills than on actual reading itself (Winograd, Wixson, and Lipson, 1989). We realize now that this is the wrong way around. Rather, we know that lots of "real" reading must be a built-in, regular component of the classroom, and the context for this can be established in kindergarten and in first grade (Anderson, Wilson, and Fielding, 1988).

One opportunity for the whole class to engage in this "real reading" simultaneously is usually referred to as Sustained Silent Reading (SSR), although, as you know, for most children in kindergarten and first grade this reading will be audible! It is also called Sustained Quiet UnInterrupted Reading Time (SQUIRT) (Cunningham, Moore, Cunningham, and Moore, 1989). Whatever you call it, it is extremely important for children to read, uninterrupted, for a period of time — a guaranteed, quiet time for the children to spend alone with their books.

The guidelines for SSR are simple; the only real adjustment throughout the year may be in the amount of time spent in SSR. Children may look at or read any reading material they choose: picture books, narratives, expository material, comic books, magazines, and so forth. There is *no talking* among the students at this time. In addition, you should read quietly yourself during SSR, thereby modeling sustained silent reading for your students. After SSR, children may share information about their reading if they wish.

The Role of Oral Reading

Oral reading is important. It begins with the *choral reading* that children do during the beginning literacy phase. In this context, oral reading is nonthreatening, enjoyable, and purposeful. Oral reading can become detrimental to students' development, however, if not used appropriately later on. Before examining how you should use oral reading, therefore, let's examine how you *shouldn't* use it.

Odds are that you've experienced how oral reading should not be used in the classroom. It should not be used in a "round-robin" fashion in which students take turns reading orally from a basal reader, going around the reading group circle. What usually happens in this situation (you may remember it!) is that instead of listening to the reading or following along in the book, each student spends most of the time looking for the part he or she expects to read orally and seeing how "hard" it is and if there are any unfamiliar words. Of course, the sequence usually gets changed along the way and the student winds up having to read a different section! "Round-robin" reading also occurs with textbooks. Each student reads one or two paragraphs orally, and on it goes throughout the chapter.

There are very good reasons why teachers have had students read this way in the past. First, particularly at the primary grade levels, teachers want to see how well the students are doing; you can tell whether or not they know most of the words by having them read orally. Second, teachers realize that students usually do not enjoy reading their textbooks and may in fact not read them. Teachers will know that the students have gone through the assigned chapter at least once if it is done in class.

So, although teachers have good reasons for using oral reading in these ways, there are other ways to determine how well students understand what they read

Used appropriately, oral reading can help students develop a better sense of the sounds, rhythms, cadences, and diversity of language. *(© Ulrike Welsch/Photo Researchers)*

and other ways to motivate them to read certain material. Having said this, just what *is* the role, if any, of oral reading?

In Chapter 6 and earlier in this chapter, we saw that reading out loud is unavoidable for most young children. Oral reading is a natural developmental phase. Language experience and shared reading experiences or Big Book activities build on this developmental phenomenon. As children pass from audible out-loud reading through whispering and on to silent reading, however, the value of oral reading should not diminish. There are three primary purposes for having students read orally: (1) to check comprehension, (2) to enhance appreciation of different genres as well as the nuances of different genres, and (3) to assess and evaluate reading development.

We have already seen how oral reading can be used to check comprehension. In the context of a DRTA, for example, a student will locate and read aloud a part of the text that supports her answer or opinion. This type of oral reading should be frequent; as is apparent, it is combined with other important strategies, such as rereading to prove a point and skimming to locate the appropriate passage. Using oral reading in this way, the teacher can check the student's ability in each of the three comprehension categories — not just the minor details.

The second purpose of oral reading is implicit in most of the activities we undertake with reading. Much of each genre scheme that students construct depends on the *way* in which language is used in different genres — on the sounds, the rhythms, the cadence of the language. Used appropriately, oral reading can develop an understanding and appreciation of these various aspects of language. There is an obvious difference in the use of language, of course, between poetry and narratives. But even within each of these genres, language functions in different ways in order to evoke different meanings. When texts are read silently, students often miss these nuances. By reading books or poems orally, students develop a better sense of the uses of language and in turn incorporate this into their silent reading. For example, the predictability of rhythms and rhymes in poetry delights young children, but for older students this same predictability becomes a parody of poetry — limited to a heavy-handed metrical beat with end-of-line rhymes. These students may benefit from also reading poetry that has more subtle rhythms and that does not end-rhyme.

The confidence to read orally before a group is in large part developed in the Author's Chair (Graves and Hansen, 1983). As we saw in Chapter 7, students first share their own writing and later may share the writing of children's authors. In both instances, of course, the children have probably read the material they will share orally to themselves several times before, an excellent experience in itself.

One of the most effective vehicles for developing an appreciation of the sounds of language is through the oral reading activity known as "Readers Theatre" (Busching, 1981; Chaparro, 1986; Stoyer, 1982). In Readers Theatre, a number of students orally read, for an audience, from a text in their hands. They take turns reading, depending on the type of text. For example, if characters are involved, each student reads a character's part; if the text is a poem, each student may read alternating lines or groups of lines.

Students will rehearse the text before presenting it, and will convey the action and emotion through their voices rather than acting it out as they would in a play or in creative dramatics. Minimal props may be used in Readers Theatre, such as masks, backdrops, and simple costumes. Students may move about, but usually it is not necessary to do so.

To illustrate, students from third grade on would delight in practicing and presenting Shel Silverstein's "Sarah Sylvia Cynthia Stout Would Not Take the Garbage Out" (1974). In this poem, Sarah Sylvia Cynthia Stout allows the garbage to accumulate, a process that Silverstein exquisitely describes. It becomes obvious in the poem that Sarah meets an unspeakable fate as the growing mound of garbage takes on monstrous proportions. Students' reading of this forty-seven-line poem could be divided between two groups of any number of students (Chaparro, 1986). The two groups of students could alternate reading two lines each, or perhaps six; the poem can be partitioned several different ways (you should make such decisions at first).

Using just this poem as an example, consider what is being highlighted and reinforced. First, there is a delight in the sounds of language through alliteration, such as the /s/ sounds in the name *Sarah Sylvia Cynthia Stout*, which is repeated throughout the poem, and through the poem's many captivating internal rhymes, such as the line ". . . Rubbery blubbery macaroni. . . ." And then there is the visual imagery of a growing mound of garbage and the dire consequences for Sarah.

Another very important type of knowledge is being developed through Readers Theatre. Because students will reread the same text several times in preparation for the presentation, fluency and reading rate develop and new words are reinforced, thus expanding and elaborating students' sight vocabularies.

Students enjoy presenting *radio plays,* which also must be read several times before sharing. The renaissance of plays on radio provide excellent models, and the students may enjoy combining the reading experience with sound effects. The most famous radio play of all time, Orson Welles's adaptation of H. G. Wells's *The War of the Worlds,* is widely available now on tape and record, and would be a marvelous introduction to the genre for intermediate level students.

When working with a group of students, whether your purpose for oral reading is to check comprehension or to develop genre schemes, *be sure that a student has read something already, usually silently, before you ask him or her to read it orally.* Why? Whenever students read orally in front of others, they naturally realize that they are "on stage" and must therefore read word-perfect. If you've ever read an unfamiliar text — whether a sentence or a page — in front of a group, you know what's on your mind: making sure you get through it without miscalling any words. Elementary students have the same concern. If they have already read the text, however, then the oral rereading is less threatening and, as I have emphasized, they have a definite purpose for reading aloud. The one exception to this rule is oral reading for assessment and evaluation purposes. Oral reading in this context will be done "in private," with the teacher.

■ Build Your Teaching Resources

Articles about Oral Reading

Additional readings that are especially relevant to this area are

Green, F. (1986). Listening to children read: The empathetic process. *The Reading Teacher, 39,* 536–543.

Manna, A. (1984). Making language come alive through reading plays. *The Reading Teacher, 37,* 712–717.

A CONCLUDING PERSPECTIVE

We have covered a lot of terrain in this chapter: the nature of reading comprehension and of word knowledge as it is applied in reading, as well as the role of the reader. The learning progression outlined here moves from beginning conventional reading to experiencing different types of texts to analyzing those texts in order both to understand the texts better and think more critically about their content and how it relates to students' lives.

Beginning conventional reading should occur in a natural context, one that gradually moves children from an experiential to an analytical perspective — all the while keeping reading enjoyable. Instruction builds on the strong foundation of children's prior knowledge about their world and about language.

After the beginning conventional reading phase, word analysis instruction in the context of reading aloud should focus on what knowledge is directly applicable in reading. More systematic word study will underlie vocabulary development and spelling; these aspects are addressed in Chapter 10.

Teachers should help students experience the different structures of and strategies for reading narrative and expository materials before emphasizing different learning strategies. In the intermediate grades, teachers play a significant role in preparing students for reading those texts, in walking them through the texts, and in consolidating knowledge gained after the reading.

Questioning and the nature of questions play a very large role in facilitating comprehension and critical thinking. The type of comprehension that a particular question taps — literal, inferential, or critical — depends on the text, the reader's prior knowledge, and the wording of the question in relation to the text.

Free reading time and oral reading are important elements in the reading instructional foundation. In the past, there has been much too little of the former and much too much emphasis on the latter — inappropriately undertaken, at that. We now understand the realistic roles each can play in reading development.

Teacher/student reading conferences are critical and extremely beneficial for instruction and for evaluation. The format of the individual conference is the foundation for group conferences, as we'll see in Chapter 9.

In the previous chapter we concluded with a comment on the creative power of writing and how, through writing, we become aware of what we believe in and the degree to which we believe in it. Many of the ideas that nurture creativity and beliefs come directly from students' reading and discussions based on reading. Many people can trace a monumental change in their lives — in their outlook, their beliefs — to the reading of a particular book. In an age where so much immediate stimulation competes with the extended, though often more compelling, world within a book, it would be wonderful if we could facilitate similar important reading experiences for our students. In this chapter we have erected the foundation for this experience; it is time now to move on and explore through reading and writing the worlds those books have to offer.

REFERENCES

Adams, M. (1990). *Beginning to read*. Cambridge, MA: MIT Press.

Anderson, R. C., Wilson, P. T., & Fielding, L. G. (1988). Growth in reading and how children spend their time outside of school. *Reading Research Quarterly, 23*(3), 285–303.

Barrett, T. C. (1976). Taxonomy of reading comprehension. In R. Smith & T. Barrett (eds.). *Teaching reading in the middle grades*. Reading, MA: Addison-Wesley.

Beck, I. (1984). Developing comprehension: The impact of the directed reading lesson. In R. C. Anderson, J. Osborn, & R. Tierney (eds.). *Learning to read in American schools: Basal readers and content texts*. Hillsdale, NJ: Lawrence Erlbaum Associates.

Beck, I. L., Omanson, R. C., & McKeown, M. G. (1982). An instructional redesign of reading lessons: Effects on comprehension. *Reading Research Quarterly, 17,* 462–481.

Busching, B. (1981). Readers theatre: An education for language and life. *Language Arts, 58,* 330–338.

Chall, J. (1989). Learning to read: The great debate 20 years later. *Phi Delta Kappan, 71,* 521–538.

Chaparro, J. (1986). Using Reader's Theatre to enhance reading comprehension. Notre Dame Reading Conference, June.

Combs, M. (1987). Modeling the reading process with enlarged texts. *The Reading Teacher, 40,* 422–426.

Cooper, J. D. (1986). *Teaching reading comprehension.* Boston: Houghton Mifflin.

Cunningham, P. M., Moore, S. A., Cunningham, J., & Moore, D. (1989). *Reading in elementary classrooms: Strategies and observations.* New York: Longman.

Davidson, J. L., & Wilkerson, B. C. (1988). *Directed Reading-Thinking Activities.* Monroe, NY: Trillium Press.

Dudley-Marling, C. (1985). Microcomputers, reading and writing: Alternatives to drill and practice. *The Reading Teacher, 38,* 388–391.

Durkin, D. (1978/79). What classroom observations reveal about reading comprehension instruction. *Reading Research Quarterly, 14,* 481–533.

Eeds, M. (1985). Bookwords: Using a beginning word list of high frequency words from children's literature K–3. *The Reading Teacher, 38,* 418–423.

Ehri, L., & Wilce, L. (1987). Does learning to spell help beginners learn to read words? *Reading Research Quarterly, 22*(1), 47–65.

Ehri, L. (in press). The development of the ability to read words. *Handbook of Reading Research.* New York: Longman.

Flood, J., & Lapp, D. (1989). Reporting reading progress: A comparison portfolio for parents. *Reading Teacher, 42,* 508–514.

Flood, J., & Lapp, D. (1986). Types of texts: The match between what students read in basals and what they encounter in tests. *Reading Research Quarterly, 21*(3), 284–297.

Freebody, P., & Byrne, B. (1988). Word-reading strategies in elementary school children: Relations to comprehension, reading time, and phonemic awareness. *Reading Research Quarterly, 23*(4), 441–453.

Gillet, J., and Kita, M. J. (1979). Words, kids, and categories. *The Reading Teacher, 32*(5), 155–175.

Goodman, K. (1987). *What's whole in whole language?* Portsmouth, NH: Heinemann.

Goodman, K., Shannon, P., Freeman, Y., & Murphy, S. (1988). *Report card on basal readers.* New York: Richard C. Owen.

Graves, D., & Hansen, J. (1983). The author's chair. *Language Arts, 60,* 176–183.

Haggard, M. R. (1988). Developing critical thinking with the Directed Reading-Thinking Activity. *The Reading Teacher, 41,* 526–533.

Hall, M. A. (1980). *Teaching reading as a language experience.* Columbus, OH: Merrill.

Hancock, J., & Hill, S. (eds.) (1987). *Literature-based reading programs at work.* Portsmouth, NH: Heinemann.

Heald-Taylor, G. (1987). Predictable literature selections and activities for language arts instruction. *The Reading Teacher, 41*(1), 6–12.

Heald-Taylor, G. (1987). How to use predictable books for K–2 language arts instruction. *The Reading Teacher, 40,* 656–661.

Henderson, E. (1981). *Learning to read and spell: The child's knowledge of words.* DeKalb, IL: Northern Illinois University Press.

Henderson, E. H., & Beers, J. W. (eds.) (1980). *Cognitive and developmental aspects of learning to spell.* Newark, DE: International Reading Association.

Holdaway, D. (1979). *The foundations of literacy.* Sydney, AUS: Ashton-Scholastic.

Hornsby, D., Sukarna, D., & Parry, J. (1986). *Read on: A conference approach to reading.* Portsmouth, NH: Heinemann.

Kimmel, S., & MacGinitie, W. H. (1985). Helping students revise hypotheses while reading. *The Reading Teacher, 38,* 768–771.

Langer, J. A. (1981). From theory to practice: A prereading plan. *Journal of Reading, 25,* 152–156.

McCallum, R. D. (1988). Don't throw the basals out with the bath water. *Reading Teacher, 42,* 204–208.

Martin, B. (1983). *Brown bear, brown bear, what do you see?* New York: Holt.

Meyer, B. (1975). *The organization of prose and its effect on memory.* Amsterdam: North-Holland Press.

Meyer, B. (1984). Organizational aspects of text: Effects on reading comprehension and applications for the classroom. In J. Flood (ed.), *Promoting reading comprehension.* Newark, DE: International Reading Association.

Morrow, L. M. (1989). *Developing literacy in the early years: Helping children read and write.* Englewood Cliffs, NJ: Prentice-Hall.

Nessel, D. D., & Jones, M. B. (1981). *The language-experience approach to reading: A handbook for teachers.* New York: Teachers College Press.

Ogle, D. (1983). K-W-L: A teaching model that develops active reading of expository text. *The Reading Teacher, 39,* 564–570.

Palincsar, A. S., & Brown, A. L. (1984). Reciprocal teaching of comprehension fostering and comprehension monitoring. *Cognition and Instruction, 1*(2), 117–175.

Pearson, P. D. (1985). Changing the face of reading comprehension instruction. *The Reading Teacher, 38,* 724–738.

Pearson, P. D., & Johnson, D. D. (1978). *Teaching reading comprehension.* New York: Holt, Rinehart and Winston.

Raphael, T. (1982). Teaching children question-answering strategies. *The Reading Teacher, 36,* 186–191.

Raphael, T. (1986). Teaching question-answer relationships, revisited. *The Reading Teacher, 39,* 516–522.

Reutzel, D. R. (1985). Story maps improve comprehension. *The Reading Teacher, 38,* 400–404.

Richgels, D., McGee, L., Lomax, R., & Sheard, C. (1987). Awareness of four text structures: Effects on recall of expository text. *Reading Research Quarterly, 22*(2), 177–196.

Shannon, P. (1988). *Broken promises: Reading instruction in twentieth-century America.* Granby, MA: Bergin and Garvey.

Silverstein, S. (1974). *Where the sidewalk ends.* New York: Harper and Row.

Smith, N. (1985). The word processing approach to language experience. *The Reading Teacher, 38,* 556–559.

Stauffer, R. (1969). *Directing reading maturity as a cognitive process.* New York: Harper and Row.

Stauffer, R. (1975). *Directing the reading-thinking process.* New York: Harper and Row.

Stauffer, R. (1980). *The language-experience approach to the teaching of reading.* New York: Harper and Row.

Stoyer, S. (1982). *Readers Theatre: Story dramatization in the classroom.* Urbana, IL: National Council of Teachers of English.

Strickland, D. S. (1988). Some tips for using Big Books. *The Reading Teacher, 42,* 966–967.

Strickland, D. S., & Morrow, L. M. (1989). Interactive experiences with storybook reading. *The Reading Teacher, 42*(4), 322–323.

Stuart, M., & Coltheart, M. (1988). Does reading develop in a sequence of stages? *Cognition, 30,* 139–181.

Sulzby, E. (1980). Using children's dictated stories to aid comprehension. *The Reading Teacher, 33*(7), 772–778.

Templeton, S. (1986). *Metalinguistic awareness: A synthesis and beyond.* In D. B. Yaden, Jr., & S. Templeton (eds.), *Metalinguistic awareness and beginning literacy: Conceptualizing what it means to read and write.* Portsmouth, NH: Heinemann.

Templeton, S. (1989). Tacit and explicit knowledge of derivational morphology: Foundations for a unified approach to spelling and vocabulary development in the intermediate grades and beyond. *Reading Psychology, 10,* 233–253.

Templeton, S., Cain, C. T., & Miller, J. O. (1981). Reconceptualizing readability: The relationship between surface and underlying structure analyses in predicting the difficulty of basal reading stories. *Journal of Educational Research, 74*(6), 382–387.

Templeton, S., & Bear, D. (eds.) (in press). *Development of orthographic knowledge and the foundations of literacy: A Memorial Festschrift for Edmund Henderson.* Hillsdale, NJ: Lawrence Erlbaum Associates.

Tierney, R. J., Mosenthal, J., & Kantor, R. N. (1984). Classroom applications of text analysis: Toward improving text selection and use. In J. Flood (ed.), *Promoting reading comprehension.* Newark, DE: International Reading Association.

Trachtenburg, P., & Ferruggia, A. (1989). Big books from little voices: Reaching high risk beginning readers. *The Reading Teacher, 42*(4), 284–289.

Vaughan, J., & Estes, T. (1985). *Reading and reasoning beyond the primary grades.* Boston: Allyn and Bacon.

White, T. G., Power, M. A., & White, S. (1989). Morphological analysis: Implications for teaching and understanding vocabulary growth. *Reading Research Quarterly, 24*(3), 283–304.

White, T. G., Graves, M. F., & Slater, W. H. (in press). Growth of reading vocabulary in diverse elementary schools: Decoding and word meaning. *Journal of Educational Psychology.*

Winograd, P. N., Wixson, K. K., & Lipson, M. Y. (eds.) (1989). *Improving basal reading instruction.* New York: Teachers College Press.

Wood, K. D. (1988). Guiding students through information text. *The Reading Teacher, 41,* 912–920.

Wood, K. D., & Mateja, J. A. (1983). Adapting secondary level strategies for use in elementary classrooms. *The Reading Teacher, 36,* 492–495.

Wysocki, K., & Jenkins, J. R. (1987). Deriving word meanings through morphological generalization. *Reading Research Quarterly, 22,* 66–81.

Yaden, D. B., Jr. (1988). A classification scheme for categorizing the types of questions that children ask during storybook read-alouds: Theoretical and empirical proofs. Paper presented at the 38th annual meeting of the National Reading Conference, December, Tucson, AZ.

Yaden, D. B., Jr., & Templeton, S. (eds.) (1986). *Metalinguistic awareness and beginning literacy: Conceptualizing what it means to read and write.* Portsmouth, NH: Heinemann.

Responding to Literature Through Reading and Writing

FOCUSING QUESTIONS

- Why is literature-based reading and writing so effective in developing students' thinking and growth in the language arts?
- How can you help students who are used to a more "traditional" curriculum effectively make the transition to a literature-based curriculum?
- How do Literature-Response Groups operate? What are some other examples of effective literature-response activities?
- What is involved in developing literature-based or themed units?

Perhaps one of the more dramatic responses to literature was once recounted by Judy Blume, author of both adult and children's fiction. She recalled one of the first books she ever read, Madeline, *by Ludwig Bemelmans (1939). Her mother had checked it out for her at the library, and when it came time to return the book, Blume hid it because she thought it was the only copy of the book in the world and she didn't want to give it up!*

INTRODUCTION

Would that every child were naturally so desperately enamored of books! In this chapter, we will be examining ways in which elementary students and literature can become better acquainted. One of our goals, as Stewig (1988) expressed it, will be to bring "the right books to the right children at the right time." Beyond this, a second goal will be to involve students in reading both *intensively* and *extensively* (Harste, Short, and Burke, 1989). That is, some texts the children will read, analyze, grapple with, and discuss at length. Others they will read just to enjoy, in the process of "compiling a personal literary history" (Peterson, 1987, p. 22). Both types of reading can develop through the types of response activities you will be arranging in your classroom.

In addition to reading and writing in response to literature that is personally gratifying and enlightening, students will be building the foundations for appreciating literature that meaningfully explores the nature of humankind. As Trelease so aptly describes: "Literature allows us to visit the heart and soul of humanity; it gives us the opportunity to listen in on what Robert Hutchins called 'the great conversation' — thoughts and values spanning thousands of years. The finest, most profound thoughts of the human species are available to us within the covers of books. It doesn't matter that Aesop, Twain, or Longfellow are centuries dead. In books, the thoughts and voices of the dead live" (Trelease, 1986, p. 70). And as C. S. Lewis succinctly defined it, good literature is "literature equally worth reading at ten and at fifty."

This is what literature can be for our students. Lesley Morrow, however, starkly portrays the reality: most teachers appear "neither to assign literature-related experiences a high priority in their classrooms nor to see [literature] as an integral component of instructional programs" (Morrow, p. 211, 1989). But there is hope. Over the past few years, a growing movement has developed that will eventually affect to various degrees how teachers teach the language arts: the movement toward *literature-based* reading and writing.

Whether literature-based reading and writing will effectively take hold in the majority of the nation's schools remains to be seen, but many educators believe we are on the verge of a monumental reorientation of reading and writing instruction, from primarily skills-based to primarily literature-based. You will be in the vanguard of this movement; you will see basal reading and English series reoriented to reflect a literature base, but as we have discussed before in this book, these materials are not the core of your instruction. *Your* knowledge base and expertise will guide what happens in your classroom.

There will also be challenges. As I have emphasized throughout the book, when you place literature in the center of teaching and learning in the language arts, you are addressing and encouraging critical thinking head-on. This approach opens up thinking and questioning by children in all grades. As the writers, publishers, and educators who support the annual Banned Book Week (a week during which the perils of censorship are underscored) have stated, "We believe . . . that what people read is deeply important, that ideas can be dangerous, but that the suppression of ideas is fatal to a democratic society. Freedom is a dangerous way of life, but it is ours." This is a rather compelling statement; although opening students up to critical thinking in response to ideas in print is challenging, it can be a heady experience for all concerned!

How will you handle issues that are potentially controversial or at least uncomfortable for you? Usually you will explore them honestly, within recognized constraints of judgment and decorum. When and whether you discuss other issues will depend on you, your students, and the standards of the community in which you teach. Anything that adult literature deals with, though, is now reflected in children's literature as well. As Cullinan (1981) sagely observed, it may perhaps be better for children to experience occasionally the "unpleasantries" of reality once removed, through literature, than to experience them directly. I would add that, for those children who tragically may experience severe and distressing situations, dealing with them in part through literature is far better than feeling powerless and confused in the face of those situations.

The issues of controversial topics, of censorship, and of the accuracy of the information provided in the books students read will always be a part of education. Objections to the books children encounter come not only from "radical" or "reactionary" fringes but also from within our midst. Sebesta (1989) cites the example of the art teacher who objected to the way great artists were portrayed through cartoons in *Rembrandt Takes a Walk* (Strand, 1986).

With respect to these issues, Sebesta suggests the following policy statement; it can reflect your own beliefs as well as, we would hope, those of your school and your school district:

Trade books for this class are selected for quality, many of them for pertinence to the curriculum. They do not ignore controversy but attempt, instead, to handle controversy with fairness and accuracy. We discuss books openly, and we attempt to evaluate them with students. We teach an open, inquiring attitude, and we do not teach that authors' messages are irrefutable. Authors are fallible, like the rest of us, but we attempt to select those who are thoughtful and knowledgeable. (Sebesta, 1989, p. 120)

In addition to everything else you must learn, you may now feel that you must become an expert in children's literature as well! Eventually, you probably *will* become an expert; for the near future, I will offer what I hope is a reassuring perspective. Yes, your goal should be to immerse your students in literature, both fiction and nonfiction. To accomplish this goal, you will need to read and learn about children's literature and become quite knowledgeable about it. As with developing expertise in any area, this will take time. In this chapter, I offer some support for you to gradually make the transition to literature-based instruction.

We will be exploring several topics related to literature-based reading and writing, bringing together everything that has been considered thus far in this text.

- We will first consider briefly the research base for literature-based reading and writing.
- In preparation for our later instructional strategies and contexts, we will review the categories of children's literature and investigate the basic elements of narratives.
- We will examine the potential for elementary students' response to literature.
- We will map out a suggested transition to literature-based reading and writing.
- We will discuss the format for literature-response groups.
- We will look at literature-response activities that effectively integrate the previous language arts strategies and emphases; it will become apparent how

the types of group discussions and questioning we reviewed earlier, for example, can be incorporated within the literature-based framework.

- ■ We will discuss how to construct and conduct literature units, using illustrative units for the primary and intermediate levels.

Foundations for Literature-Based Reading and Writing in the Classroom

From this point on the presentation of topics in this chapter will follow a progression that I suggest your teaching and your students' experiences follow, at least during your first year of teaching, and perhaps for a little while longer. With time, you will feel comfortable combining a couple of steps in this sequence. Our starting point in this chapter is the assumption that you have been reading and writing in your class for a few weeks, as well as meeting with smaller groups for DRTAs and direct teaching. In the next step, the "transition" step, you will change somewhat your procedure for read-alouds to the whole class. I will present a number of literature-response activities as a prelude to then pulling everything together — the move into literature-response groups (teacher/students and students/students) and into themed literature units.

Studies that have addressed the effectiveness of literature-based instructional programs seem to underscore one central and obvious finding: students who read more are better readers. That finding is hardly a surprise, but more important are the students' attitudes about reading and the degree to which they value reading. Their attitudes are more positive than those of students who are not exposed systematically to real literature (Cullinan, Jagger, and Strickland, 1974; Tunnell and Jacobs, 1989). Not surprisingly, students in classrooms where literature is readily available, and whose teachers place a high value on reading that literature, do on the whole tend to read more. For beginning readers in particular, intense involvement with books, supplemented by word-analysis instruction, yields better achievement than other instructional emphases (Eldredge and Butterfield, 1986). Not only are test scores and attitudes better, but the quality of students' language (Chomsky, 1972) and in many instances their reasoning (Stanovich, forthcoming) are more advanced than for students who have not been exposed systematically to real literature.

It certainly makes sense that if children read more and read *real* literature, they will be better readers and writers and will enjoy these undertakings more. Even publishers of basal reading series have been encouraging teachers not to rely solely on the series for students' reading experiences but to supplement and extend this instruction (Anderson, Osborn, and Tierney, 1984). But as we have already seen, the belief in the "discrete subskills" approach has held powerful sway in teachers' perceptions (Shannon, 1983). This belief is one that most educators hope will gradually be transformed in the next few years.

This chapter mentions a number of books and authors, mainly to give you a sampling, however limited, of the range and depth of books available. Some of these titles and their authors are considered by many people to be the best in their genre, others perhaps are not. My underlying purpose is to illustrate and, should you not yet be captivated by children's literature, to draw you in!

Categories of Children's Literature

We will spend a little time here addressing topics that are more extensively treated in a children's literature course; my purpose is to establish a foundation for further exploration. Depending on which overview of children's literature you consult, you will encounter different categorization schemes for children's literature. Most overviews, however, hold many categories in common. No category is exclusively the domain of any particular age group.

Alphabet Books

Alphabet books may teach "the basics" — that is, *print awareness* as well as the *shapes, names,* and *sounds* of the letters — but many of them work on several levels. Authors and illustrators often suggest visual metaphors and symbols that engage the older reader as well. You will find that most of these books are an enchanting visual feast, and for young children they will constitute the powerful and warm visual images that will reinforce learning these building blocks of written language. I mention here just a few of many excellent alphabet books.

Selected Alphabet Books

Anno, M. (1976). *Anno's alphabet: An adventure in imagination.* New York: Thomas Crowell/Farrar.

Baskin, H., Baskin, T., & Baskin, L. (1972). *Hosie's alphabet.* New York: Viking Press.

Isadora, R. (1983). *City seen from A to Z.* New York: Greenwillow Books.

Kellogg, S. (1987). *Aster aardvark's alphabet adventures.* New York: Morrow.

Provensen, A., & Provensen, M. (1978). *A peaceable kingdom: The Shaker abecedarius.* New York: Viking.

Wildsmith, B. (1963). *Brian Wildsmith's ABC.* New York: Franklin Watts.

Picture Books

Do the pictures tell most or all of the story in a book? If so, the book will usually be classified as a picture book — even if it has accompanying text. As we will explore later in this chapter, pictures and illustrations can provide an excellent stimulus for critical thinking. Picture books can encompass the topics and themes of the other categories of children's literature; they also comprise most of the predictable literature for primary students and some of the predictable themed literature for intermediate students. Following are some suggested titles.

Selected Picture Books

Bemelmans, L. (1962). *Madeline.* New York: Viking.

Burton, V. L. (1939). *Mike Mulligan and his steam shovel.* Boston: Houghton Mifflin.

Carrick, D. (1976). *The deer in the pasture.* New York: Greenwillow.

Emberly, B. (1967). *Drummer Hoff fired it off.* Englewood Cliffs, NJ: Prentice-Hall.

Gibbons, G. (1986). *Up goes the skyscraper!* New York: Four Winds Press.

Hoban, R. (1964). *Bread and jam for Frances.* New York: Harper and Row. [There are several books in the Frances series; they all work on both the child's level and the adult's level (particularly for parents!).]

Hoban, T. (1973). *Over, under and through and other spatial concepts.* New York: Macmillan.

Hutchins, P. (1968). *Rosie's walk.* New York: Macmillan.

Keats, E. J. (1962). *Snowy day.* New York: Viking.

McCloskey, R. (1941). *Make way for ducklings.* New York: Viking.

Rockwell, A., & Rockwell, H. (1972). *Toad.* New York: Doubleday.

Steptoe, J. (1984). *The story of jumping mouse.* New York: Lothrop, Lee, and Shepard.

Ungerer, T. (1967). *Zeralda's ogre.* New York: Harper and Row.

Van Allsburg, C. (1984). *The mysteries of Harris Burdick.* Boston: Houghton Mifflin. [Any of Van Allsburg's books are excellent; his illustrations are uniformly terrific and occasionally provocative.]

Waber, B. (1972). *Ira sleeps over.* Boston: Houghton Mifflin.

Wordless Books

Just as with picture books, wordless books — books with no accompanying text — are appropriate for intermediate as well as primary students. They can be used for any number of purposes and are powerful "concept development" tools as well as spurs to critical thinking. Again, the following list is merely a sampling.

Selected Wordless Books

Bang, M. (1980). *The grey lady and the strawberry snatcher.* New York: Four Winds Press.

Brinckloe, J. (1974). *The spider web.* New York: Doubleday.

dePaola, T. (1981). *The hunter and the animals.* New York: Holiday House. [dePaola is a well-known, excellent artist with quite a number of books to his credit.]

Krahn, F. (1968). *Sebastian and the mushroom.* New York: Delacorte Press/Seymour Lawrence.

Mayer, M. (1967). *A boy, a dog, and a frog.* New York: Dial. [This is the first in a series about these three friends by this outstanding children's illustrator.]

Parnall, P. (1970). *The inspector.* New York: Doubleday.

Ward, L. (1973). *The silver pony.* Boston: Houghton Mifflin.

Traditional Literature

This category embraces a large number of genres: nursery rhymes, fables, folk and fairy tales, myths, legends, and biblical stories. Many of these genres can be introduced through storytelling (see Chapter 5). The Bible is somewhat problematic, but fairly clear distinctions between biblical stories and particular religious interpretations can easily be made. So many of our contemporary and historical allusions are to the Bible and most of our value systems have roots there; as a result, some educators now argue that, purely apart from religious grounds, teachers have an obligation to share at least some of these stories (Peetoom, 1989).

Fables and folk tales reflect standards of behavior and belief. Often the moral is explicitly stated. In fables the main characters are usually animals; in folk tales humans predominate. These stories are basically optimistic in tone. Myths and legends usually represent a people's attempt to come to grips with more grandiose themes: creation, life, and death. Myths have attempted to account for the tremendous variety of natural phenomena that early peoples observed: the seasons; the sun, moon, and stars; storms, floods, earthquakes, and so forth. The basic narrative format in all forms of traditional literature developed and flourished as a response to the psychological and emotional needs of the listeners and readers to whom it spoke.

Selected Traditional Literature

Aardema, V. (1975). *Why mosquitos buzz in people's ears.* New York: Dial. [African]

Aesop's fables. (1981). New York: Viking Penguin. Illustrated by H. Holder.

Brown, M. (1947). *Stone soup.* New York: Scribners.

Bushnaq, I. (1986). *Arab folktales.* New York: Pantheon.

Chaikin, M. (1987). *Exodus.* New York: Holiday House.

D'Aulaire, I., & D'Aulaire, E. (1962). *D'Aulaire's book of Greek myths.* New York: Doubleday.

dePaola, T. (1987). *The parables of Jesus.* New York: Holiday House.

Gag, W. (1936). *Tales from Grimm.* New York: Coward-McCann.

Hastings, S. (1985). *Sir Gawain and the loathly lady.* New York: Lothrop, Lee, and Shepard.

Haviland, V. (ed.) (1979). *North American legends.* New York: Collins. [Native American]

Hazeltine, A. (1961). *Hero tales from many lands.* New York: Abingdon. [Includes stories from Greece, Hungary, Iran, Ireland, and Finland, for example.]

Hutton, W. (1986). *Moses in the bulrushes.* New York: McElderry Books.

Kellogg, S. (1984). *Paul Bunyan.* [Retold]. New York: Morrow.

Little, E. (1987). *David and the Giant.* New York: Random House.

Lobel, A. (1973). *Gregory Griggs and other nursery rhyme people.* New York: Greenwillow Press.

McDermott, G. (1972). *Anansi the spider: A tale from the Ashanti.* New York: Holt, Rinehart, and Winston. [African]

Perrault, C. (1976). *The sleeping beauty.* New York: Crowell.

Serwer, B. L. (1970). *Let's steal the moon.* Boston: Little, Brown. [Jewish]

Yagawa, S. (1981). *The crane wife.* New York: Morrow. [Chinese; translated by K. Paterson]

Zemach, M. (1976). *It could always be worse.* New York: Farrar, Straus, and Giroux. [Jewish]

Poetry

A poet once said that we should first listen to poetry with our hearts rather than with our ears. What he was expressing was the belief that we should not try to figure out "what it means" when we hear a poem, but simply allow it to wash over us. The effect we then feel is the true effect of poetry. Somewhat later, we can analyze *how* and *why* we experience this effect and respond to what Sebesta aptly described: ". . . the printed poem, with its unique arrangement on the page, and accompanying illustrations, may have a visual impact that, in itself, has power to arouse the reader" (1984, p. 68).

In Chapter 7 we discussed the writing of poetry and how easy it can be for students to generate poetic work. In this chapter we will explore some possibilities for using poetry with elementary students and suggest how exposure to and discussion of poetry can benefit students and complement their own writing of poetry. As was observed in Chapter 2, it so often appears that young children are natural poets, though for reasons rather different than those that motivate older poets. As teachers, it is exciting to realize that we may have a part in perhaps rejoining students with their "poetic roots." And when we do encourage close reading of a poem — as we should — we should present the activity "so that independent readers give good poetry the time, attention, and reflection needed for literary experience" (Sebesta, 1983, p. 70).

Selected Poetry Books

Adoff, A. (ed.) (1974). *My black me: A beginning book of black poetry.* New York: E. P. Dutton.

Baylor, B. (1972). *When clay sings.* New York: Scribner's.

Bierhorst, J. (ed.) (1971). *In the trail of the wind: American Indian poems and ritual orations.* New York: Farrar, Straus, and Giroux.

Blake, Q. (1983). *Quentin Blake's nursery rhyme book.* New York: Harper and Row.

Bodecker, N. M. (1976). *Hurry, hurry, Mary dear! and other nonsense poems.* New York: Scribner's.

Brewton, S., et al. (compilers) (1973). *My tang's tungled and other ridiculous situations.* New York: Crowell.

Ciardi, J. (1961). *The man who sang the sillies.* Philadelphia: J. B. Lippincott.

Coatsworth, E. (1966). *The sparrow bush.* New York: W. W. Norton.

Cole, J. (1984). *A new treasury of children's poetry: Old favorites and new discoveries.* New York: Doubleday.

Cole, W. (1964). *Beastly boys and ghastly girls.* Cleveland: Collins World.

de Gerez, T. (transl.) (1984). *My song is a piece of jade: Poems of ancient Mexico in English and Spanish.* Boston: Little, Brown.

de la Mare, W. (1979). *Collected poems.* London: Faber and Faber.

Fufuka, K. (1975). *My daddy is a cool dude.* New York: Dial.

Gardner, J. (1977). *A child's bestiary.* New York: Knopf.

Henderson, H. G. (1958). *An introduction to haiku.* Garden City, NY: Doubleday.

Hoberman, M. A. (1978). *A house is a house for me.* New York: Viking.

Hopkins, L. B. (ed.) (1970). *City talk.* New York: Knopf.

Hopkins, L. B. (1982). *Rainbows are made.* San Diego: Harcourt Brace Jovanovich.

Hughes, L. (1932). *The dream keeper.* New York: Knopf.

Larrick, N. (1974). *Somebody turned on a tap in these kids.* New York: Delacorte.

Lear, E. (1951). *The complete nonsense of Edward Lear.* Holbrook Jackson (ed.). New York: Dover.

Lee, D. (1974). *Alligator pie.* Boston: Houghton Mifflin.

Livingston, M. C. (1982). *Circle of seasons.* New York: Holiday.

Livingston, M. C. (1972). *Listen, children, listen.* New York: Harcourt Brace Jovanovich.

Lobel, A. (1974). *The man who took the indoors out.* New York: Harper and Row.

Marzollo, J. (1986). *The rebus treasury.* New York: Dial.

McCord, D. (1977). *One at a time.* Boston: Little, Brown.

Merriam, E. (1962). *There is no rhyme for silver.* New York: Atheneum.

Prelutsky, J. (1984). *The new kid on the block.* New York: Greenwillow.

Prelutsky, J. (1986). *Ride a purple pelican.* New York: Greenwillow.

Riley, J. W. (1975). *The gobble-uns'll git you ef you don't watch out!* Philadelphia: J. B. Lippincott.

Silverstein, S. (1974). *Where the sidewalk ends.* New York: Harper and Row.

Spier, P. (1969). *And so my garden grows.* Garden City, NY: Doubleday.

Strickland, D. S. (ed.) (1982). *Listen children. An anthology of black literature.* New York: Bantam.

Zim, J. (1975). *Shalom my peace.* Tel Aviv: Sabra Books.

Historical Fiction

Works in this genre are set in definite historical periods and are based on actual historical events. Historical figures may play a role, though it is usually minor. The main character is fictional, as are the supporting characters in most cases.

The range of historical fiction is wide: works from the distant past through the Vietnam War, for example, are classified in this genre. This is a powerful genre because readers not only gain a strong feel for the historical period, but they are able to identify with the main character, who is usually close to their own age. This character is therefore dealing with the same universal questions, anxieties, and hopes that are characteristic of the reader. These two aspects combine to leave young readers with a more visceral impression of the reality of the past; although period clothing may seem humorous and physical settings peculiar, such impressions fade and are overridden by a new awareness of those commonalities of human existence that really do transcend the ages.

Selected Historical Fiction

Brenner, B. (1978). *Wagon wheels.* New York: Harper and Row.

Clapp, P. (1977). *I'm Deborah Sampson: A soldier in the War of the Revolution.* New York: Lothrop, Lee, and Shepard.

Dalgliesh, A. (1954). *The courage of Sarah Noble.* New York: Scribner's.

Fox, P. (1973). *Slave dancer.* Scarsdale, NY: Bradley.

Gray, G. (1978). *How far, Felipe?* New York: Harper and Row.

Haley, G. (1973). *Jack Jouett's ride.* New York: Viking.

Lord, B. B. (1984). *In the year of the boar and Jackie Robinson.* New York: Harper and Row.

MacLachlan, P. (1985). *Sarah, plain and tall*. New York: Harper and Row.

Meltzer, M. (1976). *Never to forget: The Jews of the holocaust*. New York: Harper and Row.

O'Dell, S. (1960). *Island of the blue dolphins*. Boston: Houghton Mifflin.

O'Dell, S. (1970). *Sing down the moon*. Boston: Houghton Mifflin.

Sperry, A. (1940). *Call it courage*. New York: Macmillan.

Steucklen, K. (1974). *My brother Sam is dead*. New York: Four Winds Press.

Taylor, M. (1976). *Roll of thunder, hear my cry*. New York: Dial.

Uchida, Y. (1985). *A jar of dreams*. New York: Aladdin.

Wilder, L. I. (1932). *Little house in the big woods*. New York: Harper and Row.

Contemporary Realism

As the label suggests, this genre addresses the reality of contemporary life. Such "reality," however, is multifaceted, and this genre has matured markedly over the past twenty years or so to reflect this. Everything that adults are concerned about — and which is therefore addressed in books for adults — is now addressed in children's books as well. Books that we classify as contemporary realism deal with the many different "realities" of contemporary life that children experience: humor, tragedy, the drama of simply growing up, and more specifically, physical and mental handicaps, dysfunctional families, psychological and physical abuse, drug or alcohol addiction, single parents, crime, alternative lifestyles, racism and bigotry, pregnancy (particularly vivid for some intermediate grade students), and so on.

Through these books, elementary students can alternately escape from their concerns or they can deal with them. Again, by identifying with a main character they can realize both that having concerns or problems is quite normal and that these problems can often be worked out — and understand that they may have to accept and adjust to situations with no clear-cut resolution.

Selected Books — Contemporary Realism

Blume, J. (1981). *The one in the middle is the green kangaroo*. New York: Bradbury.

Bond, N. (1976). *A string in the harp*. New York: Atheneum.

Burch, R. (1966). *Queenie Peavy*. New York: Viking.

Byars, B. (1970). *The summer of the swans*. New York: Viking.

Cleary, B. (1983). *Dear Mr. Henshaw*. New York: Morrow.

Corcoran, B. (1974). *A dance to still music*. New York: Atheneum. [The protagonist becomes deaf.]

Cunningham, J. (1977). *Come to the edge*. New York: Pantheon.

Estes, E. (1944). *The hundred dresses*. New York: Harcourt, Brace, and World.

Fitzhugh, L. (1964). *Harriet the spy*. New York: Harper and Row.

Greene, B. (1974). *Philip Hall likes me, I reckon maybe*. New York: Dial.

Hamilton, V. (1968). *House of Dies Drear*. New York: Macmillan.

Heide, F. P. (1970). *Sound of sunshine, sound of rain*. New York: Parents Magazine Press. [The protagonist is blind.]

Holmes, B. W. (1985). *Charlotte Cheetham: Master of disaster*. New York: Harper and Row.

Klein, N. (1973). *It's not what you expect*. New York: Pantheon. [Divorce and remarriage.]

Konigsburg, E. L. (1967). *From the mixed-up files of Mrs. Basil E. Frankweiler.* New York: Atheneum.

Mathers, P. (1985). *Maria Teresa.* New York: Harper and Row.

Miles, M. (1971). *Annie and the old one.* Boston: Little, Brown.

Ness, E. (1966). *Sam, Bangs and Moonshine.* New York: Holt, Rinehart, and Winston.

Paterson, K. (1977). *Bridge to Terabithia.* New York: Crowell.

Rawls, W. (1961). *Where the red fern grows.* New York: Doubleday.

Sachs, M. (1971). *The bears' house.* New York: Doubleday.

Yashima, T. (1955). *Crow boy.* New York: Viking.

Yep, L. (1977). *Child of the owl.* New York: Harper and Row.

Modern Fantasy

This genre combines fantasy and reality but does so with logic and consistency. Consider, for example, the worlds created and developed in J.R.R. Tolkien's *The Hobbit* and in C. S. Lewis's *Narnia* books (the most famous being *The Lion, the Witch, and the Wardrobe*). Stewig expressed in part the challenge to the authors of modern fantasy: "If, in the universe the author has imagined, the frogs can speak English, there had better be a good reason why the horses cannot. Or if the goats are wearing trousers, why are the pigs' bottoms exposed to the air?" (Stewig, 1988, p. 509). As with much of traditional literature, modern fantasy is a literary playground on which primal themes are played out. Think of the range of themes and issues addressed by the now classic *Narnia* tales, for example: good versus evil, the existence of God, a Christ-figure, growing up, and interpersonal relationships among children on the verge of adolescence — to name just a few!

Literary folk tales are a subgenre of modern fantasy, reflecting certain forms of traditional literature such as legends and fairy tales. Examples are Rudyard Kipling's *Just So Stories* and the works of Hans Christian Andersen. In contrast to traditional folk tales that have been handed down through the oral tradition and that probably do not have a single author, literary folk tales have been written by known authors, though they share the same form and features as folk tales.

Modern fantasy also includes stories about animals with special abilities, as in Beverly Cleary's *The Mouse and the Motorcycle,* Robert O'Brien's *Mrs. Frisby and the Rats of NIMH,* E. B. White's *Charlotte's Web,* and Kenneth Grahame's *The Wind in the Willows.* Trips through time and space are another aspect of this category, as in Madeline L'Engle's *A Wrinkle in Time* and, to a degree, Natalie Babbitt's *Tuck Everlasting.*

A wonderful variation on the usual modern fantasy theme for both primary and intermediate students is *The Jolly Postman (or Other People's Letters)* by Janet and Allan Ahlberg, with misspelled words and delightful puns, parodied events, character insight, and so forth.

Selected Works of Modern Fantasy

Bang, M. (1977). *The buried moon and other stories.* New York: Scribner's.

Bellairs, J. (1973). *The house with a clock in its walls.* New York: Dial.

Boston, L. (1961). *A stranger at Green Knowe.* New York: Harcourt, Brace, and World.

Carroll, L. (1983). *Alice's adventures in wonderland.* New York: Knopf. Rev. ed., illustrated by S. M. Wiggins.

Cooper, S. (1965). *Over sea, under stone.* New York: Harcourt, Brace, and World. [Cooper has crafted a series of five books, each of which may be read independently but which work best read sequentially. The other four books follow.]

Cooper, S. (1973). *The dark is rising.* New York: Atheneum.

Cooper, S. (1974). *Greenwitch.* New York: Atheneum.

Cooper, S. (1975). *The grey king.* New York: Atheneum.

Cooper, S. (1977). *The silver on the tree.* New York: Atheneum.

Ehrlisch, A. (transl.) (1982). *The snow queen.* New York: Dial.

Hou-tien, C. (1977). *Six Chinese brothers.* New York: Holt, Rinehart, and Winston.

LeGuin, U. (1968). *The wizard of Earthsea.* New York: Parnassus.

Milne, A. A. (1926). *Winnie-the-Pooh.* New York: E. P. Dutton.

Rodgers, M. (1972). *Freaky Friday.* New York: Harper and Row.

Sendak, M. (1963). *Where the wild things are.* New York: Harper and Row.

Williams, M. (1983). *The velveteen rabbit.* New York: Knopf.

Informational or Nonfiction Books

The number of informational or nonfiction books for children has increased exponentially over the past couple of decades. Moreover, the content and quality of these books have improved. As we will see in this chapter, any topic you pursue with your students or that they pursue on their own will be richly enhanced by having a good many informational books on hand. Textbooks can represent the terrain to be covered in a content area, but informational books will usually be the resource that breathes life into that content. Following is just a sampling of hundreds of excellent titles.

Selected Informational Books

Aliki (1976). *Corn is maize: The gift of the Indians.* New York: Crowell.

Baylor, B. (1978). *The way to start a day.* New York: Scribner's.

Branley, F. (1973). *Experiments in the principles of space travel.* New York: Crowell. [One in a series of excellent scientific books for elementary students by the same author.]

Carrick, C. (1977). *Sand tiger shark.* New York: Seabury Press.

Charlip, R., Ancona, M. B. & Ancona, G. (1974). *Handtalk: An ABC of finger spelling and sign language.* New York: Parents Magazine Press.

Cole, J. (1976). *A chick hatches.* New York: Morrow.

dePaola, T. (1977). *The quicksand book.* New York: Holiday.

Greenfield, H. (1979). *Rosh Hashanah and Yom Kippur.* New York: Holt. [One in a series of books on Jewish holidays by the same author.]

Holling, H. C. (1957). *Pagoo.* Boston: Houghton Mifflin.

Hurd, E. T. (1973). *The mother whale.* Boston: Little, Brown.

Kamien, J. (1979). *What if you couldn't . . . ?* New York: Scribner's.

Kohl, H., & Kohl, J. (1977). *The view from the oak.* San Francisco: Sierra Club Books/ Scribner's.

Kuskin, K. (1982). *The philharmonic gets dressed.* New York: Harper and Row.

LeShan, E. (1976). *Learning to say good-bye: When a parent dies.* New York: Macmillan.

Macaulay, D. (1975). *Pyramid.* Boston: Houghton Mifflin.

Meltzer, M. (1982). *The Hispanic Americans.* New York: Crowell.

Pringle, L. (1977). *The hidden world: Life under a rock.* New York: Macmillan.

Spier, P. (1980). *People.* Garden City, NY: Doubleday.

Biography

Books in this genre tell the life stories of individuals, living or deceased. Elementary students can read biography for a number of purposes. Just as they can identify with fictional characters in contemporary realism, for example, so too can children identify with historical individuals and the conflicts they faced.

As with informational books, the number and quality of biographies written for young people have increased significantly. These include compelling new versions of the lives of individuals who you would have thought had been overwhelmingly "biographied" by now, as well as *collective biographies* that present several shorter biographies within one volume. Recently, biographies of noted minority figures have proliferated, and there are also new books that present the "victory over adversity" theme.

A list of recommended biographies and collective biographies follows.

Selected Biographies

Freedman, R. (1987). *Lincoln: A photobiography.* Boston: Houghton Mifflin.

Gherman, B. (1986). *Georgia O'Keeffe.* New York: Atheneum.

Haskins, J. (1977). *The life and death of Martin Luther King, Jr.* New York: Lothrop, Lee, and Shepard.

Lee, B. (1979). *Charles Eastman: The story of an American Indian.* Minneapolis, MN: Dillon.

Monjo, F. N. (1974). *Grand Papa and Ellen Aroon, being an account of some of the happy times spent together by Thomas Jefferson and his favorite granddaughter.* New York: Holt, Rinehart, and Winston.

Merriam, E. (1973). *Growing up female in America.* New York: Dell.

Nelson, M. C. (1972). *Maria Martinez.* Minneapolis, MN: Dillon.

Newlon, C. (1972). *Famous Mexican Americans.* New York: Dodd, Mead.

Sterling, D., & Quarles, B. (1965). *Lift every voice.* Garden City, NY: Doubleday.

Stevenson, A. (1983). *Benjamin Franklin, young printer.* New York: Bobbs-Merrill.

Sullivan, G. (1985). *Mary Lou Retton.* New York: Julian Messner.

Tobias, T. (1970). *Maria Tallchief.* New York: Crowell.

Children's Special Interests

Stewig (1988) establishes "Children's Special Interests" as a separate category even though the selections could probably be placed in the other categories we've discussed. Nonetheless, his decision is well motivated and serves to highlight those books that children list as their favorite types time and again. His concern is for children who either can read but choose not to or who are having difficulty with reading. He adopts the pragmatic approach of "hooking" such students first before trying to pull them in to the books you might wish them to experience.

Children's interests have been surveyed on a continual basis for several years (Roser and Frith, 1983, and annual surveys in *The Reading Teacher*). Remember, these are books that the *children* chose to read. More specifically, these surveys have shown that children in the primary grades prefer comical situations, family situations, school stories, animal stories, realistic adventure stories, and folk tales. We know that, in general, almost half of students at the intermediate level like mysteries; beyond this popular choice, tastes vary. More able readers like science fiction and fantasy; average readers prefer humor and adventure. Most intermediate students also prefer books dealing with interpersonal relationships, including relationships with siblings. Science books are popular, as are biographies of sports figures. It may come as a surprise that poetry is also popular among intermediate students; of the many excellent poets who write for children, Shel Silverstein is probably the best known and therefore the favorite.

The Potential for Students' Response to Literature

In Chapter 6 we sketched in broad strokes the development of literacy in children. Although we referred to the development of genre schemes as frameworks for comprehension, we have saved until now a more probing investigation. The themes of literature that you studied in high school and college are every bit as much in effect in children's literature. I've used the term *potential* to refer to students' response to literature because, as we'll see below, children are capable of more sophisticated interaction with literature than we often credit them for. How and why literature works on children can be explained from a variety of perspectives; we will explore a few of those here.

Psychosocial Roots of Response to Literature

We have discussed the structure and the reading of narratives. In Chapter 5 we touched on the value of storytelling and of reading stories aloud to students of all ages. In a psychological and social sense, children need narratives for the same reasons we adults do: to make sense of their lives and to give meaning to them. And of course this "meaning making" can work on many levels.

Stories give us frameworks for imposing order on what could otherwise be random events. They seem comfortable because they tell about things we know in some sense — perhaps tacitly, perhaps consciously. They help us rediscover or reinvent our reality and thereby understand it more deeply and meaningfully. There is always a sense of the familiar, even when the story presents quite new experiences. All of this is true because, as a poet once said, there is really only one story (Graves, 1955): there comes a day when we realize that the one story is *us*.

What psychosocial needs or themes can be addressed through experiences with literature? The psychosocial development of children has been mapped by a number of developmental psychologists, perhaps the most influential being Eric Erikson (1963). Erikson described psychosocial development in terms of *oppositions* in order to represent the ongoing "push/pull" that children experience during different developmental phases. As with Piaget's stages of cognitive development (see Chapter 2), Erikson's stages of psychosocial development are not absolute, but they do help us understand what children appear to be grappling with as they grow toward a concept of themselves, others, and their place in the world. Together with our understanding of their cognitive development, this knowledge helps us understand how and why children act, respond, and believe as they do. Our bottom line here as teachers, of course, is to use this knowledge in our moment-to-moment work with elementary students.

Erikson's stages may be characterized as follows: *basic trust/basic mistrust* (birth to two years of age); *autonomy/shame and doubt* (two to three years); *initiative/ guilt* (four to six years); *industry/inferiority* (seven to twelve years); *identity/role confusion* (twelve to eighteen years). Most of your students in the elementary grades will be in the industry/inferiority stage, developing a sense of competence and attempting to establish who they are through the things they do. Some of the students at the intermediate level will be embarking on the challenge of adolescence, in which establishing a stable sense of who and what they are is paramount. These students will need to understand that others experience what they are experiencing.

Literature will provide one of the most effective mirrors by which to facilitate this understanding. It will assist in helping to resolve the tensions between industry and inferiority, for example; scholars such as Bettelheim (1976) have explained many traditional tales such as "Hansel and Gretel" and "Jack and the Beanstalk" in terms of the underlying conflicts that children are experiencing. Our objective is to promote close, more critical reading, but it's important to realize that the value of so many of the books elementary students read lies in this simple but consequential fact: through their main characters, these books help students become more aware of their own thoughts and feelings as well as the thoughts and feelings of others.

■ Build Your Teaching Repertoire

Books about the Psychology of Literature

If you wish to explore further the psychological underpinnings of literature for children, you will enjoy the following:

Bettelheim, B. (1976). *The uses of enchantment: The meaning and importance of fairy tales.* New York: Alfred A. Knopf.

Butler, F. (1977). *Sharing literature with children: A thematic anthology.* New York: David McKay.

The essays at the end of the volume are particularly helpful.

Developmental Response to Literature

A number of researchers have investigated the nature of elementary students' responses to literature (Applebee, 1978; Barone, 1989; Cullinan, Harwood, and Galda, 1983; Eeds, 1989; Galda, 1982; Gambrell, 1986; Hickman, 1983; Morrow, 1985; Protherough, 1987; and Purves, 1972). Much of the research in children's responses to literature has been carried out within the framework of a categorization scheme first proposed by Applebee (1978). Applebee described four levels of response, each of which, he suggested, reflects the level of cognitive operations (see Chapter 2) attained by the students.

- *Retelling,* primarily characteristic of *preoperational thought,* is a simple recall of the title, beginning and ending lines or situations, and perhaps a little dialogue. There is no indication of the importance of different events; all are equally important.
- *Summary,* characteristic of *concrete operations,* does involve a recall of events in order of importance. Summaries are usually shorter than retellings.
- *Analysis,* characteristic of individuals who are either moving into or engaged in *formal operations,* uses subjective or personal responses in order to interpret the story.
- *Generalization,* also characteristic of formal operational thought, probes the theme or "meaning" of what has been read.

You can see, then, that according to Applebee higher-level response would be characteristic of intermediate grade students but not of primary. Barone (1989), however, found that most primary grade children *do* seem to be capable of higher-level responses. Although younger children cannot draw on as much personal experience as can older students, the levels at which young children are able to deal with the situations they encounter in literature nevertheless seem to be higher than previously supposed. Moreover, children who are at least at the concrete-operational stage and can summarize what they've read, recognize patterns within single-syllable words, and are becoming fluent readers (see Chapter 6) appear to be able to choose which response pattern is appropriate in a particular reading situation.

The different findings regarding the quality of elementary students' responses stem from the different contexts and ways in which their responses have been gathered. In Barone's investigation, for example, children were dealing over a period of time with the same text, a "chapter book." Therefore, there really wasn't any need for retelling to inform others of what was occurring in the text, since the students could assume that their classmates had this knowledge already. Notably, second- and third-graders who *wrote* more frequently in response to their reading were more likely to reflect in depth upon what they were reading.

The research has underscored the importance of children discussing and writing about what they are reading. When they do so — regardless of whether they are responding to shorter selections or to chapter books — they tend to give more interpretive types of responses, involving analysis and generalization. As we'll explore in this chapter, you can encourage these responses by the types of questions you pose before, during, and after the reading.

Perhaps the single most important conclusion we can draw for the classroom, based on the research into elementary students' responses to literature, is this: students should be exposed to a variety of texts — stories, chapter books, and expository selections — and they should be involved in responding to those texts through discussion and writing. For example, having a group of children read the same chapter book gives them the opportunity to get deeper into the reading *and* to assume that their classmates know what's going on in the book. Retelling or summarizing the plot becomes unnecessary; the students can proceed in their discussions to higher levels of response — to more interpretive responses, in other words. On another occasion, students may read the same short story at least twice; being thus familiar with the gist of the story they can proceed to respond in discussion and in their response journals once again at these higher levels.

Little research has been done into students' responses to expository texts; as we saw in the previous chapter, research has focused on *recall* of text content as a function of text structure (Meyer, 1984) rather than on how that content relates to students' current knowledge base, or to students' interpretation and evaluation of information. We do know that writing in a journal or learning log during and/or after reading expository material, whereby students summarize and describe how the information fits with their current knowledge, *does* significantly affect learning and retention (Applebee, 1984). Discussing what has been read will have the same effect (Alvermann and Hayes, 1989).

I noted above that informational books help "breathe life" into the content or subject matter that you and your students explore; as we saw in Chapter 4 and will explore in the units at the end of this chapter, expository or informational books will work in tandem with narratives throughout the grades. We've already examined how you will be teaching strategies for reading and writing expository material (Chapters 7 and 8). In this chapter we'll see how informational texts can be incorporated naturally into the literature-based classroom.

Literature-Based Reading and Writing

Transition to Literature-Based Reading and Writing

Literature-based reading and writing is usually built around a unit that addresses a particular topic or theme. These units involve lots of small-group and individual work. It is quite possible that your students have not been exposed to a literature-based approach to reading and writing prior to coming to your class — or even if they have, a summer vacation has intervened and they probably are not ready to jump right into small-group work. As a result, you will need transition time during which you walk the students through formats and activities that will become a critical part of instruction.

Two of these formats are the read-alouds and discussion formats presented in Chapter 5. These will be important initiating and ongoing features of your literature-based reading and writing program. Not coincidentally, there are similarities

Conducting read-alouds that follow a particular theme or that compare and contrast different themes can help you make a transition in your instruction to more fully developed thematic units. *(© Erika Stone)*

between what you do in these read-alouds and the first step in presenting a literature unit, as we will see later on.

I suggest that you get underway in the transition to literature-based reading and writing with the class as a whole. In this context you will be able to introduce the terminology, model the types of questioning, and help establish the *awarenesses* that will in turn be explored in the smaller response groups — all of which will be integral parts of your literature units. As you work with the whole class, you will begin to establish a framework and a mindset for response to literature (Monson, 1987). During read-alouds, for example, you may highlight *characterization* in one work and *setting* in another. In addition, your questions will change, increasing both in number and sophistication. I suggest that you begin with one story, then move to two or three related stories, then to a chapter book.

During this transition period you will be working out a sense of direction in your own teaching — an experience that can be both absorbing and challenging. To help you establish a foundation for your teaching plan, let me suggest that you choose read-alouds that are based in part on the ages, interests, and abilities of your students. You can sequence your presentation of read-alouds to the whole class so that you

- sample different genres.
- present different examples of a single genre.
- follow a particular theme.
- compare and contrast different themes.

By beginning on this small scale you will not only get a feel for the advantages and enjoyment inherent in a literature-based focus; you'll be developing *your* skills for what later will be an important core of your literature-based units — the read-alouds. It's fair to say that, during this transition, you will help them become aware of the potential of literature: they will be reflecting first on the particular text being read to them, then compare and contrast that text with one or two texts read previously. As the research in response to literature indicates, beginning in second grade, most students are capable of this type of interaction with texts.

Because you will be modeling reading and thinking about narratives and expository texts in your read-alouds, let's spend a little time considering the basic elements of narratives and the basic organization of expository texts.

The Basic Elements of Narratives

In Chapter 8 we discussed narratives in terms of their structure. This structure is only the framework, however, on which the author will construct the central elements of the narrative — plot, characterization, setting, theme, resolution, style, and point of view. During the elementary years, students will develop an understanding of these elements through the literature they read and the writing they produce, using that literature as a model. As the research in students' potential to respond to literature suggests, they will be able to step back to understand, appreciate, and analyze narrative elements. In a good narrative, these elements will be interwoven in a richly textured tapestry, complementing each other.

Plot   Plot is the means whereby action is developed in a story. It consists of an ordering of events and some type of conflict, or tension. Conflicts can be (1) between the main character and nature, (2) between the character and society, (3) between the character and another character, or (4) internal, within the character. Students can develop an understanding of plot by thinking about the types of conflict described in a story and discussing them. Discussing the conflicts in this way will reinforce their recall of the story's events.

Characterization   The definition of this element — how an author develops characters — is straightforward enough, but exploring the ways in which various authors develop their characters will provide some instructive and delightful insights for your students. It is a fairly natural shift from focusing on plot to focusing on characterization, because once the students identify the conflict or obstacles the character or characters must face, they can then go about discussing how the characters respond to the conflict. In so doing, they learn something about the characters themselves — their personalities, their moral fiber, and so forth.

Setting   This is the actual location and the time in which the story takes place. How an author develops the setting will depend on how important a role it will play: the setting can establish the mood, provide much of the symbolism, and contribute to the conflict in a story. We can explore setting with students by discussing why the author spends as little or as much time in establishing it. With students of any age we can discuss the mental pictures that the author helps us construct through the setting.

Theme   Theme is what the story is really about, not what happens — that is part of the plot. What underlies the elements of plot, characterization, and setting? What is the author trying to tell us? *That* is the theme. For example, the main characters in several different stories may go on a long journey that takes many years. The underlying theme in each of the stories, however, may be different. In one story, the theme may be individuality — how the main character comes to understand himself or herself in relation to the world and to others; in another the theme may involve life versus death and the inevitable necessity of accepting death. Themes may be stated explicitly, as in many fables, or they may be implicit.

Resolution   How is the developing chain of events and ensuing conflicts finally resolved? Realistically? Appropriately? The climax or resolution to the story must be satisfying in these ways; the reader may not care for how things were resolved, but if the resolution is at least plausible, then it works.

Style   Style is the manner in which the author uses language — words and sentences — to develop the story. We can talk in general or more specifically about how style underlies the development of the other elements. For example, an author may be more direct, using shorter sentences and few modifying words or phrases, or more elaborate, with sentences that are somewhat more complex (as, for example, in Virginia Hamilton's prose).

Point of View   Point of view is the stance the narrator or writer takes in the narrative. Is it "omniscient" (an impressive word for intermediate students!) — does the narrator see, know, and describe everything? Is it first person ("I"), second person ("you"), or third person ("she," "he," "they")? Authors assume a particular point of view for a reason, to get a certain effect or to establish a certain perspective.

The Basic Organization for Expository or Informational Texts

Lukens (1989) concisely describes the organization of good expository or informational books: "Breaking down the ideas into component parts that can be easily understood, the writer arranges them in coherent sequence from *simplest to most complex,* from *familiar to unfamiliar,* or from *early development to later development*" (Lukens, p. 245). As you read, examine, and select informational books to share with your students, it is important to keep this organization in mind. Your

AT THE TEACHER'S DESK: Ideas for Expository Writing

Imitation plays a critical role in learning how to read, write, and respond to expository or nonfiction selections. In Chapter 7, I presented a partial list of possibilities for expository writing; I'd like to expand those basics with the following expository formats for your students to explore (adapted from Tchudi and Tchudi, 1983):

- Thumbnail sketches:
  famous people
  places
  content ideas
  historical events
- Guess who or what descriptions
- Letters to the editor
- Letters to imaginary individuals
- Applications
- Memos
- Dialogues and conversations
- Telegrams

- Fact books or fact sheets
- Case studies:
  School problems, such as
  local issues
  national concerns
  historical problems
  scientific issues
- Reviews of television programs
- Historical "you are there" scenes
- Utopian proposals
- Practical proposals
- Dictionaries and lexicons
- Notes of options for the future:
  careers
  employment
  school
  training for the military or
  public service
- Slide show scripts
- Captions for photographs

students will become aware of this organization through continued exposure to good informational texts and as they develop in their ability to write expository material. From time to time you can comment, for example, on how a particular author develops this organization in his or her writing. For example, David MacCauley's *Unbuilding* takes readers from familiar to unfamiliar experiences with buildings. In illustration and in text, MacCauley shows how buildings are constructed, and he does so in an engaging way — by dismantling the Empire State Building in order to ship it overseas!

Expository literature is frequently given short shrift in the classroom. Often referred to as *nonfiction*, it may have a negative connotation: Beverly Kobrin observed that "Author Jane Yolen says the word *nonfiction* sounds as if it has been in a contest with fiction — and lost" (Kobrin, 1988, p. 5). All too often the term is assumed to refer to textbooks, and that's it. In fact, students are often hooked into reading and reading intensively by informational books and biographies, particularly if these books tap into their own interests. As you'll see in the sample units at the end of the chapter, expository books usually vie with fiction in your literature-based units, from the earliest years on.

Literature-Based Reading and Writing Response Groups and Group Conferences

Harste, Short, and Burke (1989) offer an excellent description of what should go on in a classroom geared to literature-based instruction: "Readers need to be involved both in reading extensively (reading a wide variety of literature without taking that reading on to response activities) and in reading intensively (reading some books with deeper responses through Literature Response Activities)" (Harste, et al., p. 150).

Literature-based response groups are an extremely important feature of your literature-based curriculum. They should be fairly natural extensions of the small groups with which you have been meeting for direct teaching in reading and writing skills, conducting DRTAs, and so forth. Through small groups and class conferences you will be facilitating your students' awareness, understanding, and appreciation of the elements and themes of narratives and poems, and of the worlds of ideas and information in expository trade books. You will do this primarily through questions that you ask directly and questions you give to groups to pursue independently. In the case of narratives and poetry, this is where the construction of meaning in a social context can truly flower; group re-constructing of the text will expand students' awareness of the potential of the text. This leads in part to what Graves (1987) has termed an "interpretive community," a kind of "group-think" (Graves, p. 198). In the next section we will look at some specific ways (including keeping response journals) your students can react to the literature they have just read. First, however, let's go over a format you can use when you divide your class into response groups.

As I noted when discussing teacher/student reading conferences in the previous chapter, your literature-response group conferences can operate with quite a bit of variability. As you know well by now, I suggest more structure at first, with gradual release of responsibility to the students over time.

Let's examine how you can set up these response groups. In preparation for small-group discussion in which you will not be involved, students prepare responses to specific questions that will tap thinking skills beginning at the *interpretive* level (see Chapters 5 and 8). You will give the students in each group a list of questions to which they will respond, and later in the week they will share these responses with the class. For example, based on the book *Bridge to Terabithia* by Katherine Paterson, you hand out the following directions and questions:

> **Decide whether each of the following statements is true or false. Each group must reach agreement, and must be prepared to support your answers with evidence from the story.**
>
> 1. **Young people react to terrible events differently than do adults.**
>
> 2. **Most boys of Jesse's age wouldn't become involved in either the real or make-believe world of Terabithia.**
>
> 3. **The relationship between Jesse and his younger sister is better than the relationship most brothers and sisters have.**

You can qualitatively increase the challenge of your questions, as the following sample questions, based on *Tuck Everlasting* by Natalie Babbit, illustrate:

Give students a dilemma:
Should Winnie have helped Mrs. Tuck escape from prison?

Present some complicating factors:
What if everyone believed they were justified in breaking the law? After all, Mrs. Tuck murdered a man (or did she?). Could Mrs. Tuck have been justified in killing "the man in the yellow suit"? (Is there ever a time when we can justify killing another human being?)

Shouldn't Winnie first attempt to explain to everyone that, if Mrs. Tuck is hanged, she will not die?

For those group conferences in which you *will* be involved, note the adjustments you will make in the basic reading-conference format introduced in the last chapter:

- *Sharing*   Students have prepared for the group conference individually or in pairs or triads. Students will share specific elements they have encountered in individual books or books read in common and discuss them in the group. In this context students can support, refute, and challenge one another's statements by locating and reading aloud appropriate excerpts from the text.
- *Questioning*   This is your opportunity to follow up and/or steer the discussion toward a different perspective.
- *Planning*   Where will the students go from here with the reading? As in the individual conference, if the student will base some extension activity or project on the book, discuss what this will entail.
- *Records*   Because the conference is the context that best provides students the forum in which to apply the skills and strategies you have been teaching, it is important to keep records of what occurs. Just as with your individual conferences, you should make notations as you are going along in the discussion and/or immediately afterwards — otherwise you run the risk of losing much of the information. Taking notes will not be easy at first, but with practice you'll find that you can jot down a few observations as you are responding to or acknowledging the students. Or, alternatively, if you and the class feel comfortable about it, you might tape the conferences.

In the sharing, questioning, and planning phases, ask questions that will help students reflect on, analyze and evaluate, and extend what they have read.

Throughout, keep this important perspective in mind: for many reasons, not all of your students will be swept up right away by literature. You will not only need to organize the appropriate environment for responding to literature but continue to model some responses yourself. Your own reactions can show your students how literature can affect readers and how experiences with one text relate to experiences with other texts. It is important to keep your responses natural, not forced. Much of this modeling can take the form of comment; that is, you can simply observe, "This book is a lot like [x] that we read several months ago" or "This author's point of view is the same as that of the author we read last week," and so forth. You then reinforce these whole-class discussions about point of view, theme, conflict, setting, and other elements in your smaller response groups and in your individual student conferences. Coming back again and again to the same points of emphasis eventually will help to draw in your reluctant or skeptical students.

A Range of Literature-Based Activities

Although I've offered the activities below in the format of a list, I do not mean to indicate they constitute simply a "grab bag." They will form an integral part of your instruction, as you will see later in the chapter. They all reflect an active, lively, and usually critical-minded approach to literature response through reading and writing. At first, you will probably be more comfortable introducing these activities independently before slowly weaving them into a whole literature-based unit. Ultimately, the experienced teacher will probably embed them almost exclusively within units.

Expand Your Teaching Repertoire

Let's begin with a reminder of activities we have already discussed that will fit well as part of literature response: Readers' Theater and creative dramatics. Creative dramatics, by the way, can be used not only as narrative pantomime but also to enact a problematic part of a reading selection; what seems problematic during the reading often becomes clear when physically acted out. Following are many more literature-based activities:

1. When examining *characterization* in discussion or through response journals, have students take the perspective of different characters. For example, how does the giant in "Jack and the Beanstalk" view the intrusion of Jack? What does the witch think about the appearance of Hansel and Gretel? In a more serious vein, how does the maid in *Summer of My German Soldier* respond after her first conversation with the German prisoner of war? (Betty Greene, the author, gives us some insight during the conversation; how does the maid's perspective change after this point?)

2. *Imitation* plays a seminal role in students' learning to write (Cramer, 1978). All writers, either by accident or design, begin by imitating the style and structure of other writers. As you share literature with your students, you will similarly find your students engaged in imitation. Take advantage of this and encourage it! You will see students creating, usually spontaneously (or after one student does it), one after another story based on a published

book or story, such as "George and Martha" (James Marshall), "The Stupids" (Harry Allard), "Encyclopedia Brown" (Donald Sobol), and on and on. You will also see imitation strictly of form, apart from content. For example, when students are studying *Aesop's Fables,* they may want to create their own fables; you can list two or three morals on the board and have each student select one and write a fable that goes with it.

3. Have students write the text for a wordless book (Moss, 1984). For intermediate students, an excellent book for this activity is Lynd Ward's *The Silver Pony,* which will yield a number of different interpretations by the students in their writing.

4. Have students make comparisons and contrasts across books they read. Galda (1987), for example, suggests using any three versions of a folk tale. She recommends the following versions of "Cinderella": *Cinderella* by Charles Perrault, retold by Amy Ehrlich and illustrated by Susan Jeffers (Dial, 1985); *Yeh-Shen* by Louie Al-ling and illustrated by Ed Young (Philomet, 1982); and *Cinderella* by Grimm, illustrated by Otto S. Svend (Larousse, 1978).

   You may have the students work on a chart in which they compare the different versions according to setting, characters, problem, magic, events, ending, titles, similarities, differences, and conclusions (Cullinan, Karrer, and Pillar, 1981). An effective follow-up activity is to have the students write their own versions of the folk tale.

5. An excellent activity to undertake after compare-and-contrast activities with different genres is to allow the students to sort a group of books according to categories. They may establish the categories; your only direction is, "Which of these books do you think belong together in some way?" Students will probably come to understand that books may in fact be classified in more than one way.

6. Have students ask their parents what books *they* remember reading. This works particularly well with primary grade students. Students and teacher will then attempt to collect as many of these books as possible, and then read and share them. Even if the parents' native language is not English, it will be fascinating to learn about the books they recall.

7. Writers develop characterization in a number of ways. To explore this development, students may do the following:

   a. Working in pairs, students can examine a story or chapter for the different ways in which a particular character is developed: through conversation, description, letters, and so forth. In Patricia MacLachlan's *Sarah Plain and Tall,* for example (appropriate for third grade and up), we learn much about Sarah through her letters before she appears in person.

   b. When students are each reading different books, have them meet in small groups to introduce the main character in their respective books, describing the character and the particular problems he or she faced. Other students may then ask questions of that character (Monson, 1987, p. 106). Each character may discuss whether his or her own problems are worse

FIGURE 9.1

A Student Rating Scale of a Character in *The Hobbit* According to Different Traits
Source: Used by permission of Thomas Nelson Australia from T. D. Johnson and D. Lewis, *Literacy Through Literature* (Portsmouth, NH: Heinemann Educational Books, Inc., 1987).

BILBO BAGGINS	very	quite	neither, both, don't know	quite	very	
good	X					bad
large				X		small
brave	X					cowardly
hot		X				cold
honest			X			dishonest

than those of the other characters. A variation on this activity is to have characters respond as though they were being interviewed on a television talk show.

c. Students can rate story characters on several traits along a continuum (good/bad, large/small, brave/cowardly, hot/cold, honest/dishonest). They should be prepared to defend ratings orally or in writing (Johnson and Louis, 1987). Figure 9.1, from Johnson and Louis, illustrates a rating scale for Bilbo Baggins in J.R.R. Tolkien's *The Hobbit*.

d. Johnson and Louis develop the application of rating scales further; Figure 9.2 is their profile of "excitement" plotted against time in the story "The Three Little Pigs" (p. 108). (Note, by the way, how this activity also teaches graphing.)

8. As students consider point of view in stories that they themselves write, you may wish to suggest they begin with the omniscient view, simply because it is easier. Later they can move on to the other types. As students experiment with other points of view — first-person point of view, character point of view, and so forth — and share these efforts with others, they will come to understand much better why authors select certain types.

9. *Response Journals* Remember from the previous chapter that two very effective applications of response journals are (1) basic dialogue format, in which the teacher responds to the student's observations, and (2) Double Entry Draft (DED) format, also involving teacher response. Once students form the habit of responding to reading in their journals, they may use their journal observations as jumping-off points for discussions with one another. You may ask them also to use their written responses as part of a more structured response activity.

a. First, have students write a synopsis or summary of what they've read. Second, ask them to jot down any personal associations they have with

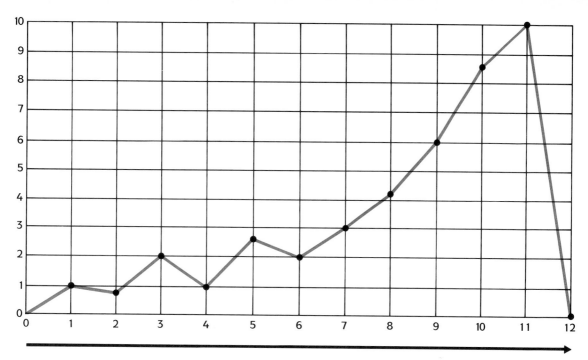

1. Pigs leave home.
2. Man with straw.
3. Wolf eats Pig 1.
4. Man with sticks.
5. Wolf eats Pig 2.

6. Man with bricks.
7. Wolf attempts Pig 3.
8. Turnip field.
9. Orchard.

10. Fair.
11. Chimney.
12. Wolf destroyed.
    Pig 3 lives happily
    ever after.

FIGURE 9.2

A Profile of "Excitement" Versus Time in "The Three Little Pigs"
Source: Used by permission of Thomas Nelson Australia from T. D. Johnson and D. Lewis, *Literacy Through Literature* (Portsmouth, NH: Heinemann Educational Books, Inc., 1987).

the reading and indicate what they believe the most important part of the text is and why. Third, have them meet in small groups to discuss this last point, prepared to support their judgment (Bleich, 1975; Temple and Gillet, 1989). This process can be used for both narrative and expository texts.

    b. An interesting twist on exploring *characterization* is to have students write entries in their response journals that a character might have written had he or she kept a journal.

10.   Once students have participated for some time in response activities and literature units (see next section), you can move their critical thinking up a notch or two by having them read or listen to a selection at least twice and then presenting questions that require real probing of the material.

    a. With a small group, present a series of questions that will reflect thinking at the *interpretive* level and beyond — in other words, questions for which there will likely be no single correct answer.

b. As you ask each question, the students first respond by writing in their journals. Then they will each share their response with the group. As they are sharing you will take notes, getting down the gist of the response. After each student has responded, you may ask questions to help the students clarify their answers and compare and contrast their responses with one another. You will then summarize the students' responses while noting where most students agreed and where there were areas of disagreement. You will then proceed to the next question.

Your questions can cover any facet of the story's elements as well as probe ethical issues — the rightness or wrongness of behavior given the specific situation in the story (Temple, 1989). Ask questions that tap central ideas, conflict, issues, and so forth first; what is important is not getting through all of the questions but rather encouraging quality responses.

11. A particularly effective activity is to publish a synopsis of a book together with the students' final responses. Other students can then compare and contrast their own reactions with those in this book (Crowley and Nelms, 1987).

12. The following approach to folk tales would tie in nicely with social studies and learning about different cultures (Norton, 1988): have a wide range of folk tales on hand, and tell students that these folk tales are the only means they have to find out about the country from which the folk tales came. Mention to students that clues may be found in the beliefs, food, music, climate, animals, and so forth in the tales.

13. Writing letters to authors is an excellent activity, although there are some constraints (see, for example, Beverly Cleary's article in *Instructor* Magazine, 1985). If the students pose questions, these should arise from genuine interest; quite often, questions that arise in response group sessions are ones that only the author can answer.

Students should do their best in writing, revising, and copying the final draft of their letters. If the students are in first or second grade, and if the teacher allows invented spellings to remain, an advisable practice is for the teacher to write a cover letter explaining why there are still misspellings (although authors may identify quite well with children, they may not be privy to the newer perspective on how children learn about the writing system!). Self-addressed, stamped return envelopes should be included as well.

14. This activity for intermediate students applies critical thinking and evaluation skills. Have students read a set of books that won the Newbery Award (given annually for the best children's fiction). Working in small groups, the students then derive what they believe are the criteria for determining which book receives the award. Then, the students may read the books nominated for the award during the current year and decide which one should win and which should receive honorable mention. They should discuss and defend their choices. After you tell them which titles in fact won, have them try to determine why a book other than their own choice was

selected (unless, of course, they picked the winner, too!). Furthermore, do they agree with the choice or not? (Watson, 1987).

Students may take a quite different perspective from their own usual perspective, which leads to an excellent writing activity. First share an example of "the other point of view." (A good prod for primary students is the book *Clyde Monster* by Robert Crowe, in which Clyde, a young monster, is afraid of the dark because *people* might be lurking about to "get him" when he's asleep. His monster parents explain that people really don't do things like that, and gradually his fear subsides. Intermediate students will enjoy the cartoonist Gary Larson's variation on this theme. Show them the "Far Side" cartoon in which two monsters sleeping under a bed imagine there are people in the bed over them.) Then have students write stories, poems, or reflections from this alternative perspective.

15. In an excellent variation on the traditional book report, have students prepare a short selection from a favorite story to read to the class. Tell them that their selection should have the effect of motivating other students to read the story or book. They may practice their oral reading by taping themselves on a cassette recorder. Then have them listen to themselves as they follow along in the text. They may continue practicing until the reading sounds natural and fluent. Then, they should share the reading with the class.

16. A book review, either written or shared orally, can add variety to book sharing or "booktalk" time. Bring in a book review clipped from the newspaper and explain that this is how many of us get our information about a book. Based often only on this information, we decide whether we wish to buy the book or check it out at the library (you can explain that *any* book should be available through a special system called the "inter-library loan system"). Discuss with the students how the reviewer has organized the review and has attempted to attract the reader's interest. Point out how the reviewer has described the book's "negatives" (if any) and what the reviewer has focused on in recommending the book.

17. Students can conduct DRTAs and DLTAs (Bear and Invernizzi, 1987; Bear and Lohman, 1988). They should meet with you beforehand to go over their plans and the follow-up questions they have prepared, and afterwards to evaluate how it all went.

18. You can make narratives "come alive" in the following ways:

    a. Arrange for a favorite author to visit the school for a day. (Note: This should not be on Young Authors' Day because it would detract from the students' efforts; see Chapter 7.) If possible, this visit can follow a whole-school focus on a particular author or theme. Authors may be contacted by writing to their publisher; most, if not all, of the initial and follow-up correspondence may be handled by the students themselves.

    b. Have a "Character Day" in which students dress up like characters from books that they have been reading.

19. Have students create an *art project* in response to their reading: dioramas, paintings, drawings, murals (individual or group), and models, all of which

Among the many ways in which students can respond creatively to literature are activities involving original illustrations, oral reading, and journal responses. *(© Elizabeth Crews)*

can represent important characters, events, settings, or significant concepts.

a. Students' drawings can be an effective response at any point in their experience of a story or book. For example, if you're reading *James and the Giant Peach* by Roald Dahl to the students, you can stop before James enters the peach and have students draw what they think it will look like inside — and what James will find there.

b. For students at any level, Romatowski (1987) suggests that teachers select from a number of texts passages that can easily be illustrated. Type each passage on a sheet of paper and distribute them. The students then "assume the role of illustrator." Have on hand several types of art media, including "magazines, wallpaper samples, old greeting cards, and yarn" (Romatowski, p. 38).

20. Have students discuss how artists choose to illustrate books. Discussing the role and composition of illustrations can highlight many of the aspects of critical thinking you have been developing through other response activities. Moreover, these discussions provide the groundwork for introducing a unit on a particular artist or comparing and contrasting two or three artists. You can focus on any book with illustrations.

a. How do the illustrations complement or work with the text?

b. How does an artist decide which scenes or events to illustrate?

c. Do artists always try to show us exactly what is there, or do they interpret what they find in the book? (You may wish to elaborate on this discussion by sharing different versions of the same story and comparing and contrasting the work of the different illustrators.)

    d. What reasons do the students believe the artist had for illustrating one scene or event more elaborately than another? (Sometimes the more elaborate illustration represents a more important event, for example.)

    e. What medium has the artist used? For example, if it is obvious that the artist has used watercolor, oils, pencil, collage, etc., you can discuss *why* the artist may have chosen a particular medium. If different media are used throughout the book, why might this be?

    f. How do the colors — or absence of color — reflect the elements of the text? (See the "Build Your Teaching Resources" bibliography after this section for a listing of books related to the role of the artist.)

21. Working in pairs, students first read a poem silently. Then one student describes to the other what it means to her. Both read the poem a second time, and then the other student explains what it means to him. If they wish, the students read the poem a third time and discuss it again. The students now write in their response journals what the poem means to them. This activity underscores the value of discussing and gradually coming to understand the potential of a poem — the different ideas it can evoke — and does so in a social context.

22. Show students how they can read poetry on their own. Rather than having them blaze through the poem when reading silently, model for your students how they can pause, go back, and play around with the sounds and images of a poem. You can do this in a "think-aloud" format, in which you read aloud as if you were reading to yourself. Pause, repeat some particularly pleasing phrase, and comment on why it pleases you (because of the alliteration, rhythm, rhyme, and so on). Or pause to comment on the image or idea a word or phrase evokes for you. Emphasize to the students that when they are reading poetry, they have the leisure to examine it more closely than they can when they are listening to it.

    After you have done this type of modeling for the students, have them look in favored poems for "lines or phrases that the poet clearly intends to be read aloud" (Sebesta, 1983, pp. 69–70) and write these down to share later.

■ Build Your Teaching Resources

Books about Illustrators and Artists

Sebesta (1987) suggests two books that are excellent for helping students conceptualize the role of the artist: *An artist* by M. B. Goffstein (1980, Harper and Row) and *Looking at art* by Alice Elizabeth Chase (1966, Crowell). The following selections also are useful resources for the classroom teacher:

Kingman, L., Hogarth, G., & Quimby, H. (eds). (1978). *Illustrators of children's books, 1967–1976.* Boston: The Horn Book.

Meyer, S. E. (1983). *A treasury of the great children's book illustrators.* New York: Abrams.

Richard, O. (1984). The visual language of the picture book. In P. Barron (ed.), *Jump over the moon*. New York: Holt, Rinehart, and Winston.

Stewig, J. W. (1988). *Children and literature*. Boston: Houghton Mifflin.

A fictional account of an artist's work is Donald Carrick's *Morgan and the artist* (1987, Houghton Mifflin). This engaging narrative may be enjoyed by second-graders on up. It works with younger students simply because the story is interesting; it works with older students on a deeper psychological level because they are able to understand that Morgan is the artist's alter ego, representing the truth in the artist's work in contrast with the commercialism.

Literature Units: Constructing and Conducting

Let's get specific: what *is* a literature unit? We referred briefly to one in Chapter 4 — the unit based on Peter Spier's book *People* (1980). Focused on a particular theme or topic and addressing specific learning objectives, a literature unit usually comprises a core selection of books that all students in the class will encounter, usually in a read-aloud format. They will read and discuss these books "intensively" (Harste, Short, and Burke, 1989). The books, building upon each other, will be read in a sequence by which students can logically develop and realize their reading goals and objectives. Occasionally, a core selection may consist of a single book, with a whole unit built around it. A number of related books to be read independently also will be available for the students.

Lasting from one to perhaps several weeks, a literature unit will include a wide range of activities in which students will analyze and apply the knowledge they develop through their interactions with the selections. The unit will involve all the language arts and quite often will involve other areas of subject matter as well. The unit will entail all of the strategies you have previously taught in the language arts: discussion, DRTAs and DLTAs, the writing process, word study (see Chapter 10), and so forth. Discussion will include the response groups we examined above, as well as individual and group conferences with you.

Before we proceed, I'd like to make a short definitional point. In your reading about literature-based units, you will see the term *theme* used interchangeably with *topic*. You've already seen, though, that *theme* can also refer quite specifically to an element of narratives. Don't let this confuse you; for our purposes, rest assured that, although I use both *theme* and *topic* myself, I will always be clear whenever I'm referring to *theme* as a literary element.

■ Build Your Teaching Resources

Sources of Ideas for Literature-Based Units

The WEB (Wonderfully Exciting Books) is an excellent resource not only because it provides reviews of recently published children's books but also because each issue presents a "Web" diagram of an exemplary instructional unit that includes suggested classroom

For Broader Study

Gods and Pharoahs from Egyptian Mythology
Warriors, Gods and Spirits from Central and South American Mythology
Seasons of Splendour—Tales, Myths, and Legends of India
Gods and Heroes from Viking Mythology
The Other World: Myths of the Celts
Greek Myths: Gods, Heroes and Monsters

Recommended References

For Deeper Study

The Power of Myth
- Primarily teacher reference; explores psychological depth of myth
Mythology for Young People
- Gives major concepts of mythology
- Has extensive annotated bibliography divided by countries
American Indian Myths and Legends
- Clear groupings of major themes and stories from main tribes

Creation

In the Night, Still Dark
In the Beginning
- Compare myths from different cultures: creation of gods and goddesses creation of man creation of earth.
- Interpret one of the creation myths through movement.
- Identify music that captures the mood and reflects the culture of a creation myth; perform a reading of the myth with musical background.

EXPLORING MYTHOLOGY
A Web of Possibilities

Nature and Native American Mythology

The Desert is Theirs and It Is Still That Way (legends told by Arizona Indian children)
- Discuss why Native Americans might make excellent advisers for EPA policies on conservation and natural resources.
They Dance in the Sky (Native American sky myths)
Raven-Who-Sets-Things-Right
How the People Sang the Mountains Up
- Use what you know about myth to create your own story to explain natural phenomena; illustrate your story.

Heroes

A Fair Wind for Troy
The Odyssey
The Gorgon's Head
Theseus and the Minotaur
- Define "hero".
- Identify your own heroes.
- Survey others to find out what kinds of heroes they choose.
- Identify modern heroes and discuss their appeal.
- Compare modern with mythological heroes.

Gods and Goddesses

The Macmillan Book of Greek Gods and Heroes
Lord of the Sky (Zeus)
The Golden God (Apollo)
The Olympians
- Research family trees of the gods.
- Create a god or goddess with powers/parents/symbols.
- Dress with the symbols of a god/goddess (winged feet of Apollo, etc.).

Mortals and Gods

Favorite Greek Myths
King Midas and the Golden Touch
- Why was Arachne turned into a spider?
- What happened to Echo after trouble with Hera?
- What is the significance of Nemesis to Narcissus?
Daughter of Earth
Song to Demeter
- Compare two stories of the goddess Demeter/Ceres.
- Find out when/why Romans took over the Greek stories.
- Explore some of the dilemmas of mythological characters through drama (e.g., assume roles of Persephone and the god of the Underworld in their conflict about her returning to her mother).

"Myths are about gods, legends are about heroes, and fairy tales are about woodcutters and princesses."

Myth in Modern Language

Words from the Myths
- Locate the myth that is the source of: a Herculean feat; Olympic games; opening Pandora's box; the Midas touch; the Trojan horse; an Achilles heel.
- What terms in our language come from myths? (names of planets; days of week and months of year; common words such as cereal, volcano, vulcanize, etc.)
- Scan advertising and product names for references to mythological characters.
Thunderbolt and Rainbow (Short descriptions of characters in mythology are paired with thought-provoking modern pictures.)
- Rewrite a mythological story for a younger audience.
- Turn classic stories into modern-day newspaper accounts, including news, sports, and society features.

FIGURE 9.3

A Sample Web of Activities: Exploring Mythology

Source: *The WEB: Wonderfully Exciting Books* (Columbus, OH: The Ohio State University, 1989), Vol. 3. No. 3. Reproduced by permission).

activities and possible readings, with annotated discussions of those readings. These webs, or units, have been constructed and used by classroom teachers.

You will find *The WEB* invaluable as you begin your teaching; certainly feel free to rely on such resources rather than always trying to construct the unit and locate materials from scratch. The sample web in Figure 9.3 and the discussion of major titles used addresses the topic of "Exploring Mythology," intended for use in the intermediate grades.
Note: *The WEB* may be ordered by writing to
The WEB, Ohio State University
29 W. Woodruff, 200 Ramseyer Hall
Columbus, Ohio 43210

Additional resources that include excellent examples of literature-based units are

Gamberg, R., Kwak, W., Hutchings, M., & Altheim, J. (1988). *Learning and loving it: Theme studies in the classroom.* Portsmouth, NH: Heinemann.

Moss, J. (1984). *Focus units in literature: A handbook for elementary school teachers.* Urbana, IL: National Council of Teachers of English.

Second edition published in 1990; although I recommend both, the first edition offers more concrete "how-to's" for the beginning teacher.

Norton, D. (1989). *The effective teaching of language arts.* Columbus, OH: Merrill.

Pappas, C., Kiefer, B., & Levstik, K. (1990). *An integrated language perspective in the elementary school.* New York: Longman.

See in particular Chapter 4.

Tchudi, S., & Tchudi, S. (1983). *Teaching writing in the content areas: Elementary school.* Washington, DC: National Educational Association.

See in particular Part II.

Steps in Constructing Units

Once they have a fair amount of experience, most teachers are able to incorporate many of the activities presented in the above section within the format of literature units. Keep in mind, however, that it is better at first to comfortably work in a few activities at a time than expect to immediately organize all the instruction in the unit.

Many school districts have developed or are in the process of developing "core" reading lists for specific grade levels. The teachers then select from these on a thematic or a topical basis. In most cases the criteria used in making these selections are very good; you will have latitude to supplement as you wish. In other districts you will rely more on your own resources. In just about all instances, though, you will be able to use, develop, and extend the literature you use.

Where core lists are available, check to determine whether they are arranged in a thematic or topical format. The lists may be arranged according to genre, and occasionally according to contributions of particular cultural groups, as in the *California Recommended Readings in Literature* (1988). Later I will list some resources you can draw upon when you construct and teach units; you will find yourself relying on them heavily when you begin constructing your own units. You will also eventually feel comfortable having your students plan their own units —

not all the time, but often enough to independently define, pursue, and summarize a particular theme or topic.

Your planning of literature units is actually an extension and elaboration of the line of thought you followed when you chose books and stories for discussion in the transition phase. You will now bring together many of the strategies and activities we have addressed thus far.

There are four main phases in constructing a literature unit (Glazer and Williams, 1979; Moss, 1984):

- Determine the goals or objectives of the unit.
- Determine the main focus (theme, topic) of the unit.
- Collect the books that will be the central works of the unit.
- Determine the primary type of activities in which the students will be engaged and plan their sequence.

Let's examine each of these phases more closely.

Determining the Unit Goals or Objectives

What do you want your students to learn? By now this is a familiar refrain: your goals and objectives will be based on (1) your knowledge of your students — their ages, interests, and social and emotional development and abilities; and (2) your knowledge of the language arts as well as the requirements of the language arts and subject matter curriculum for your school district. Recall from Chapter 4 how you can develop an overall plan for the year's instruction; it is time to bring many of these considerations to bear on the construction of your unit.

There is a lot of concern these days about the school district curriculum and basal program curriculum determining too much of what teachers teach (Goodman, et al., 1988; Shannon, 1988). Many educators feel that the students and their interests are not sufficiently included, but this concern usually dissolves when your instruction builds on reading and writing in response to literature. As you engage your students in lots of reading, writing, and discussion, you will be addressing both the interests of your students and the reading and language arts goals and objectives listed in the school district curriculum.

To stay keyed in to the interests and abilities of your students, you will rely on your general knowledge of the characteristics of students at this grade level and on what you've learned about each one of your students so far. You will have had ample time to assess their abilities across a wide range of tasks and activities. This is yet another advantage of waiting a few weeks before launching into the literature units. It also takes time for students to become familiar with classroom procedures and with the process of discussing individual stories *deeply* with you and with each other.

Determining the Unit's Focus

The main focus of each unit will be either a theme or a particular topic. It may emerge naturally out of your goals and objectives or may require a bit of thought.

For example, if your major objective is to develop awareness of one or more literary elements, then that becomes your main focus as well. On the other hand, if your major objective is to compare and contrast works within the same genre, then your *focus* will be more specific — on, for example, the role of "the fool" in folk tales, or on interpersonal relationships (the relationship between one individual and another versus one individual and a group).

We considered themes as narrative elements earlier in this chapter; following is just a sampling of the types of topics on which you can focus at the primary level (**P**), intermediate level (**I**), or both (**P, I**). As a quick glance indicates, most of these can be addressed at all elementary grade levels.

fantasy versus reality (**P**)

dreams (**P**)

toys (**P**)

city and country (**P**)

seasons (**P**)

any content area (**P, I**)

divorced families (**P, I**)

honesty (**P, I**)

genre (**P, I**)

most common folktale motifs — journey, confrontation, rescue, trick (**P, I**)

particular authors (**P, I**)

illustrators (**P, I**)

writers who write *and* illustrate their own books (**P, I**)

friendship (**P, I**)

journeys (**P, I**)

growing things (**P, I**)

interrelationships (**P, I**)

change — in humans, etc. (**P, I**)

pets (**P, I**)

stories in which heroine is problem solver (**P, I**)

stereotypes (upper **P, I**)

courage (**I**)

symbolism (**I**)

dialects (**I**)

humorous narrative (**I**)

individuality (**I**)

Collecting the Books

You will be collecting books to be read in story sessions, usually conducted with the whole class. These core selections will be read and discussed intensively. You will also be collecting books to be read independently by the students. You will, of course, look to your growing Bookfile (Chapter 5) as a possible source, but at first you will be using many other sources. In addition to prepared units such as those in *The WEB,* you will find invaluable information about books in the list below.

■ Build Your Teaching Resources

Resources for Assembling Books for Literature-Based Units

Baskin, B. H., & Harris, K. H. (1984). *More notes from a different drummer.* New York: R. R. Bowker.

Addresses handicapped learners.

Baskin, B. H., & Harris, K. H. (1980). *Books for the gifted child.* New York: R. R. Bowker.

Bernstein, J. (1983). *Books to help children cope with separation and loss.* New York: R. R. Bowker.

Brewton, J., et al. (1942). *Index to poetry for children and young people.* New York: H. W. Wilson.

Five supplements have been published; the most recent is 1983.

Children's catalog (updated annually). New York: H. W. Wilson.

Children's book review index. Detroit, MI: Gale Research.

Children's books in print (updated annually). New York: R. R. Bowker.

This bibliography is divided into subject and author.

Commire, A. (1985). *Something about the author.* Detroit, MI: Gale Research.

Dreyer, S. *The bookfinder.* Circle Pines, MN: American Guidance Service.

The elementary school library collection. New Brunswick, NJ: Bro-Dart Foundation.

Published annually; includes films, filmstrips, and other media as well.

Flowers, A. A. (ed.) (1990). *The Horn Book guide to children's and young adult books.* Boston, MA: The Horn Book, Inc.

Gillespie, J. (1985). *The elementary school paperback collection.* Chicago: American Library Association.

Greene, E., & Schoenfeld, M. (1972). *A multimedia approach to children's literature.* Chicago: American Library Association.

Hearne, B. (1981). *Choosing books for children: A common sense guide.* New York: Delacorte Press.

High interest, easy reading. (1984). Urbana, IL: National Conference on Teachers of English.

Hotchkiss, J. (1976). *African-Asian reading guide for children and young adults.* Metuchen, NJ: Scarecrow Press.

Jett-Simpson, M., and the Committee on the Elementary School Booklist (eds.). (1989). *Adventuring with books: A booklist for pre-K–grade 6.* Urbana, IL: National Conference on Teachers of English.

Kingman, L., et al. (1978). *Illustrators of children's books, 1967–1976.* Boston: The Horn Book, Inc.

Three previous volumes covering earlier illustrators have also been published.

Kobrin, B. (1988). *Eyeopener!: How to choose and use children's books about real people, places and things.* New York: Viking Penguin.

Language Arts (formerly *Elementary English*). Urbana, IL: National Council of Teachers of English.

Lass-Woodfin, M. J. *Books on American Indians and Eskimos.* Chicago: American Library Association.

Lima, C. (1985). *A to zoo: Subject access to children's picture books.* New York: R. R. Bowker.

Monson, D., and the Committee on the Elementary School Booklist (eds.). (1985). *Adventuring with books: A booklist for pre-K–grade 6.* Urbana, IL: National Conference on Teachers of English.

Posner, M. (1985). *Juvenile Judaica: The Jewish values bookfinder.* New York: The Association of Jewish Libraries.

Science and children. Washington, DC: National Science Teachers Association.

Annual list of "outstanding science trade books for children."

The Reading Teacher. Published by the International Reading Association, Newark, DE.

The IRA also publishes under separate cover the annual "Children's Choices."

Schon, I. (1983). *Books in Spanish for children and young adults.* Metuchen, NJ: Scarecrow Press.

Siegel, M. (ed.). (1984). *Her way: A guide to biographies of women for young people.* Chicago: American Library Association.

Silverman, J. (1979). *Index to collective biographies for young readers.* New York: R. R. Bowker.

Sims, R. (1982). *Shadow and substance: Afro-American experience in contemporary children's fiction.* Urbana, IL: National Council of Teachers of English.

School Library Journal. New York: R. R. Bowker Company.

Social Education. Arlington, VA: The National Council for Social Studies.

Annual list of "notable children's trade books in the field of social studies."

Subject guide to children's books in print. New York: R. R. Bowker.

Sutherland, Z. (ed.). *The best in children's books.* Appears in *The Bulletin of the Center for children's books.* Chicago: University of Chicago Press.

The WEB (Wonderfully Exciting Books). Columbus, OH: Ohio State University, Martha L. King Center for Language and Literacy.

Determining the Primary Range of Activities

This is the organizational stage for instruction. One of the best ways to begin is to brainstorm instructional ideas for the unit. A popular format for brainstorming is referred to as a "Web of Possibilities" (Cullinan, Karrer, and Pillar, 1981). According to Cullinan, et al., the idea originated in England and was popularized in the United States by Charlotte Huck. Because it is a brainstorm of ideas, remember that you certainly wouldn't do everything. You may wish to establish categories first, based on your objectives: critical thinking, writing, understanding of literary elements, art and drama activities, and so on. Alternatively, you may find that it is easier to categorize the activities after you have brainstormed. Figures 9.4 and 9.5, adapted from Huck (1979), illustrate webs based on a core work addressing the theme of feeling alone and alienated; *Crow Boy* is appropriate for primary level and *Call It Courage* is intended for the intermediate grades. A little later in the school year, your students will enjoy brainstorming ideas for their own explorations.

As you gain experience with planning and implementing units, you may wish to integrate more of your subject matter instruction into each unit. At the intermediate grade levels, of course, you will need to address many more content-related objectives (for example, those in the math, science, and social studies curricula). As you realize that you can use the unit organizational scheme for just about all of your instruction and your students' learning (Harste, Short, and Burke, 1989), you will have the confidence to implement the scheme across more of the content (see, for example, the sample unit at the end of this chapter built around the book *21 Balloons*). Once you have determined what you realistically are able to address, you should find the planning-sheet format presented in Chapter 4 to be very helpful.

Procedure for Conducting the Unit

Every day, you will read orally to the students from the core selections. The format may be similar to a DLTA in which the students make predictions orally and/or in

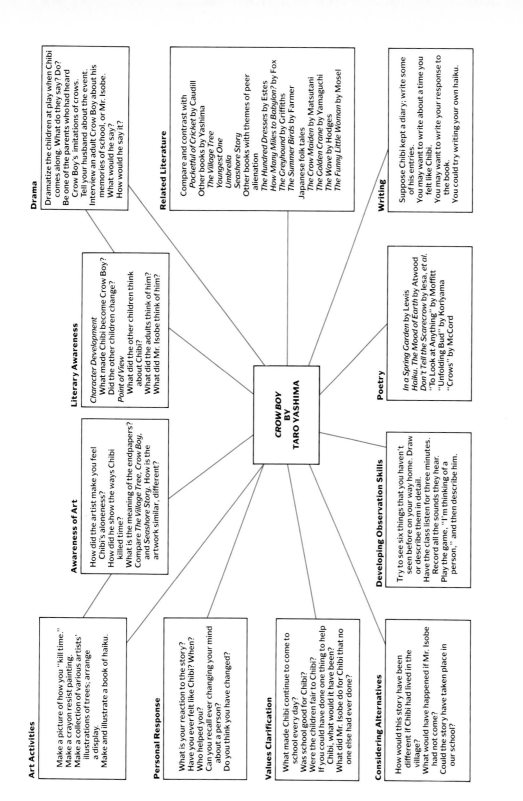

Art Activities

Make a picture of how you "kill time."
Make a crayon resist painting.
Make a collection of various artists'
  illustrations of trees; arrange
  a display.
Make and illustrate a book of haiku.

Personal Response

What is your reaction to the story?
Have you ever felt like Chibi? When?
Who helped you?
Can you recall ever changing your mind
  about a person?
Do you think you have changed?

Values Clarification

What made Chibi continue to come to
  school every day?
Was school good for Chibi?
Were the children fair to Chibi?
If you could have done one thing to help
  Chibi, what would it have been?
What did Mr. Isobe do for Chibi that no
  one else had ever done?

Considering Alternatives

How would this story have been
  different if Chibi had lived in the
  village?
What would have happened if Mr. Isobe
  had not come?
Could the story have taken place in
  our school?

Awareness of Art

How did the artist make you feel
  Chibi's aloneness?
How did he show the ways Chibi
  killed time?
What is the meaning of the endpapers?
Compare *The Village Tree, Crow Boy,*
  and *Seashore Story.* How is the
  artwork similar, different?

CROW BOY
BY
TARO YASHIMA

Literary Awareness

Character Development
What made Chibi become Crow Boy?
Did the other children change?
Point of View
What did the other children think
  about Chibi?
What did the adults think of him?
What did Mr. Isobe think of him?

Developing Observation Skills

Try to see six things that you haven't
  seen before on your way home. Draw
  or describe them in detail.
Have the class listen for three minutes.
  Record all the sounds they hear.
Play the game, "I'm thinking of a
  person," and then describe him.

Poetry

In a Spring Garden by Lewis
Haiku, The Mood of Earth by Atwood
Don't Tell the Scarecrow by Iesa, *et al.*
  "To Look at Anything" by Moffitt
  "Unfolding Bud" by Koriyama
  "Crows" by McCord

Drama

Dramatize the children at play when Chibi
  comes along. What do they say? Do?
Be one of the parents who had heard
  Crow Boy's imitations of crows.
Tell your husband about the event.
Interview an adult Crow Boy about his
  memories of school, and Mr. Isobe.
  What would he say?
  How would he say it?

Related Literature

Compare and contrast with
  Pocketful of Cricket by Caudill
Other books by Yashima
  The Village Tree
  Youngest One
  Umbrella
  Seashore Story
Other books with themes of peer
  alienation
  The Hundred Dresses by Estes
  How Many Miles to Babylon? by Fox
  The Greyhound by Griffiths
  The Summer Birds by Farmer
Japanese folk tales
  The Crow Maiden by Matsutani
  The Golden Crane by Yamaguchi
  The Wave by Hodges
  The Funny Little Woman by Mosel

Writing

Suppose Chibi kept a diary; write some
  of his entries.
You may want to write about a time you
  felt like Chibi.
You may want to write your response to
  the book.
You could try writing your own haiku.

FIGURE 9.4

A Web of Possible Activities for the Primary Grades — Exploring the Theme of Alienation

Source: *Children's Literature in the Elementary School*, Third Edition, edited by Charlotte Huck, copyright © 1979 by Charlotte S. Huck, reprinted by permission of Holt, Rinehart and Winston, Inc.

Literature Units: Constructing and Conducting   367

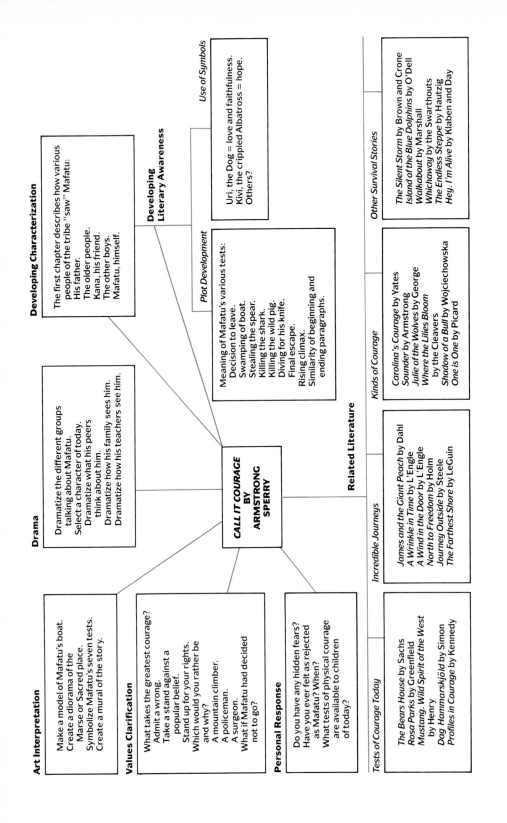

Art Interpretation

Make a model of Mafatu's boat.
Create a diorama of the
   Marae or Sacred place.
Symbolize Mafatu's seven tests.
Create a mural of the story.

Drama

Dramatize the different groups
   talking about Mafatu.
Select a character of today.
Dramatize what his peers
   think about him.
Dramatize how his family sees him.
Dramatize how his teachers see him.

Developing Characterization

The first chapter describes how various
people of the tribe "saw" Mafatu:
   His father.
   The older people.
   Kana, his friend.
   The other boys.
   Mafatu, himself.

Developing Literary Awareness

Use of Symbols

Uri, the Dog = love and faithfulness.
Kivi, the crippled Albatross = hope.
Others?

Plot Development

Meaning of Mafatu's various tests:
   Decision to leave.
   Swamping of boat.
   Stealing the spear.
   Killing the shark.
   Killing the wild pig.
   Diving for his knife.
   Final escape.
Rising climax.
Similarity of beginning and
   ending paragraphs.

Values Clarification

What takes the greatest courage?
   Admit a wrong.
   Take a stand against a
      popular belief.
   Stand up for your rights.
   Which would you rather be
      and why?
      A mountain climber.
      A policeman.
      A surgeon.
   What if Mafatu had decided
      not to go?

Personal Response

Do you have any hidden fears?
Have you ever felt as rejected
   as Mafatu? When?
What tests of physical courage
   are available to children
   of today?

CALL IT COURAGE BY ARMSTRONG SPERRY

Related Literature

Kinds of Courage

Carolina's Courage by Yates
Sounder by Armstrong
Julie of the Wolves by George
Where the Lilies Bloom
   by the Cleavers
Shadow of a Bull by Wojciechowska
One is One by Picard

Other Survival Stories

The Silent Storm by Brown and Crone
Island of the Blue Dolphins by O'Dell
Walkabout by Marshall
Whichaway by the Swarthouts
The Endless Steppe by Hautzig
Hey, I'm Alive by Klaben and Day

Incredible Journeys

James and the Giant Peach by Dahl
A Wrinkle in Time by L'Engle
A Wind in the Door by L'Engle
North to Freedom by Holm
Journey Outside by Steele
The Farthest Shore by LeGuin

Tests of Courage Today

The Bears House by Sachs
Rosa Parks by Greenfield
Mustang, Wild Spirit of the West
   by Henry
Dag Hammarskjöld by Simon
Profiles in Courage by Kennedy

FIGURE 9.5

A Web of Possible Activities for the Intermediate Grades — Exploring the Theme of Alienation

Source: *Children's Literature in the Elementary School*, Third Edition, edited by Charlotte Huck, copyright © 1979 by Charlotte S. Huck, reprinted by permission of Holt, Rinehart and Winston, Inc.

their response journals. You may have the students respond to questions that you have provided; again, responses may be both oral and written. The students' responses over time will reflect a *cumulative* process of learning (Moss, 1984) that is occurring as your students explore the literature together.

Students will read the related selections independently and discuss them in smaller groups, sometimes meeting with you for the discussions. Depending on your purpose, sometimes the groups will read the same selection (multiple copies of a book or a story in a basal reader) and sometimes each student will read a different selection. Activities can occur during the language arts block in the morning and, as appropriate, during the afternoon. You will be meeting with individuals and with groups to assess how projects are coming along and to provide feedback and help as needed.

Let's put these guidelines to work — in the following examples of literature units. The first unit is presented in a more specific day-by-day "lesson plan" format. Because of its length, the second unit (p. 375) is presented in a "two-phase" format, starting with a DLTA and culminating in a whole-class activity that also involves parents.

SAMPLE LITERATURE UNITS

Second Grade: Friendship*

The main purpose of the first unit is to help children understand their own social interactions and to help develop good peer relationships.

The dynamics of a classroom and the interactions between the children in that classroom are very important factors in the achievement of a successful school year. A friendship unit introduced early in the school year will help children develop and maintain friendships within the classroom as well as throughout the school and the community. As teachers, of course, you will at times have to deal with children who quarrel, fight, and "tattletale," and sympathize with those children whose feelings have been hurt — inadvertently or otherwise — by other children.

This unit will help children to see the world through others' eyes, to make inferences about a person's feelings and motives, and to anticipate consequences of behavior. As a group, the class will listen to stories read to them by the teacher. They will also select individual stories to read to themselves during SSR (sustained silent reading) time. For example, when children read *I'm Not Oscar's Friend Anymore* by Marjorie Sharmat, they may realize that Oscar's friend experienced feelings and misconceptions just like those they might have experienced at some time or another. This realization may help them through a similar situation in their own lives.

In this unit, the children will be guided to make inferences about the motives, feelings, and thoughts of story characters and will explore the structure and content of each story. They will compare characters and story plots from the group story sessions to characters and story plots from the individual stories they read. A major goal of the unit is to develop critical reading and

*Adapted from a unit by Patricia Sorensen, student at the University of Nevada — Reno.

writing skills and the ability to understand the relationships between friend-ships in stories and friendships in real life.

Objectives

1. To develop critical reading and writing skills
2. To develop the ability to make inferences about the motives, feelings, and thoughts of story characters
3. To compare and contrast *characters* and *plots* of different stories
4. To develop an understanding of the relationships between friendships in stories and friendships in real life

Core Books

■ Charlip, R. (1973). *Harlequin and the gift of many colors.* Chicago: Parents Magazine Press.

This beautifully illustrated story is set in fourteenth-century rural Italy at carnival time. When Harlequin's friends discover that he has no costume to wear, they each cut a piece of their own costume to give to their beloved friend. Harlequin's mother sews the pieces together to create a magnificent patchwork costume that he wears to the carnival.

■ Delton, J. (1974). *Two good friends.* New York: Crown.

Written for beginning readers, this charming story of Duck and Bear is a delightful example of maintaining a friendship by resolving differences and sharing special talents.

■ Lobel, A. (1970). *Frog and Toad are friends.* New York: Harper and Row.

Frog and Toad are two friends whose relationship is characterized by caring, sensitivity, and thoughtfulness. An "I Can Read" book. See "Related Books."

■ Marshall, J. (1972). *George and Martha.* Boston: Houghton Mifflin.

George and Martha are two not-so-delicate hippopotami who share a loving, caring, and delicate friendship. The humorous nature of their relationship is related throughout the five short chapters of the book.

Related Books (Independent Reading)

■ Baylor, B. (1977). *Guess who my favorite person is.* New York: Scribner's.

In a conversational and lyrical text, two friends play the game of naming their favorite things.

■ Eriksson, E. (1985). *Jealousy.* Minneapolis: Carolrhoda Books.

While Rosalie has the mumps, her best friend Victor starts playing with another girl, which incites Rosalie's jealousy.

■ Hallinan, P. K. (1977). *That's what a friend is.* Chicago: Children's Press.

This simple story describes friendship in rhymed text and charming illustrations.

■ Hallinan, P. K. (1973). *We're very good friends, my brother and I.* Chicago: Children's Press.

This story, told in rhyme, describes why a boy is glad to have a brother to play with, to feel sad and happy with, or just to be with.

■ Heine, H. (1982). *Friends.* New York: Atheneum.

A joyful story about three friends — Charlie Rooster, Johnny Mouse, and fat Percy, the pig — who always stick together.

■ Hoban, R. (1969). *Best friends for Frances.* New York: Harper and Row.

A story about how Frances learns to share friendship with her younger sister Gloria as well as with her other friends Albert and Harold.

■ Hoff, S. (1960). *Who will be my friends?* New York: Harper and Row.

Freddy tries to find friends after moving to a new town.

■ Kellogg, S. (1986). *Best friends.* New York: Dial Books for Young Readers.

Kathy's best friend Louise goes away to the mountains for the summer. Kathy is very lonesome until a new neighbor with a dog expecting puppies moves into the neighborhood.

■ Lionni, L. (1969). *Alexander and the wind-up mouse.* New York: Pantheon.

Alexander, a real mouse, envies his friend Willy, who is the favorite toy of a little girl, and he decides to ask a magic lizard to change him into a toy. He revises his wish, however.

■ Lobel, A. *Frog and Toad together* (1977) and *Days with Frog and Toad* (1979). New York: Harper and Row.

More stories about Frog and Toad as they spend their days together — but find sometimes it's nice to be alone.

■ Minarik, E. H. (1960). *Little Bear's friend.* New York: Harper and Row.

Little Bear and his friend Emily spend many happy days together in the summer. Little Bear later writes Emily letters after she has returned to her home.

■ Moncure, J. B. (1988). *What do you do with a grumpy kangaroo?* Chicago: Children's Press.

Tony tries to cheer up Grumpy Kangaroo by taking him to the circus and the playground.

■ Sharmat, M. (1975). *I'm not Oscar's friend anymore.* New York: E. P. Dutton.

Oscar's "former friend" relates all the reasons they aren't friends anymore until he calls Oscar and discovers that they *are* still friends.

■ Sharmat, M. (1978). *Mitchell is moving.* New York: Macmillan.

A dinosaur's exuberance about moving cools considerably when he realizes how much he will miss his friend next door.

■ Stevenson, J. (1986). *No friends.* New York: Greenwillow Books.

When his grandchildren complain that they have no friends in their new neighborhood, a wily grandpa remembers a place where he and his brother Wainey once lived.

■ Wells, R. (1973). *Benjamin and Tulip.* New York: Dial Press.

Tulip bullies Benjamin every time he passes by her house, until he finally takes the situation in hand.

■ Wildsmith, B. (1974). *The lazy bear.* New York: Franklin Watts.

The bear was good friends with all his neighbors until he took advantage of them. They finally give him a taste of his own medicine and he apologizes.

■ Zolotow, C. (1973). *Janey.* New York: Harper and Row.

This story tenderly evokes the special feeling of loss when a friend moves away.

■ Zolotow, C. (1968). *My friend John.* New York: Harper and Row.

A boy relates all the reasons why he and his friend John are best friends.

First Group Story Session

Story: *Two Good Friends* by Judy Delton. Two good friends, Duck and Bear, are very different. Duck is neat and likes to clean and Bear is messy and likes to bake. Even though they are opposites, they are best friends who learn to complement each other.

1. Conduct the story following a DLTA format. After reading, ask the following questions if they were not addressed earlier:

   a. How were the two characters different?

   b. How did they help each other?

```
              ,  19

Dear Parents:

    We are exploring the concept of friendship and want to find
out what friendship means to different people. We decided to
conduct our own original research using interviews as our
primary source of information.
    Each student in our class is to interview three people.
Your child is to write as much of the interview conversation as
possible in the exact language used. Please do not be overly
concerned about grammatical errors or with spelling at this
point. We will be "polishing" our write-ups in class.
    We will need your child's interview by_____.
    Thank you for your cooperation in this new adventure!

                                    Sincerely,

                                    Ms. O'Malley
```

FIGURE 9.6

**Explanatory Letter
to Parents**

    c.   Why do you think they are best friends?

This should lead into a discussion about what a friend is.

2. After the DLTA, have the students write their responses to the question, "What is a friend?" The previous discussion should facilitate their responses.

3. Have the students prepare for a "research paper" based on an interview to find out what other people think a friend is. Send home a letter to parents explaining the project. (See Figures 9.6 and 9.7.)

4. Over the next few days, children will interview three different people and ask them the question, "What is a friend?" (You will have discussed with them that there is no "right" answer to this question.)

5. The students record the answers, bring them back, and share them with the class.

Second Through Fourth Group Story Sessions

Stories: *Frog and Toad Are Friends,* by Arnold Lobel
         George and Martha, by James Marshall
         Harlequin and the Gift of Many Colors, by Remy Charlip

After reading each story in a DLTA format, discuss how the words and behavior of one character affected the feelings of another. For example, how did Frog

Research Paper by Merryl Nathanson

"What is a friend?"

1. Name and relation of person (relative, neighbor, friend)

Eugene Wilbur - uncle

2. Name and relation of person (relative, neighbor, friend)

Ranu Roff - neighbor

3, Name and relation of person (relative, neighbor, friend)

Vinnie Primo - friend

FIGURE 9.7

"Research" Form for Friendship Interview

help Toad, and how did Harlequin's friends help him? What did George do with the split pea soup so that he wouldn't hurt Martha's feelings? What did Martha tell George about his new gold tooth?

Independent Reading Story Selections

Through their independent reading, the students will discover new stories about friendship and relate these stories through comparison and contrast to the characters and story structure of the books that have been read aloud.

1. Display 15–25 books with friendship themes. The books range in reading levels from first through fifth grade, so that all children will be accommodated.
2. Students choose one of these books to read independently. They may of course read more if they wish.
3. During the discussion of the read-aloud books, the students can contribute points of comparison and contrast from the stories they have been reading independently. You can facilitate this process by asking about similar themes, plots, and character interactions.

Related Activities

To follow up on the interview "research paper," write a class book using the information the students obtained.

a. Have each child record the information from his or her interview paper onto a page in the class book.
b. Use either 9″ × 12″ or 12″ × 18″ white construction paper for each page. The large paper allows for written text and leaves room for children's draw-

ings. Use heavy card stock for the cover. Covers and pages should be laminated.

c. Bind the class book with loose metal rings — ¾″ or 1″ rings work best.

d. Place the completed book in the classroom book area for free choice reading.

In addition, students may select from one or more of the following activities:

1. The students can create their own stories about friendship. These can be composed primarily during the morning writing block, but the students may work on them during free time as well. Their stories will develop (of course!) according to the stages in the writing process: prewriting, drafting, revising, editing, sharing and publishing. Students will illustrate their respective friendship stories and, if they wish, compile them in a class book.

2. Working in small groups, students who have read the same book for their independent reading can transform the story into a play. Students can begin by role-playing different characters. This may be sufficient, or the students may wish to develop rehearsed dialogue, build and paint sets, make costumes, and select or create music for the play.

3. The students can dramatize a story using puppets (sock or glove puppets work best).

4. The students create a mural depicting one of the stories. Use extra large drawing paper for the background, and 9″ × 12″ or 18″ × 24″ paper for drawing and cutting out characters. The usual materials should be available: scissors, paint, brushes, felt-tipped markers. Cut out paper bubbles for dialogue. Each student can be responsible for his or her character and that character's "bubble dialogue."

Sixth Grade: *The 21 Balloons*

This unit, based upon a classic book both written and illustrated by William Pene DuBois, can last from six to nine weeks, and students will be able to exercise considerable individual choice. (Because of the degree of student responsibility involved, it is probably best to wait until the second half of the year to try this unit.) In addition, the unit ties in more directly with subject matter instruction, specifically world geography (in many school districts, a required subject in sixth grade), history, and science. For purposes of discussion, the unit will be broken down into two phases. (The unit is adapted from Bear and Lohman, 1988.)

The 21 Balloons, published in 1947 and winner of the 1948 Newbery Medal, is a fascinating and delightful fantasy about Professor Sherman, who in 1883 takes a year off to sail around the world in a balloon. He crashes, however, and winds up on the island of Krakatoa in Indonesia just before the volcano on that island erupts. Twenty families live there; up to that point they have been living in relative harmony with the volcano. Most of the book is given to describing the professor's interactions with these families — an unimaginably fantastic experience. The story continues with the tremendous eruption of Krakatoa and how the professor eventually returns home to widespread fame.

Objectives

1. To expand students' opportunities for reading and writing independently in both narrative and expository modes
2. To develop listening comprehension skills
3. To develop oral presentation skills
4. To develop and extend study skills, including note taking
5. In addition, to address specific content objectives in the school district's geography, history, and science curricula

First Phase

In order to acquaint students with the book, you begin by reading aloud the first four chapters in DLTA format. The next chapters are handled by the students themselves. Some students will be responsible for conducting the DLTA reading, and others will focus on note taking. In addition, during your reading of the first four chapters, you will set up small research groups that will investigate questions raised by the class. Following are the directions given each group of students for each activity.

Directed Listening-Thinking Activity Group
1. Read the chapter together, and find good stopping points. Find places to stop where you can ask the class what they think will happen next.
2. Write questions for each stopping point.
3. Decide what parts each of you will read orally, and practice your reading.
4. Meet with teacher to discuss your work.
5. Make your presentation.
6. Meet with teacher for an evaluation.

Students are evaluated on how well organized they were, the quality of their stopping points, their tact and politeness, and the degree to which they followed up on other students' predictions.

Note-taking Group
1. Read the chapter together and, in an outline form, list the important points.
2. Meet with teacher to share your notes.
3. Lead the class in a note-taking session following each day's reading.
4. Revise your notes to take into account additions suggested by the class.

5. Duplicate and distribute these notes before the next session.
6. Meet with teacher for an evaluation.

Students are evaluated on the basis of the accuracy, clarity, and organization of their notes, their willingness to incorporate other students' suggestions, and their promptness in distributing the notes.

Research Groups
Informal questions may be addressed, to be answered the following day after a brief investigation, such as:

- How wide is the United States?
- How many miles per day can a balloon travel?
- How long does it take to travel across country by train?
- Who was President of the United States in 1883?
- What is ballast?
- How can salt water be turned into drinking water?
- Where is Krakatoa?

More substantive issues are investigated in groups; topics are brainstormed by the students and usually include balloon travel, volcanoes, and inventions. The students will do their research, write up their findings, and make oral reports to the class. (This is an excellent time to teach about bibliographies.) Presentations are evaluated by the class.

Students exploring balloon travel will find the following books helpful:

- Briggs, C. S. (1988). *Research balloons: Exploring hidden worlds.* Minneapolis, MN: Lerner Publications.

  This book will provide an engaging twist on students' understanding of what balloons can be used for. It takes ballooning beyond transportation and explores its influence on our understanding of space. A glossary is included.

- Coombs, C. (1981). *Hot-air ballooning.* New York: William Morrow.

  Although the concepts in this book are fairly challenging, the illustrations are excellent; this book will be a gold mine for students who are really swept up in the topic.

- Scarry, H. (1983). *Balloon trip: A sketchbook.* Englewood Cliffs, NJ: Prentice-Hall.

  This text provides excellent descriptions of hot-air balloons, how they work, and what it's like to fly in them. Illustrations portray a balloonist's perspective.

Students who investigate volcanoes may do the following:

1. Invite a geologist to speak to the class on volcanoes (if no parent is available to discuss this, then contact oil companies, surveying firms, mining firms, the county agricultural extension office, or a college or university if one is close by). One or more students can summarize and write up the geologist's presentation and perhaps prepare an interview as well to pursue information in more depth. This could be published in the class or school newspaper or in the class book that represents most of the written work on volcanoes that the class will do.

2. View the videotape of the Public Broadcasting System's *Nature* program on Krakatoa.

3. Read the excellent descriptions of the formation and activity of volcanoes in *The Evolution Book* by Sara Stein (Workman Publishing, 1986). Here is an example of the power and the effect of volcanic eruptions she captures with her straightforward description of the eruption of Yellowstone in Wyoming 600,000 years ago: The ash from this one volcanic eruption "blanketed all of Wyoming, Colorado, Utah, Arizona, New Mexico, Oklahoma, Kansas, Nebraska, and South Dakota; blanketed most of North Dakota, Nevada, and California, and blanketed parts of Montana, Idaho, Louisiana, Arkansas, Missouri, Iowa, and Minnesota" (Stein, p. 283). When Krakatoa exploded, Stein notes, "its dust in the atmosphere reflected away as much as 10 percent of the sun's light as far away as Europe, and for three years" (p. 359).

    Refer also to Patricia Lauber's *Volcano: The eruption and healing of Mt. St. Helens* (Bradbury Press, 1986).

Interested students can explore the topic of inventions through the following books:

■   Ardley, N. (1984). *How things work.* New York: Wanderer.

    In addition to explaining a lot of natural phenomena, this book offers excellent descriptions of the workings of inventions. For each question, short answers are provided, followed by lengthier explanations.

■   Crump, D. (ed.). (1984). *Small inventions that make a big difference.* Washington, DC: National Geographic.

    Inventions that we take for granted (such as traffic lights) are engagingly discussed.

■   Caney, S. (1985). *Steven Caney's invention book.* New York: Workman.

    Not only are "simple" inventions discussed; Caney provides information on how to go about the business of being an inventor, including how to get a patent and market your invention.

■ Giscard d'Estaing, V. (1985). *The world almanac book of inventions.* New York: World Almanac.

Catalogues and discusses the histories of more than 2,000 inventions. Good idea book for research projects as well as for read-alouds.

Second Phase

The class now pursues intensive activities that branch farther afield from the original book itself. Three possible activities are given below.

1. The families on Krakatoa are named after the letters of the alphabet. Each month, each family prepares a meal for the other residents based on the foods from the country that begins with their letter (A = American; B = British; C = Chinese, etc.). This provides an excellent motivation for the following activity:

    a. Students will work in pairs and select the name of a country out of a hat; each pair will then research that country. (It's probably a good idea to exclude "America" for this unit!)

    b. Research will include preparing a travel brochure for their country; students may contact travel agencies as well as embassies or consulates (an excellent opportunity to apply business-letter-writing skills). If you have access to some simple graphics design software for a microcomputer, the brochure can be developed and run off using that — it's a lot easier to do than it sounds!

    c. The unit culminates in an international lunch to which parents are invited. Students prepare a dish from their country, may dress in the attire of their country, and will take a moment at the lunch to introduce their country and describe their dish.

2. Students may choose to explore books that, like *The 21 Balloons,* deal with "fabulous flights" (Huck, 1979). They can compare and contrast these books across a number of dimensions.

    Dahl, R. (1961). *James and the giant peach.* New York: Knopf.

Fleming, I. (1964). *Chitty-chitty-bang-bang.* New York: Random House. [Yes, this is the same Ian Fleming who wrote the James Bond stories!]

Lawson, R. (1949). *The fabulous flight.* Boston: Little, Brown.

L'Engle, M. (1962). *A wrinkle in time.* New York: Farrar, Straus. [Flight of a decidedly different type!]

3. Students may also elect to study the history of flight. Two excellent resources are the following:

Stoff, J. (1985). *Dirigible.* New York: Atheneum. [The conception, building, and operation of what many thought would be the aviation wave of the future.]

Zisfein, M. (1981). *Flight: A panorama of aviation.* New York: Pantheon. [Explores aviation from the very beginnings through jet aircraft. Excellent illustrations by R. A. Parker.]

4. Students may decide they'd like to read other books written and/or illustrated by William Pene DuBois. Some of them were intended for younger audiences; for these, the students may compare and contrast the writing and/or illustrations in them with those books intended for older students. This activity can lead to some intriguing insights into how authors develop narrative elements depending on the age and experience of the intended audience.

Books written by DuBois:

Bear circus. (1971). New York: Viking.
Lazy Tommy Pumpkinhead. (1966). New York: Harper and Row.
Lion. (1956). New York: Viking

Books illustrated by DuBois:

Dahl, R. (1966). *The magic finger.* New York: Harper and Row.
Godden, R. (1951). *The mousewife.* New York: Viking.
MacDonald, G. (1962). *The light princess.* New York: Crowell. [Contrast DuBois' illustrations of this fantasy with those of Maurice Sendak in the version published by Farrar, Straus (1969).]
MacLachlan, P. (1979). *The sick day.* New York: Pantheon.
Zolotow, C. (1972). *William's doll.* New York: Harper and Row.
Zolotow, C. (1974). *My grandson Lew.* New York: Harper and Row.

A CONCLUDING PERSPECTIVE

This chapter's presentation and sequence of topics about a literature-based reading and writing curriculum are based on the beginning teacher's perspective. Here is a quick recap. You first need to get a handle on reading and writing instruction in a more structured format before moving into more student-centered instruction. With experience, you will probably find that you can if you wish begin themed units on the first day of class. For starters, though, the approaches and suggestions outlined in this chapter should help you develop a feel for and confidence in the various aspects of reading and writing teaching and learning.

You also should start immersing yourself in children's literature. As a part of your immersion, ask relatives and friends to give you books for holiday and birthday presents. Join educational book clubs that give significant discounts on books. Beginning with your student teaching experience, encourage your students to order books from children's book clubs; these clubs also give dividends that you can use to purchase additional copies of particular titles (great for obtaining multiple copies of treasured titles). Remind your students: "Kids, whenever each of you orders a book or books for yourselves you're helping build our classroom collection of books. If we order multiple copies, each of you can have a copy of a chapter book to read when several students are reading it at the same time." Encourage Parent Teacher Associations or Organizations to raise money for multiple copies as well as for subscriptions to children's periodicals and teacher journals.

In summary, this chapter has pulled together most of what has been addressed throughout this book regarding strategies and emphases in reading and writing. The foundation for basing most of reading and writing instruction on real literature rests on the results of research into the potential for children's responses to literature: elementary students are capable of responding deeply and meaningfully to what they read.

Your instruction will explore the major categories of children's literature: alphabet books, picture books, wordless books, traditional literature, poetry, historical fiction, contemporary realism, modern fantasy, informational nonfiction, and biography. You will also make available plenty of books that reflect your students' interests.

I suggested a format for responding to literature by means of literature-based reading and writing response or conference groups. A "transition" to literature units allows you to try out various components of reading and writing response before coordinating everything into a unit. A wide range of literature-based activities is possible. We discussed guidelines for preparing and teaching literature units as a regular feature of your instruction and looked at resources for locating appropriate texts. The chapter concluded with two sample literature units covering grades two and six.

Greenlaw and McIntosh (1987) pointed out that "it is not enough merely to suggest good books to students; they have to be guided in strategies that will give them the knowledge and skill to explore books on their own" (Greenlaw and McIntosh, p. 111). With this observation, you are reminded of your challenge: This guidance, knowledge, and skill will develop in the context of your instruction and modeling and the effective social and literate environment in which you immerse your students.

REFERENCES

Alvermann, D., & Hayes, D. (1989). Classroom discussion of content area reading assignments: An intervention study. *Reading Research Quarterly, 24,* 305–335.

Anderson, R. C., Osborn, J., & Tierney, R. (eds.). (1984). *Learning to read in American schools: Basal readers and content texts.* Hillsdale, NJ: Lawrence Erlbaum Associates.

Applebee, A. (1978). *The child's concept of story.* Chicago: University of Chicago Press.

Applebee, A. (1984). Writing and reasoning. *Review of Educational Research, 54,* 577–596.

Barone, D. (1989). *Young children's written responses to literature: Exploring the relationship between written response and orthographic knowledge.* Unpublished doctoral dissertation, University of Nevada, Reno.

Bear, D., & Invernizzi, M. (1987). Student-directed reading groups. *Journal of Reading, 28,* 248–252.

Bear, D., & Lohman, D. (1988). Literature across the curriculum: *The 21 Balloons* in the sixth grade classroom. In J. Golub (ed.), *Focus on collaborative learning: Classroom practices in teaching English.* Urbana, IL: National Council of Teachers of English.

Bettelheim, B. (1976). *The uses of enchantment.* New York: Vintage.

Bleich, D. (1975). *Readings and feelings.* Urbana, IL: National Council of Teachers of English.

Carrick, D. (1987). *Morgan and the artist.* Boston: Houghton Mifflin.

Chomsky, C. (1972). Stages in language development and reading exposure. *Harvard Educational Review, 40,* 287–309.

Cleary, B. (1985). Dear author, answer this letter now . . . *Instructor, 95,* 22–23, 25.

Cramer, R. (1978). *Children's reading, writing, and language growth.* Columbus, OH: Charles Merrill.

Crowley, P., & Nelms, B. (1987). Literature-response logs: Making meaning, not borrowing it. In D. J. Watson (ed.), *Ideas and insights: Language arts in the elementary school.* Newark, DE: International Reading Association.

Cullinan, B. E., Harwood, K., & Galda, L. (1983). The reader and the story: Comprehension and response. *Journal of Research and Development in Education, 16,* 29–38.

Cullinan, B. E., Jaggar, A., & Strickland, D. (1974). Language expansion for black children in the primary grades: A research report. *Young Children, 29,* 98–112.

Cullinan, B. E., Karrer, M. K., & Pillar, A. M. (1981). *Literature and the child.* New York: Harcourt Brace Jovanovich.

Cunningham, P., Moore, S., Cunningham, J., & Moore, D. (1989). *Reading in elementary classrooms: Strategies and practices.* New York: Longman.

Dahl, R. (1961). *James and the giant peach.* New York: Knopf.

Eeds, M. (1989). Grand conversations: An exploration of meaning construction in literature study groups. *Research in the teaching of English, 23,* 4–29.

Eldredge, J., & Butterfield, D. (1986). Alternatives to traditional reading instruction. *The Reading Teacher, 40,* 32–37.

Erikson, E. (1963). *Childhood and society.* New York: Norton.

Freedman, R. (1987). *Lincoln: A photobiography.* Boston: Houghton Mifflin.

Galda, L. (1982). Assuming the spectator stance: An examination of the responses of three young readers. *Research in the Teaching of English, 16,* 1–20.

Galda, L. (1987). Teaching higher-order reading skills with literature: primary grades. In B. E. Cullinan (ed.), *Children's literature in the reading program*. Newark, DE: International Reading Association.

Gambrell, T. (1986). Growth in response to literature. *English Quarterly, 19,* 130–141.

Gherman, B. (1986). *Georgia O'Keeffe*. New York: Atheneum.

Glazer, J. I., & Williams, G. (1979). *Introduction to children's literature*. New York: McGraw-Hill.

Goodman, K. et al. (1988). *Report card on basal readers*. Katonah, NY: Richard C. Owen.

Graves, D. (1987). The reader's audience. In J. Hansen, T. Newkirk, & D. Graves (eds.), *Breaking ground: Teachers relate reading and writing in the elementary school*. Portsmouth, NH: Heinemann.

Graves, R. (1955). *Collected poems*. New York: International Authors.

Greenlaw, M. J., & McIntosh, M. E. (1987). Science fiction and fantasy worth teaching to teens. In B. E. Cullinan (ed.), *Children's literature in the reading program*. Newark, DE: International Reading Association.

Harste, J., Short, K., & Burke, C. (1989). *Creating classrooms for authors*. Portsmouth, NH: Heinemann.

Haskins, J. (1977). *The life and death of Martin Luther King, Jr.* New York: Lothrop, Lee, and Shepard.

Hickman, J. (1983). Everything considered: Response to literature in an elementary school setting. *Journal of Research and Development in Education, 16,* 8–13.

Huck, C. (1979). *Children's literature in the elementary school*. New York: Holt, Rinehart, and Winston.

Johnson, T. D., & Louis, D. (1987). *Literacy through literature*. Portsmouth, NH: Heinemann.

Kobrin, B. (1988). *Eyeopeners*. New York: Penguin.

Lee, B. (1979). *Charles Eastman: The story of an American Indian*. Minneapolis: Dillon.

Lukens, R. J. (1989). *A critical handbook of children's literature*. Glenview, IL: Scott, Foresman/Little, Brown.

Merriam, E. (1973). *Growing up female in America*. New York: Dell.

Meyer, B.J.F. (1984). Organizational aspects of text: Effects on reading comprehension and applications for the classroom. In J. Flood (ed.), *Promoting reading comprehension*. Newark, DE: International Reading Association.

Monjo, F. N. (1974). *Grand Papa and Ellen Aroon, being an account of some of the happy times spent together by Thomas Jefferson and his favorite granddaughter*. New York: Holt, Rinehart, and Winston.

Monson, D. (1987). Characterization in literature: Realistic and historical fiction. In B. E. Cullinan (ed.), *Children's literature in the reading program*. Newark, DE: International Reading Association.

Morrow, L. (1985). Retelling stories: A strategy for improving children's comprehension, concept of story structure, and oral language complexity. *Elementary School Journal, 85,* 647–661.

Morrow, L. (1989). Creating a bridge to children's literature. In P. N. Winograd, K. Wixson, & M. Lipson (eds.), *Improving basal reading instruction*. New York: Teachers College Press.

Moss, J. (1984). *Focus units in literature: A handbook for elementary school teachers*. Urbana, IL: National Council of Teachers of English. [2nd Edition published in 1990]

Nelson, M. C. (1972). *Maria Martinez*. Minneapolis: Dillon.

Newkirk, T. (1987). On the inside, where it counts. In J. Hansen, T. Newkirk, & D. Graves (eds.), *Breaking ground: Teachers relate reading and writing in the elementary school.* Portsmouth, NH: Heinemann.

Newton, C. (1972). *Famous Mexican Americans*. New York: Dodd, Mead.

Norton, D. (1988). *Through the eyes of a child*. Columbus, OH: Merrill.

Peterson, R. L. (1987). Literature groups: Intensive and extensive reading. In D. J. Watson (ed.), *Ideas and insights.* Newark, DE: International Reading Association.

Peetoom, A. (1989). Whole language and the Bible. *Language Arts. 66*(3), 318–322.

Protherough, R. (1987). The stories that readers tell. In B. Corcoran & E. Evans (eds.), *Readers, texts, teachers.* Upper Monclair, NJ: Boynton/Cook.

Purves, A. C. (1972). *How porcupines make love: Notes on a response-centered curriculum.* New York: Wiley.

Reed, A. (1988). *Comics to classics: A parent's guide to books for teens and preteens.* Newark, DE: International Reading Association.

Romatowski, J. A. (1987). Author! Author! In D. J. Watson (ed.), *Ideas and insights.* Newark, DE: International Reading Association.

Roser, N., & Frith, M. (1983). *Children's choices: Teaching with books children like.* Newark, DE: International Reading Association.

Sebesta, S. (1983). Choosing poetry. In N. Roser & M. Frith (eds.), *Children's choices: Teaching with books children like.* Newark, DE: International Reading Association.

Sebesta, S. (1984). Enriching the arts and humanities through children's books. In B. E. Cullinan (ed.), *Children's literature in the reading program.* Newark, DE: International Reading Association.

Sebesta, S. (1989). Literature across the curriculum. In J. W. Stewig & S. L. Sebesta (eds.), *Using literature in the elementary classroom.* Urbana, IL: National Council of Teachers of English.

Shannon, P. (1988). The use of commercial reading materials in American elementary schools. *Reading Research Quarterly, 19,* 68–85.

Stanovich, K. (in press). And because reading increases children's knowledge of the world, or their "cultural literacy," if you like. In C. Temple & P. Collins (eds.), *Children's literacy: Theory and practice in a book-rich elementary classroom.* Norwood, MA: Christopher Gordon.

Sterling, D., & Quarles, B. (1965). *Lift every voice: The lives of Booker T. Washington, W.E.B. DuBois, Mary Church Terrell, James Weldon Johnson.* Garden City, NY: Doubleday.

Stevenson, A. (1983). *Benjamin Franklin, young printer.* New York: Bobbs-Merrill.

Stewig, J. W. (1988). *Children and literature.* Boston: Houghton Mifflin.

Strand, M. (1986). *Rembrandt takes a walk.* New York: Crown.

Sullivan, G. (1985). *Mary Lou Retton.* New York: Julian Messner.

Tchudi, S., & Tchudi, S. (1983). *Teaching writing in the content areas: Elementary school.* Washington, DC: National Educational Association.

Temple, C. (1989). Reading deeply: Four approaches to a basal story. Unpublished manuscript, Hobart and William Smith Colleges.

Temple, C., & Gillet, J. (1989). *Language arts: Learning processes and teaching practices.* Glenview, IL: Scott, Foresman.

Temple, C., & Collins, P. (eds.) (Forthcoming). *Children's literacy: Theory and practice in a book-rich elementary classroom.* Norwood, MA: Christopher Gordon.

Tobias, T. (1970). *Maria Tallchief.* New York: Crowell.

Trelease, J. (1986). *The read-aloud handbook.* New York: Penguin.

Tunnell, M. O., & Jacobs, J. S. (1989). Using "real" books: Research findings on literature-based reading instruction. *The Reading Teacher, 42,* 470–477.

Vaughan, J., & Estes, T. (1986). *Reading and reasoning beyond the primary grades.* Boston: Allyn and Bacon.

Watson, D. (1987). *Ideas and insights.* Newark, DE: International Reading Association.

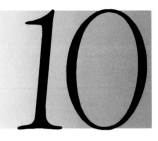

The Teaching of Vocabulary and Spelling

FOCUSING QUESTIONS

- What principles should guide your vocabulary instruction?
- Why are "word sorts" so effective in developing word knowledge?
- What are some important categories of language use, and how can they support the development of vocabulary?
- Why and how will you teach students about prefixes, suffixes, base words, and word stems?
- What are the characteristics of the stages of spelling knowledge? What features of words should students examine at each of these stages?
- How can spelling knowledge support the learning of vocabulary? How can vocabulary knowledge support the learning of spelling?

"A word," the Russian psychologist Lev Vygotsky once wrote, "is a microcosm of human experience." More recently, the poet and teacher Georgia Heard observed that "a word is like a geode: rough and ordinary on the outside, hiding a whole world of sparkling beauty inside" (Heard, 1989, p. 74). And fascinating though the study of words may be, there is much about them that has remained a mystery and a puzzle. Edgar Allan Poe wondered why the word "suspectful" did not exist in English, so he simply coined it and used it himself. It seemed quite handy, Poe believed: you could differentiate between one who suspects and one who is being suspected. Needless to say, the word didn't catch on. But English does lend itself to this type of word creation; what, after all, determines how words are formed in English? Of course, speakers of English have wondered about the spelling of English as well; Thomas Hoole commented three hundred years ago that English spelling was a "most troublesome torturer of wits." As we will see, this need not be the case.

INTRODUCTION

Ideally, we wish that our students will revel in the mysteries, meanings, and the properties of words. Much of this enjoyment may occur at the primary grade levels, particularly kindergarten through second grade. At this time, as you recall, children are becoming consciously able to step back from language — they are becoming more metalinguistically aware — and can think about the *form* of language as well as its *meaning.* These grade levels can therefore be a marvelous time for language play (Geller, 1985), which increases children's sensitivity to and understanding of words and word structure and generally communicates the potency of language. This growing sensitivity in turn provides an important part of the background knowledge so critically important for developing literacy (see Chapter 6), particularly knowledge of the information encoded in writing itself — letter/sound relationships and vocabulary knowledge — as well as knowledge of grammatical structure, or *syntax.*

Just about all young children delight in playing with language and with words. In previous chapters we have discussed ways in which teachers can help channel this natural interest by encouraging children to think about the language that they read and write. In this chapter I will discuss this exploration in terms of words in and of themselves and the underlying concepts they represent. As we examine how children become familiar with vocabulary and spelling, we will see how knowledge about *word meaning, word structure,* and the relationships between the meaning of words and their structure can be extended and elaborated. We will explore how this knowledge is developed through an examination of vocabulary learning at the primary (grades K–3) and intermediate (4–6) levels. Remember throughout that vocabulary and spelling knowledge undergird the efficiency with which students read and write. It is also important to remember that vocabulary and spelling are two sides of the same knowledge coin: knowledge about vocabulary helps spelling development, and knowledge of spelling will help to expand vocabulary.

Principles for Learning and Teaching Vocabulary

In referring to vocabulary development, Nagy (1989) suggested that learning occurs both incidentally and directly; this aptly describes spelling development as well. That is, much of students' knowledge about words will occur through wide and frequent reading as well as through informal word play and word exploration: "Increasing the volume of students' reading is the single most important thing teachers can do to promote large-scale vocabulary growth" (Nagy, 1989, p. 32). The balance of word learning will occur in direct teaching contexts, in which the teacher presents information about words and the students are actively involved in follow-up study of this information. They must further exercise this knowledge in writing.

Fundamentally, vocabulary development can be considered in terms of *elaboration,* the growth of existing concepts associated with particular words, and *expansion,* the development of new concepts and the new vocabulary that represents them. Several researchers have outlined principles for teaching vocabulary (Beck, Perfetti, and McKeown, 1982; Carr and Wixson, 1986; Graves, 1987; Johnson and Pearson, 1984; Nagy, 1989; Stahl, 1986; White, Power, and White, 1989; Templeton, 1989). Essentially these embody the following fundamentals:

- Word study should be integrated with prior knowledge and with learning in the content areas.
- Word study should involve intensive, "deep" study of *some* words, involving many exposures to the words in *meaningful* contexts, both in and out of connected text.
- Teachers should engage in direct teaching, including "a good deal of explicit teacher talk" (Graves, 1987).
- Students should be actively involved in instruction; an important side effect of this involvement is the development of favorable attitudes toward words and word learning.
- Students should be taught strategies for learning new words independently.
- Teachers should introduce words in meaning "families," so that semantic and structural relationships among the words are made explicit.
- Teachers should present word elements (affixes and word roots/combining forms) following a reasonable sequence and show the ways in which these elements combine.

Most of these principles are more applicable at the intermediate grade levels and beyond, when students' cognitive development has advanced to the point at which they can deal with increasing conceptual abstraction. Nonetheless, you will see aspects of these principles at work in much word study at the primary level as well.

Vocabulary Development in the Primary Grades

As we saw in Chapter 6, when most children first come to school, their oral vocabularies are tremendous compared to their sight or reading vocabularies. At this age, children know lots of concepts and the spoken words for them, but they don't know the corresponding words in their visual form. For children in the primary grades, a strong emphasis is on learning the *written* form of the concepts and words they already know aurally — that is, on developing their sight vocabularies. This emphasis in instruction begins to shift as children move to the intermediate grades (4–6), when their reading vocabularies typically become larger than their oral vocabularies and when their reading is becoming more and more fluent. At that point, although sight vocabulary will continue to develop, the emphasis in vocabulary instruction will be on elaborating and expanding meaning vocabulary.

In this section I'll focus on how primary grade students learn the concepts and meanings of new words and suggest some teaching applications. However, because the intermediate grades focus not only on expanding and elaborating concepts but also on learning how the visual form of words provides powerful clues to meaning, I'll give more attention to the section that follows this one. Keep in mind, though, that much of what is covered there about vocabulary development will be appropriate for many students in third grade, as well — a transitional year in many ways.

From the oral language that surrounds them, the written language brought to life through read-alouds, and the concrete examination of the here-and-now world of six-, seven-, and eight-year-olds, primary students should develop a vocabulary that is conceptually solid and rich. By reading, writing, and examining words and word structure, they will develop the essential sight or recognition vocabulary, which in turn helps make reading and writing more fluent and more rewarding.

Elaborating and Expanding Conceptual Development

I noted in Chapter 2 that the foremost vehicle for elaborating and expanding conceptual development will be meaningful experiences that are examined through purposeful and relevant discussion. As I observed earlier, "Only if children understand the familiar well can they make sense of the new." It is so easy to overlook the conceptual development that can arise from examination of the seemingly mundane. You will find, though, that your students' everyday surroundings offer the best potential for concept development. Once children examine existing, familiar concepts and begin to elaborate them, they will be better able to grasp firmly new information, concepts, and *vocabulary.*

As they move from the familiar to the new, children rely on pictures, films, records, and as much as possible, on reading and writing. They also rely on the teacher's modeling of language in general and vocabulary in particular. For example, when children are examining familiar objects in your first grade classroom, your language will direct them to consider features that perhaps they noted only tacitly before; they then have a conceptual frame that you may label with a new word and reinforce over the succeeding days. A common goldfish, for example, becomes a vehicle for talking about how different creatures breathe; once the children learn those undulating flaps on its side are called "gills," they can use the term several times during their discussion of the fish.

Teachers should also combine "hands-on " experiences with observation. In exploring new areas with primary students we rely on concrete experiences whenever possible. In math, we use real objects to illustrate the processes of combining and separating and discuss familiar terms before introducing new terms and old terms used in different ways — for example, *addition, subtraction,* or even *sets* and *borrowing* or *trading*. In science, we begin with autumn leaves or the idea of cooler temperatures before we describe how the Earth's annual trip around the sun and its tilt along its axis cause our seasons. In geography, we construct maps of the classroom (complete with a "scale of measurement") before we ask students to map their houses, their neighborhoods, and other parts of their world, incorporating all along the way the new map-related concepts and vocabulary that become essential to representing each new domain.

In the primary grades, we should also talk about words in and of themselves, showing our students that we enjoy words and find them interesting and often humorous. You can say, "Have you ever wondered about an *eggplant?* Surely it can't be made of eggs, and yet . . ." We already know we should read to our students, and much of what we share in read-alouds can be from the rhyming, songlike verses that illustrate the type of wordplay (often nonsensical) that young children enjoy (Geller, 1985). Geller's book on wordplay offers many excellent suggestions for playing with words and language at this level.

Developing Vocabulary and Concepts Through Word Sorts

Playing with words and ideas in the classroom context just described lays the groundwork for children to explore and learn about written words. Specific exploration of sight vocabulary, corresponding concepts, and knowledge about word structure can most effectively occur through *word sorts* (Barnes, 1989; Gillet and Kita, 1978; Henderson, 1981, 1990; Morris, 1982; Templeton, 1980). In this section we will consider how this word-categorization technique can elaborate conceptual development while incidentally reinforcing the learning of sight words.

Word-sort activities were briefly referred to in Chapter 8 as a type of word-bank activity. The format for word sorts is fairly standard throughout the grades; what will change is *how* the words are sorted. Word sorts utilize *known* words; students categorize these words in different ways and compare their categories with those of other students. In this way the students are involved in elaborating the concepts underlying the words they already know. They thereby become aware of word features and distinctions that had not occurred to them previously. We'll look at how the word-sort technique is applied to word structure when we discuss spelling later in this chapter.

For kindergartners and first-graders, sorting activities should begin with concrete objects and move to pictures, in order for children to understand the task and to learn from the sorting process (Henderson, 1990). For example, small colored blocks, cuisenaire rods, noodles (pasta) of different shapes and sizes, and so forth can all be sorted. Pictures can be sorted according to different concepts: large objects versus small objects, the animate versus the inanimate, tools versus toys, and so on.

When children have acquired a fair number of sight words, they can begin word sorts. The elements are simple: students categorize words written or printed on separate chips of tagboard or cardboard according to specific criteria. Word sorts may be done in a group or individually. Initially, word sorts should be introduced in a group to ensure that each child understands the fundamentals of how to sort. If the teacher is following a *language experience approach* (see Chapter 8), the words can come from the children's word banks; otherwise, the teacher simply prepares small word cards for the students. Remember, word-sort activities can focus on either the structure or the meaning of words. Let's begin with an example from first grade.

CLASSROOM EXAMPLE

The teacher has the children dump out ten to fifteen word cards, arrange them in one or two columns for easy reading, and then search them with specific criteria in mind. For example, the teacher says, "Kids, let's look for words that have to do with *big* things. The words can either stand for big things themselves or have to do with something that is big."

The words that Nathan is working with are *tank, wastebasket, bear, kangaroo, broom, mouse, book, speck, hat, zoo, green, messy, the,* and *happy.* He selects the following as words that have to do with "big":

After Nathan and the other students have selected words that they believe fit with the category, the teacher asks each student why he or she chose particular

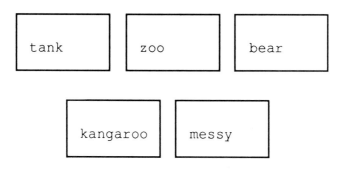

words. Curious about Nathan's inclusion of *messy*, she first asks him about *tank* and then about *messy*. He explains that his mother always tells him he makes the biggest messes of anyone she's ever seen, "and *messy* has to do with messes!"

◆ ◆ ◆

After your students understand the format for sorting according to a single category, you may suggest that they include another column or category for words that don't seem to fit, a "leftover" or "miscellaneous" category. This allows a "safety valve" (Barnes, 1989) for uncertainty. For example, on another occasion when the first-graders were sorting according to the categories "big" and "little," Michael put one of his word-bank words, *hyena*, in the "leftover" column. Although he knew that a hyena was an animal and had seen a picture of it, he was uncertain about its size.

Important thinking is going on in these sorts, not only about words but about the concepts they represent. The students must keep the criteria for one or more categories in mind and must justify their sorts in discussion afterwards. They also see that other students may have sorted the same words differently, and in the ensuing discussion will learn why. For example, in the second word sort above, Jeremy placed the word *tank* in the "small" column. His justification was that he had several small toy tanks at home.

This type of word sort is referred to as a *closed* word sort because the teacher determines the category labels. You should always begin with closed sorts, because students learn the fundamentals of the sorting process more easily at first when the labels are provided for them.

In an *open* word sort, the students decide what the categories are going to be, and sort accordingly. The criteria are up to them. In such instances, students can play "Guess My Category," which is very much like the game of "Twenty Questions": once students have sorted their words individually, they can pair up and question each other, attempting to guess the category label. Primary students familiar with word-sort techniques can become quite good at this game! Once again, the value is in the discussion generated and in the type of thinking that is going on. The thinking in this case is *inductive* because the students are examining particulars and trying to come up with a generalization.

You may by now have noticed a similarity between word sorts and other types of sorting activities discussed in this text. The visual schematic, graphic organizer, and organization for report writing (see Chapters 7 and 8) all involve making decisions about where concepts go in relation to other concepts. These activities engage basic processes of learning. Short of actually handling or experiencing the objects represented by words, in word sorts students are engaged in the active manipulation of concepts. This is why word-sort activities are such powerful learning experiences.

Vocabulary Development in the Intermediate Grades

Learning How the Structure of Words Represents Meaning

Vocabulary and spelling become very much intertwined in the intermediate grades and beyond. By learning about word elements, students develop knowledge for independent word learning and direct their attention to the ways in which word elements combine to create the meaning of a word. That is, students develop knowledge about *morphemic* or *structural analysis.* In addition, it is possible to present these elements in a general scope and sequence that is compatible with the students' levels of cognitive and word knowledge development.

Now we will look more closely at the overall processes by which word elements combine to form words. This study can be fascinating as well as instructionally beneficial. In addition to helping your students — through direct teaching — to become familiar with frequently occurring prefixes and suffixes, you should clearly demonstrate for students how to *use* their knowledge of these elements (White, Power, and White, 1989).

First we will examine how the meanings of individual words combine to create the meaning of a new, compound word. Next we will explore the basic processes in which prefixes and suffixes attach to base words and eventually to word *stems: roots* or *combining forms* — word parts that usually cannot stand by themselves as words. Once your students know how prefixes and suffixes work with base words, they will have a strong foundation for learning how these processes work with word stems, so it is generally wise to present base words before stems. The rationale for this sequence is straightforward: since stems usually cannot stand by themselves, they are not as readily understood as meaningful elements when affixes are taken away.

Morphemic Elements

When discussing morphemic elements you should keep in mind the developmental level of your students. The meanings of many prefixes and suffixes are too abstract for younger students and perhaps for many older students as well. I present a suggested instructional sequence for this material in the section on spelling (pages 425–432).

Prefixes, Suffixes, and Base Words As we noted in Chapter 8, suffixes in the form of inflectional endings — past tense (*-ed*), present progressive (*-ing*), and simple plural (*-s, -es*) — provide the first frequent morphological exposure for primary grade students. As we'll see later, these endings actually receive more explicit attention in *spelling* instruction, and are hardly as exciting to talk about as are word parts that the students can really get their teeth into. The *vocabulary* payoff will begin with the study of simple prefixes, which many students are ready to undertake beginning in the latter part of third grade.

These simple prefixes include those that represent opposites or the repeating or the undoing of an action: for example, *re-* ("again"), *un-* ("not"), and *im-* or *in-* ("not"). Although *re-* and *im-* or *in-* do not always have a single meaning, they occur so frequently with these meanings that it is wise to begin with them. The meanings of other prefixes that are invariant are usually too abstract to use when first presenting prefixes. As stressed in Chapter 8, the effect the prefix has on the base word should be discussed with students and they should clearly understand its effect; not only should they know the words *wrap* and *happy,* and un*wrap* and un*happy,* they should explicitly understand that when the prefix *un-* is added to a word it usually causes the word to change to its opposite meaning.

Once they understand a few simple prefixes, students can examine simple suffixes. Although their effect does not usually seem as dramatic as that of prefixes, suffixes serve heavy duty in the English language. Often students can appreciate the study of them more if you point out to them that it otherwise takes several words to express an idea that a suffix can represent. For example, instead of having to say "an individual who is skilled in geology," we can express the same idea by simply adding a suffix to *geology* and referring to a *geologist.* Instead of having to say "a smaller set of dining furniture," we can use *dinette;* "the state of being puzzled" becomes *puzzlement.* As explored below, you can reinforce this appreciation by having students categorize words that share the same suffix and infer the probable meaning of the suffix — and describe the effect it has on the word to which it is attached.

Many of the most frequently used suffixes in English date from Old English; you should begin your students' study of suffixes with these. As with simple prefixes, a suffix that gives its base word the opposite meaning is a good one to begin with. For primary students, *-less* ("without") fills the bill quite well. By noting the effect *-less* has when affixed to base words such as *aim, child, hope, dream,* and so forth, students can usually come up with the meaning of *-less* on their own. They can also examine the effects of the suffixes *-ly* ("like" as in awkward*ly* and bad*ly*) and *-ness* ("condition" as in sick*ness* and kind*ness*).

Appendix A presents the most frequently occurring prefixes and several of the most frequently occurring suffixes, in addition to affixes that occur less frequently but whose meanings are stable enough to allow productive exploration.

Stems: Word Roots and Combining Forms   By sixth grade, most students are usually ready to examine how several words can be formed from a single stem — how it is possible to produce several other words that are related in meaning. These "meaning families" form an important aspect of learning vocabulary. You will begin studying them with your class when you teach how several words can be derived from base words, and then you can proceed to the "subword" level and examine the word *stems* (roots and combining forms) from which innumerable words can be derived. Stems that come from Latin are termed *roots;* those that originated in Greek are termed *combining forms.*

How do you begin to talk about word stems with students? First, be sure that the students are aware of and understand fairly well how simple affixes combine with base words. Then, select a frequently occurring stem to focus on and list several words the students know that share this stem. The meaning of the stem should be clear as it functions in each of the words. Appendix A presents a list of productive stems; the most frequent of them are indicated with an asterisk.

For example, say you've chosen the word root *-spect-* ("to look") and the example words *spectator, inspect,* and *spectacles.* After listing the words on the board, here's how your discussion might go with fourth- or fifth-graders.

CLASSROOM EXAMPLE

TEACHER: "Kids, let's talk about these words for a minute. First thing we're going to do is discuss what each of them means. Okay, what's a *spectator*? Lianne?"

LIANNE: "That's someone who watches something, like a game."

TEACHER: "Okay! Thank you — now how about *inspect*? Garrett?"

GARRETT: "It's like when you check something real close for a problem, or maybe you're a detective and you're inspecting something."

TEACHER: "All right. Now for our last one, *spectacles*. You don't hear this one much anymore, but you run across it in your reading sometimes. Yes, Danny?"

DANNY: "Spectacles are like glasses you wear — it's an old word for glasses."

TEACHER: "Good! Now, these words all have something in common — does it have anything to do with their meaning?" [Lets several seconds pass.]

LIANNE: "Well, they all talk about seeing something or how you see . . ."

TEACHER: "Okay, you're really on the right track. As you *look* at these words, what is the same about all of them? Kyle?"

KYLE: "They all have the letters *s, p, e, c,* and *t* in them . . ."

TEACHER: "Now you're on to it. Do you think that these letters, *spect,* could have anything to do with *seeing*?"

A few more seconds pass, then murmurs of "Yeah, they could!" are audible. Looking around the group of students and nodding, the teacher affirms this: "Absolutely! These letters, *spect,* all stand for the same meaning, actually 'to look.' This part of the word that is the same in all of these words is called a word *root,* and it is a part of our language that came from Latin. So, *spect* means 'to look,' and when you see it in a word, it will usually stand for this same meaning.

"Let's look at a couple of our words to see how the root, *spect,* works with the rest of the word. In *spectator,* the suffix *-ator* actually means 'one who does something,' so the word literally means 'one who looks.' *Inspect* has the prefix *in-*, in this case meaning 'into,' so this word literally means 'to look into.'"

Students could also play with additional possibly unknown words: *retrospect, spectacular, respect, circumspect, spectrum.* Since these words are not so concrete, the students may have to check their hypotheses about the meaning of the words by referring to the dictionary.

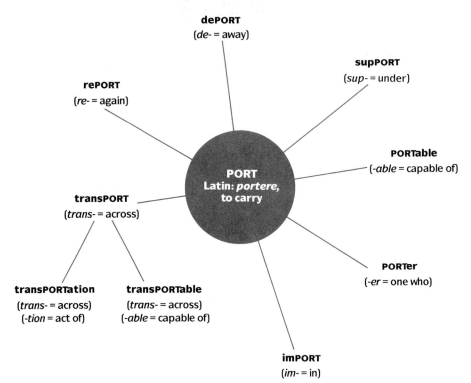

FIGURE 10.1

A Web of Words Developed from *port*

Source: Adapted from Tompkins, G., and Yaden, D. B., Jr. (1985). *Answering students' questions about words.* Urbana, IL: National Council of Teachers of English. (Diagram is taken from p. 47 of this book.) Reproduced by permission.

Talking about word roots, as above, helps set the stage for students to figure out the meanings of stems. This is an excellent way to introduce more abstract word elements. Alternatively, of course, if you feel your students are already pretty good at examining words, you may simply present a number of words that share the same stem and have the students discover the element common to them. Then they can speculate — in groups, if possible — about the meaning of the stem.

The underlying purpose of studying stems is not to memorize the meanings of dozens of stems but rather to establish a feel for stems as significant elements of words. This understanding will support the learning of many stems, it is true, but it will also help the students recognize new words as they read and learn to spell. In addition, it feeds the students' appreciation of the origin and application of words. (Appendix A can serve as a resource when you prepare activities involving stems.)

After you have discussed stems within words, then you can show your students the ways in which affixes and stems combine. After studying *-tract-,* for example, ask the students, "If you retract something that you've said, what do you do?" Then explore the longer word, *retraction,* on the board:

"Let's cover the prefix, *re-,* and what do we have left? Right, *traction.* Now let's cover the suffix, *-ion,* and what is our word root? Right again — *tract.* We've learned it means 'to pull,' so when we add *-ion* back on, we've got 'the process of pulling.' Now put *re-* back on, and we've got 'the process of pulling back.' The word appears in this sentence: 'The paper promised to publish a retraction.' This means they've printed erroneous information, so they have to 'pull back' what they said."

You could examine *abstraction* similarly. It describes the process of pulling away, which of course is what you do when you abstract information or talk about a concept at a more general, sometimes hypothetical, level.

Next, change the affixes and talk about the stem again. Here's a snippet from a sixth grade teacher's presentation: "If you say a person is easily led and changes his mind easily, you could describe him as *tractable*. What would a person who is *intractable* be like?" The teacher writes the word on the board and takes it apart, discussing each part as she does so. As before, she takes the prefix off first, discusses the meaning, then puts the prefix back on and discusses the meaning.

Usually a few "walk-throughs" of this sort will cue most intermediate students to the way in which words work. It pays, as we've noted, to begin by analyzing common words, and then to move to unfamiliar words that contain the same element.

Follow up by playing with word roots or stems in a visual schematic. Such a schematic is the beginning "word web" illustrated in Figure 10.1 (from Tompkins and Yaden, 1985). Based on the root *-port-,* the word web demonstrates at a glance the "generative" power of applying knowledge of word combinations, in this case a root and several different affixes.

Word building with stems and affixes can be reinforced easily yet enjoyably through combining word parts and discovering how many real words can be created. This can be done in a two- or three-column format, as shown below:

Prefix	Stem	Suffix
re	dict	ic
pre	tract	ion
sub	gress	able
contra	port	er/or
im	phon	ably
in	spect	ful
un	press	ation
trans	ject	

As students get caught up in playing with these important structural elements, they inevitably notice two things. First, it is possible to generate words that do not exist in English but that *could* exist; for example, "transpectable" and "intractation." Second, if we have the word *respectful,* why can't we have "predictful" or Poe's word, "suspectful" — or for that matter "constructment," "observement," or "puzzleation"? The reasons in part are historical and in part have to do with the juncture of sounds and the ease of pronunciation and with the syntactic role that the base word or word stem usually plays. These are issues that most intermediate students will choose not to pursue, but you never know when you might have a budding linguist on your hands who will only be more intrigued by this explanation and independently tackle the question!

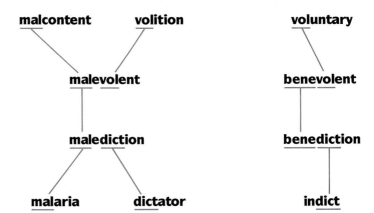

FIGURE 10.2

Part of a Larger Web of Words Formed Using Different Stems

At this point you may show students how words can be intertwined through common stems and affixes. Figure 10.2 illustrates one part of an obviously larger such "web" of words. Notice that the meanings of the stems, however, are still relatively concrete. Moreover, notice that it is possible to have more than one stem in a word, as in *benevolent: bene* and *vol.*

As you and your students look over lists of stems or examine them as they occur in words, you will notice that sometimes the spelling of the original stem has changed (for example, *ced/cess; ceiv-/-cept*). The stems still have the same origin, but sound changes within the language over the centuries have eventually led to spelling changes. As we'll see later, however, even these spelling changes may follow a predictable pattern.

If you look back at Chapter 3, toward the end, you can see how your students can learn about the processes of *derivation, compounding, back formation,* and *clipping* — four different ways words can be formed. As they examine these processes, students can learn to appreciate and understand more clearly how the combining and recombining of word parts, which they have been practicing in these activities, actually contributed historically to the growth of English vocabulary.

Etymology

The study of word origins, or *etymology,* can prove a fascinating and beneficial pursuit in terms of vocabulary development. Most of the time, the structure of words represents not only their meaning but their origins and history as well. In this section we will examine some aspects of etymology that you should explore with your elementary students.

Indo-European Roots of Words   Chapter 3 presented a brief discussion of the Indo-European language and its role in the subsequent development of so many other languages, including English. The "tracing diagram" presented in that discussion (see p. 58) illustrated how so many words have come from a single Indo-European root, *bha.*

Robinson (1989) offered a series of units built around several Indo-European (IE) roots. Through creative dramatics, discussion, reading, and writing, these units powerfully engage intermediate students, providing them with real understanding of how spoken language was first represented by written language. For example, students explore the *"bhel"* family of words (meaning "to swell") first through pantomiming a few words derived from it — *balloon, belly,* and *ball.* Later they examine other words that came from *bhel:* for example, *bulge, bulky, billow, boulder.* Students come to realize how the original meaning of *bhel* is a characteristic common to all of these words, and to words that label many other different objects and actions. Another word family is the *dhreu* family (meaning "to fall"), from which we get *drop, droop, dreary,* and *drowsy,* for example.

Despite the ways in which sounds have changed over thousands of years, usually a couple of sounds originally present in a particular Indo-European root still remain in words today. Notice that "b" and "l" remain from *bhel;* "d" and "r" remain from *dhreu.*

Words from Greek and Roman Mythology   As we've already seen, many English words that came from the Indo-European language first passed through the Greek and Roman cultures, hence the Greek and Latin languages. Many of these words were nurtured in the mythology of those cultures. Learning the stories behind the words can be fascinating and can acquaint students with some of the significant literature underlying their cultural heritage. Following are just a few of the mythological allusions underlying some of our contemporary vocabulary; many more can be explored through the references listed at the end of this section.

■ *Arachnid*

Arachnids are a class that includes spiders, a nice tie-in with science study. As with so many scientific terms from Greek and Latin, this one too has a mythological basis. Arachne was a young woman who was a very skillful weaver. She was challenged by the goddess Athena to a weaving contest. As usually happened when mortals and immortals competed, Arachne lost the contest. (Actually Athena became enraged at the scenes Arachne was weaving; you may or may not decide to share information about these scenes with students!) In humiliation, Arachne hanged herself, but Athena spared her life by turning her into a spider (arachnid), in which form her descendants to this day continue to weave.

■ *Flora, fauna*

Flora was the Roman goddess of flowers, hence our use today of *flora* to stand for all vegetation; we also use *flora* more specifically in the word *floral.* In Greek mythology her name was *Chloris,* the root of the Greek form for "green"; she lives on today in the derivations of the *chlor* stem, as in *chlorophyll.*

Faunus was the Roman equivalent of Pan, patron of shepherds and their flocks, hence guardian of all animals. The *fauns,* derived from *faunus,* were woodland creatures, half man, half goat. The Greek Pan could also be unpredictable and sometimes downright malicious; it is no coincidence that our words *panic* and *pandemonium* are derived from *Pan.* He could also be vengeful. In one version of a popular myth he was so enraged with a nymph who spurned his advances that he sent a group of shepherds into a *panic*; they tore the nymph to pieces until nothing remained but her voice — her name was *Echo*.

Changing Word Meanings   Share with your students, at least in translation, the following observation by Chaucer:

> Ye knew ek that in forme of speche is chaunge
> Within a thousand yeer, and wordes tho
> That hadden prys now wonder nyce and straunge
> Us thinketh hem, and yet they spake hem so.
>
> You know that even forms of speech can change
> Within a thousand years, and words we know
> Were useful once, seem to us wondrous strange —
> Foolish or forced — and yet men spoke them so. (Wright, 1985)

Obviously, as we saw in Chapter 3, English has changed significantly since Chaucer's day, yet even in the fourteenth century Chaucer sensed that the one great constancy of language was change. Even in the primary grades, students can get a sense of how the meanings of particular words in English have changed over the centuries. Explore with students the effects of language change as a result of migration, war, technological advance, and so forth (Dale, O'Rourke, and Bamman, 1971). Tompkins and Yaden (1985) suggest that you give students a list of words and have them research what they once meant; intermediate students can classify the changes as language scholars would.

Change of meaning for specific words can occur through (1) specialization, (2) generalization, (3) elevation, and (4) degeneration.

1. *Specialization*   This process narrows the meaning of a word. For example, *cattle* once referred to any group of four-legged animals. Similarly, *deer* originally referred to any four-legged animal. *Corpse* once referred to any body, alive or dead.

2. *Generalization*   The opposite of specialization, this process extends the meaning of words. For example, *lady* once referred only to the wife of a lord. *Ghetto* was originally the part of a city in which Jewish people lived; it now means an area of a city, usually economically depressed, where any group may be restricted. Brand names quite often become generalized: *Kleenex* now is used to refer to all tissues of a similar form and purpose, regardless of the maker. "Hoover," the name of a company that manufactures vacuum cleaners, came to mean the *act* of vacuuming as well — at least in England. I found this out (and received an insightful lesson in the diversity of purportedly similar cultures) when years ago I bought an old rug from a Brit-

ish graduate student and was told, "All you really need to do is to *hoover* it from time to time."

3. *Elevation*   Words that at one time had quite ordinary meanings have often come to mean something more exalted or *elevated* with the passing of the years. *Knight* once meant a boy, but later came to refer to one who served — often in a military capacity — a lord or king. *Mansion* once referred to a farmhouse; *angels* were simply messengers. *Nice* once meant stupid or foolish.

4. *Degeneration*   The opposite of elevation is degeneration. Many words that once had a more positive meaning now have a negative meaning or connotation. *Silly* once had a positive connotation, meaning "happy, prosperous, and blessed"; a *villain* was once merely a servant on a farm. *Stink* originally meant simply "to rise up"! *Temper* could at one time refer to any state of mind, but now it has a negative connotation, specifically of anger. *Propaganda* once referred simply to the spreading of belief; it now pertains to the spreading of belief through devious or less-than-truthful means.

Role of the Dictionary in Etymology   Dictionaries are the primary and most readily available source of etymological information. Increasingly, publishers print dictionaries for the intermediate grades that include etymological information, usually in a simplified format, which is both an advantage and a disadvantage. Such a format clearly presents the basics of a word's history, but it does not include the various forms the word has taken, including Indo-European, Greek, and Latin origins. Usually only derivations for selected words are given. Still, elementary dictionaries provide a lot of historical information that was until recently excluded in dictionaries intended for this level. Many also present an engaging, informative essay on language in general and English in particular in the front matter.

Still, intermediate students should also be shown how and encouraged to use "adult" dictionaries. The major publishers' "collegiate" editions are excellent, but if you can bring in an unabridged dictionary you will really encourage word exploration. For most entries, these dictionaries will include information about etymology and pronunciation and, whenever applicable, give a word's Indo-European root.

When your intermediate students are ready for it, present a lesson on how to interpret etymological information. Begin by *"walking through"* a few entries, talking about the information you are deriving. Choose interesting words for starters, and prime the students with a question such as "Did you know that left-handed people were once considered unlucky, even *sinister?*" Follow this up with the etymological information written on the board or prepared on a transparency.

For example, the *American Heritage Dictionary* (Second College Edition) gives the following for *sinister*:

[ME *sinistre* < OFr. < Lat. *sinister,* on the left, unlucky]

While pointing to the appropriate symbol or word, talk through the entry in this fashion: "This informs us that, in Middle English, the word *sinister* was *sinistre,* which was what the word was in Old French as well. This word in Old French came from the original word in Latin, which was *sinister.*"

After a couple of relatively easy entries, try a more involved one with the students. Following is the etymological information in the *American Heritage Dictionary* for the entry *difficulty:*

[ME *difficulte* < OFr. *dificulte* < Lat. *difficultas* < *difficilis,* difficult: *dis-,* not + *facilis,* easy.]

After such a holistic presentation, you can then explain the specific abbreviations, such as for the different languages, and what the "<" symbol means.

■ Build Your Teaching Resources

Books about Etymology

Books for Teachers

Clairborne, R. (1988). *The roots of English.* New York: Time-Life Books.

Dale, E., O'Rourke, J., & Bamman, H. (1971). *Techniques of teaching vocabulary.* Palo Alto, CA: Field Educational Enterprises.

Davies, P. (1981). *Roots: Family histories of familiar words.* New York: McGraw-Hill.

Funk, W. (1954). *Word origins and their romantic stories.* New York: Grosset and Dunlap.

Laird, H., & Laird, C. (1957). *The tree of language.* Cleveland, OH: World.

Partridge, E. (1983). *Origins: A short etymological dictionary of modern English.* New York: Outlet Book Company.

Skeat, W. (1882/1984). *A concise etymological dictionary of the English language.* Oxford: The Clarendon Press.

Tompkins, G., & Yaden, D., Jr. (1986). *Answering students' questions about words.* Urbana, IL: National Council of Teachers of English.

Watkins, C. (1987). *American Heritage Dictionary of Indo-European roots.* Boston: Houghton Mifflin.

Weekly, E. (1967). *An etymological dictionary of modern English.* New York: Dover.

Robinson, S. (1989). *Origins.* 2 vols. New York: Teachers and Writers Collaborative. (Vol. 1: Bringing words to life; Vol. 2: The word families).

Books for Students

Asimov, I. (1961). *Words from the myths.* Boston: Houghton Mifflin.

Asimov, I. (1968). *Words from history.* Boston: Houghton Mifflin.

Burningham, J. (1984). *Skip trip.* New York: Viking.

See also several other titles by Burningham, all published by Viking.

Cox, J. (1980). *Put your foot in your mouth and other silly sayings.* New York: Random House.

Davidson, J. (1972). *Is that Mother in the bottle? Where language came from and where it is going.* New York: Franklin Watts.

Hall, R. (1984). *Sniglets.* New York: Macmillan.

Hazen, B. (1979). *Last, first, middle and Nick: All about names.* Englewood Cliffs, NJ: Prentice-Hall.

Lambert, E., & Pei, M. (1959). *The book of place names.* New York: Lothrop, Lee and Shepard.

Pickles, C., & Meynell, L. (1971). *The beginning of words: How English grew.* New York: G. P. Putnam's Sons.

Sarnoff, J., & Ruffins, R. (1981). *Words.* New York: Scribner's.

Spier, P. (1971). *Gobble, growl, grunt.* Garden City, NY: Doubleday.

Wolk, A. (1980). *Everyday words from names of people and place.* New York: Elsevier/ Nelson Books.

Presenting and Reinforcing Content-related Vocabulary

Because your students will spend most of their time reading and writing, with some direct-teaching activities focusing on structural analysis and etymology threaded throughout, it may appear as though there is no time left for specific wordplay and study. But there will be: many of the activities discussed earlier also develop the learning of specific vocabulary.

Time *is* of the essence, however. You will teach some words intensively rather than many words superficially (as in the more traditional approach involving copying and memorizing of definitions). How will you select words to teach directly? As I recommended in Chapter 8, first you will look for words that are central to the major concepts and understandings in the selection or the unit. Next, you must consider these words in relation to several factors — your particular students' background knowledge and pre-existing word knowledge and also the text's presentation of the words. The meanings of some centrally important and unknown words will probably be sufficiently addressed in the context of the reading. (Note that — even for these words — you will want to follow up *after* the reading to make sure your students have gained real understanding.) You will focus your preteaching, however, on the balance of the important and unknown words — those for which context alone is not full or rich enough.

In order to prepare your students for these new words, which are really new concepts for them, in addition to following the procedure suggested in Chapter 8, you can link your preteaching to a number of other prereading activities (Blachowicz, 1986; Nagy, 1989; Nelson-Herber, 1986). Let's consider the most effective of these.

Expand Your Teaching Repertoire

1. *Structured overview*   As discussed in Chapter 8, words may be presented in a hierarchical format; a linear format may also be appropriate if the terms reflect a causal relationship, as in a science or a history unit (Marzano and Marzano, 1988; Nagy, 1989). Following is an example for a unit dealing with

the *flora* and *fauna* of Australia (an opportunity to tie in the Greek and Roman myths as described above). The overview shown in Figure 10.3 presents the fauna; the teacher has added terms the students already know in order to provide clear organization.

Based on this structured overview and your students' existing word knowledge, engage the students in general or small-group discussion. Usually, the discussion will focus on how the words are alike and how they are different, structurally as well as semantically. In this case, the new terms are *marsupials* and probably almost all of the animal names except *kangaroo* and *ostrich*. The teacher could begin the discussion with the kangaroo, describing its characteristics and suggesting that these might provide a clue to the characteristics of the other marsupials. Students will notice the shared spelling features between *wallaroo* and *wallaby*, and perhaps *wallaroo* and *kangaroo*. Might this be a clue to the relationships among these three animals? And so the discussion goes, probably accompanied by pictures of the different animals.

You might wonder why the teacher doesn't simply go ahead and show the pictures at the outset. Sometimes this may be the best strategy, but consider the benefits of having a brief discussion first. The students are actively involved in engaging whatever prior information they may have about the concepts, they are directed to examine the structure of the words for clues as to the relationships among the animals, and they are "primed" for the upcoming reading. The more students are actively engaged and made aware of the thinking strategies they are using, the more they will be likely to apply these strategies on their own.

Another means of actively engaging students in vocabulary development is to present them with the important new terms and, as Blachowicz (1986) and Anderson and Freebody (1981) have recommended, have them reflect on the degree to which they are familiar with a particular word. Encourage your students to discuss whether they (1) can define the word, (2) have seen or heard the word but cannot define it, or (3) have not seen the word and do

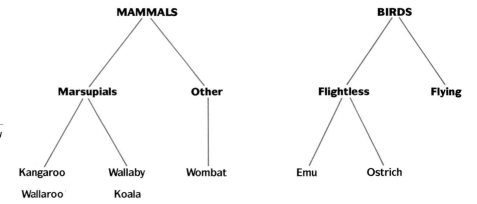

FIGURE 10.3

Structured Overview for a Unit on the Fauna of Australia — New Words Intermingled with Familiar Ones

not know what it means. Even if students are familiar with only two out of several words, that is enough to spark some predictions concerning what the students believe they will be reading about in the chapter or unit from which the words come. Notice the tie-in with the content DRTA? In the course of the discussion, you will be gaining important and necessary insights into the knowledge base of your students.

The next two activities are quite beneficial when students are partially familiar with most of the terms, and they may also be used for follow-up later in instruction.

2. *Semantic maps*   Constructing a *semantic map* (Heimlich and Pittelman, 1986; Johnson and Pearson, 1984; Nagy, 1989) is quite similar to the process involved in developing the Prereading Plan (PReP) we discussed in Chapter 8. The major differences are that with semantic mapping you use a specific visual representation (cluster or "map") and you introduce new terms. To illustrate this activity, let's take a look at how it might be used by a sixth grade teacher exploring the *21 Balloons* literature unit presented in the previous chapter.

   a. *Brainstorming*   Based on the term *volcanoes,* students suggest words that come to mind and the teacher writes these on the board.

   b. *Categorization*   After drawing an oval and writing *volcanoes* in it, the teacher involves the students in a discussion about how their suggested words can be categorized; each category represents one branch on the map (see Figure 10.4).

   c. *Teacher-added terms*   These are words that will be important in the upcoming study but that were not suggested by the students. The teacher places them in the appropriate category. This categorization orients students' understanding of the new terms (for example, *tidal wave* goes under characteristics of eruptions). In Figure 10.4, these new terms are indicated in parentheses.

   As with several other activities we have discussed, semantic mapping activates the students' prior knowledge about the concepts or topic/theme to be explored. It also affords you the opportunity to determine how much the students already know.

3. *Semantic feature analysis*   This analysis (Anders and Bos, 1986; Johnson and Pearson, 1984) allows students to examine concepts (in a semantic map, structured overview, or PReP) in relation to one another. As with any categorization activity, this involves noting comparisons and contrasts among the words (concepts).

   Figure 10.5 illustrates a semantic feature analysis for specific volcanoes. The analysis develops in this manner:

   a. Write specific features of volcanoes across the top of the grid, and the target words (in this case, names of volcanoes) down the left-hand margin. Advocates of this approach suggest that, through discussion, the students will come up with the features at the top. When you first introduce this activity, however, you should probably list these features yourself so

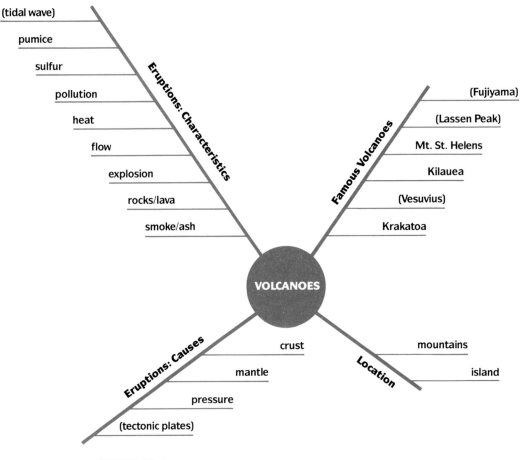

FIGURE 10.4

A Semantic Map Combining Familiar Terms Brainstormed by Sixth Grade Students with New Terms (in Parentheses) Added by the Teacher

that the students will concentrate on the analysis first rather than getting bogged down in the form. Soon after, you can involve them in the generation of features.

b. With the whole class or in small groups, discuss the matrix. The students will use the following symbols to complete each cell: a plus sign ($+$) indicates a definite relationship between the specific volcano and a feature; a minus sign ($-$) indicates the absence of the feature for that volcano; and a question mark (?) indicates more information is needed before responding.

c. After the students complete the matrix as best they can, point out that (1) they now know how much they already know about these volcanoes, and (2) they also know what they still need to find out — once again, to build bridges between the new and the known.

	On a Continent	On an Island	Explosive	Active	Extinct	Dormant
Fujiyama	–	–	?	?	?	?
Lassen Peak	+	–	?	–	–	+
Mt. St. Helens	+	–	+	+	–	–
Kilauea	– o	+	–	+	–	–
Vesuvius	–	+	+	?	–	?
Krakatoa	–	+	+	+	–	–

FIGURE 10.5

Semantic Feature Analysis

d. If most of the analysis is complete, point out to the students that the matrix now provides them with a quick means of differentiating the volcanoes: all they have to do is look down any column to see how one volcano differs from the next. To quickly summarize the features of each volcano, they simply read across each row.

The words you select for direct teaching must be reinforced in ways that require the students to *use* the words rather than simply to identify their meanings. After you have introduced these words in a meaningful context, as we have just discussed, the next two activities reinforce new words in productive ways.

4. *Word association*   Given a group of new words, students decide which one belongs with a target word they already know. For example, you can ask, "Which of our new words goes with the word *movement*?" (The words are *dormant, tectonic plates, inactive,* and *Vesuvius.*) Another question could be "Is a *wombat,* a *wallaby,* an *emu,* or a *wallaroo* most like a bear?"

Students should defend and discuss their answers. Although simple and straightforward, these exercises are nevertheless qualitatively better than those that require selecting a definition or writing a sentence. This is because students must see the new words (concepts) *in relation to other concepts* rather than simply remember them as discrete items.

Here is a good variation on the word association technique:

Could an *eruption* be an *explosion*?
Could a *cliché* be an *idiomatic expression*?
Could a *prestidigitator* be a *magician*?

5. *Sentence completion*   Students are more likely to retain the meanings of new terms if they complete a sentence with a word or phrase than they are if they make up their own sentences. For example, contrast each sentence completion below with the common student-written sentence you may otherwise get:

"You are most likely to find a *wombat* in _____ " versus "I saw a wombat."
"A *dormant* volcano is one that is _____ " versus "I like dormant volcanoes."

FULL PRONUNCIATION KEY

Sounds	Sample Words	Sounds	Sample Words
ă	as in rat, laugh	ou	as in cow, out
ā	ape, aid, pay	ŏŏ	full, took, wolf
â	air, care, wear	ōō	boot, fruit, flew
ä	father, koala, yard	p	pop, happy
b	bib, cabbage	r	roar, rhyme
ch	church, stitch	s	miss, sauce, scene, see
d	deed, mailed, puddle	sh	dish, ship, sugar, tissue
ĕ	pet, pleasure, any	t	tight, stopped
ē	be, bee, easy, piano	th	bath, thin
f	fast, fife, off, phrase, rough	*th*	bathe, this
		ŭ	cut, flood, rough, some
g	gag, get, finger	û	circle, fur, heard, term,
h	hat, who		turn, urge, word
hw	which, where	v	cave, valve, vine
ĭ	if, pit, busy	w	with, wolf
ī	by, pie, high	y	yes, yolk, onion
î	dear, deer, fierce, mere	yŏŏ	cure
j	judge, gem	yōō	abuse, use
k	cat, kick, school	z	rose, size, xylophone,
kw	choir, quick		zebra
l	lid, needle, tall	zh	garage, pleasure, vision
m	am, man, dumb	ə	about, silent, pencil,
n	no, sudden		lemon, circus
ng	thing, ink		
ŏ	horrible, pot	**Stress**	
ō	go, row, toe, though	Shown by accent marks ' and ' and by
ô	all, caught, for, paw	heavy, dark letters.
oi	boy, noise, oil	**dic·tion·ar·y** (dĭk'shə nĕr'ē)

Dictionary Use

It is perhaps a bit trite to suggest that the dictionary should be the students' "friend," but if you model a favorable attitude toward it and call upon it for timely information, you may indeed instill such an attitude in students. The dictionary should be used to supply information for those words students encounter in their independent reading that they either cannot figure out on their own or, after making an educated guess, wish to check. As we noted above, etymological information is now included in most dictionaries intended for the intermediate grades, and additional features help provide the tools students need to think about and analyze their language.

For example, dictionaries provide a major pronouncing key (see Figure 10.6) and a briefer key on every other page. For each entry, the dictionary will of course provide information about pronunciation, occasionally indicating whether a word has varied regional pronunciations. All dictionaries intended for elementary students include additional types of reference material, such as information specific to language itself: a history of the language, explanations about homographs and homophones, discussion of synonyms, an overview of how etymological information is presented, a thesaurus, and so on. One warning: use a thesaurus sparingly, because it is too easy for students to select a word randomly from a list of synonyms without reflecting on its appropriateness. You should remind the students that the thesaurus can often be helpful when they are trying to decide between two terms quite close in meaning, but that it is not the answer to their search for more colorful words. Reading widely and often is the best way to develop that source in their own heads.

In terms of attractiveness and utility, contemporary dictionaries for elementary students offer quite a bit more when compared with their forerunners. To get just a flavor of this change, refer to Figure 10.7, which is a page from a modern intermediate dictionary. Note the etymological information and the synonyms box.

In recent years, publishers have assembled dictionaries for the primary grades that are usually well done and attractive. For children who can benefit from them and who understand alphabetical order, they are most appropriate. A strong plus is their rich illustrations and informative photographs. The object or action that is pictured provides appropriate visual support for the word, while at the same time not obscuring the concept. Careful use of these dictionaries in second and third grade can favorably predispose students to the more complex dictionaries they will encounter later on.

Working with Categories of Language Use

Sometimes we talk about language for its own sake — language can be fun — but most of the time we discuss the way we use language to understand something more clearly, to make a finer distinction, or to focus on something we haven't thought about before. In the elementary grades, students will benefit from and should learn about categories of language use such as homonyms, synonyms, the

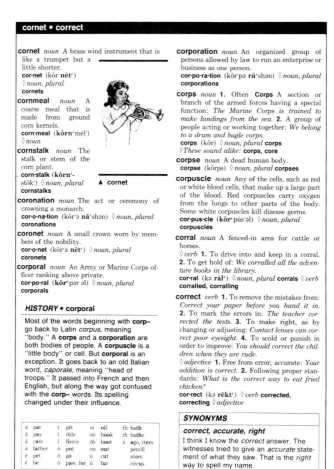

cornet • correct

cornet *noun* A brass wind instrument that is like a trumpet but a little shorter.
cor·net (kôr′nĕt′) ◊ *noun, plural* **cornets**

cornmeal *noun* A coarse meal that is made from ground corn kernels.
corn·meal (kôrn′mēl′) ◊ *noun*

cornstalk *noun* The stalk or stem of the corn plant.
corn·stalk (kôrn′stôk′) ◊ *noun, plural* **cornstalks**

coronation *noun* The act or ceremony of crowning a monarch.
cor·o·na·tion (kôr′ə nā′shən) ◊ *noun, plural* **coronations**

coronet *noun* A small crown worn by members of the nobility.
cor·o·net (kôr′ə nĕt′) ◊ *noun, plural* **coronets**

corporal *noun* An Army or Marine Corps officer ranking above private.
cor·po·ral (kôr′pər əl) ◊ *noun, plural* **corporals**

▲ cornet

HISTORY • corporal

Most of the words beginning with **corp–** go back to Latin *corpus*, meaning "body." A **corps** and a **corporation** are both bodies of people. A **corpuscle** is a "little body" or cell. But **corporal** is an exception. It goes back to an old Italian word, *caporale*, meaning "head of troops." It passed into French and then English, but along the way got confused with the **corp–** words. Its spelling changed under their influence.

ă	pat	ĭ	pit	oi	oil	th	bath
ā	pay	ī	ride	ōō	book	th	bathe
â	care	î	fierce	ōō	boot	ə	ago, item
ä	father	ŏ	pot	ou	out		pencil
ĕ	pet	ō	go	ŭ	cut		atom
ē	be	ô	paw, for	û	fur		circus

corporation *noun* An organized group of persons allowed by law to run an enterprise or business as one person.
cor·po·ra·tion (kôr′pə rā′shən) ◊ *noun, plural* **corporations**

corps *noun* **1.** Often **Corps** A section or branch of the armed forces having a special function: *The Marine Corps is trained to make landings from the sea.* **2.** A group of people acting or working together: *We belong to a drum and bugle corps.*
corps (kôr) ◊ *noun, plural* **corps**
‖ *These sound alike:* **corps, core**

corpse *noun* A dead human body.
corpse (kôrps) ◊ *noun, plural* **corpses**

corpuscle *noun* Any of the cells, such as red or white blood cells, that make up a large part of the blood. Red corpuscles carry oxygen from the lungs to other parts of the body. Some white corpuscles kill disease germs.
cor·pus·cle (kôr′pŭs′əl) ◊ *noun, plural* **corpuscles**

corral *noun* A fenced-in area for cattle or horses.
◊ *verb* **1.** To drive into and keep in a corral. **2.** To get hold of: *We corralled all the adventure books in the library.*
cor·ral (kə răl′) ◊ *noun, plural* **corrals** ◊ *verb* **corralled, corralling**

correct *verb* **1.** To remove the mistakes from: *Correct your paper before you hand it in.* **2.** To mark the errors in: *The teacher corrected the tests.* **3.** To make right, as by changing or adjusting: *Contact lenses can correct poor eyesight.* **4.** To scold or punish in order to improve: *You should correct the children when they are rude.*
◊ *adjective* **1.** Free from error; accurate: *Your addition is correct.* **2.** Following proper standards: *What is the correct way to eat fried chicken?*
cor·rect (kə rĕkt′) ◊ *verb* **corrected, correcting** ◊ *adjective*

SYNONYMS

correct, accurate, right
I think I know the *correct* answer. The witnesses tried to give an *accurate* statement of what they saw. That is the *right* way to spell my name.

FIGURE 10.7

A Page from an Intermediate Dictionary, Including Information on Synonyms and Etymology

Source: Copyright © 1986 by Houghton Mifflin Company. Reproduced by permission from *The Houghton Mifflin Intermediate Dictionary.*

distinction between denotative meaning and connotative meaning, antonyms, analogies, and figurative language.

If you are beginning to think about how to adapt activities with synonyms, denotative and connotative meanings, figurative language, homonyms, antonyms, and analogies to the teaching of your content-area vocabulary, terrific. Students should learn the labels for these different relationships and understand the underlying processes they represent, but students should also continually apply this knowledge in their acquisition of vocabulary. As we will explore in the second half of this chapter, a playful and sensitive curiosity about words can be easily incorporated within spelling instruction as well.

Synonyms

Johnson and Pearson (1984) aptly and concisely expressed the value of synonym study: "Lessons on synonyms can be powerful devices for bridging the gap in students' minds between what they know and what is new" (p. 21). Whenever you bring two synonyms together, you are not talking about two words that mean exactly the same thing. Your students should come to realize the basic economy of language. If we truly had two words that meant exactly the same thing, ultimately we would lose one of the words or it would take on a slightly different meaning. For example, think back to Chapter 3. When Old English and Danish came in contact there *were* instances of two different words standing for the same object or idea, but this situation didn't last long. In fact, it caused finer distinctions to be made within the single concept labeled, so that where we once had a single garment labeled with two words, for example, we now had two different words for two slightly differentiated garments.

By studying the fine gradations of meaning that synonymous words represent, students will learn progressively finer conceptual distinctions. During recess, for example, are they simply *loud,* or are they *garrulous, boisterous, raucous, shrill,* or *noisy*? Even terms that appear identical have different resonances in a sentence. For example, do we live *below* a particular form of government, *beneath* it, or *under* it?

The best way to begin synonym study is to categorize words that are in the same conceptual domain. The next step is to discriminate among the synonyms in actual use in the students' writing and reading. Finally, students should analyze and discuss the distinctions among lists of synonyms.

To categorize words according to a concept, the students first brainstorm words that have to do with a particular idea. For example, the word *fear* elicits the following responses from a group of third-graders: "afraid," "worried," "scared," "terrified," "frightened." The teacher discusses with the students what they think each word means and how they might use these words in their writing. This is as far as the initial discussion goes. Later on, as students are writing Halloween stories (a popular topic regardless of the teacher's intentions!), the students use these and other words to refer to the concept of fear. In reading and writing response groups, students discuss the writer's intentions in choosing one synonym over another.

Finally, the teacher discusses the concept of synonyms and helps the students develop an abstract understanding of the concept. This should be done at first in a group. The teacher begins by steering the students' discussion toward those words that are farthest apart in meaning, then moving to finer and finer distinctions: Why is *terrified* more scary than *worried*? Why is *terrified* more scary than *afraid*? or than *frightened*? This type of discrimination is challenging at first, but the teacher and the students are able to draw upon their previous discussions in reading and writing for examples and clarification.

You can further develop the students' ability to make these distinctions by having them work individually and then in pairs to rank synonymous words (Johnson and Pearson, 1984). For example, given the following format, the students will rank the words according to the scale of 1 = most intense, 4 = least intense:

_____ tiny

_____ small

_____ microscopic

_____ puny

Two students ranked the words as follows:

	Student 1		*Student 2*
2	tiny	2	tiny
3	small	4	small
1	microscopic	1	microscopic
4	puny	3	puny

Although the students agreed that *microscopic* was the most intense synonym, they differed at the other end of the scale — whether *small* or *puny* was least intense. In this case, is *puny* "smaller" than *small?* In their discussion with each other, the students offered different examples as support for their decisions; usually one student will wind up persuading the other. If there is a deadlock, however, the time to resolve it is back with the whole group. To check the majority opinion, or to resolve a problem that perhaps the whole group experienced, have your students refer to the dictionary as the final judge.

Children should study synonyms and exercise this knowledge in reading and writing throughout the elementary grades and beyond. This knowledge provides the foundation for learning and examining other types of word relationships, as we'll now explore.

Denotation and Connotation

As students think about and discuss synonyms, their discussions will naturally lead them into distinctions involving the denotative and the connotative meaning of words. *Denotation* refers to the literal meaning of a word; *connotation* refers to the feelings and emotions associated with the word, often its *implied* meaning. For example, the denotative meaning of *weak* is "lacking in strength," and its implied meaning may connote lack of character and resolve. Dictionaries often make this type of distinction by presenting literal meanings first, followed by connotative meanings.

Explain to students that we can think of words both in terms of what they literally mean, and in terms of how they affect our emotions and feelings. In this context, present word pairs for discussion and ask students to determine which word has a negative or bad connotation. Here are some sample word pairs: leave/abandon; retreat/withdraw; bold/reckless; thrifty/stingy; eat/devour; debate/argue; clever/sly; plump/fat.

To further develop understanding of these distinctions, present the students with sentences in which one word is omitted. Then ask them to substitute given words and note how each word affects the meaning differently.

Jeremy _____ down the street.

walked	sauntered	loped
strutted	ran	stumbled
lumbered		

As students move through the grades, their understanding of the uses to which denotative and connotative meaning are put will become more refined. The students can analyze propaganda techniques, sarcasm, irony, and so forth as examples of connotation and denotation at work.

Similes and Metaphors

As you read the following passage, listen for the bark of Sounder, the faithful and competent coon dog in the book of the same name by William Armstrong:

> **The trail barks seemed to be spaced with the precision of a juggler. Each bark bounced from slope to slope in the foothills like a rubber ball. But it was not an ordinary bark. It filled up the night and made music as though the branches of all the trees were being pulled across silver strings.**

Armstrong crafts his description of Sounder's bark through figurative language comprising primarily *simile* and *metaphor*. It hardly does justice to treat these aspects of figurative language so briefly here, but you can apply these basics in more depth as you explore the ways in which words are used in reading and in writing.

Similes and metaphors are the two aspects of figurative language dealt with in most depth in the elementary grades, though others are touched upon: personification, hyperbole, and occasionally synecdoche and metonymy. As with the previous categories of language, these are all effective labels and represent a convenient shorthand for talking about language.

The term *simile* comes from the Latin root *similis,* meaning "like." It is the logical place to begin considering figurative language, because it is the most explicitly signaled figure of speech. Used as a means of comparison, similes are introduced by the words *like, than, as . . . as,* or *so . . . as.* Often it is best to introduce similes to your students using *clichés* — overused, overworked similes — since some third-graders and most fourth-graders have had enough experience with language to have heard many clichés many times over. You can have them complete such clichés as:

as easy as p _____ . (pie)	as slow as m _____ . (molasses)
as dead as a d _____ . (doornail)	quick like a b _____ . (bunny)
as quick as a w _____ . (wink)	as happy as a cl _____ . (clam)

Students quite often are amazed to find out how often similes are used in literature. After a read-aloud, for example, you can note some of the similes that the author used and ask the students if they recall any. Reread a passage that has used some particularly effective similes. Consider the very first sentence of *Tuck Everlasting:* "The first week of August hangs at the very top of summer, the top of the live-long year, like the highest seat of a ferris wheel when it pauses in its turning." A popular activity for students is to keep a list of similes in their journals for a day or so and to discuss and reflect on the effect of this use of language. Being aware of similes helps the students learn how language can more precisely tap and express the feelings, senses, and ideas they experience and wish to convey.

Metaphors are comparisons or contrasts in language that are *not* explicitly signaled. Coming from the Greek (*meta,* over + *phor,* carry), metaphors "carry over" a comparison or contrast with one object, event, or person to another object, event, or person. They are powerful language devices that enable writers to express ideas in new ways. Once again, teachers should point out effective metaphors, such as this one from Norman Juster's *The Phantom Tollbooth:* "Symphonies are the large beautiful carpets with all the rhythms and melodies woven in" (Juster, 1961, p. 157).

The development of children's understanding of metaphor has been closely studied in recent years (Ortony, 1980; Winner, 1988). At first tacitly and later consciously, elementary students are quite capable of appreciating and manipulating language metaphorically. The degree to which they will do so depends on how they are brought to an awareness and then an appreciation of metaphor. The responsibility, in other words, is directly in our hands as teachers.

When students begin to learn about metaphor they are often struck with the realization that almost all language is in fact metaphorical. As we've already seen, the meaning of words extends over a period of time to include connotative as well as literal meanings. We don't want students to get bogged down at this level, though. We should focus at first on identifying instances where metaphor is used to express a thought in a fresh, new way. Fairly quickly, then, we should turn students' attention to applying their awareness of metaphor in their writing and in their reading.

Homonyms

Homonyms can provide quite a bit of fun in language study. *Homophones* (literally, "same sound") are words that sound the same but are spelled differently, as for example *pain* and *pane*. *Homographs* (literally, "same writing") are words that are spelled the same but are usually pronounced differently, such as *dove* (the bird, or the past tense of "to dive") and *lead* (the chemical element, or "to guide something along"). A third group of the larger category of homonyms is known simply *as* "homonyms" (literally, "same name"). This group includes words that are spelled and pronounced the same but that differ in meaning, such as *bat* (the mammal) and *bat* (a club used to hit baseballs).

At the second and third grade level, the category of homophones especially allows for great wordplay. Books by Fred Gwynne, such as *The King Who Rained,* highlight the silliness of confusing homophones in print. You can talk with students about what it means to write "I saw a *bare* in the woods" (oops!) or "That squirrel sure has a long *tale*" (quite a storyteller!).

Antonyms

Basically, *antonyms* refer to words that are opposite in meaning, though there are different types of opposite relationships. Antonyms can be words such as *right* and *wrong* or *yes* and *no,* with no middle ground, or they can be relative terms, such as *happy* and *sad,* which have degrees of emotion in between. Combined with synonyms, working with antonyms gives students the opportunity to make finer distinctions among relationships and to improve their critical thinking.

Analogies

After discussing the previous types of language categories and conceptual relationships, students are ready to examine *analogies*. This topic makes for challenging study, but an understanding of analogies is crucial to your students' later ability to comprehend complex relationships and logical reasoning in various subject matter areas, such as science, math, and history. Learning to apply analogical thinking, in other words, is a powerful tool that extends far beyond the simple format in which students first encounter analogies (a format, by the way, which is also used frequently in standardized tests).

Basically, analogical thinking expresses relationships among pairs of words or concepts. To begin with some simple analogies, *love* is to *hate* as *strong* is to *weak*; and *father* is to *son* as *mother* is to *daughter*. A number of analogical relationships have been identified (Johnson and Pearson, 1984). After a fair amount of work with analogies, you should involve your students in classifying analogies according to these relationships: *whole/part* as in *book : page :: table : leg*, and *temporal* or *sequential* as in *eighth : fourth :: tenth : fifth*. These examples model the higher-order thinking that will help students identify the nature of the relationship within an analogy.

The Foundations of Learning and Teaching Spelling

English spelling makes sense. This may come as a surprise to most speakers of English, including those who are good spellers. Most of us have been conditioned to expect a one-to-one match between letters and sounds in spelling, and of course this is not the case in English. However, a spelling system can serve purposes other than consistency in representing sounds, as we'll see below. Learning to spell does require effort, but the effort should be far less painful — and even enjoyable — if teachers understand how the system is structured and how children learn to spell.

Spelling plays an extremely important role in the language arts. On one level, it makes writing easier and is a courtesy to the reader (Graves, 1983). On another, more substantial level, spelling knowledge facilitates reading and writing performance (Perfetti, 1985; Henderson and Templeton, 1986): The careful examination of words that formal spelling instruction requires can beneficially affect the quality of students' reading experiences and, significantly, the quality of their writing experiences as well. The reason for this is twofold. First, spelling knowledge facilitates perception of specific words. As spelling becomes more "automatic," perception of orthographic or spelling patterns develops more generally across a growing sight vocabulary. Perfetti (1985) and others have shown that this type of perceptual development is a necessary prerequisite to efficient comprehension at both lower- and higher-order levels. Second, because spelling knowledge reflects structural and vocabulary information about words, it reinforces word-analysis strategies (see Chapter 8) and expands vocabulary.

Research in spelling has yielded some strong implications for learning and for instruction. Although for many years the learning (and teaching) of spelling was considered primarily a word-specific, rote-memory task (see Fitzsimmons and Loomer, 1974, and Hillerich, 1977, for reviews of this early research), some solid recommendations nevertheless stemmed from this view (Horn, 1969). More recent

The careful examination of words that is an important part of spelling instruction can beneficially affect the quality of students' reading and writing experiences. *(© David Strickler/Monkmeyer Press Photo Service)*

research (Hanna, Hanna, Hodges, and Rudorf, 1966; Read, 1971, 1975; Henderson, 1981, 1985, 1990; Henderson and Beers, 1980; and Templeton and Bear, in press) has demonstrated that learning to spell — indeed, learning about words at all — involves making *generalizations* from specific words, rather than simply memorizing every word as an individual unit.

As we already know, what children are able to learn and generalize about words changes throughout the elementary school years. Remember the developmental picture we painted in Chapter 6? Children's developmental word or spelling knowledge determines how they will spell words and how they will read words. This knowledge becomes increasingly more complex and abstract as children develop: most first-graders will think that words are put together by matching up letters and sounds in a left-to-right fashion; most sixth-graders will understand that letters may stand not only for individual sounds but usually carry important clues to the sounds of other letters within words and to the meaning of words. With this developmental picture, we now have a much better grasp of the ways in which children understand words at different points throughout the elementary grades. The result is a clearer sense of when and how to introduce spelling or orthographic patterns to children at different levels.

Three Principles of English Spelling

Before considering the content and the method of spelling instruction, we will examine the three principles of spelling in English. Understanding these principles will help considerably both in appreciating the way the spelling system works and

Y ou should know that, like the teaching of phonics, spelling instruction is a perennially controversial issue in education. Much of this controversy stems rightfully enough from the poorly organized spelling programs of the past, which often depended upon low-level, boring exercises. Just as with the basal reading series, some publishers in recent years have attempted to develop spelling basal programs that represent the more recent theory and practice of word learning. Some educators suggest that spelling can be learned *incidentally*, with perhaps some talk about words facilitated by the teacher or with individualized lists of words assembled by the teacher for each student (Bean and Bouffler, 1987; DeStefano and Haggerty, 1985; Wilde, 1989). This undoubtedly works for some students, but as Gamberg and her colleagues observed in their discussion of the role of spelling in a whole-language classroom, "... most children do not seem *to fully learn* conventional spelling without efforts to deliberately focus attention on it" (Gamberg, et al., 1988, p. 202, emphasis added).

In order to develop word knowledge to the level necessary for effective and efficient reading and writing, therefore, most students will benefit from the systematic exploration of words (Anderson, Hiebert, Scott, and Wilkinson, 1985; Beck, Perfetti, and McKeown, 1982). This systematic exploration can be in part presented and facilitated in a well-constructed basal spelling series.

Although research suggests that students themselves should explore words in word lists, comparing and contrasting them in ways I will discuss below, teachers will play a seminal role in this exploration. You will need to determine the levels at which your students should be

placed for such study as well as assist the students in developing their own personalized word lists — words they wish to learn how to spell. A well-constructed spelling basal (textbook) will be part of your overall word study. You may handle the text flexibly in terms of selecting activities from it and tying in these activities with your focus on word study. Again, you may find that you use the series more when you begin teaching, as you are learning more yourself and becoming a better "word-smith." Later, you may use the text primarily as a source of words for study and occasionally as a resource for particularly appropriate activities.

A well-constructed spelling series should

1. provide a scope and sequence of spelling patterns that will be a good guide for your word-study program over the elementary years.

2. provide appropriate list words that the students are familiar with through their reading and need to use in their writing; at the intermediate grade levels, some new words should be included that are related in spelling and in meaning to these known words.

3. offer instructionally sound activities that do not emphasize rote memorization but that involve students in examining words from a variety of perspectives. These activities lead to generalizations about spelling patterns that apply to many other words, not just those in the list.

4. reinforce the message that spelling is logical, is rarely haphazard, and at the intermediate levels can be tied directly to vocabulary through the "spelling-meaning connection" (Templeton, in press).

in teaching more effectively about the system. They are the alphabetic principle, the within-word pattern principle, and the meaning principle (Henderson and Templeton, 1986; Templeton, 1986).

The *alphabetic* principle states that, in English, letters represent sounds in a more or less left-to-right sequence. For example, in the word *bat,* the letter-sound correspondence is obvious: b = /b/, a = /ă/, t = /t/. In the word *grab,* the correspondence is again straightforward: g = /g/, r = /r/, a = /ă/, b = /b/. Of course, spelling is not always so straightforward; letters and combinations of letters can represent more than one sound, and one sound can be represented by more than one letter. The second two spelling principles account for this variability.

The *within-word pattern* principle demonstrates that the sounds that particular letters or groups of letters represent depend on either (1) the effects of other letters in the word on a particular sound or (2) the *position* of the sounds within words. An example of the first condition is the long vowel sound that is often indicated in words by the presence of silent letters. Long vowel sounds are often signaled by the pattern vowel-consonant-silent *e,* where the function of the final *e* is to mark the preceding vowel as long, as in c*a*ke. Another common long vowel pattern is a vowel *digraph,* in which the second, silent vowel often marks the first letter as long, as in r*ai*n. An example of the second condition is the consonant digraph *gh,* which represents different sounds in the words *cough, though,* and *ghoul.* Note, however, that the sound /f/ will never be spelled *gh* at the beginning of a word. The particular sound that *gh* stands for, then, depends on the position of the digraph within the word.

You may be wondering why these silent letters are there in the first place. Recall from Chapter 3 that English has a very rich history and that several languages have influenced our language. The original spellings of many words — in French, for example — were for the most part retained when they came into English. In a great many words, letters that are now silent were once pronounced, as with the final *e* in a word such as *make.* In many other words, silent letters remain from the original Latin spelling, or were inserted by scribes in their effort to make English appear more like Latin, as with the *b* in *debt* (based on the Latin *debitum*). Far from being troublesome, though, in terms of learning spelling and expanding vocabulary, this latter development is a bonus for readers and writers of English, as we'll see shortly.

The *meaning* principle in spelling states simply that meaning elements within words are usually spelled consistently. This principle is illustrated on a simple level by homophones, which sound alike but are spelled differently and have different meanings, and on a more abstract level by related words such as *legal/legality* and *condemn/condemnation.*

In the case of homophones, the different spellings for *tale/tail, rain/rein/reign,* and *bear/bare* help to avoid confusion in writing and in reading. Quite simply, homophones are spelled differently *because they mean different things.* For the writer and the reader, this is an asset rather than a liability of the spelling system. If *tale* and *tail* were spelled alike, for example, there might be some confusion regarding whether the writer means something that wags or something that enchants (Templeton, 1979). We know, in addition, that when the spoken word /sāl/ occurs in the context of boats or ships, it will usually be spelled *sail* (as in *sailor* and *sailboat*).

In the case of related words, the meaning principle plays its most significant role through the *spelling-meaning connection*. To get a sense of how this connection works, examine the following words:

bom*b*   bom*b*ard
mus*c*le   mus*c*ular
condem*n*   condem*n*ation
musi*c*   musi*c*ian
comple*te*   comple*t*ion

Notice how the italicized consonant letter in each word pair changes in pronunciation from the first word to the second. In the first three word pairs, a silent letter becomes sounded. In the last two word pairs, the sound that the italicized letter represents changes. Consistency in spelling despite variation in sound is a very common feature of the spelling system. Because the words in each pair are related in meaning, the spelling of these changed sounds remains constant. We can state the spelling-meaning connection this way: Words that are related in meaning are often related in spelling, *despite changes in sound*. Understanding this phenomenon powerfully aids students in spelling and, as we shall see later in this chapter, in vocabulary development.

We can gain a better appreciation of how this connection between spelling and meaning works if we attempt to spell words the way they sound. For example, let's respell some of the words that we examined above and some additional words:

define   defunition
compose   compusition
mussel   muscular
music   muzishion
legle   legality

If we did in fact spell words the way they sound, we would lose the meaning relationships that are otherwise *visually* preserved in the spelling.

The key to understanding the three principles of spelling is to examine groups of words. When we do this, we can better understand and appreciate the logic of the spelling system and realize that it is far more regular than it is often thought to be. As the within-word pattern principle and the meaning principle illustrate, this regularity exists at levels beyond a simple left-to-right, letter-to-sound match-up.

Developmental Acquisition of Spelling Knowledge

How do pupils come to understand and learn the system of spelling in English? How do they develop knowledge about the three principles just described? As mentioned above, recent research into this type of learning has offered some intriguing insights (Henderson and Beers, 1980; Hodges, in press; Read and Hodges, 1982; Templeton, 1986; Zutell, 1979). We know that learning to spell involves more than rote memorization. Although memory is certainly critical, it must be used efficiently.

We must be sensitive to where our students are along the developmental word-knowledge continuum — whether, in other words, they are conceptualizing word structure according to one, two, or all three of the principles just discussed. Otherwise we may wind up presenting them with spelling tasks at which they will surely fail, because they then will be reduced to memorizing each word as a discrete unit. This is somewhat like attempting to memorize twenty new phone numbers each week and to remember them all throughout the year!

Investigations of the development of word and spelling knowledge has demonstrated that students must construct over time the "rules" that govern spelling, just as they construct the rules for oral language. Students' understanding of spelling structure appears to follow a developmental sequence of several stages. Consistent with the sequence of stages in cognitive development discussed in Chapter 2, these stages represent the ways in which students organize their knowledge about words. As their word knowledge becomes more advanced, children reorganize the ways in which they conceptualize and exercise the spelling of words. Our understanding of this developmental sequence allows us to present certain spelling patterns and words representing those patterns for explicit instruction and examination.

Semiphonemic and Letter-Name Stages

Let's examine this development from the point at which children are writing exclusively with recognizable letters. They have moved beyond the "scribbling and drawing" phase discussed in Chapter 6, and their spelling is characterized as primarily *semiphonemic*. They represent some but not all sounds within syllables: for example, they use BD for *bird,* and WM for *worm.* Few vowel letters occur. As the children are exposed more and more to print and are read to, their *concept of word in print* develops and their spelling becomes primarily alphabetic or "letter-name." Their spelling now can be described as phonemic because they are attending to most sounds or phonemes and representing them with a corresponding letter: FETHR for *feather;* BECIM for *become;* CHRANCHRAK for *train track.* Here are some common spelling correspondences that children establish at this stage:

Long Vowels	Short Vowels	Consonant Blends
a: TAK (take)	a: SAD	/dr/: JRIV (drive)
e: SET (seat)	e: BAD (bed)	/tr/: CHREP (trip)
i: BIK (bike)	i: SET (sit)	
o: BON (bone)	o: GIT (got)	
u: SUT (shoot)	u: BOPY (bumpy)	

The children will also spell some words correctly; these will be the sight words they have acquired in their reading. Jeffrey's writing in Figure 10.8 gives evidence that he is a letter-name speller.

As several researchers have demonstrated (Beers and Henderson, 1977; Chomsky, 1979; Gentry, 1983, 1987; Kamii and Randazzo, 1985; Read, 1971, 1975; Templeton, 1980; Templeton and Thomas, 1984), the logic according to which the chil-

(This story reads:
One day one car was on the wrong side of the road, and another car came and they crashed. But the people were so scared that they couldn't look. But the people that were in the cars were O.K. The End)

FIGURE 10.8

Jeffrey's Letter-Name Writing

dren invent their spellings is consistent and in fact quite impressive — and the fascinating point about this logic is that the children cannot explain it! It is part of their *tacit* knowledge about written language (see Chapter 2). Though their invented spellings appear odd to most adults, the spellings reflect spelling strategies that are quite common among first-graders. The logic underlying these spellings is based on phonetic and articulatory or physical properties of the sounds the children are attempting to spell. However, as children learn — through reading instruction and through examination of words — how certain sounds are represented in simple words, their invented spellings begin to look more conventional. At this point, they are moving into the next developmental phase.

Within-Word Pattern Stage

As the label implies, the *within-word pattern* stage involves an understanding of the patterns to which letters and sounds correspond within single-syllable words. Sight words provide the foundation for this understanding. Most children master short vowel spellings fairly early and move on to examine the ways in which long vowels are represented. This examination requires quite some time, and as children are sorting out and learning the various ways in which long vowels can be spelled, they make some interesting spelling errors. The following spellings come from children's compositions: MAIK, MAEK, and MEAK, for the word *make*; RAUWND for *round,* and TUREN for *turn.* Jason's "79 Dungeons" story (see Figure 10.9) demonstrates this stage of word knowledge.

The children's spellings of *make* illustrate how they attempt to represent the silent letter — or as it's often called, the "marker" that indicates that the word contains a long vowel. The children may misplace this marker or, as the first word (MAIK) illustrates, include a logical marker that is correctly placed but not appropriate in this particular word. The other invented spellings above reflect students' attempts to handle vowels that are not clearly long or short — a *diphthong* in the case of RAUWND (/ow/) and an *r*-influenced vowel in the case of TUREN. As students read and examine words that evidence these letter/sound, within-word relationships, and as they exercise this knowledge in their writing attempts, they gradually come to sort out and correctly use the various spelling patterns.

Syllable Juncture Stage

Once students understand most of the basic within-word single-syllable patterns, they are conceptually ready to examine words of more than one syllable and to examine what happens at the *juncture* of syllables within words — the place where the syllables come together. At these junctures letters may be doubled, as in ba*sk*et, si*tt*ing, and begi*nn*ing; dropped (mak*e* + ing = making); or changed (gloom*y* + er = gloom*i*er). The following types of invented spellings signal that pupils are ready for systematic study of syllable patterns and affixes:

BAKEING (baking)	PALICE (palace)
STOPED (stopped)	DAFEND (defend)
SUDEN (sudden)	
NEDDLE (needle)	
CARRYS (carries)	
EQUIPED (equipped)	

In the first column, note the uncertainty about when and where to double consonants or to drop final letters. In *palace* and *defend,* notice that the errors occur in the least-stressed syllables. In many cases, the students must simply remember the spelling of the schwa sound (unstressed vowel sound) for each word.

Why does acquiring an understanding about syllable juncture depend on a firm grasp of the alphabetic and within-word pattern principles? This is because the basic clue to doubling, dropping, or changing letters depends on the structure within the joined syllables. For example, *sit* has a short vowel pattern, and when you add a suffix that begins with a vowel, you must double the final consonant in *sit.* Otherwise, you have a different word — *siting* (site + ing).

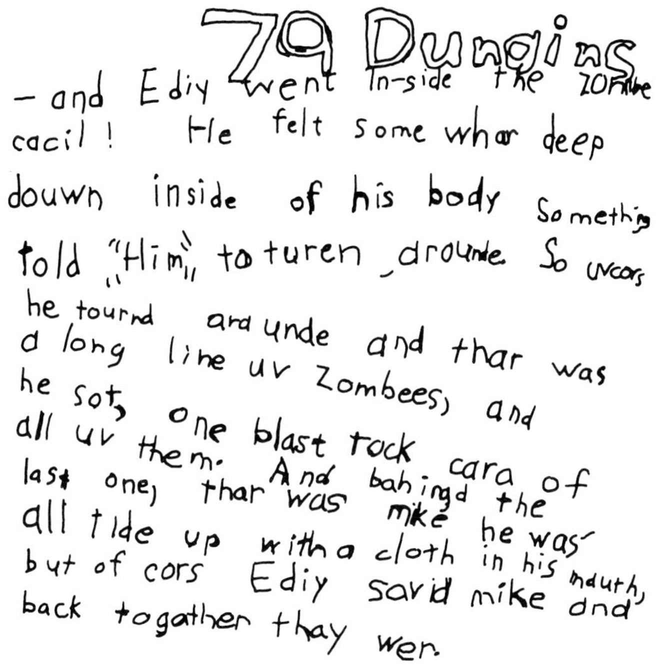

FIGURE 10.9

Jason's "79 Dungeons" Story, Demonstrating Within-Word-Pattern Spellings

(This story reads:
And Eddie went inside the zombie castle. Something told him to turn around. So of course he turned around. There was a long line of zombees. And he shot, one blast took care of all of them. And there was Mike. He was all tied up with a cloth in his mouth. But of course Eddie saved Mike and back together they were.)

Children begin to master the conventions that govern the joining of syllables, prefixes, and suffixes first in common two-syllable words and later in common polysyllabic words. Students will also notice where the stress or accent is placed within words, as well as the role that an accent can play in focusing attention on what needs to be studied in these words. Some fine-tuning of this knowledge will occur at the next stage, but most of these conventions will be learned here.

Derivational Patterns Stage

Students now are able to understand and apply fully the fundamental *meaning* principle in our spelling system: words that are related in meaning are often related in spelling as well, despite changes in sound. The following misspellings are characteristic of the *derivational patterns* stage:

INTERUPT (interrupt)   ATRACT (attract)

COMPASITION (composition)   CONDEM (condemn)

BENIFIT (benefit)   ACCOMODATE (accommodate)

This final stage reflects the broader vocabulary to which students are now exposed in their reading, a considerable input of words from the Greek, Latin, and

French linguistic legacy in English (see Chapter 3). Most of this new vocabulary will occur more frequently in print than in spoken language (Chomsky, 1970; Moskowitz, 1973; Templeton, 1979a). During this stage students extend and refine the basic spelling conventions they developed during the previous stage, primarily syllable junctures and schwa.

Word study will focus on exploring derivational relationships or spelling-sound patterns that apply to words related in spelling and meaning. As the students' vocabularies expand during the intermediate years, they will learn words that, although more abstract semantically, are highly regular in terms of the meaning principle. By fifth and sixth grade, most students are ready to formally examine the meaning principle as it applies to their growing vocabulary. Students will be examining related words such as *compete/competition, fatal/fatality, clinic/clinician,* and *judicial/adjudicate.*

At this level, you should teach and consistently reinforce the following strategy: "When you are uncertain about the spelling of a particular word, try to think of a *related* word." For example, let's say a student who is uncertain about the spelling of *advantage* has been spelling it *advantidge.* It may help him to think of the word *advantageous,* in which the sound and the spelling in the troublesome third syllable is clear — a long *a.* He can thus apply this knowledge to spell the schwa sound in *advantage.* We know that it is our responsibility to point out these relationships to students, because they usually do not make this connection on their own (Dale, O'Rourke, and Bamman, 1971; Templeton, 1989).

Occasionally the related word that may explain an uncertain spelling may not yet be part of the student's vocabulary. Teachers and students should take note of such instances; they can be turned into informal spelling *and* vocabulary lessons. For example, the fifth-grader who spells *condemn* as CONDEM, leaving off the final *n,* may be shown the related word *condemnation,* in which the *n* is clearly heard. This way the teacher not only reinforces the correct spelling of *condemn* but teaches the student a new word — and the meaning of the new word is easily derived from *condemn.* This strategy, based on drawing analogies among words, takes full advantage of the "spelling-meaning connection" in English spelling.

Formal Spelling Instruction

Formal instruction in spelling involves the systematic presentation and study of lists of words. The words are grouped or categorized according to a common pattern or principle (for example, words in which long *a* is spelled *a*-consonant-*e* or *ai,* or words in which the *-dict-* root occurs) and presented in a list. Furthermore, these words are familiar to the students from their reading. Lists should be based on words that the students use frequently in their writing and are likely to misspell; moreover, the list words should reflect the features of spelling that students are developmentally ready to examine.

In formal spelling instruction, study of the words occurs in a three- or four-day cycle, with a pretest on Monday and a posttest at the end of the week. Henderson (1985) noted that "the routine of pretest, self-correction, study, post-test, and spaced review practice is a well-established design intended to insure that a core spelling vocabulary will be memorized" (Henderson, p. 124). Study can occur in a number of ways but usually involves exercises and activities that require students to pay attention to particular elements in the words. Weber and Henderson (1989) demonstrated that students who paid attention to those elements developed word knowledge over and above the insights reading alone could give them. In other words, students do need to examine words apart from the context in which they normally occur in order to develop word knowledge more fully. This study should be complemented by word-sorting activities with list words and with additional words that reflect the same patterns.

Recent research in the development of spelling ability has identified a scope and sequence for formal, systematic study (Henderson, 1985; Henderson and Temple-ton, 1986; Schlagal, in press; Templeton, 1983, 1986). I presented this research in Chapter 8, where we discussed word analysis in the context of reading instruction. Unfortunately, spelling instruction in the past has been more likely to take the form of simply *assigning* rather than *teaching* words (Gentry, 1987). The effectiveness of such spelling lessons suffered accordingly: words that students spelled correctly on Friday's test they misspelled the following week in their writing. Your job, as we will see, will be to walk your students through a specific spelling pattern and then engage them in active exploration of the pattern. This way your students will be much more likely to apply the knowledge they acquire in the spelling lessons to their everyday writing.

At the *semiphonemic* stage, children's spelling attempts reflect their knowledge of the form and the function of print, but formal instruction in spelling at this level simply would not "take." However, at the next level, the *letter-name* stage, children are ready to begin exploring the alphabetic principle of English spelling. Table 10.1 provides an overview of the sequence of spelling instruction as a function of de-velopmental level.

TABLE 10.1 SYNCHRONIZING THE TEACHING OF SPELLING WITH CHILDREN'S DEVELOPMENTAL LEVELS OF WORD KNOWLEDGE

LETTER NAME

1. Students should be guided to examine and to learn the correct spelling of selected words they are being taught to read.
2. Through activities involving recognition, grouping, substitution, and spelling, beginning consonant elements are examined in the following order: single consonants, common consonant digraphs, and common blends.
3. Short vowel patterns (phonograms) are examined systematically. (A phonogram is the vowel and what follows within a single syllable.)
4. "Continuant" or nasal consonants that precede other types of consonants are examined (wi*n*ter, ca*m*p).
5. The most common long vowel patterns, or phonograms, are examined (m*a*ke, r*i*de).

WITHIN-WORD PATTERN

1. Additional common long vowel patterns are examined (/ā/ in b*ai*t, w*ei*ght; /ī/ in l*igh*t; /ē/ in m*ea*t, fr*ee*ze).
2. *R*- and *l*-influenced vowel patterns are studied (c*ar*d, f*er*n, f*al*l, p*ul*l).
3. Common diphthongs are introduced (h*ow*, b*oi*l).
4. Compound words are studied.
5. Through the examination of common homophones, students begin to develop an awareness of the meaning principle in spelling.

TABLE 10.1 (*cont.*)

SYLLABLE JUNCTURE

1. Common and less frequent vowel patterns in stressed syllables continue to be examined.
2. Common inflections and the ways in which they are joined to base words are examined (*-ed, -ing, -ly*).
3. The sound and the meaning of common prefixes and suffixes are analyzed (*un-, re-, -ment, -ness*).
4. The role of stress or accent is introduced in the context of homographs.
5. Unstressed syllables are examined, first in two-syllable words and later in polysyllabic words.
6. More complex prefixes and suffixes are examined.
7. The principle of consonant doubling is examined as it applies to a broader range of vocabulary.

DERIVATIONAL PATTERNS: THE SPELLING-MEANING CONNECTION

1. Silent and sounded consonant patterns are studied (colum*n*/colum*n*ist, resign/resignation).
2. Considerable attention is given to the different vowel alternation patterns, sequenced for study as follows:
   a. Long-to-short (extr*e*me/extr*e*mity, rev*i*se/rev*i*sion)
   b. Long-to-schwa (infl*a*me/infl*a*mmation, def*i*ne-def*i*nition)
   c. Short-to-schwa (exc*e*l/exc*e*llent, leg*a*l/leg*a*lity)
   d. Predictable sound/spelling alternation (con*su*me/con*sump*tion, recei*ve*-recep*tion*)
3. While the vowel-alternation patterns are studied, other accompanying consonant alternation patterns are examined:
   a. Sound change/spelling stable (musi*c*/musi*c*ian, constitu*te*/constitu*t*ion)
   b. Predictable sound/spelling alternation (explo*de*/explo*s*ion, absen*t*/absen*ce*, permi*t*/permi*ss*ion)
4. The role of Greek and Latin forms in spelling and in meaning is explored.
5. "Absorbed" or "assimilated" prefixes are examined (*ad* + tract = *at*tract; *in* + luminate = *il*luminate).

Letter Name

For children at the letter-name stage, instructional activities should involve recognition, grouping, substitution, and be focused on the elements presented in Table 10.1. The number of words examined and learned each week is small, usually no more than five. These five words will be important, though, and should therefore be carefully selected to reflect the developmental sequence.

Here are two productive activities:

■ Students note the spelling of words that show a particular type of correspondence to each other and then examine words for examples of that correspondence (e.g., all words that begin like *chip*). Words may then be grouped or categorized according to the shared feature. They may be contrasted with other words that correspond to each other in different ways: for example, contrast words that begin like *sun* with words that begin like *spin*.

■ Substitute initial consonants or consonantal elements on the same short vowel phonogram. This is really an extension of the earlier childhood game of spontaneous rhyming; children love the feeling of generating so many words that they can immediately read. Beginning with a word such as *back,* students see how many other words they can come up with by changing the first consonant (*lack, mack, rack, stack, track,* etc.). This may be done on the board, on paper, or with a commercially available product such as Ideal's Link Letters. Stauffer (1970) shared a delightful anecdote about one first-grader who, when engaged in this activity, stated that he was in "the manufacturing business." Why? "Because I'm manufacturing words!"

When children are attending to consonants or consonantal elements at the beginning of words, the groundwork is being laid for explicit examination of short vowel patterns. The same type of recognition, grouping, substitution, and spelling activities used for consonants are appropriate for vowel patterns.

At the upper end of this stage, children's experience with reading is influencing their invented spellings. These spellings will eventually include silent letters as part of long vowel spellings. This signals students' readiness to examine some conventional spellings of several of these patterns.

Within-Word Pattern

Second grade is the time during which children will develop a substantial understanding of within-word patterns. The remaining features, though introduced in second grade, will continue to be studied beyond this year. Most students will have mastered within-word pattern conventions by the beginning of fourth grade.

Students will come to understand — usually tacitly at first — that the way a sound is spelled often depends on where the sound occurs within a word. In the case of diphthongs, for example, students can examine the spelling of the /oy/ sound in the following words:

boil   toy

coin   joy

spoil   boy

foil

By comparing and contrasting these spellings, students will realize that the /oy/ sound may be spelled *oi* when it occurs in the middle of a syllable and *oy* when it occurs at the end of a syllable.

Compound words examined during this stage form the basis for later examination of morphemic elements within words. They illustrate the all-important characteristic of word-combination principles in English. It is crucial that students come to understand how the meaningful elements or morphemes within words are combined to result in the meaning of the whole word. Students can understand this process most concretely when they see how to combine separate words to form a single compound word:

coat for *rain*	= *raincoat*
ball of *cotton*	= *cottonball*
boy or *girl* who works with *cows*	= *cowboy* or *cowgirl*
shovel that runs on *steam*	= *steamshovel*

Johnson and Pearson (1984) explore the different relationships that exist between words that make up a compound word; these are enjoyable ways to demonstrate for students the many ways in which compound words can express new concepts.

Syllable Juncture

Syllable-juncture principles will be introduced gradually beginning in second and third grade, though the formal instructional focus will remain primarily on within-word patterns. In fourth grade, study of polysyllabic words is undertaken in earnest. The balance of the intermediate grades will focus on syllable-juncture conventions and prepare students in grades four, five, and six for the role that meaning will play in spelling.

The earliest point at which syllable-juncture principles may be introduced for study is toward the end of second grade, and only then for the inflectional endings -*ed* and -*ing*. These inflections are studied in third grade as well, emphasizing the role the vowel pattern plays in determining what happens at the point where the suffix joins the base. As I've already noted in connection with vocabulary development, students should be walked through the processes by which base words are affected by affixes. Use familiar words, and mention the characteristics of the spelling at the same time you discuss the effect of prefixes and suffixes on meaning. For example, although the vowel sound in a prefix such as *re-* may not be clearly heard when the word is casually pronounced, you should emphasize that the spelling should be no problem because it is tied to *meaning*.

Stress patterns for syllables within words are more obvious to students when the patterns are introduced with homographs, because the speaker's emphasis is then clearly tied to meaning. For example, the word *present* can be pronounced either as PRES-ent, when it is a noun referring to a gift that is given to someone, or pre-SENT, the verb that describes the act of giving an award to someone, for example. Similarly, you can work on a PRO-ject, or you can pro-JECT a certain image.

Once your students understand the concept of stressed syllables in homographs, the same concept can be examined in other polysyllabic words. Students should examine the words systematically, syllable by syllable, while attending to the pattern within each syllable. Often these patterns will correspond to meaning units; other times they will not. Regardless, the following example (after Henderson, 1985) illustrates how a teacher can model the effective examination or "walkthrough" of such words for the students:

1. The teacher pronounces the word *wander*, for example, and asks the students how many syllables it has.
2. The students say what letter begins the first syllable [teacher writes it on board], what letter ends the first syllable [teacher writes that on board], what letter begins the second syllable, and what letter ends the second syllable.
3. The teacher asks the students to listen to the first syllable, which is *stressed*, and to say what letter they think spells the vowel sound in the first syllable. The teacher writes the letter on the board in the appropriate place.

4. The teacher asks the students to listen as she pronounces the unstressed syllable and to offer their best guess as to the letter that stands for the unstressed vowel sound. For this word, as the teacher has predicted, they will guess the correct letter.

5. The teacher asks the students if they could be absolutely certain about the spelling of the unstressed vowel if they had not seen the word — is sound, by itself, a clue to the spelling in unstressed syllables? They should answer no, since this sound can also be spelled, *-or, -ir,* and *-ar.*

Students realize the value of closely looking at polysyllabic words such as these. The teacher asks them, if they were to study the word *wander* in order to learn its correct spelling, which part of the word would they pay attention to? This type of walk-through helps students to understand why they should attend to accent for purposes of spelling: it shows them what they already know about the spelling of a polysyllabic word (the vowel pattern in the stressed syllable) and what they need to know and therefore to pay attention to.

Toward the end of the syllable-juncture stage, students must consider both stress and syllable juncture as well as vowel pattern in deciding whether consonants are doubled at the joining of affixes and base words. To illustrate, consider the words *benefit, occur, permit, order.* When suffixes beginning with a vowel are affixed to these words, note what happens:

benefit + *-ed* = *benefited*
occur + *-ed* = *occurred*
permit + *-ed* = *permitted*
order + *-ed* = *ordered*

Students learn that what is going on here is this: for final syllables that are stressed and have a consonant-vowel-consonant (CVC) structure, the final consonant is doubled before suffixes (such as *-ed*) that begin with a vowel. If the final syllable is not stressed, then the final consonant is not doubled.

Derivational Patterns:
The Spelling-Meaning Connection

Although students have been paying attention during the syllable juncture stage to the meaning of affixes and stems and to related words (*please/pleasant, wise/wisdom, sign/signal/signature*), the role of meaning as it is represented in spelling comes into full play at the derivational patterns stage. As the examples in Appendix A illustrate, whenever possible, words should be presented in pairs or families that share a common base or stem, so that students clearly see how the changing sounds within the words are spelled consistently. Figure 10.10 shows how a fifth grade spelling basal handles this presentation.

Let's see how a sixth grade teacher might present the "long to schwa" *vowel-alternation* pattern.

Spelling-Meaning Strategy

Vowel Changes: Schwa to Short Vowel Sound

Thinking of related words may help you remember how to spell an unclear vowel sound. Read this paragraph.

> The man insisted that what he had done was **legal**. The committee questioned the **legality** of his actions and hired a lawyer.

legal
legality

Think

- How are *legal* and *legality* related in meaning?
- What vowel sound does the letter *a* spell in each word?

Here are more related words in which the same letter spells the schwa sound in one word and the short vowel sound in another.

local	normal	mortal
locality	normality	mortality

Apply and Extend

Complete these activities on a separate piece of paper.

1. Look up the words in the word box above in your Spelling Dictionary, and write their meanings. Then write a short paragraph, using one pair of words.

2. With a partner list as many words as you can that are related to *legal, local, normal,* and *mortal.* Then look on page 272 of your Spelling-Meaning Index. Add any other words that you find in these families to your list.

Summing Up When you do not know the spelling of the schwa sound in a word, the short vowel sound in a related word may help you figure out which vowel to use.

FIGURE 10.10

Instructional Activities in a Published Spelling Series

Source: *Houghton Mifflin Spelling and Vocabulary,* Level 6. Copyright © 1990 by Houghton Mifflin Company. Reprinted by permission of Houghton Mifflin Company.

CLASSROOM EXAMPLE

First, he writes *inspire* and *inspiration* on the chalkboard. He asks the students if the two words have a similar meaning. Then, he underlines *inspir* in both words.

TEACHER: "Kids, do these letters [pointing to *inspir*] stand for the same sounds in both of these words? Right, they don't! In the word *inspire,* the *i* in the second syllable has a long sound, but it changes to a schwa sound in the word *inspiration.*

"As we've seen with other types of words we've been examining, these two words are related in meaning *and* in spelling, despite differences in pronunciation. Knowing this can help you spell a word like *inspiration.* Think about it for a minute. The schwa sound in the second syllable of *inspiration* gives you no clue to its spelling — unless you think of the related word, *inspire.* In the word *inspire,* you can hear the sound in the second syllable: it's a long *i.* The spelling is obvious, and — because words that are related in meaning are often related in spelling — this long *i* is your clue to spelling the schwa sound in *inspiration.*"

Next the teacher presents other representative words in pairs: for example, *propose/proposition* and *harmonious/harmony.* In each case he discusses with the students how the stressed vowel in the second syllable of the first word is the clue to the spelling of the schwa in the second syllable of the related word.

Once students understand the spelling-meaning connection — how spelling preserves meaning among related words despite changes in sound — then they can truly benefit from more intensive examination of word stems (see earlier discussion, pages 394–398). Invariant Greek forms such as *graph* (to write), *therm* (heat), and *photo* (light) should be studied before Latin roots, which, unlike Greek combining forms, are often hidden within words and occasionally undergo spelling changes across different words. Examination of Latin roots should begin with those that occur with greater frequency and which have fairly consistent spellings (Templeton, 1983). In addition to those mentioned earlier, a few examples are *-pose-* ("to put or place," as in *position*), *-port-* ("to carry," as in *portable*), and *-dict-* ("to speak," as in *diction*).

The combination of affixes and stems should be closely examined. Here is an example of how one teacher discussed this combination in response to a particular spelling error.

CLASSROOM EXAMPLE

The teacher writes the misspelled word *interupt* on the board or on an overhead transparency.

TEACHER: "Kids, I've noticed a particular type of spelling error in many of your papers over the last two weeks, and now is a good time to talk about it. Let's begin by figuring out what's wrong with this word [points to *interupt*]. Alice?"

ALICE: "It's only got one *r*!"

TEACHER: "Right! Why should there be two *r*'s instead of one? After all, we only *hear* one 'r' sound . . ."

The teacher fields the students' responses, and if it is appropriate, offers the following walk-through: "'Interrupt' is made up of two parts, the prefix *inter,* meaning 'in between' and the word root *rupt,* which comes from a Latin word meaning 'to break.' When you put *inter* and *rupt* together, you construct a word that means 'to break in between.' If you *interrupt* someone when they're talking, you 'break in between' what they're saying."

Although they are seldom directly studied, "absorbed" or "assimilated" prefixes nonetheless form a rather large and important class of meaning-based spelling features. To illustrate prefix assimilation, you should begin with prefixes that have relatively stable meanings, and that are attached to bases or word roots that have straightforward meanings.

CLASSROOM EXAMPLE

The teacher writes the word *attract* on a transparency.

TEACHER: "Kids, we're going to explain another very common misspelling, but in doing so we're going to discover a prefix that most people don't notice. Let's take a look at the word *attract*. Actually, it's made up of the prefix *ad*, meaning 'to or toward,' and the word root *tract*, meaning 'pull.' When you put *ad* and *tract* together, two things happen. First, the word parts combine to mean 'to pull to or toward' — the meaning, actually of *attract*.

  "But look! The spelling of the prefix *ad* has changed to *at*. You can get an idea of how this happened by trying to pronounce 'adtract' so that you really notice the 'd' sound. [The teacher has students pronounce 'adtract.'] Many, many years ago when this word first came into existence as 'adtract,' it became easier for people to leave out the 'd' sound when pronouncing the word. The sound of the 'd' became absorbed into the 't' sound at the beginning of the word root *tract*. A little while later — even though only one sound, the 't' sound, could be heard where the prefix joined the word root — the spelling changed to reflect this change in sound but kept the letter 't' because it was still part of a prefix. If the last letter of the prefix had been dropped, the meaning of the prefix would have been lost."

Organization of Formal Instruction

How will you follow the sequence presented in Table 10.1 in your classroom routine? Traditional spelling research underscored the value of the "pretest/self-correct/study/posttest" format (Horn, 1969). That is, before students examine a new spelling list, they are tested on their spelling knowledge of the words. The format is as follows:

- Usually on Monday, the pretest is administered. Afterwards, students check their own paper.
- For any missed words, students look at the correct spelling, write the misspelled word correctly on the same line as the misspelled word, check the spelling, then write the word a second time. Students check this spelling, then turn the paper over and write the word from memory. (You get diminishing returns if students write the word any more than this.)
- During the week, students pay particular attention to the words they missed on the pretest in the context of other meaningful activities with words. A midweek test, often administered in a "buddy" system, with students working in pairs, can help students monitor their success with the misspelled words and focus their study for the Friday test.

In such a formal spelling approach, periodic *review* of list words is important — usually every six weeks. As a supplement to the teaching of targeted patterns and frequent and wide reading and writing, this approach will develop and reinforce the "core spelling vocabulary" to which Henderson referred (Henderson, 1985).

As with the teaching of specific skills in reading and writing, students should usually be grouped for spelling instruction. At all levels, formal spelling instruction should include examination of the list words through meaningful activities that lead to knowledge that can be *generalized* about the spelling patterns. The following list presents some very effective ideas for these activities.

Expand Your Teaching Repertoire

1. Students should keep *word study notebooks* (see Figure 10.11) that are evidence of their developing understanding of word structure. The notebooks include words they have studied as well as words they have found in word hunts in particular categories. For example, one page could contain "long *a*" words, another "short *a*" words, and so on. Notably, each category will be-

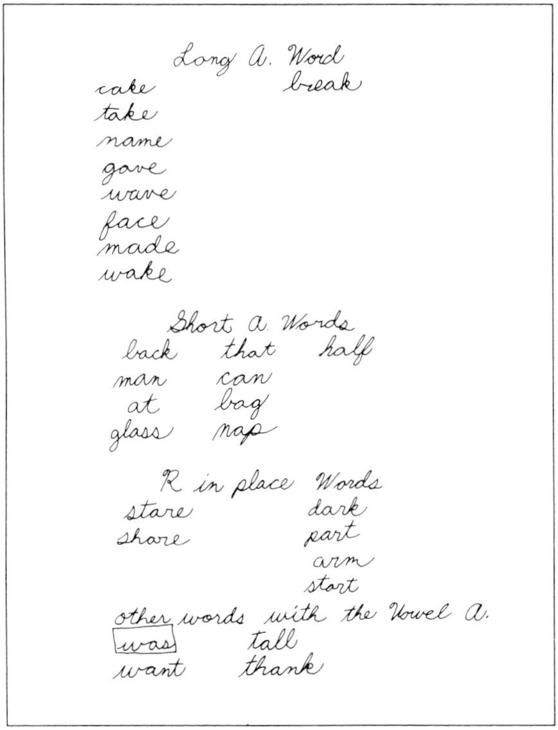

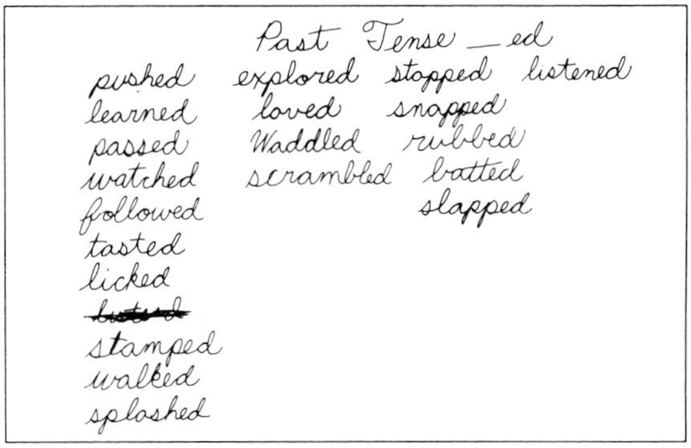

FIGURE 10.11

Children's Notebook Pages

Source: from Henderson, Edmund H., *Teaching Spelling*, Second Edition. Copyright © 1990 by Houghton Mifflin Company. Used with permission.

come further differentiated as children learn more about words. The "long *a*" page will later include words with this sound spelled according to different patterns.

2. Earlier we discussed *word sorts* with a semantic focus. Here we will examine a particularly critical application of word sorts — sorting according to spelling features. In this basic format for sorting words, we will assume that students are well into the letter-name stage or just beginning the within-word pattern stage.

   a. Begin with one category. Let's say you're going to focus on the long *i*. Place a card containing a known word with a long *i* (*hike*) at the head of a column. Each student will have a number of word cards that he or she will use in the sort. As the student looks at *and pronounces* each word, he or she will place the words that have the same vowel sound as in *hike* underneath that card; words that don't fit the pattern will go in a separate column (the "leftover" or "miscellaneous" column), headed by a blank card.

   b. After the sort is complete, ask the students to explain why they placed the words the way they did. Here is a completed sort:

hike	*Leftover words* *(blank card)*
white	stick
time	sing
smile	fish
light	wind
five	ship
slide	chin
high	slip
	give

   Let's say a student placed *wind* in the "hike" column. You had anticipated the word would be read with a short *i,* as in "the wind that blows," but this is where the student's justification comes into play. It will be clear if the student can correctly pronounce the word with a long *i.*

   You might argue against including apparent exceptions such as *give* in the sort. Usually, this is not a problem. Students learn early on that all words do not follow a particular pattern, but they also learn that most words do. They learn, that is, that a lot of words follow the *i*-consonant-*e* pattern with a long vowel sound, that a few follow the *-igh* pattern with a long vowel sound, and that a very few (such as *give*) follow the *i*-consonant-*e* pattern with a short vowel sound. It is important for students to pronounce each word as they look at it, so that they focus not only on the spelling pattern but on spelling and sound.

   c. After students are familiar with the single category and the miscellaneous column, initiate two-category sorts. For example, establish a long *i* column, a short *i* column, an "other" *i*-spelling column, and a miscellaneous column, as below.

hide	*dig*	*pink*	Miscellaneous (blank card)
time	this	think	first
slide	hiss	ink	been
drive	drip		
night	chin		
light	with		
child	kick		

d. Notice that, so far, the categories are global — long, short, other. The next step is to set up categories *within* each of these global categories. For example, the long *i* category can be differentiated into *i*-consonant-*e*, -*igh*, *i*-consonant-consonant (f*i*nd, w*i*ld, ch*i*ld), consonant-*y* (m*y*, fl*y*).

Other productive sorts involve different vowel letters that follow the same spelling pattern (for example, t*i*me versus g*a*me). Note again the *oi* versus *oy* sample word sort above (page 427). Through such sorts, students learn the effect of position on sound, and they discover the logic that underlies some apparent exceptions. By comparing words that end like *grave* and *love*, for example, they will realize that in fact no word in English ends simply in the letter *v*. The reason for this lies in the history of the spelling system; let your students investigate this particular mystery!

Whenever you believe the students are ready, initiate an "open" sort. Of course, it should be clear at first that the categories have to be based on spelling, but later the possibilities can be opened up to spelling, semantic features, and syntactic categories (see Chapter 11).

3. Earlier we discussed several meaningful activities that explore the meaning and spelling of words. These are also effective in developing vocabulary: analogies, figurative language (similes and metaphors), antonyms and synonyms, denotative and connotative meanings, and definition (making discriminative responses as well as using the words meaningfully in a composition).

■ Build Your Teaching Resources

Sources for Word Categorization Activities

The following sources offer comprehensive treatments of word-sort sequencing, activities, and monitoring:

Barnes, W. (1989). Word sorting: The cultivation of rules for spelling in English. *Reading Psychology, 10,* 293–307.

Henderson, E. (1990). *Teaching spelling.* Boston: Houghton Mifflin.

Morris, D. (1982). Word sort: A categorization strategy for improving word recognition ability. *Reading Psychology, 3,* 247–259.

Informal Spelling Instruction

In a broad sense, of course, whenever you draw attention informally to a word or words and talk about them, you are informally teaching spelling. Children will learn much from these serendipitous, spur-of-the-moment remarks. You can also respond to children's spelling efforts daily in a more systematic way. In Chapter 7 I mentioned that students certainly do not need to be evaluated on every spelling effort in every bit of writing they do. You can, however, point out and give feedback about spelling at appropriate times and for appropriate errors. Here's an example based on Figure 10.9.

CLASSROOM EXAMPLE

The second grade teacher is wandering the classroom to help as needed while most of the students are writing. She notices that Ricky has misspelled a word that he got correct on a spelling test. Kneeling beside Ricky's desk, she first compliments him on how he sounded out another word that the class hasn't yet studied; the word is *castle* and he's spelled it *cacil.* This is an excellent attempt, so this "risk" warrants a positive response. Next, the teacher simply points at *whar,* Ricky's misspelling of *where.* Earlier in the year he had gotten the word correct on a spelling test, so he should be held accountable for the correct spelling in his writing. Usually, the teacher's pointing is all that is required for Ricky to realize his misspelling. If, however, this doesn't register, then the teacher writes the word *there* on a separate piece of paper, points to it, points back to *whar,* and waits to see whether Ricky will make the connection. He does, and the teacher's impromptu lesson is finished.

What the teacher has done in this case is remind Ricky through the process of *analogy* that he does in fact know the spelling of that particular word. This type of on-line teaching is so valuable; it takes just a few seconds and it reminds students at the critical moment that they should apply the knowledge they show on the weekly spelling tests in real writing.

This type of informal response, by the way, does not usually dampen the creative sparks. It should be avoided with most first-graders, but most second-graders and older students can benefit from such occasional feedback. The students will see that learning about words also happens outside specified instructional blocks. They will pick up on your ongoing interest in words, which will help to kindle their own excitement — the all-important attitude variable in word learning!

Henderson (1985) perhaps best summed up the proper perspective on spelling that teachers can model for elementary students: "Those who set out to remember every letter of every word will never make it. Those who try to spell by sound alone will be defeated. Those who learn how to 'walk through' words with sensible expectations, noting sound, pattern and meaning relationships will know what to remember, and they will learn to spell English" (Henderson, p. 67).

A CONCLUDING PERSPECTIVE

Word study and word knowledge are multifaceted. At the very least, we now understand that children do not learn words as discrete, unrelated items. Like the concepts for which they stand, words are understood in relation to one another. We should think about vocabulary development as a process of elaborating and expanding these underlying concepts and the words that represent them. In contrast with years past, we now see that spelling development is closely tied to vocabulary development, especially in the intermediate school years.

The chapter began by placing vocabulary study in proper perspective in the overall language arts curriculum. Wide and frequent reading will help students at all grade levels expand their vocabulary, but in addition new words can and should be addressed and taught directly. The foundation for the way this may be done was laid and subsequently built on throughout the chapter.

We next addressed vocabulary development in the primary grades, emphasizing the importance of meaningful experiences accompanied by appropriate and timely oral language. We saw how sight or recognition vocabulary grows as a result of lots of reading and writing and through word-sort activities that focus on semantic features and on spelling features.

Vocabulary development in the intermediate grades is nourished by awareness and understanding of the morphemic elements that combine to form English words: affixes and word stems (word roots and combining forms). We explored the role of etymology and examined ways to teach the Indo-European, Greek, and Latin historical roots of words. Students will be interested in seeing how the meaning of words can change over time and in learning how to decipher the etymological clues in dictionaries. In addition, teachers can aid the development of content-related vocabulary by thoughtfully selecting, presenting, and reinforcing terms that students should attend to in their reading and writing and by modeling the use of the dictionary in checking meaning.

Knowing the categories we use to talk about words — synonyms, denotation and connotation, similes and metaphors, and homonyms, antonyms, and analogies — can help students develop their vocabulary. If we play our instructional cards wisely, this multifaceted approach to learning about words will draw students toward an appreciation not only of a word's underlying concept but also of the precision and beauty inherent in the relationship between a word's parts and a word's history.

Finally, we looked at the nature of the spelling system and the developmental sequence by which elementary students learn the system. Based on this theoretical and research foundation, we discussed formal and informal teaching applications. We saw that spelling study reinforces word knowledge in general as it is applied in reading and in writing. In the intermediate grades, spelling and vocabulary become intertwined through the "spelling-meaning connection," in that students recognize that words related in meaning share similar spellings. This visual preservation of meaning becomes a strategy for spelling words correctly and for expanding vocabulary knowledge.

REFERENCES

American Heritage Dictionary: College Edition (2nd ed.). Boston: Houghton Mifflin.

Anders, P., & Bos, C. (1986). Semantic feature analysis: An interactive strategy for vocabulary development and text comprehension. *Journal of Reading, 29,* 610–616.

Anderson, R. C., & Freebody, P. (1981). Vocabulary knowledge. In J. T. Guthrie (ed.), *Comprehension and teaching: Research reviews.* Newark, DE: International Reading Association.

Anderson, R. C., Hiebert, E. H., Scott, J., & Wilkinson, I. (1985). *Becoming a nation of readers.* Washington, DC: National Institute of Education, U.S. Department of Education.

Barnes, W. (1989). Word sorting: The cultivation of rules for spelling in English. *Reading Psychology, 10,* 293–307.

Bean, W., & Bouffler, C. (1987). *Spell by writing.* Portsmouth, NH: Heinemann.

Beers, J. W., & Henderson, E. H. (1977). A study of developing orthographic concepts among first graders. *Research on the Teaching of English, 11,* 133–148.

Beck, I., Perfetti, C., & McKeown, M. (1982). Effects of long-term vocabulary instruction on lexical access and reading comprehension. *Journal of Educational Psychology, 74,* 506–521.

Blachowicz, C. (1986). Making connections: Alternatives to the vocabulary notebook. *Journal of Reading, 29,* 643–649.

Carr, E., & Wixson, K. (1986). Guidelines for evaluating vocabulary instruction. *Journal of Reading, 29,* 588–595.

Chomsky, C. (1970). Reading, writing, and phonology. *Harvard Educational Review, 40,* 287–309.

Chomsky, C. (1979). Approaching reading through invented spelling. In L. B. Resnick & P. Weaver (eds.), *Theory and practice in early reading* (Vol. 2), pp. 43–65. Hillsdale, NJ: Lawrence Erlbaum Associates.

Dale, E., O'Rourke, J., & Bamman, H. (1971). *Techniques of teaching vocabulary.* Palo Alto, CA: Field Educational Publications.

DeStefano, P., & Haggerty, P. (1985). Teaching spelling at the elementary level: A realistic perspective. *The Reading Teacher, 38,* 373–377.

Egan, K. (1987). Literacy and the oral foundations of education. *Harvard Educational Review, 57,* 445–472.

Fitzsimmons, R. J., & Loomer, B. M. (1974). *Improved spelling through scientific investigation.* Des Moines and Iowa City, IA: Iowa State Department of Public Instruction and Iowa Center for Research in School Administration, University of Iowa.

Gamberg, R., Kwak, W., Hutchings, M., & Altheim, J. (1988). *Learning and loving it: Theme studies in the classroom.* Portsmouth, NH: Heinemann.

Geller, L. (1985). *Wordplay and language learning for children.* Urbana, IL: National Council of Teachers of English.

Gentry, J. R. (1982). An analysis of developmental spelling in "GYNS AT WRK." *The Reading Teacher, 36,* 192–200.

Gentry, J. R. (1987). *SPEL is a four-letter word.* Portsmouth, NH: Heinemann.

Gillet, J., & Kita, J. (1979). Words, kids, and categories. *The Reading Teacher, 32*(5), 155–175.

Graves, D. (1983). *Writing: Teachers and children at work.* Exeter, NH: Heinemann.

Graves, M. (1987). The roles of instruction in fostering vocabulary development. In M. G. McKeown & M. E. Curtis (eds.), *The nature of vocabulary acquisition.* Hillsdale, NJ: Lawrence Erlbaum Associates.

Hanna, P. R., Hanna, J. S., Hodges, R. E., & Rudorf, E. (1966). *Phoneme-grapheme correspondences as cues to spelling improvement.* Washington, DC: U.S. Government Printing Office.

Heard, G. (1989). *For the good of the earth and sun: Teaching poetry.* Portsmouth, NH: Heinemann.

Heimlich, J., & Pittelman, S. (1986). *Semantic mapping: Classroom applications.* Newark, DE: International Reading Association.

Henderson, E. H. (1981). *Learning to read and spell: The child's knowledge of words.* DeKalb, IL: Northern Illinois University Press.

Henderson, E. H. (1985). *Teaching spelling.* Boston: Houghton Mifflin.

Henderson, E. H. (1990). *Teaching spelling.* Boston: Houghton Mifflin.

Henderson, E. H., & Beers, J. W. (eds.). (1980). *Cognitive and developmental aspects of learning to spell English.* Newark, DE: International Reading Association.

Henderson, E. H., & Templeton, S. (1986). The development of spelling ability through alphabet, pattern, and meaning. *Elementary School Journal, 86,* 305–316.

Hillerich, R. (1977). *Spelling.* Columbus, OH: Merrill.

Hodges, R. E. (in press). The conventions of writing. In J. Flood, D. Lapp, J. Jensen & J. Squire (eds.), *Handbook of research in teaching English language arts.* New York: Macmillan.

Horn, T. D. (1969). Spelling. In R. L. Ebel (ed.), *Encyclopedia of Educational Research.* New York: Macmillan.

Johnson, D., & Pearson, P. D. (1984). *Teaching vocabulary.* New York: Holt, Rinehart, and Winston.

Juster, N. (1961). *The phantom tollbooth.* New York: Harper and Row.

Kamii, C., & Randazzo, M. (1985). Social interaction and invented spelling. *Language Arts, 62,* 124–133.

Marzano, R. J., & Marzano, J. S. (1988). *A cluster approach to elementary vocabulary instruction.* Newark, DE: International Reading Association.

Morris, D. (1982). Word sort: A categorization strategy for improving word recognition ability. *Reading Psychology, 3,* 247–259.

Moskowitz, B. (1973). On the status of vowel shift in English. In T. Moore (ed.), *Cognitive development and the acquisition of language.* New York: Academic Press.

Nagy, W. E. (1988). *Teaching vocabulary to improve reading comprehension.* Joint publication by National Council of Teachers of English and the International Reading Association.

Nagy, W., & Anderson, R. C. (1984). How many words are there in printed school English? *Reading Research Quarterly, 19,* 304–330.

Nelson-Herber, J. (1986). Expanding and refining vocabulary in content areas. *Journal of Reading, 29,* 626–633.

Ortony, A. (ed.). (1980). *Understanding metaphor.* Technical report no. 154. Champaign, IL: Center for the Study of Reading, University of Illinois at Urbana-Champaign.

Perfetti, C. (1985). *Reading ability.* New York: Oxford University Press.

Read, C. (1971). Preschool children's knowledge of English phonology. *Harvard Educational Review, 41,* 1–41.

Read, C. (1975). *Children's categorization of speech sounds in English.* Urbana, IL: National Council of Teachers of English.

Read, C., & Hodges, R. (1982). Spelling. In H. Mitzel (ed.), *Encyclopedia of Educational Research.* New York: Macmillan.

Robinson, S. (1989). *Origins.* (Vol. 1: Bringing words to life; Vol. 2: The word families). New York: Teachers and Writers Collaborative.

Stahl, S. (1986). Three principles of effective vocabulary instruction. *Journal of Reading, 29,* 662–668.

Stauffer, R. (1970). *The language-experience approach to the teaching of reading.* New York: Harper and Row.

Schlagal, R. C. (in press). Patterns of orthographic development into the intermediate grades. In S. Templeton & D. R. Bear (eds.), *Developmental orthographic knowledge and the foundations of literacy: A memorial Festschrift for Edmund H. Henderson.* Hillsdale, NJ: Lawrence Erlbaum Associates.

Templeton, S. (1979a). Spelling first, sound later: The relationship between orthography and higher order phonological knowledge in older students. *Research in the Teaching of English, 13,* 255–264.

Templeton, S. (1979b). The circle game of English spelling: A reappraisal for teachers. *Language Arts, 56*(7), 789–797.

Templeton, S. (1980). Young children invent words: Developing concepts of "word-ness." *The Reading Teacher, 33*(4), 454–459.

Templeton, S. (1983). Using the spelling/meaning connection to develop word knowledge in older students. *Journal of Reading, 27*(1), 8–14.

Templeton, S. (1986). Synthesis of research on the learning and teaching of spelling. *Educational Leadership, 43*(6), 73–78.

Templeton, S. (1989). Tacit and explicit knowledge of derivational morphology: Foundations for a unified approach to spelling and vocabulary development in the intermediate grades and beyond. *Reading Psychology, 10,* 233–253.

Templeton, S. (in press). Teaching and learning the English spelling system: Reconceptualizing method and purpose. *Elementary School Journal.*

Templeton, S., & Bear, D. B. (in press). *Developmental orthographic knowledge and the foundations of literacy: A memorial Festschrift for Edmund H. Henderson.* Hillsdale, NJ: Lawrence Erlbaum Associates.

Templeton, S., & Thomas, P. W. (1984). Performance and reflection: Young children's concept of "word." *Journal of Educational Research, 27,* 139–146.

Tompkins, G., & Yaden, D., Jr. (1986). *Answering students' questions about words.* Urbana, IL: National Council of Teachers of English.

Weber, W., & Henderson, E. H. (1989). A computer-based program of word study: Effects on reading and spelling. *Reading Psychology, 10,* 157–171.

White, T. G., Power, M. A., & White, S. (1989). Morphological analysis: Implications for teaching and understanding vocabulary growth. *Reading Research Quarterly, 24*(3), 283–304.

Wilde, S. (1989). A whole language perspective on learning to spell. Paper presented at the annual convention of the National Council of Teachers of English, Baltimore, Maryland, November.

Winner, E. (1988). *The point of words: Children's developmental understanding of metaphor.* Cambridge, MA: Harvard University Press.

Wright, D. (1985). *The Canterbury tales.* (transl.) New York: Oxford University Press.

Zutell, J. (1979). Spelling strategies of primary school children and their relationships to the Piagetian concept of decentration. *Research in the Teaching of English, 13,* 69–80.

CHAPTER

11

The Teaching of Grammar and Handwriting

FOCUSING QUESTIONS

- When and why should you encourage your students to pay attention to grammar and usage?
- What types of instructional strategies and activities best facilitate students' learning about sentence structure; parts of speech; and the appropriateness of dialects?
- How do students learn about mechanics, and what is your role in facilitating this knowledge?
- What is the realistic goal of handwriting instruction?
- How do you address handwriting instruction in an integrated language arts classroom?

Consider the first and last stanza of Lewis Carroll's "Jabberwocky," from Through the Looking-Glass:

'Twas brillig, and the slithy toves
  Did gyre and gimble in the wabe:
All mimsy were the borogoves,
  And the mome raths outgrabe.

Nonsense words, yes, but we can comprehend them to a certain degree because of our tacit knowledge of grammar — how words and phrases are organized within sentences. It is this tacit knowledge upon which we will base much of our instruction in grammar.

Children can develop their own understandings of the function of grammar and punctuation. One third grade pupil reflected on the function of commas *in the following way:*

"If you have a long sentence and you want to keep it there, you put a comma in to take a breath. If you were to make a new sentence, you'd change it up. One example is my last piece of writing. I said, 'We got a little lower and over the beach, I saw tiny colored dots.' Before and after the comma, they are parts of the same sentence. Like the first half of the sentence is one paragraph, and the other half is the second paragraph . . . like two edges of the same idea."*

INTRODUCTION

As we've observed throughout the book, recent developmental research has demonstrated that almost all children can write and that many enjoy writing. Moreover, developing the skills of legible handwriting, correct spelling, and proper punctuation, for example, can be incorporated within a classroom in which good writing is going on. The third grade pupil quoted above was fortunate to be in such a classroom. In classrooms where good writing is going on, creativity in writing is not sacrificed to skills, and skills are not sacrificed to creativity.

In her classic work, *Errors and Expectations,* Mina Shaughnessy observed that "matters like handwriting and punctuation . . . become important, if only because without some measure of ease, without being able to assign some operations to habit, or even to indifference, the novice writer is cut off from thinking" (Shaughnessy, 1977, p. 14). We have seen that, developmentally, children necessarily go through phases during which they attend very much to the mechanics and appearance of their writing. This should not usually be discouraged, for they will grow beyond it in time; it is part of "automating" the habit of writing so that cognitive space can be given over to thinking.

*(Calkins, 1983, p. 36).

Thus, the traditional basic skills are a necessary part of language arts not only because they allow ease of expression but also because they can be invaluable *tools* for thought and expression. For the remainder of this chapter, we will examine when and how to use these tools — and explore ways to awaken in the students themselves an appreciation of their power. Throughout our study of the traditional "basics," we should keep in mind an important observation by the linguist Ronald Wardhaugh: "Children are naturally inquisitive, and it is just as valuable for them to explore their linguistic environment as it is to explore the surrounding fields and woods or streets and stores" (1969, p. 141).

Grammar

Grammar usually refers to study or analysis of the structure of a language — how the words and phrases are organized into sentences. In the case of oral language, students will need to learn about the appropriate use of language in different social situations and contexts and the reasons for paying attention to appropriateness. In the case of written language, students will learn that most grammar and usage issues come into play during the *revising* and *editing* phases of the writing process. As students gradually become more and more familiar with the conventions of grammar and usage, most of these conventions will become automatic. But at some point the "rules" of grammar and usage must be addressed directly, and if you place them in proper perspective — as part of a real social context or as part of the revising and editing phases — then your instruction and students' learning will be relevant and fruitful. Grammar and usage do not exist apart from language as conventions to be studied separately; we attend to them only because we want to fully engage the potential of language. Once we realize how grammar and usage can help us to make meaning — to construct and express our thoughts — more creatively and effectively, then we can appreciate how they contribute to writing that is well received and well considered by readers.

Current textbooks are much better at explaining grammatical concepts than those in years past. Do not assume, however, that you can assign your students a reading on, say, predicate adjectives and trust that they will completely understand the topic. If the concept is important enough to highlight, then it is usually important enough for you first to present and discuss it with your students. You must be familiar with the conventions, vocabulary, and concepts of grammar and usage in order to do this. As with the vocabulary and concepts underlying elementary school mathematics, you must know more than what you will actually teach — you must know what will come later and why.

A Tale of Four Grammars

If you are like most individuals who have grown up going to North American schools, grammar does not top your list of favorite subjects. In fact, grammar is taught all too often as though it were a subject in itself, and although students are told that such study will help their writing, they are given little guidance in learning how this is so. There are reasons for this state of affairs, and they underlie much of what still goes on in schools.

Basically, grammar specifies how the words in a language are arranged in sentences. This notion rapidly becomes complicated, though, when you think about *how* grammar "specifies" the organization of words in sentences. It can do so in a *prescriptive* sense ("This is how a sentence must be arranged"), a *descriptive* sense ("This is what a sentence usually looks or sounds like"), or an *explanatory* sense ("This is what underlies how humans manage to make sentences").

The three major schools of thought about grammar — *traditional, structural,* and *transformational generative* grammar — each correspond to one of these perspectives. Because these three concepts have influenced instruction to various degrees over the years you should be familiar with them and know their advantages and disadvantages. You will encounter them throughout your teaching career in the curriculum and through comments and questions from parents and other members of the lay public. I will also discuss a fourth perspective — case grammar — in this section; although important, it has not yet had a major impact on instruction.

Traditional Grammar

Traditional grammar is still the best known of the three major schools of thought and probably maintains the strongest hold on contemporary practice. Traditional grammar is *prescriptive,* and its roots extend back for centuries. Recall from Chapter 3 that English language scholars once consciously attempted to make English as much like Latin as they could, changing the spellings of a number of words to reflect their presumed Latin origin. They gave this same attention to the grammar or syntax of English, which led to rules and prescriptions for usage such as "Never end a sentence with a preposition" and "Never split an infinitive." These rules are impossible to violate given the structure of Latin, and because Latin was considered the "noblest" language ever created, many scholars thought that English should follow this model. Many of our usage rules today stem directly from this period in the development of the language, as do our labels for parts of speech: nouns, pronouns, adjectives, adverbs, and so forth. The study of traditional grammar involves labeling parts of speech, identifying and labeling types of clauses, and diagramming sentences. Educationally, the assumption is that by studying the proper use of grammar and noting how sentence parts "fit together," students will learn to apply these forms in their own writing.

Structural Grammar

Structural grammar grew out of the predominant linguistic school of the first half of the twentieth century and is best represented in the works of Leonard Bloomfield (1933) and Charles Fries (1940). Rather than prescribing how language *should* work, structural grammarians thought a more realistic approach would be to look instead at how people actually use language. They identified four basic *form classes* of words based on the functions these types of words filled in sentences: nouns, verbs, adjectives, and adverbs are form classes 1, 2, 3, and 4, respectively. In contrast to the traditionalists, who defined *verb,* for example, as a word that names an action, structuralists looked at how words were used in sentences. For example, is the word *stand* a noun (a person, place, or thing) or a verb? The answer, of course, is that you can't know until you see how the word is used in a sentence, such as "*Stand* over there" or "She took a *stand* on that issue."

Structuralists applied certain tests to a word in a sentence to determine its function and form class. Nouns, for example, take only certain suffixes, occur only in certain positions (in a phrase, for example, they usually precede the verb), and are preceded only by certain *determiners* (articles such as *the, a, an;* possessives such as *his, her, their;* and demonstratives such as *this, these, those*). Structuralists also identified certain basic sentence patterns (Malmstrom, 1977). In actual use, however, *transformations* of these basic patterns occur more often.

Transformational Generative Grammar

In part, *transformational generative* grammar (TG grammar) attempts to account for these transformations in sentence patterns. TG grammar looks not so much at the sentence itself as at what must go on in a language user's head that allows him or her to generate sentences. The linguist who has been most influential in developing TG grammar is Noam Chomsky (1957, 1965, 1975). TG grammarians attempt to explain how it is that learners can produce and understand so many utterances that they have never heard before; in effect, TG grammarians attempt to describe the *finite* set of rules by which we are able to generate an *infinite* number of sentences. The theory continues to be formulated by Chomsky and others, but I will address here only those aspects that have most directly influenced language education. I should also mention that, unfortunately, in translating Chomsky's work to the classroom, educators have often misinterpreted much of the theory. At this point, however, it is less important for you to master the intricacies of the theory than to understand its application in the classroom.

TG grammar calls the basic sentence patterns in English *kernel sentences* and describes the transformations that they can undergo as language users move from the initial ideas they wish to express to the resulting spoken or written utterance. This move from idea to expression is referred to as movement from *deep structure* to *surface structure.* Kernel sentences are constructed by some simple rules in the deep structure of language that specify arrangements for elements such as noun phrases and verb phrases; these kernel sentences are then transformed by another set of rules that eventually result in a surface structure characterized by speech or writing. Despite all of the possible surface structures that can be generated with a TG grammar, the actual "core meaning" of many of these sentences may be identical. For example, although the active sentence "Herbie likes pancakes" can be transformed with a passive transformation to "Pancakes are liked by Herbie," the underlying deep structure meaning is the same.

To summarize, deep structure rules apply to the construction of basic, kernel sentences, and transformational rules then operate on these deep structures. TG grammar has directly affected instruction in several areas, including *sentence expansion* and *sentence combining.* We will explore these activities later in this chapter.

Case Grammar

A still more recent grammar, though one that has not yet directly affected instruction, is called *case grammar* (Fillmore, 1968; Chafe, 1971). Interestingly, it underlies much of the recent research in memory and text structure. I mention it here mainly because, contrary to TG grammarians, case grammarians believe that how

[handwritten note:]
TG,
Hold a thought in your head.

I like to drink water that is cold. (deep structure)

How many ways can you write this idea. Word "way" a very good

- Do posters and sentence combining & sentence expansion

rences in meaning. For example, ... e sentence, the meaning actually ... liked by Herbie," we are subtly ... ead of Herbie. Case grammarians ... e users' choices to use one type of ... t in grammar, in other words, case ... determines actual language use. ... ations between the verb and the ... the core of the sentence, and all ... ing researchers with a means of ... nships among meaning categories ... ur discussion about the develop- ... r example, the different types of ... e grammarians specify (e.g., agen- ... to the types of actions the young child performs on his or her world — which in turn establish an understanding of relationships that will come to be represented by language.

Teaching Grammar

Recall that in Chapters 2 and 6 we discussed the role and importance of *meta-linguistic awareness*. This type of awareness — thinking about language as an object — continues to develop and must be brought to bear throughout the school years. Certainly, in matters involving dialect and usage, students must be able to step back and think about the form and the context of language.

Keep in mind your rationale for this study and share it with your students: grammar and its vocabulary provide the tools for talking and thinking about language, most often language that is written and read. Attention to matters of usage allows students to learn the conventions of written language. These conventions are not just "nitpicking"; they usually allow the writer to most appropriately construct meaning so the reader will in turn construct text-appropriate meaning without confusion.

I'd like to step back for a moment and place the scope and sequence of grammar instruction within the broad context of language arts education. First, notice that there is a general parallel between the analysis and synthesis of *word* elements and the analysis and synthesis of *sentence* elements. In Chapter 10 we examined the ways in which word elements combine; here we will study the ways in which *sentence elements* combine. Just as we began our examination of word elements by looking at the base word plus simple affixes, we can begin to examine sentence elements by looking at the *subject* (the "base," if you will, or what is being high-lighted) plus the *predicate* (the "affix" that is acting on or saying something about the subject).

Second, recall how children develop in their early writing through the *preliterate* phase (moving from syllabic writing to using primarily consonants) through the *alphabetic* or *letter-name* stage (representing all sounds that they hear). This progression generally recaps the course of Western literacy from "preliteracy" through the alphabetic writing of the Greeks. We noted in Chapters 3 and 6 that young children can attain this level of development by the time they are six years old. Since, as Havelock (1983) and Papandropoulou and Sinclair (1974) observed, reflections on the *syntactic* properties of language and on parts of speech did not historically occur until about 300 years after the emergence of the alphabetic principle, we expect elementary students to begin thinking about syntax very soon after they have acquired the alphabetic principle — what it took classical scholars 300 years to understand!

With the foregoing perspective in mind, we will be examining in this chapter a scope and sequence for grammar, usage, and punctuation study. We know that elementary children can understand grammar if it is presented appropriately and in a meaningful context, but we should also be wary about beginning this instruction too soon. Appendix B can help tell you which conventions of grammar and usage most of your students have at least been exposed to at a particular grade level. Realize that most of these conventions should be mastered by the end of the elementary school years. The scope and sequence we will explore suggests approximately when most children are ready to turn conscious attention to these elements, which are often not labeled by the terms you know (for example, "predicate adjective") but are introduced in context and described in terms familiar to the students.

The logical progression for introducing parts of speech usually follows from the most concrete to the least concrete (and thus more abstract), ending with conjunctions, which have a "meaning" that is quite abstract. The general sequence is (1) proper nouns; (2) common nouns; (3) verbs; (4) adjectives; (5) pronouns; (6) articles or determiners; (7) adverbs; (8) prepositions; and (9) conjunctions. The same holds for introducing the sentence: just as was the case historically, we begin with the straightforward distinction between subject and predicate and become progressively more analytical from that point on.

As you glance over the scope and sequence for grammar, usage, and punctuation, you may be struck by the number of concepts that must be learned. This impression has led many teachers to believe that they must devote most of their language arts time to activities and exercises dealing with these skills. Remember, though, that because you will be involving your students in lots of reading and writing, there will be many opportunities for them to see examples of these concepts in real texts — texts that they read as well as ones that they write. You will teach many of these concepts directly, and you may pull examples from resource texts such as language arts or English texts for independent practice. True awareness and application of the concepts, however, will usually arise from purposeful reading and writing.

Parts of Speech

As with figurative language, the labels for parts of speech provide "handles" that make it easier to talk about words that writers use. When you first introduce these concepts, you may want to use other more familiar labels, such as "naming words" for nouns, "action words" for verbs, and "describing" or "exact" words for adjectives. This way, as we discussed in Chapter 10, the conceptual domain is developed first, and then the terms that represent the concepts are added.

Following is a lesson for introducing and teaching about a specific grammatical element or part of speech — adverbs — to a class of fourth-graders. The basic overall format, structure, and style of this lesson would work for many different grammar lessons. The objectives are to direct students' attention to adverbs so they can learn to identify adverbs as a certain type of element or part of speech, to have students learn the label "adverb," and to help them understand why it is important to understand what adverbs are.

CLASSROOM EXAMPLE

Meeting with a small group, the teacher writes the words *quickly, yesterday,* and *someplace* on the board. He then asks the students to use each word in a sentence, and he writes their sentences down on the board. The students' sentences are:

Tonya ate her lunch *quickly.*
I forgot my homework *yesterday.*
My homework is *someplace* at home in my messy room.

TEACHER: "Let's think about each of the words as they function in your sentences. Take *quickly:* it tells how something happened — in this case, how Tonya ate her lunch. *Yesterday* tells us when something happened — when the homework was forgotten. *Someplace* tells us where something happened — in this sentence, at home.

"Each of our underlined words, then, tells us something about the action in the sentence. What type of word or part of speech expresses *action*? [Students respond, "verbs."] Good. So these underlined words tell us something about the verb — the action.

"Here's the main idea, then, kids: words that tell how, when, or where the action occurs are called *adverbs.* They 'go with' the verb, even though they may be separated from the verb by other words. They are still adverbs because they answer the question how, when, or where.

"So, let's say you're working in a response group and you're giving feedback to your partner. You notice that a couple of sentences are kind of flat — they've got good verbs, but something else is not quite right. Here are a couple of examples. [Puts a transparency of part of a composition on the overhead projector. Two sentences are in brackets, and the teacher directs the students' attention to the first of these.]

"Okay, let's check out this sentence: 'My stomach twisted hard at the sight of the accident.' Now, we'd probably all agree that this sentence is on its way to being quite a strong sentence — it's going to affect the reader. Think about the action, now — the verb — and the word that tells you *how, when,* or *where* about the action. First, which word is the adverb here? [Students respond.] Good! 'Hard' tells us about the action. Does it tell us how the stomach twisted, where it twisted, or when it twisted? [Students respond.] Sure, it tells us *how* it twisted. Is 'hard' the most powerful word here — or is there another adverb the writer could use? Tracey?"

TRACEY: "Well, maybe *sickeningly* would work here?" [Students comment, "Yuck!" "Gross!"]

TEACHER: "Yeah! Judging by some of your reactions, the word *sickeningly* works pretty well here! Are there any others? Mike?"

MIKE: "How about *violently*?"

TEACHER: "Group? What do you think? Do you think *violently* would work? Okay! I think you've gotten the idea." [Proceeds with next sentence in the same fashion, then makes a general comment.]

"Okay, kids, we've got a term we can use to talk about words in our reading and writing that tell us about the verb or action, that tell us how, when, and where the action occurred. If we need feedback about descriptions in our writing or need to *give* feedback, we can use the term 'adverb' instead of having to say the long way, 'the words that talk about the action' — or 'the words that give you a better picture of what's going on.' Do you see how much easier it is just to use the term 'adverb'? The same thing goes when we're impressed in our reading by an author's description of the action; we'll have a label to place on the words that we think describe the verb well."

The teacher follows up with other examples of adverbs as necessary. Usually, if he wants to see how well the students have constructed the concept of adverbs, he asks the students to complete prepared exercises under his supervision, then to complete other exercises independently. For example, he could ask the whole group of students to look over a group of additional sentences, identify the adverb in each and justify their decisions. Then, he could ask them to go off on their own, to check sentences in books — trade books as well as books they have written — and to note the adverbs. The task could be to "find five adverbs that really help you get a good picture of the action that's going on in a sentence." After having the students work in pairs or individually, he would ask the students to come back to the group to share and discuss their adverbs and the sentences in which they were located.

Also, if the teacher is using a language arts series and if he believes it would apply appropriately for this particular concept, then he could use it to follow up the previous lesson. Figure 11.1 shows how one such text introduces adverbs; you can see how the explanation should reinforce well what the teacher has already discussed with the students.

Finally, the teacher reminds the students to keep adverbs particularly in mind in their revising, whether they are working on their own papers or responding to others. The teacher may remind the students, "There are other labels we will be learning about, and they, too, will make it much easier to talk about our writing rather than always having to use a lot of words to refer to what we mean." Emphasizing *revision* provides a more natural and meaningful context for teaching about parts of speech. Using transparencies of students' composi-

FIGURE 11.1

How Adverbs Are Introduced in One Language Arts Text

Source: *Houghton Mifflin English*, Level 4. Copyright © 1990 by Houghton Mifflin Company. Reprinted by permission of Houghton Mifflin Company.

1 | What Is an Adverb?

You know that an adjective is a word that describes a noun or a pronoun. Another kind of describing word is called an adverb. An **adverb** can describe a verb.

Adverbs give us more information about an action verb or a form of the verb *be*. They tell *how, when,* or *where*. Adverbs can come before or after the verbs they describe.

HOW: Maggie typed the letter <u>carefully</u>.

WHEN: <u>Then</u> I sealed the envelope.

WHERE: All the stamps were <u>upstairs</u>.

Study the lists below. They show adverbs that you use often in your writing. Most adverbs telling *how* end with *-ly*.

HOW	WHEN	WHERE
angrily	always	downtown
carefully	finally	inside
fast	often	off
loudly	once	out
quickly	sometimes	there
sadly	then	upstairs

Guided Practice Find the adverb that describes each underlined verb. Does the adverb tell *how, when,* or *where*?

Example: Maggie and I <u>waited</u> inside.   *inside   where*

1. The mail carrier finally <u>arrived</u>.
2. We <u>ran</u> out to meet her.
3. Maggie <u>clapped</u> her hands excitedly.
4. I quickly <u>opened</u> the gold envelope.
5. Then Maggie <u>read</u> the letter.
6. "We won the contest!" she <u>shouted</u> proudly.

 384   Unit 13:   Adverbs

---

tions (as always, with their permission), you and your class can enter into a discussion about more "exciting" or "specific" adverbs. Not all adverbs should be replaced, of course; in fact, strong, well-used adverbs should be acknowledged and discussed at the outset.

❖ ❖ ❖

The preceding example follows rather closely a direct teaching format: the teacher presents the concept and the label, the students have the opportunity to apply this information with the teacher present, and then the students apply it on their own. It is important to remember, however, that your use of this format should be flexible. Whether you follow all or some of these steps depends on the needs of a whole class, a smaller group, or a particular student.

You can reinforce awareness of and knowledge about parts of speech through a number of activities. The ones I suggest here are more like wordplay than instructional activities, which is why they work well.

Expand Your Teaching Repertoire

1. *"Silly Syntax"* In this activity, appropriate for intermediate students, sentences are constructed based on randomly selected words (Kohl, 1981; Moffett and Wagner, 1983). Importantly, the activity also helps students to elaborate their "sentence sense," an understanding of the potential of the sentence as language frame. Here's how it works.

   You set up five piles of blank 3″ × 5″ cards. Each pile is marked by a card with one of the following labels on it:

   article   adjective   noun   verb   adverb

   In the first pile, under the "article" card, place just two cards: *the* and *a.* Fill in the remaining piles by having the students write down any adjectives, nouns, verbs, and so on that they can think of. There should be about twelve cards in each pile. (If there are four players, then each player would think up three adjectives, three nouns, and so on.) Students should not let others see the words they have written. Shuffle the cards and place them face down. Each student then takes a turn successively drawing a card from each pile and reading the resulting sentence. Kohl (1981) commented that "the interest is in the created sentence, not in some final outcome of the game" (Kohl, 1981, p. 56). Students should be amused by the sentences that result and may wish to keep track of them.

   After students are familiar with the format, you may add an additional pile of linking words (*meanwhile, nevertheless, then,* and so forth), and the sentences can be linked together with delightful results. Kohl offers this example of such a sentence:

   The boring dictator spoke curiously,
   Nevertheless the slug attacked inconsiderately,
   While the energetic politician retreated warmly. (Kohl, 1981, p. 56)

2. *Compound Words* Once your students understand the concept of compound words (see Chapter 10), you may strengthen this understanding and reinforce the labels for parts of speech in an activity that generates compound words — some of them real, some of them nonsense, some of them "possible" words that at present do not exist.

   The format of this activity (adapted from Herbert Kohl) is quite simple. Label four columns with the following parts of speech: pronouns and nouns, adjectives, adverbs (and if appropriate, prepositions), and verbs. Then brainstorm with the students to come up with words that fit each category. Here is a sample:

Pronouns/Nouns	Adjectives	Adverbs/Prepositions	Verbs
cat	hard	happily	swim
him	soft	quickly	run
goose	fluffy	in	yell
foot	pretty	softly	slip
fence	green	out	look

First, ask your students to examine the columns to determine whether any existing compound words could be constructed from these lists. They will be delighted to find that, based only on their brainstorming, some real words will usually result, for example, *lookout* and *run-in.*

Second, ask the students to look for words that are close to existing compounds or that could be new compound words in their own right. Here is where the combinations become exciting, instructive, and a bit crazy! Consider the following compounds generated by a group of fifth-graders: *hardfence, slip-in, greencat, yell-quickly, run-out, soft-swim, gooselook, catyell, catlook, catslip, footswim* — their list went on and on. A definition could be written for each word; this in fact is what the above fifth-graders did, assembling a *Dictionary of Words that Almost Exist.* Of course, students can add words to this dictionary that result from other activities — complete with illustrations if they wish! Recall the word-building activities involving stems and affixes in Chapter 10. Be sure, though, that just as with real dictionaries, the part of speech the new word plays is included in the entry!

3. *Word Sorts* Word-building activities (see Chapter 10) can be combined with word sorts. For example, after students combine affixes and word stems and write down resulting words, a follow-up activity could be to have them sort the words according to base word and type of suffix. Here are two examples of word-sort activities:

   a. Using only some of the words generated by the activity on page 397 in Chapter 10, the sorted columns would be as follows.

respect			respectful .
predict	prediction		
reject	rejection		
contract	contraction		
import			importable/importation
subtract	subtraction		
transgress		transgressor	transgression
predict	prediction	predictor	
retract	retraction	retractor	

You could discuss these words in a number of ways. Let's assume that you have already gone over how the meanings of the words in the first column result from the combination of the word stem and prefix. The next step is to talk about those features that the words have in common: students may suggest suffixes, number of syllables, "hard-to-read" words (!), and so on, and you will accept all of these. You will keep challenging the students, however, until you elicit the idea of a common *function* that each of the words in a particular column serves.

For example, you will guide your students to see that, in the first column, all of the words have to do with an action of some type; then you may ask, "And what label or term do we give to words that show *action*?" (You should get a chorus of "Verbs!") In the second column, you may point out that all of the words have to do with the *result* of that action; when these words are placed in sentences their function will be that of nouns. In the third column, each of the words has to do with the person or thing that performs the action: a *transgressor* is one who transgresses; a *retractor* is someone or something that retracts. Again, you may explain, these are nouns. You and your students can discuss the few remaining words in the same way, in terms of their function, and then determine which part of speech they are.

The obvious next step in this type of word sort is to have the students come up with a generalization about the part of speech in each column based on the suffixes. Ask them, for example, "If you have a base that ends with the suffix *-ion* (or *-or* or *-ful*), what part of speech is the word likely to be?"

b. To give you a slightly different angle on the potential of word sorts, this setup allows students to determine *inductively* how to write possessive forms. You can label the columns, and then ask your students to sort words under the appropriate heading.

Singular	*Singular Possessive*	*Plural*	*Plural Possessive*
turtle	turtle's	turtles	turtles'
woman	woman's	women	women's
mouse	mouse's	mice	mice's
boy	boy's	boys	boys'
state	state's	states	states'
country	country's	countries	countries'

Note that the different patterns within the plural and the plural-possessive categories could be further partitioned. Most of the time, for example, the plural is formed by adding *s,* but sometimes, as in the case of *mice* and *women,* the plural indication is *within* the word; at other times a *y* must be changed to *ie* before the *s* is added (note how this overlaps with spelling study!).

4. *Grammatical Terms: What's in a Name?*   By engaging in this activity, your students will come to better understand the *meanings* of the terms for parts

of speech and will therefore be able to use them more fluently and fluidly. Analyzing the grammatical terms themselves will overlap effectively with your students' exploration of structural analysis. For fun, you can do this with intermediate students after they have been playing with affixes and stems for a while.

- *Pronoun* comprises a prefix, *pro,* plus the base, *noun.* Together they mean "standing in for (*pro*) the *noun.*"
- *Adjective* is made up of *ad-* ("to" or "toward") plus the stem *-ject-* ("thrown"). An adjective is a word that is "thrown toward" (that "goes with") another word — specifically, a noun.
- *Adverb,* just like *ad*jective, is a word that goes "to or toward" (i.e., goes with) the verb.

Here are some terms that we haven't directly discussed:

- A *preposition* is "positioned" *pre-* ("before") the phrase that it usually introduces.
- An *interjection* is "thrown" (*-ject*) "between" (*inter*) sentences.
- And how about *antecedent*? Combining the prefix *ante* ("before") with the word root *-ced-* ("to go") we get "to go before," which of course is the antecedent's role; it is the noun that has gone before the pronoun that refers to it.

5. *Poetry*   Remember that poetry is an extremely effective means of developing awareness of parts of speech as well as reinforcing this knowledge. Although you would probably not highlight grammar as the main focus in any poetry activity, you may refer to it in passing, and occasionally organize a form around it. The *diamante* form presented in Chapter 7, for example, is constructed partly by means of the labels *nouns, adjectives, participles.*

Noun
adjective, adjective
three participles
four nouns having to do with the subject
three participles
adjective, adjective
Noun

Recall that the diagonal in the third line indicates the point at which a contrast may be set up. A small group or whole class could create a diamante. It would begin almost as a free association, with a sense of topic and direction emerging by the third line. As students explore poetry further, they will appreciate the value of knowing the "vocabulary" of grammar as they create and respond to poetry. This metalanguage provides a means of discussing language — the "poet's paint."

Sentences

Recall our discussion in Chapters 6, 8, and 10 about the importance of studying words out of context, so that their structure becomes familiar and the students' recognition is almost automatic. The same is true for syntax. By having intermediate students attend to and manipulate phrases, we are helping them develop more automatic responses to the different structures they encounter in their reading and will employ in their writing. In this regard, Strong (1986) commented, "By attending to words, we gradually increase our naturalness in writing and reading until encoding/decoding processes are almost fully automatic and accomplished without conscious attention to syntax" (Strong, 1986, p. 3).

Much of the value of work with sentences lies in the critical thinking and reasoning skills it calls upon. Your attention to the parts of sentences and how they expand and combine will provide your students with important labels that they can use in responding to one another's writing during the revision stage. At first, you may need to meet with the whole class or small groups two to three times per week, directly discussing sentence structure; with time, meetings can drop to perhaps once a week.

Of course, reading provides the best models of varied sentence constructions. This is true of reading the children do themselves and, importantly, read-alouds by the teacher. As we saw in Chapter 5, these read-alouds "feed in" language and structure just beyond the point the children are in their own natural development. Given such immersion, many students spontaneously attempt to stretch themselves in their writing. We support this stretching and encourage other students to try it. Our only exception is with first-graders, who, for the most part, should simply be encouraged to keep the writing coming, usually without much concern for content and form.

The following developmental sequence for examination of sentences fits well with the progression from the concrete to abstract and aligns with elementary students' growing language competence and ability to reflect on language (Loban, 1976; Shaughnessy, 1977). First students develop a *concept of a sentence*. We know students have acquired this concept when they write according to basic convention and read a sentence with natural intonation. Not surprisingly, much of this understanding is tacit, but there is strong support for this underlying concept (deBeaugrande, 1985; Perfetti, 1985). As deBeaugrande observed, "Sentence boundaries often function as conceptual boundaries as well" (deBeaugrande, 1985, p. 67).

Next, students consciously attend to the *order of words* in sentences and then to the basic *subject-predicate* division. In fact, the subject-predicate distinction was the first syntactic distinction that the classical grammarians made; the subject is a "topic," and the predicate is a "comment" about that topic. In a sentence, then, you are highlighting something (the subject) and saying something about it (the predicate).

The next major step involves recognizing specific subjects and predicates in simple sentences, then expanding these kernel sentences. Later, students create still longer sentences by means of their increasingly sophisticated language facility. Along the way students note how words and phrases get attached to or embedded in kernel sentences and eventually learn how to link sentences together with logical connectives. It is also during this period — in fifth and sixth grade, for most

As students learn about sentence formation, they are reflecting upon how ideas are related; this deeper-level reasoning is really a form of critical thinking. (© Elaine Rebman/Photo Researchers)

children — that the complexity of students' written sentences can exceed the complexity of their spoken sentences.

Earlier in this chapter, where I discussed the four different grammars, I mentioned that the effects of transformational generative grammar have been most pronounced in writing instruction — specifically of sentence expansion and sentence combining. TG grammar provided the theoretical foundation for such instruction and prodded many language arts educators to look more closely at how we could develop students' abilities in this area (Hunt, 1963; Mellon, 1969). In the rest of this section, we'll look at how we can do this at the primary and intermediate levels.

Sentence expansion and *sentence combining* are two strategies for developing students' progressively more fine-tuned attention to thought and expression. For many students in second grade and most students in third grade and up, actively expanding sentences — really, expanding *thought* — is very beneficial work. Students further this skill by combining sentences: uniting whole sentences rather than simply building within them. Expanding and combining phrases in sentences helps to expand and elaborate thinking, since every manipulation brings about a different juxtaposition of ideas.

Sentence Expansion The basic strategies presented here for developing sentences in writing are equally applicable for primary and intermediate grades. An excellent activity for second and third grade students is *sentence building*. After introducing the format with a small group, have the students work in pairs. They can start with a simple sentence, and take turns adding on words. For example:

Susan likes okra.
In the summer Susan likes okra.
In the afternoon in the summer Susan likes okra with her family.
In the afternoon in the summer Susan likes okra and cornbread
with her family and her friends.
etc.

The object of this activity is obviously not to craft superb sentences but to show students how to construct sentences by adding on ideas. Later you will help them fine-tune their ideas in the context of purposeful writing. For now, sentence building is an excellent way to help primary children develop a basic concept of a sentence and become consciously aware of the potential of sentences.

Once students grasp the concept of a sentence and have a notion of word order, they can take the next step in sentence awareness: understanding the split between the subject and predicate (or, synonymously, the noun phrase and verb phrase). Developing this understanding first involves simply talking about how well the complete subject is described. For example, instead of just saying "my dog," students may think about giving a little more information about the dog: What color is he? How big? Is he friendly? In a rich literature environment, such questions in response groups will eventually lead to expanded subjects such as "My big, brown dog" and "My friendly brown dog." The expansion of complete predicates or verb phrases is similarly accomplished: Did your dog run quickly? Where did he run? Why? Many of your students may begin to expand both complete subjects and complete predicates at roughly the same time. This is great.

It is quite normal for students to take us literally when we talk about making our sentences grow. Many will write an entire composition in one or two sentences, with phrases linked by *and*. This is a suitable time to talk about breaking up the writing by taking out the "ands." (I address this type of issue later in the section on punctuation.)

As primary students gain more understanding of and control over sentence parts and become sensitive to appropriate word choice, they can benefit from actively manipulating phrases (Moffett and Wagner, 1983; Temple and Gillet, 1989). Holding large pieces of tagboard with phrases written on them, students shift their phrases around in front of the class or a smaller group. The students can literally see how many ways in which the phrases can be combined; this can develop a good sense of the *moveability* of phrases in English. For example, start with no more than three phrases on separate pieces of tagboard, such as

through the gate   **Brian rode**   **on his bike**

In a subsequent exercise, supply more than three phrases, such as

behind the garage   **before daylight**   **five cats**
had a fight   **because they weren't friends**

Of course, there will be many possible combinations. Discuss them with the students, focusing on why some are quite good, others not good at all, and still others somewhere in between. Discuss the different sense or meaning that different arrangements convey.

Sentence Combining   By itself, *sentence combining* cannot teach writing, but it can be a powerful support in writing instruction. Moreover, it can "provide a practical way of activating playful attention to written language" (Strong, 1986, p. 2).

When you introduce sentence combining, begin with short, kernel sentences. You can choose them from the students' writing, from textbooks or other nonfiction books, from fiction, or you may construct them yourself. If you choose the latter option, use the students' names — this is always a powerful motivator.

In the following classroom example, we eavesdrop on a teacher who has already introduced sentence combining to his class and who now happens to be discussing an author's descriptive language with his students. As the lesson progresses, however, he recognizes a "teachable moment" and alters his plan so that he focuses on sentence combining within the context of the original lesson. He uses sentence examples that he had already prepared for a future lesson.

CLASSROOM EXAMPLE

A group of sixth grade students has been reading Susan Cooper's fantasy, *Over Sea, Under Stone,* the first in a series of five fantasies centered in England and Wales. The fantasies become more believable and chilling because they arise out of everyday life in which evil is seen to lurk in ordinary places and people.

On this particular day, the follow-up questions the teacher has given to the group for discussion focus on how Cooper manages to draw the reader or listener into the world of the book and feel the terror of true evil. [Cooper is masterful at this, and the teacher's objective is to lead the students toward an awareness and appreciation of how Cooper uses language to describe sinister and evil entities and situations.] As we enter the classroom, the teacher has just joined a small literature-response group for a group conference (see Chapter 9).

The students are asked to share the examples they found; the teacher intends to question them further. Following are two passages from *Over Sea, Under Stone:*

And then, like the sudden snapping of a bow, the noise came.

Into the air over their heads, a dog howled: a long weird note so unexpected and anguished that for a moment they all stopped dead. It echoed slow through the harbour, a freezing inhuman wail that had in it all the warning and terror that ever was in the world. (p. 196)

The tall dark figure stopped abruptly, completely still, with its back still turned. For a moment there was absolute silence in the room. It was as if Barney had pressed a switch that would any moment bring an avalanche thundering down. He sat motionless and almost breathless in his chair. Then very slowly the figure turned. Barney gulped, and felt a prickling at the roots of his hair. Mr. Hastings was at the darker end of the room, near the door, and his face was hidden in shadow. But he seemed to loom taller and more threatening than he had ever done before, and when he spoke there was a different throb in the deep voice that paralysed Barney with fright. "You will find, Barnabas Drew," it said softly, "that the dark will always come, and always win."

Barney said nothing. He felt as if he had forgotten how to speak, and his voice had died for ever with his last words. (pp. 192–193)

The group discusses Cooper's choice of particular words or expressions to achieve her effect, such as "freezing inhuman wail," "prickling at the roots of his hair," "throb in the deep voice," and "the dark will always come, and always win."

A student comments that Cooper seems to "pack a lot" into her descriptions without going on and on. The teacher senses a productive idea germinating, so he pursues it.

TEACHER: "How does she manage to do that, Angela? Any ideas?"

ANGELA: "I think by the words she chooses, probably, just like we've been talking."

TEACHER: "Is it just the words themselves, do you think, or how she *combines* the words?"

ANGELA: "Hmm . . . they seem to fit together well . . ."

TEACHER: "How 'bout the rest of you guys? Let's think about her *sentences* . . . In these passages are they short, staccato-like, or longer?"

CLASS: "Longer!"

TEACHER: "Yeah . . . Let's look at the *ideas* she's expressing and see how she has combined them in these sentences. For example, let's take the sentence 'It echoed slow through the harbour, a freezing inhuman wail that had in it all the warning and terror that ever was in the world.' She really grabs you with that one, doesn't she? But there are a number of ways she could have expressed the idea, and she chose this way for maximum effect.

"First, think about her ideas: She's got this sound echoing through the harbor, it's echoing slowly, she says it's freezing, it's inhuman, it is a wail, it has warning in it, terror in it, and that this warning and terror is as much as was ever in the world. Wow! Let's see . . . that's at least eight separate ideas. She could have written this in separate sentences, like 'The sound was freezing and inhuman. It was a wail. It had all the warning and terror that was ever in the world.' Hmmm . . . is that as effective as the original? No? Why not?"

JUSTIN: "It kind of rolls along, the way she's got it . . . you kind of get this feeling all in one piece."

TEACHER: "That's a fascinating way to put it, Justin. I see by the other nodding heads we agree. She's combined or wrapped up some very effective words and phrases within *one* sentence that really grabs us.

"You know, when we think about having this kind of effect in our writing, we experiment with different ways of organizing the ideas. Remember when I talked to you and you practiced *sentence combining* last week? That's what we're getting at here — once we've selected the words that we want to represent our ideas, we still need to think about how to combine them to best express what we mean. Take the line Mr. Hastings says: 'The dark will always come, and always win.' Susan Cooper could have combined her ideas and said 'the dark will always come and win,' but it just wouldn't have the same effect as you get with the repetition of *always*.

"We don't have to figure all this out all at once, of course. In our first draft we just get it down, and later we can play with fine-tuning our word choice and setting up our sentences. I'd be surprised if Susan Cooper wrote these passages just this way the first time!"

[After the group has finished discussing Cooper's use of language, the teacher feels he could take the opportunity (this "teachable moment") for a brief mini-lesson on sentence combining to better "concretize" what they had been discussing.]

TEACHER: "Okay, guys, we've commented on how Cooper has a way of crafting her sentences to give us a powerful mental picture of what she's describing.

"Let's think about this sentence-combining business some more. I'm going to start with a way that you already know — but I'm doing it to make sure we all understand the strategy. Then we'll move to a more challenging strategy." [Displays the following on an overhead and takes a felt transparency marker in hand.]

Jerry plays soccer.
Jerry plays basketball. (<u>and</u>)

TEACHER: "These two sentences can be combined into one shorter sentence that doesn't repeat the same information. Watch how I use this information [points to the sentences] to combine them. [Writes *Jerry plays soccer.*] Now, I'm going to use this word [points to *and*] as my cue to combining 'Jerry plays basketball' with 'Jerry plays soccer.' I think about how I can use this cue to *combine* these sentences and not make them repeat the same information — in other words, I don't want to have to use 'Jerry plays' more than once!" [After *Jerry plays soccer* the teacher writes *and basketball.*]

"Now, I know you could have combined these sentences on your own, just the way I did, so that you come up with a shorter sentence that does not repeat information: 'Jerry plays soccer and basketball.' But remember I want you to pay attention to *how* I'm doing it, because I'm going to use this way of presenting sentences and cues when we discuss other ways of combining sentences. Let's go back over what I did: I was given two sentences [pointing] and a *cue* [points to the word *and*]. Remember, whenever you have a cue in this type of activity, it will be placed *after* the sentence in which it will be used.

"Now, whenever we do this type of activity you must be sure to read each sentence and think about how you can use the cues that are given to combine the sentences. Let's try a more challenging type of combination." [Displays the transparency with the following sentences on it:]

Kerry is eating beets.
The beets are <u>tasty</u>.
The beets are her favorite vegetable. (*that*)

Here's a way to adapt an excellent suggestion for acquiring a store of sentences you can draw on for your activities (Strong, 1986). As you go over students' compositions for purposes of evaluation, mark off with parentheses sentences that could benefit from more work. These sentences usually do not reflect the grade you assign, but they do indicate the next step your students may be ready to take in their examination of sentences and their growth in syntactic maturity. Tell the students this is your purpose, and then ask them to copy the sentence or sentences you have marked onto 3″ × 5″ cards. You can keep these on file for later use.

"We all know how much Kerry loves her beets! (As you might expect, Kerry is squinching up her face.) Anyway, let's look carefully at the sentences and the cues we're going to be working with here. [Reads the sentences.] Now, we've got two cues here that we are going to use in combining these three sentences into one sentence. Our first cue is an underlined word, *tasty,* and our second cue is the word *that.* You are going to use your cues in the order in which they are given. First I'll work on bringing together the first two sentences using *tasty* as my cue. [Writes *Kerry is eating tasty beets* on the transparency.] Do you see that by putting the adjective *tasty* before *beets* I can give exactly the same information in a shorter, tighter way than by using two sentences in which the information is repeated?

"I'm not finished, though. I still need to combine the information in this last sentence with what we've already got, but I've got the cue, *that,* to help me here. Thinking how I can use it, I'm going to finish the combined sentence this way . . ." [After *Kerry is eating tasty beets* he writes *that are her favorite vegetable.*]

"The different cue here was the underlined word *tasty.* When you have an underlined word as a cue, that means you will insert that word somewhere in the sentence you are already working on. Whenever you have our other cue [pointing to *that*] it means you will be using the cue to link another sentence onto the one you're already working with. Apply your cues in this order.

"There are usually many ways that sentences can be combined, and we're going to be playing around with a lot of them this year. This will help you think more precisely during revision about how you can craft your sentences, just as Susan Cooper did in the examples you found."

[At this point, if time allows, the teacher might have the students work with sentences he provides and be available to give feedback. If necessary, this would be followed by some additional sentences that the students would work on independently.]

Remember, it is important to follow up on this direct presentation by referring to it when appropriate in the context of real writing. Once the students are using

One aspect of grammar instruction that is both controversial and still widely used is the diagramming of sentences. Sentence diagramming may eventually fade entirely out of language arts instruction, at least at the intermediate grade level, but you will probably still encounter it in the near future. Diagramming can be a lot of fun for students who enjoy it and who are good writers. For students who don't like it, whether they are good writers or not, diagramming is drudgery and is counterproductive (Hillocks, 1986).

There is no evidence that diagramming sentences will make good writers out of less able writers; diagramming certainly does not help these students develop a positive attitude toward writing. Diagramming should probably be an elective rather than an assigned activity. Most elementary English or language arts basals have a section about sentence diagramming, usually in an appendix, and interested students can use that as their guide. They may even be intrigued by an activity my sixth grade teacher cooked up (although her primary purpose was to keep us busy, in our seats, and quiet): to diagram the preamble to the U.S. Constitution, one of the most famous lengthy sentences in the English language.

The bottom line in all teaching about sentences, however, is this: you should feel assured that the type of interplay I've described among direct teaching, reading, writing, and discussing sentences usually will provide a solid foundation for your students' growth in syntactic maturity — and with that maturity comes, of course, growth in thought.

---

the cues comfortably, then you can present sentences without cues and have the students work with them. Because everyone is an "author" in the classroom, you should capitalize on particularly effective sentences that the students craft themselves by examining and discussing them. You can also take particular sentences from the reading students are doing and discuss their structure. This can include breaking the sentences down into their constituent kernel sentences, which can impress students with the number of ideas that can be expressed in a single sentence. Finally, take care to engage in these sorts of exercises only enough to sustain interest and meet your objective; as with any such activities, their purpose should clearly support actual writing and reading and not become an end in itself.

■ Build Your Teaching Resources

Practical Information about Sentence Combining

For most students in the intermediate grades, you do not need to present sentence constructions that are more complex than those presented above. If you wish to read further in an immensely practical source for sentence combining, however, I recommend to you

Strong, W. (1986). *Creative approaches to sentence combining.* Urbana, IL: ERIC Clearinghouse on Reading and Communication Skills and the National Council of Teachers of English.

Usage

Usage usually refers to matters of word choice and appropriateness — what is preferred in the standard dialect of the language. As students learn the "vocabulary" or metalanguage of grammar, they will find matters of usage easier to discuss. For example, if you are talking about when to use *bad* versus *badly,* it is much easier for you and for the students if you can illustrate your point using the terms *adjective* and *adverb.* Put simply, *bad* is an adjective that refers to the subject of the sentence: "Sherry feels *bad*" (meaning *Sherry* is "not well"). On the other hand, *badly* is an adverb that refers to the verb: "Sherry swims *badly*" (meaning Sherry's *swimming* is "not very good").

By using the terms *adjective* and *adverb,* you can save a lot of time and confusion discussing usage, because the students will think in terms of grammatical categories rather than try to memorize specific examples or instances in which *bad* and *badly* are used. To strengthen their understanding, have the students analyze what a particular sentence means when you use an adverb instead of an adjective, and vice versa: "I feel badly," for example, describes the way in which the subject "I" goes about feeling things!

All writers must refer to a usage guide at some point, usually to settle a question about how to best arrange language according to common standards. It is important for students to realize that, although some usage elements are quite convenient to know automatically, others are considerably less vital. Consulting a usage guide is the best strategy for attending to infrequent usage questions. Basal language arts/English series texts can serve this function — for example, if a student needs to check on the correct use of *lie/lay* in a sentence he or she is writing.

Appendix C presents the common elements of usage that are addressed throughout the elementary grades. When necessary, they should be presented directly and reinforced in the revision and editing phases of writing.

Standard English and Dialects

Probably the most significant aspect of usage is the issue of standard English and variant English dialects. As we have pointed out before, the way we speak — just as the way we dress — projects who we are and gives listeners some basis from which to make judgments, fair or not, about us; that's simply human nature. It's important to help elementary students develop an awareness of the social aspect of speech.

In education, the issue is often framed in terms of "standard" versus "nonstandard" dialect, but in fact it represents a larger question: the *appropriateness* of our speech in the different contexts in which we find ourselves. As teachers, we can address the dialect issue by placing an emphasis on appropriateness. As we saw in Chapter 2, we all adjust our speech depending on the situation and the *pragmatics,* but some of us will have to work on this adjustment more than others, particularly if the dialect of American English that we speak varies significantly from the standard dialect. When we're talking to friends informally, our speech is informal — and the degree of informality can change, too, depending often on whether we are talking to friends who are of the same gender! When we are presenting information in a class, our speech is more formal — although the degree of formality depends on the professor, the course, and so forth — and on our ability to "read" the contextual cues appropriately. Linguists term these different levels of formality and informality *registers*.

You see how complex the situation can get! We all know adults who have never seemed to master the knack of reading contextual cues — the pragmatics — appropriately and who respond in an inappropriate "register." So we must be understanding of our pupils and yet be dedicated to the notion of helping them become aware of different situations, as well as the appropriate response to each one. For most children this process begins in the preschool years with parents' constant prods to say "please" and "thank you." As Elizabeth comments in Elaine Konigsberg's *Jennifer, Hecate, Macbeth, William McKinley, and Me, Elizabeth* (1967), "All my life my mother had taught me a politeness vocabulary. I didn't mind. I thought 'please' and 'thank you' made conversation prettier . . ." Of course Elizabeth and her mother are right; there is an important "politeness vocabulary" that accompanies the "rules" of social interaction.

You are the model. You model appropriate language in different situations, and you model standard English. As we saw earlier, there is no inherent "best" dialect of a language. Standard English is preferred in many situations because it is the dialect that has been spoken by those who have succeeded politically and economically in our society — the reason any dialect becomes preferred. It is the dialect in which much, though certainly not all, of the acknowledged better literature is written. It can certainly be violated in appropriate circumstances, but students had best learn to use it in those situations where other people will make judgments about them as individuals.

Rather than using the term "nonstandard" dialect, most linguists now use *variant* dialect, since it has a less negative connotation. This type of dialect, in other words, varies from standard English, usually in phonology, syntax, and vocabulary. In the best of all possible worlds, every dialect would be equally acceptable in any situation; in the real world, they are not, and it is your responsibility to assist pupils who speak a variant dialect to learn standard English. In so doing, however, realize that you will not be trying to *replace* their native dialect but you will be giving them an additional language skill. In addition to modeling standard English usage, you can involve students in several activities that teach not only standard English but socially appropriate usage as well.

Role Playing

Recall our discussion of creative dramatics in Chapter 5. It provides an excellent vehicle through which language appropriateness can be realized. Have the students role-play different situations: meeting parents' friends, meeting the school principal for the first time, buying a movie ticket, telling a friend about a particularly bothersome habit, attending a formal banquet. If you are working with children who have not been exposed directly to formal social situations, remember that they nevertheless will have some background information to draw upon; you may have to remind them of their background knowledge, but the images will be there to draw upon. You can role-play the situations both ways — as the students believe they ought to be played and, for contrast and fun, as they ought not to be played. These activities can also be excellent stimuli for writing.

Adapted Language Experience Approach

When we discussed the language experience approach (LEA) in Chapter 8, I emphasized the value of writing down *exactly* what the pupils dictate. This is important during the initial stages of LEA, given your focus on developing your pupils' concepts about print and their acquisition of a beginning sight vocabulary. Later on, however, as Gillet and Gentry (1983) suggest, you can adjust the dictated story.

1. As in the usual procedure, write down exactly what the pupils dictate.
2. Later, rewrite their story in standard English. Include most of the words they used, but change the syntax somewhat to allow for longer and/or slightly more elaborate sentences.
3. The next day, after reviewing their original story with them, show them your story. Explain that it is another version of their story. Go over it as you would with their original story — read it yourself and then choral-read it with the students. After they appear comfortable with this second version, have them compare the original with this version. Locate words that are in both stories.
4. This is an optional step. The students may produce a third version of the story, based on their first dictated version. They may work on this in pairs, each attempting to revise their first offering; your instructions should be limited to something like "see if you can say this another way."

    At no point should you make qualitative judgments about either of the first two versions. In their third version, we of course hope the students will include some aspects of the second version, but you should not force the issue if they do not. By gently working with standard English and expanded or elaborated sentences in this fashion — together with exposing students to standard English in other ways every day — you can help children move toward standard English in a nonthreatening fashion.

Read-alouds

You are probably not surprised at this mention, once again, of the value of read-alouds. One of the many values of reading aloud to children is the modeling of standard English usage. Remember that you should also read some books that model variant dialects — a touchy issue with some parents (very often the parents who themselves speak a variant dialect) — but remember that the value of this will lie primarily in two areas. First, the children who speak the variant dialect will have their pride in this dialect reinforced. Second, children who do not speak a variant dialect will learn that other dialects are valued (because they are in books), and they will get a feel for the nuances and expressive power of other dialects.

As Peter Elbow (1985) says, "The ear, in the last analysis, is the most trustworthy and powerful organ for learning syntax; and fortunately it is easiest to teach — as long as we give some time to it" (Elbow, 1985, p. 234). Many of the predictable or pattern books we discussed in Chapters 6 and 8 playfully model the structure, forms, and rhythms of standard English.

Discussion

With intermediate students, you may directly address the social issue of variant dialects and standard English. This explicit treatment often works well with role playing. Rare are the parents who will challenge you on this, but you may encounter some degree of "*I* don't need that" from some students. If you have been raised speaking primarily standard English, the students may (with some justification) challenge your credibility on this issue. For this reason, you will find it extremely helpful to invite to your classroom an adult who has mastered standard English but who can still "talk that talk" with the students. The credibility of *these* adults is unquestionable and they can be a powerful motivating force.

Identify and work on changing specific variant-dialect constructions. Once intermediate students understand the importance of using standard English in certain situations, you can survey their writing for nonstandard constructions. Identify and target for attention during revision and/or editing phases constructions that most obviously run counter to standard English usage. Point these out to each student so that he or she can learn to edit writing for variant constructions. Be sensitive here, because these constructions are perfectly consistent in the context of some variant dialects and form the core of the tacit grammar internalized by variant dialect speakers. Some examples are

Double negatives ("He don't have no . . .")
Redundant subjects ("My daddy *he* . . .")
Subject/verb agreement ("He *ask* can I go . . .")
Use of "to be" in phrases such as "He be goin'." (Interestingly, this use in Black English signals a distinction that standard English does not make: ongoing versus single-instance of behavior.)

Once again, it is important to mention that this process of targeting variant constructions must be kept in perspective; many of these constructions are common and accepted in literature, film, and contemporary music. (I reveled in the double negative myself: inspired by the lyrics coming over the radio, I imitated Elvis, to the chagrin of my primary teachers, and the Rolling Stones, to the chagrin of my high school English teachers!) Even for budding adolescents who come from a standard English background (as many of your fifth- and sixth-graders probably will) these forms are usually a harmless expression of independence from parents, schools, and adult authority. Indeed, these constructions are common among such students because their purpose is to challenge and, in some instances, to outrage. We are not denying students the right to these forms, but we are helping them understand when and where they are acceptable.

Mechanics

Mechanics have to do with capitalization and punctuation as well as matters of convention. As with parts of sentences and parts of speech, you should introduce the elements of capitalization and punctuation in a sequence that moves from concrete to more abstract.

Take *commas,* for example. Their usual function is to mark pauses — usually logical phrases — in written language. To introduce commas by discussing this usual function, however, would be too abstract for most students. Rather, this useful mark is successfully introduced in the more straightforward context of a letter, where it is set off more than it is in a regular sentence. Then, its function in separating items in a series can be explored. The following integrated lesson illustrates an instance of instruction occurring only as the need arises, making the instruction integral to students' use rather than an isolated "tacked-on" skills lesson — which grammar and usage all too often become.

CLASSROOM EXAMPLE

The purposeful context for introducing the form of a *friendly letter* will be a class project involving collecting historical information from grandparents. If the grandparents live a good distance away, then the letter is the best medium for this project — even better than the telephone. In this context the *form* of the friendly letter can be presented and discussed, and simple particulars of the form, such as the comma, can be addressed.

I. Brainstorming

The teacher brainstorms with the students what they'd like to know about when their grandparents were children. The first suggestion is "I'd like to know what it was like!" which is too broad, so the teacher narrows it down: "Think of some *examples* of what you'd like to know about." The students suggest the types of clothes their grandparents wore, the chores they had to do, what they did for play, what it was like without any TV, what school was like, and so forth.

II. Friendly Letters

Once the students have their curiosity aroused through brainstorming, the teacher introduces the friendly letter form, which includes the return address at the top, the greeting, body, and closing. Because most of the students in the class are reading *Sarah, Plain and Tall* by Patricia MacLachlan as a part of the history unit, the teacher takes advantage of the many examples of the friendly letter form in Sarah's letters to the different members of the Witting family.

The students write their first drafts of a letter to their grandparents, including a brief explanation of *why* they are asking for this information. The teacher points out the role of the comma after the greeting and after the closing (before the signature).

III. Commas

In discussions of the first drafts, the teacher notes that many children need to use the comma to separate items in a series (a common instructional objective in third grade). She selects a draft from a student who has used the comma correctly this way, makes a transparency of it, and discusses the use of the comma in a whole-class format. She then pairs up students to work on this; one member has the concept, the other doesn't. The teacher will rely on this "peer-

AT THE
TEACHER'S
DESK:
When
Punctuation
Conventions
Are Violated

What happens when punctuation is not placed where the reader has been taught to expect it? First, recall the "rule" about commas in a series: the last two items in the series are separated by a comma, and the comma comes before the conjunction that connects the items — for example, "Elvin spotted robins, cardinals, and bluejays on his way to school." In effect, what the commas do is give equal attention to each of the items in the series. As readers we thus understand that the items are of equal importance in meaning.

Now consider what happens when this convention is not followed. First, read the final stanza of Robert Frost's poem "Stopping by Woods on a Snowy Evening":

The woods are lovely, dark and deep,
But I have promises to keep
And miles to go before I sleep
And miles to go before I sleep.

Now consider the first line again. Technically, Frost has three items in a series.

But he has not separated the last two with a comma. Why not? This "error" has stirred a bit of debate among scholars, heightened by the question of whether a copy editor inadvertently omitted the comma that Frost had in fact put in the poem. Scholarly debates aside, do you notice what happens when the comma "rule" is not followed? Instead of *lovely, dark,* and *deep* each appearing as separate and distinct qualities, the latter two adjectives now connect to the word *lovely* and act to define the nature of that loveliness.

I raise this issue to make a point: of course, much of punctuation rests on convention — "that's just the way it's done" — but for a very good reason: the writer is given more opportunity to convey precisely the meaning he or she wishes to convey. Students should learn that whenever they violate a rule, they should do so purposefully. Violation of the conventions is allowable if one knows the conventions, but it may not be allowable if one is ignorant of them!

---

teaching" context to teach the concept. (Of course, if the teacher feels the whole-class presentation isn't absolutely necessary, she could skip it.)

Once again, following the guidelines for presenting new concepts and terms, you may find that you can more vividly introduce the concepts of usage by first using simpler terms for the "vocabulary" of mechanics: *capital* letters could become "big letters"; a *compound sentence* could become a "double sentence"; *parentheses* could become "half-moon marks," and so forth. Appendix D presents a suggested scope and sequence for capitalization and punctuation.

Capitalization is a fairly straightforward matter, but punctuation requires more attention, since most of it plays an important part in conveying expression and therefore meaning. Punctuation may best be taught by orally reading sentences and following the directions that the marks indicate. For example, one of the most effective strategies for directing a student's attention to the lack of — or too much — punctuation, is to read through his or her composition "honoring" the punctuation. A long sentence without commas becomes a humorous run-on that ends with a gasping teacher! Follow this up by walking through the composition again, punctuating it as you go. For example, when you get to a point where a comma is required, pause in your reading, write the comma, and continue. This procedure is so natural that, over time, it is relatively easy for the students to internalize it as a strategy. Couple this with reading to the students as they follow along with their own copies of the text, paying particular attention to your use of the punctuation as a guide. This strategy can be reinforced at a listening station, of course.

Before we move on, I'd like to make a point about editing for usage and mechanics. On-line composition requires holding a lot in one's mind; the amount of time that passes between writing the subject and writing the verb may be considerable — especially when a student has a long compound sentence in the works. In the heat of composition, agreement between subject and verb, or pronoun and antecedent, can fall by the wayside. Proofreading, though, can catch these details.

FIGURE 11.2

Presentation of Punctuation in a Language Arts Textbook

Source: *Houghton Mifflin English*, Level 4. Copyright © 1990 by Houghton Mifflin Company. Reprinted by permission of Houghton Mifflin Company.

Punctuation

End marks	**There are three end marks. A *period (.)* ends a statement or a command. A *question mark (?)* follows a question. An *exclamation point (!)* follows an exclamation.** The scissors are on my desk. *(statement)* Look up the spelling of that word. *(command)* How is the word spelled? *(question)* This is your best poem so far! *(exclamation)*
Apostrophe	**To form the possessive of a singular noun, add an apostrophe and s ('s).** baby's Russ's grandmother's family's
	For a plural noun ending in s, add only an apostrophe ('). sisters' families' Smiths' hound dogs'
	For a plural noun that does not end in s, add an apostrophe and s ('s). women's mice's children's
	Use an apostrophe in contractions in place of dropped letters. isn't *(is not)* wasn't *(was not)* I'm *(I am)* can't *(cannot)* we're *(we are)* they've *(they have)* won't *(will not)* it's *(it is)* they'll *(they will)*
Comma	**A *comma (,)* tells the reader to pause between the words that it separates.**
	Use commas to separate items in a series. Put a comma after each item in the series except the last one. Clyde asked if we had any apples, peaches, or grapes.
	You can combine two short, related sentences to make one compound sentence. Use a comma and the connecting word *and, but,* or *or.* Some students were at lunch, but others were studying.
	Use commas to set off the words *yes, no,* and *well* when they are at the beginning of a sentence. Well, it's just too cold out. No, it isn't six yet.

Proofreading for usage and mechanics requires students to read not what they meant to say but rather what they did say. Remind the students to rely on proofreading as a back-up in getting meaning across.

Again, feel free to use a basal language arts or English text as a guide to capitalization, abbreviations, and so forth. Figure 11.2 illustrates how one series presents this type of information; most often, the information will be included in an appendix.

Handwriting

In a computer-oriented age, when some people are predicting the end of any need for handwriting — or spelling, for that matter — we have at the other extreme those who believe a well-scripted hand will continue to be the best mark of sophistication and education. Once again, we find the reality somewhere in between. The need for writing in a legible script is no less important in an age of word processors, although word processors can play a very important role in the writing process. We still need to ensure that children will learn to write legibly and automatically. How we go about meeting this objective, however, is a little different than in years past.

For example, we now understand that it is important to allow children to write as much as they wish and to encourage this writing. In the past, it was commonly believed that any deviation from the exact form taught in the classroom would not only retard learning but instill (perhaps lifelong) bad habits. We now understand that, although it is important to teach handwriting directly to most students, it is not necessary to spend great amounts of time on this teaching. As with other aspects of the language arts, we know that we should spend more time on allowing students opportunities to *apply* what they are learning about handwriting. In the past, a common objective was to encourage students to try to mimic a given handwriting model. We now are more realistic, in that we aim primarily for a consistent, legible style.

Regardless of the grade level you teach, the same general guidelines for teaching handwriting will apply: (1) Be consistent. (2) Be a good model in your own handwriting. If you aren't confident of your ability, practice the forms presented in this chapter or the exercises in a handwriting book, or both. (3) Clearly display the model of the style you are teaching in your classroom. Most teachers put these models above the chalkboard or at least at about that height in the classroom. An additional aid for primary students is to have a model taped to their desk or table. (4) Emphasize *real* writing tasks.

I've already stated in earlier chapters that students should not focus as much on the "surface" of their compositions during the drafting stage; this holds for handwriting. They will save their best handwriting for final copying of a composition for publication. This does not mean, however, that messy and illegible handwriting during drafting is acceptable; it is not, because others will have difficulty reading it, and thus responding to the content of what the student has written. If legible handwriting is "automated," then it can be hurried during the drafting phase and still be read by others. Let students know, in other words, that legibility is always the objective, but that in final editing and copying tasks they should do their very best.

As we will explore below, the content of handwriting instruction is straightforward. Students first learn *manuscript* writing — more commonly referred to as "printing" — and then they learn *cursive,* or "real writing," as primary students usually call it. It is important to understand what children are learning about the "surface" of written language. This is where we will begin, because only if we understand the child's contribution to the task of learning handwriting will we present the appropriate instructional tasks at the appropriate time.

Handwriting in Preschool and Kindergarten

In Chapter 6 I pointed out that preschool children can learn much about print even though they are far from being literate in a conventional sense. Young children learn about the *directionality* of print, they understand that letters are somehow different in important ways from pictures, and they begin to develop prerequisite knowledge for understanding how alphabetic characters are used and combined. In Clay's terminology (1975), at this point children understand two important principles in writing.

1. *The* recurring *principle*   Children's writing shows that they understand that a limited number of characters (letters) *recur* again and again, as in four-year-old Megan's writing:

2. *The* generativity *principle*   Children's writing demonstrates that they realize that not just one but several forms recur over and over. This limited number of forms is combined and recombined in different sequences; they can *generate,* in other words, a seemingly limitless series of different sequences. Following is a sample from four-year-old Derek's writing:

With continued observation and experimentation, children show in their writing that they are experimenting with what is "allowable" as a letter and what is not — what Clay termed the *flexibility* principle. When you stop and think about it, this is no easy task. Look at five-year-old Jeffrey's writing, and then I'll discuss what he's doing:

Notice the *E*-like letters and the *M*-like forms? Jeffrey is picking up on the specific features of letters in the written language that surrounds him. This requires more than a simple process of differentiation, however, because Jeffrey will also have to understand that some forms can vary quite a bit and still be the same letter, yet others can vary only a little and be different letters. To illustrate the first type of letter, consider these different forms of lower-case *a*:

$$a, a, a.$$

To illustrate the second type of letter, consider the lower-case *p, d, b,* and *q,* and the upper-case *M* and *W.* In all other situations, objects in the world do not change identity when they turn around or flip over, but with letters such as these, identity *does* change. So, children must not only learn the distinctive features of letters but the orientation of these features as well.

In early handwriting development, then, we have an excellent illustration of the "global to more finely differentiated" pattern that Bissex discussed (1980). Depending on the culture in which children spend their first few years, their early handwriting will display the general features of that culture's writing system even before showing evidence of letterlike characters. This is what Bissex referred to as the "universal to more culture-specific" developmental pattern. Recall from Chapter 6 the rather dramatic demonstration of this from Harste, Burke, and Woodward (1984) when they contrasted the early handwriting of an English-speaking child with that of Arabic-speaking and Hebrew-speaking children.

For a couple of reasons, I've gone over handwriting development in children before the point at which formal instruction begins. One reason has to do with *readiness* for formal instruction in first grade; the other has to do with the *context* in which these understandings have developed. Let's take context first. We've already talked a lot about it, but let's step back and admire what children such as Megan, Derek, and Jeffrey have done: with very little outside input about what to pay attention to in writing, they have abstracted the significant features of letters. They have done so through *observing* written language around them and *constructing* approximations of that writing. Over time, their approximations will reflect more and more the quite specific characteristics of English letters. Allowed to observe and encouraged to experiment, these children have probably learned more — and enjoyed the learning more — than if we had sat them down and attempted to explain what the letters were and how to make them. We will do well to bear this fact in mind when we later teach directly about handwriting.

Handwriting Styles

There are a number of handwriting styles, some of which are illustrated in Figures 11.3 and 11.4. As is apparent, most of the variation among styles is within cursive script. Research does not clearly demonstrate which is easiest to learn, though all are easy on the eye. The current question regarding ease of learning involves contrasting D'Nealian script (Thurber, 1981) with other types. Notice the slope and curvature of the D'Nealian manuscript style in both upper and lower case? The rationale for teaching D'Nealian is that the transition from manuscript to cursive is supposed to be easier. Compare D'Nealian manuscript with D'Nealian cursive. Most of the cursive letters can be made by adding one or two simple strokes to the manuscript letters, which are already familiar.

The research is not very helpful in determining whether one style of handwriting is better than another. There is even some question about whether manuscript (printing) should be taught first; children perhaps should move right into cursive. On the other hand, one point of view argues for teaching manuscript and forgetting all about cursive, since many individuals can write manuscript as fast as cursive (Hildreth, 1960). This is one issue on which tradition may always win out: manuscript will be taught in first grade and cursive will be taught later, either in the second half of second grade or in third grade.

I would argue that there are good reasons for teaching manuscript first. First of all, manuscript letters look more like letters in books. Second, the letters are easier to write given the children's small-muscle dexterity — cursive is more demanding. Third, when children learn about the shape and composition of manuscript letters in handwriting instruction, this knowledge should strongly support word knowledge through the bonding of print to sound and meaning.

Teaching Manuscript and Cursive Writing

For most children, instruction in manuscript writing begins in first grade. How do you determine when children are ready for more direct teaching? Following are guidelines for determining such readiness:

- *"Play writing" must be clearly developed.*

  This criterion is the single best indicator that a child is ready to benefit from direct teaching in handwriting (Nathan, Temple, Juntunen, and Temple, 1989). You will be able to determine this early in the school year through observations of the children's writing and drawing. Are identifiable letters recombined and arranged in a linear fashion across an unlined sheet of paper? If so, the child is ready for some direct teaching.

- *Hand dominance must be established.*

  By first grade, most children have clearly established a preference for their right or left hand. A very few children are still as likely to use one hand as the other. With these children, offer objects to them so that they are likely to grasp them with their right hands (it is, after all, a right-handed world, and if they can learn to use their right hand more often, matters will be easier in

FIGURE 11.3

The Zaner-Bloser Model of Handwriting

Source: Used by permission of the publisher, Zaner-Bloser, Inc., 1459 King Ave., Columbus, OH 43212.

the long run). On the other hand, never attempt to change a left-hander; although they will have to learn to cope with the right-handed world, they will be able to do so with fewer problems than if you try to change them!

■ *Children must be able to use crayons, brushes, scissors, and pencils in a number of different tasks.*

These implements all require small-muscle dexterity, and a good way to see how well these small muscles can operate is to observe a child using these

FIGURE 11.4

The D'Nealian Model of Handwriting

Source: Scott, Foresman and Company, Glenview, IL. Reproduced by permission.

implements for several tasks. If the child is awkward, then hold off formal instruction, although you should continue to involve him or her in a wide range of small- and large-muscle tasks. These may include activities that are letter-oriented, such as drawing on the chalkboard and making different shapes with clay, in sand, or in shaving cream. As with all skill development, cognitive as well as motor, the more experience a child has with implements such as paintbrushes, scissors, and crayons, the less he or she will need to attend directly to the task, trying to think about several things at once. Once they have automated these composite movements, the children can benefit from your direct teaching.

- *Children should be able to copy simple shapes.*

    This of course is a more challenging task than generating shapes of one's own. If children seem to have a fair amount of difficulty with copying, then certainly hold off on the handwriting instruction. This ability, by the way, will develop more readily and less painfully if pupils are given few copying tasks and more opportunity to develop the small muscles further.

When children are ready according to these criteria, you can usually move directly to systematic teaching of handwriting. Furthermore, you probably do not need to use the large "primary pencils" so popular in first grade. Most children can use good old No. 2 pencils, just like the rest of us. You should make one adjustment, though: because the children will need to learn how to grip, move, and apply pressure to the paper, do not sharpen these pencils to a fine point. I can guarantee that the point will break — if someone is not punctured by the point first!

Pause for a minute to respect what these youngsters will be learning how to do: gripping, pressing, and moving, while trying to think about what they are doing. Their experience is not unlike my first experience — and perhaps yours — in learning how to handle a tennis racket: gripping it, wielding it, trying to make it do what it was designed to do, and thinking about the whole process. Allow the children plenty of opportunities to use pencils in their drawing and spontaneous writing. During this time, encourage them to hold the pencil at the bottom, where the paint is, and not any closer to the point. Once they have a feel for holding and using the pencil, you can begin formal instruction. This is an important step in learning, in which sight, touch, movement, and hearing (visual, tactile, kinesthetic, and auditory) abilities are all involved.

For both manuscript and cursive handwriting, the pencil or pen should be held in a way that is comfortable and that allows fluid writing without causing undue muscle fatigue. Encourage both right- and left-handers from the beginning to hold the pencil between the forefinger and index finger, supported by the thumb, which rests naturally and firmly against the pencil. For many children, this will be quite different from their usual grip, in which all but the little finger are pressed against the pencil. Although this gives the "feel" of firmness, it causes premature fatigue.

Figure 11.5 illustrates how the paper should be positioned for right-handers and for left-handers. Note that these positions prevent the writer's hand from covering the line during the writing. Left-handers, by the way, will likely constitute from five to ten percent of your classroom. If you are right-handed, invite a left-hander to your classroom to model letter formation for them; this could be another teacher or, more often, an older student. If the left-hander's paper is positioned as in Figure 11.5 and if the end of the pencil or pen is aimed at the student's left shoulder, then the writing will be comfortable and neither the line on which the child is writing nor any previous line will be obscured.

Prior to instruction, draw lines on the board or on a transparency that are like the lines on the children's paper. For manuscript, the 8½″ × 11″ paper with the line design shown in Figure 11.6 is appropriate. For cursive writing, the same design, though smaller, will be fine. After Furner (1969) and Fairchild (1987), here is the suggested sequence for directly teaching handwriting:

1. *Modeling and Guided Observation*   Draw the letter you are introducing, and talk about how and what you are doing, so your students will know what to attend to. Refer to where you begin, where you stop, the number of strokes involved, how large you are making each line, circle, or semicircle, and so on.
2. *Application and Verbalization*   The students follow your guide, talking through the process of forming the letter, just as you did in the first step.
3. *Comparison with the Model*   After students complete the letter, they should compare what they did with your model. As necessary, repeat the first step.

How much time should you spend? In the primary grades, ten to fifteen minutes a day is appropriate. This includes all three steps and assumes a fair amount of time given to the second and third steps. At the intermediate grades, less time is necessary, and after the first few weeks of the school year you may find that two periods a week are quite sufficient.

For *manuscript* writing, organize the sequence of letters to introduce according to shared features (Furner, 1969; Temple and Gillet, 1989), for example, "circle letters," "straight-line letters (*l*)," "point letters (*v, w*)," "tail letters (*j, g, y*)," and

FIGURE 11.5

Positioning the Paper for Right- and Left-handed Children

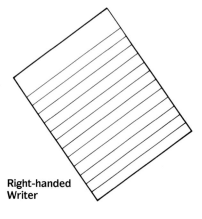

Right-handed Writer

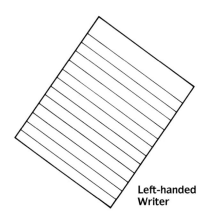

Left-handed Writer

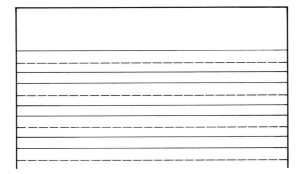

FIGURE 11.6

Lined Paper for Handwriting Lessons

"hump letters (*m, n*)." (Most handwriting programs are organized this way.) Similarly, for *cursive* writing, group letters that share similar features: *m* and *n, y* and *g, a* and *c,* and so on.

Continually remind students about why you are spending time on learning handwriting. In a writing-process classroom, the need for legibility is apparent, but do not take your purpose for teaching handwriting for granted: make it explicit to the students. In the intermediate grades and beyond, the students will be taking notes during presentations and during their reading; and there will be times when a handwritten note or letter is more fitting than a word-processed one, and when a letter is more appropriate than a quick phone call. Students who insist that a word processor is all they need should be reminded of these other writing situations. Just as with other aspects of revision and editing, put compositions on transparencies so that you can discuss features of the handwriting with the whole class. If you want to examine poorer handwriting, choose your examples from writing by students in previous years — not by current students.

Evaluating Handwriting

In teaching and evaluating handwriting, Barbe and others (1984) suggest that you focus on what they term the "six elements of legibility": letter formation, size and proportion, spacing, slant, alignment, and line quality. Let's consider each briefly.

- *Letter formation* refers to the way the letters are formed. Definite strokes are made in a certain order, and the direction and order of the strokes reflects the easiest, least awkward manner of letter formation. In cursive writing, the connecting strokes between letters are also highlighted.

- The *size and proportion* of letters reflects the developmental characteristics of handwriting throughout the elementary grades. When children first begin to write manuscript, the size of their letters is comparatively large, and upper-case letters are twice as large as lower-case. When the transition to cursive occurs, this proportion remains the same. With time, though, the lower-case letters will become even smaller and the proportion between upper- and lower-case letters will be three to one.

- *Spacing* refers to both the spaces between letters (in manuscript) and between words. In manuscript, there should be approximately one letter space between words and two between sentences. The spacing within words in cursive should obviously not be too "stretched" or "bunched"; the criterion is consistent spacing.

- ■ *Slant* should be consistent as well — vertical for manuscript and slanted to the right for cursive. Ideally, both right- and left-handed students' cursive writing should slant slightly to the right.
- ■ *Alignment* simply means that the letters should sit on the line and that upper-case letters are the same size and lower-case letters are the same size.
- ■ *Line quality* is the consistent quality of the thickness, darkness, and direction of the lines. Students should move their pencils or pens in a manner that results in even, fluid, and uniform strokes.

As I mentioned earlier, students should realize that all of the writing they do need not evidence high standards of handwriting quality: the *purpose* of the writing determines the necessary standard. When they do evaluate their own handwriting, however, they should attend to the following elements:

1. Correct formation of letters
2. Letters neatly sitting on the baseline and touching either the midline or topline
3. Even spacing between letters and words
4. Correct slant of letters (or up-and-down for manuscript)

For students whose handwriting is consistently below acceptable standards, continue direct teaching but always bear in mind Shaughnessy's wise recommendation:

FIGURE 11.7

Calligraphy

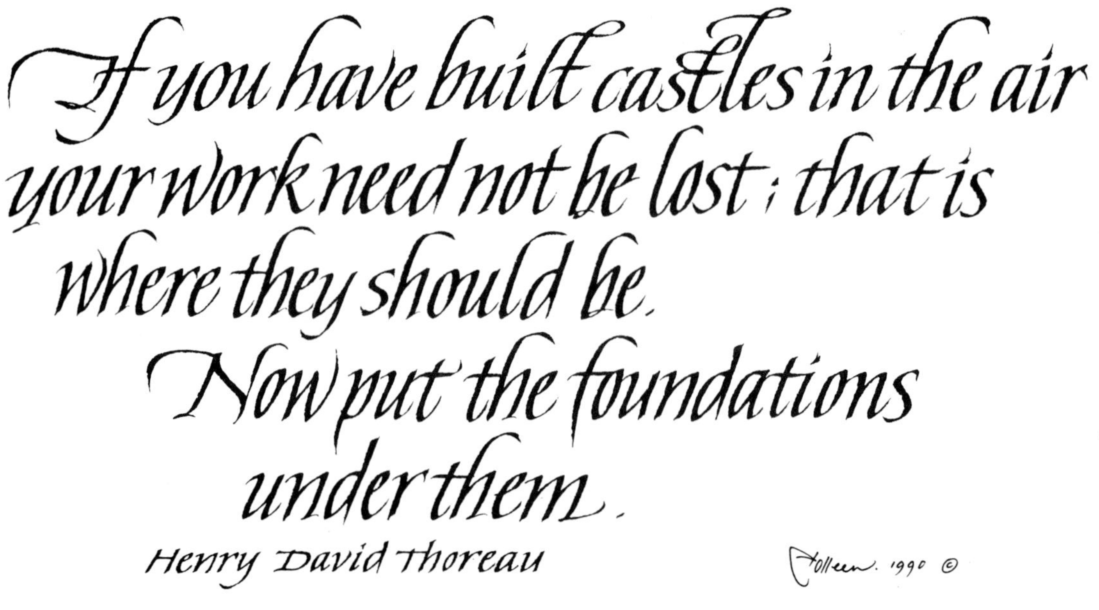

If you have built castles in the air your work need not be lost; that is where they should be. Now put the foundations under them.

Henry David Thoreau

Colleen. 1990 ©

"... [the] answer to this is practice — writing and more writing, preferably in modes that encourage a flow of words (journals, free writing, notations or observations), until the pen seems a natural extension of the hand, and the hand of the mind itself" (Shaughnessy, 1977, p. 16).

Maintaining Interest in Handwriting

Handwriting as a subject can be of considerable interest to many students. As part of an integrated unit or a learning center, or as an adjunct to handwriting instruction, you may wish to introduce calligraphy, graphology, and other methods by which humankind has written over the centuries.

Calligraphy (from the Greek *kallos* meaning "beauty," literally "beautiful handwriting") is a style of writing that often is used to embellish signs, announcements, greeting cards, and so forth. Actually, the style and strokes originally came from China. Figure 11.7 illustrates this style. Here are some references that describe how to do calligraphy.

■ Build Your Teaching Resources

Books about Calligraphy

Cataldo, J. W. (1969). *Words and calligraphy for children.* New York: Reinhold. (Out of print, so contact your library.)

Wolff, D. (1975). *Chinese writing.* New York: Henry Holt.
The second half of the book focuses on calligraphy.

Graphology is the "astrology" of handwriting. Nonetheless, many students become fascinated by the pseudoscience of attempting to determine the characteristics of an individual by analyzing his or her handwriting. Many detective novels for intermediate students include a graphology element, and of course Sherlock Holmes raised the pseudoscience to a fine art! (Holmes is a fascinating read for some upper intermediate students. Start them on *The Hound of the Baskervilles* — probably one of the best examples of "wholesome" terror!).

Finally, recall the references in Chapter 3 to hieroglyphics; these are well worth students' attention. An exciting spin-off from the study of hieroglyphics is having students develop their own hieroglyphic-type script.

A CONCLUDING PERSPECTIVE

I have defined grammar and usage, the mechanics of capitalization and punctuation, and handwriting as the traditional "basics." Traditionally they have been important; traditionally they have not been fun. They are still important; they need not, however, be dull. Learning them must be purposeful — and learning them can be interesting.

Grammar deals with the study or analysis of the structure of a language — how the words and phrases are organized into sentences. Three grammars have influenced our classroom practices: traditional, structural, and transformational generative; a fourth, case grammar, may yet influence instruction. We looked at the scope and sequence of parts of speech and sentence elements and examined appropriate and purposeful ways of presenting them in the classroom. We also explored the development and teaching of sentence structure in writing, focusing on sentence expansion in the primary grades and sentence combining in the intermediate grades.

Usage deals with the application of grammatical knowledge in accordance with the conventions of the language, as defined by the standard dialect of the language. We discussed the issue of standard versus variant dialects in English. The role of standard English should be emphasized, and presented within a context that underscores appropriate usage in the appropriate context. We looked at mechanics, including capitalization and punctuation, in the critical context of how they affect meaning.

The latter part of the chapter traced the nature and teaching of handwriting from the preschool years through the direct teaching of manuscript and cursive writing. Going beyond the functional role of a consistent and a legible script, you can help your students develop an interest in handwriting as a subject through calligraphy and graphology.

I can think of no more appropriate way to conceptualize and summarize the role of all the traditional "basics" than to quote Mina Shaughnessy once again: we need to focus appropriately on these basics in our instruction "... until the pen seems a natural extension of the hand, and the hand of the mind itself" (Shaughnessy, 1977, p. 16).

REFERENCES

Barbe, W., Wasylyk, T., Hackney, C., & Braun, L. (1984). *Zaner-Bloser creative growth in handwriting (grades K–8)*. Columbus, OH: Zaner-Bloser.

Bissex, G. (1980). GYNS AT WRK: A child learns to write and read. Cambridge, MA: Harvard University Press.

Bloomfield, L. (1933). *Language*. New York: Henry Holt.

Calkins, L. (1983). *Lessons from a child*. Portsmouth, NH: Heinemann.

Chafe, W. (1971). *Meaning and the structure of language*. Chicago: University of Chicago Press.

Chomsky, N. (1957). *Syntactic structures*. The Hague: Mouton.

Chomsky, N. (1965). *Aspects of the theory of syntax*. Cambridge, MA: MIT Press.

Chomsky, N. (1975). *Reflections on language*. New York: Pantheon.

Clay, M. (1975). *What did I write?* Portsmouth, NH: Heinemann.

deBeaugrande, R. (1985). Sentence combining and discourse processing: In search of a general theory. In D. Daiker, A. Kerek, and M. Morenberg (eds.), *Sentence combining: A rhetorical perspective*. Carbondale, IL: Southern Illinois University Press.

Elbow, P. (1985). The challenge for sentence combining. In D. Daiker, A. Kerek, and M. Morenberg (eds.), *Sentence combining: A rhetorical perspective*. Carbondale, IL: Southern Illinois University Press.

Fairchild, S. (1987). Handwriting as a language art. In C. Personke and D. Johnson (eds.), *Language arts instruction and beginning teaching.* Englewood Cliffs, NJ: Prentice-Hall.

Fillmore, C. (1968). The case for case. In E. Bach and R. T. Harms (eds.), *Universals in linguistic theory.* New York: Holt, Rinehart, and Winston.

Fries, C. (1940). *American English grammar.* New York: Appleton-Century.

Furner, B. (1969). Recommended instructional procedures in a method emphasizing the perceptual-motor nature of learning in handwriting. *Elementary English, 46*(8), 1021–1030.

Gillet, J., & Gentry, R. (1983). Bridges between standard and non-standard English with extensions of dictated stories. *Reading Teacher, 36*(4), 360–364.

Harste, J., Burke, C., & Woodward, V. (1984). *Language stories and literacy lessons.* Portsmouth, NH: Heinemann.

Havelock, E. (1983). *The literate revolution in Greece and its cultural consequences.* Cambridge, MA: Harvard University Press.

Hildreth, G. (1960). Manuscript writing after sixty years. *Elementary English, 37,* 3–13.

Hillocks, G. (1986). *Research in written composition.* Urbana, IL: National Council of Teachers of English.

Hunt, K. W. (1963). *Grammatical structures written at three grade levels.* NCTE Research Report No. 3. Champaign, IL: National Council of Teachers of English.

Kohl, H. (1981). *A book of puzzlements: Play and invention with language.* New York: Schocken.

Latham, E. C. (ed.) (1969). *The poetry of Robert Frost.* New York: Holt, Rinehart, and Winston.

Loban, W. (1976). *Language development: Kindergarten through grade twelve.* Urbana, IL: National Council of Teachers of English.

Malmstrom, J. (1977). *Understanding language: A primer for the language arts teacher.* New York: St. Martin's Press.

Mellon, J. C. (1969). *Transformational sentence-combining: A method for enhancing the development of syntactic fluency in English composition.* NCTE Research Report No. 10. Champaign, IL: National Council of Teachers of English.

Moffett, J., & Wagner, B. (1983). *Student-centered language arts and reading, K–13.* Boston, MA: Houghton Mifflin.

Nathan, R., Temple, F., Juntenen, K., & Temple, C. (1989). *Classroom strategies that work: An elementary teacher's guide to process writing.* Portsmouth, NH: Heinemann.

Papandropoulou, I., & Sinclair, H. (1974). What is a word? Experimental study of children's ideas on grammar. *Human Development, 17,* 241–258.

Perfetti, C. (1985). *Reading ability.* New York: Oxford University Press.

Shaughnessy, M. (1977). *Errors and expectations.* New York: Teachers College Press.

Strong, W. (1986). *Creative approaches to sentence combining.* Urbana, IL: National Council of Teachers of English.

Temple, C., & Gillet, J. (1989). *Language arts: Learning processes and teaching practices.* Glenview, IL: Scott, Foresman.

Thurber, D. (1981). *D'Nealian handwriting (grades K–8).* Glenview, IL: Scott, Foresman.

Wardhaugh, R. (1969). *Reading: A linguistic perspective.* New York: Harcourt, Brace, and World.

Weaver, C. (1979). *Grammar for teachers: Perspectives and definitions.* Urbana, IL: National Council of Teachers of English.

C H A P T E R

Assessment and Evaluation of Students' Instructional Needs

FOCUSING QUESTIONS

■ What distinguishes *informal* from *formal* evaluation in the language arts?

■ What is "portfolio assessment," and why is it the most effective basis for evaluating student development? What types of information will you include in the portfolio for each of the language arts?

■ When, why, and how will you group your students for instruction in the language arts?

■ How is formal assessment in reading and writing changing, and how will it be different from what it has been?

It was the end of my very first year of teaching. Teachers were required to administer a group of standardized reading achievement tests to all children — whether or not they could actually "read" in a conventional sense. Ricky, one of my first-graders, could read a little; in fact, he had begun to move right along in April once he had acquired a concept of word in print (at the time I didn't know about "concept of word in print" — I only knew that the magic moment had finally come around for Ricky). He was excited and feeling good about himself, which was especially gratifying for me because Ricky had really been trying all year.

Now, however, it was the end of May and time for testing. Deep down, Ricky knew what the testing meant. After looking in despair at the first couple of pages on the test, he also knew he could not do much of anything on the test. So he sat at his desk throughout the testing time, not making a sound, while tears rolled down his cheeks.

INTRODUCTION

Anyone who has taught for even one week has met someone like Ricky. Most likely, we have experienced Ricky's total sense of incapacitation ourselves in some testing situation. It can be frightening enough in a high school chemistry class, but especially devastating for elementary students trying to learn how to read. For me the frustration remains, because I was never able to apologize to Ricky, or to the many other similar children who came after him.

Experiences such as these have led many educators to argue against standardized testing; many support outright elimination of it. We will consider such issues in this chapter, but as you will see our main focus will be on assessment and evaluation in your classroom — for purposes of determining students' growth, making instructional decisions, and assigning grades.

Perspectives and Definitions

Although we will consider both informal and formal assessment and evaluation in this chapter, I will emphasize informal strategies — the types of classroom-based, day-to-day means of observing and collecting information that provide more relevant and valuable insight into your students' growth. I'll emphasize the areas of spoken language, reading, writing, and spelling or word knowledge.

Let's begin with the basic question: what are assessment and evaluation? Although these terms are used differently by different people, the ways I will use them in this chapter reflect widely held definitions. *Assessment* is selecting and administering particular tasks in order to gather information about individuals or groups. *Evaluation* is analyzing and synthesizing the information that has been gathered in order to make decisions about individuals or groups. Both assessment and evaluation can be informal or formal.

Informal assessment and evaluation rely upon information that you collect in the regular classroom and are based primarily on the ongoing reading, writing, and discussion in which your students engage. Informal assessment may also include particular tasks that you have the students complete — a tape of their oral reading, for example, or a spelling inventory. You will use informal assessment and evaluation for various important instructional purposes: when you wish to pinpoint students' strengths and weaknesses, when you want to form groups in the classroom, and as you continually determine how much students have learned from lessons or tasks so that you can plan the next instructional steps.

Because informal assessment and evaluation grow directly out of the students' day-to-day work, informal strategies are by far the best means of determining both student growth and your instructional direction. Evaluation for the purpose of assigning grades — an inevitability in most schools — can also be based on informal assessment.

Formal assessment and evaluation, most familiar to the lay public, involve administering and interpreting standardized or *norm-referenced* tests to see how well large groups of students are doing; this is the type of test that bedeviled Ricky. Formal assessment and evaluation are usually used when the purpose is to determine how much students nationwide are learning in reading, for example, or to meet district-mandated regulations. In other words, national, regional, state or provincial, and local assessments of student learning most often rely on the less precise formal standardized measures.

Before we look further at these informal and formal settings, let's consider what a test is. Technically, a *test* is an existing task or set of tasks through which students' knowledge is assessed and evaluated. You can use tests both informally and formally; norm-referenced tests as well as tests of your own design will be part of your assessment and evaluation. Typically, formal assessment always involves a test, whereas informal assessment can also include an instructional task used diagnostically through teacher observation.

The word *test* of course carries a lot of negative connotations, provoking anxiety at least, and at worst causing intimidation. In part for this reason I will not use the term *test* often in this chapter, but you need to understand its precise meaning, despite whatever personal feelings about tests you may entertain!

Informal Assessment and Evaluation

As a teacher, you will find that informal assessment and evaluation are your most important and useful tools. You will use the techniques of informal assessment throughout the year in conferences with individual students, for example, and in your record-keeping during group reading conferences. Informal assessment allows you more authentic insight because it is based on ongoing daily activities in the language arts.

You will use informal assessment for the following two major purposes:

1. *As an early measure of identifying a particular student's skills and knowledge, which in turn helps with grouping.* As noted in Chapter 4, assessment and evaluation is a continuing process that helps teachers determine specific abilities and characteristics of their students. It is the basis of grouping for some instruction, such as assessing the concept of word in print among beginning first-graders and administering a spelling inventory to determine word knowledge among students at any grade level.

2. *As an ongoing measure of determining how well individual students and the class as a whole are responding to and learning from specific instructional situations and lessons.* This keeps the instructional cycle going, of course, in the sense that it enables you to judge new strengths and weaknesses, possibly new grouping arrangements, and the effectiveness of instruction.

As we have seen throughout this book, whenever you interact with students individually or in groups, you pick up information about the degree to which they are developing, understanding, and applying knowledge about reading, writing, and speaking and listening. Here we will discuss how to organize this information, applying the vocabulary of assessment and evaluation.

You will be what Yetta Goodman called a "kid-watcher" (Goodman and Goodman, 1989). That is, through authentic reading, writing, and discussion activities you will be gaining truer insight into your students' developing learning. Indeed, the mistakes or "miscues" you observe them making in reading, writing, spelling, and so forth "often show their underlying competence, the strengths they are developing and testing the limits of" (K. Goodman, 1987, p. 41). From time to time you will also "set the stage" a bit by presenting specific tasks to students and then observing their response: how they sort words, for example, or discuss a piece of literature in terms of theme and setting. Often you will prepare informal tests or assessments to check on their understanding — a list of questions, for example, to which each student in a group will respond.

Important aids in classroom assessment and evaluation are the "portfolios" that you will set up for each student. In fact, *portfolio assessment* is a popular concept in language arts, and rightly so (Au, Scheu, Kawakami, and Herman, 1990; Mathews, 1990; Pikulski, 1990; Wolf, 1988, 1989). Just as artists develop portfolios to represent a range of their best work, so too will each student have a portfolio or file that contains samples of his or her learning efforts (Valencia, 1990). The portfolio provides an extremely helpful basis for students' evaluation of themselves and for your evaluation of your students. It usually will include

- samples of work selected by the student and the teacher.
- observational notes by the teacher.
- the student's own assessment.
- progress notes contributed by both teacher and student, often written collaboratively.

To assemble their portfolios students select compositions, for example, that they believe best represent their work in a particular genre. This selection process involves self-evaluation as they reflect on why particular pieces are most representative of what they have learned. The students keep a record of books that they have read, and you keep a record of the observations you make during individual and group reading and writing conferences. We'll explore portfolio assessment for writing and for reading below, with examples.

Oral Language

As we saw in Chapter 2, most of children's basic syntactic structures and phonological system are developed before formal schooling begins. Development will continue during the school years, of course, but with a major difference, as Wells noted: "what is learned and the order in which it is learned becomes progressively more dependent on experience" (Wells, 1986, p. 32). This is where you come in. Through all the language-based activities you offer them, students have the opportunity to develop further the structure, vocabulary, and use of language. How can you keep track of this development? Again, informal assessment provides your best information.

You can assess children's development in language structure and vocabulary through group and one-to-one interactions. You should always include some assessment of the students' use of spoken language when they are working together without your direct involvement. Make notes on the following:

- Do they speak clearly, expressing themselves through syntax and vocabulary appropriate to the task? Or do they rely on stock phrases and responses, reluctant to elaborate when their meaning is unclear?

- Are they able to rephrase appropriately when their meaning is not clear? Or do they rely on another student or students to explain for them?

- Do they usually comprehend others, or do they appear often confused? If the latter, do they really *listen* to others or do they appear to be distracted when others are speaking?

- Do they play with using language structures and vocabulary that come from their reading and/or your read-alouds?

- Are younger first- and second-graders still using some sounds incorrectly? This is not unusual, but it should be investigated by a speech therapist if it persists. Usually the child has not further differentiated the rules governing the articulation of the sound. For example, common phonemes that are still incorrectly used at these early levels are /w/ instead of /r/ ("vewy" instead of "very") and /th/ instead of /s/ ("thaw" instead of "saw").

- In the context of discussion groups, do they contribute freely? Do they attend to what others are saying? Do they respect the guidelines according to which the group operates?

Informal, impromptu writing conferences offer an excellent opportunity to observe and evaluate an individual student's development in writing. *(© David Pratt/Positive Images)*

You may include most observations in each student's assessment portfolio and directly discuss your comments with the student if improvement is needed — as, for example, in attending to what others are saying.

In summary, although you will attend closely to each student's command of the systems of language — syntax, phonology, and semantics or vocabulary — you will be increasingly interested throughout the elementary grades in students' *use* of this information. As you recall from Chapter 2, the students will be refining their pragmatics, their awareness of the different contexts in which language is used and the conventions that govern language appropriateness.

Writing

Portfolio Assessment in Writing

You may make daily observations about each student's development in the writing process as you observe the student working in groups, with a partner, and individually. You will also acquire information through conferences with each student. As you go through a morning working with several students, it helps to have an easy means of noting and saving this evaluative information. Rowe, Harste, and Short (in Harste, Short, and Burke, 1989) suggest that you carry a clipboard with one-inch gummed labels on it; you can then write your observations for a particular student on one label, date it, and at the end of the day put the label in the child's writing folder on the "Evaluation" page. This information can be periodically reviewed, preferably with the student, and transferred to the writing portion of the assessment portfolio.

An assessment portfolio neatly eliminates the classic concern about "grading" every piece of writing that students compose. Of course, you already know from your understanding of the writing process that it would be counterproductive to grade everything because ultimately this would stifle students' creativity and undermine their risk-taking. Following are guidelines for your evaluation:

■ Do not evaluate every composition. Decide how many written compositions you will be evaluating each grading period. The number will depend on the particular genres and forms of writing emphasized.

■ Base a good portion of the grade on compositions that the students wish to submit for grading. These compositions will most often be published pieces. The students will be keeping drafts and completed pieces in a writing folder, so by leafing through their folders they will be able to make their selections fairly easily. Their selections will then be put in their assessment portfolios.

■ Evaluate both content and mechanics. Make sure the criteria for each area are clear to the students, for these criteria will change depending on the type of

FIGURE 12.1

Sample Evaluation Form Using a Point System

```
NAME_____          DATE_____

TYPE OF WRITING_____

        Skills Checked                           Rating Scale

        _____

        _____

        _____

        _____

        _____

        _____

        _____

        _____


        Comments:                               Total_____
```

writing being evaluated. You may use a point system, provide comments, or do both. Much of your evaluation will be holistic, based on consideration of the overall composition in terms of content and mechanics. You may also provide some focused evaluation, considering one or two specific elements in content and/or mechanics. Figure 12.1 shows a sample evaluation form that uses a point system. Note that the rating scale is left blank so that you may assign a greater number of points for some criteria than for others. For example, you may decide to rate correct spelling on a scale of 1–5, and clear paragraph sequencing on a scale of 2–10. Figure 12.2 shows a completed evaluation form for fifth grade in which the first score is for content and organization and the second is for mechanics.

Let's examine the following suggested criteria for evaluating writing in grades one through six.

First Grade   You will be fortunate indeed if you teach in a system that does not require you to assign letter grades during first grade. Most systems either require letter grades or at best require them after the first grading period. Remember, your evaluation at this point will be of the child's process, not product. Mark the

FIGURE 12.2

Completed Evaluation Form Using a Point System

NAME _Keith_   DATE 4/28

TYPE OF WRITING _Persuasive letter_

Skills Checked		Rating Scale				
Reasons clearly stated	2	4	6	⑧	10	
Reasons in order (strongest to weakest/ weakest to strongest.)	1	2	③	4	5	
Each reason supported	2	4	⑥	8	10	
				Total 17/25		
spelling	1	2	3	4	⑤	
punctuation	1	2	3	4	⑤	
sentence structure	1	2	3	④	5	
correct letter format	2	4	6	⑧	10	

Comments: _Good thinking, Keith. Good improvement on spelling & punctuation. Should add more support for your reasons._   Total 22/25 following three points *always, sometimes,* or *rarely* (adapted from Nathan, Temple, Juntunen, and Temple, 1989):

- Does the pupil write during writing time?
- Does the student use appropriate strategies for getting his or her writing going?
- Does the student participate when writing is shared (e.g., during Author's Chair activities)?

Second Grade   In second grade the evaluative focus is still primarily on process. Note that some additional points have been added (adapted from Nathan, Temple, Juntunen, and Temple, 1989).

- Does the pupil write during writing time?
- Does the student use appropriate strategies for getting his or her writing going?
- Is the student serious about teacher/student and student/student conferences?
    - a.   Does the student listen to other students' drafts and offer helpful feedback?
    - b.   Does the student consider feedback from other students and from the teacher?
- Does the student show an understanding of the difference between revising and editing?
- Does the student participate when writing is shared?

If you must evaluate the product in second grade, the only mechanical aspects you should probably attend to are the following:

- Is the handwriting legible?
- Does the first word in each sentence begin with a capital letter and does each sentence end with a punctuation mark?

Third Grade   Students' understanding of the steps in the writing process can really take off during third grade. If the first two grades have emphasized process and involved the students in lots of reading and writing, then we can expect third-graders to appreciate the value of revision, for example, and we can evaluate their developing attempts to fine-tune their writing. Accordingly, we can evaluate more aspects of their writing in terms of both process and product.
Evaluate the process of writing according to the following points:

- Does the pupil write during writing time?
- Does the student use appropriate strategies for getting his or her writing going?
- Is the student serious about teacher/student and student/student conferences?
    - a.   Does the student listen to other students' drafts and offer helpful feedback?

    b.   Does the student consider feedback from other students and from the teacher?

■ Does the student show appropriate revision strategies?

■ Does the student show appropriate editing strategies?

■ Does the student participate when writing is shared?

■ Does the student use other sources of information available in the classroom such as checklists and guidelines, informational materials, dictionaries, appropriate sections of the English or language arts text?

Evaluate the products of writing according to the following points:

■ Is the handwriting legible?

■ Does the first word in each sentence begin with a capital letter and does each sentence end with the appropriate punctuation mark?

■ Are commas used appropriately?

■ Are words used appropriately and effectively?

■ Are different forms of writing used appropriately (e.g., stories, expository or transactional writing)?

■ Is the composition appropriately partitioned into paragraphs?

You can evaluate additional specific skills on an ongoing basis. For example, if you emphasize the use of order words to clarify the sequence of events, you would evaluate a composition on this particular aspect.

Fourth, Fifth, and Sixth Grades   All of the process and product points to which you attend in third grade continue to pertain in the intermediate grades. Depending on the school or district in which you teach, the number of writing-related skills that are evaluated in final products during or after third grade usually grows considerably.

    Not all aspects of writing will be taught explicitly, but for any one child those that are needed should be focused on. As noted in Chapter 4, you will not need to memorize scope and sequence guidelines for all the grades; a general grasp will be sufficient for now. As you anticipate your own classroom teaching, you should know that a scope and sequence of grade-appropriate skills will usually be available in the teacher's edition accompanying the English or language arts program in use in your school. Many districts also publish such skills under their Curricular Objectives for the Language Arts. You will find these guidelines useful during your first year or two, and then you will know them almost automatically. If required, you may include a skills checklist in each student's portfolio to mark off throughout the year.

    Figure 12.3, "Fate of a Serf," represents another evaluative record of a student's understanding and creative integration of information. While studying cathedrals, a fourth grade class became interested more generally in life during the Middle Ages, and this illustration was part of a student's contribution to the project exploring this topic (Gamberg et al., 1988). It illustrates the variety of completed

FIGURE 12.3

Example of Fourth Grade Student's Work that Could Be Included in an Assessment Portfolio

Source: Gamberg, R., Kwak, W., Hutchings, M., Altheim, J., & Edwards, G. (1988). *Learning and loving it: Theme studies in the classroom.* (p. 78). Portsmouth, NH: Heinemann. Reproduced by permission of Johannes Graham.

compositions that can more broadly — and validly — represent writing development and the kinds of learning that are occurring in the classroom.

Reading

Grouping and Making Initial Decisions

Chapter 4 presented guidelines for grouping students for reading instruction. Since that time, you have digested a lot of information about the language arts. Let's consider grouping in light of evaluation, to clarify the rationale for small instructional groups. You will eventually have a variety of groups in your class; most of them will be heterogeneous groups, but for some direct teaching the children will

*AT THE
TEACHER'S
DESK:
Grouping
Students for
Reading
Instruction*

Traditionally, grouping has had an ironclad finality to it. Once students were placed in a reading group in first grade, for example, they stayed in that ability group throughout their elementary school years. The "crows" in first grade would still be the "crows" in the intermediate grades, and the "swans" would always be the "swans." This very real fact has led many educators to question the value of grouping at all, and there is some research that supports large-group or whole-class instruction (Rosenshine and Stevens, 1984). Nevertheless, I encourage you to group students for reading instruction, particularly in the primary grades, for two major reasons. First, for many of your teaching and learning objectives, you can interact more effectively with a smaller number of students than with a whole class. Second, you will be better able to offer developmentally appropriate instruction. You should also feel assured that once students have learned how to work collaboratively on assigned tasks, even those groups not meeting with you at a particular moment will be able to keep productively busy.

be grouped homogeneously. Organizing these latter groups is the issue I would like to address at greater depth here.

Informal assessment and evaluation will help you form reading groups that will be the initial basis for both reading and writing instruction. Since writing, unfortunately, is not emphasized nearly as much in the elementary grades as is reading, you are quite likely to have students who read rather well but who have not developed accordingly in their writing. In terms of their peers, then, students do not have to "catch up" in writing nearly as much as is often the case in reading. In addition, much of the knowledge underlying writing is developed in the context of reading instruction.

In first grade, you will work with smaller groups of children using the strategies provided by the language experience approach (see Chapter 8). Much instruction will occur when all of the children are together, but your initial grouping will offer language development and print awareness activities to those children who need them. In second grade and up you can group students based on reading proficiency and on actual reading situations (Cunningham et al., 1989). During the first week or two of school, as the students readjust to the school setting, observe their book choices during sustained silent reading, and notice how they handle content books whenever necessary. Also spot-check individually: ask a student you have a hunch about to read a paragraph aloud to you, for example. After this readjustment, bring together several students who you believe are of similar ability. Go through a Directed Reading-Thinking Activity with them, observing each student's willingness to make predictions, accuracy in prediction, ability to support a position by referring to and/or locating relevant information in the text, reading rate, and response to your questioning. In the intermediate grades you should probably conduct both narrative and content DRTAs. Repeat this procedure with two other groups of students you have tentatively grouped according to ability; you will probably find that a few students need to be moved to a different group. Point out that you will be

Teachers should make use of many informal observations gleaned during lessons such as Directed Reading-Thinking Activities in order to form evaluations about students' knowledge. (© David Strickler/TSW/Click Chicago Ltd.)

doing a lot of group work this year, and that these groups for reading are one part of this work — they will allow you to work more closely with smaller groups of students. Your students will still perceive that reading ability is the underlying criterion for these reading groups, but your attitude and the students' subsequent work with many other students will soften this distinction.

Informal Reading Inventories (IRIs)

You will need additional information about some students when you are making initial grouping decisions. Traditionally, an excellent means of obtaining this information has been through an *informal reading inventory* (IRI). The administration of these inventories can also serve other important purposes, as we shall see.

In addition to identifying word-analysis knowledge and strategies, an IRI can provide a tentative picture of a student's reading comprehension. For the trained reading specialist, an IRI can be a gold mine of initial information to refer to throughout the year. Knowledge about IRIs may be useful to you early in your teaching career for the following reasons:

■ *You may use them early on, in addition to observing the whole class, to learn about students who appear to be behind the others in reading.*

Although informal reading inventories may be increasingly replaced by knowledgeable teachers who can apply good "kid-watching" skills, they are

AT THE
TEACHER'S
DESK:
Under-
standing
Reading Levels

In Chapter 8, I mentioned Hansen's description (1987) of the different levels of books with which children interact: "the one I'm working on," "challenge," and "easy" books. These labels correspond to the *reading levels* of instructional, frustrational, and independent.

Although we want students to be doing lots of reading at their *independent level* (where they understand at least 90% of the material and know 99% of the words), our teaching efforts will be focused primarily on the *instructional level.* Recall that students reading at their instructional level are encountering some difficulty; although they comprehend at least 60 percent or so of what they read, they may not know 5 to 6 percent of the words. Material that is at students' *frustrational level* contains too many unknown words; students are able to comprehend at best only about 50 percent of what they read. Though you may teach a particular skill using material that is at students' independent level, you should make sure that they have the opportunity to apply it at their instructional level as well.

and have been a significant aspect in reading education. Traditionally, IRIs have been used by reading resource teachers and some classroom teachers.

■ *You may eventually use them with all students to check on strengths and weaknesses.*

As we'll explore later in this chapter, this is an important part of your assessment portfolio in reading.

■ *You may use them with actual instructional materials to better match students and curriculum materials.*

See Barr, Sadow, and Blachowicz (1990) for an excellent discussion of how to use the IRI procedure with instructional materials. Your familiarity with published IRIs will help you adapt their format to your print-based curricular materials, and you can use longer passages from textbooks and narratives.

■ *The skills you develop in administering and evaluating IRIs will be extremely helpful in your day-to-day instruction.*

Although you will probably use an IRI sparingly in your own classroom, the basics will serve you very well in your general instruction. For example, learning the types and marking system for oral reading errors or miscues will come in handy in day-to-day observation of your students' reading.

An informal reading inventory yields three major types of information about a student's reading: word knowledge in isolation and in context, comprehension in oral and in silent reading, and oral reading fluency. Informal reading inventories do have limitations; they are not as "natural" or authentic a reading task, and they do not sample across larger segments of texts and several different types of reading. On the other hand, if there is good rapport between the teacher who is administering the IRI and the student, then the results do provide a good indication of a student's reading "power." A number of published informal reading inventories are available, and most major basal reading series have included one. This latter type is primarily used for placement purposes, but you can still use it to gain some insight into a student's reading abilities.

The basic format of an IRI is a series of (1) word lists and (2) graded reading passages. The word lists at each grade level contain words that usually appear in basal readers for the first time at that level. Two reading passages are included for each grade level, one to be read orally and one to be read silently. It is possible to determine fairly accurately a student's reading levels using an IRI, but of more interest and benefit to you will be the specific information it yields about the student's word knowledge and comprehension. You need information about the student's power in these areas in order to target the type of instruction he or she needs. Let's look at the procedure for administering an IRI.

Have the student read graded word lists to determine (a) where the student should begin reading in the graded reading passages; (b) the student's ability to identify immediately words in isolation; and (c) the student's strategies for figuring out words not immediately identified — this also gives information about the student's level of word knowledge and demonstrates whether the student reasons systematically, guesses, or does a little of both. The graded oral and silent passages will give you information about the student's (a) reading level; (b) comprehension, both through recall and direct questioning; (c) strategies of word recognition in context; and (d) oral reading fluency. Most published informal reading inventories will print the criteria for determining reading level on the same page as the passage to be read.

If you have the time, check comprehension by asking the student to retell what he or she has read ("Tell me what happened in this story" or "What is this story/ this passage about?"). If the student gives one or two short statements, probe further with "Tell me more about that" (avoid asking, "*Can* you tell me more about that?" — a subtle but important distinction). Some IRIs have a list of important points that the student should usually recall in a retelling, and you can simply check these off. If the student does not recall some points, probe a bit with questions provided in the IRI that may elicit the information. Most readers, even poorer ones, usually comprehend more than they recall in a retelling; thus the follow-up questions are important.

Another way to check comprehension is to bypass the retelling and go directly to the questions that accompany the IRI passage. This is a less comprehensive assessment, but it will still give you a reasonable appraisal of the student's comprehension, and you may probe more intensively on another occasion.

Note how naturally the student reads aloud: is it word by word, by phrases (although haltingly), in a monotone, or with more natural inflections? This information is best preserved, of course, on tape. A taped record will be dramatically helpful later on when students, and parents, compare the initial oral reading to the most recent oral reading.

Excellent in-depth discussions of informal reading inventories are provided in books by Barr, Sadow, and Blachowicz (1990) and Johnson, Kress, and Pikulski (1987). In addition to these texts, I recommend the following informal reading inventories.

Build Your Teaching Resources

Informal Reading Inventories

The published informal reading inventories listed below are some of the best currently available. It may be helpful to refer to *Informal Reading Inventories* by Johnson, Kress, and Pikulski (cited above) before reviewing these inventories. In order to get a "feel" for administering IRIs, as well as to gain valuable insights into the reading process, select an inventory and administer it to a child, preferably in the intermediate grades, who is having difficulty in reading. (Do not, however, use this first administration to provide diagnostic/instructional suggestions for the classroom teacher.)

Burns, P. C., & Roe, B. D. (1989). *Informal reading inventory.* Boston: Houghton Mifflin.
Ekwall, E. (1986). *Ekwall reading inventory.* Boston: Allyn and Bacon.
Johns, J. L. (1985). *Basic reading inventory.* Dubuque, IA: Kendall/Hunt.
Silvaroli, N. (1990). *Classroom reading inventory.* Dubuque, IA: Wm. C. Brown.
Woods, M. L., & Moe, A. J. (1985). *Analytical reading inventory.* Columbus, OH: Merrill.

Portfolio Assessment in Reading

We've already gone over an important part of the framework in which you can evaluate your students' reading competence: group and individual conference. Let's look more closely at how you can gather the information you need and keep track of it. In addition to samples of students' writing and relevant evaluations, the assessment portfolio will include the following information about students' *reading:* (1) attitudes and understandings about reading; (2) responses to literature tasks, which assess growth in reading comprehension; and (3) a "running record" (Clay, 1979) of students' application of word-analysis skills in context.

Attitudes and Understandings About Reading   You will be able to keep track of how students feel about reading and their motivation to read through your conferences with them and by having them keep a *vocabulary reading log* that you will check from time to time. To develop this Reading Log, place a "Reading Log" sheet in each student's portfolio. The students will record the title, author, and date(s) for each book they read. You may place a separate sheet in the portfolio on which you summarize and evaluate the students' voluntary reading. From time to time you should look over the students' reading logs and plan individual conferences to discuss the types of genres and/or authors they prefer. Au et al. (1990) suggest your log for each student include the following information: number of books read, reading levels of the books (independent, instructional, frustrational), types of genre read, favorite book, favorite author, and any comments you wish to enter about a student's voluntary reading — for example, "Reads every day" or "Often selects books on higher reading level but seems to get information and enjoyment from them," and so forth.

During individual conferences, as Roehler, Duffy, and Meloth (1986) suggest, three extremely effective questions that you can ask students are: (1) What did you learn about reading today? (2) How do you do it (apply the strategy or information you learned)? (3) When and why should you use it for reading? Their responses will keep you abreast of the procedural and self-knowledge the students apply in reading. You may also note particular responses students make during group conferences and enter them later in their individual portfolios.

Responses to Literature Tasks Your assessment also will include information you glean daily from your students' written responses and spoken comments during individual and group conferences. Through the students' retellings and your own judicious probing, you will note their use of strategies for approaching different texts and setting reading purposes. Watch carefully for these strategies and attend to any comments about them in discussions. Encourage students to measure their growth in reading knowledge by comparing their earlier and more recent responses to literature. You may also use their responses to discuss explicitly what you will be focusing on in upcoming instruction.

You may wish to record your comments on the type and nature of reading responses that students enter in their journals. This is information that you gain by interacting regularly with students through their journals. Figures 12.4 and 12.5 are examples of responses from one student's journal. Eldon, a second-grader, wrote each response during his reading of a chapter book. Included in his portfolio, they illustrate his development in writing, spelling, and reasoning in relation to his reading.

Figure 12.4 (September 24) is his response shortly after beginning Beverly Cleary's *Dear Mr. Henshaw.* Figure 12.5 (March 3) is his response toward the end of reading Roald Dahl's *Danny the Champion of the World.* Although the second response strikes us initially as somewhat disjointed, remember that this is an unedited, first-impression response. Comparing the nature of the two responses, we can see that the second is qualitatively richer. Rather than giving a straightfor-

FIGURE 12.4

Second-grader's Journal Response to a Chapter Book, Included in His Assessment Portfolio (September)

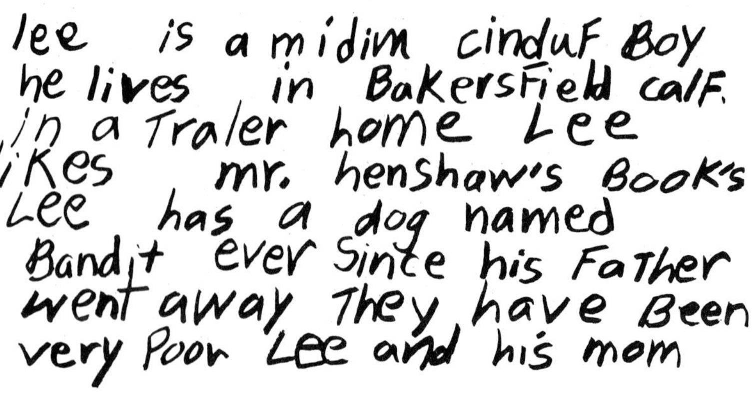
lee is a midim cinduf Boy
he lives in BakersField calf.
in a Traler home Lee
likes mr. henshaw's Book's
Lee has a dog named
Bandit ever Since his FaTher
went away They have Been
very Poor Lee and his mom

(This journal entry reads:
Lee is a medium kind of boy. He lives in Bakersfield, California in a trailer home. Lee likes Mr. Henshaw's books. Lee has a dog named Bandit. Ever since his father went away they have been very poor, Lee and his Mom.)

FIGURE 12.5

Second-grader's Journal Response to a Chapter Book, Included in His Assessment Portfolio (March)

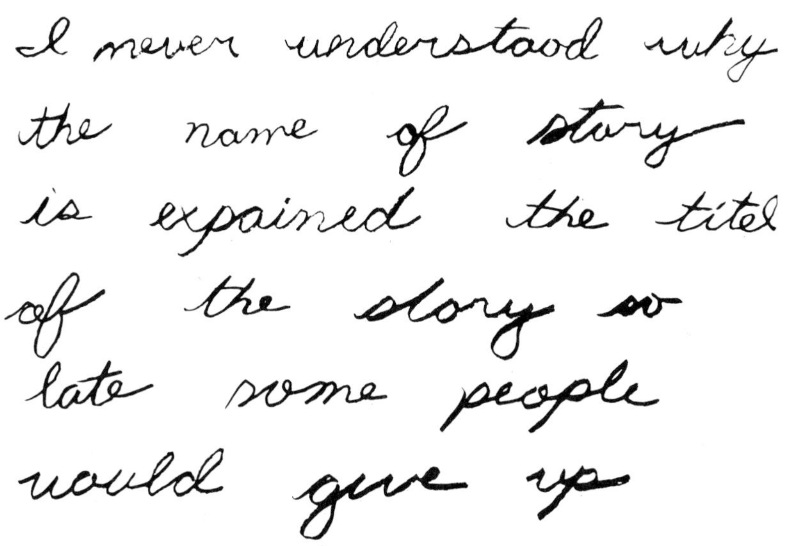
I never understood why the name of story is expained the titel of the story so late some people would give up

(This journal entry reads:
I never understood why the name of story is explained the title of the story so late some people would give up.)

ward description of things, as does the first response, the second response shows that Eldon has "stepped outside" his own reading and enjoyment of the book to reflect on a broader phenomenon that characterizes many books, not just *Danny the Champion of the World*: the wording of *titles,* what they mean, and when the reader finally (if ever!) figures out the meaning. As Eldon points out, a lot of children may indeed "give up" on their reading if they are merely wondering why a book has a particular title.

You can summarize the understandings, skills, and strategies you have been teaching by including a checklist in each assessment portfolio. It will reflect reading objectives that you formulate in line with the general goals of your state, province, or district school system. The specific reading tasks you present will tap understanding and application of reading skills and concepts.

Running Record Clay's "running record" (1979, 1985) is a modification of a procedure used in informal reading inventories and miscue analysis (Goodman, Watson, and Burke, 1987). Basically, this type of record details a student's development of word-analysis ability in context, as well as reading fluency and expression throughout the school year and across the grade levels. The procedure for gathering and recording information is similar to that for an IRI.

Clay suggests that you have a student orally read one passage at his or her independent level, one passage at the instructional level, and one passage at the frustrational level. Following along in your own copy of the passage being read, you record the errors or "miscues" that the student makes. Later you determine what sources of information the student is or is not applying when encountering an unfamiliar word: is the student primarily relying on visual and/or phonic cues, syntactic cues, semantic cues, or some combination of these? Excellent descriptions of running records may also be found in Pinnell (1985) and in Lipson and Wixson (1989).

It is possible to get quite involved in interpreting oral reading miscues, according to rather extensive procedures (Goodman, Watson, and Burke, 1987). Your time is limited, but with practice and experience you can make some fairly accurate judgments about a student's application of word-analysis skills. Figure 12.6 lists a relatively straightforward categorization of error types and shows how to mark them quickly as the student reads.

Omissions refer broadly to any phrase, word, or part of a word that is left out. *Insertions* are additions to what is on the page; they also can be words or parts of words. *Substitutions* are words that are read in place of words on the page; they may be meaningful substitutions or mispronunciations that do not make sense. For example, a meaningful substitution would be a student's reading *jet* instead of *airplane* in the following sentence: "Jerry looked up and saw the airplane in the sky." A nonmeaningful substitution would be the word *ask* instead of *airplane*. Often-

FIGURE 12.6

Types of and Marking for Oral Reading Errors ("Miscues")

1. Omissions are scored by drawing a circle around the word or phrase omitted. [Example]

    There were no toys ⊙left⊙ in the room.

2. Insertions are indicated by drawing a caret (∧) and writing in what the student said.

    In those days there was always a need for ∧more protection from one's enemy.

3. Substitutions are marked by drawing a line through the word or phrase on the page and writing the substitution above it.

    Harry tried to ~~release~~ please himself as quickly as he could.

    Harry tried to release himself as ~~quickly~~ fast as he could.

4. Repetitions are marked with an arrow or a wavy line; Draw Ⓡ and to indicate repeated words.

    In the meantime, all of the chickens had escaped.
    (change order) (Or, In the meantime, all of the chickens had escaped.)

5. Corrections are indicated with a check mark (✓) or with a ©, and it is important to write what the original miscue was, however:

    Several times he tried to go✓ get back into the boat.
    (Or, Several times he tried to go©get back into the boat.)

6. Punctuation is marked with a circle if omitted and appropriate punctuation marks if the voice indicates a different punctuation than what is on the page: Write in the punctuation miscue

    Why didn't she return to her home after the fire? ∧
    The townspeople said it was because she was afraid something could still happen to her. They would never know the real reason.

times the substitution *could* make sense if you stretched the situation a bit — say, if the student read *answer* instead of *airplane*. Usually, however, a pattern emerges; the substitutions either make sense or don't and reflect the student's attention to the appearance of the word on the page. *Repetitions* are words and phrases that are repeated. *Corrections* are miscues that the student goes back to correct. Often repetitions and corrections occur together, since in correcting a miscue the student rereads the phrase in which it occurred. *Punctuation* errors occur when a student omits or wrongly interprets punctuation, such as continually ending a declarative sentence with a rising intonation, as for a question.

In counting the miscues that a student makes, you should always take off for (a) omission of words or phrases but not for omission of punctuation, (b) insertions, and (c) substitutions. You usually do not take off for the other errors, although some educators disagree about whether to count repetitions. I suggest that you not count repetitions, but if a student is excessively repeating words you should determine whether it interferes with comprehension.

Place a copy of the passages the student reads, with your markings, in the assessment portfolio, and attach a summary sheet indicating the number and type of errors or miscues for each passage. This is valuable information for you in planning instruction as well as an excellent means of noting development. In your ongoing day-to-day work, you may add to this summary page as you notice a student's particular miscues and self-correction strategies. This information will often be handy in your individual reading conferences.

Spelling

Recall from Chapter 10 that spelling, far from being mere memorization of letter sequences, reflects a wide range of word knowledge. Assessing spelling knowledge, therefore, gives you considerable insight into your students' overall word knowledge in reading and in writing.

Forming Initial Judgments of Students' Knowledge

Your initial assessment will provide valuable information about your students' word knowledge and about appropriate placement for word study. Just as there are different levels of reading proficiency in your classroom, there are different levels of spelling or word knowledge, and students should be placed accordingly.

Most basal spelling series have an initial placement test, which you can use to gain a sense of the different ability levels in your class. If you wish a more comprehensive assessment, the lists in Table 12.1 will be an excellent resource for you. They can act as a spelling inventory and will help you determine students' independent, instructional, and frustrational levels in spelling. Because of the criteria by which the words are selected, the lists also give you excellent insight into an individual student's word knowledge (Henderson and Invernizzi, 1984). Both for placement tests in spelling basals and for this Qualitative Spelling Inventory, use the following scores to determine instructional levels (Betts, 1946; Henderson, 1990): independent level = 90% and above; instructional level = 50% to 90%;

TABLE 12.1 WORD LISTS FOR QUALITATIVE SPELLING INVENTORY

LEVEL I (GRADE 1)	LEVEL II (GRADE 2)	LEVEL III (GRADE 3)	LEVEL IV (GRADE 4)	LEVEL V (GRADE 5)	LEVEL VI (GRADE 6)
bump	batted	find	square	enclosed	absence
not	such	paint	hockey	piece	civilize
with	once	crawl	helmet	novel	accomplish
trap	chop	dollar	allow	lecture	prohibition
chin	milk	knife	skipping	pillar	pledge
bell	funny	mouth	ugly	confession	sensibility
shade	start	fought	hurry	aware	official
pig	glasses	comb	bounce	loneliest	inspire
drum	hugging	useful	lodge	service	permission
hid	named	circle	fossil	loyal	irrelevant
father	pool	early	traced	expansion	conclusion
track	stick	letter	lumber	production	invisible
pink	when	weigh	middle	deposited	democratic
drip	easy	real	striped	revenge	responsible
brave	make	tight	bacon	awaiting	accidental
job	went	sock	capture	unskilled	composition
sister	shell	voice	damage	installment	relying
slide	pinned	campfire	nickel	horrible	changeable
box	class	keeper	barber	relate	amusement
white	boat	throat	curve	earl	conference
	story	waving	statement	uniform	advertise
	plain	carried	collar	rifle	opposition
	smoke	scratch	parading	correction	community
	size	tripping	sailor	discovering	advantage
	sleep	nurse	wrinkle	retirement	cooperation
			dinner	salute	spacious
			medal	treasure	carriage
			tanner	homemade	presumption
			dimmed	conviction	appearance
			careful	creature	description

Source: E. H. Henderson and M. Invernizzi, "Qualitative Inventory of Word Knowledge." McGuffey Reading Center, University of Virginia. Used with permission.

frustrational level = below 50% — although Morris, Nelson, and Perney (1983) suggest 40% (be flexible in interpreting students' scores that fall between 40% and 50%).

I suggest that you assess students' spelling for purposes of instructional placement beginning in second grade. Either with the whole class or in smaller groups, begin by telling the students that you are going to ask them to spell some words and that their spelling will not be graded. If they are uncertain about the spelling of any word, they should do the best they can; it is important that you see how they go about spelling when they aren't sure of a word. Pass out sheets of paper and administer the words from the list in Table 12.1 that is one grade level below that of your students. Collect these and then administer the list that is from their grade level (for younger students this can be done the next day). If necessary, give a third list from the grade level just above. To a very few students, those who have done exceptionally well or rather poorly, give additional lists (either two grade levels above or below, depending on performance). Usually the three lists will identify the spelling levels of most of your students. On the average, the instructional level for most students will correspond to their grade level, and a few will be a grade above or below. It is important for those few to continue their study using appropriate words; it is unrealistic and unfair to require the less able students to be accountable for twenty words taken from a level far beyond where they are, or to ask excellent spellers to work tediously with twenty words they already know.

To illustrate, let's discuss how you can use spelling assessment in a first grade classroom. You are concerned with appropriate placement at the beginning of the year, but your approach to assessment will be different from that in later grades. That is, you won't be dealing with reading levels or spelling levels but with determining the students' understanding of basic print conventions and familiarity with print material. As I have emphasized, your assessment should arise from the actual literacy experiences in which you involve your first grade students: from the language experience approach to dictated stories, from predictable (big) books, and from writing. You will be gathering information about children's basic understanding of print conventions, concept of word in print, knowledge of sight words, and level of spelling knowledge (semiphonemic, letter name, within-word pattern). Because word knowledge is so critical at the primary level, assessing it through spelling can underscore the other types of information you are gathering.

Bear and Barone (1989) have shown that word knowledge as assessed through spelling is a powerful indication of beginning and transitional readers' general reading competency. I refer you to their article for a comprehensive treatment of assessment based on spelling proficiency, but see Table 12.2 for the portion of their diagnostic list that is appropriate for first and second grade (representative spellings for each level of word knowledge are included). Note that you should discontinue administering the list when a student misspells five words in a row. Students who test primarily at the letter-name stage will be word-by-word readers, and those who test primarily at within-word pattern will be moving toward fluency. In first grade, the range of stages will usually be from preliterate through within-word pattern.

TABLE 12.2 DEVELOPMENTAL SPELLING LIST FOR FIRST AND SECOND GRADE WITH REPRESENTATIVE SPELLINGS BY STAGE OF WORD KNOWLEDGE

| | REPRESENTATIVE SPELLINGS | | |
WORD TO SPELL	Semiphonemic Stage	Letter-Name Stage	Within-Word Pattern Stage
bed	b, bd	bad	bed
ship	s, sp, shp	sep, shep	sip, ship
drive	frv, drv	griv, driv	drieve, drive
bump	b, bp, bmp	bop, bup, bomp	bump
when	w, yn, wn	wan, whan	wen, when
train	j, t, trn	fran, chran, tan,	traen, trane, train
closet	k, cs, clst	tran	clozit, closit
chase	j, cs	clast, clost	case, chais, chase
float	f, vt, ft	tas, cas, chas	flowt, flote, float
beaches	b, bs, bcs	fot, flot	bechise, beches, beaches
preparing		bechs, becis	preparng, preypering
popping			popin, poping
cattle			catel, cattel, cattle
caught			cot, cote, cought, caught

Source: D. R. Bear and D. M. Barone, "Using Childrens' Spellings to Group for Word Study and Directed Reading in the Primary Classroom." *Reading Psychology,* Vol. 10, #3, pp. 275–292, 1989. Reproduced by permission of the authors.

Let's face the issue you will inevitably be puzzling over from your first day of teaching on, if not before. In most school systems you have to assign grades. How do you do it in line with the philosophy put forth in this book?

We first broached this issue in Chapter 4, so you may wish to glance back at that discussion. Put simply, what you have taught is what you evaluate. If the students know why they are being involved in certain activities and being taught certain things, then they know what you are focusing on for evaluation. Be frank and discuss this at the beginning of the year. You are grading *process,* which they will keep tabs on themselves, as well as *product.* Reassure your students that they will know what they will be graded on because you will be discussing the grading together.

In the context of openly discussing evaluation with your students, you will have the opportunity to help them learn how to set challenges for themselves, as well as meet challenges that you encourage them to attempt. At grading time you can discuss with them the degree to which they, and you, believe they have met those challenges. Importantly, they should come to see their grades as reflecting what they accomplish, not how their work compares to that of others. Comparison is a part of life, of course, but students will be better prepared for it if they feel good about themselves and what they have accomplished.

Ongoing Assessment and Evaluation

The type of analysis discussed above will not only help you to determine the level at which your students should begin word study (see phonics in Chapter 8 and word sorting in Chapter 10), but it can also serve as a tool for ongoing assessment throughout the year.

In addition, you can stay abreast of students' developmental spelling or word knowledge during the year through weekly assessments with lists constructed according to the criteria presented in Chapter 10 and through informal observation of students' writing. Samples of students' writing that you place in their assessment portfolios — particularly spontaneous writing — will also provide ongoing information.

Formal Assessment and Evaluation

Traditionally, assessment and evaluation have been conducted formally, which is partly why many educators have been so concerned about testing: formal assessment is quite removed from the more "authentic" literacy activities in which students should be daily engaged. The usual purpose of formal assessment is to provide comparative information about groups of students — information that, of necessity, can only be gained through tests administered to whole groups at a single administration. Formal testing provides very little information about individual students — the type of information teachers need in order to provide appropriate instruction. (Although there *are* individual formal tests, at bottom they usually yield less valuable information about students than that obtainable through informal assessment.)

There are reasons, though, that formal or *norm-referenced* testing is still a significant part of our educational world. Our society relies on "numbers" in many ways; quantitative information will always at least give the illusion of precision. So, when the nation — or your local school board — wants to know how well schoolchildren are doing, they will want to see the bottom line expressed in numbers.

Significant new efforts are under way to change both the nature of large-scale assessments and the public's perception of educational testing, and these efforts should begin to have some effect in the next few years (Clay, 1990; Pikulski, 1990; Valencia and Pearson, 1987; Simmons, 1990; Teale, 1988). We might be able to begin this change by collecting *more* information from *fewer* students across the nation. This way, we could include what have until now been considered informal assessments — authentic writing and reading tasks across a range of different purposes. Ultimately, this type of assessment and evaluation would take about as much time as the current large-scale assessments, but it should yield much more helpful, insightful, and valid information than the current norm-referenced tests, which by design can sample only superficially at best.

It is a reality, however, that large-scale formal or norm-referenced tests will continue to be used in the near future, so we will examine them in this section as well as look at a "new generation" of such tests already being developed. An extensive vocabulary is associated with standardized assessment. I will avoid most of it here, except to point out some basic concepts.

Standardized refers to the procedure by which the test is administered: the person giving the test, usually the teacher, exactly follows the directions in the test administration manual, right down to the wording of the directions and the moment at which the test booklet is opened. There's a reason for this strict procedure. Any variation in presentation — say, for example, in explaining a point further — could affect the test performance of the students by giving them an edge that other students wouldn't have. It would then become extremely difficult to make comparisons among the groups.

Norm-referenced means that the scores obtained on the standardized test are "referenced" or based on the *normal curve*. The normal curve is often referred to as the bell-shaped curve because that is the shape the distribution of scores of a large number of students will take when the scores are plotted. Usually, a very large number of students take the test before it is published; the scores of all students who later take the test are then based on this distribution of scores — on this bell curve.

What are some of these scores? *Standardized* or *normal-curve equivalent* scores tell you where on the normal curve a student has scored — how far above or below the mean (the average). These scores in turn can be expressed as *stanines* (another way of saying where the student scored on the curve), *percentiles* (how many students scored above and below a particular student), and *grade-equivalent scores*. This last type of score is widely misunderstood; it is supposed to represent a student's performance in terms of grade level (for example, 4.5 means performance equivalent to the fifth month of fourth grade). The greatest error in interpreting this score is assuming that a student whose grade-equivalent score is 4.5 should automatically be placed in a basal reader appropriate for a student in the middle of fourth grade. In fact, you need much more information about the student's skills in order to make an appropriate placement, information that comes from informal assessment.

Thus, we're back to the limitations of standardized norm-referenced tests. Although these tests do give a general picture of a student's knowledge and skill in relation to that of other students, they do not give valuable information about the individual student's instructional needs. Such information can be obtained only from individual informal tests or activities. Remember that you will often be in the position of explaining to parents the purpose and results of formal norm-referenced reading and language arts tests. You should be familiar with these tests, therefore, and know what the various types of scores mean. But parents should also understand that these tests are not the be-all and end-all of their child's ability and that you do not make important instructional decisions solely on the basis of these scores.

Reading

Traditional Standardized Group Tests

As I mentioned, there is considerable debate about the value of norm-referenced tests — specifically of reading tests. Whereas real reading usually involves large chunks of text, formal standardized tests usually have shorter segments, often only one paragraph long, which does not allow students to get their teeth into a selection. In addition, standardized group tests attempt to "control for" background information by including passages that may be of little interest or concern to elementary students; thus we do not see how well the students are able to apply their background knowledge. (Below we will see how some large-scale testing in reading is changing to address these concerns.) Standardized reading tests usually have subtests labeled "comprehension," "word analysis," "vocabulary," and so forth. More extensive achievement tests such as the Stanford Achievement Test have several additional subtests in listening, spelling, language, and so on.

The "New Generation" of Standardized Group Tests

Recently, many reading and language arts educators in several states (for example, California, Illinois, Maryland, Michigan, and Virginia) and at the national level (National Assessment of Educational Progress) have undertaken to construct standardized group tests in reading that do not have many of the same shortcomings as the traditional norm-referenced tests. Assuming that standardized group tests will always be an educational fact of life, these educators believe that the challenge is not to attempt to eliminate all such testing but to make group testing as realistic and valid as it can be (Wixson, Peters, Weber, and Roeber, 1987). The tests they are formulating represent recent concepts about the reading process: the reader, the text, and the context must all be considered. I'll present two examples here that illustrate the new trend in assessing reading: the National Assessment of Educational Progress (Educational Testing Service, 1989) and the Illinois Goal Assessment Program for Reading (Illinois State Board of Education, 1990).

Since 1969 the National Assessment of Educational Progress has conducted an ongoing nationwide assessment in several curricular areas. The 1990 assessment approaches the testing of reading in a new way: passages are selected and test items constructed to reflect two major concepts — *mode of comprehension* and *type of text*. Mode of comprehension includes two subareas, *constructing meaning* and *extending or examining meaning*. This distinction captures the two basic purposes for which readers read: (1) to get the "gist" of a selection and (2) to read more deeply, analyzing ideas and extending information gleaned from the selection to other situations and realms of knowledge. Roughly speaking, this distinction reflects the difference between literal and inferential comprehension on the one hand and critical comprehension on the other. *Type of text* refers to the distinction between narrative texts ("literary comprehension") and expository texts ("informational comprehension" and "document literacy" of graphs, charts, maps, directions, etc.). Figure 12.7 shows an informational comprehension selection appropriate for grade four, together with questions based on the passage that reflect different "modes" of reading. The passage, taken from a science textbook appropriate for this grade level, includes features of expository material, such as subheadings and italicized terms.

Developers of the Illinois Goal Assessment Program for Reading have similarly analyzed the reading process and have generated questions that assess aspects such as background knowledge of a topic, knowledge of different comprehension strategies, attitudes about reading, and context of reading. Selections are much longer than on traditional tests, and students are encouraged to refer back to a selection whenever necessary to respond to items. Figure 12.8 shows a sample assessment of reading strategies (Illinois State Board of Education, 1989, p. 9).

These two examples from a national and a state assessment in reading should illustrate the shape and content that large-scale standardized group assessment probably will assume over the next few years. The gap should be narrowing, in other words, between what we know about the reading process and how we assess that knowledge in standardized group tests.

Writing

Standardized Group Tests

Somewhat ironically, large-scale formal assessment of writing has been more realistic in recent years than it has been of reading. The technique most often used is termed *holistic* evaluation. You will recognize similarities between large-scale holistic assessment and your own classroom assessment. As Chapter 7 suggested, you evaluate the *product* of your students' writing in terms of the features a particular type of writing should evidence, and these features should be clear to the students because they have been emphasized in your teaching. In addition, however, you will assess the students' writing *process*.

Living in an Environment

GRADE 4

Where you live is important. In fact, the survival of all living things depends on where they live. The surroundings of a living thing are called its *environment.* Your environment includes all the living and nonliving things that affect your life.

Ecosystems — A marsh ecosystem has several types of plants and animals. All of the same type of organisms living in a certain place make up a *population.* The populations may be large or small. The marsh grass is one population of plants. The heron, crab, and raccoon each belong to different animal populations.

All of the different populations in a given area make up a *community.* The marsh community includes many kinds of plants, mammals, birds, fish, insects, amphibians, and mollusks. These living things in a community depend on many nonliving things in their environment. Air, moisture, soil, and light are just a few nonliving things that living things need to survive.

A community and its nonliving things are called an *ecosystem.* An ecosystem can be as large as an ocean or as small as a puddle. A marsh is one example of an ecosystem.

Nonliving Things — Populations that live in the same ecosystem have common needs, such as water and shade. You would not find a water lily growing in a desert. Nor would you find a cactus growing in a pond. These plants would live in ecosystems that fit their needs. The nonliving things in an ecosystem often determine the ecosystem's community, and they can limit the type and size of a community.

Feeding Relationships — The feeding relationships in an ecosystem limit the size of populations. Food relationships begin with plants, since plants use energy from sunlight to produce their own food. For this reason, plants are known as *producers.*

The food stored in plants is eaten by animals, such as zebras. And these animals are eaten by other animals, such as lions. Therefore, zebras are *consumers* of plants, and lions are consumers of zebras. A consumer is an organism that feeds on other plants or animals. *Predators* are animals that hunt, kill, and eat other animals, which are called *prey.* For example, lions are predators and zebras are prey.

How can these feeding relationships limit the size of different populations? Suppose people kill many lions. With fewer lions to hunt zebras, the zebra population can increase rapidly. The zebras graze more, killing the grasses. With less grass to eat, many zebras may die.

—— **Questions 1–5 refer to the article on pages 49-50.** ——

Mode of Reading: Constructs Meaning

1. Which of the following best tells the central purpose of this passage?

   (A) Sunlight is the most important factor in an ecosystem.
   *(B) Living things in an ecosystem depend on each other and on nonliving things.
   (C) The size of a population in an ecosystem is important for survival.
   (D) Feeding relationships depend on the number of predators in an ecosystem.

2. What is an ecosystem?

   (A) All of the living things in an area
   (B) All of the nonliving things that a community needs
   *(C) The different populations and nonliving things in an area
   (D) The nonliving things and water in an area

3. What do the living things in an ecosystem have in common?

   (A) They all eat the same food.
   *(B) They need many of the same non-living things.
   (C) They are all similar in size.
   (D) They are all predators.

4. Why are plants known as producers?

   (A) Plants provide food for other living things.
   *(B) Plants make their own food.
   (C) Plants provide oxygen for the ecosystem.
   (D) Plants are eaten by predators.

Mode of Reading: Extends or Examines Meaning

5. What will happen if too many predators in an ecosystem are killed?

   (A) The grasses will not be eaten.
   (B) The oxygen supply will be limited.
   (C) Producers will not be able to make enough food.
   *(D) The amounts of different kinds of food in the ecosystem will be changed.

*Correct answers for multiple-choice items are indicated by an asterisk (*).

FIGURE 12.7

A "New" Standardized Test of Reading Comprehension

Source: Passage: "Ecosystems," *Addison-Wesley Science,* Grade 5, by Barman, et al. Copyright © 1989, Addison-Wesley Publishing Company, Menlo Park, CA. Reprinted by permission. Test: "Information Comprehension," Grade 4 (Living in an Environment) from *Reading Objectives 1990 Assessment,* April 1989, The Nation's Report Card, The National Assessment of Educational Progress (NAEP), pp. 49–51.

Reading Strategies Section

Questions 33 to 42 are about useful things to do when you read. First, read the problem in the box. Then, look carefully at the reading activities below and judge how helpful each one would be.
CHOOSE ONLY ONE ANSWER FOR EACH ACTIVITY.

> You have just read "How Plants Help People." Imagine that while discussing it with your classmates you are asked to give your opinion about the point the author was trying to make.

Now think carefully . . .

How much would it help your classmates if you said . . .	Won't Help At All (A poor summary)	Will Help a Little Bit (A fair summary)	Will Help Quite a Bit (A good summary)	Will Help a Whole Lot (An Excellent summary)
33. "It is about how it took millions and millions of years to make coal and oil. We use oil and coal to heat the buildings we live in and to make the nylon clothing we wear."	O	O	O	O
34. "It is about how people get all the food they eat from plants that grow on the highest mountain tops. These plants are also used to heat our homes and to keep cheese from turning to mold."	O	O	O	O
35. "It is about how plants give us many important things that we need to live. Plants and people help one another to survive."	O	O	O	O
36. "It is about how people eat the roots of carrots and the meat from animals. People also use paper to make books. They like to see pretty flowers."	O	O	O	O
37. "It is about how people cannot live without plants because plants give us oxygen to breathe, food to eat, clothing to wear, fuel to keep us warm, lumber to build our houses, and medicine to help make us well."	O	O	O	O

> You have just read "How Plants Help People." Imagine that in 2 minutes you will take a test to show how well you understand the story. This means you don't have time to reread the whole story. However, you want to make sure you understand how all the ideas in the story fit together.

Now think carefully . . .

How much would it help if you were to . . .	Won't Help At All (A poor strategy)	Will Help a Little Bit (A fair strategy)	Will Help Quite a Bit (A good strategy)	Will Help a Whole Lot (An Excellent strategy)
38. start to reread the story from the beginning?	O	O	O	O
39. reread the part of the story about the parts of plants we eat?	O	O	O	O
40. look quickly through the paragraphs?	O	O	O	O
41. look up the meanings of the words "plants" and "people" in the dictionary?	O	O	O	O
42. reread the part of the story about how plants give us oxygen?	O	O	O	O

FIGURE 12.8

A "New" Standardized Test of Reading Strategies

Source: Sample *1989 Illinois Goal Assessment Program, Reading, Grade 3.* (Springfield, IL: Illinois State Board of Education, 1989). Reprinted by permission. *Note:* The results of data analyses of statewide assessment results for 1988 and 1989 have led to further revisions in the formatting of these tests; the format shown here will be changed.

In holistic assessment, compositions are read for their overall organization and effect. The criteria for rating are determined by a group of evaluators after reading a small sample of compositions from the larger batch that will be evaluated. The ratings are expressed numerically (for example, 0 to 4, with 4 being "best" and 0 being "poorest"). In total holistic scoring, the rater considers all aspects of the composition — meaning, coherence, spelling and grammar — and makes an over-all rating of the piece. Statewide writing assessments are usually conducted this way (for example, the California Assessment Project [1989] and the Texas "TEAMS" writing evaluation), and the National Assessment of Educational Progress has used this format in the past.

Table 12.3 (Millett, 1990) presents general criteria for holistic scoring. Figure 12.9 illustrates two compositions by fifth grade students that have been holistically scored based on a 0–4 point scale for *descriptive* writing. The task was to write a description of an old, abandoned house, and an illustration of the house was pro-vided for the students.

Primary trait scoring, or *focused holistic* scoring, is similar to holistic scoring in that the overall composition is considered and rated, but this time more specifically in terms of the features of a particular type of writing. For example, the California Assessment Project assesses several different types of writing at the intermediate grade levels and beyond. Whether *persuasive* piece or business letter, all writing is scored according to the primary traits the type of writing should contain. The National Assessment of Educational Progress evaluates writing in terms of (1) task accomplishment (primary trait scoring) and (2) overall fluency (general holistic scoring).

TABLE 12.3 HOLISTIC SCORING GUIDE

SCORE VALUE	EXPLANATION
0	Papers in this category cannot be scored for one reason or another. Papers that are blank, that respond to an assignment different from the one given, that merely comment on the assignment, that only copy or rephrase the assignment, or that are illegible would all be included in this category.
1	Papers in this category attempt to deal with the assignment, but they fail to do so adequately. These papers are too general, abrupt, or refer to the assignment only indirectly.
2	Papers in this category respond to the task set up in the assignment, but they do so in a way that is sketchy, inconsistent, and incomplete. There are gaps or other problems in the organization. Vocabulary may be too general and the paper lacking in the detail necessary to convey the purpose clearly and exactly. The reader has a basic idea of what the writer is trying to say but has to make many inferences.
3	Papers in this category fulfill the requirements of the assignment, although the reader might encounter a little confusion from time to time. The paper is generally well organized so that the reader does not need to make a lot of inferences. These papers include sufficient details so that the reader understands the writer's message.
4	Papers that merit this highest score are well organized, complete, and explicit. These papers include all of the strengths of the 3 category, but they are more clearly and consistently presented. The reader grasps the writer's message easily without having to make inferences. The writer uses a varied and exact vocabulary that enhances as well as clarifies the message.

Source: *Teaching the Writing Process: A Guide for Teachers and Supervisors* by Nancy Carlyon Millett. Copyright © 1990 by Houghton Mifflin Company. Reprinted by permission of Houghton Mifflin Company.

> ### The Old House
>
> Old houses are sort of interesting. I like to think about the people who lived there. When did they live there? Did they have kids? Theres an old house on the other side of town. My Mom says some people named Rider lived there once.

Score: 0

Explanation: The writer writes about old houses in general and one that is located nearby. The writer makes no attempt to describe the pictured house.

> ### The Old House
>
> The house is so old that the porch is practicaly falling over. It would be dangerus to stand on it. because the roof might cave in on you. The front door is hanging and looks ready to fall off too. Two windows by the door are boarded up. One of the top windows over the porch is broken, and one of them has a shutter hanging down. All the shutters have little hearts in them. Some of the shingels on the roof are turned up and some are missing. There is a brick chimny and a television antena that looks like a coat hanger. The yard is a mess. I bet this house has been empty a long, long, time.

Score: 4

Explanation: This paper is unified, well organized, and clearly detailed. The writer describes the features of the house in a logical and consistent manner, using exact words and vivid images.

FIGURE 12.9

Holistically Scored Compositions in a Fifth Grade Standardized Group Writing Test

Source: *Teaching the Writing Process: A Guide for Teachers and Supervisors* by Nancy Carlyon Millett. Copyright © 1990 by Houghton Mifflin Company. Reprinted by permission of Houghton Mifflin Company.

A CONCLUDING PERSPECTIVE

This chapter has provided a quick overview of informal and formal assessment in important areas of the language arts. You can use informal assessment with your whole class as well as with individuals to identify strengths and weaknesses and to group students. I stressed throughout that informal assessment and evaluation in the classroom yields information that is of most use to you. On the other hand, you must know the purpose and limitations of formal assessments in order to communicate effectively with parents about these aspects of their children's performance.

Large-scale formal standardized assessments in reading can be useful if they are meant to give a general picture of the performance of large groups. Traditional standardized tests, however, do not assess reading as validly as do more recently developed tests, such as several state-level tests and the new National Assessment of Educational Progress.

The types of writing assessments that have been used on a large scale can be applied in the classroom as well. You can adapt holistic scoring to reflect the overall coherence, content, and mechanics of a composition and to assess the specific features of different types of writing (primary trait or focused holistic scoring).

REFERENCES

Au, L. H., Scheu, J. A., Kawakami, A. J., & Herman, P. A. (1990). Assessment and accountability in a whole literacy curriculum. *The Reading Teacher, 43,* 574–578.

Barr, R., Sadow, M., & Blachowicz, C. (1990). *Reading diagnosis for teachers.* New York: Longman.

Bear, D., & Barone, D. (1989). Using children's spellings to group for word study and directed reading in the primary classroom. *Reading Psychology, 10*(3), 275–292.

Betts, E. (1946). *Foundations of reading instruction.* New York: American Book Company.

Clay, M. M. (1979). *Reading: The patterning of complex behaviour.* Auckland, New Zealand: Heinemann.

Clay, M. M. (1985). *The early detection of reading difficulties* (3rd ed.). Auckland, New Zealand: Heinemann.

Clay, M. M. (1990). What is and what might be in evaluation. *Language Arts, 67,* 288–298.

Cunningham, P. M., Moore, S. A., Cunningham, J. W., & Moore, D. W. (1990). *Reading in elementary classrooms: Strategies and observations.* New York: Longman.

Gamberg, R., Kwak, W., Hutchings, M., Altheim, J., & Edwards, G. (1988). *Learning and loving it: Theme studies in the classroom.* Portsmouth, NH: Heinemann.

Goodman, Y., Watson, D., & Burke, C. (1987). *Reading miscue inventory: Alternate procedures.* Katonah, NY: Richard C. Owen.

Goodman, K., & Goodman, Y. (eds.). (1989). *The whole language evaluation book.* Portsmouth, NH: Heinemann.

Hansen, J. (1987). *When writers read.* Portsmouth, NH: Heinemann.

Harste, J., Short, K., & Burke, C. (1989). *Creating classrooms for authors.* Portsmouth, NH: Heinemann.

Henderson, E. H., & Invernizzi, M. (1984). *Qualitative inventory of word knowledge.* Charlottesville, VA: McGuffey Reading Center, University of Virginia.

Henderson, E. H. (1990). *Teaching spelling.* Boston: Houghton Mifflin.

Johnson, M., Kress, R., & Pikulski, J. (1987). *Informal reading inventories.* Newark, DE: International Reading Association.

Lipson, M. Y., & Wixson, K. K. (1989). *Student evaluation and basal instruction.* In P. N. Winograd, K. K. Wixson, & M. Y. Lipson (eds.), *Improving basal reading instruction* (pp. 109–139). New York: Teachers College Press.

Mathews, J. K. (1990). From computer management to portfolio assessment. *The Reading Teacher, 43,* 420–421.

Millett, N. C. (1990). *Teaching the writing process: A guide for teachers and supervisors.* Boston: Houghton Mifflin.

Morris, D., Nelson, L., & Perney, J. (1983). Exploring the concept of "spelling instructional level" through the analysis of error-types. *Elementary School Journal, 87,* 181–200.

Nathan, R., Temple, C., Juntenen, K., & Temple, F. (1989). *Classroom strategies that work: An elementary teacher's guide to process writing.* Portsmouth, NH: Heinemann.

Pikulski, J. J. (1990). The role of tests in a literacy assessment program. *The Reading Teacher, 43,* 686–688.

Pinnell, G. S. (1985). Helping teachers help children at risk: Insights from the Reading Recovery Program. *Peabody Journal of Education, 62,* 70–85.

Pinnell, G. S. (1985). Ways to look at the functions of children's language. In A. Jaggar & M. Smith-Burke (eds.), *Observing the language learner.* Newark, DE: International Reading Association and Urbana, IL: National Council of Teachers of English.

Roehler, L. R., Duffy, G. G., & Meloth, M. B. (1986). What to be direct about in direct instruction in reading: Content-only versus process-into-content. In T. E. Raphael (ed.), *Contexts of school-based literacy* (pp. 79–96). New York: Random House.

Rosenshine, B., & Stevens, R. (1984). Classroom instruction in reading. In P. D. Pearson et al. (eds.). *Handbook of reading research.* New York: Longman.

Simmons, J. (1990). Portfolios as large-scale assessment. *Language Arts, 67,* 262–268.

Teale, W. H. (1988). Developmentally appropriate assessment of reading and writing in the early childhood classroom. *Elementary School Journal, 89,* 172–183.

Valencia, S., & Pearson, P. D. (1987). Reading assessment: Time for a change. *The Reading Teacher, 40,* 726–733.

Valencia, S. (1990). A portfolio approach to classroom reading assessment: The whys, whats, and hows. *The Reading Teacher, 43,* 338–340.

Wells, G. (1986). *The meaning makers.* Portsmouth, NH: Heinemann.

Wixson, K. K., Peters, C. W., Weber, E. M., & Roeber, E. D. (1987). New directions in statewide reading assessment. *The Reading Teacher, 40,* 749–755.

Wolf, D. P. (1988). Opening up assessment. *Educational Leadership, 45* (4), 24–29.

Wolf, D. P. (1989). Portfolio assessment: Sampling students' work. *Educational Leadership, 46*(7), 35–39.

Diversity in the Language Arts Classroom

FOCUSING QUESTIONS

■ What are some important issues related to the labeling of children with special educational needs?

■ How has our understanding of school success and failure with respect to students who are culturally or linguistically diverse evolved?

■ Why are simple events such as storytelling important for teachers to understand?

■ What are the strengths and weaknesses of bilingual and English as a Second Language programs?

■ What are the requirements for special education programs as defined by PL 94–142?

■ What are some strategies that enhance the learning of all students, and in particular students with special needs?

Deltrea, Wilfredo, and Shiromani are three children who wrote about their first days in public school in the United States:*

Deltrea — "When I first started school, kids called me and Delton bad names — bad words like 'Blackie' and 'Monkey.' That almost made me go crazy, but I didn't say nothing. It's not fair for people to call names. You could hurt somebody's feelings or make them mad. Now when I hear them call names, I say, 'Cool it!' Because they ain't being friendly to other people.

One day I saw a boy in my class acting ugly to a new kid. Tim hit David and he said, 'Chinese boy, you can't hardly talk English!' I said, 'Don't do that!' But Tim done it again anyway. David started crying. And I beat Tim up. That's when David and me started being friends."

Wilfredo — "We came to San Francisco right before school started. On the first day of school, I met Jose. He is mexicano. He introduced me to my teacher and some other kids in the class. He stayed with me the whole day. We talked in Spanish. I was so glad he was there!"

Shiromani — "I went to school, but nobody talked to me there. A boy said, 'You're stupid. You don't know English. I don't like you.' I didn't say anything to him. But I wanted to say, 'You're ugly. When you came to this world, you didn't speak English, either.'

I was lonely in America. Even the Hindu people in America were different. Some of them don't want to talk Hindi, only English. That means they want to forget where they're from. I don't want to be just American. I want to be my own, too. I like to be Fiji."

INTRODUCTION

These voices express the concerns of the culturally and linguistically different children who could be a part of your future classroom. The stories they tell help us to understand the academic, social, and emotional upheaval that such children encounter when they begin school in an American classroom. How will you respond to these culturally and linguistically different children, or to children who are classified as different because of special academic or physical needs? You need to consider these questions, for you can expect to have children in your class that are in some way thought to be different from the majority of children who are enrolled in school.

This chapter will address diversity within the regular classroom. We will begin with an overview of the various perspectives about culturally and linguistically diverse children. Next, we will consider students with special education needs. Finally, we will discuss classroom strategies for language arts instruction that will enable all your students to view themselves as competent and successful learners.

*(Yee, S. and Kokin, L., 1977; pp. 10–11; 25; 50)
Note: This chapter was contributed by Dr. Diane Barone, University of Nevada, Las Vegas.

Instructional Overview

Teachers sometimes worry that students with special needs will require extraordinary teaching measures. They often suspect that the extra attention such students require will dilute the time that they can spend with other children in the class. You should feel relieved to know that instructional strategies and practices for students with special needs are in most instances the same quality teaching strategies that you will normally use in your regular instruction. As Ysseldyke and Algozzine observe, "For the most part, the things we do to plan, manage, deliver, and evaluate instruction for students who are exceptional are the same as those we do for nonexceptional students" (Ysseldyke and Algozzine, 1990, p. 356). They add to this idea a statement that is important to remember as we teach: "All students — both exceptional and nonexceptional — are more alike than they are different" (p. 35).

Even after being assured that most students learn in the same way and that your instruction will require only minor adaptations, you may still feel apprehensive about addressing all the different needs of your students. You may have heard that children who have dialects or are learning English as a second language present unique difficulties in the classroom. Schools in California, more than schools in most other states, have large numbers of students who are dialect speakers or are learning English as a second language. The *English–Language Arts Framework* (1987) published by the California State Department of Education recommends that teachers working with culturally and linguistically diverse schoolchildren should select "activities and processes involving the reading of good literature, writing about important ideas, and discussing topics which have meaning to their lives." Reading and writing about the characters and events in quality children's books "[helps] all students, regardless of their heritage or language skills" (p. 14).

You may also have heard that poor, inner-city children have difficulty learning in a classroom, but you should know that there are also many examples of school success for these students. Harste directly addresses your concerns about this population of students: "Poor kids learn in the same way as rich kids. Our best research evidence suggests that most regular education students learn in the same way as most special education students, and vice versa. This finding must be kept in mind when considering a policy favoring children coming from certain kinds of homes but recommending a different, often more structured program for students labeled poor or culturally disadvantaged or special (Stephens, 1986)" (Harste, 1989, p. 47).

The above discussion should confirm for you that in most of your teaching you will be using strategies considered appropriate for all students, even those who are culturally and linguistically diverse or have special education needs. Many of the teaching strategies that we will consider in this chapter have been presented throughout this book as models for effective language arts teaching, so they should sound and feel very familiar to you. In this chapter you will rethink some of these language arts strategies and note their particular effectiveness in dealing with the learning needs of your diverse students.

Culturally and Linguistically Diverse Students

Certain areas of the country contain greater numbers of culturally and linguistically diverse students than do other areas; California, Florida, New York, and Texas have the majority of these students at present (Olsen, 1989). However, when Olsen (1989) surveyed the statistics collected on students who are still mastering spoken and written English, he found this population represented to some extent in every state. Enright and McCloskey write that "the trend is toward the creation of linguistically different households in a growing number of communities across all regions of North America" (Enright and McCloskey, 1988, p. 4). And while we may feel that this trend is in the very distant future, Dunn (1987) states that by 2000, one of every three students will be a member of a minority group.

Although linguistically and culturally diverse students are spread throughout the United States, a closer look at the demographics of California show the different facets of this population. Cortes (1986) estimates that "between 1980 and the year 2000, California's Hispanic population is likely to increase by 109 percent (to 9.5 million), the Asian-American population by 90 percent (to 3 million), and the black population by 35 percent (to 2.4 million), while the non-Hispanic white population should increase by less than 13 percent (to 17.8 million)" (p. 9). Narrowing the focus from the whole state of California to the city of Los Angeles, Cortes reports that in the Los Angeles Unified School District, 50 percent of the children in kindergarten through second grade are Hispanic. Bill Honig, state superintendent of schools in California, commented in 1989 in the *Reno Gazette Journal* (Reno, NV) that the number of students in California who have only beginning skills in English doubled during the 1980s. He added that the 742,559 students who are classified as novice English speakers speak 45 different languages. You may not begin your teaching career in an area of the country, like California, that has a large number of children learning English as a second language. But the statistics and predicted trends almost guarantee that sometime during your career you will be teaching several culturally or linguistically diverse children, even if you work in South Carolina, which reports fewer than 100 children learning English as a second language (Olsen, 1989).

Doubtlessly children are and will continue to start school either without or with very minimal abilities in speaking, reading, and writing English. Remember, however, the great variety among these students. For example, some children arrive in the United States having had considerable school experience in their native country. If these children are already reading and writing in their native language, their skills will quickly transfer as they learn to read and write in English (Barnitz, 1985; Hudelson, 1984). Other children, such as the sons and daughters of migrant workers and refugees, have had few experiences with formal schooling; their adjustment to American schools is usually more difficult. They not only have to learn to speak English but also need to learn how to read and write for the first time in this second language, a much harder task than the one facing the first group of children.

In determining how best to teach these children, educators are often influenced by the prevailing political notions. Early in this century, the metaphor of the melting pot was the guiding principle in schools. Children were expected to disregard and

Children from many varied cultural, social, and ethnic backgrounds will make up your classes; you have a wonderful opportunity to grow personally and professionally from working with them. *(© Jeffry Myers/Stock Boston)*

forget their native language and quickly learn English. Recall from Chapter 1 that the melting pot metaphor is inappropriate now. People can retain the qualities of their ethnic backgrounds and still be considered part of the American culture. Children are no longer expected to abandon their first language as they learn English. The statements given by the children at the beginning of this chapter vividly illustrate how important it can be to retain some sense of an original culture.

The terminology associated with persons who are learning English as a second language continues to change. Enright and McCloskey (1988) point out the negative connotations of many terms, such as "non–English speaking" and "limited English speaking," and prefer the more positive terms "first language students" for native English speakers and "second language students" for students learning English as a second language. Tiedt and Tiedt (1986) dislike the term "culturally disadvantaged." They argue that most of us would qualify as culturally disadvantaged because we are familiar with only one culture. We need to be aware of these broader terms and how they often emphasize qualities students may lack rather than ones they possess.

Terms that refer to ethnic groups are also being examined. For example, once considered appropriate, the term *Oriental* is no longer acceptable; *Asian American, Chinese American,* and *Japanese American* are used instead. Other preferred terms are *Afro-American, African American,* or *black American,* and *Chicano* or *Mexican American. Native American,* while accepted, is not very specific; most members of this ethnic group prefer to be identified with a specific tribe, such as Navajo or Paiute (Tiedt and Tiedt, 1986).

My objective in this discussion is to convey to you the present importance of developing a sensitive attitude toward culturally and linguistically different children. You will need to call upon the same type of sensitivity when we investigate the terms that refer to children with special education needs. Ramsey cautions that "as social values and the relationships among groups change, labels and descriptions will continue to evolve. . . . Readers are encouraged to continue to be sensitive to what messages are implied by specific terms and to modify their language to reflect the changing identities and relationships" (Ramsey, 1987, p. 16).

Research on Success or Failure in School

In general, when researchers study the school success or failure of culturally and linguistically diverse students, most of their reports present a very pessimistic view. This depressing outlook pervaded most of the early research about students with special needs. Currently, several researchers are closely investigating those groups of students who, despite their cultural and linguistic differences, perform well in school (Gibson, 1983; Ogbu and Matute-Bianchi, 1986; Ortiz and Yates, 1983). We will take a closer look at the statistics related to school success and/or failure, and then we will examine why such a pessimistic view has been presented and why it is changing.

Ogbu and Matute-Bianchi (1986) state that language minorities, such as Native Americans and Mexican Americans, experience persistent school failure. Cortes quotes pessimistic statistics about the success rate or lack of success of many of these culturally and linguistically different children: in California, "Hispanic students who were enrolled in ninth grade in Fall 1979 had lost over 14 percent of their class. The 1979 Hispanic class of tenth graders had lost almost 29 percent by Fall 1981, and the graduating class of June 1981 had 31 percent fewer Hispanics than it did in Fall 1980" (Cortes, 1986, p. 12). The statistics are equally as bleak for elementary school youngsters. African Americans, Mexican Americans, and many other cultural and linguistic minorities tend to be one or two grade levels below their classmates in reading as measured by standardized tests (Cazden and Mehan, 1989; Delpit, 1986; Hakuta and Gould, 1987; Kagan, 1986; NAEP, 1981; Ogbu and Matute-Bianchi, 1986; Penfield, 1987). Ortiz and Yates (1983) and Rueda (1987) also remind us that second language learners are overrepresented in special education categories, particularly that of "learning disabled."

We have evolved in our understanding of this situation. Early researchers attempted to account for lack of success in school by ascribing intellectual inferiority to certain racial or ethnic groups. It has since been well documented, however, that cultural bias in the making of standardized tests is what causes certain groups to score lower in IQ and other measures (Sue and Padilla, 1986). Mercer (1979), for example, found that blacks and Hispanics who had assimilated the values and attitudes of the mainstream culture had higher IQ scores. One of the most devastating results of this now discredited belief in the fixed intellectual capacity of certain groups was that teachers were not seen as particularly effective in helping members of these groups to succeed in school.

A second view suggested that the minority culture itself was deficient, partially due to the historical effects of prejudice and discrimination. Stereotypical patterns of behavior often associated with one group or another were claimed as responsible for the individual child's lack of success in school. Given this perspective, schools had two choices in remedying this situation. One was to instruct the student and parents so that they would be less deficient in school-related skills. Head Start is an example of a program established to compensate and eliminate deficiencies before children began formal schooling. The other choice was to attempt to eliminate prejudice and discrimination through integration in schools and across schools (Sue and Padilla, 1986).

Gradually a third explanation — cultural mismatch — was elaborated. This concept suggests that each culture is unique in some respects and that the skills of one culture may not be particularly functional within a second culture. Thus, for example, the cooperation emphasized in Hispanic cultures would not apply well to the competitive nature of much of life in the United States, but the work ethic emphasized in Chinese and Japanese cultures would. Cultures, however, are not as one-dimensional as this explanation assumes, and the interactions between cultures are very complex and cannot be outlined so easily. Another problem is that this explanation subtly suggests that the characteristics of one culture are better than another. The classroom result is that teachers primarily emphasize the learning of English. They see English, and English only, as the key to success in the American workplace (Sue and Padilla, 1986).

Our current understanding, described by the term *contextual interaction,* suggests that there is no one single answer as to why so many culturally and linguistically diverse children do not achieve in schools. This approach insists that no cultural group is more "deficient" than any other and that students who are acquiring aspects of a second culture should not be expected to abandon or ignore characteristics of their first culture. The school and community work together, and both change so that students have a better chance at school success (Sue and Padilla, 1986).

Working within the perspective of contextual interaction, Heath (1983, 1986) and Wells (1986) suggest that the primary reason for school failure is a mismatch of teaching and learning expectations between the teacher and the culturally and linguistically different child. Heath studied children in the Piedmont Carolinas, and Wells observed children in Bristol, England. Although these studies occurred in very different geographic locations, the results and conclusions are similar; in both cases teachers were not building from the language strengths exhibited by culturally and linguistically diverse children at home. The teachers in these studies ignored the language competencies that children brought to school and focused on what they perceived to be the children's language deficiencies in accomplishing school tasks.

Effects of Varied Literacy Experiences

Heath (1983) spent ten years carefully describing the differences among storytelling and other literacy events in two communities, "Roadville" and "Trackton" (not the real names of the communities). Roadville residents, predominantly Anglo-American, expect their children to tell stories that are accurate, exact renditions of actual events. Most often these stories are retellings of events that combine into good stories and contain a moral. Heath reports that "children in Roadville are not allowed to tell stories, unless an adult announces that something which happened to a child makes a good story and invites a retelling. When children are asked to retell such events, they are expected to tell non-fictive stories which 'stick to the truth'" (1983, p. 158).

In contrast, Trackton children, who are predominantly black, tell stories that exaggerate the real event. Heath describes the stories told by Trackton residents as being based "on an actual event, but they creatively fictionalize the details surrounding the real event, and the outcome of the story may not even resemble what indeed happened" (1983, p. 166). When these children arrive together at school, among their other unique qualities will be this very different concept of a story: "For Roadville, Trackton's stories would be lies; for Trackton, Roadville's stories would not even count as stories" (Heath, 1983, p. 189). As you probably recognize, each of these definitions of storytelling is limited and would need to be extended by the teacher. Heath noted that the success or failure of particular children in school very much depended on how well the child's literacy behavior matched the teacher's expectations. The above example suggests that the Roadville children's understanding of story will better match the teacher's concept of story. Thus, something as simple as storytelling routines can support or interfere with school success.

Wells (1986) studied the language development of a group of 32 English-speaking children for five years. At the conclusion of the study he noted that all of the children in this sample had adequate language competency to succeed in school, even a child named Rosie, who had never had a story read to her at home. The difficulty that many of these children had in school, Wells notes, arose from different expectations about school talk. Those children whose home language better matched the teacher's expectations about teacher-student talk were more successful in school.

Consider again a statement first referred to in Chapter 5.

If the culture of the teacher is to become part of the consciousness of the child, then the culture of the child must first be in the consciousness of the teacher. (Bernstein 1971, p. 49)

Particularly after you have worked with culturally or linguistically diverse students, Bernstein's words give a new perspective to the notion of a "child-centered" classroom. They remind us that in order to be successful in teaching, we must build on each child's unique strengths rather than focus on perceived individual deficiencies.

Cazden, Heath, and Wells all suggest that teachers need to broaden their

Although, as we've seen, the reasons for the success or failure of culturally and linguistically different children in our classrooms are quite complex, it is important for you as a teacher to remember that each child in your class comes to school with unique literacy strengths. As a teacher you have two choices in the attitude that you share with your students about their differences. You can see the cultural and linguistic differences that children bring to school as a problem. Your job as a teacher then becomes the eradication of these differences. I'm sure you have already guessed that this is *not* the attitude advocated in this book.

I would like you to consider the teaching of culturally and linguistically diverse students a wonderful opportunity for social, academic, and personal growth. Your diverse students should serve as resources to help you and all your other students understand one another in a richer way. Through discovering a broader world view, your class as a whole could investigate the similarities shared by all the world's people. I will focus on the specifics of multicultural explorations later in this chapter.

classroom instruction so that all children can be successful at developing literacy abilities. These researchers mainly studied children who were culturally different and spoke variant dialects of English. The sensitivity that they recommend teachers develop about the children in their classrooms will be even more critical to develop for second language learners, since the cultural and linguistic differences will be even greater.

As we saw in Chapter 1, poverty is a factor that must also be included in this discussion. From the statistics cited above, we realize that many culturally and linguistically diverse students are living in the barrios and the inner-city neighborhoods of major cities. Many of them come from poor families, a circumstance that certainly may influence their success or failure in school. Children living in poverty usually participate in fewer story-reading sessions, for example, than children who are more well off (Heath, 1982; Teale, 1986). The reasons for this are complex. Many poor families often are headed by a single parent who works during the day or night and must also fulfill the role of chief caregiver. Obviously these parents have less time — not to mention energy — to spend with children. They are often unaware of the importance of reading to preschool children and become more involved with their child's reading only after formal instruction in school begins. Parents who are themselves unable to read in English or in their native language, or who do not have a supply of books in their native language, cannot share in book-reading experiences with their children.

What implications do home literacy experiences have for the child's education? If we compare the number of hours low-income families and middle-income families spend in literacy endeavors, we'd expect the middle-income child to have significantly more experiences with storybook reading. Recall the concept of mismatched expectations in the classroom. If the teacher teaches to a typical middle-income child's understanding of storybooks, a low-income child in the class may be very confused. Even if the low-income child has a highly developed notion of oral story from home literacy experiences (Egan, 1987), the teacher may never be aware of this strength.

Kozol (1988) extends our view of poor children by considering the difficulties that homeless children have in surviving life, let alone succeeding in school. He describes the hotels for the homeless in New York City as very depressing places, and his observations of homeless inner-city children are very dismal. By contrast, Taylor and Dorsey-Gaines (1988) share a more positive view of literacy in inner-city families. They describe the extraordinary effort that some low-income families make to support the literacy development of their children, checking homework and quizzing the child on content, and very much taking part in the child's school learning experience.

Historical Perspectives on Second Language Education

We often think that the dilemma of how to educate second language learners is a recent concern, but as Tiedt and Tiedt (1986) indicate, second language acquisition has been an issue in American education since the early 1900s. Interestingly, major political events often change the philosophy underlying second language instruction. Before World War I, for example, classes routinely met on Saturday to teach children languages other than English. Following World War I, popular attitudes toward foreign language instruction changed and "English only" was mandated in schools. Later still, the launch of Sputnik resulted in increased concern for math and science classes and a renewed need for students to speak foreign languages.

In addition to the historical events that altered foreign language instruction, a change occurred in U.S. immigration patterns. One pattern was first noticed in Florida, as an influx of Cuban immigrants arrived in the early 1960s. The children of these immigrants, Spanish-speaking youngsters, were quickly enrolled in the public schools. As a result of the influx of Spanish speakers in the school population, Dade County, Florida, began a bilingual program in 1963, which provided instruction in Spanish for Cuban children. (Bilingual programs include instruction in a child's native language and in English.)

Over the next several years, more and more second language students entered schools throughout the nation. In 1968 the federal government passed the Bilingual Education Act, which contained a special provision that recommended bilingual programs in schools, along with recommending educational programs for students with physical handicaps and students living in rural areas. As states were establishing bilingual programs, the Supreme Court in 1974 decided in *Lau* v. *Nichols* that schools must provide education to students in languages that meet their educational needs. To comply with this decision, schools "began plans to teach students in their native language, whether it be Yupik or Tagalog, and to provide ESL [English as a Second Language] programs specifically designed for each group" (Tiedt and Tiedt, 1986, p. 18). This Supreme Court decision significantly reinforced the importance of multicultural perspectives on the part of teachers and schools.

Challenges to Bilingual and ESL Programs

The bilingual emphasis so dominant in the 1960s and 1970s is currently being challenged in several states. In 1981, a senator from California tried to have English declared as the official language of the United States. Several states have recently passed or attempted to pass bills and resolutions making English the official language of the state. Speaking directly to educators in 1986, Secretary of Education William Bennett proposed that education for second language learners not include their home language. Instruction for second language learners is still molded by political and philosophical beliefs. The questions of which language to use in instruction and how best to teach second language learners continue to be debated, often on the front pages of our nation's newspapers as political leaders argue the merits for or against "English only" curriculums.

In schools, bilingual programs or English as a Second Language (ESL) programs nevertheless proceed. Supporters of bilingual education argue for academic instruction in a child's first language as the child learns English. Hudelson (1984) states that this approach makes sense, because teachers build on the child's first language literacy when they teach reading, writing, or any other subject area. The child can grow in knowledge of other content areas as he or she learns English. Wong-Fillmore (1982) points out that it takes between five and seven years for children to become proficient in the second language. The lengthy period of time required to become competent in speaking and learning through English suggests that children are not fully developing in their understanding of other academic subjects during this period. Bilingual education is philosophically grounded in providing instruction in a child's first language concurrently with English instruction, so that a child does not lag behind in knowledge of other subjects.

Criticism of bilingual instruction, beyond patriotic concerns, points at a lack of teachers who are bilingual and able to conduct classes in a child's first language. This problem is more easily solved in areas where the students all speak the same second language. Think back, however, to the earlier example of language diversity in California; in order to provide bilingual education for this state's students, there would have to be teachers proficient in 45 languages! The demands are still more complicated. The children who speak each language are most likely spread all over the state, so the teacher fluent in a Cantonese dialect, for instance, may find that children who require instruction in this language live in separate cities and towns and are in various grades. In addition, second language learners in any one school generally speak more than one language, and those who do speak the same language often speak variant dialects. How can teachers conduct classes in all of these languages and dialects?

A second criticism of bilingual instruction is that it isolates second language students from the other members of the school for a considerable amount of time. Educators worry that this separation will hinder the second language learner's social and emotional adjustment to the new culture. Parents of children learning English as a second language also often object to bilingual education on this basis; they want their children to quickly become a part of the new culture and this means becoming proficient in the new language.

In response to the difficulties in establishing bilingual classrooms, many schools have adopted English as a Second Language teaching strategies. Often, when second language students first arrive at the public school, they are placed in special classes to help them develop a few words of English. When students are proficient in these few words and phrases, they become members of a traditional class and receive support in the special class for a brief portion of each day. Sometimes these students also receive support in the regular classroom through the use of a bilingual aide. The aide explains to the child in his or her first language what the teacher is teaching. The majority of the child's instruction, however, is in English. Children in ESL programs have as their primary goal the learning of English and as their secondary goal the learning of subject matter.

ESL programs may be a pragmatic solution to the problem of educating second language learners, but critics make us aware of the limitations of this approach. Krashen (1981) states that the second language learner may never catch up academically, since while the child is learning English, he or she is not learning the traditional subject matter taught at a specific grade level. Or the child may be proficient enough in English to be a part of the classroom lesson but find it difficult to understand more abstract ideas in English. A second criticism of ESL programs is that the child's first language is never developed fully and the child does not become truly bilingual. Finally, the lack of the home language in school subtly suggests to the child that his or her first language is not fitting for educational purposes.

The above discussion should help you understand the complexity of educating children who are learning English as a second language. Bilingual and ESL programs have advantages and certainly disadvantages for students. Hakuta and Gould indicate that whereas bilingual and ESL programs differ in the importance they place on the child's first language, they agree on the primary goal — "the development of the students' English to the level of participation in all-English classrooms" (Hakuta and Gould, 1987, p. 39). This goal implies that students, in addition to learning to speak English, are developing the ability to learn academic concepts through English. As a teacher you will want to focus on this primary goal for second language learners or dialect speakers and facilitate their use of their first language and their new language when it is appropriate to do so. For instance, children need to be able to converse in school talk, home talk, friend talk, store talk, and so on (Gee, 1987). All students need to have enough flexibility in their language use so they can adapt their level of discourse as the situation demands. They should also have enough facility with English so they can consider abstract and concrete issues related to instruction.

Whether the school in which you eventually teach offers a bilingual or an ESL program, the chances are great that you will have students who are in the process of acquiring English. Stein (1986) indicates that of the total student population just beginning to speak English, 90 percent are taught in "English only" classrooms. To complicate this situation, only about 6 percent of regular classroom teachers have taken even one course in how to teach these second language students (Waggoner and O'Malley, 1985). Before you become frustrated and a bit overwhelmed at what you can do as a teacher of second language learners, remember the discussion at the beginning of this chapter. The strategies that you will use with these children

AT THE
TEACHER'S
DESK:
*Second
Language
Learners*

People who are suddenly called on to communicate with individuals proficient in another language often resort to strategies that we use with a child who is just beginning to learn to talk. They speak more slowly and loudly, and they often shorten their thoughts to holophrastic speech: "Here?" "Sit." "Food." If we constantly adjust our speech in this way with children in our class, they may feel that we are angry with them. Think about your own reactions to spoken language: if you don't understand the words that someone is saying, a change in the speaker's phrasing to deliberate, terse command may imply anger on the part of the speaker. This is most definitely not the message that we are trying to convey to our students.

A second concern in teaching children who are proficient in another language has to do with preserving a sense of their own intelligence or brightness. This concern was vividly illustrated when I asked a fluent Spanish speaker to conduct a Directed Listening-Thinking Activity with an undergraduate class in reading. The students in the class, who were allowed to speak only in Spanish, became very frustrated when they didn't understand the teacher and when they found it difficult to communicate. Later they said that they were unable to express their ideas in a second language and that, overwhelmingly, they felt "dumb." Remember that these students were successful learners — college juniors and seniors. How must a young child, who is just beginning as a learner, feel in this same situation? It is very important to remember the frustration that second language learners experience as they try to communicate and learn in a new language.

are often the same quality teaching strategies that you will already be using with the other students in your class. We'll consider these strategies after discussing the other students with special needs in your classroom.

Students with Special Education Needs

You may be considering becoming a full-time teacher of children with special education needs, although as a regular classroom teacher, you will also teach these children. Students who are having difficulty learning in the regular classroom are often referred by their teacher to specialists, who conduct a battery of tests to determine if the child qualifies for special programs (Ysseldyke and Algozzine, 1990). In many cases these students spend a portion of their day in a special class and the remainder of the day in a traditional classroom. The current emphasis is to keep these children in the regular classroom as much as possible, a practice referred to as *mainstreaming*.

Ysseldyke and Algozzine (1990) and Kirk and Gallagher (1989) indicate that about 4.5 million children receive special education services in the United States.

These children represent about 10 percent of the total school enrollment. Unfortunately, the statistics related to school success are equally as bleak for students with special education needs as they are for culturally and linguistically diverse students. Twenty-five percent of students with special education needs drop out of school; in urban schools this rate can be as high as 65 percent. Most of the students with special education needs (40 percent) who are leaving school come under the category of emotionally disturbed (Ysseldyke and Algozzine, 1990).

As for culturally and linguistically different students, the labels for students with special education needs abound. Teachers need to realize that the labels change and that many of the labels themselves result in bias. In a discussion of the effects of labeling, Ysseldyke and Algozzine state that "teachers expect students labeled mentally retarded to perform poorly in reading, writing, and mathematics, students labeled emotionally disturbed to be disruptive and difficult to teach, and students labeled learning disabled to perform poorly on a complex visual-motor task" (Ysseldyke and Algozzine, 1990, p. 89). Whereas terms and labels may facilitate discussion about a child or a group of children, teachers need to be cognizant of the child who is often buried beneath the label and the characteristics that make him or her a unique individual.

Historical Perspectives on Special Education

Considering individual needs and educating each child to his or her maximum potential was not always an ideal in education. Up to the late 1800s, children and adults with special education needs were generally placed in poorhouses. They were set apart from the rest of society. In keeping with this practice of separation, residential schools for the deaf, blind, and retarded were established during the mid-1800s. Children who exhibited more minor learning difficulties generally were not provided with special academic support.

Surprisingly, most of the laws and initiatives related to special education have occurred during the last 25 years. Public Laws during the 1960s provided grants for teacher training, for education of children with special needs, and for resource centers to improve the education of children with physical handicaps. Then in 1975, PL 94-142 was passed. This law required states to provide a free education to all children with physical handicaps between the ages of three and eighteen. PL 94-142 is responsible for many of the special education programs that we consider routine today.

PL 94-142 defined several key principles related to special education services. While the law never specifically mentioned mainstreaming, mainstreaming practices are closely associated with it. Mainstreaming implies that a student with special education needs will receive instruction in a regular class whenever possible; in addition, the student may receive instruction in a special class, if necessary. It follows from the mainstreaming concept that children should be placed in the least restrictive environment: spending as much time in a regular classroom setting as possible. In most schools students with special education needs routinely move between a regular classroom and a resource room (a classroom and teacher who provide special services). Other principles included in PL 94-142 are

- *Zero Reject.* All children who qualify for special services must receive them. There can be no waiting lists.

- *Nondiscriminatory Evaluation.* Children must receive individual evaluation, and the evaluation must consider the child's unique cultural and linguistic background. In some cases this means that the child will be evaluated in his or her native language. Each child must be re-evaluated every three years.

- *Parent Participation.* Parents must consent to the evaluation, approve the special education placement, and participate in designing the child's individual educational program (IEP).

- *Individualized Education Program.* An individualized educational plan (IEP), which includes the child's current performance and yearly goals, must be developed for the child. (See Figure 13.1 for a portion of an IEP created for a second-grader who was experiencing difficulties in reading and writing.)

- *Due Process.* The family has a right to disagree with the decisions concerning their child. They may have the child evaluated by a professional outside the school or seek other legal help to settle their dispute. (Kirk and Gallagher, 1989; Orlich et al., 1985; Ysseldyke and Algozzine, 1990)

Legislation has continued to expand services to students with physical handicaps. In 1975 the Education for All Handicapped Children Act (Sect. 619) provided grants to states for services to children between the ages of three and five. Then in 1986, Public Law 99-457 mandated services to all children with physical handicaps and children deemed to be at risk for achieving educational success from birth to age five (Kirk and Gallagher, 1989). Preschool classes are currently being added to public schools as educators attempt to provide services to these young at-risk children. The goal of many of these classes is to facilitate these children's social and academic development so that they do not qualify for special education services when they enter kindergarten, an objective very similar to that of Head Start. Directors of these programs often utilize community members and parents to help locate and identify these young children. Several preschool programs include children who have been the victims of drugs, a new at-risk category.

Court decisions (Ornstein and Levine, 1989) have supported the federal laws. *The Mills vs. Bd. of Education* case in 1972 stated that if there were not sufficient funds to cover all the needs of the school district, then all programs should be cut back in a district, not just special education programs. In 1979, *Larry v. Riles* supported the use of appropriate tests that considered a child's cultural and linguistic background before a child could be labeled as a special learner. These cases and others indicate the judicial support given to the provision of appropriate education for all learners.

Individualized Education Program (IEP)
Hidden Valley School District

Student: *Mary Ryan* Age: 7 Grade: 2

Date: *September 1991*
(reevaluation of instructional goals due Feb. 1992)

Instruction: *30 minutes per day in resource class*
remainder of day in regular class

Instructional Goals:

I. *Develop beginning reading skills*
  A. *Language Experience activities (1 per week)*
    1) *build sight vocabulary to 25 words*
    2) *build fluency through repeated readings*
    3) *develop concept of word by pointing to words while reading*
    - *Evaluation - Mary will be able to read any language experience*
      text fluently.
        Mary will be able to identify, without context,
        25 sight words collected from language experience
        texts.

  B. *Predictable Stories*
    1) *Comprehension through retelling of story*
    2) *repeated readings for fluency*
    3) *concept of word through word pointing*
    - *Evaluation - Mary will be able to retell a previously*
      read predictable text.
        Mary will fluently read a predictable text.

  C. *Word Study*
    1) *concept sorts*
    2) *initial consonant sorts*
    - *Evaluation - Mary will sort a group of pictures by*
      initial consonants.
        Mary will sort sight words by initial
        consonants.

II. *Develop beginning writing skills*
  A. *journal writing (daily)*
  B. *writing activities related to stories*
  C. *story writing*
    - *Evaluation - Mary will be able to write a story about*
      a self-selected topic.
        Mary will be able to write about a story that
        she has read or has been read to her.

FIGURE 13.1

A Portion of an Individualized Education Program
Source: Diane Barone. Used with permission.

Categories of Special Education in the Public Schools

Now that we have examined a general history of special education in the United States, let's look at the kinds of students who are certified for these special services. Children who qualify for special education services in the public schools fit many different categories.

First, Ysseldyke and Algozzine (1990) group three types of students together — those with learning disabilities, those who are gifted and talented, and those with speech and language impairments — because this grouping represents the majority of children receiving special education. As an elementary teacher you can expect that most of the students with special education needs who are placed in your class will come from this grouping of high-prevalence categories.

Before 1960 children with *learning disabilities* were classified in many ways, as emotionally disturbed, mildly mentally retarded, neurologically impaired, and so on. Children labeled as learning disabled represent the fastest-growing category of special education, for several reasons. One is that parents accept this term more easily than they do other labels, and another is that often more federal money is allocated for learning disabled programs than for remedial programs (Kirk and Gallagher, 1989). Children qualify as learning disabled because there is a discrepancy between the grade level they are at and their academic performance. The definition of *learning disabled* excludes children who are below grade level in performance due to physical handicaps, mental retardation, emotional handicaps, or economic or cultural environments.

Gifted and talented students are included when exceptional students are discussed, but PL 94-142 does not define this category as one that must be served. The federal government offers grant support for gifted and talented programs, but states and local school districts decide how these monies will be allocated. Children who are labeled as gifted and talented often perform in academic subjects or in the arts at levels beyond what is normally expected of their peers.

Children with *speech and language impairments* have difficulty communicating because of speaking or listening difficulties and therefore exhibit problems in reading and other subject areas in the curriculum. Most of these children do not exhibit any physical symptoms. Children with cleft palate, cerebral palsy, or a facial birth defect are among the exceptions (Orlich et al., 1985).

Ysseldyke and Algozzine (1990) include in the next major grouping the moderate-prevalence categories, children who are *mentally retarded* and children who are *emotionally disturbed*. Children are usually identified as being mentally retarded through the results of IQ testing; since 1973, children or adults who score below 73 on an IQ test are considered mentally retarded. IQ testing is only one component of the evaluation process, however. Children would need to score in the lowest 2 to 3 percent on an intelligence test, have difficulty learning basic literacy and math skills, and have difficulty adapting to their home or school environment to qualify as mentally retarded (Kirk and Gallagher, 1989).

Often children who are determined to be mentally retarded come from families living in poverty. Remember that earlier in this chapter we discussed the poor results that cultural minorities may exhibit on IQ tests. Ysseldyke and Algozzine (1990) support these earlier observations and extend them to all children living in poverty in the following passage:

> **Children who grow up in environments where resources and experiences are limited can develop intellectually at a very slow rate. Poor children as a group tend to earn lower scores on intelligence tests, one criterion for placement in classes for students who are mentally retarded. The end product is classes comprised heavily of youngsters from poor families. As we've come to recognize the relationship between tests scores and economic status (and that has taken a very long time — longer in some communities than in others), our thinking about mental retardation has changed, as has our thinking about the factors that cause retardation. (p. 165)**

These authors discuss the factors that cause retardation, such as the diet of pregnant mothers, prematurity, lead poisoning, neglect, and heredity. Boyer (1987) elaborates on the relationship between hunger and brain development. A developing fetus requires a diet that contains proteins, vitamins, and minerals, and most poor pregnant mothers have diets that do not include these elements. He goes on to say that the human brain develops very rapidly during a child's first year; poor children, who constitute 40 percent of all persons living in poverty, have inadequate diets and often suffer from malnutrition.

Children who are emotionally disturbed exhibit unusual behavior over an extended period of time. These children might misbehave, refuse to interact with other children, or perform other behaviors not thought to be typical of their peers. The persistent behavior problems exhibited by these children interfere with their academic performance. Ysseldyke and Algozzine (1990) indicate that the majority of children (80 percent) referred for testing for this category are boys in the intermediate grades.

The final grouping listed by Ysseldyke and Algozzine describes children who exhibit characteristics that fit the low-prevalence categories: children with *orthopedic handicaps and other health impairments;* children with *severe or multiple handicaps;* children who are *hard of hearing* or *deaf;* and children who are *visually handicapped* or *blind.* Most of these students are identified by the medical profession long before they are ready for formal schooling. At some time in your teaching career you may have children from this low-prevalence category in your classroom. Some school districts choose to bus children with similar handicaps to one or more schools in a district, so you may have a deaf child mainstreamed into your classroom, for instance, for part of the day. This child would also spend part of his or her day in a special class that focuses specifically on learning strategies for the deaf. For example, in Takoma Park, Maryland, a blind first-grader named Olivia Norman attends a regular class full-time. Olivia's teacher has adapted her classroom and teaching strategies so that Olivia can fully participate, and Olivia is supported by a visiting teacher who helps her with Braille (Viadero, 1989). This situation may seem unusual, but it demonstrates the flexibility with which educators are attempting to solve the problem of how to best educate youngsters with physical handicaps.

Strategies for Instruction

Now that we have considered some types of student diversity possible within a classroom, we will look at what you can do as a regular classroom teacher to support the language arts learning of all the children in your class. It is important to remember that the majority of the students in your classroom with special education needs will come from the high-prevalence categories (Ysseldyke's and Algozzine's first major grouping), and to a lesser degree from the moderate-prevalence grouping. This means that most of the language arts activities and strategies that you share with your regular education children will be appropriate for your students with special needs. Your activities will be structured so that all children can successfully participate in the teaching and learning experience. You will only need to make significant adaptations to your language arts teaching if you find that your class includes students from low-prevalence categories (Ysseldyke's and Algozzine's third grouping). In these situations, school staff are usually trained and supported in their endeavors to help you teach these particular children. In addition, I refer you to the following excellent references, which directly discuss the instruction of children in the low-prevalence groups.

■ ## Build Your Teaching Resources

Books about Special Education Instruction

Ford, A., Schnorr, R., Meyer, L., Davern, L., Black, J., & Dempsey, P. (eds.). (1989). *The Syracuse community-referenced curriculum guide for students with moderate and severe disabilities.* Baltimore, MD: Paul H. Brookes.

Orelove, F. P., & Sobsey, D. (1987). *Educating children with multiple disabilities.* Baltimore, MD: Paul H. Brookes.

Snell, M. E. (1987). *Systematic instruction of persons with severe handicaps.* Columbus, OH: Merrill.

We will first consider some general strategies in classroom organization, reading, writing, and theme unit implementation and then we will discuss specific activities directly related to language arts instruction. In many cases they will already be familiar to you, for effective teaching strategies are appropriate for all of the learners in your classroom.

Classroom Organization and Overall Considerations

Cooperative Groups

Barnes (1975) tells us that "pupils' talk is important, in that it is a major means by which learners explore the relationship between what they know, and new observations or interpretations which they meet" (Barnes, 1975, p. 81). If the teacher organizes his or her lessons mainly through a lecture format, the teacher will be doing most of the talking. The alternative would be for the teacher to routinely incorporate small-group instruction, which often includes cooperative learning strategies and, as a result, more student talk. The use of cooperative learning in small groups is strongly recommended for all students and especially for diverse students (Barnes, 1975; Cazden, 1989; Enright and McCloskey, 1988; Heath, 1986; Kagan, 1986; Pinnell and Matlin, 1989; Rigg and Enright, 1986; Topping, 1989; Ysseldyke and Algozzine, 1990).

Cooperative groups make a lot of sense when we are educating children who are very diverse. (See Chapter 4 for a full description of cooperative groups.) The small group provides a more intimate and safe forum for expressing ideas. Each child has a greater opportunity to talk than during whole-class instruction, and thus a greater chance to practice English and refine or clarify understandings. The use of small groups facilitates the acceptance of the diverse child into the regular classroom because it helps other students realize, perhaps tacitly, that these individuals have important ideas to contribute (Johnson and Johnson, 1975; Kohn, 1986; Slavin, 1979, 1980, 1986). Kagan expressed the advantages of cooperative groupings for all students this way:

> In contrast to the peer relations in the traditional classroom is the positive interdependence among team members in cooperative classrooms. The success of any team member leads to increased rewards (grades, recognition, pride) for the others. Students in this structure naturally begin hoping for their teammates to do well. They begin to adopt a prosocial attitude toward their teammates, which probably generalizes to others as well. (1986, p. 250)

Moll (1986) integrates the importance of cooperative groups with Vygotsky's concept of a "zone of proximal development." Vygotsky observed that students can accomplish problem-solving tasks beyond their individual competence when working in heterogeneous groups. Moll realized that even in groups, however, no child will be able to acquire knowledge much beyond his or her current level of understanding. Let's look at two examples that illustrate Moll's idea. One child in Matthew's writing response group did not understand the part in Matthew's story when the villains drilled a hole through the ground and escaped to China. Matthew had to use a globe to explain what he meant. The child who questioned the story then was on the way to acquiring this new understanding. Remember, however, that group work can help a child push only a bit beyond his or her present level of knowledge. The word "zone" is very important to this concept. The second example will expand on this word's critical significance. Craig, a member of a group of students convened to work on long-division problems, is still trying to learn simple multiplication. Certainly Craig's membership in this group will not result in his mastery of the process of long division. Moll has applied this concept of a "zone of proximal development" only to the teaching of second language learners, but we can readily see how his ideas can extend as well to the teaching of students with special education needs.

Peer Tutoring

Peer tutoring, particularly during reading and math, is another highly recommended small-group strategy that helps all children learn — especially diverse students. You can form pairs in all sorts of ways, but it's wise to avoid pairing the student most proficient in reading or math with the student least proficient in reading or math. These pairs often find it very difficult to work together. A better strategy is to rank the students in the class with respect to math and reading ability. Then divide the class into two halves. Now you can match the most proficient reader with a child who is at the top of the lower half of students, a pairing that functions much better.

In these paired sessions, the tutee could read a story to the tutor, with the tutor supplying help when necessary. These partners could also write reports and stories together. Another strategy might be to form partnerships between students from different classes or grades and have the older student read or write with younger students. Both members of the partnership benefit from this activity, since the more able partner receives additional practice and the chance to be the expert and the less able partner has a willing partner for practice (Topping, 1989). If you form partnerships in both of these ways, all students in your class will feel responsible for another student's learning and have the additional confidence-building benefit of being the expert.

For example, in one school, the kindergarten class was linked with third grade writing partners. One afternoon a week, each third-grader visited his or her kindergarten partner and read aloud a story that had been practiced especially for the kindergarten friend. Following the reading, the two children would talk about the story, and the third-grader would record the kindergartener's thoughts. Another partnership, a first and fifth grade pairing, was established in that same school for a short-term research project. Each first-grader chose an animal that he or she wanted to know more about. The first grade teacher then enlisted the fifth-graders to help the first-graders locate and read pertinent material about that animal. The fifth-graders were rewarded when they watched their first grade partners share the animal information at a special gathering.

Comprehensible Input

Krashen (1981) described the process by which second language learners acquire a new language. In this discussion, Krashen focused on a concept called comprehensible input, which is very similar to Vygotsky's "zone of proximal development": the teacher presents information to the student that is just a little beyond his or her current competence in any subject area. While Krashen is not necessarily concerned with group functioning, he does suggest that teachers consider their own language, the child's background knowledge, the method of presentation (concrete or abstract), and other important elements, since information or language way beyond a child's competence can appear to be nonsense if the child can make no sense of it. As with Vygotsky's observations, Krashen's ideas can extend to fit the needs of your diverse students. Let's look at two examples that suggest how you might apply the concept of comprehensible input to the language you use in the classroom.

First, Heath (1978) illustrates the difficulty that second language learners, in particular, can have in understanding some "simple" directions given by the teacher. Heath portrays the following typical classroom episode:

> [Teacher and students working at a table with boxes and objects of different shapes.]
>
> Hold the red box *up*.
> Put the blue circle *in* the red box.
> Hold the sheet of brown paper *over* the red box.
>
> In this reading setting, the students are learning to deal with a paradigm: they learn to display, to be exact, and — most important — to pay attention to the examiner's actions. They learn to learn by following directions; they probably learn little about the meaning of prepositions — the explicit focus of the lesson.
> Contrast the use of prepositions in the following routine expressions as the teacher attempts to maintain classroom control throughout the day:
> We've got to get *over* this habit of everyone stopping at the water fountain on the way to lunch.
> Let's put the scissors *up* now.
> Are we all *in* line?
> Hold your work at your desk until the reading circle is *over*. (1987, p. 17)

Heath's example vividly demonstrates just how confusing it is for a child to learn a second language. The other learners in the class may have an equally difficult time with these "simple" directions. No wonder children periodically give their teacher a look that suggests they are totally lost. If you are sensitive to the nuances of language, you will realize the difficulties a child may be having in trying to sort out exactly what a word means and exactly when it means that.

Enright (1986) provides a second example of the importance of thinking about language when working with diverse students. During a summer practicum, Enright observed an ESL intern, Molly, as she changed her language and instruction to aid the learning of her students. Molly's class had 16 primary students who spoke six different languages and four students who were native English speakers. Molly made some major adaptations.

First, Molly began to see classroom language as performing both a language teaching as well as a subject-matter teaching function. Seeing this, Molly then

began to use more and more small group and individualized activities in place of full group activities. Finally, Molly adapted her view of her own role in the classroom from viewing herself as a language giver to viewing herself as a language facilitator and user with her students. (p. 122)

The adaptations that Molly made were strategies that you already consider essential for quality instruction. These types of adaptations will certainly enhance the learning of all your diverse learners.

Reading

Teachers often feel that reading instruction is difficult to provide to children who are culturally and linguistically diverse or who have special education needs. They worry that children who read below grade level will have difficulty with the stories in their curriculum. They are concerned that the cultural backgrounds of the students will interfere with their comprehension of American children's stories. And they wonder about how to teach a child who speaks very little English to read. We will address these concerns as we look once again at some very familiar strategies that now seem particularly appropriate in teaching your diverse students to read.

Language Experience Approach

The language experience approach (Dixon and Nessel, 1983; Feeley, 1983; Moustafa, 1987; Sutton, 1989) is recommended for learners with special needs because the language of the child becomes the bridge to the more formal reading and writing of the classroom. Besides providing this bridge to more formal reading and writing, LEA has other benefits as well. Children can share their own personal experiences as the dictations develop. This focus on self is particularly important for children experiencing emotional difficulties and for children with physical handicaps. The language experience approach allows children to share stories from home, another way of informally helping the child make the transition to school. The process of taking an LEA dictation involves the children in extended talk about a topic. Working in small groups helps students with special needs build confidence in the importance of their ideas and develops understandings about a topic that they might not risk talking about with the whole class. Perhaps most important, LEA provides time for a small group of students and the teacher to work together closely and to grow in mutual understanding.

The language experience approach is not only appropriate for young beginning readers and writers. Teachers who work with older students also must determine exactly how to include below-grade-level readers and second language learners into their curriculums. Finding appropriate reading materials for older beginning readers is often more difficult than it is for younger students, since the older students are sensitive about their learning, and supplying them with picture books can be discouraging and embarrassing. LEA allows such a child to fully participate in thinking with the rest of the class as his or her reading proficiency develops. The dictations the child creates are highly motivating and relevant because they are

*AT THE
TEACHER'S
DESK:
Thinking and
Language
Experience*

One of the dilemmas in working with students with special needs is to provide activities that tap their cognitive capabilities. While picture books are wonderful, not many fifth- or sixth-graders want to spend a lot of time with books that focus on colors, numbers, or baby animals. Even if they are interested in these topics they may want to explore them at a more sophisticated level. This is where the language experience approach comes in. You want to keep your below-level readers involved in the higher-level thinking and discussing that is occurring in class and to assure them that their ideas are worthwhile.

One strategy is to have the student create his or her own text about the topic being studied. You, a parent, or another child could read the pertinent chapter or section of chapter into a tape recorder. The student could then listen to this tape and dictate to a partner the ideas he or she found to be important. This dictation now becomes the child's text. Through this minor adjustment, your students with special needs will fully participate in regular class activities, and their knowledge of subject matter will not lag behind as they build power in reading.

---

centered on the same topics that the class is studying. (For a detailed account of using LEA with second language learners, see Dixon and Nessel, 1983.)

Carlsen (1985) further suggests that students who are hearing impaired participate in an activity or a field trip before dictating an LEA. The combination of real experience and the written record helps the deaf child understand vocabulary and sentence structure and aids reading development. In fact, as you know, combining real experience with writing makes sense for all the learners in your class, whatever their reading level.

Reading Aloud, "Narrow Reading," and Repeated Readings

One of the ways to help "special" children become readers and writers is to share a variety of literature with them (Hough, Nurss, and Enright, 1986; Ramsey, 1987; Sutton, 1989). You will want to read aloud to beginning readers predictable books and books that are well illustrated. These books, based so often on rhymes and songs, help acquaint children with storybooks. Older students, who may read so slowly and laboriously that they fail to appreciate a story, can stay more involved with stories by listening to the teacher's oral reading. Perhaps once you have read a story to the class, your less proficient readers might attempt to read the book themselves, feeling more confident about their abilities.

Wordless books take on a new importance for learners with special needs. Dixon and Nessel (1983) specifically recommend wordless books for children who are learning English as a second language. These authors suggest that the child supply his or her own oral text for the picture story, which then can be written down using LEA or can be tape-recorded for other listening experiences. Wordless books

Many effective regular language arts strategies, such as predictable books and repeated reading, will work well with your students with special needs. *(© Jerry Howard/Positive Images)*

can enable parents who do not speak or read and write English to "read" aloud with their children, using their first language to share the story. Parents who do speak English but are unable to read can also share stories this way.

Another strategy recommended for diverse students is called "narrow reading" (Krashen, 1981). In "narrow reading" a child experiences several works of one author or several books on a single topic. A child who reads several works by Beverly Cleary, for instance, would find the first book the most difficult to read but subsequent books easier. While reading the first book, the child has an opportunity to become familiar with the author's writing style and vocabulary. Since many authors employ the same characters and settings in book sequels, the child has only to focus on the new plot while reading a second or third book in the series. To each new book the child brings more background knowledge about the characters and the author's style. To do "narrow reading" on a single topic, share with students books that vary in complexity from very simple, introductory texts to more complete discussions. The children build background knowledge from each book and can bring it to bear on subsequent books. This strategy helps below-grade-level readers develop a fuller understanding of the topics being studied in class.

Repeated reading of the same dictated text, story, or poem allows the student to come to the text focused only on meaning. On second and subsequent readings the child recognizes the sequence and the vocabulary of the story and doesn't need to give as much attention to these details. Second language learners and below-level readers have a better chance of forming predictions after a second or third reading of a story (Krashen, 1982; Sutton, 1989; Wong-Fillmore, 1982). You should try to choose books that are particularly interesting or that easily provide for a second focus. For example, during the first reading of *The Doorbell Rang* (Hutchins, 1986), the children could listen to discover what happens to the cookies and who appears at the door. During the second reading you could ask students to focus on the mother to discover the difficulties she has in keeping the floor clean.

Another way to encourage repeated reading is through paired reading: children practice a story with a partner so that they can then read it to a third child. Many times teachers have older students choose a picture book to read to a kindergarten or first grade child; the practice reading sessions that occur before the sharing let the older reader experience truly fluent reading. Readers Theatre is another excellent forum that requires children to repeatedly reread a story for an informal performance.

A very important advantage of this strategy is that children's comprehension becomes deeper on successive readings. Children talk more about familiar stories and develop a greater understanding of the story (Martinez and Roser, 1985; Morrow, 1987; Yaden, 1988). Morrow (1987) explains that after hearing a story once, children often talk about the illustrations. After subsequent readings, children comment on and question the plot and characters. These extra readings let all of the children in your class — even the least proficient reader — understand the importance of discovering the meaning of a story.

Finally, I'd like to note that the strategies of reading aloud and repeated readings have been incorporated into a special remedial program for at-risk first-graders. Reading Recovery, a program initiated to bring first-graders up to grade level reading, emphasizes the importance of reading to children and of the repeated reading of stories. In each tutoring session, the teacher includes the reading of a story and the repeated reading of a favorite story or a dictation. These shared-reading experiences are seen as critical elements in helping at-risk first-graders develop literacy skills (Pinnell, Fried, and Estice, 1990).

Critical Thinking and Problem Solving

Throughout our discussion of teaching and learning experiences for students with special needs, I have indirectly referred to the development of children's thinking and problem-solving skills. In the process of helping their diverse students, teachers may be so intent on developing basic reading and writing skills that they neglect the child's imagination. You will be able to teach your diverse students to read and write more effectively, however, if you do engage their critical thinking and problem-solving knowledge.

Cooperative groups are a vital forum in which children can formulate their ideas about issues. As each child listens to the others, the group comes to a consensus about a topic and the youngsters build trust that encourages them to risk sharing personal thoughts and ideas. It is important to integrate your learners with special needs into many groups so that each student can learn from a variety of perspectives; no one group should be composed of all the diverse students in your class.

For example, an activity as simple and concrete as brainstorming all of the different ways to cure hiccups can allow students to discover the similarities and differences in behavior across cultures. In one case, four first-graders, Ryan, Ann, Carlos, and Atina, brainstormed all the ways that they knew about curing hiccups. Atina said that her father scared her by jumping up and down. Ryan asked if that really worked; he thought that a drink of water would be better. Atina stubbornly responded that being scared worked more quickly than drinking water. Carlos said that his sister pinched him when he had hiccups. At that point, all of the students agreed that pinching might work — but that they would rather try another remedy! The discussion continued in this way for another ten minutes, when the teacher brought all the groups together so that they could share their information.

The discussion that occurs during these small group experiences should be at a level that enables all the children to participate. If the topic is quite abstract, perhaps one group activity could be to have each child share a concrete example of the idea. Say, for instance, that the children are each given the job of acting out a specific emotion displayed by a character in a book they are reading. Following this simple drama activity, the children create drawings of this emotion. This helps the below-level reader or second language learner understand the more abstract elements in a story, and all the children will realize the wide range of ideas elicited from a single emotion.

You can hone children's thinking skills by having them make predictions before and while they read, which keeps them involved in achieving meaning. Costa and Marzano (1987) suggest that children compare and contrast the similarities and differences among several stories they have read. Use very specific vocabulary when you ask your students to make comparisons — simply saying, "Let's look at these stories" is too general. Specific terms such as *compare* and *contrast* help focus a child's thinking and allow him or her to concentrate on the problem-solving requirements of a task.

Perhaps one of the most important ideas to remember in fostering the critical-thinking skills of your diverse students is to design assignments that allow for a variety of responses. And though each child's response may vary, every student should be able to support his or her viewpoint through concrete examples. This ability will probably be part of your criteria in evaluating students. Smith makes the observation that since "modern attitudes tend to accept events, without judgment about their value, students and adults may drift along quite nicely as mere observers, not as critical thinkers. When those same people read, they will continue to be passive — unless their teachers or friends jolt them into changing" (Smith, 1989, p. 424). You and all of the children in your class will be responsible for "jolting" one another into more active, charged activities in thinking.

Writing

Hudelson (1984) emphatically states that second language learners can write in English before they have mastered the oral and written systems of English. Hudelson and others discovered that reading and writing develop as children participate in the process of composing text. Not surprisingly, writing is also recommended for your students with special education needs. Rhodes and Dudley-Marling indicate that many of these students "have plenty to say if they would only leave behind their nearly paralyzing concern about conventions, spelling in particular" (Rhodes and Dudley-Marling, 1988, p. 114). You will begin your writing instruction by helping students move beyond these self-imposed roadblocks, recognizing that "writers cannot concentrate on generating ideas and using conventions correctly at the same time" (Rhodes and Dudley-Marling, 1988, p. 114). To develop your students' writing fluency, these authors recommend the use of self-selected topics, journal writing, and several drafts before considering correctness.

Children who are writing in English as they learn English often include elements of their first language in their stories. Figure 13.2 includes two responses to the story *Buenas Noches,* written by two first-graders in a predominantly Hispanic classroom. The teacher read the story to the children in Spanish, and then the children wrote about it in Spanish using invented spelling and illustrations. (The teacher provided a Spanish and an English translation for us.) These children are still predominantly using Spanish when they write; the relationship between their invented spelling and the conventional Spanish provided by the teacher is clear.

Figure 13.3 comes from a second grade class studying a unit on insects. The teacher asked the children to write about what insect they might like to be and what they would do as that insect. As the figure shows, a second-grader wrote a story about being a bug and flying over people, schools, trees, parks, and stores. She thought it would be okay to be a bug during the day but at night she would turn back into a person. Notice that her story is relatively easy to read and that the carry over from her first language is the use of "de" for *the.*

Teachers sometimes worry that permanent writing confusion may develop for students who mix their home language and English. Edelsky (1982), Nathenson-Majia (1989), and Urzua (1987), who have studied the writing of second language learners, note that the children use what they know about their first language when learning a second language and that they follow the spelling development strategies described in Chapter 10 when writing English. Their invented spelling may have characteristics unique to their first language — for example, "de" for *the,* "es" for *s* ("estop"), or "ch" for *sh* ("wach") for Hispanic children (Nathenson-Majia, 1989) — but these features will disappear as the children become more proficient readers and writers of English. Hayes and Bayruth (1985) caution that these errors will not disappear overnight but that "the errors are not a cause for alarm, and teachers should not correct them. Children learning English as a second language will make errors, but as they become more proficient, as their production increases, as they read and write more, the number of errors will decrease" (Hayes and Bayruth, 1985, p. 102).

(This reads:
El pajarito grito,
"ph, ph, ph, ph, ph.")

(The bird shouted,
"ph, ph, ph, ph, ph.")

(This reads:
Alli hay gorriones.
Hacen "ti.")

(There are the robins.
They say "ti.")

FIGURE 13.2

Story Responses Written by Two Hispanic First-graders

Strong support for the reading and writing strategies described above comes from a demonstration school in California. The Fair Oaks School, which has a student population 85 percent Hispanic, 10 percent other minorities (Filipino, black, Asian), and 5 percent white, began a program a number of years ago to change its grim statistics: the students were three to four years below grade level as measured by an achievement test. The core ingredient of the new program was to have students read and write each day, and today the majority of students test at grade level. (To read more about this school, see Bird, 1989.)

Dialogue Journals

As interactive writing experiences, dialogue journals are recommended for all students, especially for the diverse students in your class (Gutstein, 1989; Hayes and Bayruth, 1985; Peyton and Seyoum, 1989; Staton, 1983, 1988; Sutton, 1989). These journals allow for personal communication between you and your students. Many

Tania Tamay

If I was a bug I con fly
and se de pipov and de shools
and de tres and de parges and de
gauses and de stors and de boics and de
son I loic to bi o bug but
and de nait ay tor bag to a purse
n.

FIGURE 13.3

**Story Written by a
Second-grader
Whose First
Language Is Spanish**

(This story reads:
   If I was a bug I can fly and see the people and the schools and the trees and the
parks and the houses and the stores and the bikes and the sun. I like to be a bug but in
the night I turn back to a person.)

times students with special education needs feel distant from classmates and from the teacher; this distance is especially noticeable with older students who have experienced several years of academic failure. By having children communicate directly with you about interesting ideas that they find in books, for instance, you can show through your response that you truly value their ideas. You may even be able to share a similar personal experience that lets students know you are a "real person" in addition to being their teacher.

Dialogue journals combine many of the practices we have discussed that support literacy development — comprehensible input, writing experience, the intimacy of working in small groups. The child initiates the writing, and the responder builds on the content of the original entry, taking the child slightly beyond his or her original understandings. In addition, dialogue journals stress the communicative nature of the writing task; the child develops his or her writing abilities in order that another child or the teacher can read the communication.

Staton (1983) provides two examples of dialogue journals. The first is from a student who is learning English as a second language, and the second is from a university student who is hearing impaired.

STUDENT'S ENTRY: Ms. Reed, I like dis room and I like you Bekes you are a good teshir and teach my English. I like evryBety.

TEACHER'S RESPONSE: Everybody likes you, too, Laura. Did you read the book? We will read every day. (p. 1)

STUDENT'S ENTRY: I know what identify and identity mean but I want to make sure that I have understand what those means but these are different meaning.

TEACHER'S RESPONSE: First thing: identify is a verb, identity is a noun.
    "Identify" means to name something or someone, or point out someone or something. Example: I will identify the man who robbed me (meaning I will name him or point him out).
    "Identity" is when someone or something is already named or pointed out. Example: The police know the identity of the man who robbed me. His name is Bob Smith. (p. 6)

In the first example the teacher welcomes the student and gives her a nudge to read a book. She helps the child understand the routine of the class by telling her that they will be reading each day. In the second example the student is trying to clarify her understanding of two words. The teacher carefully clears up the student's misconceptions. Interactive writing can also occur between students in the class or from other classrooms. The students might converse about their classes in general and about the books they are reading or the stories they are writing. These informal opportunities at communicating through writing will spark reading and writing development in all of your students.

Computers

Computers are exciting tools that can enhance classroom instruction. Using simple word-processing programs, children of varying abilities can write stories on a computer (Hummel and Balcom, 1984). You might first pair up students who each have different strengths and weaknesses. Each child contributes sentences to the story. Sam and Amanda, for instance, decide on a setting for their story and perhaps write the first sentence together. Then Sam writes a sentence. Amanda uses Sam's sentence as a jumping-off point and continues the story. Then it's Sam's turn again. This process continues until the story is completed. One benefit of using the computer in this way is that it eliminates the difficulty that the children may have in reading each other's handwriting. Just using a computer can itself be rewarding; children enjoy seeing their writing take shape on a screen and are less inhibited about engaging in and revising this writing.

Children find a computer particularly helpful when they are creating a newsletter. They can compose their articles directly at the computer and, as a group, revise and edit on the screen. This group revision and editing should polish the work of even your most reluctant writer. Once your students develop proficiency with a simple word-processing program, they may want to move to a more sophisticated software package that lets them incorporate graphics into their newsletters. Group projects such as class newsletters help all students feel that they are an important part of the class and build positive relationships between home and school.

Another creative computer project makes use of a modem as a classroom teletype. Two bilingual classes, one in Connecticut and one in California, jointly published a newsletter edited by both classes (Sayers, 1989). The students wrote drafts in their own classrooms; during the evening the drafts were sent, via the computer modem, to the partner school. The students' work then was edited and read by an audience beyond the limits of their own classroom. The children also learned about each other's schools, cities, and states.

Educational software developers are designing programs that let students interact with a story on the screen — for example, to use problem-solving skills to extricate a character from some predicament. In order for the program to incorporate the suggested remedy, the children must type their directions into the computer, which is a clever way to integrate reading, writing, and thinking. Another computer application for the classroom is CD-Rom technology, which connects a CD player to a computer; children can access compact disks containing catalogues and encyclopedias, and often music and art. One sample disk plays some of Mozart's music as the screen displays information about the composer. This type of computer technology certainly can benefit the diverse learners in your class.

When you select software for your in-class computer, ask your computer dealer to demonstrate the program. Be critical about the programs you select. Many educational software packages are just worksheets moved to a computer, filled with reading and writing skill activities once seen only in workbooks. Unfortunately these types of programs are often recommended for students with special education needs. You should make sure that the activities students do on computers match the activities that you ask them to do without computers. You want your students to be engaged in real reading and writing and to practice critical thinking and problem solving when they use the computer.

Thematic Units

Integrated, thematic organization of curriculum is recommended for all the learners in your classroom, particularly those with special needs. Kirk and Gallagher (1989) even suggest this type of instruction for children who are mentally retarded. Based on variations from a specific topic, thematic units give children many opportunities to explore a concept and to more actively participate in their own learning. Thematic units also reinforce Krashen's idea of "narrow reading," since students explore a topic in depth rather than just being exposed to it (Edelsky, 1986; Enright and McCloskey, 1988; McCloskey, 1987). Children are encouraged to read many books on a topic as they discover other ideas related to the theme.

Egan (1987) offers a way to organize thinking within thematic units that should prove helpful to your diverse students. He suggests that students explore topics by thinking about their opposites. Children could approach the general topic of fire, for instance, by comparing its beneficial and detrimental effects. Egan specifically suggests a history curriculum built around binary opposites. Western culture thus might be considered as the "struggle for freedom against tyranny, for peace against violence, for knowledge against ignorance, for power against powerlessness, and so on" (Egan, 1987, p. 467). Theme units that allow children to extend their thinking between two poles help students with special needs come to a fuller understanding of abstract ideas. These discussions should certainly be lively as children express their different views.

■ Build Your Teaching Resources

Thematic Planning

Chapter 9 gives you the specifics of developing a thematic or literature-based unit. To explore thematic planning in more detail, you may want to examine the following books:

Moss, J. (1984). *Focus units in literature: A handbook for elementary school teachers.* Urbana, IL: National Council of Teachers of English.

Moss, J. (1990). *Focus on literature: A context for literacy learning.* Katonah, NY: Richard C. Owen.

> Moss explores thematic units for first through sixth grades. Each unit includes discussion and writing suggestions appropriate for all learners. Moss also provides an extensive list of independent reading materials that relate to the theme, including books of varying difficulty. You should be able to find a book for each student in your class. Some of the themes are "Pig Tales," "The Sea," and "Wish Tales."

Enright, D. S., & McCloskey, M. (1988). *Integrating English.* Reading, MA: Addison-Wesley.

> Enright and McCloskey detail how to create the social, physical, and academic environments that support learning using thematic organization. Their book specifically focuses on the second language learner.

Involving Parents

Schools that have large populations of learners with special needs and that are considered successful at meeting the needs of these students all have close ties with parents. Sometimes these connections involve teachers in learning more about the home culture so they can make adaptations in the classroom. For example, in the KEEP program (Au, 1980) teachers in Hawaii incorporated into their reading curriculum the "talk story" format so familiar to the children. Children produced narratives developed by more than one student at the beginning of the reading lesson, and the focus of instruction shifted from decoding to comprehension. With these simple additions to the curriculum, the children grew in their reading competency. Heath (1982) describes a similar adaptation made by teachers in the Carolinas. When they included in classroom work some of the story structures the children experienced at home, the academic performance of the children increased. In each of these examples, teachers discovered the home literacy strengths of the children and added these to the classroom curriculum. Without requiring an immense amount of time and energy, these simple additions resulted in increased academic performance for children who are not often successful in school.

One program spearheaded by James Comer in New Haven (Comer, 1987) was developed to enhance the academic and social success of at-risk students and was grounded in "the understanding that suggestions and interests of parents, teachers, and other participants must be taken seriously, and that representatives of these groups must have meaningful roles in the school program" (Comer, 1987, p. 16). Nevertheless, teachers are often reluctant to invite parents into the curriculum. Typically, parent help is requested only for chaperoning a field trip. Rasinski (1989) offers advice on how to better integrate parents into the reading program. He suggests that committees of parents and teachers design at-home reading programs and that both parents and teachers coordinate all reading activities.

Tiedt and Tiedt (1986) describe other less direct methods of including parents. Specific activities can welcome children and involve parents in the curriculum. On a September bulletin board, for example, the teachers and students write "Welcome" in many different languages. Later each of the children develops a "Me" collage for the display. In the collage each child includes his or her birthplace, baby pictures, favorite things, names of siblings, and so on. (See Figure 13.4 for one example of such a collage.) Building on this activity, the children investigate their names. The study can expand to the origin of surnames and to naming customs, including the transformation their names undergo in different languages (for example, John, Jan, Johan, Juan, Jean, Giovanni, etc.). As the authors point out, these activities often require expert advice from home. Children need to check with parents about how they were named, why they moved to the United States, and on other important facts. These activities allow parents to participate informally and indirectly in the school curriculum. They also foster important discussion between the child and his or her parents and may motivate parents to become more active participants in the school.

FIGURE 13.4

"ME" Collage

William Bennett directly addressed the importance of parent involvement in schools. He boldly stated:

> Some people contend that we cannot expect much from parents who lack education, money, or a solid grasp of the English language. Yet for generations, our schools have successfully taught the children of immigrants and refugees who insisted on making the fearful trip to meet the teacher because they knew school was important; the children of working-class people who did not know how to read very well but who made sure that their children completed their lessons each night; and the children of the poor, hopeful that their families could escape poverty by learning. Today, millions of low-income and ill-educated parents do their utmost to further their children's education. Saying that poor parents cannot help because they are poor is snobbism of the worst sort, and it is wrong." (1986, p. 11)

Bennett certainly makes it clear that parents are to be included in the educational process. He goes on to specifically suggest ways of supporting parents in their attempts to help their children. Bennett looks to the local library and to neighborhood members to organize story hours so that children whose parents cannot read can still participate in read-aloud discussions. He recommends that schools find creative ways to include parents. One school in eastern Arizona provided baby-sitters and transportation so that parents from the San Carlos Apache Reservation were able to attend school functions. Teachers from a New Hampshire school who wanted to improve communication with the parents of children with physical handicaps devised a "Communication Notebook" for each child. Teachers and parents used the notebooks to write about these students' growth and problems; these daily chats helped the school and parents cooperate more closely.

Many teachers are unsure about how to deal with parents who do not speak English. They may recommend that parents try to use the little English they have acquired when speaking to their children, in hope that the parents and the children will learn English together. Unfortunately, this recommendation is not in the best interest of the child who is learning English as a second language. Since these parents are often very limited in English proficiency, the child will not be participating in a full range of language activities. Heath (1986) recommends that parents use their strongest language so that children become aware of the multiple opportunities to use language. She says that "those students who have the most diverse, well-developed, and extensive language use (even in a language other than English) will be best prepared to learn a rich and powerful English in schools" (Heath, 1986, p. 26).

As a teacher, though, you will still be faced with the difficulty of communicating with parents who do not speak English. You may want a bilingual student or adult to translate the notes you send home. This way parents can read your messages in their strongest language. You might also have a child create a tape in the parents' native language explaining some of the events happening in school. Remember that the child will probably need to borrow the tape recorder to play the message at home. For parent conferences, you will want to arrange for an older child or a bilingual member of the community to help you communicate. Remember to have

FIGURE 13.5

**Examples of
Environmental Print**

samples of the child's work, since referring to these should make the conference go more smoothly.

Homework is another aspect to consider. Enright and McCloskey (1986) suggest that you give children more than one night — preferably a week — to complete homework assignments. Recognize that the children in your classroom come from all types of homes and may return from school to discover that their parents won't be available to help with homework. Sometimes, too, special family events compete with homework time. Flexibility in allowing assignments to be completed over two or three days should result in a better rate of homework completion.

Expand Your Teaching Repertoire

Below are some specific instructional activities that you can assimilate into your classroom. These are individual ideas that will help you as you first begin to plan instruction for your diverse students.

1. Children can participate in a search for environmental print in and around the school. They will notice that writing is everywhere (Enright and Mc-Closkey, 1988) and that they can read it. (See Figure 13.5 for examples of common environmental print.) You might also ask students to look for international signs so that they realize there are common ways of communicating across languages. A driver's education booklet would be a likely resource for some of these signs.

2. Include books in your classroom library that are written in different languages or different dialects. There are many books available in Spanish, for

example. All children will enjoy comparing the words written in another language, and they might even discover that many of the words are similar. You can also include books from the child's home. While you might not consider books bought in a grocery store to be great literature, these books are in many homes, and children might select them because they are familiar and provide connections to home reading.

3. Your students can perform a research study that involves interviewing parents, friends, and other children in the school. They might try to discover what the first day of school was like for individuals of all ages and then create a time line that shows how going to school has changed. Another question children might ask the adults they interview is how people learned to drive and what were the rules for getting a license. The students could investigate the changes in driving laws in the United States. They might also compare the driving laws of other countries. The list of possible questions is endless; to narrow the possibilities, you might develop questions that relate to your thematic unit.

4. Parents and children might share a special night. The parents and children could cook and share a dish that has significance in their family. The child might bring a special object from home and then explain its significance to himself or herself and the family. This type of evening would help reduce the anxiety that usually accompanies family trips to school (Ramsey, 1987), and everyone certainly would get to know each other a bit better.

5. Ramsey (1987) and Tiedt and Tiedt (1986) suggest that teachers incorporate special holidays and important events from other cultures into the classroom. Teachers and students might celebrate Chinese New Year and Cinco de Mayo, for example. Inclusion of special cultural events could occur monthly throughout the school year.

6. When children create class books, they can include a Braille script or a translation to another language on each page. They might tape their story so that other students can read along in English or in some other language. Tapes and books can be shared with parents through a checkout system. Parents or other community members might even respond to the story on cards provided in the book.

7. The *California English–Language Arts Framework* (1987) provides models of integrated language arts lessons that make provisions for all students. One example describes a unit on weather for intermediate grades. The unit is introduced by reading Steven Kellogg's *Paul Bunyan* and a Chinese tale called *The First Snow*. The children then research weather using various books and newspapers. The unit includes many reading and writing activities and, what is particularly interesting, literature from many different countries. Another unit focuses on the feelings of being handicapped; it includes books such as Helen Keller's *The Story of My Life* and Elizabeth Speare's *The Witch of Blackbird Pond*. The children participate in many activities that sensitize them to the difficulties of having a handicap. For example, they try to block out sight and sound for one hour before reading about Helen Keller. Rather than fo-

cusing on each handicap and creating a list of related difficulties, the students experience feelings that are common across handicaps. In this unit the students spend time considering prejudice and how it affects persons with handicaps and others considered to be different.

Children's Literature Related to Diversity

You are probably familiar with books about Martin Luther King, Jr., Frederick Douglass, and Helen Keller. Teachers tend to read these to children during a special unit, perhaps on black history or on people who have successfully lived with handicaps. Books that include characters from diverse populations often are shared only during these special units; during other story-reading sessions, Anglo-American children and their culture predominate. You will want to include in your classroom on a much more regular basis literature that describes cultural, linguistic, academic, and physical diversity.

Katherine Lasky (1990), in an article on the dilemmas of writing historical fiction, shared a school experience of her daughter.

> **In Cambridge, Massachusetts, where my children go to school, January is Black History Month. My own personal feeling is that black history should be taught every month, with perhaps an emphasis in January because of Martin Luther King's birthday. My little girl, a second grader now, became confused last year. She thought all black history had taken place in the month of January and that was it. (p. 160)**

We certainly don't want to contribute to this type of confusion on the part of children. It is important for children to become engaged daily with books that represent all of the diversity among the world's children.

Beyond the special units just mentioned, you can use thematic units to share books that represent all cultures. For example, in a unit on economics you could read Cleary's *Ramona and Her Father,* Hazen's *Tight Times,* and Greenfield's *Grandmama's Joy.* Ramona is an Anglo-American child growing up in a middle-class family, the male character in *Tight Times* is Hispanic and has an urban background, and Greenfield's Rhondy is a black American child living in the city. In a unit on grandparents or older people you might read Miles's *Annie and the Old One,* Mathis's *Hundred Penny Box,* and dePaola's *Nana Upstairs and Nana Downstairs.* These books represent three very different cultures, but children can discuss these stories thoroughly without explicitly realizing this. Your students do not need to be made aware of these cultural differences in any formal way. What is important for them to realize is that common emotions are shared by all humans, regardless of their particular cultural background. By sharing literature that deals with themes common to humanity, children will focus on the likenesses among members of various cultures rather than on the differences.

■ Build Your Teaching Resources

Resources for Children's Literature Related to Diversity

Tiedt, P., and Tiedt, I. (1986). *Multicultural teaching.* Boston: Allyn and Bacon.

   This provides lists of books representative of different cultures, including many nonfiction books.

California State Department of Education. (1986). *Recommended readings in literature.* Sacramento, CA: California State Department of Education.

   This resource book accompanies the *California English–Language Arts Framework.* It has several sections dealing with multicultural literature and a complete section of children's books written in other languages.

Sutherland, Z., & Arbuthnot, M. (1986). *Children and books.* Glenview, IL: Scott, Foresman.

   This shares many types of children's literature. One section deals with literature representing children who are mainstreamed into classrooms.

   Patricia Ramsey (1987) presents a checklist for evaluating children's books with particular emphasis on racism and sexism. As you prepare to read any book to your students, you might consider these elements.

1. Check the illustrations. Look for stereotypes and what people are doing.
2. Check the storyline. What are the standards for success? Do minorities have to exhibit extraordinary skills to be successful? Who is responsible for resolving the problems?
3. Look at lifestyles. Who is living where? Are all the minority children living in a ghetto or barrio?
4. Weigh the relationships between people. Who is subservient?
5. Note the heroes and heroines.
6. Consider the effects on a child's self-image.
7. Consider the author's and illustrator's background.
8. Check out the author's perspective. What cultural, social, and economic perspectives does the book portray?
9. Watch for loaded words.
10. Look at the copyright date. Books in the early 1960s often depict African Americans from an Anglo-American point of view.

■ Build Your Teaching Resources

Children's Literature Books Related to Diversity

The books in this reference list are divided into two categories: multicultural literature and literature for and about children with special education needs. I've chosen these books because they describe situations typically experienced by all children. You can include these types of books in your classroom regularly. Occasionally, particularly with respect to literature about children with special education needs, a book will focus on a child's daily routine and how he or she copes with a handicap.

Multicultural Literature

Picture Books

Bang, M. (1983). *Ten, nine, eight.* Harmondsworth, Middlesex, England: Puffin Books.

Barth, E. (1971). *The day Luis was lost.* Boston: Little, Brown.

Baylor, B. (1975). *The desert is theirs.* New York: Scribner's.

Baylor, B. (1982). *Moon song.* New York: Scribner's.

Brown, M. (1989). *Baby animals.* New York: Random House.

Bunting, E. (1982). *The happy funeral.* New York: Harper and Row.

Bunting, E. (1988). *How many days to America.* Boston: Clarion.

Caines, J. (1973). *Abby.* New York: Harper and Row.

Clifton, L. (1978). *Everett Anderson's nine month long.* New York: The Trumpet Club.

Clifton, L. (1980). *My friend Jacob.* New York: Dutton.

dePaola, T. (1973). *Nana upstairs and nana downstairs.* New York: Putnam.

Desbarats, P. (1968). *Gabrielle and Selena.* New York: Harcourt, Brace, Jovanovich.

Ets, M. (1959). *Nine days to Christmas.* New York: Viking.

Ets, M. (1963). *Gilberto and the wind.* New York: Viking.

Feelings, M. (1974). *Jambo means hello: Swahili alphabet book.* New York: Dial.

Feelings, T., & Greenfield, E. (1981). *Daydreamers.* New York: Dial.

Goble, P., & Goble, D. (1978). *The girl who loved wild horses.* New York: Bradbury Press.

Greenfield, E. (1974). *She come bringing me that little baby girl.* New York: Lippincott.

Greenfield, E. (1977). *Africa dream.* New York: T. Crowell.

Greenfield, E. (1980). *Grandmama's joy.* New York: Philomel Books.

Greenfield, E. (1988). *Nathaniel talking.* New York: Black Butterfly Children's Books.

Havill, J. (1986). *Jamaica's find.* New York: Scholastic.

Hazen, B. (1979). *Tight times.* New York: Penguin Books.

Hill, E. (1967). *Evan's corner.* New York: Holt, Rinehart and Winston.

Isadora, R. (1979). *Ben's trumpet.* New York: Greenwillow.

Keats, E. (1962). *The snowy day.* New York: Viking.

Keats, E. (1967). *Peter's chair.* New York: Harper and Row.

Keats, E. (1969). *Goggles!* New York: Macmillan.

Keats, E. (1974). *Dreams.* New York: Macmillan.

Lee, J. (1987). *Ba-nam.* New York: Henry Holt.

Levinson, R. (1985). *Watch the stars come out.* New York: Dutton.

Lexau, J. (1966). *The homework caper.* New York: Harper and Row.

Lexau, J. (1968). *The rooftop mystery.* New York: Harper and Row.

Lexau, J. (1968). *Striped ice cream.* New York: Lippincott.

Mathis, S. (1975). *The hundred penny box.* New York: Viking.

McDermott, G. (1975). *Arrow to the sun.* New York: Viking.

Miles, M. (1971). *Annie and the old one.* Boston: Little, Brown.

Ness, E. (1963). *Josefina February.* New York: Scribner's.

Politi, L. (1963). *Rosa.* New York: Scribner's.

Politi, L. (1973). *The nicest gift.* New York: Scribner's.

Pomerantz, C. (1989). *The chalk doll.* New York: Lippincott.

Robison, D. (1976). *Anthony's hat.* New York: Scholastic.

Rylant, C. (1985). *The relatives came.* New York: Bradbury Press.

Sonneborn, R. (1970). *Friday night is papa night.* New York: Viking.

Spier, P. (1980). *People.* New York: Doubleday.

Steptoe, J. (1969). *Stevie.* New York: Harper and Row.

Turkle, B. (1972). *The adventures of Obadiah.* New York: Viking.

Udry, J. (1966). *What Mary Jo shared.* New York: Whitman.

Udry, J. (1970). *Mary Jo's grandmother.* New York: Whitman.

Walter, M. (1990). *Two and too much.* New York: Bradbury Press.

Yashima, T. (1955). *Crow boy.* New York: Viking.

Yashima, T. (1958). *Umbrella.* New York: Viking.

Zolotow, C. (1974). *My grandson Lew.* New York: Harper and Row.

Intermediate Multicultural Literature

Bess, C. (1982). *Story for a black night.* Boston: Houghton Mifflin.

Bulla, C. (1953). *Eagle feather.* New York: T. Crowell.

Cleary, B. (1975). *Ramona and her father.* New York: Dell.

Galbraith, C. (1971). *Victor.* New York: Knopf.

George J. (1972). *Julie of the wolves.* New York: Harper and Row.

Gilson, J. (1985). *Hello, my name is scrambled eggs.* New York: Lothrop, Lee and Shepard.

Greene, B. (1974). *Philip Hall likes me. I reckon maybe.* New York: Dial.

Greenfield, E., & Little, L. (1979). *Childtimes: A three-generation memoir.* New York: T. Crowell.

Hamilton, V. (1974). *M. C. Higgins, the great.* New York: Macmillan.

Howard, E. (1988). *Her own song.* New York: Atheneum.

Jackson, J. (1968). *Tessie.* New York: Harper and Row.

Krumgold, J. (1953). *And now Miguel.* New York: T. Crowell.

Lord, B. (1984). *In the year of the boar and Jackie Robinson.* New York: Harper and Row.

O'Dell, S. (1967). *The black pearl.* Boston: Houghton Mifflin.

Panetta, G. (1971). *The shoeshine boys.* New York: Grosset and Dunlap.

Paterson, K. (1988). *Park's quest.* New York: The Trumpet Club.

Pinkwater, M. (1975). *Wingman.* Dodd, Mead, and Co.

Surany, A. (1964). *Ride the cold wind.* New York: Putnam.

Taylor, M. (1976). *Roll of thunder, hear my cry.* New York: Dial.

Taylor, M. (1987). *The gold Cadillac.* New York: Dial.

Taylor, T. (1969). *The cay.* New York: Doubleday.

Thomas, D. (1970). *Mira! Mira!* New York: Lippincott.

Walter, M. (1990). *Mariah keeps cool.* New York: Bradbury Press.

Yep, L. (1975). *Dragonwings.* New York: Harper and Row.

Folk Literature and Fairy Tales

Aardema, V. (1960). *Tales from the story hat: African folktales.* New York: Coward-McCann.

Aardema, V. (1975). *Why mosquitoes buzz in people's ears.* New York: Dial.

Aardema, V. (1981). *Bringing the rain to Kapiti plain: A Nandi tale.* New York: Dial.

Aardema, V. (1984). *Oh, Kojo! How could you!* New York: Dial.

Anderson, B. (1979). *Trickster tales from prairie lodgefires.* Nashville, TN: Abingdon.

Aruego, J., & Dewey, A. (1988). *Rockabye crocodile.* New York: Greenwillow.

Baylor, B. (1976). *And it is still that way: Legends told by Arizona Indian children.* New York: Scribner's.

Cleaver, E. (1985). *The enchanted caribou.* New York: Atheneum.

DuBois, W. (1972). *The hare and the tortoise and the tortoise and the hare: La liebre y la tortuga y la tortuga y la liebre.* New York: Doubleday.

Dyer, V. (1982). *The brocade slipper and other Vietnamese tales.* Reading, MA: Addison-Wesley.

Esbensen, B. (1988). *The star maiden*. Boston: Little, Brown.

Ginsburg, M. (1988). *The Chinese mirror*. New York: Harcourt, Brace, Jovanovich.

Goble, P. (1988). *Her seven brothers*. New York: Bradbury Press.

Griego, M. (1981). *Tortillitas para mama: And other nursery rhymes*. New York: Holt, Rinehart and Winston.

Hamilton, V. (1985). *The people could fly*. New York: Knopf.

Hamilton, V. (1988). *In the beginning*. New York: Harcourt, Brace, Jovanovich.

Haviland, V. (1959). *Favorite fairy tales told in France*. Boston: Little, Brown.

Haviland, V. (1961). *Favorite fairy tales told in Ireland*. Boston: Little, Brown.

Haviland, V. (1965). *Favorite fairy tales told in Italy*. Boston: Little, Brown.

Leaf, M. (1987). *Eyes of the dragon*. New York: Lothrop, Lee and Shepard.

Louie, A. (1982). *Yen-Shen: A cinderella story from China*. New York: Philomel Books.

McDermott, G. (1972). *Anansi the spider: A tale from the Ashanti*. New York: Holt, Rinehart and Winston.

McDermott, G. (1974). *Arrow to the sun, a Pueblo Indian tale*. New York: Viking.

Mikolaycak, C. (1984). *Babushka*. New York: Holiday House.

Mosel, A. (1972). *The funny little woman*. New York: Dutton.

Musgrove, M. (1976). *Ashanti to Zulu*. New York: Dial.

Phang, R., & Roth, S. (1984). *Patchwork tales*. New York: Atheneum.

Roy, C. (1972). *The serpent and the sun: Myths of the Mexican world*. New York: Farrar, Straus and Giroux.

Sadler, C. (1982). *Treasure mountain: Folktales from southern China*. New York: Atheneum.

Stamm, C. (1990). *Three strong women*. New York: Viking.

Steptoe, J. (1984). *The story of jumping mouse, a Native American legend*. New York: Lothrop, Lee and Shepard.

Steptoe, J. (1987). *Mufaro's beautiful daughters*. New York: Lothrop, Lee and Shepard.

Uchida, Y. (1949). *The dancing kettle*. New York: Harcourt, Brace, Jovanovich.

Yolen, J. (ed.). (1986). *Favorite folktales from around the world*. New York: Pantheon.

Young, E. (1989). *Lon Po Po*. New York: Philomel Books.

Zhang, X. (1984). *Monkey and the white bone demon*. New York: Viking.

Poetry

Adoff, A. (ed.). (1970). *Black out loud: An anthology of modern poems*. New York: Macmillan.

Adoff, A. (1973). *Black is brown is tan*. New York: Harper and Row.

Adoff, A. (1981). *OUTside INside poems*. New York: Lothrop, Lee and Shepard.

Adoff, A. (1982). *All the colors of the race*. New York: Lothrop, Lee and Shepard.

Baron, V. (ed.). (1969). *Here I am: An anthology of poems written by young people in some of America's minority groups*. New York: Dutton.

Baylor, B. (1969). *Before you come this way*. New York: Dutton.

De Gerez, T. (1984). *My song is a piece of jade*. Boston: Little, Brown.

Demi. (1986). *Dragon kites and dragonflies*. New York: Harcourt, Brace, Jovanovich.

Giovanni, N. (1984). *Spin a soft black song*. New York: Hill and Wang.

Greenfield, E. (1978). *Honey I love: And other poems*. New York: T. Crowell.

Hopkins, L. (ed.). (1986). *Best friends*. New York: Harper and Row.

Hughes, L. (1967). *Don't turn your back*. New York: Knopf.

Maher, R. (1977). *Alice Yazzie's year*. New York: Coward-McCann.

Morrison, L. (1988). *Rhythm road: Poems to move to*. New York: Lothrop, Lee and Shepard.

Pomerantz, C. (1982). *If I had a paka*. New York: Greenwillow.

Turner, A. (1986). *Street talk*. Boston: Houghton Mifflin.

Literature for and About Students with Special Education Needs

Baldwin, A. (1978). *A little time.* New York: Viking.

Byers, B. (1970). *The summer of the swans.* Harmondsworth, Middlesex, England: Puffin.

Carlson, N. (1990). *Arnie and the new kid.* New York: Viking.

Cleaver, V., & Cleaver, B. (1973). *Me too.* New York: Lippincott.

Clifton, L. (1980). *My friend Jacob.* New York: Dutton.

Cohen, M. (1983). *See you tomorrow, Charles.* New York: Greenwillow.

Coutant, H. (1983). *The gift.* New York: Knopf.

Fanshawe, E. (1975). *Rachel.* New York: Bradbury Press.

Goodsell, J. (1965). *Katie's magic glasses.* Boston: Houghton Mifflin.

Heide, P. (1970). *Sound of sunshine, sound of rain.* New York: Parents Magazine Press.

Little, J. (1968). *Take wing.* Boston: Little, Brown.

MacLachlan, P. (1979). *Through Grandpa's eyes.* New York: Harper and Row.

Peterson, J. (1977). *I have a sister my sister is deaf.* New York: Harper and Row.

Rabe, B. (1981). *The balancing girl.* New York: Dutton.

Raskin, E. (1972). *Spectacles.* New York: Atheneum.

Riskind, M. (1981). *Apple is my sign.* Boston: Houghton Mifflin.

Roy, R. (1985). *Move over. Wheelchairs coming through.* Boston: Houghton/Clarion.

Slepian, J. (1980). *The Alfred summer.* New York: Macmillan.

Slepian, J. (1981). *Lester's turn.* New York: Macmillan.

Smith, D. (1975). *Kelly's creek.* New York: T. Crowell.

Sullivan, M., and Bourke, L. (1980). *A show of hands.* New York: Harper and Row.

Taylor, T. (1981). *The trouble with Tuck.* New York: Doubleday.

A CONCLUDING PERSPECTIVE

We began this chapter on diversity in the language arts classroom with an overview of culturally and linguistically diverse students. We reviewed some of the research into the experiences these children have in school and considered the historical and political events, laws, and judicial decisions that have shaped and changed ideas about educating diverse students. We then similarly investigated the educational history and experiences of students with special education needs. The second half of the chapter focused on general instructional strategies and learning activities recommended for your diverse students. Most important, we looked at ways you can develop these children's critical thinking and problem-solving skills as you build their reading and writing abilities. The chapter concluded with a bibliography of children's literature that describes and values children's differences while portraying emotions all people share.

From a teacher's point of view, the diversity of children so common in today's classrooms offers a myriad of learning opportunities. Along with these opportunities comes the day-to-day challenge of teaching culturally and linguistically diverse children and children with special education needs. As you try some of the strategies or specific activities suggested in this book, you may experience periods of uncertainty. Think back to our earlier discussions about risk taking in Chapters 1 and 4: you will be taking risks as you try to provide instructional activities that meet the academic needs of all of your students. On most days your risks will pay off — and you will feel exhilarated by what your students are able to accomplish. On some days things will not go as well. But these days would happen even if it were possible for every student in your class to be somehow exactly the same.

Through your personal and instructional sensitivity, you will feel satisfied that you are offering each of your diverse students his or her rightful place as a contributing, thinking member of the classroom. The successful learning experiences you provide will result in meaningful instruction that allows your students to develop as readers, writers, listeners, and speakers. In addition to growing in literacy, your students will gain self-esteem and increase their understanding and appreciation for all the world's people.

REFERENCES

Au, K. (1980). Participation structures in a reading lesson with Hawaiian children: Analysis of a culturally appropriate instructional event. *Anthropology and Education, 11*(2), 91–115.

Barnes, D. (1975). *From communication to curriculum.* New York: Viking Penguin.

Barnitz, J. (1985). *Reading development of nonnative speakers of English.* Georgetown: Center for Applied Linguistics.

Bennett, W. (1986). *First lessons: A report on elementary education in America.* Washington, DC: U.S. Government Printing Office.

Bernstein, B. (1971). *Class, codes, and control.* (Vol. 1). London: Routledge and Kegan Paul.

Bird, L. (1989). *Becoming a whole language school: The Fair Oaks story.* New York: Richard Owen Publishers.

Boyer, E. (1987). Early schooling and the nation's future. *Educational Leadership, 44*(6), 4–6.

California State Department of Education. (1987). *English–Language arts framework.* Sacramento, CA: California State Department of Education.

Carlsen, J. (1985). Between the deaf child and reading: The language connection. *The Reading Teacher, 38*(5), 424–426.

Cazden, C. (1988). *Classroom discourse: The language of teaching and learning.* Portsmouth, NH: Heinemann.

Cazden, C., & Mehan, H. (1989). Principles from sociology and anthropology: Context, code, classroom, and culture. In M. Reynolds (ed.), *Knowledge base for the beginning teacher* (47–57). New York: Pergamon Press.

Cleary, B. (1977). *Ramona and her father.* New York: Dell.

Comer, J. (1987). New Haven's school community connection. *Educational Leadership, 44*(6), 13–16.

Cortes, C. (1986). The education of language minority students: A contextual interaction model. In *Beyond language: Social and cultural factors in schooling language minority students* (pp. 3–33). Los Angeles, CA: Evaluation, Dissemination and Assessment Center.

Costa, A., & Marzano, R. (1987). Teaching the language of thinking. *Educational Leadership, 45,* 29–33.

Coutant, H. (1974). *First snow.* New York: Knopf.

Delpit, L. (1986). Skills and other dilemmas of a progressive black educator. *Harvard Educational Review, 56*(4), 379–385.

dePaola, T. (1973). *Nana upstairs and nana downstairs.* New York: Putnam.

Dixon, C., & Nessel, D. (1983). *Language experience approach to reading (and writing).* Hayward, CA: The Alemany Press.

Dunn, L. (1987). *Bilingual Hispanic children on the U.S. mainland: A review of research on their cognitive, linguistic, and scholastic development.* Circle Pines, MN: American Guidance Services.

Edelsky, C. (1982). Writing in a bilingual program: The relation of L1 and L2 texts. *TESOL Quarterly, 16,* 211–228.

Edelsky, C. (1986). *Writing in a bilingual program: Habia una vez.* Norwood, NJ: Ablex Publishing.

Egan, K. (1987). Literacy and the oral foundation of education. *Harvard Educational Review, 57,* 445–472.

Enright, S. (1986). Use everything you have to teach English: Providing useful input to young language learners. In P. Rigg & S. Enright (eds.), *Children and ESL: Integrating perspectives* (pp. 115–162). Washington, DC: Teachers of English to Speakers of Other Languages.

Enright, S., & McCloskey, M. (1988). *Integrating English.* Reading, MA: Addison-Wesley.

Feeley, J. (1983). Help for the reading teacher: Dealing with the limited English proficient (LEP) child in the elementary classroom. *The Reading Teacher, 36*(7), 650–655.

Gee, J. (1987). What is literacy? Paper presented at the Literacy Assistance Center, New York.

Gibson, M. (1983). *Home-school-community linkages: A study of educational equity for Punjabi youths.* Washington, DC: National Institute of Education.

Greenfield, E. (1980). *Grandmama's joy.* New York: Philomel Books.

Gutstein, S. (1989). Dialogue journals and language minority students. Paper presented at the National Association for Bilingual Education, Miami, FL.

Hakuta, K., & Gould, L. (1987). Synthesis of research on bilingual education. *Educational Leadership, 44*(6), 38–46.

Harste, J. (1989). *New policy guidelines for reading.* Urbana, IL: National Council of Teachers of English.

Hayes, C., & Bayruth, R. (1985). Querer es poder. In J. Hansen, T. Newkirk, and D. Graves (eds.), *Breaking ground: Teachers relate reading and writing in the elementary school* (pp. 97–110). Portsmouth, NH: Heinemann.

Hazen, B. (1979). *Tight times.* New York: Penguin.

Heath, S. (1978). Teacher talk: Language in the classroom. *Language in education 9: Theory and practice.* Arlington, VA: Center for Applied Linguistics.

Heath, S. (1982). What no bedtime story means: Narrative skills at home and school. *Language in Society, 11,* 49–76.

Heath, S. (1983). *Ways with words.* Cambridge: Cambridge University Press.

Heath, S. (1986). Sociocultural contexts of language development. In *Beyond language: Social and cultural factors in schooling language minority students* (pp. 143–186). Los Angeles, CA: Evaluation, Dissemination and Assessment Center.

Hough, R., Nurss, J., & Enright, D. (1986). Story reading with limited English speaking children in the regular classroom. *The Reading Teacher, 39*(6), 510–514.

Hudelson, S. (1984). Kan yu ret an rayt en ingles: Children become literate in English as a second language. *TESOL Quarterly, 18*(2), 221–235.

Hummel, J., & Balcom, F. (1984). Microcomputers: Not just a place for practice. *Journal of Learning Disabilities, 17,* 432–434.

Hutchins, P. (1971). *The doorbell rang.* Boston: Houghton Mifflin.

Johnson, D., & Johnson, R. (1975). *Learning together and alone: Cooperation, competition, and individualization.* Englewood Cliffs, NJ: Prentice-Hall.

Kagan, S. (1986). Cooperative learning and sociocultural diversity: Implications for practice. In *Beyond language: Social and cultural factors in schooling language minority students* (pp. 231–298). Los Angeles, CA: Evaluation, Dissemination and Assessment Center.

Keller, H. (1903). *The story of my life.* New York: Doubleday.

Kellogg, S. (1984). *Paul Bunyan.* New York: Morrow.

Kirk, S., & Gallagher, J. (1989). *Educating exceptional children.* Boston: Houghton Mifflin.

Kohn, A. (1986). How to succeed without even vying. *Psychology Today, 20,* 22–28.

Kozol, J. (1988). *Rachel and her children: Homeless families in America.* New York: Crown Publishers.

Krashen, S. (1981). The case for narrow reading. *TESOL Newsletter, 15*(6), 23.

Krashen, S. (1982). *Principles and practices in second language acquisition.* London, England: Pergamon Press.

Lasky, K. (1990). The fiction of history: Or, what did Miss Kitty really do? *The New Advocate, 3*(3), 157–166.

Martinez, M., & Roser, N. (1985). Read it again: The value of repeated readings during storytime. *The Reading Teacher, 38*(8), 782–786.

Mathis, S. (1978). *The hundred penny box.* New York: Viking.

McCloskey, M. (ed.). (1987). *Turn on units.* Atlanta, GA: State of Georgia Board of Education.

Mercer, J. (1979). In defense of racially and culturally nondiscriminatory assessment. *School Psychology Digest, 3,* 89–95.

Miles, M. (1971). *Annie and the old one.* Boston: Little, Brown.

Moll, L. (1986). Writing as communication: Creating strategic learning environments for students. *Theory into Practice, 25,* 102–108.

Morrow, L. (1987). Promoting inner-city children's recreational reading. *The Reading Teacher, 41*(3), 266–275.

Moustafa, M. (1987). Comprehensible input plus the language experience approach: A longterm perspective. *The Reading Teacher, 41*(3), 276–287.

Nathenson-Majia, S. (1989). Writing in a second language: Negotiating meaning through invented spelling. *Language Arts, 66*(5), 516–526.

National Assessment of Educational Progress. (1981). *Literacy in America: A synopsis of National Assessment findings.* Denver, CO: Education Commission of the States.

Ogbu, J. (1978). *Minority education and caste: The American system in cross-cultural perspective.* New York: Academic Press.

Ogbu, J., & Matute-Bianchi, M. (1986). Understanding sociocultural factors: Knowledge, identity, and school adjustment. In *Beyond language: Social and cultural factors in schooling language minority students* (pp. 73–142). Los Angeles, CA: Evaluation, Dissemination and Assessment Center.

Olsen, R. (1989). A survey of limited English proficient student enrollments and identification criteria. *TESOL Quarterly, 23*(3), 469–488.

Orlich, D., Harder, R., Callahan, R., Kravas, C., Kauchak, D., Pendergrass, R., & Keogh, A. (1985). *Teaching strategies: A guide to better instruction.* Lexington, MA: D.C. Heath.

Ornstein, A., & Levine, D. (1989). *Foundations of education*. Boston: Houghton Mifflin.

Ortiz, A., & Yates, J. (1983). Incidence of exceptionality among Hispanics: Implications for manpower planning. *NABE Journal, 7,* 41–54.

Oxenbury, H. (1987). *Buenos noches*. Barcelona, Spain: Editorial Juventud.

Penfield, J. (1987). ESL: The regular classroom teacher's perspective. *TESOL Quarterly, 21*(1), 21–39.

Peyton, J., & Seyoum, M. (1989). The effect of teacher strategies on students' interactive writing: The case of dialogue journals. *Research in the Teaching of English, 23*(3), 310–334.

Phillips, S. (1972). Participant structures and communicative competence: Warm Springs children in community and classroom. In C. Cazden, V. John, & D. Hymes (eds.), *Functions of language in the classroom* (pp. 370–394). New York: Teachers College Press.

Phillips, S. (1983). *The invisible culture: Communication in classroom and community on the Warm Springs Indian Reservation*. New York: Longman.

Pinnell, G., & Matlin, M. (1989). *Teachers and research: Language learning in the classroom*. Newark, DE: International Reading Association.

Pinnell, G., Fried, M., & Estice, R. (1990). Reading recovery: Learning how to make a difference. *The Reading Teacher, 43*(4), 282–295.

Ramsey, P. (1987). *Teaching and learning in a diverse world*. New York: Teachers College Press.

Rasinski, T. (1989). Commentary: Reading and the empowerment of parents. *The Reading Teacher, 43*(3), 226–231.

Reno Gazette Journal, December 30, 1989. Pupils from non-English-speaking backgrounds double. 24.

Rhodes, L., & Dudley-Marling, C. (1988). *Readers and writers with a difference: A holistic approach to teaching learning disabled and remedial students*. Portsmouth, NH: Heinemann.

Rigg, P., & Enright, S. (1986). *Children and ESL: Integrating perspectives*. Washington, DC: Teachers of English to Speakers of Other Languages.

Rueda, R. (1987). Social and communicative aspects of language proficiency in low-achieving language minority students. In H. Trueba (ed.), *Success or failure: Linguistic minority children at home and in school* (pp. 185–197). New York: Harper and Row.

Sayers, D. (1989). Bilingual sister classes in computer writing networks. In D. Johnson and D. Roen (eds.), *Richness in writing* (pp. 120–133). New York: Longman.

Slavin, R. (1979). Effects of biracial learning teams on cross racial friendships. *Journal of Educational Psychology, 71,* 381–387.

Slavin, R. (1980). Cooperative learning. *Review of Educational Research, 50*(2), 315–342.

Slavin, R. (1986). Learning together. *American Educator, 10*(2), 6–13.

Smith, C. (1989). Prompting critical thinking. *The Reading Teacher, 42*(6), 424.

Staton, J. (1983). Dialogue journals: A new tool for teaching communication. *ERIC/CLL News Bulletin, 6*(2), 1–2, 6.

Staton, J. (1988). ERIC/RCS report: Dialogue journals. *Language Arts, 65*(2), 198–201.

Stein, S. (1986). *Sink or swim: The politics of bilingual education*. New York: Praeger.

Stephens, D. (1986). *The integration of reading and writing: A collaborative study of change in a special education classroom*. Unpublished doctoral dissertation, Indiana University, Bloomington, IN.

Sue, S., & Padilla, A. (1986). Ethnic minority issues in the United States: Challenges for the educational system. In *Beyond language: Social and cultural factors in schooling language minority students* (pp. 35–72). Los Angeles, CA: Evaluation, Dissemination and Assessment Center.

Sutton, C. (1989). Helping the nonnative English speaker with reading. *The Reading Teacher, 42*(9), 684–688.

Taylor, D., & Dorsey-Gaines, C. (1988). *Growing up literate: Learning from inner-city families.* Portsmouth, NH: Heinemann.

Teale, W. (1986). Home background and young children's literacy development. *Emergent literacy.* Norwood, NJ: Ablex.

Tiedt, P., & Tiedt, I. (1986). *Multicultural teaching: A handbook of activities, information, and resources.* Boston: Allyn and Bacon.

Topping, K. (1989). Peer tutoring and paired reading: Combining two powerful techniques. *The Reading Teacher, 42*(7), 488–494.

Urzua, C. (1987). You stopped too soon: Second language children composing and revising. *TESOL Quarterly, 21*(2), 279–297.

Viadero, D. (1989). Side by side. *Teacher Magazine, 1,* 40–46.

Waggoner, D., & O'Malley, J. (1985). Teachers of limited English proficient children in the United States. *NABE Journal, 9*(3), 25–42.

Wells, G. (1986). *The meaning makers.* Portsmouth, NH: Heinemann.

Wong-Fillmore, L. (1982). Language minority students and school participation: What kind of English is needed? *Journal of Education, 16*(4), 143–156.

Yaden, D. (1988). Understanding stories through repeated read-alouds: How many does it take? *The Reading Teacher, 41*(6), 556–560.

Yee, S., & Kokin, L. (1977). *Got me a story to tell.* San Francisco, CA: St. John's Educational Threshold Center.

Ysseldyke, J., & Algozzine, B. (1990). *Introduction to special education.* Boston: Houghton Mifflin.

Appendix A

Frequently Occurring Affixes and Word Stems*

Prefixes			Examples
Number			
amphi	(Gr.)	both	amphibian, amphitheater
mono*	(Gr.)	one	monorail, monarch
uni*	(Gr.)	one	uniform, unicycle
bi	(L.)	two, twice	bicycle, bimonthly
di	(G.)	two	dioxide, diphthong
tri	(L.)	three	triangle, tripod
quad	(L.)	four	quadruped, quarter
quin	(L.)	five	quintet, quintuplets
penta	(L.)	five	pentagon, pentangle
sex	(L.)	six	sextet, sextant
hexa	(L.)	six	hexagon
sept	(L.)	seven	September
octa	(L.)	eight	octopus, October
nov	(L.)	nine	November
non	(L.)		nonagon
dec	(L.)	ten	decade, December
poly	(L.)	many	polygon, polysyllabic
semi	(L.)	half	semicircle, semiannual
milli	(L.)	1/1000	millisecond, millimeter
multi	(L.)	many	multicolored, multiply
Opposite			
dis	(L.)	opposite	disconnect, discomfort
im*	(L.)	not	immovable, impartial
in*			incorrect, inactive

*Indicates most frequently occurring, based on Becker, W.C., Dixon, R., & Anderson-Inman, L. (1980). *Morphographic and root word analysis of 26,000 high frequency words.* Technical report 1980–1981. Eugene, OR: University of Oregon; Francis, W.N. & Kucera, H. (1982) *Frequency analysis of English usage: Lexicon and grammar.* Boston: Houghton Mifflin; and Thorndike, E.L. (1941) *The teaching of English suffixes.* New York: Bureau of Publications, Teachers College.

Prefixes			Examples
il			illegible, illiterate
ir			irregular, irreplaceable
ob	(L.)	against	obstruct, objection
un	(L.)	not	undone, unsure

Place in Time or Space

ante	(L.)	before	antedate, antecedent
com*	(L.)	together, with	compose
col*			collaborate
cor*			correspond
e	(L.)	out	eject, erupt
ex			extract, excerpt
exo			exoskeleton, exoderm
extra	(L.)	outside, beyond	extraordinary, extracurricular
inter*	(L.)	between, among	international, interrupt
intra	(L.)	within	intrastate, intramural
intro	(L.)		introspect, introvert
mid	(L.)	middle	midway, midwestern
para*	(G.)	beside	paragraph, parasite
per*	(L.)	through	permanent, perpetual
peri*	(G.)	around, near	perimeter, periscope
post	(L.)	after	postgame, postscript
pre*	(L.)	before	prewar, predict
pro*	(L.)	in front	program, prologue
sub	(L.)	under, below	submarine, subtract
super*	(L.)	over, above	supernatural, supersede
syn	(G.)	together, with	synonym, synchrony
syl			syllable, syllabus
sym			symphony, sympathy
trans*	(L.)	across, over	transcontinental, transfer

Size

macro	(G.)	large	macroscopic, macrocosm
micro*	(G.)	small	microscope, microphone

Other

de	(L.)	down, away	depopulate, detract
dis	(L.)	apart from	dismiss, dislocate

Prefixes

			Examples
hyper*	(G.)	over, beyond	hyperactive, hypersensitive
hypo*	(G.)	under, too little	hypodermic, hypoactive
im	(L.)	in, into	immigrate, implant
in			intake, incision
il			illuminate, illustrate
mal	(L.)	bad	malpractice, malady
mis	(OE)	bad	misbehave, mistake
pro	(L.)	in favor of	pro-American, proslavery, pro-civil rights
pro		forward	progress, project
proto	(G.)	first	prototype
pseudo	(G.)	false	pseudonym, pseudoscience
re	(L.)	again	reread, readmit
re		back	retract, refund
retro	(L.)	back	retrorocket, retrospection

Suffixes

		Examples
able, ible	can be done, inclined to	workable, credible peaceable, terrible
ance, ence	state of	tolerance, confidence
ation	process, action, state of, result of	consideration, decoration occupation
en	made of, to make	soften, wooden
er, or, ar	one who	runner, creator, vicar
ful	full, full of	hopeful, forgetful
hood	state, quality	falsehood
ic	of the nature of, characterized by	angelic, volcanic
ion	act, process, state of, characterized by	construction, revolution ambition, suspicion
ish	having the qualities of	childish
ist	person who	geologist, pianist
less	without	hopeless, childless
ly	like	happily, forgetfully

Suffixes

Suffixes		Examples
ment	action or process, state of	development, government puzzlement, amazement
ness	condition	kindness
ship	skill, condition	friendship
ward	towards	forward, leeward
y	full of	sandy

Stems

Stems			Examples
aqua	(L.)	water	aquaduct, aquarium
aud	(L.)	hear	auditory, auditorium
bene	(L.)	good	benefit, benevolent
bio*	(G.)	life	biology, biography
cap	(L.)	head	capital, decapitate
cav	(L.)	hollow	cavern, excavate
ced	(L.)	go, yield	precede, concede
cess	(L.)	go, yield	process, incessant
chron(o)	(G.)	time	chronicle, chronometer
cide*	(L.)	kill	insecticide, homicide
circ*	(L.)	ring	circle, circular
cis*	(L.)	cut	incision, scissors
civ	(L.)	citizen	civic, civilization
cogn	(L.)	know	cognitive, recognize
crat	(G.)	rule	democrat, autocrat
cred	(G.)	believe	incredible, discredit
demos	(G.)	people	democracy, epidemic
dent	(L.)	tooth	dentist, trident
dict*	(L.)	say	dictate, contradict
div	(L.)	separate	division, divorce
duce*	(L.)	lead	introduce, induce
duct	(L.)		aqueduct, reduction
equ*	(L.)	equal	equality, equator
fac	(L.)	to do, make	factory, facility
fect*	(L.)	to do, make	perfect, defect
flect	(L.)	bend	deflect, reflect
flex		bend	flexible, reflex
fract	(L.)	break	fracture, infraction
fuse*	(L.)	pour	transfusion, diffuse
gene*	(L.)	birth	generation, progeny
gen	(L.)	of the same class	gentry, gentlemen

Stems			Examples
geo	(G.)	earth	geometry, geology
gno*	(G.)	know	diagnose, agnostic
gram	(G.)	written	grammar, telegram
graph*	(G.)	write	telegraph, autograph
gress*	(L.)	move	progress, aggression
hom	(G.)	man	homage, homicide
hydr	(G.)	water	dehydrate, hydrant
ject*	(L.)	throw	reject, projectile
junct	(L.)	join	conjunction, juncture
kilo	(G.)	one thousand	kilometer, kilowatt
lect*	(L.)	gather	collect, select
leg	(L.)	law	legal, legislate
leg*	(L.)	read	legible, legend
liber	(L.)	free	liberate, liberty
liter	(L.)	letter	literature, literate
loc	(L.)	place	locate, local
log	(L.)	speech	dialogue, prologue
lum	(L.)	light	illuminate, luminous
luna	(L.)	moon	lunar, lunatic
magni	(L.)	great	magnify, magnificent
mare	(L.)	sea	marine, maritime
mater	(L.)	mother	maternal, maternity
math	(L.)	learning	mathematics, polymath
matur	(L.)	ripe	maturity, immature
mis*	(L.)	send	mission, missile
mit	(L.)	send, allow	transmit, permit
medi*	(L.)	heal	medicine, remedial
mode*	(L.)	manner, measure	model, moderate, mode
mort	(L.)	death	mortal, mortuary
nat	(L.)	born	natural, native
neo	(G.)	new, modern	neoclassic, neophyte
opt	(G.)	sight	optical, optometrist
pater	(L.)	father	paternal, patriarch
ped*	(L.)	foot	pedal, pedestrian
pend*	(L.)	hang	pendulum, suspend
phon*	(G.)	sound	telephone, phonics
photo	(G.)	light	photograph, photosynthesis
port*	(L.)	carry	transport, portable
polis	(G.)	city	metropolis, police
pos*	(L.)	place	position, preposition
press*	(L.)	force	pressure, oppression

Stems

Stems			Examples
rect*	(L.)	straight, right	correct, rectangle
sacr	(L.)	devote	sacrament, sacred
scope	(G.)	watch	periscope, telescope
scrib	(L.)	write	inscribe, describe
script			scripture, manuscript
sist*	(L.)	stand	insist, persist
spect*	(L.)	look	inspector, spectacle
spire*	(L.)	breathe	respiration, expire
stru*	(L.)	build	construct, instruct
tain, ten		hold	retain, contain, detention, tenacious
tele	(G.)	distant	telescope, television
terra	(L.)	earth	terrestrial, terrace
tract*	(L.)	pull	tractor, abstract
ven*	(L.)	come	convention, convene
vent	(L.)	wind	vent, ventilation
vert*	(L.)	turn	convert, invert
vid, vis	(L.)	see	video, evidence, vision, visible
voc	(L.)	call	vocal, evocative
vol	(L.)	will	voluntary, volition

Appendix B

Scope and Sequence for Introduction and Reinforcement of Grammatical Elements and Terms

ELEMENT	GRADE 1	GRADE 2	GRADE 3	GRADE 4	GRADE 5	GRADE 6
Sentences						
Declarative			x	x	x	x
Interrogative			x	x	x	x
Exclamatory			x	x	x	x
Imperative				x	x	x
Simple			x	x	x	x
Compound				x	x	x
Parts of Sentences						
Complete Subject	x	x	x	x	x	x
Simple Subject				x	x	x
Compound Subject					x	x
Complete Predicate	x	x	x	x	x	x
Simple Predicate				x	x	x
Compound Predicate					x	x
Predicate Nouns						x
Predicate Adjectives						x
Direct Object					x	x
Prepositional Phrase						x
Parts of Speech						
Nouns						
Definition	x	x	x	x	x	x
Singular Forms	x	x	x	x	x˙	x
Plural Forms	x	x	x	x	x	x
Possessive Forms				x	x	x
Common and Proper	x	x	x	x	x	x
Appositives						x
Pronouns						
Definition			x	x	x	x
Personal			x	x	x	x
Possessive				x	x	x
Interrogative						x
Antecedents					x	x

ELEMENT	GRADE 1	GRADE 2	GRADE 3	GRADE 4	GRADE 5	GRADE 6
Verbs						
Definition	x	x	x	x	x	x
Action	x	x	x	x	x	x
Main				x	x	x
Helping or Auxiliary		x	x	x	x	x
Regular			x	x	x	x
Irregular	x	x	x	x	x	x
Forms of *to be*	x	x	x	x	x	x
Linking					x	x
Present Tense	x	x	x	x	x	x
Past Tense	x	x	x	x	x	x
Future Tense					x	x
Perfect Tenses						x
Contractions		x	x	x	x	x
Adjectives						
Definition	x	x	x	x	x	x
Proper						x
Forms of Comparison	x	x	x	x	x	x
Predicate Adjectives						x
Articles			x	x	x	x
Prepositional Phrases as Adjectives						x
Adverbs						
Definition				x	x	x
Forms of Comparison					x	x
Negatives				x	x	x
Prepositional Phrases as Adverbs						x
Prepositions						
Definition						x
In Phrases						x
Objects of Prepositions						x
Conjunctions						
Definition						x
Coordinating				x	x	x

Appendix C

Scope and Sequence for Introduction and Reinforcement of Elements of Usage

ELEMENT	GRADE 1	GRADE 2	GRADE 3	GRADE 4	GRADE 5	GRADE 6
Sentence Usage						
Run-ons			x	x	x	x
Fragments					x	x
Verb Usage						
Subject/verb: Present Tense	x	x	x	x	x	x
Subject/verb: Helping verbs				x	x	x
Subject/verb: Forms of *to be*	x	x	x	x	x	x
Irregular verbs	x	x	x	x	x	x
Pronoun Usage						
Agreeing with Antecedents					x	x
Pronouns or Contractions?				x	x	x
Adjective/Adverb Usage						
Adjectives or Adverbs?				x	x	x
Forms of Comparison	x	x	x	x	x	x
Selecting Correct Article			x	x	x	x
Double Negatives				x	x	x

Appendix D

Scope and Sequence for Introduction and Reinforcement of Mechanics

ELEMENT	GRADE 1	GRADE 2	GRADE 3	GRADE 4	GRADE 5	GRADE 6
Capitalization						
First word in sentence	x	x	x	x	x	x
Proper nouns	x	x	x	x	x	x
First word of greeting or closing in letter		x	x	x	x	x
Title of people		x	x	x	x	x
Titles of books, poems, stories, reports, songs, articles			x	x	x	x
Abbreviations		x	x	x	x	x
First word of direct quotation			x	x	x	x
Punctuation						
Period						
After statement	x	x	x	x	x	x
After command or request				x	x	x
After abbreviation		x	x	x	x	x
Question Mark						
After interrogative sentence	x	x	x	x	x	x
Exclamation Mark						
After exclamatory sentence			x	x	x	x
Comma						
After greeting in friendly letter		x	x	x	x	x
After closing in a letter		x	x	x	x	x
To separate names of city and state		x	x	x	x	x
To separate day from year		x	x	x	x	x
In a series			x	x	x	x
In direct address				x	x	x
In a compound sentence				x	x	x
After introductory words				x	x	x
With appositives						x
Apostrophe						
In contractions		x	x	x	x	x
To show possession			x	x	x	x

ELEMENT	GRADE 1	GRADE 2	GRADE 3	GRADE 4	GRADE 5	GRADE 6
Quotation Marks						
With other punctuation			x	x	x	x
Colon						
For a list					x	x
Underlining						
In Titles				x	x	x

Appendix E

Recommended Computer Software for the Language Arts

The programs listed in this appendix are just a sampling of a wide range of available programs. They are recommended because they actively engage students in reading and writing and do not involve mere "skill and drill."

Writing

Bank Street Writer III. Scholastic Software, Scholastic, Inc., P.O. Box 7502, 2531 E. McCarty Street, Jefferson City, MO 65102.

Appropriate for third grade and above, this word processing program has proven itself over the years as one of the easiest to learn and use by elementary-school students.

Explore-A-Story. D.C. Heath/Collarmore Educational Publishing, 125 Spring Street, Lexington, MA 02173.

Intended for beginning readers, this program allows students to compose their own versions of popular stories. The program also includes artwork that students may select to illustrate their stories.

The Print Shop. Broderbund Software, 17 Paul Drive, San Rafael, CA, 94903-2101.

Because it is so easy to use, *The Print Shop* is appropriate for users from the elementary grades on up. It can be used to embellish final drafts as well as for a variety of other purposes. It will fit directly into your writing curriculum at the sharing/publishing stage.

Success Stories Guide and the *Writing Solutions Guide.* LIST Services, 10810 Harney Street, Suite 202, Omaha, NE, 68154.

Intended to support all aspects of the writing process, these programs represent creative approaches that teachers have applied successfully in the classroom.

Reading

BookBrain. Oryx Press, 2214 North Central at Encanto, Phoenix, AZ 85004.

This program conducts an interest survey with the student and then suggests books in which the student may be interested.

FrEdWriter (Free Educational Writer). Computer Using Educators (CUE), P.O. Box 271704, Concord, CA 94527-1704.

The appeal of this simplified word processing program is twofold. First, it is very easy to use; and second, it is inexpensive and may be copied as many times as you wish. There are several additional packages you may obtain that augment FrEdWriter and that offer additional ideas and possibilities for classroom applications.

"Hypertext" and "Hypermedia" Programs.
B&B Soundworks, 1040 S. Daniel Way, San Jose, CA 95101.
Voyager Company, 2139 Manning, Los Angeles, CA 90025.

These two companies have produced "hypertext" and "hypermedia" programs that involve stories and poems. Hypertext and hypermedia coordinate information among a number of computerized sources — graphics, text, and sound — and allow users to interact in productive ways with the information. At present, these programs have been developed primarily for older students, but innovative programs are just beginning to appear for elementary students. (See the following informative article by J. S. Blanchard & C. J. Rottenberg: Hypertext and hypermedia: Discovering and creating meaningful learning environments. *The Reading Teacher, 43,* 656–661.)

MacWrite. Apple Computer, 20525 Mariani Avenue, Cupertino, CA 95014.

MacWrite is a powerful and accessible word processing program that meets the needs and competencies of the user, from first grade on up. The one disadvantage is that it is currently available only for the Macintosh computer.

Magic Slate. Sunburst Communications, 39 Washington Avenue, Pleasantville, NY 10570.

Appropriate for second grade and up, this is an easy word processing program that offers different type sizes in which to work, accommodating different levels of user expertise.

Quill. D.C. Heath, 125 Spring Street, Lexington, MA 02173.

Appropriate for third grade and up, this word processing program is partitioned into different functions, including prewriting, editing, and an electronic mailbag.

The Semantic Mapper. Gainesville, FL: Teacher Support Software.

This program efficiently generates student-created semantic maps or other structural components of text (such as episodes).
Each title selected is annotated so students can form preliminary ideas about a book before they seek it out. An excellent feature of this program is the availability of searches according to author, subject matter, or title.

KidTalk. First Byte Software, 2845 Temple Street, Long Beach, CA 90806.

This program was designed from a language-experience-approach perspective. The computer will "read" out loud the child's dictation.

The Literary Mapper. Gainesville, FL: Teacher Support Software.

This program already includes the format for character, setting, and action mapping, and will complement the reading of any story or book.

Reading Comprehension Early Reading. Houghton Mifflin Educational Software Division, P.O. Box 683, Hanover, NH 03755.

This package presents several real literature stories and folktales appropriate for beginning readers. Each page on the screen is illustrated, and the program will pronounce any words about which the students are uncertain. Questions are embedded in each selection, encouraging a prediction strategy; they are printed on the screen and may be pronounced.

Success with Reading. New York: Scholastic.

This program ties in response activities with trade books.

Super Story Tree. New York: Scholastic.

This program allows students to interact with a popular story in a "hypermedia" format.

You can stay abreast of developments in software capability as well as of specific new software packages through the following resources.

The columns "Reading Technology" in *The Reading Teacher* and "On-Line" and "DISKovery" in *Language Arts*

The journals *Computers and the Schools, Computers, Reading, and Language Arts,* and *T.H.E. Journal* (Technological Horizons in Education)

Name Index

Subject Index

Ability groups, 105, 119
Academic environment, *see* Classroom, academic environment of
Adjectives, 452, 453, 454
Adverbs, 452, 453, 454
Advertisements, in propaganda lesson, 138
Alphabet, development of, 59, 61
Alphabet books, 333
Alphabetic fashion, word structure understood in, 195
Alphabetic principle, of spelling, 418
Alphabetic writing, 191–194, 448
Alphabetizing, 288
American Dictionary of the English Language (Webster), 70
American English, 70–71
Analogies, 415, 423, 424, 436
Analysis, 344
Analytic phonics, 291
"Ands", in sentences, 458
Anglo-Saxon, Old English and, 63
Animals, stories about, 339–340
Antecedent, 455
Anticipation, listening in, 135
Antonyms, 414
Arrival at school, 89–90
Articles, 452
Artists, books about, 359–360
Art project, in response to reading, 357–358
Assertive Discipline, 92–93
Assessment, 485; *see also* Formal assessment and evaluation; Informal assessment and evaluation
Assessment portfolio, 113
Authoring cycle, of writing, 222
Authors: invited to school, 357; students writing to, 356
Author's Chair: oral reading and, 322; for sharing writing, 224, 225

Back formation, vocabulary changed with, 72, 398

Background knowledge, 387; development of, 194; in intermediate grades, 205–206; in reading, 183
Bandwagon, as propaganda, 136
Banned Book Week, 330
Basal programs, for spelling, 417
Basal reading series, 275, 277; literature supplementing, 332
Base words, 211, 293, 394
Bay Area Writing Project (BAWP), 221
Becoming a Nation of Readers (Anderson, et al.), 86, 87
Bed-to-bed stories, 203, 204
Before, during and after sequence, as illustrated by the DRTA, 297–299; as illustrated by the CDRTA, 302–304, radio and, 18
Beginning reading, 277–289; experiences with print for, 277; predictable texts for, 278–280; *see also* Language experience approach
Beginning of school day, 90
Bible, biblical stories versus, 334–335
Big Books, 278–279, 321
Bilingual Education Act, 525
Bilingual programs, 525–528; *see also* Culturally and linguistically diverse students
Binding students' books, 246–247
Biography, 341
Biology, development and, 29
Black English, 71, 467
Blending, vocabulary and, 73
Blind, *see* Visually handicapped
Board games, word bank and, 288
Bodily-kinesthetic intelligence, 32
Bookfile: of books read aloud, 141; for literature unit books, 364
Booklets, sent to parents, 114
Book reports, 357
Book reviews, 357
Books, development of, 65–66; *see also* Children's literature; Literature unit

Book talk: beginning knowledge of, 187; book review for, 357
Brain, thought and language development and, 30–31
Brainstorming: for categorizing words, 411; for description, 250; with diverse students, 542; for interviewing, 253; for literature unit, 366, 367, 368; for persuasion, 251; as prewriting activity, 236, 237–238; in semantic mapping, 405; in small-group discussion, 156, 157; for thematic unit development, 112
Brown Bear, Brown Bear (Martin), 278
Bulletin boards, 85, 100, 115

Calendar, by students, 114
California Assessment Project, 512
California English-Language Arts Framework, 552–553
California Reading Initiative, 275, 276
Canada, English language in, 71
Canterbury Tales, The (Chaucer), 65, 66
Capitalization, 469
Card games, word bank and, 288
Case grammar, 447
Categorization: of experiences, 6; in semantic mapping, 405, 406
Cause and effect, in expository texts, 206
CD-Rom technology, for diverse students, 447
CDRTA, *see* Content Directed Reading-Thinking Activity
Celts, Old English and, 63
Censorship, teacher and, 331
Chancery, scribes and, 65–66
"Character Day," 357
Characterization, in narratives, 178, 254, 347; "Character Day" for, 357; literature-based activity for, 352, 353–354; response journals for, 355

Children's literature, categories of, 333–342; alphabet books, 333; biography, 341; contemporary realism, 338–339; historical fiction, 337–338; informational, 340–341; modern fantasy, 339–340; picture books, 333–334; poetry, 335–337; special interests, 341–342; traditional, 334–335; wordless books, 334; *see also* Literature-based reading and writing

Children's special interests, as literary genre, 341–342

Children's storytelling, 168–169

Choral reading, 320

Cinquains, 260

Clarification, questions for, 156

Classbook, in literature unit, 374, 375

Classroom: environment as meaningful, 21, 25, 26, *see also* Classroom, academic environment of; Classroom, social environment of; example of, 79; integrated instruction in, 79, 82–83; physical environment of, 83–86; risk taking in, 79–80; talking in, 80–82

Classroom, academic environment of, 99–122; evaluating learning and, 112–113, 118, 119–120, 122; example of, 115–122; goal setting and, 99–100, 116, 117; parents and, 113–115, 117, 118, 120, 122; scheduling and, 100–105, 116, 117–118, 119, 121; thematic units and, 100, 110–112, 118, 119, 122; *see also* Grouping

Classroom, social environment of, 20, 86–99; groupings, 82, 84, 85; home and community, 97–99; rules, 87–91; transitions, 89–91; *see also* Discipline, in classroom

Clean-up procedures, 90

Clipping, vocabulary and, 73, 398

Closed word sort, 392

Clustering: for description, 250; for persuasion, 251; for prewriting, 233–236

Cognitive development, 29, 34–37, 50–51; brain and, 30–31; communication potential and, 30–34; concepts, 34–35, 36–37; metacognition, 37; patterns in, 33–34; response to literature and, 344–345; schemes, 34, 35–36; universal features in, 31; *also* Intelligence

Coherence, of narrative structure, 179

Collaborative learning, 240

Collaborative poetry, 257–259

Collection of work, 90–91

Collective biographies, 341

Combining forms, 394, 431; *see also* Stems

Commas, 468–469, 470

Commercials, in propaganda lesson, 138

Communication potential, 30–34, 129

Compare-and-contrast activities, across books, 353

Comparison, in expository texts, 206

Comparison portfolio, 113

Compositions, 471–472; *see also* Writing

Compounding, vocabulary and, 72, 398

Compound words, 427–428; for structural analysis concept, 292; teaching, 452–453

Comprehensible input, for English as a Second Language students, 536–538

Comprehension, *see* Reading comprehension

Computers: for diverse students, 546–547; as information source, 18–19; writing and, 265–267

Concentration, for creative dramatics, 161–162

Concepts: categorizing words and, 411; in cognitive development, 34–35, 36–37; elaborating and expanding development of, 389–392, of word in print, 199, 200, 201, 420; *see also* Vocabulary

Concrete operations, summary of story in, 344

Conferencing, reading taught with, 256, 273–274, 499–500; in literature-based reading and writing, 350–351

Conferencing, writing taught with, 219, 221–222, 226–232; guidelines for, 226–227, 231–232; in literature-based reading and writing, 350–351; questions for, 229–232; response group, 227–229; student/student, 219, 227, 231–232, 233; teacher/student, 229–231

Conflicts, in plot, 347

Connotation, 412–413

Consonant digraph, 418

Consonants, 291

Construction, in listening, 133

Contemporary realism, 338–339

Content: of language arts, 4–6; of written language, 176

Content-area vocabulary, 403–409, 410

Content Directed Reading-Thinking Activity (CDRTA), 302–305, 405

Content schemata, 205–206

Context, 8–14; of early language learning, 48–49; information society as, 13–14; language systems and, 38, 40; multicultural world as, 9–12; *see also* Social context

Context clues, 293–294

Contextual interaction, school failure of culturally and linguistically diverse children and, 522

Continuity, in lessons, 92

Contracts, for subject areas, 104

Controversial topics, 330–331

Cooperative grouping, 108–109, 122; for diversity in classroom, 535–536, 542

Created sounds, 134

Creative comprehension, 185

Creative dramatics, 128, 157–170; children's storytelling, 168–169; concentration for, 161–162; definition, 158–159; drama, 170; examples of, 157–158; fingerplay, 164; grouping for, 160; improvisation, 169–170; as literature-based activity, 352; materials for, 159–160; pantomime, 166–168; puppetry, 164–165; quieting activities for, 163; relaxation for, 160–161; simple movement for, 162–163; space and organization for, 159–160; trust for, 162; usage taught with, 465–466

Creative pantomime, 168

Critical comprehension, 185, 186, 296, 297, 314

Critical listening, 135

Critical thinking, 7–8; antonyms and synonyms for, 414; for diverse students, 541–542; as literature-based activity, 355–357; metacognition, and, 37; radio and, 18; teaching, 8–9

Culturally and linguistically diverse students, 518, 519–528; comprehensible input for, 536–538; instructional strategies for, *see* Diversity in classroom; as opportunity, 524; statistics and trends on, 519; success or failure in school of, 521–522; terms for, 520–521; varied literacy experiences, 523–524; *see also* English as a Second Language students

Culture, 9–11; *see also* Diversity in classroom

Cumulative folders, 107
Cuneiform, 60
Curriculum guides, 99, 100, 111
Cursive, 472, 474–479

Danish, Old English and, 63–64
Deaf, special education for, 533
Decentering, 36, 40
Deck stacking, as propaganda, 136–137
D.E.D., see Double-entry draft format
Deep structure, in transformational generative grammar, 446
Degeneration, word meanings and, 401
Denotation, 412–413
Derivation, vocabulary and, 72, 398
Derivational constancy, word knowledge and, 196, 211
Derivational patterns stage, of spelling, 423–424, 426, 429–431
Description, as expository writing, 179, 206, 250
Descriptive sense, of grammar, 445
Desk arrangement, 83–84
Details, in outline, 312
Determiners, in grammar, 446
Development, 9; see also Cognitive development; Language development; Reading, development of; Writing, development of
Diagramming sentences, 463
Dialects, usage and, 464–465; see also Culturally and linguistically diverse students; Variant dialects
Dialogue format, of response journals, 354
Dialogue journal: diverse students and, 544–549; in sharing stage of writing process, 248–249
Diamantes, 260, 455
Dictated composition, 256
Dictated-experience chart, 281–285
Dictations, see Language experience approach
Dictionaries, 70; for content-related vocabulary, 409, 410; in etymology, 401–402
Dictionary of the English Language (Johnson), 70
Dictionary of Words that Almost Exist, 453
Differentiation, in cognitive development, 35
Digraphs, 418
Diphthongs, 422
Directed Listening-Thinking Activity (DLTA), 104, 145–148, 298; for children's storytelling, 168–169;

for reading to students, 280; for storywriting, 256
Directed Reading-Thinking Activity (DRTA), 119, 145; Content, 302–305, 405; in literature unit, 360, 366, 372–373, 376; for narrative text comprehension, 297–301; oral reading and, 321; for reading evaluation, 495–496; students and, 357
Directionality of print, 189
Direct teaching, 21–22, 24; for oral communication skills, 131; for propaganda, 138–139; for reading, 272; for writing, 219–220
Discipline, in classroom, 91–97; Assertive Discipline, 92–93; care from teacher and, 94; continuity and momentum in lessons and, 92; expectations of teacher and, 95; guidelines for, 94–97; having fun with students and, 96; help from teacher and, 95–96; ignoring behavior and, 96; journals for, 95; logical consequences approach, 93–94; mistakes as natural and, 95; overlapping and, 92; proximity of teacher and, 94; signal for attracting attention for, 96; in small-group discussion, 156–157; teacher effectiveness training, 93; withitness and, 91–92
Discussion: in literature-based reading and writing, 345; with small group, 153–157; for usage, 467
Distribution of materials, 90–91
Diversity in classroom, 9–12, 517–518; children's literature and, 553–557; computers for, 546–547; contents of language development and, 48; cooperative groups for, 535–539, 542; critical thinking and problem solving and, 541–542; dialogue journals for, 544–546; homework and, 551; language experience approach for, 538–539; "narrow reading" for, 540; parents and, 548–551, 552; peer tutoring for, 536; reading aloud for, 538–539, 541; reading instruction and, 538–542; repeated readings for, 541; specific instructional activities for, 551–553; thematic units for, 547–548, 553; writing with, 543–547; see also Culturally and linguistically diverse students; Special education
DLTA, see Directed Listening-Thinking Activity
D'Nealian cursive, 474, 476

D'Nealian manuscript, 474, 476
Double-entry draft (D.E.D.) format: in dialogue journals, 249; for response journals, 354
Double negatives, in variant dialects, 467
Drafting stage, of writing, 182, 219, 222–223, 239–240, 252–254
Drama, in creative dramatics, 170
Dramatics, see Creative dramatics
Drawing: in development of writing, 190, 191; as prewriting activity, 233; in response to reading, 358
DRTA, see Directed Reading-Thinking Activity
Due process, in PL 94–142, 530

Editing, 182, 219, 223–224, 243–245, 444, 470–471
Education for All Handicapped Children Act, see PL 94–142
Elaboration: questions for, 156; vocabulary and, 388
Electronic mail, writing and, 267
Electronic media, see Computers; Film; Radio; Television
Embedded contexts, 8
Emergent literacy, 187; see also Reading, development of; Writing, development of
Emotionally disturbed, special education for, 532–533
End of the day, 91
English: Black, 71, 467; principles of spelling, 416, 418–419; standard, 465; see also Language
English-Language Arts Framework, 518
English as a Second Language (ESL) students, 525–528; comprehensible input for, 536–538; parents and, 549–550; writing for, 543–544; see also Culturally and linguistically diverse students
Environment, development and, 29
Environmental print, 188, 551
Epistemic writing, 209–210
Errors and Expectations (Shaughnessy), 443
ESL, see English as a Second Language students
Etymology, 398–403
Evaluation: definition, 485–486; for grouping, 107; of learning, 112–113, 118, 119–120, 122; literature-based activity for, 356–357; parent conferences and, 113; report cards for, 113; word meaning changes through, 401; see also Formal assessment and

Evaluation: definition (*cont.*)
evaluation; Informal assessment
and evaluation
Examined experience, oral language
and, 130
Expansion, vocabulary development
and, 388
Expectations of teacher, discipline
and, 95
Experiences: oral language and, 130;
vocabulary and, 389; *see also*
Background knowledge
Expert, student as for expository
writing, 251–252, 253
Explanatory sense, of grammar, 445
Expository texts: comprehending,
302–312; Content Directed
Reading-Thinking Activity for,
302–305; graphic post-organizers
for, 309–310; interactive reading
guides for, 308–309; outlining for,
309, 311–312; prereading plan
for, 305–306; road maps for, 306–
308
Expository texts: development of,
202; organization for, 348–349;
students' responses to, 345; *see
also* Expository texts,
comprehending; Informational
books; Literature-based reading
and writing; Textbooks
Expository writing, 177, 178–179,
206, 250–254; across curriculum,
262–263; description, 250;
epistemic writing in, 209–210;
exposition, 250–251; ideas for,
349; interviewing for, 252–254;
persuasion, 251; print material for,
254; student as expert for, 251–
252, 253
Expression, as form of expository
structure, 179
Expressive voice, 196, 198

Fables, 335
Fairy tales, 256, 334
Figurative language, 413–414
Film, as information source, 17
Fingerplays, 164
First person point of view, 348, 354
Flashbacks, 194
Flexibility principle, of handwriting,
193, 472–473
Fluency of reading, 202, 322
Focus, of literature unit, 363–364
Focused holistic scoring, of writing,
512
Focus lessons, for writing, 220
Folk tales, 335; comparisons and
contrasts among, 353; literacy,
339; social studies tied with, 356;

storywriting learned with, 256;
traditional, 335, 339
Form, of written language, 176
Formal assessment and evaluation,
506–513; limitations of, 508;
normal curve and, 507; of reading,
508–509, 510–511; scoring, 507,
508; standardized, 507; of writing,
509, 512–513
Formal operations, story and, 344
Form classes of words, 445–446
Foster grandparents, as helpers in
classroom 98–99
Foxfire (Wiggington), 252
Free reading, 319–320
French: English spelling and, 67;
Middle English and, 64–65
Friendly letter, 468–469
Friendship, literature unit on, 369–
375
*From Communication to
Curriculum* (Barnes), 80–81
Frustrational level, of reading, 497
Fun, with students, 96
Functional shift, vocabulary changed
with, 72
Function words, 45
Furniture, in classroom, 83–85
"Future shock", 13

Generalization: as response to
literature, 344; word meaning
changes through, 400–401
Generative principle, of
handwriting, 193, 472
Genres, students classifying articles
according to, 353; *see also*
Children's literature, categories of
Genre schemes, 176; development
of, 187, 194–195; in intermediate
grades, 206–210; oral reading
and, 321–322; in writing, 181,
182, 198, 217, 218
Germanic, 57
Gifted and talented, special
education for, 532
Gifts, sent to parents, 114
Glittering generality, 136
"Global village," world as, 14
Goal setting, in classrooms, 99–100,
116, 117
Grade-equivalent scores, 507–508
Grading, 112–113; *see also*
Evaluation
Grammar, 444–463; case, 447;
definition, 444, 445; descriptive
sense 445; explanatory sense,
445; prescriptive sense of, 445;
structural, 445–446; teaching,
447–448, *see also* Parts of
speech; traditional, 445;
transformational generative, 446,

467; *see also* Sentences;
Mechanics; Usage
Grammatical structure, *see* Syntax
Grapheme/phoneme relationships,
291
Graphic post-organizers, 309–310
Graphology, 481
"Great Vowel Shift", 67–68
Greek: alphabet, 61; English
language and, 67, 68; words from
mythology of, 399–400
Group conferences, in literature-
based reading and writing, 350–
351; *see also under* Conferencing
Group experience charts, 281–285
Grouping, 84, 85, 105–112, 119;
ability, 105, 119; characters
studied in, 353–354; for creative
dramatics, 160; discussion, 153–
154; evaluation for, 107;
heterogeneous, 105, 107, 119;
homogeneous, 105, 106; literature
study group, 108; partnerships,
122; physical space and, 109;
purposes, 105–106; for reading,
494–496; social dynamics of, 109;
special interest, 107–108; spelling
instruction, 433; student talk and,
82; trust in, 162; whole-class, 118;
whole-group, 119, 122; *see also*
Cooperative grouping
Group Investigation, groups formed
with, 109
"Guess My Category," 392

Haiku, 261
Hand dominance, handwriting and,
474–475
Hands-on-experiences, for
vocabulary, 390
Handwriting, 471–481; calligraphy,
480, 481; cursive, 472, 474–479;
developmental pattern of, 473;
evaluating, 479–481; flexibility
principle of, 472–473; generative
principle of, 472; graphology, 481;
maintaining interest in, 480, 481;
manuscript, 472, 474–479; in
preschool and kindergarten, 472–
473; readiness for, 473, 474–475,
477; recurring principle of, 472;
styles, 474, 475, 476; teaching,
471, 474–475, 477–479
Head Start, 530
Hearing, listening distinct from, 133
Hearing impaired: dialogue journals
for, 545–546; special education
for, 533
Herd movement, 163
Heterogeneous groups, 105, 107,
119
Heuristic language, 132

Historical fiction, 337–338
Holidays, teaching with diverse students, 552
Holistic scoring, of writing, 509, 512–513
Homework, diverse students and, 551
Homogeneous groups, 105, 106, 495
Homographs, 414
Homonyms, 414
Homophones, 414, 418
Hypotheses testing: children and, 34, 43; on language, 46

Ideographic systems, *see* Logographic systems
Illinois Goal Assessment Program for Reading, 509, 511
Illustrations, literature-based activity with, 358–359
Illustrators, books about, 359–360
Imaginative language, 132
Imitation, as literature-based activity, 352–353
Immigration, English and, 71
Improvisation, 169–170
Independent level, of reading, 497
Independent reading, in literature unit, 374
Individual conferences, 499–500
Individual dictations, 286
Individual education program (IEP), in PL 94–142, 530, 531
Individual invention, of movement activities, 163
Indo-European, 56–57, 58; roots of words from, 398–399
Industry/inferiority stage, 343
Inferential comprehension, 185, 186, 296, 314
Informal assessment and evaluation, 486–505; of oral language, 488–489; portfolio assessment, 487–488; purposes of, 487; of spelling, 503–506; *see also* Reading, informal assessment and evaluation of; Writing, informal assessment and evaluation of
Informal learning situations, 131
Informal reading inventory (IRI), 496–499
Informal teaching, 22, 24, 25
Informational books, 340–341; in literature-based classroom, 345; organization for, 348–349
Information processing, writing process and, 181, 182
Information society, 13–14
Information sources, 14–20; computers, 18–19; film, 17; print, 14–16; radio, 18; social

relationships, 19–20; television, 16–17
Informative language, 132
Insertions, as reading miscues, 502, 503
Instructional level, of reading, 497
Instrumental language, 132
Integrated language arts instruction, based on interrelationships, 128–129; defined, 5; focused on reading, 272; planning teaching around, 79, 82–93, 102, 103; projects part of, 104; and teaching grammar and mechanics, 468–469; *see also* Literature-based reading and writing; Literature units; Response groups; Response journals; Thematic units
Integrated Language Perspective in the Elementary School, An (Pappas, Kiefer, Levstik), 112
Integration, in cognitive development, 35
Intelligence: development of, 29; multiple, 32–33, 159
Intent, in writing, 222
Interactional language, 132
Interactive model, in reading, 184
Interactive reading guides, for expository texts, 308–309
Interests of children, as literary genre, 341–342
Interjections, 455
Internalization, in writing, 222–223
Interpretation, narrative pantomime and, 168
Interviewing: with diverse students, 552; for expository writing, 252–254
Invented spellings, 199–200, 211, 421, 422
IRI, *see* Informal reading inventory

Jigsaw approach, groups and, 108
Journals: discipline and, 95; in intermediate school years, 209; as learning logs, 262; learning and retention and, 345; similes in, 413; in writing, 226, 247–248; *see also* Dialogue journals; Response journals

KEEP program, 448
Kernel sentences, 446, 456
Knowledge, 6–7; phonological, 41–42; procedural, 6, 7, 206; self-, 6, 206; topical, 6, 7–8; transformed, 7

Language: as basis of language arts, 8; dialects, 464–465; functions of,

38–40, 132; heuristic, 132; informative, 132; meaningful, 48; oral reading and aspects of, 321–322; personal, 132; regulatory, 132; whole, 5; *see also* Language development; Language heritage; Language systems; Oral communication; Oral language; Written language
Language development, 29–30, 37–51; from birth to two years, 43–45; brain and, 30–31; communication potential and, 30–34; contexts of, 48–49; factors facilitating, 48–49; metalinguistic awareness and, 50; observing, 46; parents and, 49; patterns in, 33–34; in preschool years, 42–50; questions, 47; reasons for examining, 29; teacher and, 47–48; from two years to five years, 45, 47–48; universal features in, 31
Language experience approach (LEA), 280–289, 321; group experience charts for, 281–285; "how-to's" of, 286; individual dictations in, 286; for special education, 538–539; teaching resources for, 288–289; for usage, 466; word banks in, 287–288; word sorts and, 391
Language heritage, 54–57; American English, 70–71; books on, 73–74; classroom example for, 57–59; derivational patterns stage of spelling and, 423–424; of English language, 63–71; etymology and, 398–401; Indo-European, 56–57, 58; Middle English, 64–68; Modern English, 63, 68–70; Old English, 63–64, 65; oral language development, 55–56; spelling and, 418; teaching resources on, 73–74; vocabulary changes, 72–73, 398; written language development, 59–62
Language systems, 38–40; *see also* Phonology; Semantics; Syntax
Language use, categories of, 409–415; analogies, 415, 436; antonyms, 414; denotation and connotation, 412–413; homonyms, 414; metaphors, 413, 414; similes, 413; synonyms, 410–412
Larry v. *Riles*, 530
Latin: English language and, 67, 68; Old English and, 63; spelling and, 418; words from mythology of, 399–400

Laughing, with students, 96

Lau v. *Nichols*, 525

LEA, *see* Language experience approach

Learning: neurobiology of brain and, 31; social context of, 20

Learning disabled, special education for, 532

Learning log, 345

Learning Together, 108–109

Lecture demonstration, 152

Left-handers, teaching handwriting to, 487–488

Legends, 335

Letter-name stage, 226; of spelling, 200, 420–421, 425, 426–427; of word knowledge, 196; of writing, 448

Letters: to authors, 356; commas taught by, 468–469

Library: for thematic unit, 111; *see also* Children's literature, categories of; Literature units

Linguistically diverse children, *see* Culturally and linguistically diverse students

Linking words, 452

Listening, 133–138; in anticipation, 135; critical, 135; to natural and created sounds, 134; propaganda and, 136–138; to sequences, 134; storytelling and, 148–150; to voices, 134; *see also* Reading aloud

Literacy, *see* Reading; Writing

Literacy experiences, culturally and linguistically diverse students and, 523–524

Literal comprehension, 185, 186, 296, 314

Literary folk tales, 339

Literature-based reading series, 275, 276

Literature-based reading and writing, 329–383; activities for, 352–359; challenges of, 330; developmental response to literature and, 344–345; effectiveness of, 332; elements of narratives, 347–348; expository texts and, 348–349; foundations of, 332–342, *see also* Children's literature, categories of; goals of, 329, 331; group conferences in, 350–351; response groups in, 350–351; response to literature and, 342–345; transition to, 345–347; *see also* Literature unit

Literature study group, 108

Literature unit, 360–380; around story element, 256; books

collected for, 364–365; day-by-day "lesson plan" format, 369–375; description of, 360; focus of, 363–364; goals and objectives of, 363; procedure for conducting, 366, 368; range of activities for, 366, 367, 368; samples of, 369–380; sources of ideas for, 360–362; steps in constructing, 362–366; "two-phase" format, 375–380; *see also* Thematic units

Logical consequences approach, to discipline, 93–94

Logical-mathematical intelligence, 32

Logographic systems, 60–61

Logographs, words as, 199

Long vowel sound, 418

"Mailbag" feature, in QUILL, 267

Main idea: children's concept of, 283; in outline, 312

Mainstreaming, 528

Manuscript, teaching, 474–479

Mapping, *see* Clustering

Marker, in spelling, 422

Meaning: in case grammar, 447; in drafting stage of writing, 222

Meaning, making: brain and, 31; children and, 29, 50, 183; psychology of literature and, 342; talking and, 20; thought and language and, 6

Meaning principle, of spelling, 418–419, 423

Mechanics, 467–471

Media, *see* Information sources

Mentally retarded: special education for, 532–533; thematic units for, 547

Mental map, questions and, 319

Metacognition, 37: metalinguistic awareness and, 50; reading in intermediate grades and, 206

Metacognitive knowledge, *see* Self-knowledge

Metalanguage, 49, 50

Metalinguistic awareness, 8; language development and, 50; teaching grammar and, 447; word identification and, 290

Metaphors, 413, 414

Microcomputers, writing and, 265–267; *see also* Computers

Middle English, 64–68

Mills vs. Bd. of Education, 530

Mini-lesson, writing and, 220

Minnesota Educational Computing Consortium (MECC), 267

Minority groups, *see* Culturally and linguistically diverse students

Mirroring, 162

Miscues, in reading, 501–503

Mistakes, as natural, 95

Mode of comprehension, in National Assessment of Educational Progress, 509

Modeling, by teacher, 21–22, 24, 131, 220, 272, 316–317

Modern English, 63, 68–70

Modern fantasy, 339–340

Momentum, in lessons, 92

Morphemes, 210–211, 289, 292

Morphemic analysis: in intermediate school years, 210–211; in word identification, 292; word meaning and, 393–402

Morphemic elements: base words, 211, 293, 394; prefixes, 211, 293, 393–394, 431–432, 454; compound words and, 427–428; roots, 211, 293, 394, 398–399, 431; stems, 394–398, 431, 454; suffixes, 211, 293, 393, 394, 454

Movement activities, 162–163

Multicultural society, 9–12; *see also* Diversity in classroom

Multiple intelligences, 32–33, 159

Music, for simple movement activities, 163

Musical intelligence, 32

Mythology, 335; words from Greek and Roman, 399–400

Name calling, as propaganda, 137

Name game, language development and, 43–44

Narrative pantomime, 168

Narratives: characterization, 7, 347, 352, 353–354, 355, 357; comprehending, 297–302; Directed Reading-Thinking Activity for, 297–301; elements of, 254, 347–348; literature-based activity for, 357; literature-based response groups for, 350; plot, 178, 254, 347; point of view, 348, 354; psychosocial needs of children and, 342; resolution, 254, 348; setting, 178, 254, 255, 348; specific elements focused on for, 302; story maps for, 301; storytelling and, 148; style, 348; theme, 178, 348; *see also* Literature-based reading and writing; Poetry; Stories

Narrative structure, 176, 177–178. *See also* Narratives; Poetry; Stories

"Narrow reading," 447, 540

National Assessment of Educational Progress, 206, 508, 509, 510, 512

National Writing Project, 221

"Pretend to be and do" pantomimes, 167

"Pretend to do" pantomimes, 167

Previewing, for reading informational material, 304

Prewriting, 182, 219, 222, 232–238; brainstorming for, 236, 237–238; clustering for, 233–236; drawing for, 232; for interviews, 252–254; of story writing, 255; stream-of-consciousness writing for, 236–237

Primary trait scoring, of writing, 512

Print, concept of word in, 199, 200, 201, 420

Printed material, as information source, 14–16

Print information, in reading, 184

Printing, see Manuscript

Printing press, 65, 66–67

Print resources, for expository writing, 254

Prior knowledge, comprehension and, 185–186

Problem, in plot, 254

Problem and solution, in expository texts, 206

Problem solving, for diverse students, 541–542

Procedural knowledge, 6, 7; for effective communication, 133; metacognition and, 37; reading in intermediate grades and, 206

Procedures, 87–91, 102

Productions, plays in children's magazines for, 170

Professional organizations, 23

Pronouns, 453, 455

Pronunciation, later Middle English period and, 67–68

Proofreading, 241, 470–471

Propaganda, 136–138, 401

Prosody, 42

Protolanguage, 39

Proximity of the teacher, discipline and, 94

Psychosocial development of children, literature and, 342–343

Publishing, see Sharing

Punctuation, 180, 195, 469–470

Puppetry, 164–165

Qualification, questions for, 156

Qualitative Spelling Inventory, 503, 504

"Question-Answer Relationships" (QARs), 313–319

Questions, 312–319; appropriate, 318; in conferences for writing, 229–232; for critical thinking, 355–356; importance of, 312–313; informative language and,

132; in language development, 47; in literature-based group conference, 351; in literature-based reading and writing, 344, 346; for literature-based response groups, 350; "Question-Answer Relationships," 313–319; in small-group discussion, 156; in teacher/student reading conference, 274; in teaching reading, 312–313; when to ask, 318–319

Quieting activities, for creative dramatics, 163

Quill, "Mailbag" feature in, 267

Radio, as information source, 18

Radio plays, 170, 322–323

Rating scale, of characters, 354, 355

Read-Aloud Handbook, The (Trelease), 140

Readers Theatre: as literature-based activity, 352; oral reading and, 322; plays in children's magazines for, 170; repeated reading encouraged by, 541

Readiness, for handwriting, 473, 474–475, 477–478

Reading aloud, 138–148; bookfile for, 141; books for, 142–144; Directed Listening-Thinking Activity as, 145–148; example of, 139; guidelines for, 140–142; in literature-based reading and writing, 345–347; modeling reading and, 272; similes and, 413; for special education, 538–539, 541; for usage, 464; varied sentences for, 456; see also Oral reading

Reading to children, 188–189

Reading comprehension, 185–186, 271, 294; creative, 185; critical, 185, 186, 296, 297, 314; inferential, 185, 186, 296, 314; literal, 185, 186, 296, 314; narratives, 297–302; oral reading checking, 321; in primary school years, 202; prior knowledge and, 185–186; "Question-Answer Relationships" for, 313–319; skills and strategies for teaching, 295–297; teaching resources for, 297; see also Expository texts, comprehending; Vocabulary

Reading, development of, 196; background knowledge and, 183, 205–206; in intermediate school years, 205–211; in preschool years, 187–189; in primary school years, 194–195, 197, 199–203; sight vocabulary, 197; text schemas and, 206; transitional

reading, 201–202, 203, 264; word knowledge, 199–201

Reading experiences, oral reading and, 321

Reading, informal assessment and evaluation of, 494–503; attitudes and understandings about reading and, 499–500; grouping, 494–498; informal reading inventory, 496–499, "new generation" of standardized group tests of, 508–509, 510–511; portfolio assessment, 499–503; responses to literature tasks and, 500–501; running record, 501–503; traditional standardized group tests of, 508

Reading levels, 497

Reading Log, 499

Reading process, 183–186; components of, 185–186, see also Reading Comprehension; Word knowledge; description of, 183; interactive nature of, 183–185; models of, 184–185; text model, 183; verbal efficiency theory of, 185

Reading rate, 202, 322

Reading Recovery, 541

Reading skills, 272–273

Reading, teaching, 271–327; basal reading series for, 275, 277; conferencing for, 273–274; direct teaching for, 272; free reading, 319–320; in integrated language arts program, 272–277; literature-based reading series for, 275, 276; materials for, 275–277; modeling for, 272; oral reading, 320–323; see also Beginning reading; Questions; Reading comprehension; Word identification

Records: in literature-based group conference, 351; running, 501–503; in teacher/student reading conference, 274

Recurring principle, of handwriting, 193, 472

Redundant subjects, in variant dialects, 467

Regulations, in classroom, 87–91, 116, 118

Regulatory language, 132

Rehearsing, see Prewriting

Relaxation, for creative dramatics, 160–161

Renaissance, English language and, 67, 68

Repetition: in poetry, 259; in reading to children, 189; for special education, 541

Report cards, 506
Research groups, in literature unit, 377–379
Resolution, in narratives, 254, 348
Response groups: in literature-based reading and writing, 350–351; student/student conferences as, 219; synonyms in, 411; writing taught with, 227–229
Response journals: dialogue format, 354; double-entry draft format, 354; in intermediate school years, 209; as literature-based activity, 354–355; for literature-based response groups, 350; for literature tasks, 496–497; poetry meaning in, 359; response to questions in, 356
Retelling, as response to literature, 344
Revision: grammar and usage and, 444; parts of speech and, 451; of poetry, 261–262
Rewards, in Assertive Discipline, 93
Rhymes, children and, 43; see also Poetry
Risk taking, in classroom, 79–80
Road maps, for expository text comprehension, 306–308
Role playing, usage taught with, 456–466, 467
Roots, 394; from Indo-European, 398–399; in intermediate school years, 211; spelling-meaning connection and, 431; in word identification, 293; see also Stems
Rotation organization, 119; for subject areas, 104
Routines, 87–91, 102, 117–118
Rules, see Regulations, in classroom
"Running record," for informal assessment and evaluation of reading, 501–503

Scheduling, 100–105, 116, 117–118, 119, 121
Schemas, in cognitive development, 34, 35–36; see also Genre schemes
Scores, for formal assessment and evaluation, 507
Scribbles, in writing, 190, 191
Scribes, 156; of fourteenth century, 65–66
Second language education, see English as a Second Language students
Self-evaluation, of written composition, 263
Self-knowledge, 7; metacognition and, 37; reading in intermediate grades and, 206

Semantic feature analysis, 405–407
Semantic maps, 405, 406
Semantics, 40–41, 43; development of, 45, 46, 47; in reading, 184
Semiphonemic stage, of spelling, 200, 420, 425
Semiphonemic word knowledge, 196, 200
Sentence completion, 408
Sentences, 456–463; acquiring store of, 462; from ages two through five, 47; "ands" in, 458; combining, 456, 457, 459–463; concept of, 456; developmental sequence for, 456–457; diagramming, 463; expansion, 446, 447–449; introducing, 448; kernel, 446, 456; moveability of phrases and, 458–459; order of words in, 456; predicate, 448, 456, 458; subject, 448, 456, 458; subject-predicate division in, 456; word bank and, 288
Sequence: children recalling, 134; in expository texts, 206
Setting, in narratives, 178, 254, 255, 348
Shakespeare, for elementary students, 170
Sharing, in writing process, 150–152, 182, 219, 224, 232, 245–249; Author's Chair for, 223, 245; binding students books for, 246–247; dialogue journals for, 248–249; journals for, 247–248; in literature-based group conference, 351; student-directed, 152; synopsis of books, 356; teacher-directed, 151–152; in teacher/student reading conference, 273–274
"Show-and-tell", see Sharing
Sight vocabulary, 389, 420; development of, 197; in language experience approach, 286; within-word pattern stage of spelling and, 421; word sorts for, 390–392
"Silly Syntax", 452
Similes, 413
Slavery, American English and, 71
Small-group discussions, 153–157, 345
Small-muscle dexterity, handwriting and, 475, 477
Snob appeal, as propaganda, 137
Social context: language development and, 44; learning and, 20
Social dynamics, of groups, 109
Social environment, see Classroom, social environment of

Social relationships, as information source, 19–20
Spanish: American English and, 71; in poetry, 259
Spatial intelligence, 32
Speaking, see Oral communication; Oral language
Special education, 518, 528–534; books about, 534; categories of, 532–534; for emotionally disturbed, 532–533; for gifted and talented, 522; for hearing impaired, 533; historical perspectives on, 529–531; instructional strategies for, see Diversity in classroom; for learning disabled, 532; literature on, 558; mainstreaming and, 528; for mentally retarded, 532–533; for physically handicapped, 533; PL 94–142 and, 529–530; PL 99–457 and, 530; for speech and language impaired, 532; success or failure of, 529; terminology for, 529; for visually impaired, 533
Special interest groups, 107–108
Special interests of children, as literary genre, 341–342
Specialization, word meaning changes through, 400
Speech and language impaired, special education for, 532
Spelling, 203, 387, 415–437; activities for, 433–435; alphabetic principle of, 418; derivational patterns stage, 423–424, 425, 429–431; developmental knowledge of, 419–424; formal instruction for, 424–435; foundations for learning and teaching, 388, 415–416; informal assessment and evaluation of, 503–506; informal instruction for, 436–437; initial judgments of students' knowledge of, 503–505; invented, 199–200, 211, 421, 422; letter-name stage of, 200, 420–421, 425, 426–427; meaning principles of, 418–419, 423–424; ongoing assessment and evaluation of, 506; "pretest/self-correct/ study/posttest" format, 424–425, 432–433; semiphonemic stage of, 200, 420, 425; series for teaching, 417; spelling-meaning connection, 424, 426, 429–431; standardized, 69–70; of stems, 398; suffixes and, 393; syllable juncture stage, 422–423, 426, 428–429; three principles of, 416, 418–419; within-word pattern stage, 203,

Spelling (*cont.*)
205, 418, 421–422, 423, 425, 427–428; *see also* Vocabulary
Spelling books, origin of, 69
Spelling-meaning connection, 417, 419, 426, 429–431
SQUIRT, *see* Sustained Quiet UnInterrupted Reading Time
SSR, *see* Sustained Silent Reading
STAD, *see* Student teams achievement divisions
Standard English: usage, 464–465; variant dialects versus, 467
Standardized scores, 507
Standardized tests, 486, 507; *see also* Formal assessment and evaluation
Stanines, 507
Stems, 394–398, 431, 454. *See also* Roots
Stereotypes, moving beyond, 12
Storage, 84–85, 115–116
Stories, 177–178; concepts of, 187; development of, 195; elements of, 178, 254, 347–348, *see also* Characterization; organization of, 255; psychosocial needs of children and, 342; structure of, 178; teaching writing, 254–256; *see also* Narratives
Storybooks, 188–189
Story grammar, 194
Story maps, 301
Storytelling, 148–150: by children, 168–169; with culturally or linguistically diverse students, 523; psychosocial needs of children and, 342; for traditional literature, 344
Strategy lessons, 220
Stream-of-consciousness writing, as prewriting activity, 236–237
Stressed syllables, language development and, 43
Structural analysis of words: in intermediate school years, 211; word identification and, 292; word meaning and, 393–402
Structural grammar, 445–446
Structure, in classroom, 88
Structured overview, for content-related vocabulary, 403–405
Structured-process writing, 218
Student-directed sharing, 152
Student/student conferences, for writing, 219, 227, 231–232, 233
Student teams achievement divisions (STAD), groups formed with, 108
Style, in narratives, 348
Subject, of sentence, 448, 456, 458

Subject area, time for, 104
Subject/verb agreement, in variant dialects, 467
Substitutions, as reading miscues, 502–503
Suffixes, 393, 394; in intermediate school years, 211; teaching, 454; in word identification, 293
Sumerians, logographic systems of, 60, 61
Summary, 344
Supply areas, 84, 115–116
Supporting ideas, in outline, 312
Supreme Court: English as a Second Language and, 525; special education programs and, 530
Surface structure, in transformational generative grammar, 446
Surnames, origin of, 65
Sustained Quiet UnInterrupted Reading Time (SQUIRT), 320
Sustained Silent Reading (SSR), 116, 118, 120, 272, 320
Sustained writing, 264
Syllable juncture stage: of spelling, 422–423, 426, 428–429; of word knowledge, 196, 211
Syllabication: development of concept of, 193; knowledge of in intermediate school years, 211; in word identification, 292
Syllabic systems, 61
Synonyms, 410–412
Syntactic properties, of language, 448
Syntax, 40, 41, 43, 387; development of, 45, 46, 47, 187, 194, 448; in reading, 183, 184
Synthetic phonics, 291

Talking: in classroom, 80–82; as information source, 19–20
Teacher: conception of, 22–24; placement of desk of, 85
Teacher-added terms, in semantic mapping, 405, 406
Teacher effectiveness training, 93
Teacher evaluation, of written composition, 263
Teacher planning sheet, for thematic unit planning, 111
Teacher/student reading conferences, 273–274
Teaching, *see* Direct teaching; Informal teaching
Teaching resources: on calligraphy, 481; on Content Directed Reading-Thinking Activity, 305; on diversity, 554–557; on etymology,

402–403; on illustrators and artists, 359–360; on informal reading inventories, 499; on language experience approach, 288–289; on language heritage, 73–74; on literature-based units, 360–362, 364–366; on oral communication, 135; on oral reading, 323; on outlining, 312; on poetry, 262; on predictable texts, 279–280; on read-alouds, 142–144; on reading comprehension, 297; on sentence combining, 463; on special education, 558; on storytelling, 150; on thematic planning, 558; on word categorization, 435–436; on word identification, 292
Telegraphic stage, of language development, 45
Teletype, computer for, 447
Television, 16–17
Tension, in plot, 254
Testimonial, as propaganda, 136
Tests, *see* Evaluation
Texas "Teams" writing evaluation, 512
Textbooks: goal setting with, 99–100, 117; for reading instruction, 275–276; for thematic unit planning, 111; for writing, 221; *see also under* Expository texts
Text model: in primary school years, 202–203; in reading process, 183
Text schemes, 206–210
TG grammar, *see* Transformational generative grammar
Thematic units, 100, 110–112, 118, 119, 122; on diversity, 553; for special education, 547–548; *see also* Literature units
Theme: booklet based on, 114; for classroom, 100; in narratives, 178, 348
Thesaurus, 409
They All Want to Write (Burrows), 217
Think-alouds, for independent poetry reading, 359
Third person point of view, 348
Thought: as basis of language arts, 6–8; development of, 29; *see also* Cognitive development
Timed word bank review, 288
Time and space, books on trips through, 339–340
Title, children's concept of, 283
"To be," in variant dialects, 467
Topical knowledge, 6, 7–8; direct teaching for, 22; for effective communication, 133

Writing process (*cont.*)
Revision; Sharing; Writing,
teaching
Writing, teaching, 216–269;
classroom organized for, 264–
265; comfort with writing and,
225–226; computers for, 265–
267; conferencing for, 219, 221–
222, 227–232; direct teaching for,
219–220; evaluation, 263–264;
genre schemes and, 217, 218;
materials and space for, 221, 265;
modeling for, 220; as natural or
structured process, 218–219;
sustained writing, 264; textbooks
and prepared materials for, 221;
time for, 264–266; voices and,
217, 218; *see also* Expository
writing; Narrative writing; Writing
process
Writing workshops, groups for, 106
Written language, 5; development
of, 42, 59–62; oral language
development and, 49

Yearly plan, 100
Young Authors Conference, 246

Zero reject, in PL 94–142, 530
Zone of proximal development,
comprehensible input and, 536,
537

An Invitation to Respond

We would like to find out a little about your background and about your reactions to *Teaching the Integrated Language Arts.* Your evaluation of the book will help us to meet the interests and needs of students in future editions. We invite you to share your reactions by completing the questionnaire below and returning it to: *College Marketing, Houghton Mifflin Company, One Beacon Street, Boston, MA 02108.*

1. Please tell us your overall impressions of the text.

	Excellent	*Good*	*Adequate*	*Poor*
a. Was it written in a clear and understandable style?	——	——	——	——
b. Were difficult concepts well explained?	——	——	——	——
c. How would you rate the Classroom Examples?	——	——	——	——
d. How comprehensive was the coverage of major issues and topics?	——	——	——	——
e. How does this book compare to other texts you have used?	——	——	——	——
f. How would you rate the *At the Teacher's Desk* feature?	——	——	——	——
g. How would you rate the study aids at the beginning and end of each chapter and the Resource lists within each chapter?	——	——	——	——

2. Can you comment on or illustrate your above ratings? _____

_____

_____

_____

3. What chapters or features did you particularly like? _____

_____

_____

_____

4. What chapters or features did you dislike or think should be changed? _____

_____

_____

5. What material would you suggest adding or deleting? _____

_____

_____

_____

6. What was the title of the course in which you used this book? _____

_____

_____

7. Are you an undergraduate student? _____ If so, what year?

_____

8. Are you a graduate student? _____ If so, have you taught before? _____

9. Have you taken any other courses in education? If so, which courses?

_____

_____

10. Do you intend to keep this book for use during your teaching career? _____
Why or why not? _____

_____

11. Did you like the physical appearance of this book? _____ Did you
find that the design of the text made using and finding material simple or
difficult? _____ Why or why not? _____

12. We would appreciate any other comments or reactions you are willing to
share. _____

_____

_____